SOCIAL MEDIA
STRATEGY

MARKETING, ADVERTISING, AND
PUBLIC RELATIONS IN
THE CONSUMER REVOLUTION

THIRD EDITION

Keith A. Quesenberry
Messiah University

ROWMAN & LITTLEFIELD
Lanham • Boulder • New York • London

Executive Editor: Elizabeth Swayze
Editorial Assistant: Dina Guilak
Higher Education Channel Manager: Jonathan Raeder

Credits and acknowledgments for material borrowed from other sources, and reproduced with permission, appear on the appropriate pages within the text.

Published by Rowman & Littlefield
An imprint of The Rowman & Littlefield Publishing Group, Inc.
4501 Forbes Boulevard, Suite 200, Lanham, Maryland 20706
www.rowman.com

6 Tinworth Street, London SE11 5AL, United Kingdom

British Library Cataloguing in Publication Information Available

Library of Congress Cataloging-in-Publication Data
Names: Quesenberry, Keith A., 1971– author.
Title: Social media strategy : marketing, advertising, and public relations in the consumer revolution / Keith A. Quesenberry, Messiah University.
Description: Third edition. | Lanham : Rowman & Littlefield, [2021] | Includes bibliographical references and index.
Identifiers: LCCN 2020007483 (print) | LCCN 2020007484 (ebook) | ISBN 9781538138168 (cloth ; alk. paper) | ISBN 9781538138175 (paperback ; alk. paper) | ISBN 9781538138182 (epub)
Subjects: LCSH: Internet marketing. | Internet advertising. | Social media. | Internet in public relations.
Classification: LCC HF5415.1265 .Q46 2021 (print) | LCC HF5415.1265 (ebook) | DDC 658.8/72—dc23
LC record available at https://lccn.loc.gov/2020007483
LC ebook record available at https://lccn.loc.gov/2020007484

∞™ The paper used in this publication meets the minimum requirements of American National Standard for Information Sciences—Permanence of Paper for Printed Library Materials, ANSI/NISO Z39.48-1992.

Brief Contents

Detailed Contents

PART III: Choose Social Options for Target, Message, and Idea

Preface

I first began teaching a dedicated social media strategy college course in 2012. This was after seventeen years of working in the marketing communications industry where the second half of that career was spent integrating social media into traditional marketing, advertising, and public relations. At the same time I started a career as a professor, I began researching social media, looking at the scholarship and theories around this topic. Those years of researching social media, years in the industry using social media in plans and campaigns, and years of teaching cross-discipline social media undergraduate and graduate courses in multiple business and communications schools informed and guided the first edition of this book.

The goal of the first edition was to develop a broad-based strategic approach to social media that went well beyond the up-to-the-minute social media networks, features, and tips reported in the trade press or professional blogs. These are excellent resources for latest developments, but I found that this piecemeal method didn't provide enough guidance to fully teach a strategic, integrated approach to social media. A collection of articles didn't provide a clear process for developing a social media plan for a specific organization with their unique challenges, opportunities, and goals. I wanted more than a business book, which can be very valuable but is often narrow in subject or only offers one person's path to success. I wanted more than a textbook, which can be heavy on theory but light on practical application. The goal was to bridge the gap between scholarly research and professional practice, combining theory and academic research with business research and applied industry examples.

I knew there was value in having a deeper dive into the background and context of social media that explained how we got here, why it is so troublesome to many professionals, and where we are headed. Social media is too complicated a subject and too disruptive to traditional business and communications methods to not explore and understand core differences. Social media also brings together siloed academic disciplines and business departments in more intensive ways than ever before. A social media book must be cross-disciplined. Social media is too big for one corporate or college department.

The first edition was written to provide a strategic approach that would be relevant beyond this month's hyped-up social media platform, feature, or algorithm change. A social media strategy isn't built on Meerkat and Vine or Facebook and Instagram. Platforms come and go or change their rules, and target audiences become more or less active on different and more social platforms. What makes a social media plan strategic is that it can be effective no matter the social platform. Social media strategy must also include social platforms that the student or businessperson may not be active on personally. A broad array of relevant social media must be considered—not just the most popular or familiar. The first edition outlined a strategic process with these goals in mind that was based on business objectives, target audiences, big ideas, and social media channel categories that can last.

Why then a second and now a third edition? Through teaching, consulting, and feedback over many semesters and several years, related topics and resources have been discovered that help create a fuller and more complete look at social media and the strategic process. Based on student and instructor feedback, what and how concepts are presented and explained have also been adjusted to increase comprehension and ensure alignment with professional practice. The third edition also updates statistics, features, tactics, and social media platform options. Yet the core strategic process from the first edition remains the same, with key pieces added and other areas simplified and optimized. For a look at that strategic process, please see the introduction.

Although social media platform statistics and features are being updated in this edition, tomorrow Facebook will adjust its business pages and Instagram will add a new feature. That is why a checklist is included at the end of every chapter. Each "Chapter Checklist" acknowledges the fact that social media specifics change quickly and provides a checklist directing readers to find the latest developments in important areas from that chapter. It also reminds readers to check the website PostControlMarketing.com, where significant developments are added on a regular basis, such as updates on the top social media platforms by category or insights into key new developments such as TikTok or hiding likes. Each chapter also has updated cases and examples of brands applying social platforms and key concepts to professional practice. There are thirty-eight fresh new brand examples throughout the text from Pura Vida, Hydroflask, and GoPro to Mack Trucks, KLM, and John Deere.

Numerous topics and sections have been added to many chapters. In total more than 125 key concepts have been added, appearing in each chapter as bolded key terms with definitions and explanation. A new section, "Key Concepts" has been added to the end of every chapter as a summary review of all key concepts covered and defined in the chapter in the order they were covered. In addition, all key terms have been included in an alphabetical glossary with more than 340 concepts and definitions. Instead of limiting ethics discussion to only the final chapter, key ethical considerations have been added to each chapter. Each fourth chapter question specifically addresses a social media ethics question appropriate to a key situation from that chapter.

Chapter 1 now includes a new section on the maturing of social media, presenting statistics that point toward social media moving past a high-growth stage of new users and new platforms. Examples are presented and the implications for strategy are explained. With this comes important new defined terms such as daily active user (DAU) versus monthly active user (MAU). A new table illustrates the importance of considering MAU and DAU engagement rate and generational differences on five top social media platforms. A new box explores broadcasting versus narrowcasting. Three new theories had been added and explained as a theoretical basis for understanding of social media. Social capital theory is explained along with the related concepts of social influence and social proof.

Chapter 2 adds to its discussion of the fragmentation of mass media segmented audiences as applied to target audience. The impact of mass media fragmentation is illustrated with a new table showing the decline of what is considered a hit. The concept of long tail is introduced along with discussion of mass appeal products and services versus horizontal segmentation aimed at consumers' variable tastes. The chapter gets a new box dedicated to the subject of social media command centers. The pros and cons of command centers are presented along with recommendations for determining whether and how to create one. Chapter 2 also has a new section, "Mobile First Media," that discusses the transition of consumers' media consumption to mobile. Mobile marketing is defined along with the concept mobile first strategy and the importance of delivering a mobile first customer experience.

Chapter 3 now has a dedicated section on careers in social media. Content has expanded to include top social media job titles and descriptions plus salary information with links to social media online job databases, summarized in a new table. Freelancers and solopreneurs are discussed as well as descriptions of the various types of outside agencies that provide social media services and the multiple departments in an organization that social media may be housed. The opportunities for journalist social media content developers has also been included. An important new box section has been added dedicated to social media manager mental health. The unique opportunities and challenges of a career in social media is discussed. This includes possible negative effects, stress, and burnout. Two social media professionals' tips are included to prevent possible mental health effects and to avoid social media burnout.

The strategic process presented in chapter 4 remains the same but has added additional perspective from Simon Senek's popular TED Talk, "Start with Why," also known as the Golden Circle theory. Discussion of targeting goes beyond generations, market, and audience to include more perspectives. For the public relations perspective, the terms "stakeholders" and "publics" are now defined and explained. Firmographics is defined and explained for targeting in a business-to-business context. Nonprofit marketing is defined and how targeting can vary for charities and nonprofits is explained. The importance of brand voice, value proposition, and a brand style guide are emphasized. The differences between a slogan and tagline and social media monitoring and social media listening are explained.

Chapter 5 gets a new section, "Social Media Marketing Cycle," which explains how marketing funnels and the old AIDA model have changed with social media and a fragmented buyer's journey and how that impacts social strategy, content, and measurement. This provides opportunity to also discuss the various social media organization models. To expand upon the discussion of account planning, actionable insights, and storytelling leading up to a big idea, a standard creative brief framework is added. The importance of corporate social responsibility (CSR) is discussed along with examples of companies using a CSR message in their social media. For improved brainstorming and idea generation, a five-step creative process is also presented.

With the growing importance placed on social media return on investment, chapter 6 has a new section explaining how to create a social media measurement plan. With that comes a new discussion of multichannel and omnichannel marketing, brand positioning, perceptual maps, brand equity, reach, and impressions. A new table is added comparing social media ad campaign objectives to common social media ad buying options such as CPM and CPC. The growth of direct sales in more social media platforms is also introduced by defining and explaining social commerce. Chapter 6 now ends with the addition of a new box section defining and presenting an outline of a social media strategic plan. This provides important context presenting the outline of the social media plan that the book is designed to produce in chapter 14 and following the three-step social media plan in appendix A.

Chapter 7 begins with a new table that summarizes questions to consider when selecting social platforms for a strategic social media plan. Facebook Watch and Facebook Portal are now defined and discussed. Chapter 7 also adds definition and explanation of the growing area of conversational commerce. Chapter 8 has a new section on the social platform TikTok, a new table of popular TikTok video trends, and brand examples such as Sony Pictures' *Jumanji* release. It also newly discusses of the impact of over-the-top media (OTT) as more people cut the cord to cable, switching to streaming TV services. Chapter 9 adds consideration of the social live video platforms of Twitch and YouTube Live along with the concept of hashtag hijacking. It also has a new table with the advantages and disadvantages of social live video. Chapter 10 removes the StumbleUpon platform and adds new case examples with L'Oréal, Hot Wheels, and *The Economist*.

Chapter 11 has a new table summarizing organizational uses for social data analysis. It also gets a new box section on the strategy of surprise and delight social media. The important consideration of diversity marketing is now discussed for content marketing and social media. In the crowdsourcing section, the term "crowdfunding" has been added and defined. The sociology term "parasocial relationships" is now discussed to further explain unique influence and emotional bonds that can be formed in podcasts between publisher and listener. The theory section of local search has added the concept of competency trap for greater understanding of practical application.

Chapter 12 has an updated and expanded section on personas and user-generated content. Explanation of personas is expanded and added as part of the social media strategic process. Personas are also tied to jobs to be done theory as important concepts to create more effective content. The content marketing section adds explanation of search engine optimization and search engine marketing. Evangelism marketing is also expanded with the strategies of gamification, employer advocacy, and employer branding. This includes a new table summarizing the benefits of employer advocacy programs. Malcom Gladwell's *Tipping Point* concepts for evangelism marketing have additions, supported with comparison of Seth Godin's *Ideavirus* concepts. The influencer marketing section is expanded with explanation of differences and how to use advocates, brand ambassadors, and influencers. Influencers have been further defined into mega-influencers, macro-influencers, micro-influencers, and nano-influencers.

Chapter 13 has added a new section on crisis communication and reputation management along with explanation of net promoter score, flame war, and faupology. The differences between traditional crisis communication and social media crisis communication is discussed as well as new considerations for social media crisis strategies, processes, and response. A new case example of the Crock-Pot *This Is Us* presents social media crisis communication in action. A new box section discusses the implications of a crisis the scale of COVID-19 has on social strategy and is unique from traditional crisis communications. Online reputation management is also defined with respect to how it is different from crisis communication. Best practices for online reputation management are also added.

Chapter 14 now has a new section on social media content creation. This section covers best practices in the writing and design of effective social media posts, images, and video. It adds topics such as active and passive voice, landing page, negative space, rule of thirds, evergreen content, A/B testing, and engagement rate. A new box discusses the challenges and opportunities of dark social in more depth. A new section on artificial intelligence defines terms such as "automation," "drip marking," "machine learning" (ML), and "natural language processing." It also discusses the opportunities and challenges in the various ways AI is helping and could help social media professionals.

Finally, chapter 15 has six new case examples including a new box section, "The FTC Takes Action," providing recent actions against companies for violating social media regulations. Important new guidelines and laws have been added and explained, including the FTC Statement on Deceptively Formatted Native Ads and the FTC Consumer Review Fairness Act. The new California Consumer Protection Act (CCPA) is explained and discussed as setting up unprecedented privacy protections in the United States similar to those provided in the General Data Protection Regulation for European Union citizens. The five rights granted by CCPA are highlighted in a new table. Along with CCPA, the California Bot Disclosure Law has been added and discussed as a new standard in the United States for using bots in social media. The ethics and etiquette section of this chapter has been divided into two new sections of Social Media Ethics and Social Media Etiquette.

The social media strategic process has been tweaked and explained in further detail with a new clear and concise social media plan outline for major subhead sections of Brand, Industry, and Competitor; Business Objectives and Target Audience; Social Media Audit; Social Strategy Big Idea; Recommended Social Platforms; Creative Content and Calendar; Policies, Guidelines, and Requirements; Social Media Analytics; and Social Media Budget. More than fifty new figures have been added throughout the text to put social media use, statistics, and concepts into visual perspective with photos, tables, and graphs.

Surveys indicate technology platform experience is an important skill for new hires. Therefore links to key outside online support materials, courses, and professional certification badges have now been embedded into the text appearing in each chapter with the concepts, strategies, and platforms that they support. These key links are easily identified with an underline followed by the URL. More than fifteen links to professional support resources provide excellent opportunities for additional in-depth learning in key areas instructors want to emphasize. They also provide opportunities for students to personalize their learning in areas of interest to prepare for specific career goals and earn professional certifications and badges in technology platforms that demonstrate knowledge to prospective employers.

The new "Careers in Social Media" section in chapter 3 includes links to more than ten online job databases to view current social media positions' job descriptions, titles, and requirements. These include the current top online job databases, professional discipline online job listings, and top online sites providing freelance social media projects. Chapter 4 now has links to social media platform training and certifications including Hootsuite, Meltwater, and Cision. Chapter 6's emphasis on social media integration and measurement is supported with links to Hootsuite's Social Marketing training and certification and HubSpot's Social Media training and certification. Chapter 7 includes a link to Facebook Blueprint training and certification courses for additional learning in Facebook, Instagram, Messenger, and WhatsApp.

Chapter 8 highlights Twitter Flight School, Snapchat Explore, Pinterest Academy, and Google Ads Video training and certification to support social media strategies on Twitter,

Snapchat, Pinterest, and YouTube. Chapter 13 adds a link to Salesforce's Trailhead training and credentials for additional learning on this enterprise social media CRM platform. The content marketing and B2B social selling section also includes links to HubSpot's Inbound Sales training and certification and Hootsuite's Social Selling training and certification. Chapter 14's new section on social media content creation provides links for additional learning and support for the Adobe Creative Suite, including Adobe Spark through LinkedIn Learning and Adobe Education Exchange and Canva platform and design training through Canva Design School. Links also provide opportunities to learn through YouTube Creator Academy and earn the YouTube Certification.

Other previous sections have been updated as well. Each "Theoretically Speaking" section has additional practical professional practice examples or considerations to further connect theory to practice. In addition to the new cases and examples, each previous "Mini Case" section has updates to explain what the brand is doing today. For further in-depth analysis and practice of these real cases new instructor support materials are available called case briefs.

Case briefs take the cases presented in the book and add additional information about the brand's current business situation with real performance data and graphs. Challenges and opportunities are presented as fictionalized situations placing students in potential professional roles after graduation or later in their careers. They are asked to provide solutions and recommendations in a real-world context where decisions have not yet been made. The ten new case briefs align with key mini cases in the text and take that brand story forward. Cases are written to focus on possible solutions around key concepts, strategies, and platforms as they are learned in chapters throughout a semester. Unlike case studies where the decisions were made and outcomes known, case briefs set up possible situations where recommendations must be made without hindsight. Enough background context and current research is provided to get students started, but solutions must be found and supported on their own, setting up the opportunity for robust and in-depth class discussion.

The ten case briefs are available to instructors through the publisher's website along with updated chapter outlines, updated chapter-by-chapter test banks, revised example assignments, and revised example syllabi for undergraduate and graduate courses online and in person. New PowerPoint slides include key points for each chapter. More than ten downloadable templates and guides are also provided to support key strategic tools in the text. For students and instructors who prefer digital texts, an eBook is available on the Rowman & Littlefield publisher website (https://rowman.com) as an alternative to the printed editions. For a complete look at the book, what it covers, and how it is structured, please see the introduction.

Acknowledgments

I would like to thank Leanne Silverman at Rowman & Littlefield for shepherding the first edition of this book to publication and Elizabeth Swayze for guiding the second; Bruce Bendinger, who told me that I should write it; and Michael Coolsen, who has helped me bridge the professional practice and academic research worlds.

Of course, there is more to life than this. I also am a proud husband and father. Thank you to my family for their love and support. Without you this book surely would not have been possible.

And all of life takes faith which comes from the one above.—John 8:32

Introduction

It is hard being a business or communications professional these days. Just when you think you have it figured out, the rules change. You like the idea of social media and know you have to do it. Who doesn't like direct access to your consumer and everything being measurable? But there is something uniquely challenging about social media strategy and integration. The old strategies and methods of business, marketing communications, advertising, and public relations don't easily apply to this interactive and highly influential medium. You can't simply add it to the communications mix as another channel or outlet for your brand message. Yet every year there is greater pressure to integrate social media, do it well, and prove success through social analytics.

So you search. You turn to Google for the top social media tips for success. We like lists because they make us feel that social media can be a simple add-on: just follow these ten steps and you'll succeed! Yet a Google search of "social media tips" returns 1.9 billion results.[1] This is up from 146 million in 2017 when the second edition of this text was published.[2] Read some of these lists and you find that few tell you to do the same things. Tomorrow hundreds more tips will be published. Now suddenly all those simple tips are no longer so simple. On top of that it feels like there are new platforms, features, content, and algorithms happening all the time. In social media we don't have an information problem. We have an information overload problem.

The truth is there is no one-list-fits-all social media strategy. No matter how hard we search for that ultimate top-ten list, we will never find it. The issue with articles like "The Best Social Media Marketing Tells a Story,"[3] "Top 6 Social Media Marketing Tips for Businesses,"[4] "Social Media Marketing: How Do Top Brands Use Social Platforms?"[5] or "TikTok Hit 1.5 Billion Downloads"[6] is that you can't build a social media plan out of them. The fact that more than half of the top brands are using Pinterest or Snapchat does not mean it's appropriate for your organization.

Even if you did use Snapchat, how would you use it? What would you post there? How would that tie into what you're doing on Facebook and Instagram? Is it a good idea to tell a story in social media? Yes. But what story do you tell and where? Everyone is talking about TikTok, but is it right for your target audience, brand message, and organizational goals? These are answers that cannot be found in a blog post or news article about the latest social media platform, tactic, tool, or case. What worked for IBM, BMW, or Nike will probably not work the same for a regional bank, tech startup, nonprofit, or packaged good.

In the past eight years companies have spent 10 percent more on digital marketing than traditional advertising. Successful organizations today must engage with the digital consumer on multiple devices and platforms to capture their attention as non-digital channels continue to lose reach and ROI. This changing environment has also resulted in a doubling of marketing spending on brand building in the last five years. Christine Moorman and Lauren Kirby of the CMO Survey explain:

> Brands compete for distracted consumers' attention and wallet share in a noisy marketplace, characterized by new incumbents, business transformation, a 24/7 news and media cycle and millions of digital platforms. Thus, brand building is critical to counteract the lack of simple, consistent ways to reach consumers as individual digital platforms and techniques rise and fall in popularity. The No. 1 use for social media reported in the February survey was brand awareness and brand building.[7]

Social media is an excellent tool for creating and growing brand communities. Beyond brand building social media is also seen as a valuable tool for acquiring new customers, introducing new products and services, retaining current customers, offering promotions, engaging with employees, and marketing research.[8]

But how do you navigate all the changes, challenges, and cross-discipline uses of social media? A successful social media strategy needs to be built upon a framework that is unique to the brand, its products, services, and customers. You must start in a place rooted in a brand's distinct situation and drive a strategy of choosing social platforms and creating content based on business objectives and target audience. Otherwise you are simply chasing 1.9 billion different people's top social media tactics that may or may not work for your organization and situation. Only when a unique strategy is developed from the beginning will those tips and lists become useful by focusing only on the advice and insight that applies.[9]

In the consumer digital revolution analytics is more important than ever, but so is creativity. Research-based theories are needed, but they must be put into the context of professional practice. Practice must be explained, but not from one discipline's perspective. Integration of academic disciplines and business departments is required. What follows is a cross-discipline field guide to social media strategy. It draws from the best in academic research and professional practice cutting through the hype to set a strategic mindset and take advantage of the exciting opportunities of social media. Whether you are a business, marketing, advertising, public relations, or communications professional, or a professor or student, you'll learn the context, process, and tools needed to create a comprehensive, unique, and practical social media strategy.

Social Media Strategy: Marketing, Advertising, and Public Relations in the Consumer Revolution is a blueprint for the practice of business and communications in a digital world where the consumer has taken control. The game has changed and you need a new plan. The consumer revolution is not about giving up or giving in; it is about adjusting methods to effect change, support traditional efforts, and leverage consumer influence for the good of the brand whether it's a small business, large corporation, or nonprofit organization. Spending on social media is expected to double over the next five years.[10] Ensure you have a solid social media strategy to invest it wisely.

How to Use This Book

This book consists of fifteen chapters divided into five parts. Part I (chapters 1–3) provides an overview of social media. It defines the topic, looks at its scale, and covers the background and context for how we arrived at our current situation of a maturing social media landscape. It explains how this has led to new career opportunities and new organizational structures. It sets a theoretical foundation with various concepts from social capital and social influence to social proof and social presence. Part I also explores the shift in communications and technology that has led to a rise in consumer influence and a decline in mass media, and how business and communications professionals must respond with a shift in perspective from control to engagement in an increasingly mobile first environment.

Part II (chapters 4–6) then explains a systematic process for creating a social media strategy and integrating it into traditional business or nonprofit marketing, advertising, and public relations practice. It explains how to translate personal social media use into strategic social media use for a brand. This part covers business objectives, target audience, social media audits, big ideas, the creative process, and storytelling. It also explains the changes in the purchase funnel and buyer's journey, the role of paid social media and integration across disciplines in integrated marketing communications. It sets up the importance of analytics, data-driven decision making, and having a measurement plan with details such as connecting social media ad campaign objectives to social media ad buying options. The outline for a social media strategic plan is introduced as guideposts for completion of the strategic process working toward a final strategy in chapter 14. The theoretical backgrounds for market segmentation, observational research, and communication disciplines are explored.

Part III (chapters 7–10) explores eight categories of social media: social networks and social messaging; blogs and forums; microblogging and media sharing; geosocial; live video; ratings and reviews; social bookmarking; and social knowledge. Within each category the top three social platforms are defined and explained, including users, content, possible strategies, and paid social media opportunities. The objective is to select the right social media channels for brand objectives, strategy, and target audience. The purpose is also to explore social media platforms and consider options that the reader may not be personally active on. These chapters expand notions of social media from just the popular social networks to include all forms of social media that impact organizations.

Part IV (chapters 11–13) looks at how social media is affecting and influencing multiple areas of business and organizations outside of the marketing and communications silos. It explains five strategies for the marketing, advertising, and public relations functions to integrate with other organizational departments for social media success. This includes social media insights, crowdsourcing, content marketing, influencer marketing, social care, and social selling. This part also covers related topics such as personas, user-generated content, advocates and brand ambassadors, reputation management, and crisis communication. Theoretical concepts are considered including competency traps and consumer-brand relationships.

Part V (chapters 14–15) pulls every concept and process together to create and implement a complete social media plan or campaign for a business or organization. Chapter 14 provides an outline for writing a comprehensive social media strategic plan and explains the importance of selling the plan to key stakeholders through education and presentation. This part also adds key elements for strategy execution such as best practices in content creation, content calendar, social media metrics, social media budgeting, and artificial intelligence. The final chapter adds key implementation considerations in the area of social media law, regulation, and ethics including consumer data privacy and security. Positive and negative societal impacts of social media are considered. This final part also addresses the importance of and a system for personal branding considering social media etiquette and professionalism. Related theoretical concepts of uses and gratification and elaboration likelihood model are included.

Each chapter follows a similar format with a chapter "Preview" providing personal context and strategic insight to introduce the topic, "Theoretically Speaking" sections dig deeper into theory behind practice, and "Mini Cases" show theory and strategy applied in brand case studies. Graphs, tables, charts, and photos throughout bring examples and research to life while providing valuable templates and guides for practical application. Each chapter ends with a "Chapter Checklist" to guide updates into how stats, strategies, or options may have changed since publication. "Key Concepts" provides an ordered summary review of key terms defined in the chapter. Questions for discussion and exercises provide opportunities to explore topics further as discussion prompts or written assignments. More than one hundred figures are included throughout the text to illustrate social media use, statistics, and concepts with photos, tables, and graphs.

Links to software training courses, certifications, and badges are embedded in relevant chapters for additional applied learning of technology skills valuable to employers. These optional resources provide an opportunity for customized earning by student interests or instructor course objectives. For example, one student or instructor may want to focus on additional content creation training and certifications such as Adobe Creative Cloud or YouTube Creator Academy while others may be interested in more in-depth analytical or digital marketing training with Google Analytics Academy or Salesforce Trailhead CRM training. Some may want to emphasize a specific social media monitoring and listening platform. Therefore, links to software training and certification such as Hootsuite Academy, HubSpot Academy, Cision University Program, and Meltwater Masterclass are included. A summary of social media and digital marketing training and certification options is included at the end of the Social Media Tools and Resources list in appendix B.

The Social Plan (parts 1–15) functions as a built-in workbook that provides a consistent overall assignment throughout the book, applying key concepts to current professional situations as they are learned. The Social Plan pulls all theories, concepts, strategies, and examples together into a unified step-by-step process to develop a social media strategy plan and presentation for a brand, product, service, or organization. Each step can serve as weekly assignments or can be combined into a smaller number of reports leading up to a final plan or social media campaign.

Appendix A presents a three-part method to developing, presenting, and executing a social media strategy plan or campaign. It is a condensed version of the individual chapter plan sections organized into an easy-to-follow three-step process. Appendix B concludes with a categorized list with description and links to online social media tools and resources to be used in the planning process and for social media implementation. Finally, an alphabetical listing and definition of key social media–related terms is provided in a glossary, and the index provides an easy guide to find where keywords are located in the chapters.

The result is fifteen relatively concise chapters explaining the core principles and main concepts of social media aimed at developing the skills needed to plan, execute, and measure social media strategies and tactics in professional practice. Important theoretical foundations, scholarly influence, and societal impact are presented throughout, but the focus remains on training students to think like social media professionals practicing social media on the job.

For more resources related to the book including downloadable templates and guides plus updates on current social media stats, strategies, platforms, and resources, visit the website Post Control Marketing at http://www.postcontrolmarketing.com. For instructor support materials including chapter outlines, test banks, templates, guides, example assignments, example syllabi, PowerPoint slides, eBook, and decision-based case briefs, visit the publisher website at https://rowman.com.

Notes

1. Google search, "Social Media Tips," accessed November 22, 2019, https://www.google.com/search?client=firefox-b-1-d&q=social+media+tips.

2. Google search, "Social Media Tips," accessed August 22, 2017, https://www.google.com/search?safe=strict&q=social+media+tips&oq=social+media+tips&gs_l=psy-ab.3..0i7i30k1l3j0i20k1.7312.7832.0.8438.2.2.0.0.0.0.117.190.1j1.2.0....0...1.1.64.psy-ab..0.2.190...0.CU7jy_LDakE.

3. Tom Devaney and Tom Stein, "The Best Social Media Marketing Tells a Story," Forbes.com, July 23, 2013, http://www.forbes.com/sites/capitalonespark/2013/07/23/the-best-social-media-marketing-tells-a-story.

4. "Top 6 Social Media Marketing Tips for Businesses," Digiblog.in, October 17, 2019, digiblog.in/blog/top-6-social-media-marketing-tips.

5. Lisa Mahapatra, "Social Media Marketing: How Do Top Brands Use Social Platforms? [Charts]," IBTimes.com, August 9, 2013, http://www.ibtimes.com/social-media-marketing-how-do-top-brands-use-social-platforms-charts-1379457.

6. Isobel Asher Hamilton, "TikTok Hit 1.5 Billion Downloads, and Is Still Outperforming Instagram," BusinessInsider.com, November 18, 2019, https://www.businessinsider.com/tiktok-hits-15-billion-downloads-outperforming-instagram-2019-11.

7. Christine Moorman and Lauren Kirby, "Top Marketing Trends of the Decade," CMOSurvey.com, August 15, 2019, https://cmosurvey.org/wp-content/uploads/sites/15/2019/08/2019CMOsurvey_ebook.pdf.

8. Moorman and Kirby, "Top Marketing Trends."

9. Keith Quesenberry, "There Are No Top 10 Best Rules for Social Media Marketing," Post ControlMarketing.com (blog), August 26, 2013, http://www.postcontrolmarketing.com/?p=1270.

10. Christine Moorman, "The CMO Survey February 2019 Results," CMOSurvey.com, accessed November 22, 2019, https://cmosurvey.org/results/february-2019/.

PART

I

An Overview of
Social Media

The Scale and Scope of Social Media

The old paradigm was pay to play. Now you get back what you authentically put in. You've got to be willing to play to play.[1]

—Alex Bogusky

PREVIEW

Think about how often you access Wikipedia. How many articles did you view this week? Take a quick look at your web history and see the number of Wikipedia pages you have visited in the past month. Wikipedia is one of the most popular websites on the internet whether accessed through desktop or mobile. Many of us today simply take access to this information for granted, not even thinking about how that information is created and by whom. The truth is that Wikipedia is both social media sourced and a social media channel. Thus, it is appropriate to start a book on social media with mention of Wikipedia. This social encyclopedia is an enormous tool for students and professionals alike, yet professor William Badke appropriately summed up the often-contradicting opinions about the resource saying, "Often banned by professors, panned by traditional reference book publishers and embraced by just about everyone else, Wikipedia marches on like a great beast."[2]

Wikipedia can be controversial because it somewhat replaces formal, professionally written, "for pay" encyclopedia publications. Some see it as a group of amateurs writing whatever they want, while others see it as an amazing collection of the wisdom of the crowd that is constantly fact-checked and continually changing to remain current. The truth is most likely somewhere in between. Ultimately, there needs to be a balance in use of Wikipedia. A total ban ignores reality and a valuable source of information. Yet everyone, professional, professor, or student, should also be mindful about an over-reliance on any single reference source.

The American Library Association expressed concern about this over-reliance after the Wikipedia Black Out Day in 2012 when a student was quoted as saying, "If Wikipedia is gone, I don't even know how to research anymore." Over the years various governments have also perceived Wikipedia to be a threat. In 2017 Turkey's communications ministry blocked access to Wikipedia, citing a law for protection of public order, national security, and the well-being of the public.[3] As of 2019 Wikipedia is still fighting to return to Turkey in the country's high court and launched a social media campaign with the hashtag #WeMissTurkey.[4] While some seek to ban or limit Wikipedia, others see great potential. Many publishers can now imagine the upside of Wikipedia linking to their content as an opportunity to reach greater audiences.[5] Whatever a person's opinion about Wikipedia and social media in general, one thing is certain: social media is here to stay and will only grow in scale and scope.

The Rise of Social Media

There is something unique about social media. Alex Bogusky of the Crispin Porter + Bogusky advertising agency described it as playing versus paying for attention and reach. What is social media? Wikipedia explains that **social media** is interactive computer-mediated technologies that facilitate the creation and sharing of information, ideas, and other forms of expression via virtual communities and networks. As noted, Wikipedia is social media itself and can change over time as people add, subtract, correct, and generally debate over entries. Click on the "Talk" button next to "Article" in the top left of a Wikipedia entry and you will find discussion about the entry. For example, on March 6, 2012, one contributor said that the social media entry was "in a *dreadful* state. It is pretty much unreadable at the moment." The social media Wikipedia entry has been edited more than two hundred times by just under two hundred editors since it first appeared on July 9, 2006. Click on the "View History" tab (at the top right of the page next to Search) to view a comprehensive list of revisions and dates.[6]

As the definition states, social media is all about creating and sharing information and ideas, whether it's Wikipedia entries or Facebook updates about favorite football teams, fabulous cheesecakes, and what famous people wore to an awards show. As more and more people created their own personal and professional content online, it began to grow in amount and importance comparable to corporate- or organization-produced content. As views of amateur content have increased over time, a transfer of power has occurred. Social media has risen in both amount and attention, shifting content from a conventional publisher-centric model to a more user-centric one.[7] **User-centric** means having more control, choices, or flexibility where the needs, wants, and limitations of the end user are taken into consideration.[8] This is a term that can apply to many industries and disciplines from media to marketing. Philip Kotler, Hermawan Kartajaya, and Iwan Setiawan in *Marketing 4.0* have in turn called for the practice of **human-centric marketing** where brands behave like humans treating customers as friends.[9]

This shift in power is especially evident in journalism. In the past, the main form of communication with a journalistic publication from consumer to publisher occurred through letters to the editor. Of those submitted letters, only a few would have been published. Now most publications enable blog-style commenting on their articles and enlist many more contributors to their publications through blog articles and commentary. Many personal blogs have risen to professional publication status and more and more people are getting their news from social media platforms. News is also now shared in social networks where comments, likes, and shares occur and are measured. News reporting and news dissemination have both shifted over time from traditional print, radio, and television.

In 2018, Pew Research Center reported that nearly two-thirds of adults in the United States (68 percent) got their news from social media channels such as Facebook, YouTube, and Twitter. This was up from 62 percent in 2016.[10] In a Reuters Institute survey of thirty-eight countries across the globe, more than half prefer to access news through search engines, social media, or news aggregators with younger audiences more likely to use social media. Across all adults in the United States, 46 percent use social media as a news source, with 45 percent in Australia and 40 percent in the United Kingdom.[11] Increasing reliance on social media as a news source has raised concerns; some have questioned influence in US elections and the Brexit campaign in the United Kingdom. These issues will be discussed further in chapter 15, Social Media Law, Ethics, and Etiquette. For organizations, this means

Figure 1.1. Turning to social media for news impacts society and business in many ways.

© Tero Veslainen / iStock Photo

fewer opportunities for traditional public relations media outreach and traditional advertising placement. While consumers worldwide increasingly turn to social media for news, 40 to 50 percent are also using ad-blocking software.[12]

Social media has really changed the professional practice and business of journalism. Anthony Adornato, author of *Mobile and Social Media Journalism*, says, "The use of mobile and social media tools for gathering info, distributing stories, and engaging audiences, that's just what multimedia journalism is now."[13] Social proof has also become the judge of success; now each article can be measured for social shares, views, and links. And each digital article becomes dependent on engagement, whether as comments on the article itself or on social channels where the article is shared or comments are shared to the journalist's social channels. While journalists must be more versatile, news stories increasingly are being sourced to guest contributors and the number of journalists are being cut. Employment in US newsrooms dropped 25 percent in the last decade, with the number of newsroom employees in newspapers dropping 47 percent.[14] Increased social engagement with professional journalists and amateur journalism has often made it increasingly difficult to determine fact from opinion.

Beyond news we also have turned our attention to social media as direct sources of information. We already discussed the influence of Wikipedia and how it is sourced, monitored, and edited by the crowd. WikiLeaks is another example of the rising influence of social media. **WikiLeaks** is an international nonprofit that collects news leaks and classified media by anonymous sources and publishes them on its website. WikiLeaks has been very controversial but has influenced major events and situations around the world. For example, WikiLeaks obtained and published information that had significant implications with regard to the 2016 US presidential election campaign, impacting candidates Bernie Sanders, Hillary Clinton, Donald Trump, and others.[15]

In early 2017 WikiLeaks published files revealing the CIA's secret cyber hacking tools, causing possible threats to national and global security.[16] By late spring 2017 a huge cyber attack occurred in the United Kingdom, Spain, and other European countries that spread globally. "WannaCrypt" blocked people from their data unless they paid a ransom and seriously hit the United Kingdom's National Health Service. It is believed that the malicious software was developed from emails stolen from the US National Security Agency and reportedly released on WikiLeaks.[17] WikiLeaks claims its own influence as being cited in more than twenty-eight thousand academic papers and US court filings, formal UN documents, the European Court of Human Rights, and UK courts. WikiLeaks is still under investigation as hackers associated with the organization are being summoned to testify before grand juries in the United States.[18] It is important to note that WikiLeaks is not affiliated with Wikipedia.[19]

From social network use and social news to social information sourcing, it appears that we have become a more social society. Yet it is important to note that the rise in new technology didn't create a rise in our desire for social interaction. Social interactions have always occurred. In the past, humans did not need social networks to be social. We always found ways to socialize in community without technology. This desire was expressed well in the movie *Castaway*, when the main character is stranded alone on an island after a plane crash. Craving social interaction, he makes friends with and begins talking to a volleyball named Wilson.[20]

What makes social media different are the software applications that have built communities and networks so that social interactions can now occur virtually and in real time.[21] Some research has even indicated that we may prefer "virtual" communication through social media because it requires less emotional involvement, cognitive effort, and brain activation.[22] However, this shift did take time and an evolution of technology. The big rise in social commentary online did not occur with the invention of the internet or even the first version of the World Wide Web. It happened specifically with the advancement in features and capabilities called Web 2.0.

Early internet communication was limited to passive viewing of content on static pages. Companies and organizations created web pages, but they were more like digital brochures. Businesses and organizations wrote and designed corporate websites that they planned would remain the same for the next several years. Interactivity was limited to email on a contact page. However, a shift in capability happened in the first few years of the twenty-first century that changed everything. This shift was so dramatic it was called Web 2.0, a term popularized in 2004 by open-source software advocate Tim O'Reilly and implying a comprehensive new software release of the World Wide Web, taking it from version 1.0 to version 2.0.

Yet the web's inventor, Tim Berners-Lee, says there was no technical update to the web. He argues that he always envisioned the web as "a collaborative media, a place where we could all meet and read and write." What did change was the development of web browser technologies such as Ajax and JavaScript that enabled live two-way communication, plus Flash, which brought multimedia audio and video content to websites. Whether a person sides with O'Reilly or Berners-Lee, **Web 2.0** is the common term used to designate the collective technology changes in the way web pages were made and used that took them beyond the static pages of earlier websites.[23]

Web 2.0 takes on many forms such as social networking sites, blogs, wikis, forums, photo- and video-sharing sites, collaborative tagging, social bookmarking, ratings, and reviews. Today Web 2.0 has even grown to include live streaming video on platforms such as Twitter, Facebook, Instagram, LinkedIn, and Twitch plus augmented reality experiences with 3D lenses in Snapchat.[24] For Tim O'Reilly's early list of Web 1.0 versus Web 2.0 examples, see table 1.1.[25] Please note that his list today has been revised and can be viewed on the O'Reilly Media website.

Social media depends on web-based technologies and now mobile technology to create highly interactive platforms for co-creating, sharing, discussing, and modifying user-generated content. These universal changes have significantly affected the way individuals, communities, and organizations communicate.[26] The old model of larger organizations communicating to a mass number of individuals started to break down with Web 2.0. Suddenly individuals had a way to communicate directly to other individuals. They also had the potential to skip traditional gatekeepers to reach a mass audience. For businesses and organizations, this change was disruptive. As Web 2.0 expanded consumer influence, the communication power of enterprise and traditional publications diminished. This raised great concerns for marketing communications professionals.

Erich Joachimsthaler and David Aaker foresaw the problem in a 1997 *Harvard Business Review* article titled "Building Brands without Mass Media." Even before social media, the

Table 1.1. Tim O'Reilly's List of Web 1.0 vs. Web 2.0 Examples

Web 1.0		Web 2.0
DoubleClick	vs.	Google AdSense
Ofoto	vs.	Flickr
Akamai	vs.	BitTorrent
mp3.com	vs.	Napster
Britannica Online	vs.	Wikipedia
personal websites	vs.	blogging
evite	vs.	upcoming.org and EVDB
domain name speculation	vs.	search engine
page views	vs.	optimization
screen scraping	vs.	cost per click
publishing	vs.	web services
content management	vs.	participation
systems	vs.	wikis
directories (taxonomy)	vs.	tagging ("folksonomy")
stickiness		syndication

Source: James Governor, Duane Nickull, and Dion Hinchcliffe, "Chapter 3—Web 2.0 Architectures," *Web 2.0 Architectures* (Sebastopol: O'Reilly Media, 2009), accessed February 16, 2015, http://oreilly.com/web2/excerpts/web2-architectures/chapter-3.html#tim_apostrophy_s_list_of _web_1.0_vs._web.

authors were concerned with rising media fragmentation and increased communication channels that enabled consumers to bypass advertising for entertainment and news. They sought alternative methods to brand building beyond mass-media advertising.[27] With the rise of social media, Joachimsthaler and Aaker's concerns have come true.

The psychological basis of social media adds further context to the rise of social media. Multiple disciplines including sociology have studied the idea of social capital. Different disciplines and scholars have approached social capital theory in diverse ways and definitions vary based on context. For the purposes of social media strategy, a broad definition will be used based on sociologist Pierre Bourdieu's theory of capital. Bourdieu saw capital as not simply an economic concept but also related to cultural, social, and symbolic relationships. **Social capital theory** is a broad concept recognizing the power of an individual to exert influence on a group or individual to mobilize resources.[28]

With the advent of social media networks you can see how social capital becomes more important. This is especially apparent when looking at social media counts such as followers, likes, views, and subscribers where an individual can amass a larger group of people upon whom to exert influence through social networks. This is further explained through the concept of **social influence**, which is any process from which a person's attitudes, opinions, beliefs, or behavior are altered or controlled by a form of social communication.[29] More directly, the theory of social capital and concept of social influence have been applied to social media through the concept of social proof. **Social proof** is the concept that if larger numbers of people endorse something then other people are more likely to believe that it

Figure 1.2. Social capital, social influence, and social proof help explain social media.

© Just Stock / iStock Photo

is correct, influencing their attitudes and actions.[30] In social networks where organizations depend upon individuals sharing brand messages, literal social proof counts become important. Not only do they measure influence, but they also help increase it.

As Alex Bogusky indicates in his quote at the beginning of the chapter, marketers and advertisers cannot buy attention in a social media channel as they can for a traditional advertising channel. Even with the paid social media options available today, marketers, advertisers, and public relations professionals can only buy "reach" into some social media channels—they cannot buy attention. The content still must be valuable or good enough to draw consumers' engagement and to generate further reach through additional sharing. An uninteresting social media post boosted or paid to appear in someone's newsfeed scrolls by faster than a thirty-second TV commercial. Only brand content of value, whether marketer- or consumer-generated, is effective in gaining attention in social media. As Bogusky says, "You get back what you authentically put in."[31]

The Size of Social Influence

As people's attention and time have shifted to online activity, organizations have been able to monitor consumer actions and decisions. The increase in digital activity has increased a marketer's ability to collect consumer data. **Big data** refers to massive amounts of data so large or complex they are difficult to process using traditional data processing applications. It includes data such as transactions, email, messages, activity logs, and social media text.[32] Big data has become a buzzword in recent years for good reason. According to industry reports, by 2013, 90 percent of all of the world's data was created in the previous two years and of that, 80 percent was content created from social media sources such as Facebook, Instagram, and YouTube.[33] The entire digital universe is expected to reach forty-four zetta-bytes in 2020. That is forty times more bytes than there are stars in the observable universe or 44,000,000,000,000 gigabytes.[34]

Not only has the amount of information collected been dramatic, but this data has also dramatically impacted business. A *Forbes* global survey titled "Data Driven and Digitally Savvy: The Rise of the New Marketing Organization" found organizations that are leaders in data-driven marketing are almost three times more likely to have increased revenue (55 percent versus 20 percent) than their laggard counterparts. The authors of the study argue that increased data and analysis is creating a growing advantage gap between data-driven and traditional marketing approaches.[35]

The amount of digital data is growing fast, and so are the social media platforms that are creating much of it. One illustration of the pace of growth is to compare how long different media took to reach 50 million users. For example, it took radio thirty-eight years to reach 50 million users. The pace quickened with television. After TV was introduced in the 1950s, it took thirteen years to reach 50 million users. Yet today the pace of adoption in social media is tremendous. After Facebook's introduction, it only took the social network three and a half years for 50 million users to open accounts.[36]

Facebook has surpassed two billion monthly active users, a number reached in just thirteen years.[37] But this amazing growth is not limited to Facebook alone. Instagram has reached more than one billion monthly users. Instagram users doubled from 500 million in just two years from 2016 and 2018.[38] YouTube has more than two billion monthly active users[39] and Twitter has more than 321 million users.[40] Snapchat has grown to more than 306 million users in less than five years.[41] Business has become very social as well, considering LinkedIn now has more than 303 million monthly active users and it grew at a faster rate than any other social platform in 2019. And these social platforms are driving a significant number of people to organization websites. Social media has grown to drive between 20 and 30 percent of referral traffic becoming just as important as search.[42] **Referral traffic** is the number of website visits of people clicking on a hyperlink from another website. Referral traffic to websites is important; it sends potential customers to brand websites. Having more referral links can also help you rank higher in search engine results pages such as Google to drive more search traffic to your website.[43]

The enormous size of social media and the data it generates presents an immense opportunity. A study conducted by Forbes Insights and Turn (see figure 1.3) found that social media data is an important part of data-driven marketing campaigns. Demographic data drives most marketing efforts (62 percent), but social metrics (34 percent) are now being collected ahead of traditional brand surveys (31 percent) and even **customer rela-tionship management (CRM)** data (31 percent),[44] which uses systems to better manage data and interactions with customers and potential customers with a focus on long-term relationships.[45] Social media is integral to big data business practice. As indicated in the

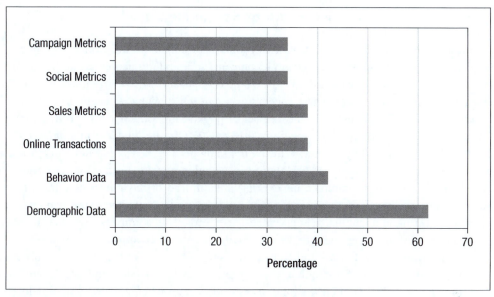

Figure 1.3. Types of Data Collected for Data-Driven Marketing

Source: Paul Alfieri, "Data Driven and Digitally Savvy: The Rise of the New Marketing Organization," Forbes Insights and Turn, 2015, https://images.forbes.com/forbesinsights/StudyPDFs/Turn-The_Rise_of_the_New_Marketing _Organization-REPORT.pdf.

Forbes report, the companies that are taking advantage of social media research are gaining a competitive advantage for their actions.

Research into electronic word-of-mouth (eWOM) suggests that it is seen as a reliable source of information, significantly affects the perceived value of a firm's offering, and has a direct relationship with loyalty intentions.[46] In other words, social media supercharges the potential of word-of-mouth and word-of-mouth is one of the most effective business tools. Business and communications professionals have always known this, but up until the creation of social media, word-of-mouth simply did not scale. Today we have seen consumer-produced YouTube videos garner views once only obtainable through a TV media buy, and some consumer-created blogs have monthly subscriptions larger than top publications such as *Time* magazine and the *New York Times*. Word-of-mouth on Web 2.0 scales.

Liquid Plumr®'s "Will it clog?" campaign demonstrated the power of word-of-mouth winning a Shorty Award for multi-platform partnership. The brand found that top-of-mind awareness in the category was dominated by competitor Drano® and sales of Liquid Plumr® were not growing despite category growth. After researching the consumer's path to purchase they discovered that when facing a clog, consumers searched Google to find DIY solutions that were not fixing the problem and then they would go to the store to buy Drano® because it was top of mind. The campaign tapped popular YouTubers VAT19, to produce challenges of the product facing common clogs. The YouTube videos were promoted on the brand website, in display ads, a promoted trend on Twitter, and TV commercial integration with Jimmy Kimmel Live. The campaign generated more than 75 million impressions and produced the brand's best market share growth in years.[47]

The Maturing of Social Media

Obviously, social media is not a fad and has become mainstream. Of the world's 7.6 billion people, 57 percent are on the internet and 45 percent, or 3.5 billion people, are active social media users, a number that grew from just 37 percent in 2017. As the number of global internet users increases, so does social media use with each growing 9 percent in 2018. In the United States, 70 percent of adults use social networking sites, but for the first time this number did not grow year to year from 2018 to 2019. In the United Kingdom, active social media users grew only 2 percent during the same period.[48] This indicates a maturing of social media use as total growth has slowed in certain countries, putting more pressure on individual platforms to compete for existing users instead of relying on new users for growth. A larger majority of new user growth could shift to less saturated world markets.

This maturing and shifting of social media user growth is confirmed in a Facebook report announcing 8 percent user growth in 2019. Upon further inspection it is revealed that growth in the United States and Canada was only 1 percent and Europe saw only 2 percent growth. In contrast, Facebook new user growth was 12 percent in the Asia-Pacific.[49] Many thought Snapchat would lose a lot of users to Instagram when it added Snapchat-like features. Instagram did grow but Snapchat users have remained consistent. In a social media maturity stage, it seems that people may add new social platforms but are keeping their existing ones. In fact, the average global social media user age sixteen to thirty-four years has nine social media accounts. Even fifty-five to sixty-four-year-olds now have an average of five social media accounts.[50] Another sign of the maturing of social media comes from

Figure 1.4. Social media users of all ages now average 5 to 9 social media accounts.

© Big Tuna Online / iStock Photo

eMarketer's 2019 Time Spent with Media Report. US daily time spent with social media fell one minute in 2018 after a combined increase of thirteen minutes in 2016 and 2017. eMarketer expects daily time spent with social media to remain flat at one hour, fifteen minutes through 2021.[51] This means that social networks will become even more competitive with each other for users' time.

As marketing, advertising, and public relations professionals it is now becoming more important to focus not only on total users and demographics of social platform users, but also the frequency of use on these platforms. A new statistic to consider over monthly active users and user demographics is daily active users. The question to ask may no longer be "What social media platform is my target audience on?" but instead "What social media platforms are my target audience most active in?" As a result, when looking at individual social media platforms later in the book we will not only consider monthly active users (MAUs), but also put those numbers into more context by considering daily active users (DAUs). **Monthly active users (MAUs)** is the total number of unique people who have interacted with an app or website in a month.[52] **Daily active users (DAUs)** is the total number of unique people who interact with a an app or web page in day.[53]

Table 1.2 shows a comparison of monthly active users to daily active users worldwide for top social media networks. Looking at daily engagement rate is useful to see which social channels have the most active users. Globally the social platforms with the most users in order are (1) Facebook, (2) YouTube, and (3) Instagram. But if you look at global daily engagement, the top social platforms in order are (1) Snapchat, (2) Facebook, and (3) Twitter. Yet only looking at engagement rate for all global users can be deceiving. Table 1.2 also adds demographics and narrows by specific country use. The last column shows daily engagement

Table 1.2. Comparison of Monthly Active Users to Daily Active Users in Top Social Networks

Social Network	Monthly Active Users	Daily Active Users	Overall Daily Engagement Rate	Generation Z Daily Engagement Rate
Facebook	2.4 billion	1.5 billion	66.2 percent	34 percent
YouTube	2 billion	99 million	49.5 percent	63 percent
Instagram	1 billion	500 million	50.0 percent	65 percent
Snapchat	306 million	203 million	66.3 percent	51 percent
Twitter	250 million	139 million	55.6 percent	24 percent

Sources: Simon Kemp, "Digital in 2019," wearesocial.com, 2019, https://wearesocial.com/global-digital-report-2019; Facebook, "Number of Daily Active Facebook Users Worldwide as of 2nd Quarter 2019 (in Millions)," Chart, July 24, 2019, Statista, accessed September 13, 2019, https://www.statista.com/statistics/346167/facebook-global-dau/; Omnicore, "YouTube by the Numbers: Stats, Demographics & Fun Facts," Omncore.com, September 5, 2019, https://www.omnicoreagency.com/youtube-statistics/; Amy Gesenhues, "Mary Meeker: Social Media Usage Is Flat Globally, Mobile Ad Spend Continues to Climb," MarketingLand.com, June 12, 2019, https://marketingland.com/mary-meeker-social-media-usage-is-flat-globally-mobile-ad-spend-continues-to-climb-262403; Snap Inc., "Number of Daily Active Snapchat Users from 1st Quarter 2014 to 2nd Quarter 2019 (in Millions)," Chart, July 23, 2019, Statista, accessed September 13, 2019, https://www.statista.com/statistics/545967/snapchat-app-dau/; Twitter, "Number of Monetizable Daily Active Twitter Users (mDAU) Worldwide from 1st Quarter 2017 to 2nd Quarter 2019 (in Millions)," Chart, July 26, 2019, Statista, accessed September 13, 2019, https://www.statista.com/statistics/970920/monetizable-daily-active-twitter-users-worldwide/; eMarketer, "Most Popular Social Networks and Apps According to Gen Z Social Media Users in the United States as of January 2019, Based on Daily Usage," Chart, August 16, 2019, Statista, accessed September 13, 2019, https://www.statista.com/statistics/306947/us-teens-social-media-apps-dau/.

by Generation Z (thirteen to twenty-one-year-old) social media users in the United States. The highest daily engagement for US Gen Z users in order are Instagram, YouTube, and Snapchat. In contrast, the most popular social networks accessed by US moms in order are Facebook, Pinterest, and then Instagram.[54] As you can see there is no one strategy for success in social media. One platform or technique is not the answer. The best social media strategy must be created uniquely based on your organization's specific business objectives, target audiences, and geographic markets.

Another sign of the maturing of social media is the increase in spending on paid social media. Social media used to be thought of as "free marketing." This is no longer the case if you want to remain effective and drive results. While use of social media marketing in the United States barely rose just 1 percent in the past two years (90 percent to 91 percent),[55] spending on social media advertising rose 48 percent ($18.6 billion to $34.9 billion).[56] An example of what a maturing social media strategy looks like is the Fortune 100 company John Deere. They had been using social media effectively for eight years. Yet social was still seen by management as "free marketing," where the brand would post all the content they had, when they had it, on all their existing social channels. In more recent years this approach to social started seeing diminished returns. In Twitter the amount of content they pushed out increased by 33 percent, but engagement dropped 33 percent and their organic reach eroded to just .001 percent.

Recognizing the maturing of social media, they advanced their strategy. Instead of using social to saturate their audience with the same content on the same channels, they are now adding social channels and using paid social to target the right audiences at the right time in the right social platforms. They have also expanded their social strategy, adding employee advocacy, executive communication, user-generated content, 24/7 social customer service, and influencer marketing. They are moving beyond the free marketing mindset and making the business case for social media connecting it to business objectives and using analytics to measure outcomes. Jen Hartmann, the public relations and social media manager at John Deere, says, "we're a 180 year old company. If we're going to be around for the next 180 years, we have to continue introducing the latest technologies and innovations."[57]

This maturing is also captured in a *Marketing Land* series, "Welcome to the next era of social media marketing." The author, Amy Gesenhues, says, "if brands want to thrive in this new era of social advertising, they will have to recognize conversations as only one piece of the puzzle." In this new era user growth has slowed, paid social is evolving to be more competitive, machine learning is optimizing campaigns, consumers are expecting more creative that they can connect with, messaging is driving more one-to-one relationships, and social commerce is exploding, putting more pressure on delivering a unique customer experience via social channels. Social media strategy has become more important than ever.[58] Social media author and consultant Jay Baer says, "If your social media strategy is older than a year, you don't have a strategy."[59]

Despite recent backlashes against social media, privacy concerns, and calls for deleting accounts, it looks as if social media will most likely continue to mature instead of decline and remain an important part of any organization's strategy for success. As an article in *Psychology Today* by Liraz Margalit indicates, "digital communication is so often easier than communicating face-to-face."[60] Social media is ubiquitous and has reached mass appeal. To

MINI CASE

Kony 2012

Perhaps no other case study demonstrates both the enormous potential and possible pitfalls of social media success better than what happened to the organization Invisible Children upon releasing their video KONY 2012 on YouTube. In only six days it reached one hundred million views and more than fifty thousand comments to become the most viral video in history.[a] This internet-released documentary reached Hollywood blockbuster distribution in less than a week.[b] And it had the support of Hollywood-caliber stars such as Rihanna, Taylor Swift, Justin Bieber, Oprah Winfrey, and Kim Kardashian without any influencer marketing payouts.

The thirty-minute documentary told the story of Joseph Kony, an African warlord who has been kidnapping and killing citizens in his country for more than two decades. The film urged people to support the nonprofit and help the cause. A big response would seem like a blessing; however, the response was so enormous that the organization's email system broke and the computer system crashed, locking its sales force out of the online store. Also, due to the tremendous rise in buzz, Invisible Children cofounder Jason Russell flew nonstop between media appearances, managing only two hours of sleep in four days.

The organization did benefit with more than triple its previous year's revenue, but the instantaneous fame and pressure ended up being too much to bear for Russell.[c] The same buzz that can spread a message so quickly can also draw harsh and very public criticism. In less than two weeks, Russell had a highly publicized mental breakdown that took a toll on him and his family personally as well as the professional image of the entire organization. In the short term, the nonprofit greatly increased its efforts in Africa, but by 2014 the charity found itself in debt and struggling to survive.[d] By December of that year they officially announced that most of the staff and Jason Russell would stop working for the organization. The challenge of having an enormous viral hit is surviving the mass attention and then following up with something just as captivating to keep the momentum going.

[a] Todd Wasserman, "'KONY 2012' Tops 100 Million Views, Becomes the Most Viral Video in History [STUDY]," Mashable.com, March 12, 2012, http://mashable.com/2012/03/12/kony-most-viral.
[b] Derek Thompson, *Hit Makers: How to Succeed in an Age of Distraction* (New York: Penguin, 2017), 194.
[c] Claire Suddath, "'Kony 2012': Guerrilla Marketing," BusinessWeek.com, August 30, 2012, http://www.businessweek.com/articles/2012-08-30/kony-2012-guerrilla-marketing.
[d] Kristof Titeca and Matthew Sebastian, "Why Did Invisible Children Dissolve?" WashingtonPost.com, December 30, 2014, https://www.washingtonpost.com/news/monkey-cage/wp/2014/12/30/why-did-invisible-children-dissolve/?utm_term=.a73ed779c430.

many marketers, advertisers, and public relations professionals, this is still a scary thought because social media strategy is so very different from traditional communication in marketing. Social media cannot simply be added as another marketing communications outlet. Integrating social media requires an entire shift in mindset—one that is more oriented to the consumer or user. Philip Kotler, Hermawan Kartajaya, and Iwan Setiawan in *Marketing 4.0* describe this as a shift from value proposition messages to useful and valuable content.[61]

Social Media Change Leads to Opportunity

Marketing, advertising, and public relations practitioners can and should be excited about this change because it comes with increased capabilities and untapped opportunities. The shift to a user-centric model represents a huge opportunity for organizations that have struggled to buy awareness in the old, expensive, publisher-centric mass media model. In the past, budgets have been an overwhelming deciding factor in a brand's share of voice. A large advertising budget bought increased brand awareness. Today, big brands with small budgets, small businesses, startups, and nonprofits can use social media to help level the awareness playing field. Social media strategy can make a difference at almost any budget level. The viral spread via consumer views and shares plus the earned media opportunities that spread views and shares even further are what make a difference in driving visibility to reach mass audiences.[62] Even paid social media can be done on a small budget and is highly targeted and measurable.

Social media also makes traditional marketing, advertising, and public relations efforts more effective. Integration is key and running a marketing, advertising, or public relations plan with social media pays off in real business results. A study published in the *Journal of Marketing Research* found that electronic word-of-mouth by customers delivers nearly twice as much customer acquisition compared to traditional marketing.[63] Other research has proven social media's positive effect on sales through a synergistic effect when combined with traditional marketing actions. A study of a large, US consumer packaged-goods food company found that social media was especially effective in increasing sales when combined with

Figure 1.5. Viral spread via social networks levels the brand awareness playing field.

© Gremlin / iStock Photo

Broadcasting vs. Narrowcasting

An important concept to understand that represents the shift that has occurred with the consumer digital revolution is broadcasting and narrowcasting. **Broadcasting** is a general message delivered to a large group. **Narrowcasting** is a specialized message delivered to small group.[a] The traditional model for acquiring customers has been a broadcast approach relying heavily on mass media advertising. Brands generally know who their customers are and target messages based on broad categories of consumers such as age, income, or education. While a broadcast approach attracts what seems to be impressive large groups of customers, the value of that large group is usually fairly low. Why? Not everyone in the large group was the right fit for the brand product and service.

An alternative method of customer acquisition is a narrowcast approach. Instead of focusing on a broader target, customer narrowcasting goes further to identify the most valuable customer. This means not just identifying the customers who are most likely to be interested in the product, but the customers who are most likely to become your best customers who will purchase from your more frequently and be the most loyal. Many organizations with a customer relationship management system have the data available to identify key characteristics of customers who are more likely to spend more and purchase more often. Mike Ferranti, founder and CEO of online-marketing agency Endai Worldwide, calls these your highest value targets. With new digital technologies such as programmatic advertising, database marketing, and predictive analytics, narrowcasting is possible.[b] It is also made possible through social media by targeting messages to niche groups via hashtags, social network groups, forums, and blogs, and through influencers.

Narrowcasting is also more likely to be shared in social media. Research by Alixandra Barasch and Jonah Berger compared how audience size affected what people share. They found that narrowcasting encourages people to share content that is useful to the message recipient. When broadcasting messages to a larger group, people tend to focus on self. This tendency was found to apply whether the person was sharing with acquaintances or strangers. Both these conditions can apply in social media where consumers and brands can communicate in both narrowcasts (direct messages [DMs], messaging apps, private posts) and broadcasts (public posts on social apps and websites).[c]

Social media professionals can apply these insights by first identifying and targeting more niche audiences in social media. Then they can consider audience size in crafting messages. An example of this is when customers with brand service problems will often post public complaints as self-focus to broadcast their dissatisfaction. Then when the brand responds and wants to offer genuine help, the conversation often moves to other-focus in DM or messaging. Similarly, a happy customer will broadcast a public post about the product as self-focus for a group to see they are part of the brand community. Brands will normally first be other-focused, responding individually with a direct reply. Once a relationship is formed, the brand may ask the consumer for permission to share the post on a broader scale by republishing it on their brand account. Some brands today even pay to boost these customer posts to reach larger audiences in crowded social networks.

[a] "'Narrowcasting' vs. 'Broadcasting,'" Merriam-Webster.com, accessed November 20, 2019, https://www.merriam-webster.com/words-at-play/broadcasting-and-narrowcasting.

[b] Mike Ferranit, "Customer Value: Narrowcasting vs. Broadcasting," TargetMarketingMag.com, March 15, 2016, https://www.targetmarketingmag.com/post/customer-value-narrowcasting-vs-broadcasting/all/.

[c] Alixandra Barasch and Jonah Berger, "Broadcasting and Narrowcasting: How Audience Size Affects What People Share," *Journal of Marketing Research* 51, no. 3 (June 2014): 286–299.

in-store promotions and product sampling. Increased brand exposure and brand engagement with social media users helped to make consumers more responsive to timely marketing actions.[64] Integration of social media also helps improve business-to-business sales. A study in *Industrial Marketing Management* found that a salesperson's use of social media improved their communication and responsiveness, leading to improved customer satisfaction.[65]

How do you take advantage of social media's powerful benefits? All organizations, big brands, small startups, or nonprofits must learn to play a new game with new rules. Alex Bogusky reminds us that social media doesn't allow brands to buy their way in. Buying reach for a paid social media post is still a one-way conversation, which drops the word "social" from social media. Everyone must play the social media game by following a very different set of rules. What are those rules? That is what this book will lay out—a systematic process for ensuring strategic action in social media.

With millions of Google search results, there is no one "Top 10 Best Social Media Marketing Rules." Yet there is a shift in mindset and a strategic framework that can be followed to integrate social media into organizations to supercharge marketing, advertising, and public relations efforts and meet organizational goals. Success takes more than opening a lot of social media accounts. It is very tempting to jump into social media by opening accounts in every new social network and app, but even the largest enterprises don't have enough time and resources to win at every social media platform or channel. Like all marketing, strategy is needed to focus limited resources. Researching and developing a solid game plan is the only way to win. Take the time now to step back and see the strategic forest for the social media trees. Build a solid framework with a well-researched and thought-out social media plan. Don't head into this new marketing communications game without a new playbook. Play the right way and the rewards can be immense.

This is an exciting time to be a marketer, advertiser, public relations professional, or entrepreneur. Best-selling business-book author Seth Godin captured this excitement well when he said, "If you can make it clear to consumers that you have a better offer, it's infinitely easier to acquire a million customers than ever before."[66] Big data is a big opportunity. The scale and scope of social media are enormous, and it will only continue to grow. If marketing communications professionals learn to think differently and utilize social media correctly, they can exploit this scale and scope for the benefit of their organizations.

Theoretically Speaking:
Interactivity and Two-Way Communication

Professor John Deighton of Harvard Business School defines **interactive marketing** as the ability to address the customer, remember what the customer said, and then address the customer in a way that illustrates that the organization remembers what the customer told them.[67] Deighton's definition comes from the marketer's perspective, but what do consumers view as interactive? Researchers Sally McMillan and Jang-Sun Hwang tell us that study into interactivity has been defined by using multiple processes, but three elements tend to appear as the basis of a consumer's perceived interactivity of marketing and advertising communication: direction of communication, user control, and time.[68]

First, interactivity must enable two-way communication that provides mutual conversation and the ability to offer feedback. Other researchers, Brian Massey and Mark Levy, take this notion further, stating that interactivity provides interpersonal communication and a friendly interface that leads to positive word-of-mouth for companies.[69] Second, user control is also seen as a key characteristic of interactivity. In general, the web has given users this control through more content and navigation options than traditional media. Third, the perception of interactivity is important to consider. This perception is impacted by the time or the speed at which messages can be delivered. The longer a consumer waits for a response, the less interactive the communication is perceived to be. In *The Art of Human-Computer Interface Design*, Chris Crawford captures this thought, stating that interactivity means the computer does not inhibit the user by slowing communication.[70] Today this also means that the marketer is not slow to respond to the consumer.

As you integrate social media channels and strategy into traditional marketing, these three elements of interactivity should be considered. When comparing and analyzing marketing, advertising, and public relations strategies and options, consider how the decision will increase or decrease consumer perception in two-way communication, user control through options, and response time. This interactivity and interpersonal communication through social media can help build brand communities and create a brand culture that leads to positive word-of-mouth for businesses and organizations. **Brand community** is a group of people with social relations structured around being admirers of a brand.[71] The real power in social media is much more than simply providing connections to consumers. The real benefits come from building community through those connections.

To apply these theoretical concepts to real life, go on a social channel and directly engage with three competing brands of the product or service you may be purchasing soon. Monitor and record each brand's response under the categories of direction of communication, user control, and time. Did the brand respond (two-way communication) or not respond (one-way communication)? Are you offered multiple ways to communicate with the company that are convenient for you (user control)? How long did it take for them to respond (time)? How did difference in response change your perception of each brand and impact purchase intent?

Chapter 1 Checklist

Social media can change quickly. Visit Post Control Marketing (http://www.postcontrol marketing.com) for updates, but also use this chapter checklist to briefly check how social media statistics in this chapter have changed since publication.

- ✓ What is the current percentage of global social media users and users in the United States and other countries? Has growth slowed, stalled, or even declined?
- ✓ How have daily active users for top social media networks changed? What about for specific demographic and country users?
- ✓ How many social media accounts does the average user have? How has this changed among age groups?

SOCIAL PLAN PART 1

Discover and Explore

The first part of the social media plan is to become familiar with the types of social media and various social media features. Based on the definition of social media given in this chapter, search and identify various social media channels. Go beyond the well-known networks such as Facebook, YouTube, and Instagram. After identifying several digital social channels, explore the features unique to each and use those features to determine social media categories. In other words, what is the main activity on the platform? Why does it exist? Finally, provide examples of how organizations could take advantage of each social channel. If you are not already on a channel, the best way to learn the most about a social media platform is to open an account and become a user. After exploration report the following:

1. Based on the definition of social media, list five different websites or apps that you feel are social media platforms. Explain why you chose each one.
2. Explore each as a social media marketing channel and explain the features, capabilities, and user characteristics.
3. Look at each channel's features, determine the main differences between each, and place the channels into categories such as photo sharing or news aggregation.
4. Explain three ways an organization could use each channel for marketing communication.

For a condensed version of the social plan see appendix A: Three-Part Social Plan.

KEY CONCEPTS

social media

user–centric

human–centric marketing

WikiLeaks

Web 2.0

social capital theory

social influence

social proof

big data

referral traffic

customer relationship management (CRM)

monthly active users (MAUs)

daily active users (DAUs)

broadcasting

narrowcasting

interactive marketing

brand community

QUESTIONS FOR DISCUSSION

1. Going back to the *KONY 2012* case study, what do you think Jason Russell and Invisible Children could have done differently to avoid the problems they had? What could they have done to ensure a better future for the organization?

2. Find a startup that has achieved enormous success. What role did social media play in the organization's rise? Did they use one or multiple social media platforms? Was social media the only method of promotion or was it integrated with traditional media?

3. Research a company that has gone out of business or is struggling. How did the organization's lack of social media integration or adaptation to changing technology contribute to its demise?

4. Ethics should be considered with every social media action. As discussed, big data can be very valuable, but are there right and wrong ways to use it? You work for a hospital system and your customer database includes health information such as illness diagnosis. Should you use that data to better target customers with specific services in Facebook ads?

ADDITIONAL EXERCISES

1. Visit the Wikipedia page "List of Social Networking Websites" (http://en.wikipedia.org/wiki/List_of_social_networking_websites). Scroll down the list. How many have you heard of? Start to think about which of these social networks would attract the potential customers of a specific brand, and where those potential customers may be most active. Think daily use versus monthly use. Are there social sites where customers are active, yet the brand is not?

2. How big is social media? Research the number of subscribers or viewers of traditional media such as top newspapers, magazines, and TV shows. Now look up the number of active users of the top social networks. How do the numbers compare? To take this analysis one step further, look up the cost of an advertisement to reach those viewers or readers in traditional media advertising. Compare that to the cost of a paid social media post to reach a similar number of viewers or users.

Notes

1. "Alex Bogusky Quotes and Sayings," Inspiring Quotes, accessed November 3, 2019, https://www.inspiringquotes.us/author/8817-alex-bogusky.

2. William Badke, "What to Do with Wikipedia," *Online* 32, no. 3 (2008): 48–50.

3. Can Sezer and David Dolan, "Turkey Blocks Access to Wikipedia," Reuters.com, April 29, 2017, http://www.reuters.com/article/us-turkey-security-internet-wikipedia-idUSKBN17V06Q.

4. Suzan Fraser, "Turkish High Court to Review Wikipedia Appeal against Ban," ABC News, September 11, 2019, https://abcnews.go.com/Technology/wireStory/turkish-high-court-review-wikipedia-appeal-ban-65533286.

5. Henrietta Thornton-Verma, "Reaching the Wikipedia Generation," *Library Journal* 137, no. 7 (2012): 32–40.

6. "Social Media," Wikipedia, last modified on September 11, 2019, http://en.wikipedia.org/wiki/Social_media.

7. Terry Daugherty, Matthew S. Eastin, and Laura Bright, "Exploring Consumer Motivations for Creating User-Generated Content," *Journal of Interactive Advertising* 8, no. 2 (2008): 16–25.

8. "Definition of User-centric," *PC Magazine*, accessed September 11, 2019, http://www.pcmag.com/encyclopedia/term/59259/user-centric.

9. Philip Kotler, Hermawan Kartajaya, and Iwan Setiawan, *Marketing 4.0: Moving from Traditional to Digital* (Hoboken, NJ: Wiley, 2017), 109.

10. Katerina Eva Matsa and Elisa Shearer, "News Use Across Social Media Platforms 2018," Pew Research Center, September 10, 2018, https://www.journalism.org/2018/09/10/news-use-across-social-media-platforms-2018/.

11. Nic Newman, Richard Fletcher, Antonis Kalogeropoulos, and Rasmus Kleis Nielsen, "Reuters Institute Digital News Report 2019," Reuters Institute, accessed September 12, 2019, https://reutersinstitute.politics.ox.ac.uk/sites/default/files/2019-06/DNR_2019_FINAL_0.pdf.

12. Irfan Ahmad, "Global Ad Blocking Behavior 2019 [Infographic]," SocialMediaToday.com, April 2, 2019, https://www.socialmediatoday.com/news/global-ad-blocking-behavior-2019-infographic/551716/.

13. Cited in Alexander Frandsen, "Journalism Schools Need to Focus on Data, Local News, Social Media and Business Models. Here Are Some That Are," Story Bench, May 16, 2019, https://www.storybench.org/journalism-schools-need-to-focus-on-data-local-news-social-media-and-business-models-here-are-some-that-are/.

14. Elizabeth Grieco, "U.S. Newsroom Employment Has Dropped by a Quarter Since 2008, with Greatest Decline in Newspapers," Pew Research Center, July 9, 2019, https://www.pewresearch.org/fact-tank/2019/07/09/u-s-newsroom-employment-has-dropped-by-a-quarter-since-2008/

15. "WikiLeaks," Wikipedia, last modified on August 18, 2019, https://en.wikipedia.org/wiki/WikiLeaks.

16. Greg Miller and Ellen Nakashima, "WikiLeaks Says It Has Obtained Trove of CIA Hacking Tools," WashingtonPost.com, March 7, 2017, https://www.washingtonpost.com/world/national-security/wikileaks-says-it-has-obtained-trove-of-cia-hacking-tools/2017/03/07/c8c50c5c-0345-11e7-b1e9-a05d3c21f7cf_story.html?utm_term=.def8e4e69819.

17. James Titcomb and Cara McGoogan, "Cyber Attack: Latest Evidence Indicates 'Phishing' Emails Not to Blame for Global Hack," *The Telegraph*, May 15, 2017, http://www.telegraph.co.uk/technology/2017/05/15/nhs-cyber-attack-latest-authorities-warn-day-chaos-ransomware/.

18. Rachel Weiner and Ellen Nakasima, "Hacker Linked to WikiLeaks Says He's Been Brought to Virginia for Testimony," WashingtonPost.com, September 3, 2019, https://www.washingtonpost.com/local/legal-issues/hacker-linked-to-wikileaks-says-hes-been-brought-to-virginia-for-testimony/2019/09/03/3a46600c-ccce-11e9-87fa-8501a456c003_story.html?noredirect=on.

19. "What Is WikiLeaks," WikiLeaks.org, November 3, 2015, https://wikileaks.org/What-is-Wikileaks.html.

20. *Cast Away* (2000), IMBd, accessed September 11, 2019, https://www.imdb.com/title/tt0162222/.

21. "Social Media," Wikipedia.

22. Liraz Margalit, "The Psychology Behind Social Media Interactions," *Psychology Today*, August 29, 2014, https://www.psychologytoday.com/blog/behind-online-behavior/201408/the-psychology-behind-social-media-interactions.

23. "Web 2.0," Techopedia.com, accessed August 30, 2019, https://www.techopedia.com/definition/4922/web-20.

24. Keith Quesenberry, "2019 Social Media Update: Top Social Media Channels By Category," May 20, 2019, PostControlMarketing.com, https://www.postcontrolmarketing.com/2019-social-media-update-top-social-media-channels-by-category/.

25. James Governor, Duane Nickull, and Dion Hinchcliffe, "Dissecting Web 2.0 Examples: Chapter 3—Web 2.0 Architectures," in *Web 2.0 Architectures* (Sebastopol, CA: O'Reilly Media, 2009), accessed September 11, 2017, http://oreilly.com/web2/excerpts/web2-architectures/chapter-3.html#tim_apostrophy_s_list_of_web_1.0_vs._web.

26. Lowell D'Souza, "What Does 'Interactive Marketing' Mean?" MarketingBones.com, April 2, 2010, http://marketingbones.com/what-does-interactive-marketing-mean.

27. Erich Joachimsthaler and David Aaker, "Building Brands without Mass Media," *Harvard Business Review*, January–February 1997, https://hbr.org/1997/01/building-brands-without-mass-media.

28. Tristan Claridge, "Bourdieu on Social Capital—Theory of Capital," SocialCapitalResearch.com, April 22, 2015, https://www.socialcapitalresearch.com/bourdieu-on-social-capital-theory-of-capital/.

29. "Social Influence," OxfordRefernce.com, accessed December 4, 2019, https://www.oxfordreference.com/view/10.1093/oi/authority.20110803100515197.

30. Margaret Rouse, "Social proof," WhatIsIt.TechTarget.com, January 2017, https://whatis.techtarget.com/definition/social-proof.

31. "Alex Bogusky Quotes and Sayings," Inspiring Quotes.

32. "Definition of: Big Data," *PC Magazine*, accessed September 12, 2019, http://www.pcmag.com/encyclopedia/term/62849/big-data.

33. Michele Nemschoff, "Social Media Marketing: How Big Data Is Changing Everything," CMSWire.com, September 16, 2013, http://www.cmswire.com/cms/customer-experience/social-media-marketing-how-big-data-is-changing-everything-022488.php.

34. Jeff Desjardins, "How Much Data Is Generated Each Day?" World Economic Forum, April 17, 2019, https://www.weforum.org/agenda/2019/04/how-much-data-is-generated-each-day-cf4bddf29f/.

35. "New Report Shows Data-Driven Marketing Drives Customer Engagement & Market Growth," Forbes.com, January 8, 2015, http://www.forbes.com/sites/forbespr/2015/01/08/new-report-shows-data-driven-marketing-drives-customer-engagement-market-growth.

36. "Reaching 50 Million Users," Visually, accessed November 3, 2019, http://visual.ly/reaching-50-million-users.

37. Josh Constine, "Facebook Now Has 2 Billion Monthly Users . . . and Responsibility," Techcrunch.com, June 27, 2017, https://techcrunch.com/2017/06/27/facebook-2-billion-users/.

38. Leo Sun, "Are Social Media Users Abandoning Facebook and Instagram?" USA-Today.com, September 12, 2019, https://www.usatoday.com/story/tech/2019/09/12/are-social-media-users-abandoning-facebook-and-instagram/40113681/.

39. Mansoor Iqbal, "YouTube Revenue and Usage Statistics (2019)," BusinessofApps.com, August 8, 2019, https://www.businessofapps.com/data/youtube-statistics/.

40. Hamza Shaban, "Twitter Reveals Its Daily Active User Numbers for the First Time," WashingtonPost.com, February 7, 2019, https://beta.washingtonpost.com/technology/2019/02/07/twitter-reveals-its-daily-active-user-numbers-first-time/.

41. Simon Kemp, "Digital in 2019," wearesocial.com, 2019, https://wearesocial.com/global-digital-report-2019.

42. Craig Zevin, "Pinterest, Google, & Instagram Big Winners as Facebook Share of Visits Falls 8% in 2017 [Report]," Shareaholic.com, February 22, 2018, https://www.shareaholic.com/blog/search-engine-social-media-traffic-trends-report-2017/.

43. "What is Referral Traffic and Why Is It Important?" Visitor-Analytics.io, April 3, 2018, https://www.visitor-analytics.io/blog/what-is-referral-traffic-and-why-is-it-important/.

44. Paul Alfieri, "Data Driven and Digitally Savvy: The Rise of the New Marketing Organization," Forbes Insights and Turn, 2015, https://images.forbes.com/forbesinsights/StudyPDFs/Turn-The_Rise_of_the_New_Marketing_Organization-REPORT.pdf.

45. "Customer Relationship Management—CMR," Investopedia.com, April 23, 2019, https://www.investopedia.com/terms/c/customer_relation_management.asp.

46. Thomas W. Gruen, Talai Osmonbekov, and Andrew J. Czaplewski, "eWOM: The Impact of Customer-to-Customer Online Know-How Exchange on Customer Value and Loyalty," *Journal of Business Research* 59, no. 4 (2006): 449–456.

47. "Will it clog?" ShortyAwards.com, accessed September 20, 2019, https://shortyawards.com/11th/will-it-clog-2.

48. Kemp, "Digital in 2019."

49. Sun, "Are Users Abandoning Facebook and Instagram?"

50. "Average Number of Social Media Accounts per Internet User as of June 2019, by Age Group," We Are Social, DataReportal, and Hootsuite, July 18, 2019, https://www.statista.com/statistics/381964/number-of-social-media-accounts/.

51. Debra Aho Williamson, "US Time Spent with Social Media 2019," eMarketer.com, May 30, 2019, https://www.emarketer.com/content/us-time-spent-with-social-media-2019.

52. "Monthly Active User (MAU)," BareMetrics.com, accessed November 13, 2019, https://baremetrics.com/academy/startups-know-monthly-active-users.

53. "Daily Active User (DAU)," BareMetrics.com, accessed November 13, 2019, https://baremetrics.com/academy/daily-active-user.

54. "Most Popular Social Networks Accessed by Mothers in the United States as of January 2018," Edison Research, May 10, 2018, https://www.statista.com/statistics/629250/leading-social-networks-among-us-moms/.

55. "Social Media Marketing Usage Rate in the United States from 2013 to 2019," eMarketer, November 27, 2017, https://www.statista.com/statistics/203513/usage-trands-of-social-media-platforms-in-marketing/.

56. "Social Media Advertising—United States," Statista, accessed September 23, 2019. https://www.statista.com/outlook/220/109/social-media-advertising/united-states.

57. Jay Baer, Adam Brown, and Jen Hartmann, "How a 180 Year Old Brand Made A Huge Social Media Pivot," Social Pros Podcast, ConvinceAndConvert.com, August 2, 2019 https://www.convinceandconvert.com/podcasts/episodes/how-a-180-year-old-brand-made-a-huge-social-media-pivot/.

58. Amy Gesenhues, "Welcome to the New Era of Social Media Marketing," MarketingLand.com, June 24, 2019, https://marketingland.com/welcome-to-the-next-era-of-social-media-marketing-262718.

59. Baer, Brown, and Hartmann, "180 Year Old Brand."

60. Margalit, "Psychology Behind Social Media Interactions."

61. Kotler, Kartajaya, and Setiawan, *Marketing 4.0.*

62. Amelia Burke, "Planning and Evaluating Digital Media Campaigns for the Public Sector," *Social Marketing Quarterly*, May 22, 2011, http://www.socialmarketingquarterly.com/planning-and-evaluating-digital-media-campaigns-public-sector.

63. Julian Villanueva, Shijin Yoo, and Dominique M. Hanssens, "The Impact of Marketing-Induced versus Word-of-Mouth Customer Acquisition on Customer Equity Growth," *Journal of Marketing Research* 45, no. 1 (2008): 48–59.

64. V. Kumar, JeeWon Choi, and Mallik Greene, "Synergistic Effects of Social Media and Traditional Marketing on Brand Sales: Capturing the Time-Varying Effects," *Journal of the Academy of Marketing Science* 45, no. 2 (2017): 268–288.

65. Raj Agnihotri, Rebecca Dingus, Michael Y. Hu, and Michael T. Krush, "Social Media: Influencing Customer Satisfaction in B2B Sales," *Industrial Marketing Management* 53 (2016): 172–180.

66. Kim Bhasin, "Seth Godin Explains the True Power of Consumers Today," BusinessInsider.com, June 11, 2012, https://www.businessinsider.com/seth-godin-explains-the-true-power-of-consumers-today-2012-6.

67. John A. Deighton, "The Future of Interactive Marketing," *Harvard Business Review* 74, no. 6 (1996): 151–160.

68. Sally J. McMillan and Jang-Sun Hwang, "Measures of Perceived Interactivity: An Exploration of the Role of Direction of Communication, User Control, and Time in Shaping Perceptions of Interactivity," *Journal of Advertising* 31, no. 3 (2008): 29–42.

69. Brian L. Massey and Mark R. Levy, "Interactivity, Online Journalism, and English-Language Web Newspapers in Asia," *Journalism & Mass Communication Quarterly* 76, no. 1 (1999): 138–151.

70. Chris Crawford, "Lessons from Computer Game Design," in *The Art of Human-Computer Interface Design*, edited by B. Laurel (Reading, MA: Addison-Wesley, 1990), 103–111.

71. Albert M. Muniz Jr. and Thomas C. O'Guinn, "Brand Community," *Journal of Consumer Research* 27, no. 4 (2001): 412-432.

CHAPTER

2

Shifting Influences and the Decline of Push Marketing

The buying of time or space is not the taking out of a hunting license on someone else's private preserve, but is the renting of a stage on which we may perform.[1]

—Howard Gossage

PREVIEW

If I gave you a pen and paper and asked, "What's your story?" what would you write? What would your father or mother write? How about your grandmother or brother, best friend, teacher, boss, favorite celebrity, or the neighbor you've never met? In 2009, Brandon Doman started doing just this in a coffee shop to help us explore the universal truths, desires, and experiences that make us all human. "The Strangers Project" continues today with more than twenty-five thousand true stories being shared online at stangersproject.com.[2] When someone says, "I have a story," we all lean in. Everyone has a story and we all have a desire to know each other's stories through social interaction.

Social interaction is the process of reciprocal stimulation or response between two people.[3] Interaction or being social is central to being human. Even our understanding, meaning, and memory of the world is centered on human interaction and story. Psychology researchers Stephen Read and Lynn Miller remind us of this insight in "Stories Are Fundamental to Meaning

30

and Memory: For Social Creatures Could It Be Otherwise?"[4] Story is a powerful device for marketing communication that many in business often overlook.

Researchers have argued that stories are central to human interaction because they provide useful memory structures.[5] Yet Read and Miller take this thought further, saying that stories serve as important social goals that help enable successful social interaction. British anthropologist and evolutionary psychologist Robin Dunbar found that stories are powerful enablers for group identity and social cohesiveness.[6] Researchers John Tooby and Leda Cosmides have established that stories help with conformity to group norms and values, which in turn enables greater cooperation.[7] In other words, humans are social, just all want to get along, and stories help us make sense of the world, remember what we learned, and feel like part of the crowd.

Social media is an excellent platform to tell stories and provides an ideal space to fulfill the human need for interaction. It is a powerful tool that serves to bring groups of people together for conformity, cooperation, memory, and meaning. Over time social media posts and comments end up telling group and individual stories. A marketer who understands this can bring people together for conversation within their brand story and build brand community. Thus, brand participation in social media can provide a powerful tool for marketing, advertising, and public relations. The rise of social media is the story of the rise of a powerful new persuasive and pervasive communications medium.

When Push Comes to Shove

Howard Gossage understood that a prospective customer was not a target to be hunted, but an audience for which you performed. He was an innovative copywriter active during the Creative Age of advertising in the 1950s and 1960s and is credited with many innovations in industry practice. He was honored by trade publication *Advertising Age* as the twenty-third-most-influential advertising person of the twentieth century behind Dan Wieden and David Kennedy of Nike "Just Do It" fame. Gossage understood the human need for interaction and story a half-century before social media was even conceived. Gossage was said to have started his advertising agency to create riveting conversations with consumers.[8]

What is conversation exactly? **Conversation** is defined as an informal talk involving two people or a small group of people.[9] How could Gossage create conversations with consumers through the one-way communication of ads in traditional media? A conversational style can be created with writing that is similar to an oral discussion. In his day, Gossage was talking about creating a conversation with customers in print and television advertising with perhaps radio, outdoor, and direct mail. Gossage knew that good advertising copy was written like a spoken conversation. Now many marketers have the opposite approach in that they are often writing in styles and tones that are not conversational within the two-way medium of social media.

The problem today with the Gossage quote that opens this chapter is that it has become harder and harder to buy people's time and space. No matter how much a marketer or advertiser talks, it is not much of a conversation if no one reads or hears the message. Advertisers may still rent the stage to present their messages, but when they look out into the crowd, there are a lot fewer people in the audience. The advertising stage has traditionally been mass media print publications and television shows, but the number of readers and viewers has been dropping. This declining audience also applies to public relations practice where getting that big news story about a brand isn't as big when fewer people are reading or viewing the traditional news publication or news show. Journalist outreach and traditional journalistic-style press releases to mass media is a practice with diminishing returns.

Pew's Project for Excellence in Journalism reports that single-copy sales of magazines fell for four consecutive years starting in 2007 and dropped a staggering 9 percent in 2011. Paid subscriptions also dropped 2.5 percent during that same period. Newspapers did not fare much better. The number of newspapers in the United States fell 16 percent from 1,611 in 1990 to 1,350 in 2012. Daily and Sunday circulation dropped 30 percent from 1990 to 2010.[10] The news for newspapers hasn't gotten any better in recent years. US newspapers continue to suffer from steep declines in circulation. More recent statistics include a 12 percent decrease in daily circulation and a 13 percent decrease in circulation in 2018. From a high in the late 1980s and early 1990s, both daily and Sunday newspaper circulation has fallen more than 50 percent. After some years of growth, even traffic to newspaper websites has leveled off.[11]

TV media is losing advertising audience at an even more alarming rate. Research by Morgan Stanley reports there was a 50 percent collapse in average broadcast network TV audience ratings from 2002 to 2012. The story gets worse when advertisers realize that they were paying more than 50 percent more in terms of average cost per million (CPM) during the same period.[12] Not only are marketers losing audience; they are also paying more for fewer viewers. Some may call this insanity—doing the same thing over and over yet expecting different results.

More recent statistics show this decline continues and could get worse with younger audiences as they abandon ad-supported television for streaming. All four major broadcast networks—CBS, FOX, NBC, and ABC—saw their average primetime audience of adults eighteen to forty-nine drop 27 percent from 2017 to 2019, losing 2.6 million viewers in two years. Not a single network had a show reach a 2.0 rating in 2019, which is only 2 percent of the TV viewing population. NBC came the closest with 1.8 but ABC only managed a 0.9. Despite declining reach, 2019 ad sales revenue increased due to the principles of supply-and-demand economics. As the supply of national TV audiences shrink, the demand for national TV ad placements by marketers has not, pushing up unit costs.[13]

The story in cable doesn't get much better for traditional advertising placement or traditional public relations earned media opportunities. Increased bandwidth in cable has led to further segmentation of mass audiences. Specialized channels have increased dramatically. Just looking at the "Cs" on a typical cable channel listing illustrates the depth and specialization of this expansion with genres such as the Cartoon Network, Church Channel, Comedy Central, Cooking Channel, and Crime & Investigation Network.[14] By 2014 the average US TV home received 189 channels and tuned in to 17 of those channels per week.[15] Outside of the Super Bowl, mass audience rarely exists in television anymore. By 2016 the problem had become so apparent that one advertising TV buyer was quoted in *Advertising Age* as saying, "The numbers have shrunk so much in the last 10 years that you almost have to put the 'broad' in 'broadcast' in air quotes. Between the fragmentation and all the time-shifting, there are almost no big-reach vehicles left, unless you have the money to spend on football."[16]

Derek Thompson reports in *Hit Makers* that in 2000 there were 125 scripted series and fewer than three hundred reality shows. By 2015 those numbers tripled to four hundred scripted series and nearly one thousand reality series. The old standard for a hit TV show was a Nielsen rating of 20, where one-fifth of TV homes watched it. In 1979, marketers had twenty-six hit shows to advertise on, but by 1999 they only had *ER* and *Friends*. By 2015 no shows reached a 20 rating and the definition of a hit narrowed to a 2.0 rating, or just 2 percent of the country. As seen above, in 2019 no broadcast show could even hit that mark.[17] By 2019 the top two morning news shows, NBC's *The Today Show* and ABC's *Good Morning America*, both only had a 0.9 rating, reaching a mere one million viewers.[18] Now new streaming services are further dividing attention with options from Hulu, AT&T, YouTube, Apple+, Disney+, and more. There are no more mass audiences for advertising or public relations. We have become a society of niche audiences (see table 2.1).

As we have shifted from mass audiences, so have we shifted from mass appeal products and services. Niche audiences isn't only a communications strategy. It is also a business strategy. Chris Anderson, editor in chief of *Wired* magazine, predicted this movement toward niche markets and niche audiences in his 2004 *Wired* article and 2006 book called *The Long Tail*. Anderson describes his theory as:

> The theory of the Long Tail is that our culture and economy is increasingly shifting away from a focus on a relatively small number of "hits" (mainstream products and markets) at the head of the demand curve and toward a huge number of niches in the tail. As the costs of production and distribution fall, especially online, there is now less need to lump products and consumers into one-size-fits-all containers. In an era without the constraints of physical shelf space and other bottlenecks of distribution, narrowly-targeted goods and services can be as economically attractive as mainstream fare.[19]

A general definition of Anderson's theory of the **long tail** refers to the large number of products that sell in small quantities, as contrasted with the small number of best-selling products.[20] It is important to note that not everyone agrees with the long tail applying in all circumstances. Wharton researchers Serguei Netessine and Tom F. Tan have found that the Long Tail effect holds true in some cases but may not hold true in all cases when factoring

Table 2.1. The Definition a of Hit TV Show Based on Nielsen Ratings

	TV Shows over 20 Rating (old hit standard)	TV Shows over 2 Rating (new hit standard)
1979 Season	26 shows	
1999 Season	2 shows	
2015 Season	0 shows	10 shows
2019 Season	0 shows	0 shows

Sources: Derek Thompson, *Hit Makers: How to Succeed in an Age of Distraction* (New York: Penguin, 2017), 194; Lisa de Moraes, "Full 2015-16 TV Season Series Rankings: 'Blindsopt,' 'Life In Pieces' & 'Quantico' Lead Newcomers," Deadline.com, May 26, 2016, https://deadline.com/2016/05/tv-season-2015-2016-series-rankings-shows-full-list-1201763189/.

in expanding product variety and consumer demand. There is a limit to the tail and mass appeal products can retain their importance.[21]

For more on this concept of appealing to variabilities versus universals, see *Tipping Point* author Malcom Gladwell's popular TED Talk video, "Choice, happiness and spaghetti sauce," at https://youtu.be/iIiAAhUeR6Y. Gladwell shares lessons learned from the food industry, where they found there is no one perfect spaghetti sauce. Only perfect spaghetti sauces. Having choice, or more narrowly focused products on consumers' variable tastes, is what leads to consumer happiness and sales success. This choice can also be called horizontal segmentation.[22] The concepts of narrowly defined target markets and audiences will be addressed again in chapter 4 when selecting target audiences for social media plans and in chapter 13 with social care and social sales in focusing efforts on your best customers following the Pareto principle or 80/20 rule.

Mobile First Media

As if these trends were not challenging enough for marketing communications practice, another development has further deteriorated audience attention. When marketers look out at these diminished audiences, they see a third screen distracting them. Illuminated smartphones and tablets are constantly spewing news updates, posts, tweets, check-ins, messages, or simply funny cat videos that divide attention. A survey of worldwide internet users found that one-third (31 percent) are browsing the internet while watching TV and nearly one-fifth (19 percent) are participating in online discussions. Another fifth of respondents are actually using smartphones or tablets with TV to watch two or more programs at the same time.

These multitasking, attention-grabbing activities all increased from 2 percent to 8 percent from 2014 to 2016.[23] Another study by Samsung Research found that of the time spent multitasking on a device, only 10 percent was related to the content played on the TV.[24] By definition, **attention** is the selective narrowing or focusing of consciousness and observance on something.[25] Attention is becoming a rare commodity today. Divided attention has simply become a normal state of mind for most people.

Overall, people's attention is shifting from traditional to digital media. For the first time, in 2013 US time spent per day with online and mobile media surpassed time spent with traditional media such as television, radio, and print (see table 2.2).[26] By 2019 for the first time, US TV penetration among adults fell below internet penetration and consumers spent more time on mobile devices than watching TV. Average daily time spent on traditional TV viewing has dropped to 3.35 hours, with digital media increased to 6.35 hours—a full 3 hours more.[27] The United States may be leading this digital revolution, but other countries are seeing similar shifts. In the United Kingdom daily time spent on smartphones surpassed TV in 2017,[28] and in Canada daily time spent with digital media passed traditional media in 2019.[29] Even if marketers manage to find a small portion of their target audience through traditional media, messages are not guaranteed to reach them because their heads are turned down toward their mobile devices.

Digital media started with desktop and laptop computers, but more and more activity is shifting to mobile. What defines mobile? **Mobile media** is a personal, interactive,

Table 2.2. Time Spent per Day with Major Media by US Adults from 2010 to 2013

	2010	2011	2012	2013
Digital	*3:11*	*3:49*	*4:33*	*5:16*
–Online	2:22	2:33	2:27	2:19
–Mobile (nonvoice)	0:24	0:48	1:35	2:21
–Other	0:26	0:28	0:31	0:36
TV	*4:24*	*4:34*	*4:38*	*4:31*
Radio	*1:36*	*1:34*	*1:32*	*1:26*
Print	*0:50*	*0:44*	*0:38*	*0:32*
–Newspapers	0:30	0:26	0:22	0:18
–Magazines	0:20	0:18	0:16	0:14
Other	*0:45*	*0:37*	*0:28*	*0:20*
Total	**10:46**	**11:18**	**11:49**	**12:05**

Source: "Digital Set to Surpass TV in Time Spent with U.S. Media," eMarketer .com, August 1, 2013, http://www.emarketer.com/Article/Digital-Set-Surpass-TV -Time-Spent-with-US-Media/1010096.

Note: Hours and minutes spent with each medium regardless of multitasking.

internet-enabled, and user-controlled portable platform for the exchange of information.[30] As technology continues to change, scholars will most likely debate what constitutes mobile media. However, all agree that mobile has helped contribute to the end of traditional mass communication.

In 2019, for the first time, US consumers spent more time on their mobile devices than watching TV, with 70 percent of that time on smartphones. The average smartphone user in the United States now spends three hours and ten minutes on their device. Apps account for 90 percent of smartphone time, and the largest share of content consumed in apps is digital audio, social media, and digital video.[31] Consumers in the United Kingdom are ahead of the United States, spending three hours and thirty-seven minutes on their smartphones a day.[32] Consumer time and attention is increasingly moving to mobile and advertisers' budgets are following. WARC's Global Ad Trends reports predicts mobile ad spending to hit $165.7 billion in 2019, a nearly 10 percent increase in two years, making it the largest ad channel.[33] **Mobile marketing** includes advertising delivered via mobile devices and use of mobile technology to create personalized promotion.[34]

Traditional one-way "push marketing" channels are disappearing or dividing, mass audiences are dwindling, and consumers are tuning out with ever-increasing digital distraction. Yet marketers continue with more effort to push more messages through. The increased growth and segmentation of media combined with the increase of new forms of advertising has created an enormous amount of media clutter.

In the 1970s, it is said that the average person saw roughly five hundred advertising messages a day.[35] Some forty years later, this has increased ten times to the mind-numbing average of up to five thousand ads a day.[36] Some digital marketing experts estimate this

Figure 2.1. A mobile first strategy responds to people's shift in media consumption.

© Marco Piunti / iStock Photo

number to have climbed to 10,000 ads a day with the increase in digital and social media advertising.[37] Some have questioned the accuracy of these numbers, but anyone spending time searching the internet or scrolling their social media newsfeed can see the clutter for themselves. The numbers are rough estimates, but the overall problem remains that the number of advertisements and marketing messages we are exposed to is increasing as more of the empty space around us is being crowded with more ads.[38] When push comes to shove, perhaps it is time that marketers need to stop shoving so much. How? The opposite of push is pull. For further insights into the concept of push versus pull marketing, see the "Push versus Pull" box below.

This switch in media consumption to mobile devices has led to a movement and strategy called mobile first. **Mobile first strategy** started as designing websites for smaller smartphone and tablet devices but has expanded to delivering a mobile first customer experience.[39] A mobile first strategy first applied mainly to website design and utilized mobile friendly adaptive design. But a mobile first mentality has expanded into a strategy encompassing many areas of a business or organization. Mobile first strategy now focuses on designing mobile first experiences for both customers and employees as the primary method for conducting business built on mobile operating systems and touch screen interface. In social media many of the early social networks such as Facebook and YouTube were first developed for the desktop and later adapted to mobile design and apps. Other social networks like Instagram and Snapchat were built as mobile apps, first taking advantage of smartphone features such as cameras, GPS, and notifications.

A mobile first strategy shifts the focus from businesses and organizations pushing out messages to consumers to brands pulling in the consumer's attention with experiences that deliver value. People want the convenience of shopping, conducting business, reading news, getting customer service, communicating, and connecting on the go. As Daniel Newman points out in *Forbes*, a mobile first strategy means:

1. Delivering your business anywhere on smartphones, tablets, and watches.
2. Thinking ahead to a mobile-only consumer for future generations.
3. Creating easier communication for customers and employees.
4. Building relationships with stakeholders through social media and chat.[40]

Howard Gossage was said to be ahead of his time. Eerily, he may have been further ahead than people thought. It is hard to believe that this 1960s advertising copywriter could have seen the future of social media. Yet there is something to learn from his desire to have conversations with consumers. Perhaps he knew that at heart, we are all social creatures prone to distraction, and we were like this even before the current glut of media and

 Push versus Pull

What are push and pull marketing? The American Marketing Association describes the traditional **push strategy** as a manufacturer enticing other channel members to carry a product, versus a **pull strategy** that aims marketing efforts at the end consumer to persuade the consumer to request the products from retail channels.[a] In this sense the difference is really between trade (business to business) or consumer (business to consumer) communication.

However, a push strategy is not to be confused with **push marketing**, which is focused on interrupting potential customers, usually through the purchase of ads. In contrast, **pull marketing** attempts to attract the customer to brand communication by providing valuable content, which is usually delivered via social media.[b] In social media, pull marketing can be used for both consumer (business to consumer) and trade (business to business) communication. With the ever-increasing problem of ad clutter, pull marketing through social media offers an antidote to the annoyance of more ads showing up in unexpected places that people eventually get used to and ignore or find ways to block over time. In *Marketing 4.0* Philip Kotler, Hermawan Kartajaya and Iwan Setiawan describe how marketers can participate further through community marketing. **Community marketing** is when companies don't control the conversation in social media directly but facilitate the discussion with the help of loyal customers.[c]

[a] American Marketing Association, "Dictionary," accessed February 16, 2015, https://www.ama.org/resources/Pages/Dictionary.aspx?dLetter=P.
[b] Gary Garth, "Pull Marketing vs. Push Marketing: Definition, Explanation & Benefits," WhiteSharkMedia.com (blog), July 27, 2012, http://blog.whitesharkmedia.com/why-every-small-mid-sized-business-focus-pull-marketing.
[c] Philip Kotler, Hermawan Kartajaya, and Iwan Setiawan, *Marketing 4.0: Moving from Traditional to Digital* (Hoboken, NJ: Wiley, 2017), 109.

marketing clutter. Gossage is also the one who said, "Nobody reads ads. People read what interests them. Sometimes it's an ad."[41] For those who want to master social media marketing, this sentiment is truer now than ever.

Mass Media to Consumer Communication

Seth Godin, marketer, entrepreneur, and author of *Idea Virus, Purple Cow* and other influential marketing books, says, "Conversations among the members of your marketplace happen whether you like it or not."[42] Here he captures a key truth about consumers—they like to talk and like to talk about brands. **Word-of-mouth** communication is when people share information about products or promotions with friends and is one of the oldest forms of marketing.[43] Deliver a good product or service, and the customer talks to his or her friends and family, generating awareness for the brand and delivering increased sales for free. Of course, this same personal communication system also works in reverse. If the customer had a bad experience, they are likely to tell friends and family not to buy. In the past, this was not a huge problem because the delivery system was small. People only had so many friends and they had to make an effort to visit, run into them by the watercooler, or call them to pass on the information one or a few at a time.

Today, the definition of "friend" has changed and the delivery system has enlarged. Of the more than two billion people on Facebook, each has an average of 338 "friends," and they can communicate with those friends quickly and easily from almost anywhere in the world.[44] On Twitter, the average user has 707 followers.[45] How many friends or connections do you have on your various social networks? The rise of social media networks, mass adoption by the public, and portability of access through expanding Wi-Fi and cellular broadband have dramatically increased the influence of consumer word-of-mouth. Now 90 percent of US adults eighteen to twenty-nine years old use social-networking services on their phone, with 69 percent of people fifty to sixty-four doing the same.[46]

The power of the consumer voice has grown quickly through social media. In 2004, a new trade group was launched to establish standards and best practices. The Word-of-Mouth Marketing Association (WOMMA) was the official trade association dedicated to word-of-mouth and social media marketing.[47] The Association of National Advertisers (ANA) acquired WOMMA in 2018.[48] *McKinsey Quarterly* reports that word-of-mouth is the primary factor behind 20 to 50 percent of all purchase decisions. When that recommendation comes from a trusted friend conveying a relevant message, that recommendation can increase likelihood of purchase up to 50 times.[49]

This spread of consumer influence is shifting power from institutions to individuals. One example is twenty-three-year-old Molly Katchpole. In 2011, she led a consumer revolt against Bank of America's new five-dollar monthly debit card fee. From links on Facebook and Twitter she garnered more than ten thousand signatures for her Change.org online petition. ABC News and other media outlets picked up the story and pushed signatures up to thirty thousand. After weeks of bad publicity, Bank of America gave in and revoked the fee. Verizon also bowed to social media–empowered consumers when it decided to revoke its new two-dollar convenience charge for debit card payments.[50]

Consumer social media activism is still going strong with the public turning their concerns to food policies at companies such as Gatorade, Taco Bell, Trader Joe's, McDonald's, and Starbucks. For example, New York mom Renee Shutters used social media to raise awareness about artificial dyes in M&M's, which can cause hyperactivity in kids. After 217,000 consumers shared her protest, Mars listened and responded with the president and CEO of Mars saying, "Our consumers are the boss and we hear them."[51] Weber Shandwick and KRC Research conducted a study of this new wave of social media–fueled activism. They say that there has been an increase in the frequency, intensity, and visibility of consumer activist events described as "wallet activism." Wallet activism can take the form of both boycotts and buycotts. **Boycott** is when consumers avoid purchasing a company's products as a show of disapproval. **Buycott** is when consumers purchase a company's products in show of support. Their survey of consumer activists in the United States and United Kingdom found that 77 percent believe social media has made the actions of buycotts more effective while 75 percent believe social media has made the actions of boycotts more effective.[52]

Using social media as an outlet to rant or rave about a product, service, or organization is growing. Yet people are not just complaining. They expect a response and they expect it fast. Only 32 percent of people who complain on social media are happy with how fast businesses are responding. Now nearly 40 percent expect a reply within an hour, yet the average business response time is five hours.[53] This may require more resources, but no response is a negative response. Social media expert Jay Baer says, "Ignoring your customers only tells them that you don't care."[54] And ignoring consumers in social media has become a big deal because so many current and potential customers are active on social media.

How big is this consumer voice? As of 2019, 90 percent of US online adults aged eighteen to twenty-nine used social network sites, with 82 percent of thirty- to forty-nine-year-olds active there as well. But these users are not just young adults. People older than sixty-five have quadrupled their presence on social networks from 7 percent in 2010 to 40 percent by 2019. Plus, this increased social activity spreads beyond Facebook to multiple social networks and apps. More than 73 percent of US adults now also use YouTube, 37 percent use Instagram, 28 percent use Pinterest, 27 percent use LinkedIn, 24 percent use Snapchat, and 22 percent use Twitter.[55] In 2019 there were 3.4 billion active social media users globally or 45 percent of the total world population.[56]

What are these socially active consumers talking about? On social networking websites they are just as likely to share their opinion (26 percent), what and how they are doing (26 percent), and links to articles (26 percent) as they are to share products and services they like (25 percent).[57] Why? Researchers have found that people place a high value on opportunities to share their thoughts and feelings. In experiments, self-disclosure produced activity in the brain in areas associated with rewarding outcomes. It is especially rewarding for people to find opportunities to disclose their thoughts to others—something social media is especially good at providing.[58]

Forrester Research reports that consumers create 500 billion social media product and service influence impressions on one another annually.[59] Through social media posts, blog posts, comments, ratings, and reviews, consumers command a powerful voice in brand communication. The increased consumer voice through social networks is very influential. A Nielsen study reveals that eight in ten (83 percent) of global consumers trust

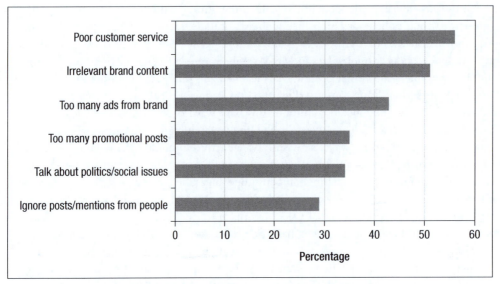

Figure 2.2. Why Consumers Unfollow Brands on Social Media

Source: "The Sprout Social 2019 Index, Edition XV: Empower and Elevate," SproutSocial.com, accessed September 21, 2019, https://sproutsocial.com/insights/data/index/.

recommendations from people they know and two-thirds (66 percent) trust consumers' opinions posted online. Trust in unknown people's opinions is now at the same level of trust as editorial content such as newspaper articles (66 percent) and trust in forms of paid online advertising is 48 percent and lower.[60] Another global survey, the Edelman Trust Barometer, found that 74 percent of people actually use one or more strategies to avoid advertising.[61]

How do you become the content that consumers want to share? Some insight can come from research into why consumers unfollow brands on social media. See figure 2.2 for the results of Sprout Social's Social Index Edition XV: Empower and Elevate. Top reasons for consumers to unfollow a brand include poor customer service, content that is not relevant to them, and too many ads and promotional content. Consumers also may not like too much talk about politics and sensitive social issues from the brand. And they don't like brands that do not respond to people who are posting about and mentioning the brand. Keep these insights in mind when creating a social media strategy to become a part of the word-of-mouth discussion happening in social media around your brand.[62]

This social media word-of-mouth has also been linked to sales. A study in the *Journal of Marketing Research* found that purchase decisions can be influenced by others' opinions and that increased positive online word-of-mouth volume produces increased sales impact.[63] Word-of-mouth through social media such as Twitter has also been linked to increased box office revenue for movies,[64] and Twitter with consumer reviews has been shown to impact sales of new video games.[65] Yet many marketing plans and budgets still devote the majority of their time and money to traditional advertising. Perhaps that is why spending on social media is expected to rise 73 percent over five years from just over 11 percent of

MINI CASE

Sony Europe

As a demonstration of how opposite social media thinking can be from traditional marketing, this case shows how Sony Europe succeeded by leveraging an online community through social media instead of simply pushing advertising content through the new channel. As more and more consumers were asking customer service questions via social media, Sony faced an enormous challenge, considering they have thousands of different products.

In response, Sony Europe created an online community of Sony users and began to identify and reward the most valuable super-fans. **Super-fans** are a company's most active online consumers who answer forum questions, write in-depth blog posts, and provide valuable feedback without collecting a fee. Sony's fifty super-fans were invited to product launches, offered new products, and given all-expenses-paid trips to biannual super-fan conferences. The result is thousands of customer questions answered every year with an 85 percent solve rate that saves the company millions in support costs.[a]

Why do super-fans provide all this free product support and marketing buzz even before they are found and rewarded by companies such as Sony? Self-presentation theory explains motivations behind human behavior to project an image of oneself to other people. These actions are activated by the presence of other people observing behavior such as in an online community. Many people want to be perceived as knowledgeable, helpful, and friendly—especially in front of an audience. This audience pleasing motivates people to want to help others learn about a brand and solve problems around a product for the reward of feeling better about one's self-image.[b] Online brand communities provide an audience that super-fans want to please. Instead of trying to control unofficial brand or product communication, smart marketers encourage fan communities and reward the most active users to help them grow. Today Sony continues this strategy with examples like Sony PlayStation interactive forums where gamers can control their experience and interact with others with similar interests about the product and brand.[c]

[a] Jeremy Taylor, "Social CRM Cast Study: Sony Europe Creates a Community of Super-fans," OurSocialTimes.com, May 14, 2014, http://oursocialtimes.com/social-crm-case-study-sony-europe-creates-a-community-of-super-fans.

[b] Erving Goffman, *The Presentation of Self in Everyday Life* (New York: Doubleday Anchor, 1959).

[c] Anna Johansson, "Why Building a Community Is the Best Thing You Can do for Your Brand (and How to Do It)," Inc.com, February 27, 2018, https://www.inc.com/anna-johansson/why-building-a-community-is-best-thing-you-can-do-for-your-brand-and-how-to-do-it.html.

US marketing budgets to nearly 20 percent by 2024.[66] And this is why global social media advertising spending nearly doubled from 2017 to 2019 and is expected to grow to $111 billion in 2020, surpassing all other forms of digital advertising including search, banner, video, and classifieds.[67]

All this growth in social media presents an enormous opportunity. But some view it as a threat. Empowered consumers generating and sharing their brand comments and content do not fit neatly into traditional models of marketing and communications strategy.[68] Most

Social Media Command Center

Many brands today have recognized the importance of the consumer voice and have invested in a social media command center. A **social media command center** is a branded social media monitoring room acting as a central, visual hub for social data. These centers tend to be set up in high-profile locations within company offices. Gatorade built their mission-control center in the middle of the marketing department at their Chicago headquarters. Radian6 (now part of Salesforce) and IBM partnered with the sports beverage brand to build a custom war room that monitors the brand in real time across social media.[a]

GM (General Motors) built a social media command center in their Detroit headquarters that is described as a "high-energy, state-of-the-art engagement environment featuring dozens of wireless work stations, multiple collaboration rooms and 18 HD monitors that display a wide variety of social feeds." GM's twenty-six full-time social media advisers average more than six thousand monthly interactions for in-market presale and customer care. The command center covers 150 owned social channels from the car brands of GM, Chevrolet, Buick, GMC, and Cadillac while also monitoring eighty-five earned media sites like automotive fan forums.[b] As an indication of the importance of social listening, Target's mission-control-style monitoring room is called "guest central" and is on the C-Suite floor of their Minneapolis headquarters only steps from the CEO's office.

What are the benefits of a social media command center? Talkwalker says that a command center has some unique benefits over simple social media monitoring. The benefits of a command center are that it:

1. *Breaks down data silos.* A command center can help promote collaboration among departments, changing the way data is shared across the company.
2. *Makes more informed decisions.* A command center can also help you see the big picture and help you optimize strategy based on real-time insights from consumers and competitors.
3. *Facilitates access to data.* A command center presents important data in large visualizations for all to see. It gets data out of spreadsheets into a form that can be easier to understand.
4. *Showcases results.* A command center provides visibility for your digital efforts and displays how the brand is perceived by consumers in social media and all brand experiences.[c]

Despite all these benefits, social media command centers can be expensive to build and require a lot of staff time and expense. William Comcowich of Glean.info says, "PR and marketing teams can issue quick, on-target responses from a regular office—or from home. With the help of messaging apps like Slack, teams can now collaborate remotely. For multinational organizations, the non-centralized approach . . . enables localization with multiple languages and with better cultural focus and sensitivity."[d] Following COVID-19 restrictions, many companies may have more employees work at home permanently.

Are they worth the time and money? Research firm Gartner asked this question and said that organizations should carefully consider the value of these highly visible investments. Organizations should not invest in a command center until they first integrate their social media processes, data, and content with their multichannel marketing strategy and other important departments such as customer care, corporate communications, PR, and human resources. Discover and focus on critical metrics to ensure you are collecting and measuring what really counts. Integrate strategies, data, and measurement across departments first, then add the room, screens, and real-time visualization. For more on this topic see "Social Media Measurement Plan," figure 6.6.

Gartner says, "A simple relocation of the social team into a command center, without a view toward supporting the entire marketing strategy and customer journey, will only shine a brighter light on this divide." But a social media command center can benefit the right organizations (see figure 2.3). Gartner suggests four guidelines to follow in determining if a command center is worthwhile:

1. Identify the use cases where the center will improve performance, such as crisis management, event marketing, customer care.
2. Talk to teams from various departments to determine if they would value a command center environment.
3. Secure commitment and support from key leaders and teams across various departments in the organization.
4. Evaluate an estimate of the investment against use cases versus improving existing capabilities, communication, and virtual collaboration.[e]

[a] Adam Ostrow, "Inside Gatorade's Social Media Command Center," Mashable.com, June 15, 2010, http://mashable.com/2010/06/15/gatorade-social-media-mission-control.

[b] David Mingle, "Shhhh! Customer Listening in Progress," CIOReview.com, April 28, 2017, https://customer-experience-management.cioreview.com/cxoinsight/shhhh-customer-listening-in-progress-nid-24218-cid-118.html.

[c] Albane, "7 ways a social media command center will empower your brand," Talkwalker.com, August 3, 2017, https://www.talkwalker.com/blog/social-media-command-center-for-your-brand#.

[d] William Comcowich, "Are Social Media Command Centers Worth the Cost?" Glean.info, June 29, 2017, https://glean.info/social-media-command-centers-worth-cost/.

[e] Chris Pemberton, "Are Social Media Command Centers Worth the Investment?" Gartner .com, September 29, 2016, https://www.gartner.com/smarterwithgartner/are-social-media -command-centers-worth-the-investment/.

marketing principles and communication strategies still operate on a marketer, advertiser, or public relations control model. Social media breaks brand communication control and thus breaks the traditional model that most have learned and practiced. Going back to Seth Godin's quote, whether you like it or not the control model has to change. Organizations can no longer keep their heads in the sand pretending they still have control. Simply ignoring social conversation will not work.

The good news is that if marketers and their advertising and public relations partners choose to enter the social conversation through engagement, it can be very effective. **Engagement** is involvement, interaction, intimacy, and influence between an individual and a brand.[69] Engagement is effective. WOMMA reports that 78 percent of consumers indicate being influenced by a brand's social media posts.[70] Compare this to the Nielsen report of only 48 percent of consumers trusting traditional online advertising. Marketers and advertisers need to learn to talk and interact with consumers in a very different way if their brands are to have a chance in this highly transparent, consumer-empowered environment.[71]

Figure 2.3. Is a social media command center a good investment for every organization?

© Web Substance / iStock Photo

As Philip Kotler, Hermawan Kartajaya, and Iwan Setiawan say, "The essence of Marketing 4.0 is to recognize the shifting roles of traditional and digital marketing in building customer engagement and advocacy."[72]

Public relations professionals should especially be equipped to handle the challenge and opportunity of building customer engagement and advocacy in social media. The public relations profession has always been about engagement, storytelling, and conversation. The difference is a shift in focus from PR writing of the past when journalistic standards and the AP Stylebook drove content creation in the form of traditional press releases. Katie Winchell in *Public Relations Tactics* described this well, saying, "PR writing was aimed mostly at journalists who were in turn reporting to a passive readership." Then Web 2.0 happened and Winchell continued, "Your brand is being evangelized, dismissed, measured and documented in real time online . . . it's time to join the conversation and show your company or client cares—a mission perfectly suited for the PR professional."[73]

Edelman, the largest public relations agency in the world, won a Shorty Award for client Playtex introducing a new product innovation by leveraging the power of storytelling, engagement, and conversation in social media. The campaign titled "The World's Most 'Extra' Tampon" won in the categories of health and fitness and comedy video with a gold distinction in humor. Playtex was losing market share to new brand competitors and needed to evolve their product, increase awareness of the new innovations, and make the brand relevant again to millennial women. Edelman helped the brand partner with D'Arcy Carden, who plays Janet on the TV show *The Good Place* to create an SNL-style parody ad poking fun at all the unnecessary extras that come with the new competitor brands. The video trended on Instagram's Discover page, earning 184 million impressions in just two days. Social conversation around Playtex increased 182 percent with 98 percent of comments being positive.[74]

Theoretically Speaking: Social Presence and Media Richness

What are the theories behind this phenomenon of social media? Researchers Andreas Kaplan and Michael Haenlein propose that social presence theory and media richness theory are key elements of social media.[75] **Social presence theory** states that media differ in the degree of social presence (acoustic, visual, and physical contact) they allow between two communication partners. Social presence is influenced by the intimacy (interpersonal versus mediated) and immediacy (asynchronous versus synchronous) of the medium. Social presence is thought to be higher for interpersonal (face-to-face discussion) than mediated (television) and for synchronous (live chat) than asynchronous (email) communications. The higher the social presence, the larger the social influence that the partners have on each other's behavior.[76] It is not hard to see how this theory predicts social media to be more influential than traditional media whether for personal or marketing, advertising, and public relations communication.

Closely related is **media richness theory,** which states that media differ in the degree of richness they possess—the amount of information they allow to be transmitted in a given time. If a medium is richer (it can transmit more information), it will be more effective in communication. Social media is rich in its ability to transmit text, images, sound, and video, and it can transmit this information instantaneously in both directions to or from anyone around the world. Think about the amount of media richness the average consumer has on their smartphone these days. One social media platform such as Facebook alone is rich in many media options for posting, commenting, and sharing text, images, sound, video, emojis, illustrations, and graphics. Marketers who apply these theories to social media versus traditional media such as print, radio, and television will quickly see how advanced this communication medium is in terms of its potential for effectiveness.[77]

An example of media richness is a Gatorade "video everywhere" media strategy that crossed channels with the launch of "Sisters in Sweat" on multiple platforms. The campaign uses the richness through a short film on YouTube following a young girl and her soccer ball through a fantastical animated world featuring Mia Hamm, Mallory Pugh, and Dr. Seuss. In just four months the film attracted 23 million views.[78] The campaign extends media richness through a Snapchat AR (augmented reality) lens that uses the rear-facing camera of smartphones to immerse users with the feeling they are in this magical world. The portal lens gives consumers the viewpoint of getting into the game, scoring the winning goal, and learning the power of sport from Gatorade through augmented reality. The campaign is also supported on Twitter for live engagement and the brand was exploring options on TikTok.[79]

Gatorade also branded a new mobile app called Highlights. The app focuses on the brand's core teen athlete audience to help them create exciting short-form video highlight clips of themselves. It allows the addition of Gatorade brand color motion stickers, text, and graphics to create splashy looping videos that can be shared easily to other social media platforms such as Instagram, Snapchat Stories, and TikTok. Gatorade observed their targets' behavior online and in person through sports camps, tournaments, and schools, noticing their high consumption of sports highlight clips. The brand saw an opportunity to add media richness to a behavior their audience was already doing online. The app helps amateur athletes look a little more like the pros and the Gatorade brand gets more exposure through user-generated content (UGC), creating a win-win situation.[80] Observational research was valuable to Gatorade to understand their target audience. This type of observational research is explained in chapter 5 under Theoretically Speaking: Ethnographic Observational Research. Gatorade also had to have a well-defined, narrow target market to make this effort a success. Identifying target markets and target audiences will be covered in chapter 4.

Chapter 2 Checklist

Social media can change quickly. Visit Post Control Marketing (http://www.postcontrol marketing.com) for updates, but also use this chapter checklist to briefly check how social media statistics in this chapter have changed since publication.

✓ What is the current time spent per day by major media? Has it changed significantly? If you market in a different country, has the decline in traditional mass media and rise in time spent with digital media followed a similar pattern?

✓ What types of information do people share in social media? Have the categories shifted? Are there new ones?

✓ Have advertising trust numbers shifted? Are opinions of strangers in social media still more trustworthy than all forms of online advertising, brand websites, or traditional media like journalism?

 SOCIAL PLAN PART 2

Adding to the Noise

Is an organization adding to the clutter? In the earliest stages of a social media plan, the goal is to start getting a sense of a brand's image in the marketplace. Take an inventory of all marketing and advertising activities and messages. Then determine how "pushy" the brand's marketing communication has become. Is the brand heavily reliant on push marketing through traditional media? In social media, is the brand intrusive with one-way sales-focused posts, or are posts helpful and responsive? Make a list or spreadsheet of all consumer touch points in traditional, digital, and social media. Analyze the type of messages the company is promoting in each, and report the answers to the following questions:

1. Is the communication company-focused or consumer-focused?
2. Is the information useful, newsworthy, entertaining, or valuable?
3. Do consumers perceive the message as an unwanted interruption or a welcome message?
4. Take an inventory of all brand marketing and advertising activities and rate the "pushiness" of brand communication. Is the brand over-reliant on traditional media? Are they using social media as more of a one-way communication channel? On a scale of 1 to 10, how much is the brand contributing to media clutter?

For a condensed version of the social plan see appendix A: Three-Part Social Plan.

KEY CONCEPTS

social interaction	pull marketing
conversation	community marketing
long tail	word–of–mouth
attention	boycott
mobile media	buycott
mobile marketing	super-fans
mobile first strategy	social media command center
push strategy	engagement
pull strategy	social presence theory
push marketing	media richness theory

QUESTIONS FOR DISCUSSION

1. How much do you think consumer conversations actually influence purchasing decisions? Can you quantify this influence or find research that proves it?
2. Howard Gossage said we should not try to hunt our target audience, but instead entertain. Describe three of your favorite TV commercials or advertising videos and describe three of your least favorite. List characteristics of each category. What makes one group of ads more favorable than the other?
3. This chapter discusses evidence of media clutter such as the number of cable channels available in the average household. Now new shows are being created in ever-increasing streaming channels such as Netflix, Hulu, Amazon Prime, Disney+, and Apple+. In what ways are marketers of these TV shows using social media to grab and hold viewers' attention?
4. Ethics play an important role in social media management. Do you feel it is OK to reward super-fans or brand advocates with free products and special offers? How do you decide who gets rewarded and who doesn't? What about direct payment for posting?

ADDITIONAL EXERCISES

1. Type in the Google search box a brand name and "+ complaints." Then hit return. How many customers are talking about the company? What are they saying—is it positive or negative? Where are they saying it? Now narrow the search to news, video, and blogs. Repeat the same search on Twitter. Read reviews of the company on retail or review sites. Remember that the internet is one of the first places people turn when seeking information about a brand, product, or service. With this in mind, what is the overall image of the brand when you take into account official brand communication and social media content?
2. Take a day and log your activity on your devices (desktop, laptop, smartphone, tablet). How many times a day do you check your devices, by device? Categorize each interaction by purpose, such as reading email, texting, reading news, checking social media, and posting or commenting on social media. Note the time of day and time in minutes. Then add up the total for the day in each category. What percentage of your time is spent on your devices and

what percentage of your time is spent on social media? How does this compare to your traditional media usage? Do the results surprise you? What do they say for marketers? What do they say to you personally? As an alternative, just look at the Screen Time stats on your iPhone or Digital Wellbeing stats on your Android phone and ask the same questions.

Notes

1. Howard Gossage, *The Book of Gossage* (Chicago: Copy Workshop, 2006), 20.

2. Brandon Doman, "The Strangers Project," accessed September 16, 2019, http://strangers project.com/.

3. Pam M. S. Nugent, "Social Interaction," Psychology Dictionary.org, accessed September 16, 2019, http://psychologydictionary.org/social-interaction.

4. Stephen J. Read and Lynn C. Miller, "Stories Are Fundamental to Meaning and Memory: For Social Creatures Could It Be Otherwise?" in *Knowledge and Memory: The Real Story: Advances in Social Cognition, Volume VII*, edited by R. S. Wyer Jr. (New York: Psychology Press, 2014).

5. Robert C. Schank and R. P. Abelson, *Scripts, Plans, Goals, and Understanding* (Hillsdale, NJ: Lawrence Erlbaum Associates, 1977).

6. Robin Dunbar, "Co-evolution of Neocortex Size, Group Size and Language in Humans," *Behavioral and Brain Sciences* 16, no. 4 (1993): 681–735.

7. John Tooby and Leda Cosmides, "The Psychological Foundations of Culture," in *The Adapted Mind: Evolutionary Psychology and the Generation of Culture*, edited by Jerome H. Barkow, Leda Cosmides, and John Tooby (New York: Oxford University Press, 1992).

8. David Klein, "Ad Age Advertising Century: An Introduction," AdAge.com, March 29, 1999, http://adage.com/article/special-report-the-advertising-century/ad-age-advertising-century -introduction/140147/.

9. "Conversation," Merriam-Webster.com, accessed September 16, 2019, http://www.merriam -webster.com/dictionary/conversation.

10. Rick Edmonds, Emily Guskin, Tom Rosenstiel, and Amy Mitchell, "The State of the News Media 2012," Pew Research Center, accessed September 16, 2019, http://assets.pewresearch .org/wp-content/uploads/sites/13/2017/05/24141622/State-of-the-News-Media-Report-2012 -FINAL.pdf.

11. "Newspapers Fact Sheet," Pew Research Center, July 9, 2019, http://www.journalism.org/ fact-sheet/newspapers/.

12. Jim Edwards, "BRUTAL: 50% Decline in TV Viewership Shows Why Your Cable Bill Is So High," BusinessInsider.com, January 31, 2013, http://www.businessinsider.com/ brutal-50-decline-in-tv-viewership-shows-why-your-cable-bill-is-so-high-2013-1#ixzz2f5VViddn.

13. Anthony Crupi, "Ratings Bombshell: In Two Years, Network TV Demos Plummeted 27 Percent," AdAge.com, January 28, 2019, https://adage.com/article/media/c3/316390.

14. "Verizon Fios Channel Lineup," Verizon.com, accessed September 16, 2019, http://www .verizon.com/home/fiostv/.

15. "Changing Channels: Americans View Just 17 Channels Despite Record Number to Choose From," Nielsen.com, May 6, 2014, http://www.nielsen.com/us/en/insights/news/2014/changing -channels-americans-view-just-17-channels-despite-record-number-to-choose-from.html.

16. Anthony Crupi, "Where TV Ratings Go from Here," AdAge.com, April 18, 2016, http:// adage.com/article/media/ratings/303574/.

17. Derek Thompson, *Hit Makers: How to Succeed in an Age of Distraction* (New York: Penguin, 2017), 194.

18. Tony Maglio, "'GMA' Beats 'Today' Show for First Weekly Ratings Win in 4 Years," TheWrap.com, August 20, 2019, https://www.thewrap.com/gma-beats-today-show-ratings-good-morning-america/.

19. Chris Anderson, "About Me," Long Tail blog, accessed December 4, 2019, https://longtail.typepad.com/about.html.

20. "Long Tail," Lexico Oxford, accessed December 4, 2019, https://www.lexico.com/en/definition/long_tail.

21. "Rethinking the Long Tail Theory: How to Define 'Hits' and 'Niches,'" Knowledge.Wharton.UPenn.edu, September 16, 2009, https://knowledge.wharton.upenn.edu/article/rethinking-the-long-tail-theory-how-to-define-hits-and-niches/.

22. Malcom Gladwell, "Choice, happiness and spaghetti sauce," TED Talk, January 16, 2007, https://www.youtube.com/watch?v=iIiAAhUeR6Y&feature=youtu.be.

23. "More People Are Multitasking While Watching TV," eMarketer.com, November 16, 2016, https://www.emarketer.com/Article/More-People-Multitasking-While-Watching-TV/1014726.

24. Auriana Shokrpour and Michael J. Darnell, "How People Multitask While Watching TV," Proceedings of the 2017 ACM International Conference on Interactive Experiences for TV and Online Video (2017), 11–19.

25. "Attention," Merriam-Webster.com, accessed September 16, 2019, http://www.merriam-webster.com/dictionary/attention.

26. "Digital Set to Surpass TV in Time Spent with U.S. Media," eMarketer.com, August 1, 2013, http://www.emarketer.com/Article/Digital-Set-Surpass-TV-Time-Spent-with-US-Media/1010096.

27. Mark Dolliver, "Time Spent with Media 2019—US," eMarketer.com, May 30, 2019, https://www.emarketer.com/content/us-time-spent-with-media-2019.

28. Bill Fisher, "Time Spent with Media 2019—UK," eMarketer.com, May 30, 2019, https://www.https://www.emarketer.com/content/uk-time-spent-with-media-2019.

29. Paul Briggs, "Time Spent with Media 2019—Canada," eMarketer.com, May 30, 2019, https://www.emarketer.com/content/canada-time-spent-with-media-2019.

30. Ran Wei, "Social Media: Coming of Age with a Big Splash," *Mobile Media & Communication* 1, no.1 (2013): 50–56.

31. Yoram Wurmser, "US Time Spent with Mobile 2019," eMarketer.com, May 30, 2019, https://www.emarketer.com/content/us-time-spent-with-mobile-2019.

32. Fisher, "Time Spent with Media 2019—UK."

33. David Murphy, "Mobile Ad Spend to Hit $165.7bn in 2019: WARC," MobileMarketing Magazine.com, February 2, 2019, https://mobilemarketingmagazine.com/mobile-ad-spent-to-hit-1657bn-in-2019-warc.

34. Will Kenton, "Mobile Marketing," Investopedia.com, October 6, 2019, https://www.investopedia.com/terms/m/mobile-marketing.asp.

35. Steuart Henderson Britt, Stephen C. Adams, and Allan S. Miller, "How Many Advertising Exposures per Day?" *Journal of Advertising Research* 12 (December 1972): 3–9.

36. Louise Story, "Anywhere the Eye Can See, It's Likely to See an Ad," NYTimes.com, January 15, 2007, http://www.nytimes.com/2007/01/15/business/media/15everywhere.html.

37. Ron Marshall, "How Many Ads Do You See in One Day?" RedCrowMaarketing.com, September 10, 2015, https://www.redcrowmarketing.com/2015/09/10/many-ads-see-one-day/.

38. "The Myth of 5,000 Ads," Choice Behavior Insights at Hill Holiday, accessed September 16, 2019, http://cbi.hhcc.com/writing/the-myth-of-5000-ads/.

39. Margaret Rouse, "Mobile First," SearchEngineComputing.TechTarget.com, July 2014, https://searchmobilecomputing.techtarget.com/definition/mobile-first.

40. Daniel Newman, "What Does A Mobile-First Digital Transformation Strategy Look Like?" Forbes.com, May 29, 2019, https://www.forbes.com/sites/danielnewman/2018/05/29/what-does-a-mobile-first-digital-transformation-strategy-look-like/#423156b5f3c0.

41. Gossage, *Book of Gossage.*

42. Seth Godin, "What Every Good Marketer Knows," SethGodin.com (blog), May 9, 2005, http://sethgodin.typepad.com/seths_blog/2005/05/what_every_good.html.

43. American Marketing Association, "word-of-mouth," accessed February 16, 2015, https://www.ama.org/search/?s=Word-of-mouth.

44. Aaron Smith, "6 New Facts about Facebook," Pewresearch.org, February 3, 2014, http://www.pewresearch.org/fact-tank/2014/02/03/6-new-facts-about-facebook/.

45. Ryan MacCarthy, "The Average Twitter User Now has 707 Followers," Science of Social Sales Blog, KickFactory.com, June 23, 2016, https://kickfactory.com/blog/average-twitter-followers-updated-2016/.

46. "Social Media Fact Sheet," PewInternet.org, June 12, 2019, https://www.pewinternet.org/fact-sheet/social-media/.

47. "About WOMMA," Womma.org, accessed September 16, 2015, http://womma.org/about-womma/.

48. "ANA Influencer Marketing," ana.net, January 1, 2018, https://www.ana.net/content/show/id/womma.

49. Jacques Bughin, Jonathan Doogan, and Ole Jørgen Vetvik, "A New Way to Measure Word-of-Mouth Marketing," *McKinsey Quarterly* 2 (June 2010): 113–116.

50. Jeff Howe, "How Hashtags and Social Media Can Bring Megacorporations to Their Knees," TheAtlantic.com, June 8, 2012, http://www.theatlantic.com/business/archive/2012/06/the-rise-of-the-consumerate/258290.

51. Pulin Modi, "With Social Media Help, Consumers Find Their Voice on Food Policy," HuffingtonPost.com, February 16, 2016, http://www.huffingtonpost.com/pulin-modi/with-social-media-help-co_b_9243108.html.

52. "Battle of the Wallets: The Changing Landscape of Consumer Activism," Webershandwick.com, May 2018, https://www.webershandwick.com/wp-content/uploads/2018/05/Battle_of_the_Wallets.pdf.

53. Jay Baer, "New Research Shows How Fast Companies Have to Be in Social Media," ConvinceandConvert.com, accessed September 16, 2019, https://www.convinceandconvert.com/hug-your-haters/new-research-shows-how-fast-companies-have-to-be-in-social-media/

54. Jay Baer, "4 Reasons to Answer Every Complaint on Social Media," Adweek.com, April 6, 2017, http://www.adweek.com/digital/jay-baer-guest-post-4-reasons-to-answer-every-complaint-on-social-media/.

55. "Social Media Fact Sheet," PewInternet.org, June 12, 2019.

56. Simon Kemp, "Digital in 2019," wearesocial.com, 2019, https://wearesocial.com/global-digital-report-2019.

57. "Majority (71%) of Global Internet Users 'Share' on Social Media Sites," Ipsos.com, September 17, 2013, https://www.ipsos.com/en-us/majority-71-global-internet-users-share-social-media-sites.

58. Diana I. Tamir and Jason P. Mitchell, "Disclosing Information about the Self Is Intrinsically Rewarding," *Proceedings of the National Academy of Sciences of the United States of America* 109, no. 21 (2012): 8038–8043.

59. Josh Bernoff, "Spotting the Creators of Peer Influence," AdAge.com, April 20, 2010, http://adage.com/article/digitalnext/marketing-spotting-creators-peer-influence/143372.

60. "Global Trust in Advertising," Nielsen.com, September 28, 2015, http://www.nielsen.com/us/en/insights/reports/2015/global-trust-in-advertising-2015.html.

61. Richard Edelman, "In Brands We Trust? 2019 Edelman Trust Barometer Special Report," Edelman.com, 2019, https://www.edelman.com/sites/g/files/aatuss191/files/2019-07/2019_edelman_trust_barometer_special_report_in_brands_we_trust_executive_summary.pdf.

62. "The Sprout Social 2019 Index, Edition XV: Empower and Elevate," SproutSocial.com, accessed September 21, 2019, https://sproutsocial.com/insights/data/index/.

63. Yubo Chen, Wang Qi, and Jinhong Xie, "Online Social Interactions: A Natural Experiment on Word-of-Mouth versus Observational Learning," *Journal of Marketing Research* 68 (April 2009): 238–254.

64. Hyunmi Baek, Sehwan Oh, Hee-Dong Yang, and JoongHo Ahn, "Electronic Word-of-Mouth, Box Office Revenue and Social Media," *Electronic Commerce Research and Applications* 22 (2017): 13–23.

65. André Marchand, Thorsten Hennig-Thurau, and Caroline Wiertz, "Not All Digital Word of Mouth Is Created Equal: Understanding the Respective Impact of Consumer Reviews and Microblogs on New Product Success," *International Journal of Research in Marketing* 34, no. 2 (2017): 336–354.

66. "The CMO Survey: Highlights & Insights Report," CMOSurvey.com, February 2019, https://cmosurvey.org/wp-content/uploads/sites/15/2019/02/The_CMO_Survey-Highlights-and_Insights_Report-Feb-2019-1.pdf.

67. "Digital Advertising Spending Worldwide from 2017 to 2023, by Format (in Million U.S. Dollars)," Statista, November 30, 2018, https://www.statista.com/statistics/456679/digital-advertising-revenue-format-digital-market-outlook-worldwide/.

68. Sean Corcoran, "Revisiting the Meaning of Engagement," Forrester.com, April 12, 2011, http://blogs.forrester.com/sean_corcoran/11-04-12-revisiting_the_meaning_of_engagement.

69. Andreas M. Kaplan and Michael Haenlein, "Users of the World, Unite! The Challenges and Opportunities of Social Media," *Business Horizons* 53, no. 1 (January–February 2010): 59–68.

70. "WOMMAPEDIA," Wommapedia.org.

71. Mandy Ewing, "Integrated Marketing Communications Measurements and Evaluation," *Journal of Marketing Communications* 15, no. 2–3 (2009): 103–117.

72. Philip Kotler, Hermawan Kartajaya, and Iwan Setiawan, *Marketing 4.0: Moving from Traditional to Digital* (Hoboken, NJ: Wiley, 2017): 54.

73. Katie Winchell, "Writing the Conversation: How Social Media Is Redefining PR's Content Creation," Public Relations Tactics Apps: prsa.org, February 1, 2010, https://apps.prsa.org/Intelligence/Tactics/Articles/view/8509/1007/Writing_the_conversation_How_social_media_is_redef#.XX9ghCUpAWo.

74. "The World's Most 'Extra' Tampon," ShortyAwards.com, accessed September 20, 2019, https://shortyawards.com/11th/playtex-the-extra-newcomer.

75. Kaplan and Haenlein, "Users of the World, Unite!"

76. John Short, Ederyn Williams, and Bruce Christie, *The Social Psychology of Telecommunications* (Hoboken, NJ: Wiley, 1976).

77. Richard L. Daft and Robert H. Lengel, "Organizational Information Requirements, Media Richness, and Structural Design," *Management Science* 32, no. 5 (1986): 554–571.

78. "Gatorade: Every Day Is Your Day ft. Mia Hamm and Mallory Pugh," YouTube.com, June 4, 2019, https://www.youtube.com/watch?v=xQkSyv_arYY.

79. Kristina Monllos, "Gatorade Now Has a 'Video Everywhere' Media Strategy—and a New AP Snapchat Lens," Digiday.com, June 17, 2019, https://digiday.com/marketing/gatorade-now-video-everywhere-media-strategy-new-ar-snapchat-lens/.

80. Natalie Koltun, "Campaign Trail: How Gatorade Elevates UGC with an App for Teen Athletes," July 19, 2019, MarketingDive.com, https://www.marketingdive.com/news/campaign-trail-how-gatorade-elevates-ugc-with-an-app-for-teen-athletes/558898/.

Point of View from Control to Engagement

As the distracted consumer flits back and forth between watching TV, texting their friends, looking up information on actors, or just aimlessly surfing while the TV's on in the background, getting through to them with marketing messages on any device becomes harder and harder.[1]

—Sean Carton

PREVIEW

When is the last time you shopped in a department store, in-store or online? What did you purchase? If you are like most people, you probably have purchased a wide variety of goods and services in person and online with ease in the last couple of days. Many take for granted the fact that anything you want can be found quickly, along with prices and reviews, and purchased with the touch of a button, with easy returns if you don't like it or it doesn't fit. We have come a long way in retailing.

At the beginning of the twentieth century, John Wanamaker opened what would become the first department store. Seen as a pioneer in marketing and integral to the establishment of the profession of advertising, Wanamaker started his stores in Philadelphia and later expanded to cities such as New York, London, and Paris. Known as "The Grand Depot," the twelve-story Wanamaker's in Philadelphia famously took up an entire city block. The store pioneered the now-standard retail practices of fixed prices and money-back guarantees, expressed then as a revolutionary principle: "One price and goods returnable." A devout Christian, Wanamaker believed that if everyone was equal before God, then they should all be equal before price. This retail pioneer also started the practice of advertising and hired the first full-time advertising copywriter, John E. Powers.[2]

Despite John Wanamaker's marketing philosophy and strong belief in the power of advertising, he is also well known for a phrase that is still talked about today: "Half the money I spend on advertising is wasted. The trouble is, I don't know which half."[3] As more and more marketing, advertising, and public relations becomes digital, more and more consumer actions are becoming trackable. Perhaps all the advancements in measurable digital marketing and big data have made this statement less applicable today. If John Wanamaker were alive, would he still say it? How far have we advanced in advertising practice and performance?

The Mass Media Age Is Over

In chapter 2 we saw statistics that pointed toward the decline in mass media in various forms of traditional print and broadcast media to new digital forms. This decline has in turn impacted the practice of many professional careers, including journalism as previously discussed. Here we will discuss more specifically how this shift has impacted the marketing communications professions of advertising and public relations.

Figure 3.1. Today individuals can attract a mass audience through social media.

© Grinvalds / iStock Photo

From the Super Bowl to *Mad Men,* advertising has become more visible in popular culture, but with the advancement of digital media the practice of advertising has undergone nothing short of a revolution. **Advertising** is defined as the placement of announcements and persuasive messages in time or space purchased in mass media.[4] The basis of the advertising profession was to craft persuasive messages and then purchase space in mass media to reach a large audience. Following this formula, advertising became a very effective marketing communications tactic for well over a hundred years.

Yet the advertising industry and the marketing professionals who hire advertising firms have gone through dramatic changes in the past few decades. The changes occurred in bits and pieces but came to a more noticeable head in 2009 when the eighty-year-old leading trade publication *Advertising Age* boldly announced, "The Ad Age Is Over." The article "Cannes Swept by PR, Integrated, Internet Winners" explained that for the first time in history the top prize in the most prestigious advertising-industry award show went to an advertisement made for the internet rather than television. The film jury handed its sole Grand Prix to an internet film for Philips Electronics.[5]

In that same year, a tourism campaign for Queensland, Australia, took the first Public Relations Grand Prix along with new Direct and Cyber Cannes award categories. David Lubars, then chief creative officer of BBDO North America and president of the Cannes film and press juries, predicted, "The way the world is heading is voluntary engagement."[6] These were signs that the future of marketing communications was here. Mass marketing was moving into a new digital environment where the consumer had more involvement and control; thus more integrated communication efforts were needed to reach a more fragmented target audience. Mass media was diminishing and the method of persuasion transforming. Marketers and advertisers have entered a new age of engagement where they have less influence over all the messages consumers read, hear, and watch about their brands. Marketing departments and the advertising agencies they hire continue to move from controlled push marketing to more interactive engagement marketing.

A similar shift in public relations practice started to occur around the same period. **Public relations** creates and maintains the goodwill of the public, such as customers, employees, and investors, through nonpaid forms of media.[7] A sign in the beginning was a blog post titled "Die! Press Release! Die! Die! Die!" in which ex–*Financial Times* journalist Tom Foremski called for an end to the spin and spend on traditional public relations press releases.[8] That same year public relations agency SHIFT Communications developed the **Social Media Press Release**, which is an easy-to-scan document containing text and multimedia elements that are simple to share and that offers links to a collection of relevant information.[9] Brian Solis, digital analyst and developer of the Conversation Prism visual map of the social media landscape, saw similar dramatic changes in public relations practice. In 2009 he described a shift from public relations 1.0 of "top down" standard press release writing, account management, and standard pitching to public relations 2.0 with a "bottom up" approach of experts in fields and tools engaging with consumers through listening and monitoring, content creation and story development, community management and engagement, plus influencer identification and management.[10] A recent study of journalists found that more than half (53 percent) of US journalists don't rely on press releases and of those who do only 3 percent rely on those sent by traditional newswires.[11]

MINI CASE
Queensland Tourism

In 2009 Tourism Queensland challenged its advertising agency to deliver a global campaign that would raise awareness of the islands of the Great Barrier Reef across cultures and backgrounds. With a relatively small budget, the effort tapped into a universal desire and wrote an employment ad for "The Best Job in the World."[a] The recruitment ads were placed in fifteen countries and described a six-month contract paying $150,000 (£75,000) to live in a rent-free luxury home on Hamilton Island and blog about the experience. Candidates had to upload an application video to islandreefjob.com. The public voted for the final sixteen, who were interviewed in person.

The campaign garnered worldwide media attention through traditional advertising and public relations and benefited from the power of word-of-mouth and social media engagement with the consumer. Results included more than 8 million website visitors, 34,000 video applications from 197 countries, a 67 percent increase in Facebook fans, and a 93 percent increase in Twitter followers. The public relations value was estimated to be nearly $400 million, and more than 9,000 passengers booked trips to Queensland following the campaign.[b]

Tourism Queensland has continued their track record of social media innovation. For example, years after "The Best Job in the World," one campaign used social listening for a surprise and delight effort that selected unknowing travelers on the ground in Queensland for impromptu customized trip enhancements. The trips were shared in social media—generating stories, comments, and views ultimately resulting in 2.5 million earned media impressions to #ThisIsQueensland or @Queensland.[c]

[a] "The Best Job in the World," iab.net, accessed September 18, 2019, http://www.iab.net/media/file/Sample_Case_Study.pdf.

[b] Tourism Queensland, "'Best Job in the World' Social Media Campaign," UTalkMarketing.com, April 12, 2010, http://www.utalkmarketing.com/pages/article.aspx?articleid=17349&title=tourism-queensland-%E2%80%98best-job-in-the-world%E2%80%99-social-media-campaign.

[c] "Case Study: How Tourism and Events Queensland's Innovative Online Listening Campaign Added 'Surprise & Delight' to Visitor Experiences via Twitter," DestinationThink.com (blog), April 13, 2016, https://destinationthink.com/case-study-tourism-events-queensland/.

If the ad age is over, traditional public relations practices are diminishing, and new media is gaining so much attention, should marketers simply drop marketing communications in traditional media and move to all interactive digital and social media engagement marketing? Research says no. A study published in the *International Journal of Integrated Marketing Communications* analyzed integrated marketing communications touchpoints used in 421 Effie Award–winning campaigns from 1998 to 2010. Like Cannes, Effie Awards are prestigious awards for advertising, public relations, and marketing professionals, except that winners are also chosen primarily based on proven results. Effie campaigns are marketing success stories that are awarded for effectiveness. Each entrant submits verifiable data that demonstrates the campaign has delivered real business results by meeting its marketing objectives.[12]

The research found that in twelve years of Effie Award–winning campaigns, there was an overall increase in the number of marketing or consumer touchpoints from an average of two (such as TV and print) to six (such as TV, print, radio, public relations, interactive, consumer involvement). Additionally, it was found that traditional media such as TV has not been replaced by the new digital media. Instead, emerging media has been added to traditional advertising media to ensure success.[13] As mass media has fragmented, marketing communications has had to spread its persuasive messages over more and more places to reach the same audience and achieve successful results. See table 3.1 for a list of examples of Effie Award–winning marketing campaigns and their increased touch-point usage over the

Table 3.1. Effie Award Winners by Touch Point from 1998 to 2010

Year	Sponsor and Title	Touch Points	Touch Point Categories
1998	Maytag, "Keeping Your Cool"	1	TV
1999	YoCrunch, "Smooth & Crunchy"	2	Radio, Retail
2000	Volkswagen, "New Jetta Launch"	3	TV, Radio, Interactive
2001	Maybelline, "Maybe She's Born with It"	4	TV, Print, Sponsorship, Retail
2002	*LA Times*, "Connecting Us"	5	TV, Radio, Print, OOH, Retail
2003	Bud Light, "Great Lengths"	6	TV, Radio, Print, Interactive, OOH
2004	Yahoo Search, "The New Yahoo"	7	TV, Radio, PR, Interactive, OOH, Guerrilla
2005	Breathe Right, "Back in the Sack"	8	TV, Radio, Print, Direct Mail, PR, Interactive, Guerrilla
2006	Infinity Broadcasting, "How Far Will You Go?"	9	TV, Radio, Print, PR, Interactive, OOH, Retail, Consumer
2007	Saab, "Born from Jets"	10	TV, Radio, Print, Direct Mail, PR, Interactive, OOH, Retail
2008	Mayfield Dairy, "Nurture Milk Launch"	11	TV, Print, Direct Mail, OOH, PR, Direct Email, Design, Interactive, Retail, Guerrilla, Consumer
2009	Dos Equis, "The Most Interesting Man in the World"	12	TV, Radio, Print, Direct Email, PR, Design, Cinema, Interactive, Sponsorship, Retail, Guerrilla, Consumer Involvement
2010	Clear Wireless, "Welcome to the Future"	13	TV, Radio, Print, Direct Mail, Direct Email, PR, Cinema, Interactive, OOH, Trade, Sponsorship, Retail, Guerrilla

Source: Keith A. Quesenberry, Michael K. Coolsen, and Kristen Wilkerson, "IMC and the Effies: Use of Integrated Marketing Communications Touchpoints Among Effie Award Winners," *International Journal of Integrated Marketing Communications* 4, no. 2 (2012): 60–72.

Note: OOH = out-of-home advertising sources such as billboards and transit ads.

twelve-year study period. More recent research confirms that this multi-touchpoint approach is more effective. The 2019 Edelman trust barometer confirms this previous IMC research. As consumers see a message repeated across channels, their trust in that message increases from 66 percent trust with one touchpoint to 97 percent trust with six touchpoints.[14]

How should marketers respond to this new multi-touchpoint, engagement reality? Marketing communications professionals, whether they approach social media from the marketing, advertising, or public relations discipline, need to adjust their perspective from a strict, top-down control strategy to a more participative and interactive one.[15] As Jeff Howe said in *the Atlantic,* "Now, a brand's success has everything to do with the global, real-time, 24/7, electronic conversation taking place around it. As consumers gain leverage, corporations are learning to obey."[16] Yet practicing marketing, advertising, and public relations in this post-control marketing world doesn't mean all brands and organizations are simply at the mercy of the consumer. There is room for strategy and influence and even greater opportunity for success.

Whether you view this shift in perspective as obeying the consumer or choosing to change, organizations must let go of the traditional message-control model. Empowered consumers generating and sharing their own brand content do not fit neatly into traditional models of marketing communications strategy and practice.[17] Some estimate that consumers are now generating at least a quarter of all messages about a brand on the web. This shift requires a strategic change much bigger than simply purchasing more consumer touchpoints or reaching more journalists for more earned media stories with advertiser-crafted sell messages and highly spun public relations news releases. Social media is a different medium where users have very different expectations. Traditional advertising is built upon purchasing consumer attention through interruption, and traditional public relations is built upon influencing journalists to get a message out through news. To be effective in social media, the brand must build interest and engagement with consumers directly in the social media channel.

Social media is not a quick add-on, like picking up another advertising channel such as TV, radio, and billboards, or holding an event, or sending out a release about a new feature. Social media must be approached in a separate way, but still be integrated into traditional marketing communication. Yet social media goes beyond the disciplines of advertising, public relations, and even marketing itself. When brands open a social engagement channel, they will also find questions and interactions with consumers that have more to do with other business units such as operations, customer service, and human resources. A social media strategy affects the entire business organization. Consumers see brand social media accounts as one place to get all their needs including product information, but also nonmarketing needs such as customer service, sales account information, and even human resources–focused employee or recruitment requests.[18] Therefore, any truly effective social media strategy must be built from the ground up, integrating all business units.

Marketing communications professionals must be careful not to underestimate the extent of this change from control to engagement. This seemingly simple adjustment in mindset can make a vast difference in practice. A shift of this magnitude occurred with the rise of a new discipline: integrated marketing communications (IMC). IMC arose out of a desire and need for marketers to integrate messages for consistency across traditional media channels and marketing communications disciplines. This was a change in the way managers thought about marketing to improve efficiency of promotional communication. Later it also became an effective tool to combat the proliferation of media clutter and build awareness in light of decreasing mass media audience.[19] Marketers could no longer rely on reaching their target markets by buying mass audience attention in one or two places or gaining a couple of high-profile news stories in traditional media. **Integrated marketing communications (IMC)** seeks to align and coordinate all marketing communications delivered to consumers to present a cohesive whole that persuades consumers to purchase.[20]

With IMC, communications touchpoints are managed together for consistency and greater impact. Yet even this system and strategy has broken down with the increased consumer adoption of social media. Integrated marketing communications is no longer enough because social media is not just another organization-controlled touchpoint. The consumer has a more powerful voice and therefore has a say in brand communication (see figure 3.2). Today consumers create communications about businesses and organizations—good, bad, and indifferent—that organizations cannot directly control. Consumers have their own mass media channels that brands cannot buy and traditional marketing practices don't account adequately for this social media–empowered consumer.[21] Hence, even an integrated

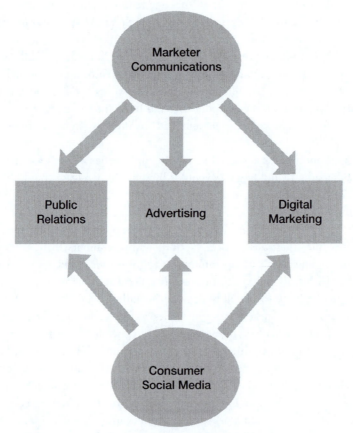

Figure 3.2. Control marketing is breaking down.

marketing communications approach must evolve into an engagement model centered on a more powerful, influential, and demanding consumer.

Therefore, organizations must now do more than create consistent marketing messages pushed out to consumers through traditional communications disciplines. Both company-generated messages and consumer-generated communications should be integrated through engagement to create one cohesive marketing strategy. Social media creates conversations with consumers rather than one-sided strictly persuasive or sales-oriented brand messages.[22] Social media requires creating content the consumer values and will choose to engage with and share. Seth Godin calls this permission marketing, describing it as "the privilege (not the right) of delivering anticipated, personal and relevant messages to people who actually want to get them."[23] This phrase has also now become a legal term with new privacy regulations put in place and will be discussed further in chapter 15.

When you let consumers in, they can say anything about the brand to anyone listening or reading. Because the marketer cannot predict what the customer will say, the strategies must also be more flexible and nimbler, accounting for more immediate adjustment, response, and inclusion of other business units like customer service, sales, and human resources. Campaigns and messages cannot be crafted over months. They need to be delivered live in the moment.

This shift in perspective does not mean social media marketing is not persuasive. The business objectives to sell a product or service or gain support for a nonprofit organization remain the same, but the method to achieve those results needs to change. Interrupting sell messages should be balanced with content of value that attracts the audiences. Push sell messages should be supplemented with two-way consumer communication that involves them in the brand. News stories by journalists should be supported with consumer-generated brand content that is encouraged and shared. Consumer complaints about products and services should be noted and addressed. Again, this shift in mindset and strategy is not about completely giving up all control of a brand; it is about changing methods to maintain control and influence in a new consumer-centered social media reality.

From Communication Interruption to Engagement

What feeling do you get when you're walking down the street or through the mall and a person stops to interrupt you and deliver a polished sales speech? You try to tell them that you are not interested. You try to tell them what you actually want, but they don't listen and instead of talking with you, they keep talking at you with product feature after product feature until you agree to buy or you simply run away. This can happen in social media.[24]

What would a marketer or advertiser do if they could not interrupt their audience? How would that change their marketing-communication message, strategy, and tactics? The answers to these questions require a new model of marketing. This new model requires both interaction and integration of all information between the company and consumer.[25] Moving beyond traditional integrated marketing communications, brands must now take a step back to include all sources of brand messages. The big difference now is that this not only includes brand communication produced by different business departments or marketing partners, but also all consumer-generated brand content. Think of this new role as less of an integrated communications creator or controller and more of an integrated communications manager. In this new role, communications professionals must also move from an overall emphasis on interruption to more of an engagement perspective. When thinking about reaching a target audience with brand messages, traditional interruptive advertising and traditional public relations media placement still plays a role, but engagement should be a key consideration.

With the rise of the third screen and simultaneous digital and social media usage, it can be hard to tell if anyone is really paying attention to traditional media channels. As author Sean Carton says in a *ClickZ* article on the distracted consumer, "In a media marketplace that's increasingly fragmented and deficient in consumer attention, social media is one place where people tend to spend lots of time engaged with content and opinions."[26] To succeed today, marketing communications professionals must draw interest from the consumer where their attention is shifting, and must do it in a way to which they will respond.

If mass media is losing consumer attention and that attention is shifting to social media, then organizations must follow to maintain brand attention. In this sense, social media is not a development taking away control from the marketing, advertising, and public relations professional. If brands learn to play by the new engagement rules, social media represents an opportunity to maintain control. Social media integration just may be the glue that can hold the professional practice of marketing, advertising, and public relations together in this new age of interactive media. Web 2.0 was not developed to destroy advertising, public relations, or traditional marketing. Marketing communications professionals must simply evolve with these developments into matching practices of Marketing 2.0, Advertising 2.0, and Public Relations 2.0.

What if marketers thought of the consumer as less of a target to be sold to and more of a coauthor of the brand?[27] Professor John Deighton of Harvard Business School argues that the digital interactive transformation of marketing has become one of consumer collaboration. This new marketing model now includes a consumer's use of digital media or user-generated content that lies beyond the control of marketers. Deighton states, "The shift from broadcasting to interaction within digital communities is moving the locus of control over meanings from marketer to consumer and rewarding more participatory, more sincere and less directive marketing styles."[28] Philip Kotler, Hermawan Kartajaya, and Iwan Setiawan say we've moved into a new era of Marketing 4.0 where these customer communities are the new consumer segments of old marketing.[29] In an almost counterintuitive way, marketing communications professionals must give up brand control in order to maintain it. Learning to give up control and engage with the consumer more than competitors could reward a marketer and their organization with a competitive advantage.

One way to gauge the impact of these changes is to add to traditional marketing performance measurements such as market share communications measurements like share of voice. **Share of voice** is your brand social media mentions divided by total competitive brand social media mentions.[30] For further indication look at the sentiment of those social media comments. **Sentiment analysis** is identifying and categorizing opinions in a piece of text, determining if the attitude expressed is positive, negative, or neutral.[31] Is your brand being talked about more or less than competitors in social media? Does your brand have

Figure 3.3. Consumer social feedback contributes to brand perception and awareness.

© Tolgart / iStock Photo

higher or lower positive to negative social media sentiment compared to competitors? Social media management company Lithium suggests that these measurements can be indicators of brand loyalty, which contributes to brand sales. Therefore, improving share of voice and increasing positive to negative brand mentions above competitors in social media can be a factor in contributing to market share.

In a *PR Week* article titled "Earned Media Measured: How to Prove Your Worth," Cision suggests that public relations firms measure the impact of their campaigns with new measurements for earned media. It is no longer about news story clippings but measuring the output of earned media that reflects the new converged media reality that proves the value of PR outside of traditional discipline silos. This starts with understanding business objectives and then crafting research and measurement strategies around measuring those objectives, including earned media coverage, social media monitoring, and website analytics. Cision's Tom Ritchie says this approach makes it easier to "communicate to the decision maker and the c-suite in a way that makes more sense to them."[32]

To gain this social media and overall business advantage, new marketing practices should aim to manage and integrate all brand-related communication, whether organization-created or consumer-generated, through more of a two-way conversation. Part IV of this book will explain in more detail how this engagement goes beyond marketing, advertising, and public relations practice to other organizational areas. To be the most effective, social media management and strategy must include other business units or disciplines such as research, product development, customer service, sales, and human resources.

To be effective, social media management must also understand how social media fits into the bigger picture of marketing and business objectives. Social media actions and even overall strategies and plans can exist on their own, but without an understanding of the marketing and business behind them, they could be acting in vain. Even communication-focused disciplines such as advertising and public relations must embrace the need for broader marketing and business knowledge. A survey of global corporate social media professionals found that 90 percent say social media is considered an important part of their marketing strategy and 80 percent say that social media is an important part of their business strategy.[33]

This means that social media professionals must make the business connection not only by speaking the language of social media but also by translating social media activity into business action. Most C-Suite or top-level senior executives (CEO, CFO, CIO, COO, etc.) don't care about social media account follower numbers. To get approval and funding for social strategies, marketing communications professionals need to understand and measure the broader business goals such as sales, market share, awareness, customer retention, leads, and so forth. Learn to speak the language of business to create and measure more effective communications plans that prove your worth.

Social media professionals must also see the connection beyond their discipline. When a brand opens a two-way communication channel with a customer, the customer does not distinguish between marketing and nonmarketing messaging, but rather views the brand as one whole. In the new consumer collaboration model, companies become hubs for the constant flow of brand discussion as they monitor, respond to, and facilitate consumer buzz, and integrate consumer social feedback into other organizational activities. IMC should evolve from integrated marketing communications to integrated communication management where marketer and consumer both contribute to the brand's messaging, promotion, and its products and services.

Marketing 2.0, Advertising 2.0, and Public Relations 2.0 recognize the power of the consumer social media voice to create and spread brand messages, improve operations and customer service, leverage influencers, communicate with key stakeholders such as employees and investors, recruit new employees, and provide valuable product, service, and marketing insight to supplement traditional research. An article in *AdNews* by Amaury Tréguer sums up this thought nicely with the title "Time to Let Consumers Be the Voice of Brands."[34] Consumer brand social media is too powerful to ignore. An Olapic consumer trust survey found that 70 percent of US respondents and 53 percent of European respondents indicated that they are more likely to buy a product after seeing a positive or relatable consumer-generated image of it.[35]

Adjusting to this transformation is challenging. It requires changes in strategy, tools, and organization, but there is reward for the organizations that embrace the shift in mindset and implement a social media strategy correctly. Research into electronic word-of-mouth communication (eWOM) suggests that it is seen as a reliable source of information, increases the perceived value of offerings, and improves loyalty intentions.[36] Other research has found that participation in company or brand social networks enhances value co-creation by customers and customer stickiness. **Customer co-creation** is simply the joint creation of value by the company and customer.[37] **Customer stickiness** is the increased chance to utilize the same product or service that was bought before.[38] The authors of the research indicate that brand social networks are an important competitive marketing channel and play an important role in business enterprise.[39] Thus, the consumer voice generates brand awareness, increases brand value, and builds loyalty. In social media, loyalty is contagious. Businesses and organizations have always known word-of-mouth is the best form of advertising. Now through social media it has finally reached the scale and scope to be a significant business objective–reaching strategy.

Listening to what customers, competitors, critics, and supporters are saying is key to getting results from social media campaigns. How does someone listen? **Homegrown monitoring** is using search engines and going to each social media platform to find and manually track and analyze brand social media conversation.[40] This includes simply typing into the Google search box the brand or product name with the word "complaint" or "love," performing a blog search, and searching names and hashtags in each social media network. Discover what people are saying who have tweeted a company, product, or CEO's name. Find public support forums, fan clubs, and sites such as Yelp or TripAdvisor, and check the ratings and reviews on retail sites like Amazon.com. Do the same search for competitors as well. Be sure to locate all brand social media accounts and find conversations that are happening on social media platforms where the brand doesn't currently have an official presence.

Professional monitoring is using one or multiple software tools to track and analyze brand social media conversation in one or multiple social media platforms.[41] Professional monitoring is possible when social media platforms give access to their API (application program interface) to third party software developers. Professional monitoring doesn't always mean paid. There are numerous free social media monitoring tools and paid options often offer free basic accounts with fewer features or free, limited trials. This is especially suitable for students, small businesses, and startups. Yet homegrown monitoring efforts don't scale. If an organization is serious about social media and has a budget for it, it should invest in a paid social media–monitoring service and content-management system. Partnering with a vendor will save time in collecting data, delivering new content, and creating reports.

Costs for paid social media monitoring vary widely from $20 a month to $10,000 a month or more, based on needs, time, and long-term strategy for listening, content publishing, analytics, integration, and reports.[42] This expense could also be divided among departments. For example, chapter 13 details how real-time social media monitoring can turn into a real asset for customer service. See appendix B, "Social Media Tools and Resources," for a listing of the major tools available with both paid and free social media listening options. For the most up-to-date list, visit postcontrolmarketing.com/links.

GoPro is an expert at customer co-creation. To jumpstart the launch of the new HERO7 Black, the brand challenged the GoPro brand community to help them create the most epic highlight reel ever made. The featured content creators would share $1 million in contest winnings. While previous product highlight videos were shot by their in-house team, they believed the new camera features enabled anyone to capture professional-looking shots. Users were encouraged to share their clips with the social media hashtag #GoPro-MillionDollarChallenge. The brand's social media community managers engaged with fans through comments, reposting across YouTube, Facebook, Instagram, and Twitter and featuring the best on GoPro's owned channels. In the end the brand crowdsourced their product highlight video from 25,000 submissions with fifty-six creators from twenty-two countries making the final cut. Each took home nearly $18,000 for their efforts. The video earned over three million views across YouTube and Facebook and picked up earned media mentions in news articles and broadcasts.[43]

Careers in Social Media

As a result of these changes, growth and demand for employees with social media skills has increased greatly with many new career possibilities. A McKinley Marketing Partners survey of marketing companies looking to hire found that the top in-demand marketing skills were digital marketing (59 percent) compared to the bottom category of product marketing (25 percent). The top skills in demand within digital marketing include digital advertising, content creation and curation, content strategy, and social media. Despite the active demand for digital skills at 59 percent, the available supply of active job seekers with digital skills is only 19 percent, representing a 30 percent gap. This is certainly a problem for companies trying to attract those employees. But it represents a big opportunity for marketing communications professionals or students who can demonstrate that they have that knowledge and those skills.[44]

Figure 3.4. Social media skills are required in many professions and office environments.

© Iovro77 / iStock Photo

The story is the same in the advertising and public relations industries. An *Advertising Age* article by Maureen Morrison explained that digital skills are no longer a plus but are expected and says that ad agency leaders "need to be steeped in the digital landscape and everything that goes along with it: social platforms and their data, ad formats and attribution models."[45] Public relations firms are also emphasizing social media skills. A survey of public relations firms by Gould+Partners asked what they require of new hires. Under the category of preferred knowledge, social media practices was number one (88 percent) followed by public relations practices (69 percent).[46] Having social media skills has become essential for any marketing communications professional.

Yet there are also a host of new job roles focused on social media with many options inside the field itself. And there are many types of organizations where these social media job roles are being employed. It is useful to consider the different roles that may match your interest and skills and the type of work environment that you may prefer. Specific social media roles and titles are still evolving, but the most common ones will be discussed.

Social media strategists plan an organization's social media strategy, ensuring the strategy connects to larger objectives and integrates marketing, advertising, and public relations. Strategists often utilize tools like social media audits to improve social media content and measure performance to report results to management. The average salary for social media strategists in the United States is $68,000.[47] The next position is more action oriented. **Social media marketing managers** manage the creation and execution of an organization's social media strategy, which can include the overall brand presence and specific campaigns. At larger organizations they have people under them to help with implementation and day-to-days tasks. At smaller organizations social media managers may also implement the strategy they manage. The average salary for social media managers is around $54,000.[48]

Other roles are more on the front lines of social media. **Social media community managers** create and foster social media communities built around a brand through direct engagement as a person advocating for the brand on social media channels. They monitor and respond to conversations happening across social media platforms or may be assigned to specific social networks. The average salary of social media community managers is $54,000. **Social media coordinators** plan, implement, and monitor a brand's social media strategy to meet organizational objectives working with content creators, internal departments, and external partners to measure and improve performance.[49] The average salary for social media coordinators in the United States is around $45,000.[50] **Social media specialists** focus on implementation of social media strategy, writing social copy, scheduling social content, and tracking social media key performance indicators (KPIs) while staying up to date on the latest trends in social media. The average salary for a social media strategist in the United States is $41,000.[51]

Other social media roles are focused on creating content. **Social media copywriters** plan, create, and analyze channel-specific brand social media written content, building content calendars, writing guidelines, and finding internal and external sources. The average salary for a social media copywriter in the United States is $50,000.[52] **Social media graphic designers** create and maintain visual brand assets and find and create appropriate images and graphics for various social media channel content. The average salary for a social media graphic designer in the United States is $46,000.[53] **Social media video specialists** capture, edit, and produce videos for brand assets and specific social media channel content. The average salary for a social media video specialist in the United States is $47,000.[54]

Some social media roles are oriented toward more specialized areas. **Influencer relations managers** identify, build, and manage mutual relationships with relevant celebrity, macro, and micro influencers to create and share brand social media content. The average salary for an influencer relations manager in the United States is $60,000.[55] **Social media analysts** focus on social media measurement by developing systems, processes, and reporting methods that gather and analyze social media metrics to make better-informed decisions and optimize strategies, tactics, and content.[56] The average salary for a social media analyst in the United States is $49,000.[57] A **content marketing manager** plans, creates, and measures all digital content including social media and other content such as eBooks, email, search, and display ads to drive traffic to brand websites.[58] The average salary for a content marketing manager in the United States is $66,000.[59]

It is also important to mention hybrid roles where professionals trained as journalists are getting jobs as social media content developers for news brands and companies. A **journalist social media content developer** uses journalism skills to promote news brands or create news-style content for corporate brands in social media. As mentioned earlier in the chapter, traditional journalist newsrooms are shrinking but social media journalists are in demand whether using social media to promote news content or to create newsworthy social media content for businesses and organizations. According a survey by Curata, the

Figure 3.5. Social media professionals can work from home as freelancers or solopreneurs.

© Deagreez / iStock Photo

greatest missing skill in today's content marketers is the ability to create content. Increasingly brands are seeking journalists to fill these social media content roles as skilled researchers, writers, editors, interviewers, multimedia storytellers, and fact checkers.[60]

There is an option where social media professionals can work for themselves. **Social media freelancers** provide the services of specific social media roles on a project or campaign basis versus as a full-time employee.[61] This could also be called being a social media solopreneur. A **solopreneur** is an entrepreneur who runs a business without full-time employees. Being a solopreneur often means you can work from home and set your own hours; it provides the most flexibility. For example, a social media writer could work on projects for a brand to write content for a social media campaign from a social media manager at a company. Or a social media strategist could provide consulting services to a brand and create a social media strategy. If the brand wants the content to be executed, the solopreneur could then bring in additional freelance social media writers and designers to complete the campaign.[62] The average rate for a social media freelancer in the United States is $60 an hour.[63]

To get the best idea of current positions, duties, and requirements, visit an online job database and search available positions with the keywords social media. Some options include

- LinkedIn Jobs at https://www.linkedin.com/jobs/
- Indeed at https://www.indeed.com/
- ZipRecruiter at https://www.ziprecruiter.com/
- Glassdoor at https://www.glassdoor.com/index.htm
- SimplyHired at https://www.simplyhired.com/.

Also consider the jobs boards for the major professional organizations where social media professionals may work:

- American Marketing Association at https://jobs.ama.org/
- Public Relations Society of America at https://jobs.prsa.org/
- American Advertising Federation at http://jobs.aaf.org
- Association of National Advertisers at https://www.ana.net/jobpostings.

For an idea of the type of freelance social media work available, search sites like

- Upwork at https://www.upwork.com/
- Flexjobs at https://www.flexjobs.com/
- Fiverr at https://www.fiverr.com/
- LinkedIn Profinder at https://www.linkedin.com/profinder
- Freelancer at https://www.freelancer.com/
- Guru at https://www.guru.com/.

Finally, for those hybrid journalism social media content jobs, search on the job boards above for employers seeking people with journalism skills. Also look for hybrid positions on Journalism Jobs at https://www.journalismjobs.com/.

Another consideration for careers in social media management is that these roles often present unique challenges from other jobs that may be more behind the scenes at an organization. The key is being aware of the challenges and having a plan in place to avoid getting burned out in your social media career. See the box: Social Media Manager Mental Health for more information on these unique challenges and best practices to avoid burnout.

 ## Social Media Manager Mental Health

Social media professional Thea Neal posted an article on LinkedIn asking the question, "Should you ask your social media manager if they're okay?" The answer is yes. A social media career can be fun, exciting, and rewarding, but it also can come with its own unique stresses. As Neal points out, the internet isn't always a fun place. You may be hated online because you represent that brand. Increasing studies are coming out attributing negative health effects from social media use and social media professionals may spend the most time in these environments. The field is also still very new and is changing all the time; you must keep up. Thus, many professionals can find themselves with increased responsibilities without necessarily increased staff. It is also hard to leave your work at the office when social media is 24/7/365 days a year. Your professional brand standards can creep into your personal social media, making personal posting work.[a]

Yet social media offers amazing opportunities that allow organizations and individuals to reach audiences instantly across the globe, enabling more than ever to succeed. As a social media professional you can make a real difference in people's lives and help organizations meet their objectives. It is rewarding knowing your hard work is making a difference and seeing the numbers that prove it. Social media can be a lot of fun, creating content and engaging with people. But how do you avoid the negative effects and stresses? Olga Rabo of Iconosquare suggests six mental health survival tips for social media managers:

1. *Don't multitask.* Set up dedicated time for separate activities.
2. *Unfollow accounts.* Only take in content that contributes to your mission and joy.
3. *Stop being hooked on likes.* Quality engagement matters more and they're addictive.
4. *Be aware of triggers.* Minimize pressure to respond and unnecessary notifications.
5. *Browse mindfully.* Only go on social media with a purpose and interact with positive content.
6. *Reduce use.* Set time limits. It makes you more productive and increases well-being.[b]

Emma Brown at Hootsuite has a related but different perspective that provides additional considerations that can apply to anyone for professional and personal use. Brown suggests seven ways to avoid social media burnout:

1. *Set boundaries.* Have social media–free times and turn off work streams after work.
2. *Give your eyes a rest.* Eye strain can lead to irritated eyes, neck/back pain, and headaches.
3. *Get up and move.* Walk (without your phone) regularly for mental and physical health.
4. *Get some sleep.* Sleep (without devices in bed) is healthy and makes you more productive.
5. *Structure your time.* Assign parts of your day to specific activities (such as one-hour blocks).
6. *Delete apps.* Make your phone your personal device. Manage brand social on your laptop.
7. *Digital detox.* Take digital free time off for a night or weekend to recharge.[c]

Whether your title has the term *social media* in it or not, most professional marketing, advertising, and public relationship jobs today require engagement with social media. Even part-time responsibilities can cause stress. Be sure to consider these suggestions and others. Olga Rabo reminds us that "social media is meant to be social. It's meant to connect with other people, not lose ourselves in feeds and letting likes and notifications get the best of us."[d]

[a] Thea Neal, "Should You Ask Your Social Media Manager If They're Okay?" LinkedIn.com, June 11, 2018, https://www.linkedin.com/pulse/should-you-ask-your-social-media-manager-theyre-okay-thea-neal.
[b] Olga Rabo, "Social Media and Mental Health: 6 Survival Tips for Social Media Managers," Blog.Iconosquare.com, July 11, 2019, https://blog.iconosquare.com/social-media-and-mental-health/.
[c] Emma Brown, "7 Ways for Social Media Marketers to Avoid Social Media Burnout," Blog.Hootsuite.com, February 19, 2019, https://blog.hootsuite.com/ways-to-avoid-social-media-burnout/.
[d] Rabo, "Social Media and Mental Health."

Besides specific social media roles, there are various types of organizations within which social media professionals can work. We have already discussed working on your own as a freelancer or solopreneur. The **marketing department** is the department in an organization that promotes the business and drives sales of products and services.[64] Many social media positions today are hired in-house at the company or organization, working directly in the marketing department. A social media professional at a company could also be housed in the corporate communications department, and some companies are creating separate social media departments that work with other departments including marketing, communications, sales, customer service, and human resources. Many companies also hire outside firms to help will the planning and implementation of social media.

A **public relations agency** is hired by organizations to conceive, produce, and manage unpaid messages to the public through media to change public actions by influencing opinions.[65] PR agencies often provide services to their clients such as strategy development, messaging, media relations, content marketing, social media marketing, event planning, crisis communication, and influencer relations.[66] An **advertising agency** is hired by organizations to conceive, produce, and manage paid commercial messages through TV, outdoor, ratio, print, digital, and social marketing to promote products and services. Ad agencies can be hired to produce a single ad campaign or may be agency of record for a brand, providing multiple integrated services in an ongoing relationship as a brand partner providing strategy, implementation, and measurement.[67]

A **digital marketing agency** is hired by organizations to conceive, produce, and manage brand assets through digital media including website, mobile, and digital ads to promote products and services. Digital agencies often focus on services such as website design and development, apps, search engine optimization, search and display advertising, social media and email marketing, content creation, online lead generation, plus mobile apps and campaigns.[68] A **social media agency** is hired by organizations to conceive, produce, and manage the presence of a brand through social media channels such as social networks, messaging apps, blogs and forums, podcasts, ratings, and reviews. Social media agencies often focus on social media strategy, content creation, community management, paid social

Table 3.2. Social Media Professional Job Roles, Organizations, and Job Databases

Social Media Job Roles	
Social media strategist	Social media video specialist
Social media marketing manager	Influencer relations manager
Social media community manager	Social media analyst
Social media coordinator	Content marketing manager
Social media specialist	Journalist social media content developer
Social media copywriter	Social media freelancer
Social media graphic designer	Social media solopreneur

Social Media Organizations	
Marketing department	Social media agency
Public relations agency	News organization
Advertising agency	Solopreneur
Digital marketing agency	

Job Databases (Search Social Media)	
LinkedIn Jobs (linkedin.com/jobs)	**Freelance**
Indeed (indeed.com)	Upwork (upwork.com)
ZipRecruiter (ziprecruiter.com)	Flexjobs (flexjobs.com)
Glassdoor (glassdoor.com)	Fiverr (fiverr.com)
SimplyHired (simplyhired.com)	LinkedIn Profinder (linkedin.com/profinder)
AMA (jobs.ama.org)	Freelancer (freelancer.com)
PRSA (jobs.prsa.org)	Guru (guru.com)
AAF (jobs.aaf.org)	Journalism Jobs (journalismjobs.com)
ANA (ana.net/jobpostings)	

advertising, influencer engagement, social listening, measurement and monitoring, promotions, and crisis management.[69] Finally, journalists could be hired for social media content developer roles for news organizations. While most of the time these agencies are outside firms, some companies have hired employees to form their own inhouse PR, advertising, and digital departments. For a summary of social media roles, organizations, and job databases, see table 3.2.

The CMO Survey reports that nearly one-fourth (24 percent) of a company's social media activities are performed by outside agencies. This has increased from just 17 percent in 2017, but it also means that three-fourth of social media activities are performed inside a company. This makes sense when you consider how important social media has become, impacting departments across the company and often requiring live response.

While social media knowledge is important in any job related to marketing communications today, most social media–specific jobs are inside companies and organizations themselves. The great opportunity here is to marry your interest in social media with your passion for another field. Perhaps you love sports. Focus your knowledge and efforts on social media in sports and look for social media jobs at sports teams, leagues, college athletic departments, or e-sports brands. Are you really into fashion? Focus your knowledge and experience on social media in fashion and look for social media positions at fashion brands or fashion retailers. No matter your interest, from cars and tech to health and nonprofits, chances are that brands in that industry need social media professionals.[70] Also remember that if you end up in or pursuing another job in any of these departments or agencies, social media may be part of your job and your understanding of social media will be a benefit; it will improve social media integration with your key function and make you a more valuable employee and prospect.

Theoretically Speaking: The Four Ps to the Four Cs

A basic principle in marketing is the **Four Ps**, which divides the marketing mix or function into four interconnected parts: product, price, promotion, and place (distribution).[71] The Four Ps concept was first introduced by Jerome E. McCarthy and then popularized by Philip Kotler, the Father of Modern Marketing.[72] This traditional Four Ps view of marketing has been taught since the 1960s. However, in the 1980s Gordon Bruner and other scholars started to argue that the Four Ps were no longer adequate to describe the new breadth of marketing applications. Bruner proposed a new marketing mix termed the Four Cs of concept, channels, costs, and communication.[73] The Four Cs were said to address changes in marketing tools and consumer perspectives.

Around the same time, the concept of integrated marketing communications (IMC) was introduced by Don E. Schultz and other scholars. The practice of IMC argues for the integration of what were previously seen as separate methodologies: advertising, sales promotion, direct marketing, and public relations. IMC seeks to align and coordinate all marketing communications delivered to consumers to present a cohesive whole that persuades consumers to purchase.[74] IMC is also said to focus on consumer-centric communication to meet the needs and desires of the customer.

More recently, Robert Lauterborn has further refined the Four Cs concept, emphasizing the value of customers and the importance of convenience and relationships. The **Four Cs** can be explained as consumer not product, cost not price, convenience not place, and communicate not promote. In this shift in perspective from marketer to consumer, value defines the product in the marketplace instead of product features. In this perspective, consideration is paid to the customer's needs, limited money, and shopping experience, and communication becomes more interactive and relational.[75]

Phillip Kotler, who was integral in founding the concept of the Four Ps, now acknowledges that the concept of marketing mix has evolved to include customer participation. In his book *Marketing 4.0* with Hermawan Kartajaya and Iwan Setiawan, he proposes that the Four Ps should be redefined as a connected marketing mix of the Four Cs of co-creation, currency, communal activation, and conversation.[76] Whether you believe that the Four Ps are relevant or not, and no matter which new definition of the Four Cs you embrace, it is clear that the marketing mix has changed and marketers' strategies must change along with it. In the GoPro HERO7 launch campaign explained above, what difference does it make to understand marketing from this new perspective? Would GoPro be as successful if they had a more traditional product, price, place, and promotion marketer perspective?

Chapter 3 Checklist

Social media can change quickly. Visit Post Control Marketing (http://www.postcontrol marketing.com) for updates, but also use this chapter checklist to briefly check how social media statistics in this chapter have changed since publication.

- ✓ How have the definitions of marketing, advertising, and public relations changed? Are these traditional disciplines evolving and/or merging?
- ✓ Have the roles and organizations of social media professionals changed? Are there new job titles and responsibilities? Do most social media professionals work in company departments or agencies? Which departments and which agencies?
- ✓ Is the concept of the Four Ps in marketing still the standard? Has there been greater adoption of the Four Cs? Which specific Cs are professionals using?

 SOCIAL PLAN PART 3

Quantifying Engagement

Ask and answer these questions: Is the brand integrating the consumer's voice into the organization? In what areas are consumers being integrated and engaged, and how much? In this part of the social media plan, visit all the active social media accounts for the brand, product, or service. Visit each account and scroll down the posts. Who is talking? Is it only the brand or are consumers responding? When consumers do respond, does the brand respond back? Is the brand fixing customer-support problems via social media? Has the brand ever considered or used consumer product or service ideas given in social media feedback? Conduct this research and then report findings in these areas:

1. List all brand social media channels with account names and active brand participants.
2. Gauge the interaction by quantifying brand versus consumer posts.
3. Provide example responses in each category: customer support, product/service ideas, promotions, and appreciation.
4. Explain any evidence that the brand has acted on customer social media contributions such as improving the product or service or using brand content.
5. List possible social media channels where the brand's consumers are active but the brand is not.

For a condensed version of the social plan see appendix A: Three-Part Social Plan.

KEY CONCEPTS

advertising

public relations

social media press release

integrated marketing communications (IMC)

share of voice

sentiment analysis

customer co-creation

customer stickiness

homegrown monitoring

professional monitoring

social media strategist

social media marketing manager

social media community manager

social media coordinator

social media specialist

social media copywriter

social media graphic designer

social media video specialist

influencer relations manager

social media analyst

content marketing manager

journalist social media content developer

social media freelancer

solopreneur

marketing department

public relations agency

advertising agency

digital marketing agency

social media agency

Four Ps

Four Cs

QUESTIONS FOR DISCUSSION

1. The distracted consumer is a marketing problem, but also a human one. In the book *The Shallows: What the Internet Is Doing to Our Brains,* Nicholas Carr presents research arguing that the internet is physically changing our brains and reducing attention spans.[77] How distracted are you? Do you find your attention span waning?

2. What are your thoughts on integrated marketing communications? Is it always necessary, or do you believe a campaign could still be a success by using only one touchpoint, such as TV or just social media?

3. What opportunities are out there for marketing, advertising, and public relations professionals with social media skills? Do some job searches and find the top titles for social media pros. Make a list of required skills and responsibilities. If you found your dream job, plan to acquire those skills as you work your way through this book.

4. Ethics is important in social media. Co-creation sounds like a great concept, but can companies go too far? TikTok has grown quickly via paid social media ads on other social networks. Some users have been surprised to see their personal videos being used in those ads. TikTok claims it was in the user agreement. Is this ethical?

ADDITIONAL EXERCISES

1. Go back to the John Wanamaker quote: "Half the money I spend on advertising is wasted. The trouble is, I don't know which half." Do you believe this statement is still true today? Find evidence, tools, and research that prove Wanamaker wrong. How do you know advertising works today? Is 100 percent of advertising spending not wasted, or has the percentage changed, and, if so, to what? You can also attempt this for public relations. What percentage of public relations spending can be proven to be effective and not wasted?

2. Perform a content analysis of all of the commercials seen during one TV show. Which commercials mention social media and what social media channels are included? Be sure to

capture all the ways social media is integrated into the commercial messages. Do the social media icons simply appear at the end of the commercial or do the brands ask the viewer to do something?

Notes

1. Sean Carton, "Marketing to the Distracted Consumer," ClickZ.com, October 24, 2011, http://m.clickz.com/clickz/column/2119225/marketing-distracted-consumer.

2. "John Wanamaker (1838–1922) Retailer, Philadelphia," AdAge.com, accessed September 20, 2019, http://adage.com/article/special-report-the-advertising-century/john-wanamaker/140185.

3. "John Wanamaker," AdAge.com.

4. "Advertising," AMA Dictionary, accessed September 20, 2019, https://marketing-dictionary.org/a/advertising/#cite_ref-1.

5. Laurel Wentz, "Cannes Swept by PR, Integrated, Internet Winners," AdAge.com, June 29, 2009, http://adage.com/print?article_id=137630.

6. Wentz, "Cannes Swept by PR."

7. "Public Relations," BusinessDictionary.com, accessed October 1, 2019, http://www.businessdictionary.com/definition/public-relations.html.

8. Tom Foremski, "Die! Press Release! Die! Die! Die!" SiliconValleyWatcher.com, February 27, 2006, http://www.siliconvalleywatcher.com/mt/archives/2006/02/die_press_relea.php.

9. Sarah Sherik, "The Difference between Social Media News Releases and Traditional Press Releases," PRNewswire.com, January 24, 2013, http://www.prnewswire.com/blog/the-difference-between-social-media-news-releases-traditional-press-releases-6116.html.

10. Brian Solis, "The State of PR, Marketing, and Communications: You Are the Future," Briansolis.com, June 8, 2009, http://www.briansolis.com/2009/06/state-of-pr-marketing-and/.

11. "Shareability, Credibility, & Objectivity: The State of Journalism in 2018," Muck Rack & Zeno Group, accessed October 8, 2019, https://info.muckrack.com/journalistsurvey.

12. Keith A. Quesenberry, Michael K. Coolsen, and Kristen Wilkerson, "IMC and the Effies: Use of Integrated Marketing Communications Touchpoints among Effie Award Winners," *International Journal of Integrated Marketing Communications* 4, no. 2 (2012): 60–72.

13. Quesenberry, Coolsen, and Wilkerson, "IMC and the Effies."

14. Richard Edelman, "In Brands We Trust? 2019 Edelman Trust Barometer Special Report," Edelman.com, 2019, https://www.edelman.com/sites/g/files/aatuss191/files/2019-07/2019_edelman_trust_barometer_special_report_in_brands_we_trust_executive_summary.pdf.

15. Keith A. Quesenberry and Michael K. Coolsen, "How to Integrate Social Media into Your Marketing Strategy: Best Practices for Social Media Management," *Advertising Age Research Reports*, May 20, 2013, http://adage.com/trend-reports/report.php?id=74.

16. Jeff Howe, "How Hashtags and Social Media Can Bring Megacorporations to Their Knees," TheAtlantic.com, June 8, 2012, http://www.theatlantic.com/business/archive/2012/06/the-rise-of-the-consumerate/258290.

17. Gordon C. Bruner II, "The Marketing Mix: Time for Reconceptualization," *Journal of Marketing Education* 11, no. 2 (1989): 72.

18. Keith Quesenberry, "Social Media Is Too Important to Be Left to the Marketing Department," HarvardBusinessReview.com, April 19, 2016, https://hbr.org/2016/04/social-media-is-too-important-to-be-left-to-the-marketing-department.

19. Michael Ewing, "Integrated Marketing Communications Measurements and Evaluation," *Journal of Marketing Communications* 15, no. 2–3 (2009): 103–117.

20. Don Schultz, Charles H. Patti, and Philip J. Kitchen, *The Evolution of Integrated Marketing Communications* (Abingdon, Oxon: Routledge, 2013).

21. Quesenberry and Coolsen, "How to Integrate Social Media."

22. Thorsten Hennig-Thurau, Edward C. Malthouse, Christian Friege, Sonja Gensler, Lara Lobschat, Arvind Rangaswamy, and Bernd Skiera, "The Impact of New Media on Customer Relationships," *Journal of Service Research* 13, no. 3 (2009): 311–330.

23. Seth Godin, "Permission Marketing," Seths.Blog, January 21, 2008, https://seths.blog/2008/01/permission-mark/.

24. Keith Quesenberry, "Treat Customers as Co-authors, Not Targets, and Hit a Marketing Bullseye," Entrepreneur.com, November 12, 2015, https://www.entrepreneur.com/article/252209.

25. Quesenberry and Coolsen, "How to Integrate Social Media."

26. Carton, "Marketing to the Distracted Consumer."

27. Quesenberry, "Treat Customers as Co-authors."

28. John Deighton and Leora Kornfeld, "Digital Interactivity: Unanticipated Consequences for Markets, Marketing, and Consumers," Harvard Business School, September 26, 2007, http://www.hbs.edu/faculty/Publication%20Files/08-017_1903b556-786c-49fb-8e95-ab9976da8b4b.pdf.

29. Philip Kotler, Hermawan Kartajaya, and Iwan Setiawan, *Marketing 4.0: Moving from Traditional to Digital* (Hoboken, NJ: Wiley, 2017), 109.

30. Katie Sehl, "Social Share of Voice: What It Means and How to Get More of It," Hootsuite.com, April 22, 2019, https://blog.hootsuite.com/how-to-increase-share-of-voice/.

31. "Sentiment Analysis," OxfordDictionaries.com, accessed September 20, 2019, https://en.oxforddictionaries.com/definition/sentiment_analysis.

32. Cited in Eleanor Kahn, "Earned Media Measured: How to Prove Your Worth," PRWeek.com, April 24, 2018, https://www.prweek.com/article/1462887/earned-media-measured-prove-worth.

33. Jack Edgar, "The State of Corporate Social Media Briefing 2016," Incite-Group.com, accessed September 20, 2019, http://1.incite-group.com/LP=8265.

34. Amaury Tréguer, "Time to Let Consumers Be the Voice of Brands," AdNews.com, May 26, 2017, http://www.adnews.com.au/opinion/time-to-let-consumers-be-the-voice-of-brands.

35. "Consumer Trust Report," Olapic.com, accessed November 3, 2019, http://www.olapic.com/keep-it-real/.

36. Thomas W. Gruen, Talai Osmonbekov, and Andrew J. Czaplewski, "eWOM: The Impact of Customer-to-Customer Online Know-How Exchange on Customer Value and Loyalty," *Journal of Business Research* 59, no. 4 (2006): 449–456.

37. Christine Crandell, "Customer Co-Creation Is the Secret Sauce to Success," Forbes.com, June 10, 2016, https://www.forbes.com/sites/christinecrandell/2016/06/10/customer_cocreation_secret_sauce/#7813b7045b6d.

38. "Customer Stickiness," Knowledge@Wharton High School, February 28, 2011, http://kwhs.wharton.upenn.edu/term/customer-stickiness/.

39. Mingli Zhang, Lingyun Guo, Mu Hu, and Wenhua Liu, "Influence of Customer Engagement with Company Social Networks on Stickiness: Mediating Effect of Customer Value Creation," *International Journal of Information Management* 37, no. 3 (2017): 229–240.

40. Charlene Li and Josh Bernoff, *Groundswell, Expanded and Revised Edition: Winning in a World Transformed by Social Technologies* (Boston: Harvard Business Review Press, 2011).

41. Li and Bernoff, *Groundswell.*

42. Li and Bernoff, *Groundswell.*

43. "GoPro Million Dollar Challenge," ShortyAwards.com, accessed September 20, 2019, https://shortyawards.com/11th/gopro-million-dollar-challenge-2.

44. "2018 Marketing Hiring Trends Report," McKinleyMarketingPartners.com, April 17, 2018, https://mckinleymarketingpartners.com/resources/ebooks/2018-marketing-hiring-trends-report/.

45. Maureen Morrison, "How Account Management Was Reborn: The Account Manager Is More Powerful than Ever," AdAge.com, May 2, 2016, http://adage.com/article/agency-news/dad-s-account-man/303804/.

46. Gould Partners, "What PR Agencies Require of New Junior AEs," CapitolCommunicator.com, July 10, 2015, http://www.capitolcommunicator.com/what-pr-agencies-require-of-new-junior-aes/.

47. Maxwell Gollin, "10 Social Media Job Titles (and What They Actually Mean)," Falcon.io, March 5, 2019, https://www.falcon.io/insights-hub/case-stories/cs-social-media-management/10-social-media-job-titlesand-what-they-actually-mean/.

48. Gollin, "10 Social Media Job Titles."

49. "Free Download: 37 Ready-to-Use Marketing Job Descriptions," HubSpot.com, 2019, https://offers.hubspot.com/ready-to-use-marketing-job-descriptions.

50. "Social Media Coordinator Salaries," Glassdoor.com, last modified September 17, 2019, https://www.glassdoor.com/Salaries/social-media-coordinator-salary-SRCH_KO0,24.htm.

51. Gollin, "10 Social Media Job Titles."

52. "Average Copywriter with Social Media Marketing Skills Salary," PayScale.com, accessed September 19, 2019, https://www.payscale.com/research/US/Job=Copywriter/Salary/0f9956ed/Social-Media-Marketing.

53. "Average Social Media Manager with Graphic Design Skills Salary," PayScale.com, accessed September 19, 2019, https://www.payscale.com/research/US/Job=Social_Media_Manager/Salary/23a4e789/Graphic-Design.

54. "Average Video Specialist Salary," PayScale.com, accessed September 19, 2019, https://www.payscale.com/research/US/Job=Video_Specialist/Salary.

55. "Influencer Relations Manager Salaries," Glassdoor.com, accessed September 19, 2019, https://www.glassdoor.com/Salaries/influencer-relations-manager-salary-SRCH_KO0,28.htm.

56. "Free Download: 37 Ready-to-Use Marketing Job Descriptions."

57. "Average Social Media Analyst Salary," PayScale.com, accessed September 19, 2019, https://www.payscale.com/research/US/Job=Social_Media_Analyst/Salary.

58. "Free Download: 37 Ready-to-Use Marketing Job Descriptions."

59. "Average Content Marketing Manager Salary," PayScale.com, accessed September 20, 2019, https://www.payscale.com/research/US/Job=Content_Marketing_Manager/Salary.

60. "Content Marketers Desperately Need More Journalists," Curata.com, accessed December 2, 2019, http://www.curata.com/blog/content-marketers-need-journalists/.

61. "Freelance," Dictionary.com, accessed November 3, 2019, https://www.dictionary.com/browse/freelance.

62. Tyler Horvath, "What is a Solopreneur?" Solopreneurinstitute.com, January 29, 2019, https://www.solopreneurinstitute.com/what-is-solopreneur/.

63. Jeff Bowdoin, "How Much to Charge for Social Media Management? (Freelancers and Consultants)," BlogSocialMediaStrategiesSummit.com, May 15, 2018, https://blog.socialmediastrategiessummit.com/how-much-charge-social-media-management/.

64. Karen S. Johnson, "Description of a Marketing Department," Smallbusiness.Chron.com, March 11, 2019, https://smallbusiness.chron.com/description-marketing-department-56409.html.

65. "Public Relations Firm (PR Firm) Definitions," AgencyFinder.com, accessed September 20, 2019, https://www.agencyfinder.com/define-your-ideal-agency-for-us/public-relations-firm-definition/.

66. Shannon Furey, "What Services Do PR Firms Provide? 6 Public Relations Tactics to Help Your Business Grow," Business2Business.com, August 14, 2018, https://www.business2community .com/public-relations/what-services-do-pr-firms-provide-6-public-relations-tactics-to-help-your -business-grow-02107942.

67. "Advertising Agency Definitions," AgencyFinder.com, accessed September 20, 2019, https://www.agencyfinder.com/define-your-ideal-agency-for-us/what-is-an-advertising-agency -and-how-does-it-operate/.

68. Digital Agency Network, "What Is A Digital Agency?" DigitalAgencyNetwork.com, May 20, 2018, https://www.agencyfinder.com/define-your-ideal-agency-for-us/what-is-an -advertising-agency-and-how-does-it-operate/.

69. "Social First. Social Only. Social Partners," IgniteSocialMedia.com, accessed September 20, 2019, https://www.ignitesocialmedia.com/services/.

70. "The CMO Survey: Highlights & Insights Report," CMOSurvey.com, February 2019, https://cmosurvey.org/wp-content/uploads/sites/15/2019/02/The_CMO_Survey-Highlights-and_ Insights_Report-Feb-2019-1.pdf.

71. "Four Ps," AMA Dictionary, accessed September 20, 2015, https://marketing-dictionary .org/m/marketing-mix/.

72. Teo Graca, "The Evolution of Advertising—Social Media Has Taken Charge," Advertising Advocates.com, accessed September 20, 2019, http://articleadvocates.com/articleadvocates/display .cfm/6623.

73. Neelima Mahajan, "The Thinker Interview with Philip Kotler, the Father of Marketing," CKGSB Knowledge, October 8, 2013, http://knowledge.ckgsb.edu.cn/2013/10/08/marketing/ philip-kotler-four-ps-model-marketing-still-king.

74. Don Schultz, Charles H. Patti, and Philip J. Kitchen, *The Evolution of Integrated Marketing Communications* (Abingdon, Oxon: Routledge, 2013).

75. Lucian J. Lombardi, "The 4Cs of Marketing," *LIMRA's Marketfacts Quarterly* 29, no. 4 (2010): 71–90.

76. Kotler, Kartajaya, and Setiawan, *Marketing 4.0*, 50–51.

77. Nicholas Carr, *The Shallows: What the Internet Is Doing to Our Brains* (New York: Norton, 2010).

PART

II

A Strategic Process for Social Media

A Foundation for Social Media Strategy

You should never go to battle before you've won the war on paper.[1]

—Philip Kotler

PREVIEW

Do you have goals for your life? I am sure most people reading this automatically said yes. Perhaps general aspirations popped into your head. You would like to be successful in your career, perhaps have a family, and even retire early. Or maybe you just want to be able to get through this week. Beyond these vague ideas, have you taken the time to write down specific goals for your future?

For years, consultants have been telling a story about Yale's graduating class of 1953. Researchers reportedly surveyed the seniors and found that only 3 percent had specific, written goals for the future. Twenty years later, researchers polled the surviving members of the class and found that the 3 percent with goals had accumulated more wealth than the other 97 percent of the class combined! This is a fascinating story, but in 1996 Lawrence Tabak reported in *Fast Company* that it was completely untrue.[2] In fact, Yale University Library received so many requests for the study that they now report on their website that they have determined no "goals study" ever occurred.[3]

However, the nonexistence of the Yale study motivated Gail Matthews of Dominican University to conduct her own. In a survey of 149 participants, Matthews found that those who wrote goals actually accomplished significantly more than those who did not.[4] Despite the true or untrue status of the Yale story, taking the time to plan and have specific written goals is important and leads to better results.

Plans, Campaigns, and Goal Setting

So far, this book has looked at the history and definition of social media and noted the changes in mass media, marketing, advertising, and public relations. This has provided valuable background and context to establish how persuasive, influential, and disruptive social media has become. There is a strong argument for why organizations should be active in social media. Of course, most businesses have heard this message and many have in fact responded. As of 2016, 98 percent of Fortune 500 corporations had a presence on LinkedIn, 89 percent were on Facebook, and 91 percent had Twitter accounts.[5] Yet as Philip Kotler points out, going into the social media battle and having a plan are very different actions.

Knowing an organization should be active in social media and even having social media accounts is not difficult. Many sources have published articles and videos on how to set up social accounts quickly and easily. A brand may have had a Facebook page for a decade or more, but learning to use that page effectively is an entirely different game. It is a game entrepreneurs, marketers, advertisers, and public relations professionals cannot win unless they take the time to plan an effective strategy. What are the different aspects or forms of strategy?

At the very top, a **strategy** is the high-level connection between an effort or function and organization requirements. A social media strategy links social media actions to organization requirements such as attracting customers and generating sales or performing customer care and generating leads for salespeople. A **strategic plan** details the specific tactics that will be used to help meet specific objectives over a period of time.[6] Therefore, a social media plan details how all social media components will help meet objectives specifically over a period such as a year. A **strategic campaign** is a focused, tactical effort to meet one aspect or specific objective of a plan often on a shorter time frame.[7] For example, one aspect of a year-long social media plan could be a six-month campaign to promote user-generated content submissions to award a prize.

Since 2014 chief marketing officers' progress toward linking social media to marketing strategy has increased only 5.7 percent and the number who are able to quantitatively show the impact of social media on their business has increased only 9.5 percent.[8] Why? Having a Twitter page and updating it with corporate press releases or promotions is not a winning social media strategy. This is treating social media as simply another traditional media channel to push out controlled marketing communications messages. Used the wrong way, a Facebook, Instagram, or Twitter page simply becomes another outlet to add to advertising clutter like digital billboards or bathroom-stall advertising.

There is also evidence that brands are not moving well beyond main social platforms to strategically add social channels well suited to their business goals and target audience. Of the high percentage of Fortune 500 companies on LinkedIn, Facebook, and Twitter, only 63 percent are on Instagram, just over half (53 percent) have corporate blogs, just 32 percent have a brand presence on Pinterest,[9] and just 10 percent have Snapchat accounts.[10] Only 48 percent of Fortune 500 CEOs are active on social media.[11] Yet today success depends on having a multichannel social media strategy. For example, 90 percent of people say Pinterest helps them decide what to purchase, 78 percent say they want to see content from brands on the platform, and 66 percent buy something after seeing a brand's pins.[12] Snapchat can be the ideal place to reach younger target markets like millennials. The fantasy sports pro- vider FanDuel used Snap Ads, Story Ads, and Filters to reach consumers in the platform. The Snapchat campaign drove a 7.2 percent increase in first deposits, an 8.9 percent increase in registrations, and increased ad awareness and favorability.[13] Instagram has played an inte- gral role in helping brands such as Gatorade, which saw a 3 percent increased household penetration and 4 percent increased sales.[14] Businesses that have prioritized blogging are thirteen times more likely to receive positive return on investment.[15] Without a strategy or revaluating a strategy that hasn't been updated in years, success in social media will at best be unknown and at worst lead to decreasing returns.

How should brands communicate in these new social media outlets? They must go back to the very beginning of marketing. A **market** is defined as a place where products are bought and sold.[16] The best-selling book *The Cluetrain Manifesto* reminded us that marketing originated in traditional physical markets. In those open squares, "markets are conversations, talk is cheap, silence is fatal."[17] Old-time markets began as a place where people talked about what they cared about and the goods on the table between them. As the distance between producer and consumer grew, a gap between our business voice and our authentic voice appeared.

Marketing became an applied science to engineer responses through calibrated stimuli— control marketing. Social media bridges that gap and brings the consumer and merchant back to the table in a personal conversation. Consequently, for social media success, organizations need to start with a customer-centric marketing strategy.

As the physical market turned into the marketing discipline, a gap opened between producer and marketing communications professional. When the person talking to the customer made the product and ran the business, business goals were readily apparent to them. They most likely had objectives to sell a certain amount of product by the end of the day, week, month, and so forth. Today a gap has opened between the business manager, owner, or producer and the marketing manager and social media professional. Often they are speaking different languages and their goals and objectives don't align. This is where many social media efforts go wrong from the very beginning. As social media expert Jay Baer of Convince & Convert says, "The goal is not to be good at social media. The goal is to be good at business because of social media."[18]

Social media is not an end unto itself. The biggest mistake a marketer, advertiser, or public relations professional can make is to place their social media strategy objectives too low. Don't get caught in the trap of immediately going to easy objectives based on low- er-level social metrics. Yes, it makes sense to have a brand presence in social media because your target market is there and you want to engage them. Yet simply setting a goal of higher followers and objectives on existing social platforms is, as marketing expert Jon Gatrell puts

Figure 4.1. Social media plans need to start with business objectives to prove ROI.

© Sarinya Pinngam / iStock Photo

it, "viewing social media as both the beginning and the end." This is not only extremely limiting for your social media plan but also fails to recognize the reason upper-level managers or owners of the organization or business are paying you to develop and implement a social media strategy in the first place.[19]

A **goal** is simply something that a person or group is trying to achieve.[20] An **objective** is a goal expressed in specific terms.[21] Goals and objectives should be business- or organization-driven, but they can vary widely. A goal could be a straight increase in sales of a product or service, or an increase in donations or volunteers for a nonprofit. Perhaps a brand is suffering from a negative image and goals would pertain to changing consumer perception. A startup may want to increase general awareness, or an established company may need to increase awareness of social responsibility efforts or a new product. Social media strategy and this process applies to nonprofits and charities just as much as for-profit business. **Nonprofit marketing** is strategies to spread the message of a nonprofit brand and solicit donations and volunteers to meet organization objectives.[22]

How do you know what these important higher-level business goals and objectives are? Sometimes the manager, client, or business owner will know and give this to you from the beginning. But often managers get caught up in day-to-day operations and have trouble expressing a multitude of needs as one, two, or even three clear and concise organization or business objectives. Also the situation may have changed because objectives were set in a dated business or marketing plan. Perhaps you are new to the company as an outside consultant or agency or have worked for the company for a while and have struggled to connect social media action with overall business strategy and business impact. You are not alone. Nearly half of social media marketers say their greatest challenge is developing a strategy that supports business goals. Without that foundation it becomes a real struggle to prove ROI.[23]

Return on investment (ROI) is measuring the profitability of an investment as a ratio between the net profit and the cost of investment.[24] ROI is important in social media strategy because social media professionals must justify their role to bosses and clients, proving that social media action helps to meet business needs. Knowing your social media ROI also helps you secure the budget you need for social media campaigns and helps you know if those campaigns are working so you can make adjustments and optimize results.

In any of these instances it is best to start with a brand summary of the current product and service offering and existing sales and marketing strategy. Then perform a situation analysis to discover relevant market, consumer, trend, and competitor data. This will help ensure that your social media campaigns and overall plan aligns with company goals. Follow this process to know your message, your audience, and your medium to develop a social strategy that supports measurable business objectives.

Situational Analysis, Target, and Objectives

A brand summary and situation analysis can uncover problems and opportunities to set accurate and relevant business objectives and discover strategies to help meet those objectives. One of the most basic strategic processes in marketing is a situation analysis. **Situation analysis** consists of components used to analyze an organization's environment that impacts an organization's ability to achieve its objectives.[25] Begin by collecting internal and external information. What type of information should be captured?

Gather primary and secondary data about:

1. History and vision/mission of the organization
2. Brand, industry, competitor performance/trends over time
3. Current marketing tagline, design, and voice for brand
4. Target market and key target audience(s)
5. Business objectives (follow SMART guidelines)
6. Social brand/consumer/competitor talk (social media audit)

Even if you work for an organization, it is important to remind yourself of the history of the organization and ground your work in an understanding of the vision of the brand, what it stands for, and the core principles that should direct all action. This can often get lost in day-to-day operations. You can think of this as the backstory. People buy for rational and emotional reasons that can come from the organization's origin. Make sure you understand the company's human side of starting in a garage, the experience that gave the founder the idea for the company, or the childhood dream come true. Big companies can benefit from showcasing humble roots.[26]

Consultant, author, and speaker Simon Sinek is known for giving one of the most popular TED Talks (56 million views between Ted.com and YouTube). In "Start with Why" he explains that people don't buy what you do. They buy why you do it. The difference between very successful companies like Apple and others is that they start with "why." Do you know the "why" of the organization?[27] To make money is not a sustainable answer for employees or customers. What does the company stand for and where is it headed? Think of solving a greater problem, spreading a bigger message, supporting a cause, community, or the environment or being the absolute best at something specific. Steve Jobs said about Apple, "We're here to put a dent in the universe."[28] He didn't say they were here to be the world's most valuable brand. Sinek's **Golden Circle** is a concept that seeks to discover a person's or organization's purpose by asking why, how, and what by starting with why in the center of three concentric circles.[29]

Don't underestimate the importance of "why" or the vision of an organization. Take time to discover or remind everyone the organization's vision. **Vision** is an organization's reason for existence, where it is headed, and what impact it wants to make in the world.[30] Once you know "why" make sure you also know "how." This is the second phase of Sinek's concept of the Golden Circle. How does the organization make the vision come to life?[31] What differentiates them from the competition? This is often expressed in a mission, which can be a more specific statement of vision. Many companies have a mission statement found on their websites and in annual reports. A **mission statement** is a written declaration of an organization's core purpose and focus that tends to remain unchanged over time.[32]

The final phase of Sinek's Golden Circle is "what."[33] Ensure you know exactly what the organization is selling and promising to the customer, including specific product and service offerings, lines and versions. Do they sell one product or many? How is the product delivered to customers? Are the products or services available in one channel or multiple channels? Is it sold online or in physical stores, direct from the brand or through retailers or brokers? You need to know where to direct customers for sales. It is also important to know pricing strategy. Does the brand operate on a low-price strategy or a premium pricing model? Do customers purchase it once or is it a monthly subscription? If it is an app or service, is there a free version or free trial?

Another "what" to understand is the organization's recent performance, industry trends, and key competitors. Companies don't operate in a vacuum and industry and competitor factors should be considered. What industry is the brand in? Is the overall industry or category growing or declining? Are there major trends driving the industry and consumer demand? Who are their main competitors? How do they compare in market share and sales over recent years? Was the brand formerly dominant and has declined or is it an up-and-comer trying to catch the dominant brands? There is usually one main competitor below or above a brand that they are either trying to stay ahead of or surpass.

Where do you find this information? Many organizations have existing primary research that is very useful for this analysis. If you are not an employee, some of this information can be found on corporate websites and in industry trade association reports. There is a wealth of secondary research available as well. Consider company profile databases such as Standard & Poors, International Directory of Company Histories, and Hoovers. Annual reports can usually be obtained from corporate websites. MarketLine and SRDS (Standard Rate & Data Service) provide valuable reports and research insight. Mintel is one of the leading research firms that gathers consumer, trend, market, and competitor data for analysis in valuable industry reports. MRI-Simmons provides US consumer data on more than 500 product categories and 8,000 brands.[34] Statista is a global statistics portal with more than 60,000 diverse topics of data and facts from more than 10,000 sources onto a single professional platform. PrivCo is also a good resource for private company data. Check with university and public libraries for access to valuable databases.

Always start with existing research, but there may be a need for new research to make informed strategic decisions or to ensure objectives are measurable. **Secondary research** discovers information previously researched for other purposes that is publicly available. **Primary research** is new research to answer specific questions, and can include questionnaires, surveys, or interviews.[35] Start with secondary research to see what is available and discover what primary research you may need to fill the gaps. Sometimes secondary research is free, but often you must pay for individual reports or subscribe to services to access this data. Depending on your organization, the value of these reports and subscriptions can outweigh the cost and is normally less expensive than conducting primary research.

Smart research is an investment to help avoid costly mistakes down the road. Too often, marketers and other communications professionals skimp on research up front only to succumb to the old adage, "There's never enough money to do it right the first time, but always enough to do it twice." Even informal primary research can be gathered economically. It doesn't take a lot of effort to write and field an online survey. Consider fielding informal independent research via tools such as SurveyMonkey or Google Docs and Twitter or Instagram polls.

Don't forget the business trade press, which can share valuable developments and insights. And many research companies such as Gartner, Nielsen, and Forrester issue press releases that highlight key findings. Sometimes the trade press will obtain research reports and write articles about highlights. Product industry trade organizations often conduct research and issue reports for their members. Other organizations such as the Pew Research Center and US Census Bureau issue data and reports free of charge. For information, insights, and best practices specific to social media, look to outlets such as Social Media Examiner, Social Media Today, and SmartBrief. Facebook releases consumer research reports through Facebook IQ and Think with Google provides marketing research and digital trends.

The next "what" to know is current marketing communications activity. Is there an existing advertising, public relations, or IMC campaign that is running? Does the brand have certain imagery, or a spokesperson who appears in all marketing promotion material? Is there a current tagline or slogan? What's the difference? A **slogan** is a sentence or long phrase that expresses a company or product goal. A **tagline** is a short, memorable phrase repeated in marketing messages about a company or product.[36] Nike's slogan could be "Inspiration and innovation for every athlete in the world," while their tagline is "Just do it."[37]

What are brand standards you may have to follow? In social media, brand voice is especially important to understand. **Brand voice** is the personality used in brand communication that usually remains consistent,[38] whereas tone is an attitude that comes across in a specific situation. A brand can have an overall tone of playful or witty that matches a casual brand voice, but in certain circumstances the tone might need to adjust to being more serious and empathetic in a national or brand crisis or in a customer service situation with an angry customer. Also, different audiences on different platforms may call for variations of brand voice. Visual identity must be considered as well. Some brands have trademarked their colors, such as Pullman brown for UPS, T-Mobile's magenta, and John Deere's green and yellow.[39] Finally, is there an established spokesperson? You probably cannot imagine a new social media effort for M&M's that doesn't include the M&M's characters Red, Yellow, Blue, Green, Orange, and Ms. Brown. Often these brand standards are expressed in a style guide. A **brand style guide** is a document that defines a brand and makes it understandable and replicable through visual and content style.[40]

Another important "what" to understand is the brand's target market and its target audiences. Who needs the brand's products and services most? Who are the purchase decision makers and who are the purchase influencers? Successful companies focus on the people most likely to benefit from and be attracted to their brand, products, services, and message. Will the social strategy better reach a current target audience or will the social media strategy be part of an effort to reach new target audiences? For a reminder of the importance of narrowly defined target markets and audiences see chapter 2 where Chris Anderson's theory of *The Long Tail* was discussed along with Malcom Gladwell's "Choice, happiness and spaghetti sauce."

Identify a target audience or multiple target audiences for the social media communications effort. Note that a target audience may be different from a target market. A **target market** is identified in business and marketing plan objectives and represents a group of people who share common wants or needs that an organization serves.[41] On the other hand, a **target audience** is a group of people identified as the intended recipient of a communications message.[42]

Figure 4.2. Understanding your target audience is an important part of social strategy.

© Adamakaz / iStock Photo

A nonprofit may have a target market of people in need to whom it provides services and a target audience of people who provide support through donation of time or money.[43] There may be target audiences that are not in the target market but that influence end users to make conversion or purchase decisions. This is important in social media, where a quarter of consumers may influence the purchases of the rest.[44] The important decision here is to identify the group that is most likely to respond positively to the effort and directly or indirectly contribute to helping meet organization goals and overall business objectives. A narrowly focused message stands out, and reaches and motivates an audience. General messages addressing everyone get lost in the crowd.

Gatorade understands that one of their target audiences is teen athletes, which drove the insights for the "video everywhere" campaign discussed in chapter 2. They learned this the hard way years ago after shifting to a mass-market advertising campaign targeting men eighteen to forty-nine that positioned Gatorade as hydration for everyone—both athletes and nonathletes. Going after the broad market led to a sales decline of 10 percent in 2008 while competitor Powerade grew 13 percent. The core athlete audience felt that the brand had left them. Marketer Sarah Robb O'Hagan dug into their research and discovered high school athletes made up 15 percent of customers and marathoners made up another 7 percent. Yet that 22 percent combined for 46 percent of all sales. Only when the brand switched back to focusing on high school athletes and endurance athletes and away from mass advertising to niche digital marketing did sales return. If you try to be everything for everyone, you'll end up not being anything for anyone.[45]

Sometimes targeting a niche audience helps you reach mass sales. The fact that you target a small group doesn't mean that they will be the only ones who purchase the product. Often targeting a niche group makes the product or service more attractive to those outside the group. A related topic will be discussed in chapter 13 in focusing efforts on the top 20 percent of customers with relation to social care and social sales as supported by the Pareto principle or 80/20 rule.

If you are a marketer at a business or a marketing communications professional working for the business, it is always good practice to verify that the target audience is really who you think. BSquared social media agency found this out for a client. The brand defined their target audience from social media follower data. They had the most followers from eighteen- to twenty-four-year-olds and defined this as their target market and audience. BSquared dug in deeper, adding social listening data based on keywords of people talking about the brand in all social channels—not just at the brand-on-brand pages. They also added social media and digital advertising data that tracked sales and found that the next two older demographic groups actually contained 90 percent of their buyers compared to only 10 percent of the eighteen- to twenty-four-year-olds purchasing products.[46]

An example of a target market not matching a target audience is Old Spice (see "Mini Case: Old Spice New Target"). Here the marketer and its advertising agency selected women as the target audience for a campaign where the target market, the main users of the product, was men. Research revealed that women made or influenced the buying decision more than the male users of the product.[47] There may also be multiple target audiences to reach the same business objective. For example, a college may have an objective to maintain or increase undergraduate enrollment. The target market for this objective would be high school students. Yet, research tells marketers that parents are also influential in the college

MINI CASE

Old Spice New Target

In 2010 the men's body-wash category was growing, but Old Spice's sales were slipping. Procter & Gamble's research found that women purchased 60 percent of men's body washes. For the first time, Old Spice marketing was targeted to women with its "The Man Your Man Could Smell Like" campaign.[a] It received a lot of attention, but did it deliver business results?

In the first three months, Old Spice captured 76 percent of all online conversations about male body-wash brands, with more than half of that coming from women. This resulted in Old Spice becoming the #1 all-time most viewed and #2 most-subscribed branded channel on YouTube. The six-month campaign generated 1.7 billion total impressions, and sales more than doubled versus the prior year, with an increase of 125 percent.[b] In this case having a different target audience from the target market for the product was a better strategy. Also notice that success was ultimately expressed in sales increases. Social media views, likes, comments, and shares were the specific strategy and tactics to get there.

Today Old Spice has expanded its product line to include deodorant, body wash, hair care, beard products, and swag such as "socks for your manly man feet." The brand has also added eCommerce branded under the Old Spice Barber Shop that includes exclusive online-only products. For social media they have kept a focus on the three main social channels of YouTube, Facebook, and Instagram.[c]

[a] "Old Spice Campaign Is Not Only Great, It Sells—Now #1 in U.S. in Both Dollar and Volume Share," CampaignBrief.com, July 16, 2010, http://www.campaignbrief.com/2010/07/old-spices-campaign-is-not-onl.html.
[b] "Old Spice Case," Effie Awards, accessed February 17, 2015, http://www.apaceffie.com/docs/default-source/resource-library/oldspice_case_pdf.pdf?sfvrsn=2.
[c] "Old Spice Barber Shop," OldSpice.com, accessed November 3, 2019, https://oldspice.com/.

decision. Therefore, the enrollment social media strategy could include a primary target audience of school students with a secondary target audience of parents of high school–age children. Dig into the numbers. Don't rely on assumptions or single data points to determine target market and target audience.

In defining a target market and target audience for a social media effort, narrow the selection by more closely defining who is most likely to respond to the brand, product, service, or organization or who current makes up the majority of sales. See table 4.1 for possible variables and bases of segmentation. Demographic and psychographic variables are normally the most important. Yet depending on the organization, geographic and behavioral variables can play an important role. For a national brand with national distribution, geographic segmentation may not apply. But for a sports team it would make more sense to focus around the region where the sports team is located. You don't have to define all variables and bases—only those that are relevant.

Demographic variables can include information such as age range, gender, geographic location, ethnic background, marital status, income, and education.[48] When possible,

Table 4.1. Variables and Basis of Segmentation

Geographic	Demographic	Psychographic	Behavioral
Basis such as region, climate, population density, and growth rate	Basis such as age, gender, ethnicity, education, occupation, income, and family	Basis such as values, attitudes, and lifestyle	Variables such as usage rate, price sensitivity, brand loyalty, and benefits sought

quantify these designations with specific numbers, such as women aged twenty-five to thirty-four. Not only does this ensure that one person's interpretation of middle age is the same as someone else's, it will also match advertiser and publisher standards for buying media. Most agree that eighteen- to twenty-four-year-olds have more in common with each other in terms of interests, needs, and desires than they do with forty-five- to fifty-four-year-olds. Age ranges for target markets and target audiences usually follow time periods associated with stages in the family life cycle. The **family life cycle** is the stages people pass through from childhood to retirement that usually represent different needs and desires.[49] Stages can include child, preteen, teenager, young single adult, young married with no children, married with young children, older married with children, older married with no children, and older single. This can be broken down further into age ranges such as under six, six to ten, eleven to twelve, thirteen to seventeen, eighteen to twenty-four, twenty-five to thirty-four, thirty-five to forty-nine, fifty to sixty-four, and sixty-five-plus.[50]

Another factor to consider is **generational targeting,** when organizations target broader age groups such as baby boomers, generation Xers, or millennials because they may have similar desires compared to previous generations. **Psychographic variables** consist of internal factors such as values, attitudes, interests, lifestyle, and behavior.[51] For example, not all eighteen- to twenty-four-year-old male millennials are equally interested in rugby, robotics, or running. Define the target audience utilizing both of these types of information. An example target audience could be "Twenty-five- to thirty-four-year-old married women professionals with young children living in urban and suburban areas interested in staying fit and active."

It should be noted that business to business (B2B) target markets and audiences are usually segmented with different variables sometimes called firmographics instead of demographics. These can include company size, industry, geographic market, and business needs such as price, quality, delivery, and sustainability. A B2B target audience can include variables focused on people with certain job titles, and professional organizations or interests.[52] **Firmographics** is data used to segment organizations into meaningful categories for business-to-business marketing.[53]

Sometimes a social media strategy needs to communicate to an individual or group not directly related to the target market for the product or service. This is often the case in corporate communication and public relations efforts to manage the reputation of a company, improving relations with employees, investors, or suppliers. This can also include issues management with community groups such as nongovernmental organizations (NGOs), media relations with journalists and other thought leaders or influencers, and communicating to regulators or political leaders about issues impacting the operation of an organization. In these cases additional target audiences would be added to a social media strategy to include people not directly involved in the purchase or purchase decision and lie outside the sales funnel or customer journey in marketing. In these situations the recipients of these messages are often referred to as stakeholders or publics.[54]

These terms related to target audience are often associated with the public relations discipline where stakeholders and publics are often the focus of campaigns and strategies. In general a stakeholder is identified based on its relationship to the organization and publics are identified based on their relationship to message. **Stakeholders** have been defined as any people who have an influence or interest in an organization's success. Common stakeholders include employees, customers, shareholders, communities and suppliers. **Publics** have been defined as the audiences identified to receive messages from an organization. Common publics include employees, customers, shareholders, communities, political leaders, etc. Often these are divided into internal and external publics or stakeholders. Communication to employees would be considered an internal audience while communication to customers would be considered external. Identifying publics or stakeholders follows a similar segmentation process as identifying target audience and will therefore be referred to as target audience throughout the book to represent both target market and key stakeholders or publics.[55]

Once data is gathered to complete a situation analyses it can be organized, summarized, and gathered into a visual overview through a SWOT summary, often called SWOT analysis. Not to be confused with situation analysis, a SWOT analysis is one component of a situation analysis at the end of the process to access all that was uncovered.[56] **SWOT analysis (or SWOT matrix)** is a process and visual overview for identifying an organization's strengths, weaknesses, opportunities, and threats to analyze the internal and external factors impacting success.[57] Start with a blank SWOT template such as the one shown in figure 4.3.

Identify and organize internal strengths and weaknesses and external opportunities and threats from information collected in the situation analysis. **Internal factors** are the factors that occur within an organization and impact the approach and success of operations. **External factors** consist of a variety of factors outside the organization that organizations typically don't have direct control over.[58] Summarize the facts that may be helpful or harmful to the organization as short bullet points in each quadrant of the SWOT matrix graphic. List only the most relevant and important factors to highlight the big picture; do not include all the details. The details should have already been covered in the situation analysis; do not introduce new information. If it is important it should be included and supported by research in the situation analysis first.

What could some SWOT bullet point summaries look like? Internal strengths could be a new product, quality of service, area of expertise, or location and convenience. Internal weaknesses could include lack of experience in a new industry, products with no real difference from competitors, inconvenient locations, poor-quality products or service, or poor brand reputation. Examples of external threats could be a new competitor or new competitor product, more convenient and better service, new regulations, or declining consumer demand. Example opportunities could include developing markets such as online sales, new services or industry trends, overseas opportunities, new consumer market segments, or competitors leaving.[59] From this big picture SWOT summary of the current environment,

	Helpful	Harmful
Internal	**S** Strengths	**W** Weaknesses
External	**O** Opportunities	**T** Threats

Figure 4.3. SWOT Analysis (Matrix) Graphic Template

identify internal factors that match external factors. For example, match internal strengths with external opportunities. Try many combinations. There is no one right answer, but several promising strategies should start to emerge. There will be varying degrees to which an organization's resources and capabilities match external factors to form a strategic fit.

For an example of how this could all fit together, consider a hypothetical sports apparel company. The company's internal strengths could include established manufacturing capabilities, strong traditional distribution channels, and brand awareness. Internal weaknesses include undifferentiated products and declining sales and market share in current markets. External threats to the sports apparel company are new upstart brands selling yoga and casual sports clothing and new online distribution models leveraging social media commerce. On the other hand, external opportunities include new markets of increased online sales and consumer trends of increasing interest and sales in athleisure. From this you could identify a strategy to leverage current strengths in manufacturing and brand awareness with opportunities of growing interest in athleisure to market a casual sportswear line targeted to a new target market of consumers interested in this trend with a new online sales model directed through social media channels where the target audience spends the majority of their media time. This would lead to setting specific business objectives such as increasing sales and expanding share in the new market.

In a written plan or presentation, explain what you saw in the SWOT matrix graphic in short narrative paragraph form. Make sure the reader sees what you are seeing and knows what challenges and opportunities have been revealed. These revelations should lead to relevant business objectives in line with the organizational vision and mission and be the basis for a solid strategic direction for the social media plan.[60] Whether performing a situation analysis on a brand, product, service, individual, for-profit, or nonprofit, goals should always be expressed as organizational objectives following SMART guidelines. **SMART objectives** are specific, measurable, achievable, relevant, and timely.[61] Expressing goals as quantified objectives that follow SMART guidelines ensures that they are measurable and thus success can be proven and effort can be justified (see box).

When setting objectives for a social media strategy, don't make the mistake of focusing on smaller social media activity such as "likes" or comments—sometimes called vanity metrics. Always start with larger overall business-oriented objectives such as increasing sales, generating leads, or improving customer satisfaction. Your business objectives should not be social media–focused tactics like "Within six months, open an Instagram account and post a minimum of five times a week." A good business objective following SMART guidelines could be more like "Increase sales by 20 percent to sixteen- to twenty-four-year-olds within twelve months." Opening an Instagram account and posting a minimum of five times a week may be a part of your social media strategy and tactics to help meet that business objective. Goals are long-term changes you'd like to see, objectives turn goals into measurable metrics on a specific smaller time frame, strategy is the way you will meet the objectives, and tactics are what you will use to implement the strategy. Research from Sprout Social indicates that marketers' top business goals for social media are to increase brand awareness, increase sales, increase leads, increase community engagement, grow brand audience, and increase web traffic. You turn these goals into objectives by adding specific numbers and time frames following the SMART guidelines based on what was found about your specific brand in the situation analysis.[62]

Different organizational objectives and target markets may require very different social media tools and social media channels from sales and awareness to customer service and lead-generation objectives. Don't start with current brand social media accounts and simply set higher follower or engagement KPI metric objectives. Existing channels may be wrong for the current objective and were started for very different reasons. New social media channels may be ideal but were never considered. Customer service may be on a separate social media software tool from marketing, but now integration is needed. Start with business objectives from the beginning and keep an open mind about adding and subtracting social media tools and social media platforms as the brand, industry, and consumer research indicates.

Later in chapter 14, after selecting social media platform channels and social media tools, we will discuss how to connect business goals to specific social media channel KPIs and metrics as a way to measure success, optimize efforts, and prove ROI. Starting with larger overall business objectives ensures your social strategy will be relevant to company executives or the business owner and other business departments. It will help ensure that your social media actions are contributing to the **bottom line**, which is the line at the bottom of a financial report showing profit or loss.[63] Obviously not everything in social media is directly attributable to sales. Yet the more you can connect social media plan actions to revenue generation the better.

Be sure to translate social media actions into the language of the people who have to approve and fund your social media plan. Aim to tell the bigger story of how social KPIs and metrics align with higher-level objectives that matter to everyone in the business. Through the situation analysis, you should uncover problems or opportunities that will identify what these business objectives need to be or confirm the business objectives communicated to you. The situation analysis also lays the groundwork for the social media strategy needed to meet those objectives. For now, focus on getting the business objectives right. Don't

Objectives Should Meet SMART Guidelines

How do you turn a goal into something measurable? Make it an objective relevant to your brand expressed in a concise statement following SMART guidelines. Each objective should be a single sentence that meets all five requirements of S-M-A-R-T acronym categories, not separate objectives or sentences for each S-M-A-R-T requirement. In most cases there is no need to explain how each objective meets these requirements or to label them "SMART objectives." They are simply your "business objectives" written to follow these guidelines.

- **Specific:** If the objective is to increase sales, express this in terms of an exact percentage or dollar increase. If the objective is to increase awareness, state it in concrete terms such as a percentage of awareness among a target market.
- **Measurable:** A specific objective is useless unless it can be measured. If the objective is to increase awareness by 40 percent, current awareness levels must be known and there must be a plan to collect awareness levels later.
- **Achievable:** A sales increase of 400 percent is exciting, but is it feasible? Perhaps there isn't even the production capacity to meet that objective. If objectives are too big, they are setting up the plan for failure. Are the necessary resources and support available?
- **Relevant:** Objectives must match a specific organization's mission, goals, and current situation. What problems or opportunities were discovered in the situation analysis? Specifics found in that brand and market research such as a trending sales, market share, target market, or brand awareness numbers are where you should look.
- **Timely:** Because you are setting business objectives for a social media plan, set a deadline that matches the plan time frame. A year is a good standard to align with most marketing plans, annual financial reports, and budgets. Additionally, experts recommend that social media plans be revalued every year. Set the specific number based on historical data over that time frame. How much has the brand or competitors increased or decreased in the past in a year? Exceptions are plans for event marketing, product launches, or political campaigns with a set start and end date.

To identify these business objectives, consider questions such as: What numbers must the company meet? How does management judge success? What big issue is challenging the brand? Hootsuite explains that real business goals tend to come from the three categories of business conversions, brand awareness, and customer experience.[a] Don't write business objectives focused on social media vanity metrics such as likes or followers. Focus on bottom-line measures that address the business challenges and opportunities found in your brand summary and situation analysis. Also don't explain how you will meet the business objectives in the objectives or as separate objectives. That is the purpose of the larger social media plan that will explain the strategies and tactics you will use to meet the business objectives.

[a] Sarah Dawley, "Do Vanity Metrics Matter on Social Media? Yes (and No)," Hootsuite.com (blog), May 30, 2017, https://blog.hootsuite.com/vanity-metrics/.

worry about followers, likes, or even specific social platforms. Later in the book and in the social media plan you will identify the best social media strategies (chapters 5–6), channels (chapters 7–10), and tactics (chapters 11–13) to meet the business objectives. Once these are decided, in chapter 14 we will connect specific social media KPIs and metrics to each business objective in a social media measurement plan as an ongoing system to measure ROI.

In *The Art of War*, Sun Tzu taught that true strategy was not planning by working through an established list, but rather responding to changing conditions.[64] The same thought applies when developing a social media strategy. The process may need to adjust to the situation. In some organizations, the target audience may be fixed. Start there and work back toward setting objectives and performing the situation analysis. Or the target audience may change in the midst of the process as new information and insight is discovered. And business objectives may change as new challenges and opportunities are uncovered. No matter, at the end of the situation analysis you should have a deeper understanding of the "why," "how," and "what" of the organization. Then you can better understand the organizations value proposition. **Value proposition** is the value a company promises to deliver to customers, telling them what it stands for, how it operates, and why it deserves their business.[65] Knowing the value proposition informs objectives, strategy, and tactics. This ensures your social strategy starts in the right place and direction.

Listening to what people are saying in a social media audit may change the target audience or business objectives. Remain flexible and respond to changing conditions yet stay rooted in a solid foundation that meets the organization or business objectives, matches brand vision and mission, leverages research insight, and maintains communications focus. Take Philip Kotler's advice in formulating the plan to win the battle on paper, but follow Sun Tzu's foresight in keeping it flexible and be willing to use an eraser.

Listen with a Social Media Audit

Ernest Hemingway said that he learned a great deal from listening carefully, yet most people he knew never listened.[66] A shortcoming of many marketing, advertising, and public relations people is that they like to talk. Maybe this is a characteristic that drew them into the field. Being able to talk serves them well in convincing people to bet millions on marketing, advertising, and public relations ideas. Yet listening is an important skill that is a key to social media success.

The creators of brand communication may not be seeking a Nobel Prize in Literature like Hemingway, but getting the crowds to like and share brand content is surprisingly similar to developing a best-selling novel. Edward Moran and Francois Gossieaux performed a study of more than five hundred companies and found that, to increase chances of success, marketers developing a social media strategy must first listen to what online communities are saying about their products and where they are saying it.[67]

Furthermore, not listening can get organizations into big trouble. In 2006, Dave Carroll composed a song about United Airlines' mishandling of his $3,500 guitar and their refusal to compensate him. Within one week, the video received three million views, 19.5 million by 2019, and earned media coverage from news outlets such as CNN, the *Wall Street Journal*, the BBC, and the *CBS Morning Show*.[68]

Figure 4.4. A social audit takes time but leads to valuable strategic insights.

© Ijuba Photo / iStock Photo

The magazine *Fast Company* reported that Carroll contacted United for nine months with calls and emails, but only after the video's success, and United Airlines' stock price drop of 10 percent, did the company try to make things right.[69] Carroll wrote a book about the experience called *United Breaks Guitars: The Power of One Voice in the Age of Social Media.* United, like other airlines, has made great strides since then by significantly expanding customer service via social media. Unfortunately, they didn't completely learn that old policies must also be updated.

In 2017 a similar incident happened when Dr. David Dao was violently removed from Flight 3411 to make room for United flight crews and the cell phone footage of the incident went viral.[70] With global social media adoption greatly increased since 2009 and the many more social channels with video capabilities, this video racked up hundreds of millions of views within days, attracting more than 100 million views on China's Weibo alone. After a huge social media backlash, negative news coverage, and a loss of $1.4 billion in stock evaluation, the airline apologized and eventually changed their crew travel policy.[71]

Listening in social media is important. Social media listening should not be confused with social media monitoring. **Social media monitoring** is identifying and responding to brand mentions in social media to improve customer engagement. Many organizations use social media monitoring software algorithms to monitor, filter, and prioritize conversations to identify actionable ones, positive impact, and negative sentiments. **Social media listening** is collecting data from brand social mentions and broader relevant conversations to improve strategy.[72] Philip Kotler, Hermawan Kartajaya, and Iwan Setiawan in *Marketing*

4.0 describe social listening and monitoring as a form of digital anthropology. It can be used in content marketing evaluation, identifying leads and prospects in social selling, and identifying complaints and negative sentiment for crisis communication and reputation management. It can also be a key tool in customer relationship management, provide valuable competitive intelligence, and supplement traditional market research methods.[73]

For more details on social media monitoring and listening, see Hootsuite Academy's Hootsuite Platform training and certification at https://education.hootsuite.com/courses/platform-training. **Hootsuite Academy** is an online education site offering free and paid training courses and professional certifications.[74] Another resource for social media monitoring and listening platform training is the Meltwater Masterclass training at https://meltwater.com/masterclass/resources. **Meltwater Masterclass** is free online training for monitoring and analyzing social media.[75] Additionally, social media monitoring and listing platform training is available with Cision training and certification at https://www.cision.com/us/resources/university-program. **Cision University Program** offers free training courses and professional certification.[76]

The initial step in listening is a social media audit. A **social media audit** is a systematic examination of social media data. In this phase of social media planning, think of the social media audit as taking a snapshot of all social media activity in and around a brand and then evaluating the information gathered. It is a social situational analysis that includes both internal company social media actions and external consumer and competitor social media activity.

First, listen to what the brand is publishing on its social accounts and what consumers are saying about the brand, product, service, organization, and key personnel in any social platform. Also listen to what is being said by and about the brand's main competitors. Listen with an outside perspective to what the organization and its employees are currently saying on official corporate social media accounts and unofficial or personal accounts. A combination of internal and external social talk data will help identify challenges or problem areas within the current social media environment. The audit will also identify possible opportunities that may become significant parts of a strategic plan.

Second, organize the collected data and make it accessible for meaningful analysis. To accomplish this, use a social media audit template (see table 4.2). The template provided is divided into three key areas of talk for listening and analysis: company, consumer, and competitor. In each area, gather information and record what is found into "W" categories. These categories come from the principle of the **Five Ws**, by which journalists are directed to find out the who, where, what, when, and why of a news story.[77]

Data collection and analysis should occur in these key categories: who—company, consumers, competitors; where—social media channel (YouTube, Facebook, Pinterest, etc.) and environment (describe the look and feel); what—type of content (articles, photos, videos, questions, etc.) and sentiment (positive, negative, neutral); when—frequency of activity (number of posts, comments, views, shares, etc. per day, week, or month); why—purpose (awareness, promotion, complaint, praise, etc.). Note that the number of rows under each "Who" (company, consumer, competitor) will vary based on the number of brand and competitor social accounts and the number of social media platforms or channels where consumer brand talk is found. It is often best to create a table and add additional rows as

Table 4.2. Social Media Audit Template

Who	Where Channel/Environment	What Content/Sentiment	When Date/Frequency	Why Purpose/Performance
Company				
Consumer				
Competitor				

additional brand accounts are found and significant consumer talk is discovered on various social media platforms.

If the brand has an official social media account (such as Facebook, Twitter, Pinterest, etc.) you place it under "Company" with its own row for insights. This is where you describe what the company is doing on those platforms. Under "Consumer" you should list all the social platforms where consumers are participating in discussion about the brand. If they are engaging on an official company social media account, list it here and provide those insights in a row (such as Facebook and Pinterest). Also search the brand name and see what people are saying aside from the official account and be sure to include that discussion as well.

If a brand has an account on a social platform and there is no consumer engagement (such as Twitter) then list it under "Company," but don't list it under "Consumer." This may be a platform the brand will want to close. Search main platforms where the brand doesn't have an account (such as Instagram). Are consumers talking about the brand? List that platform in a row under "Consumer" and describe what is being said. There may be a brand community but no official brand account and they may want to add this platform. For "Competitor" you don't need to go as far in depth to capture insights. Simply list each official brand account on a row and describe what the brand is doing and what their customers are doing on those channels.

To be effective, the audit need not track down and collect each digital conversation. The objective of the social media audit is not to capture every mention but to gather a snapshot of the social talk—enough to get an accurate picture of what is currently happening in the social space. Still, be sure to gather a complete picture. Take the time to uncover conversation on all social media platforms, not just where the brand and competitors already have official accounts. It may be useful to pause and take a look at the table of contents, part III, chapters 7 through 10, to ensure you are considering all possible social channels in the listening phase of the social audit. Also search for social media brand alternates or fake accounts that may have been created by brand fans or brand haters.

For current company social media efforts, it is important to determine purpose and note key performance indicators (KPIs), if any. A **KPI** is simply a key indicator that is used as a type of performance measurement.[78] Try to determine the purpose of each social channel. For example, why does the organization have a Pinterest page and how is success being measured? For some this may be easy to answer and for others it could be a wake-up call. "Because everyone else is using it" is not an acceptable answer. A brand social media account should exist to support higher-level business objectives.

In the social media audit template, larger organizations may have to divide the "Company" category further into departments, offices, or employees. Perhaps several departments or local offices are each operating their own company social media account, or numerous high-profile employees are active in talking about the organization on their personal accounts—such as a CEO. It is important to capture what each is communicating and to discern whether they are presenting a unified brand image and collect any content performance data you can access. If you haven't before, collect a list of account owners and passwords, unauthorized accounts, and so forth.

When determining the "Why" or purpose of a communication channel, dig deep and find a strategic reason that directly supports the organizational mission or business objectives.

If a strategic purpose cannot be found for being in a specific social media channel, then it needs to be reevaluated. Is maintaining the social media account worth the organization's time and effort?

What could the results of a social media audit look like and find? Let's say a company currently has a Twitter and Tumblr account. They are sharing text with links on Twitter and photos with links on Tumblr to drive traffic to their website. They want to increase website traffic, especially unique visits for more conversions. The audit reveals they have little engagement with these brand posts. Consumers are tweeting on the brand account and mentioning the brand, asking questions, and seeking help, but the brand is not responding. Consumers are not discussing the brand on Tumblr; however, they found that customers are actively sharing photos about the brand on Instagram despite the brand not having an official account. The company's main competitor is on Twitter and is sharing a lot of photos and videos with links and hashtags and are tweeting twice as much per day. The competitor also has an Instagram brand account where they share photos, text, and hashtags, driving consumer engagement.

In this example, Tumblr is not driving traffic or engagement and the brand should consider shutting it down. Based on positive consumer brand activity on Instagram and the competitor's success, they should consider an Instagram account. Their Twitter presence could be improved with more visual content and by adding social media customer care to respond to customer questions and complaints. They should also consider increasing frequency of posts based on consumer activity and competitor success. Negative customer issues should be resolved and the brand should look at creating more valuable content on more appropriate channels for the target market from insights gathered in the social media audit.[79] See appendix B, "Social Media Tools and Resources," for a listing of the major tools available with both paid and free social media listening options. For the most up-to-date list, visit postcontrolmarketing.com/links.

Even if a brand is already monitoring social media on a day-to-day basis, they should perform a regular social media audit every twelve months. As Jay Baer said in chapter 1, "If your social media strategy is older than a year, you don't have a strategy."[80] After social conversation data has been collected and categorized into company communication, consumer communication, and competitor communication, it must be analyzed. Like any audit, data needs to be examined to formulate a judgment. What is the data saying? Does it point to any opportunities? Are there any trouble spots? How is the existing social media activity performing in terms of helping to meet organizational goals and business objectives?

How can social media help meet business objectives? The Cotton Council International wanted to grow global US cotton sales under the Cotton USA brand through a business to business (B2B) effort. Two niche B2B target audiences were identified as Mills & Manufactures and Brand & Retailers in seventeen countries speaking twelve different languages. Through LinkedIn and Facebook the brand's advertising agency Cramer-Krasselt used social ads to target and retarget decision makers by job title, level, industry, and geography. Social media was integrated into a complete digital effort including website, email, video, white papers, and articles. The integrated highly targeted campaign to B2B resulted in growth in export sales that exceeded the goal by 137.5 percent.[81]

Figure 4.5. Social media changes quickly and social strategy should be evaluated regularly.

© Zakokor / iStock Photo

Theoretically Speaking: Market Segmentation

What is the foundation for having and identifying a target audience? Many have heard the saying, "Birds of a feather flock together." This holds true in most people's personal experiences. They tend to gravitate toward like-minded individuals. It also holds true in marketing, advertising, and public relations. **Market segmentation** is a process of "grouping potential customers into sets that are homogeneous in response to elements of the marketing mix."[82] Wendell Smith introduced the concept in 1956,[83] and then Russell Haley in 1968 expanded segmentation bases to include psychographic variables.[84] Market segmentation is a valuable strategic tool to help organizations focus marketing activities on target segments. This activity helps concentrate limited resources to make them more impactful.

Traditionally, market segmentation has fallen into two approaches. **Commonsense market segmentation** is when managers use a single segmentation criterion, such as age, to split consumers into homogeneous groups. On the contrary, **data-driven market segmentation** is when managers analyze more complex sets of variables to split consumers into homogeneous groups. Commonsense segmentation is simple and easy, but a business basing its strategy on more data-driven approaches with more psychographic and demographic bases for segmentation will perform better.[85] The more research-driven segmentation bases brands uncover, the tighter and more successful the target audience and social media efforts will be.

In an interesting twist of segmentation, Kevin Kelly, founding executive editor of *Wired* magazine, put forth the theory of one thousand true fans in 2008, predicting the future of online business before the creation of crowdfunding sites like Kickstarter. Kelly says, "To be a successful creator you don't need millions. You don't need millions of dollars or millions of customers, millions of clients or millions of fans. To make a living as a craftsperson, photographer, musician, designer, author, animator, app maker, entrepreneur, or inventor you need only thousands of true fans."[86] Put this theory to the test. Was the Gatorade case given in this chapter a fluke? Can you find a case study where a brand is today successfully making mass appeal products and services, targeting a truly general mass audience?

Chapter 4 Checklist

Social media can change quickly. Visit Post Control Marketing (http://www.postcontrol marketing.com) for updates, but also use this chapter checklist to briefly check how social media statistics in this chapter have changed since publication.

- ✓ What percentage of Fortune 500 companies are on the top social media channels? Have the percentages gone up or down? Are they spreading out to more social networks?
- ✓ Are there new social media listening tools? What are the latest free and paid options?
- ✓ Are social media command centers still popular and valuable? Is brand social monitoring and listening happening at the brand headquarters or at communication partners like advertising agencies, digital marketing firms, or public relations firms?

SOCIAL PLAN PART 4

Objectives, Target, Situation Analysis, and Audit

In this part of the social media plan, first perform a situation analysis. Gather information about the history, vision, and mission of the organization. Detail current marketing efforts including any spokespeople, slogans, taglines, and important brand standards that must be maintained. Define the target market and key target audiences. Also capture brand performance, industry trends, and key competitors. Identify quantified and time-bound business objectives and then collect current social media talk from and about the brand and competitors in a social media audit. This part of the plan is about identifying where the business or organization wants to go and where it is currently. Cover these areas in this report, following the process and tools outlined in this chapter:

1. Summarize brand history vision and mission.
2. Detail brand performance over time, industry trends, and key competitors.
3. Describe current marketing identifying key themes, images, and taglines.
4. Define a target audience with multiple bases of segmentation.
5. Identify overall business objectives that follow SMART guidelines.
6. Perform a social media audit, report results in an audit table, and describe insights gained.

For a condensed version of the social plan see appendix A: Three-Part Social Plan.

KEY CONCEPTS

strategy

strategic plan

strategic campaign

market

goal

objective

nonprofit marketing

return on investment (ROI)

situation analysis

Golden Circle

vision

mission statement

secondary research

primary research

slogan

tagline

brand voice

brand style guide

target market

target audience

demographic variables

family life cycle

generational targeting

psychographic variables

firmographics

stakeholders

publics

SWOT analysis (SWOT matrix)

internal factors

external factors

SMART objectives

bottom line

value proposition

social media monitoring

social media listening

Hootsuite Academy

Meltwater Masterclass

Cision University Program

social media audit

Five Ws

KPI

market segmentation

commonsense market segmentation

data-driven market segmentation

QUESTIONS FOR DISCUSSION

1. Is increasing the number of brand social media accounts a good objective? Why or why not? What might be a good business objective for the sports apparel company example given with the SWOT analysis discussion in this chapter?

2. Does Simon Sinek's Golden Circle concept hold up in real context? Base your answer on real examples of successful and unsuccessful companies that focus on "Why" or seem to only focus on "What."

3. How should brands respond to negative comments on social media? Should the brand ignore comments, dispute them, or try to censor them?

4. Ethical decisions in social media happen in a very public forum. "Birds of a feather flock together," may hold true in behavior, but at what point does customizing the message to a target segment pass ethical boundaries? What is the difference between celebrating differences and playing upon stereotypes in social messages?

ADDITIONAL EXERCISES

1. Find an organization's business plan, marketing plan, or corporate "About Us" web page. Look at the mission, objectives, and/or target market. Now look at their social media

efforts. Do they match? Everything done in social media should be checked to ensure it is in line with organizational vision and mission. Every social effort should help meet business objectives and be focused on talking to and with the right target audience. If there is a disconnect between the stated mission and current social media activity, which should be updated?

2. Log on to Twitter or Facebook and look at the streams of several large businesses in a specific industry, such as cellular service providers. Look at companies such as Verizon, AT&T, T-Mobile, and Boost. Are most of the tweets from the marketer? Do they respond to customers, and how? Are there a lot of complaints? What are most about? Is the channel active? How many followers does each have? Quantify and compare engagement. In just a few minutes you should form a quick assessment of efforts and gain some key insights. Which of the competitors is doing the best job?

Notes

1. Philip Kotler, "Kotler's Quotes," accessed September 23, 2019, http://www.pkotler.org/kotlers-quotes.

2. Lawrence Tabak, "If Your Goal Is Success, Don't Consult These Gurus," FastCompany.com, December 31, 1996, http://www.fastcompany.com/27953/if-your-goal-success-dont-consult-these-gurus.

3. "Yale Business Answers Now," Library.yale.edu, accessed September 15, 2017, http://faq.library.yale.edu/recordDetail?id=7508&action=&library=yale_business&institution=Yale.

4. Gail Matthews, "Summary of Goals Research," Dominican.edu, accessed September 15, 2017, http://www.dominican.edu/academics/ahss/undergraduate-programs-1/psych/faculty/fulltime/gailmatthews/researchsummary2.pdf.

5. Nora Ganim Barnes, Allison Kane, and Kylie Maloney, "The 2018 Fortune 500 Target Millennials and Seek Uncensored Expression," Umassd.edu, last modified July 3, 2019, https://www.umassd.edu/cmr/research/social-media-research/2018-fortune-500.html.

6. Jonathan M., "Marketing Campaign vs. Strategy—What's the Difference?" LinkedIn.com, July 2, 2019, https://www.linkedin.com/pulse/20140702092918-117874168-marketing-campaign-vs-strategy-what-s-the-difference.

7. "Marketing Plan vs. Marketing Campaign," ImagineConsulting.com, April 11, 2017, https://www.imaginemediaconsulting.com/blog-all-posts/staysocialcampaign.

8. "The CMO Survey: Highlights & Insights Report," CMOSurvey.com, February 2019, https://cmosurvey.org/wp-content/uploads/sites/15/2019/02/The_CMO_Survey-Highlights-and_Insights_Report-Feb-2019-1.pdf.

9. Barnes, Kane, and Maloney, "2018 Fortune 500 Target Millennials."

10. Abbie S. Fink, "LinkedIn Most Popular Social Media Network for Fortune 500 Companies," HMAPR.com, July 18, 2018, https://hmapr.com/linkedin-social-media-fortune-500/.

11. Chloe Taylor, "These CEOs Have the Strongest Social Media Presence, Survey Shows—Here's Why That Matters," CNBC.com, June 17, 2019, https://www.cnbc.com/2019/06/17/these-ceos-have-the-strongest-social-media-presence-survey-shows.html.

12. "Here's How People Shop on Pinterest," Business.Pinterest.com, March 8, 2018, https://business.pinterest.com/en/blog/heres-how-people-shop-on-pinterest.

13. "FanDuel Drives Full-Funnel Success Using a Multi-Product Strategy on Snapchat," ForBusiness.snapchat.com, accessed September 20, 2019, https://forbusiness.snapchat.com/inspiration/fanduel-drives-full-funnel-success-using-a-multi-product-strategy-on.

14. "Gatorade," Business.Instagram.com (blog), accessed September 23, 2019, https://business.instagram.com/success/gatorade-2/.

15. Olivia Allen, "6 Stats You Should Know about Business Blogging in 2015," HubSpot.com (blog), July 28, 2017, https://blog.hubspot.com/marketing/business-blogging-in-2015.

16. "Market," Merriam-Webster.com, accessed September 23, 2019, http://www.merriam-webster.com/dictionary/market.

17. Rick Levine, Christopher Locke, Doc Searls, and David Weinberger, *The Cluetrain Manifesto: The End of Business as Usual* (Cambridge, MA: Perseus, 2000).

18. Jay Baer, "Five Shifts to Fix Your Social Media Metrics," @jaybaer, Medium.com, June 30, 2015, https://medium.com/@jaybaer/five-shifts-to-fix-your-social-media-metrics-bbe763c9d954.

19. Jon Gatrell, "Why You Need a Business Strategy, Not a Social Strategy," ConvinceandConvert.com, February 1, 2016, http://www.convinceandconvert.com/social-media-strategy/why-you-need-a-business-strategy/.

20. "Goal," Merriam-Webster.com, accessed September 23, 2019, http://www.merriam-webster.com/dictionary/goal.

21. "Objective," Merriam-Webster.com, accessed September 23, 2019, http://www.merriam-webster.com/dictionary/objective.

22. Will Kenton, "Nonprofit Marketing," Investopedia, February 22, 2018, https://www.investopedia.com/terms/n/nonprofit-marketing.asp.

23. "The Sprout Social 2019 Index, Edition XV: Empower and Elevate," SproutSocial.com, accessed September 21, 2019, https://sproutsocial.com/insights/data/index/.

24. "Return on Investment," Wikipedia.com, last modified September 19, 2019, https://en.wikipedia.org/wiki/Return_on_investment.

25. "Situation Analysis," Investorwords.com, accessed October 18, 2019, http://www.investorwords.com/19336/situation_analysis.html.

26. Keith Quesenberry, "Visualize Your Marketing Strategy to Form a Solid Foundation for All Marketing Communication," PostControlMarketing.com, October 12, 2016, https://www.postcontrolmarketing.com/visualize-your-marketing-strategy-to-form-a-solid-foundation-for-all-marketing-communication/.

27. Dave Chaffey, "Start with Why: Creating a Value Proposition with the Golden Circle Model," SmartInsights.com, March 22, 2019, https://www.smartinsights.com/digital-marketing-strategy/online-value-proposition/start-with-why-creating-a-value-proposition-with-the-golden-circle-model/.

28. "Steve Jobs Quotes," GoodReads.com, accessed September 21, 2019, https://www.goodreads.com/quotes/950437-we-re-here-to-put-a-dent-in-the-universe-otherwise.

29. Simon Sinek, "The Golden Circle: Presenter Slides and Notes," SimonSinek.com, accessed November 13, 2019, https://simonsinek.com/product/share-the-golden-circle-presenter-slides-and-notes/.

30. Meg Prater, "Why Your Brand Needs a Tagline, Slogan, Vision and Mission," Brandfolder.com, accessed September 21, 2019, https://brandfolder.com/blog/tagline-slogan-vision-mission.

31. Simon Sinek, "Start with Why—How Great Leaders Inspire Action," TEDxPugetSound, YouTube.com, September 28, 2009, https://www.youtube.com/watch?v=u4ZoJKF_VuA&vl=en.

32. "Mission Statement," BusinessDictionary.com, accessed September 23, 2019, http://www.businessdictionary.com/definition/mission-statement.html.

33. Sinek, "Start with Why."

34. "Essential Consumer Intelligence," MRISimmons.com, accessed October 7, 2019, https://www.mrisimmons.com/.

35. "Business Case Studies," Businesscasestudies.co.uk, accessed September 15, 2017, http://businesscasestudies.co.uk/food-standards-agency/market-research-and-consumer-protection/primary-and-secondary-research.html#ixzz3IgNvWPPI.

36. Emelda M., "Difference Between Taglines and Slogans," DifferenceBetween.net, accessed September 23, 2019, http://www.differencebetween.net/business/difference-between-taglines-and-slogans/.

37. Prater, "Why Your Brand Needs a Tagline."

38. Melissa Lafsky, "Brand Voice Doesn't Mean What You Think It Means, But You Still Need One," Contently.com, March 5, 2015, https://contently.com/2015/03/05/brand-voice-doesnt-mean-what-you-think-it-means-but-you-still-need-one/.

39. Kim Bhasin, "Can You Identify These 12 Brands by Their Trademarked Colors Alone?" BusinessInsider.com, February 1, 2012, http://www.businessinsider.com/can-you-identify-these-12-brands-by-their-trademarked-colors-alone-2012-2.

40. Liz Moorehead, "Brand Guide vs. Style Guide: What's the Difference?" ImpactBND.com, January 30, 2015, https://www.impactbnd.com/blog/brand-guide-vs.-style-guide.

41. "Target Market," BusinessDictionary.com, accessed September 23, 2019, http://www.businessdictionary.com/definition/target-market.html.

42. "Target Audience," BusinessDictionary.com, accessed September 23, 2019, http://www.businessdictionary.com/definition/target-audience.html.

43. Erica Tambien, "The Difference between a Target Market & Target Audience," eHow.com, November 15, 2012, http://www.ehow.com/about_6747097_difference-target-market-target-audience.html.

44. "WOMMAPEDIA," wommapedia.org, accessed September 15, 2017, http://www.wommapedia.org.

45. Jason Feifer, "How Gatorade Redefined Its Audience and a Flagging Brand," FastCoCreate.com, May 22, 2012, http://www.fastcocreate.com/1680819/how-gatorade-redefined-its-audience-and-a-flagging-brand/; Caroline Beuley, "The Digital Strategy Driving Gatorade's Growth," Prophet.co, August 9, 2016, https://www.prophet.com/2016/08/gatorade-digitally-enabled-business-growth-strategy/.

46. Mark Schaefer and Brooke Sellas, "Key Takeaways on the Future of Marketing—Episode 174," BusinessGrow.com, Marketing Companion Podcast, October 13, 2019, https://businessesgrow.com/podcast-the-marketing-companion-2/.

47. "Old Spice Campaign Is Not Only Great, It Sells—Now #1 in U.S. in Both Dollar and Volume Share," CampaignBrief.com, July 16, 2010, http://www.campaignbrief.com/2010/07/old-spice-campaign-is-not-onl.html.

48. "Demographic Variables," BusinessDictionary.com, accessed November 3, 2019, http://www.businessdictionary.com/definition/demographic-variables.html.

49. "Family Life Cycle—Topic Overview," WebMD.com, accessed September 23, 2019, https://www.webmd.com/parenting/tc/family-life-cycle-topic-overview.

50. "Demographic Targeting," KnowOnlineAdvertising.com, November 1, 2017, http://www.knowonlineadvertising.com/targeting/demographic-targeting/.

51. Roger A. Kerin and Steven W. Hartley, *Marketing: The Core*, 7th ed. (Boston: McGraw-Hill/Irwin, 2017).

52. Margaret Rouse, "Firmographic Data," WhatIs.TechTarget.com, September 2016, https://whatis.techtarget.com/definition/firmographic-data.

53. Rouse, "Firmographic Data."

54. "Corporate Communication," Wikipedia.com, last modified September 25, 2019, https://en.wikipedia.org/wiki/Corporate_communication.

55. Brad. L. Rawlins, "Prioritizing Stakeholders for Public Relations," InstituteForPR.org, March 2006, https://www.instituteforpr.org/wp-content/uploads/2006_Stakeholders_1.pdf.

56. Margaret Rouse, Mary K. Pratt, and Linda Tucci, "SWOT Analysis (Strengths, Weaknesses, Opportunities and Threats Analysis)," SearchCIO.TechTarget.com, accessed September 23, 2019, http://searchcio.techtarget.com/definition/SWOT-analysis-strengths-weaknesses-opportunities -and-threats-analysis.

57. "SWOT Analysis," Investopedia.com, accessed September 23, 2019, http://www.investo pedia.com/terms/s/swot.asp.

58. Neil Kokemuller, "What Are Internal & External Environmental Factors That Affect Business?" SmallBusiness.Chron.com, accessed September 23, 2019, http://smallbusiness.chron.com/ internal-external-environmental-factors-affect-business-69474.html.

59. "SWOT Analysis," MarketingTeacher.com, accessed November 13, 2019, https://www .marketingteacher.com/swot-analysis/.

60. "SWOT Analysis," MarketingTeacher.com.

61. George T. Doran, "There's a S.M.A.R.T. Way to Write Management's Goals and Objectives," *Management Review* 70, no. 11 (1981): 35–36.

62. Brent Barnhart, "How to Set (and Achieve) Meaningful Social Media Goals," SproutSocial .com, October 10, 2019, https://sproutsocial.com/insights/social-media-goals/.

63. "Bottom Line," Merriam-Webster.com, accessed September 23, 2019, https://www.merriam -webster.com/dictionary/bottom-line.

64. Sun Tzu, *The Art of War,* accessed September 23, 2019, http://www.gutenberg.org/ ebooks/132.

65. "Value Proposition," Investopedia.com, accessed September 21, 2019, https://www.investo pedia.com/terms/v/valueproposition.asp.

66. "Ernest Hemingway Quotes," BrainyQuote.com, accessed September 23, 2019, http://www .brainyquote.com/quotes/authors/e/ernest_hemingway.html.

67. Edward Moran and Francois Gossieaux, "Marketing in a Hyper-Social World: The Tribalization of Business Study and Characteristics of Successful Online Communities," *Journal of Advertising Research* 50, no. 3 (2010): 232–239.

68. John Deighton and Leora Kornfeld, "United Breaks Guitars: Case Study," *Harvard Business Review,* June 2010, http://hbr.org/product/united-breaks-guitars/an/510057-PDF-ENG.

69. Ravi Sawhney, "Broken Guitar Has United Playing the Blues to the Tune of $180 Million," FastCompany.com, July 7, 2009, http://www.fastcompany.com/blog/ravi-sawhney/design-reach/ youtube-serves-180-million-heartbreak.

70. John Beckett, "United Airlines PR Disaster: What you Can Learn from Their #FAIL," Devumi.com (blog), April 21, 2017, https://devumi.com/2017/04/united-airlines-pr-disaster -what-you-can-learn-from-their-fail/.

71. Benjamin Zhang, "United Made a Major Change to Ensure the Nightmare of Flight 3411 Doesn't Happen Again," BusinessInsider.com, April 14, 2017, http://www.businessinsider.com/ united-airlines-policy-change-prevent-david-dao-2017-4.

72. Amanda Welgrove, "What's the Difference Between Social Monitoring and Social Listening?" Sprinklr.com (blog), November 14, 2017, https://blog.sprinklr.com/difference-between -social-monitoring-and-social-listening/.

73. Philip Kotler, Hermawan Kartajaya, and Iwan Setiawan, *Marketing 4.0: Moving from Traditional to Digital* (Hoboken, NJ: Wiley, 2017), 111.

74. "Hootsuite Academy," Education.Hootsuite.com, accessed November 15, 2019, https:// education.hootsuite.com/.

75. "Masterclass Resources," Meltwater.com, accessed November 15, 2019, https://www.melt water.com/masterclass/resources/.

76. "University Resources," Cision.com, accessed November 15, 2019, https://www.cision .com/us/resources/university-program/.

77. John Kroll, "Digging Deeper into the 5 W's of Journalism," *International Journalist Network*, November 21, 2013, http://ijnet.org/en/blog/digging-deeper-5-ws-journalism.

78. Todd Wasserman, "What Is a Key Performance Indicator?" Mashable.com, March 11, 2013, http://mashable.com/2013/05/11/kpi-definition.

79. Keith Quesenberry, "Conducting a Social Media Audit," *Harvard Business Review*, November 18, 2015, https://hbr.org/2015/11/conducting-a-social-media-audit.

80. Jay Baer, Adam Brown, and Jen Hartmann, "How a 180 Year Old Brand Made A Huge Social Media Pivot," Social Pros Podcast, ConvinceAndConvert.com, August 2, 2019 https://www.convince andconvert.com/podcasts/episodes/how-a-180-year-old-brand-made-a-huge-social-media-pivot/.

81. "U.S. Cotton: The Cotton the World Trusts," ShortyAwards.com, accessed September 23, 2019, https://shortyawards.com/11th/us-cotton-the-cotton-the-world-trusts.

82. J. M. Choffray and G. L. Lilien, "Industrial Market Segmentation," in *Market Planning for New Industrial Products*, edited by J. M. Choffray and G. L. Lilien (New York: Wiley, 1980), 74–91.

83. Wendell R. Smith, "Product Differentiation and Market Segmentation as Alternative Market-ing Strategies," *Journal of Marketing* 21, no. 1 (1956), 3–9.

84. Russell I. Haley, "Benefit Segmentation: A Decision-Oriented Research Tool," *Journal of Marketing* 32, no. 3 (July 1968): 30–35.

85. Sara Dolnicar and Friedrich Leisch, "Using Graphical Statistics to Better Understand Market Segmentation Solutions," *International Journal of Market Research* 56, no. 2 (2014): 207–230.

86. Kevin Kelly, "1,000 True Fans," The Technium, March 4, 2008, https://kk.org/ thetechnium/1000-true-fans/.

Customer Experience and Customer Engagement

We think our job is to take responsibility for the complete user experience. And if it's not up to par, it's our fault, plain and simply.[1]

—Steve Jobs

PREVIEW

How many friends do you have? Right away the number of friends you have on Facebook or the number of followers you have on Instagram or Twitter may pop into your head. But if you were asked this question as recently as ten years ago, your answer would be very different and probably not in the hundreds. Back then friends meant people you see in person and whom you trust to share private details of your life.

Social networks began with the intention of being a private conversation between "friends." Yet today any complaint or random thought that used to be shared personally between closer friends is now published in mostly a public and searchable forum. Facebook Search allows any user to search for people, posts, photos, places, pages, groups, apps, and events on Facebook.[2] It is also just as easy for a Facebook friend to repost to their network or take a screen grab and post anywhere something that was originally only posted to friends or followers.[3]

Researchers from Cornell University and Facebook discovered how influential these posts could be. On average, twice as many Facebook posts contain positive words (47 percent) as negative words (22 percent). However, this study found that people who had positive words removed from their news feeds made fewer positive posts and more negative ones and people who had negative words removed made fewer negative posts and more positive. The research was based on the concept of emotional cognition.[4] **Emotional cognition** is a psychological phenomenon in which a person or group influences the emotions and behavior of another through conscious or even unconscious emotions.[5] This study emphasizes the importance of fixing organizational problems that may be creating negative brand social talk.

Fix Operations, Product, and Service Issues

Let's say that through social media monitoring or listening research, an organization discovers a serious customer service issue that is causing a lot of negative social media comments from customers. Or perhaps there is a substantial quality issue in product delivery that continues to show up in customer ratings and reviews. Many marketers could easily say that this is a customer service department or operations responsibility. In the new social media landscape, these issues become marketing, advertising, and public relations concerns even if these business functions don't have direct control over the issue. Steve Jobs may have been talking about user interfaces or operating systems, but the same thought applies to marketing communications professionals who must now take responsibility for the entire user experience with a brand.

Customer service is the process of ensuring customer satisfaction, often while performing a transaction, taking a sale, providing post-purchase support, or processing a returned product or service.[6] Customer service can take the form of personal interaction, a phone call, or an internet chat, usually provided by customer service representatives. **Operations** are jobs tasked with converting inputs such as materials, labor, and information into outputs such as goods, services, and value-added products that can be sold for a profit.[7] In general, operations make what consumers buy, marketing gets the customers, and customer service keeps those customers happy.

Why should marketing get involved in an operations or customer service issue? Marketing, advertising, and public relations professionals make product and service claims or promises to consumers. When the product, service, or experience doesn't live up to that promise, the wrong communication has been delivered. If the message, product, or service is not adjusted, then any new efforts to increase social media talk will only increase negative communications. If marketing, advertising, or public relations does not address the root cause, it is merely setting itself up for failure in meeting its own objectives and goals.

Advertising creative director Jerry Della Femina once said, "Nothing kills a bad product faster than good advertising. Everyone tries the thing and never buys it again."[8] Today, this happens even faster, because every bad customer experience can be instantly told to hundreds or thousands of people through social media channels. Plus, once social media posts or comments are published, they do not disappear like a negative newspaper print article, TV report, or personal interaction by the watercooler. Social media is forever and is only a Google or social media search away. For a marketing department to reach its ultimate objectives, it must involve itself in other departments of the organization. Prevention is the best medicine.

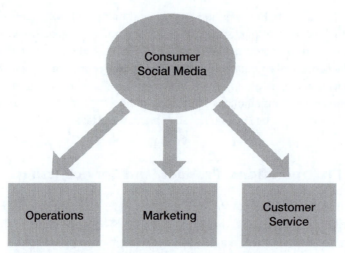

Figure 5.1. Social media impact all business units.

For years organizations have been set up with dedicated business functions in departments such as accounting, marketing, and human resources. These units or "silos" often have separate goals, leadership, and resources. This can lead to a silo mentality where each department rarely interacts with other business units. In many ways the power and influence of social media is forcing down these disciplinary or business-unit silos.

Consumers don't see organizations as separate operating units with independent budgets, management, goals, and objectives. Consumer conversations in social media impact all business units (see figure 5.1). This is the main message in part IV of this book, "Integrating Social Media across Organizations." Marketing simply cannot be only about marketing anymore and must work across strategic business units. A **strategic business unit (SBU)** is a fully functional and distinct unit that develops its own strategic vision and direction.[9] Today, marketers, advertisers, and public relations professionals need to be concerned about other business functions. The good news is that if marketing becomes the social media expert in an organization, it becomes more valuable to all business units and will earn a larger role in the entire organization. This means a seat or more prominent seat for social media in the corporate suite, as evidenced by Target's social media command center being on the same floor as the executive offices in their corporate headquarters in Minneapolis. Some organizations are forming new organizational structures where a separate social media department or center has been created to work with and serve marketing, advertising, public relations, customer service, corporate communications, human resources, information technology (IT), and other departments.

Many companies have determined that they need a hub or center of excellence that organizes social media strategy, governance, technology, policy, and process for social activities. Altimeter Group has found that social media is structured inside an organization in five common ways. **Social media organization models** are the five ways social media is categorized within an organization including decentralized, centralized, hub and spoke, multiple hub and spoke, and holistic. Decentralized would be an organization without a formalized governance where everyone is doing social media on their own. Centralized, hub and spoke, and multiple hub and spoke are all forms of a social media center of excellence (CoE) where the CoE either controls all social media for all aspects of the business, controls some aspects but shares responsibility with individual units, or controls the main aspects but shares responsibility with groups of units. Holistic represents a stage beyond a center to when social media excellence is interwoven into every aspect of an organization.[10]

No matter how social media is organized or where it is located in an organization or partner firm, if there is a discrepancy between product or service promise and delivery, a change must be made. In some instances the marketing, advertising, and public relations message needs to be adjusted to lower expectations and promise a less-ambitious customer experience. No matter what improvements are made, perhaps the organization simply can't meet overzealous communications expectations. At other times, social media listening will uncover a customer service, product, or operations issue that needs to be fixed no matter what the communications message. The key is to not move forward with a new social media strategy until adjustments are made.

In a ten-year analysis, Altimeter Group found that the number one cause of social media crises was exposure to a poor customer experience.[11] Every organization most likely has numerous competitors ready to take advantage of any weakness. Consider negative social media talk as an early-warning system to get any product or service issues right before they cause real and long-lasting damage.

As the collectors of this information, marketing and its communications partners must sometimes be the bearers of bad news. Communicate to and engage with other organizational departments to try to resolve the issues as soon as possible. Fix them before more consumers find out. Fix them and go out of the way to make it right with current customers. In turn, they will most likely reward the organization with positive talk. **Silo syndrome** is when a department or function, like marketing, develops its own culture and has trouble working with other functions such as operations, customer service, or sales.[12] Breaking down silos is not an easy task. Philip Kotler, Hermawan Kartajaya, and Iwan Setiawan in *Marketing 4.0* say, "collaboration works best when companies merge different channel teams, along with their goals and budgets."[13] If this hasn't happened yet in an organization, it is still the social media professional's job to start collaboration and coordination with other strategic business units from the very beginning of the social media strategy process.

Steve Cody, CEO of Peppercomm public relations, talks of company-crushing, social media–driven uprisings, saying, "People are pissed because they feel no one's listening to them. And often, no one *is* listening to them." If people are mad, listen to them and fix it—no matter the root of the problem. If the CEO said something wrong in a comment, encourage the CEO to apologize or correct it. If people are upset about ingredients in a product, change them or explain them better.

Changing the problem is what happened with lean, finely textured beef. "Pink slime" was a filler made from meat scraps that used to comprise many beef products such as fast-food hamburgers. The industry considered this an acceptable ingredient until ABC News ran a series that triggered a social media backlash, protest, and boycott targeted toward elementary schools, supermarkets, and restaurants. Those companies listened and contacted operations, and then manufacturing adjusted its process and dropped producers of pink slime from the supply chain. The negative social talk died down.[14] Unfortunately, it is not clear whether lean, finely textured beef was an acceptable food ingredient. In 2017 Beef Products Inc., the manufacturer of "lean, finely textured beef," filed a defamation suit against ABC. Both sides quickly agreed to a confidential settlement, but ABC stood by its reporting, saying that it did nothing wrong.[15]

Social Media Marketing Cycle

How do we fit this idea of very influential post-purchase consumer action into the marketing process? We must adjust some of our marketing processes. A central concept of marketing is the purchase funnel, by which companies move prospective consumers from awareness to consideration and finally purchase through marketer-generated activity. **Purchase funnel** is a model that illustrates a customer journey toward purchase from awareness to interest, desire, and action.[16] In each step, the number of consumers gets smaller. Traditional purchase funnels tend to ignore user-generated activity after purchase, when consumers use the product or service and then talk about it on social media, cycling back to the consideration phase where prospective customers read posts, comments, ratings, and reviews. Social media conversation is so powerful because it has a unique ability to influence the consideration phase of this traditional marketing purchase funnel through the social media consumer feedback.

The **social media feedback cycle** is social media connecting post-purchase social media conversation back to the purchase process, where social media is the product of

Figure 5.2. Social media's unique position changes the traditional purchase funnel.

© People Images / iStock Photo

operations based on the expectation given in marketing communication.[17] A television advertisement is good at generating awareness, but when consumers are really contemplating a purchase, they go to the internet to see what other consumers think. This is where they see post-purchase consumers talking on social media about their experience with the brand, product, or service. The talk can be positive or negative and it carries more influence than marketing's traditional consideration phase point-of-purchase materials such as in-store posters. Acknowledging and implementing this additional phase in the purchase funnel process represents a key shift in thinking to be successful in social media strategy.

The original purchase funnel, also known as a marketing, sales, customer, buying, or conversion funnel, is based on the AIDA model first developed in the late 1800s by E. St. Elmo Lewis to explain how personal selling works. Later it was taken up by marketing and advertising theorists and professionals to analyze and measure the customer's journey to purchase. The **AIDA model** is a hierarchy of effects model that indicates how marketing, advertising, and sales people should move consumers through the stages of awareness, interest, desire, and action.[18] It is illustrated as a funnel because the number of potential prospects decreases with each stage and tactics change from branding and mass media advertising to sales promotion and personal sales.[19]

The problem with the funnel is that it stops at purchase and does not map out post-purchase customer stages that influence repeat purchase and referral. McKinsey research has found that two-thirds of the touchpoints during the active-evaluation phase of purchasing now involve consumer-driven activities such as internet reviews and word-of-mouth recommendations from friends and family—post-purchase consumer activity not accounted for in the funnel.[20]

This social media–fueled feedback loop has shifted power from seller to buyer. Search and social has enabled people to create their own paths to purchase via dozens or even hundreds of touchpoints. In fact, Google's research has found that no two purchase journeys are exactly alike. The consumer is at the center of their own unique customer journey.[21] The sales, marketing, advertising, and public relations people are no longer the exclusive providers of information about their products and services. Derek Thompson in *Hit Makers* describes this consumer revolution well, saying, "The gatekeepers had their day. Now there are simply too many gates to keep."[22]

However, this doesn't mean consumers don't want marketing or that marketing communications professionals have lost all influence. Research indicates consumers want to engage with brands, but they want it to be more of a two-way relationship. Salesforce's State of Marketing report found 79 percent of people are willing to share their data in exchange for contextualized engagement, 88 percent will do so for personalized offers,[23] and 70 percent say connected processes, such as seamless handoffs, situation-specific engagement, and needs anticipation, are important to their customer journey.[24] It's no longer about being a gatekeeper; it is about joining the community of consumers who are already talking about your brand.

Consumer engagement is key in a new customer-centered buyer journey. In our digital era the marketing funnel is more like a circular system. The consumer is at the center controlling much of their own buyer journey while influencing other consumers on the path to

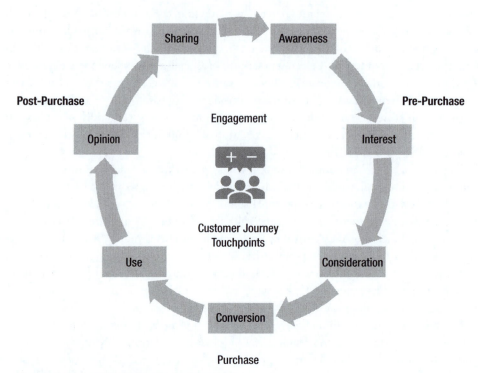

Figure 5.3. Social Media Marketing Cycle

purchase. The marketer joins the conversation via engagement as a guide, not a gatekeeper. This can be seen in the marketing cycle illustrated in figure 5.3.

The customer journey no longer follows a linear path of predictable marketing tactics that move consumers down a funnel of awareness toward purchase. A Facebook ad or blog post may appear in the consumer's feed or search results to generate awareness or could be the touchpoint they engage with right before conversion. A customer service interaction with a current customer on Twitter may recruit a new customer as well as a customer rating, and review on Amazon or TripAdvisor may influence a conversion.

The engagement in the middle of this marketing cycle can impact any part of the journey at any time. Positive or negative interactions and comments can pull more customers in or push more customers out, entering any stage of this new circular path to purchase. The customer is at the center of this journey, but the brand can still join in and help guide the path. After purchase, customers use the product or service, form an opinion, and share that experience through social media. This user-generated content (UGC) is found by perspective customers via search and social networks feeding back into the marketing cycle influencing their awareness, interest, consideration, and conversion stages.

The brand engages with potential customers through varied touchpoints along the journey from pre-purchase awareness, interest, and consideration to purchase conversion followed by post-purchase use, opinion, and sharing. These touchpoints become the tactics of social marketing strategy that now puts the customer in the center where the marketer, advertiser, public relations professional participates in a brand community. Different messages become important at each stage where traditional brand, category, product/service, and sales promotion still play a role in awareness, interest, consideration, and conversion, but customer service, loyalty, and advocacy are added through use, opinion, and share stages to recognize the importance of post-purchase activity. The **social media marketing cycle** is a model for the customer journey that includes influential post-purchase customer social media, putting the customer at the center of the process where the marketer participates in a brand community through engagement in customer touchpoints.

Joseph Jaffe is one of the first people to describe this new ecosystem in his book *Flip the Funnel: How to Use Existing Customers to Gain New Ones.* What is amazing is that this book was published in 2010, before social media really took off. His latest book, *Built to Suck*, predicts the downfall of corporations because most still have failed to embrace this new reality. Marketers need to move away from corporate centric first customer thinking to customer centric best customer thinking built around a brand experience community. Jaffe calls this conversational marketing.[25] In *Marketing Rebellion: The Most Human Company Wins*, Mark Schaefer calls it human centered marketing.[26] And marketing expert Seth Godin describes the new reality in the title of his latest book, *This is Marketing: You Can't Be Seen Until You Learn How to See.*[27] The social media marketing cycle helps you see your brand community in social media and strategically participate to meet organizational objectives.

The inbound marketing firm HubSpot describes this new perspective as moving from a funnel to a flywheel where the marketer's role is to add force to the areas that have the most positive impact and decrease friction in areas with the most negative impact. Doing so will increase the size of your flywheel, adding more customer promoters. A flywheel uses the momentum of your happy customers to drive referrals and repeat sales. It brings customer relationship management to social media marketing where your own customers become part of your sales force.[28]

Trust is at the center of any good relationship and is at the center of the social media marketing cycle. Edelman's Trust Barometer research reports that 67 percent of consumers said they would stop buying from companies they don't trust. How do you build trust? Edelman found that the best way to build trust is to lead with peer (social media UGC, influencers, employee advocacy, ratings/reviews, etc.) and amplify with owned, social, and paid. In other words, to build customer relationships marketers must remove themselves from the command of a marketing funnel and put consumers in the center of a social media marketing cycle. Trust starts with listening in a customer-centered social strategy.[29]

Trust built through connected consumer relationships has its rewards. Edelman also found consumers that trust brands reward them by buying their brand first (53 percent), staying loyal (62 percent), advocating (51 percent) for the brand and defending (43 percent) the brand. Social media and the connected consumer disrupted the purchase funnel where marketing people played gatekeeper, but they still play an important role as guide in the new customer-empowered journey built around engagement in the brand community.[30]

Content creation also takes a laser focus on customers and their changing needs. When developing content, flip from a brand-first to customer-first mindset. Consumers' needs and behaviors are different when they're not actively seeking to buy, when they become interested in buying, and after they have become customers—different stages of the buying cycle. Marketers, advertisers, and public relations professionals should create content for the pre-purchase, purchase, and post-purchase consumer.[31]

Rosalia Cefalu of HubSpot suggests that different employees from various departments are best suited for communicating with customers in these different stages. Distributing social responsibilities across departments to the most relevant people makes communication more effective and efficient, making one-on-one social media engagement more scalable. As will be discussed in chapter 13, setting up a cross-department social care team can help generate customer engagement throughout the buying cycle to gain new customers, repeat purchases, loyalty, and brand advocates.[32] How can brands optimize each of these stages with social media monitoring through active listening, publishing, and response?

For the pre-purchase stage, seek consumers who are in the market to buy but who have not yet purchased. Listen to social media for people using the right keywords, such as mentions of the brand, competitors, industry, or specific products and services. Marketing and advertising professionals could create relevant messages and valuable content to attract fans and followers and monitor conversations to engage with those responding. Public relations or corporate communications professionals could be looking for larger industry or corporate issues and identify journalists or bloggers for media outreach. As explained in chapter 13, social selling has become an important part of sales strategy. Thus, for a business-to-business (B2B) company, sales professionals could leverage this stage by creating and sharing valuable content and answering questions to generate leads.

In the purchase stage, look for consumers seeking purchase information. Marketing, advertising, and public relations professionals could help answer questions and provide additional information, but sales representatives may be better suited to deliver more relevant engagement. In a business-to-consumer (B2C) company, the sales team may interact with customers on social media to facilitate a sale. With a B2B brand, salespeople could address the question of qualified leads, helping them toward conversion.

In the post-purchase stage, brands want to keep current customers happy. Listen for brand customers seeking help. Marketing, advertising, or public relations people can play a role, but resolving product and service issues is best addressed by customer service representatives. As explained in chapter 13, these satisfied customers are likely to share their positive experiences, leave ratings and reviews, or make additional purchases, all of which help turn customer service into a marketing function. In B2B, sales representatives should follow up with existing customers, ensuring that they are happy and thus encouraging referrals and additional sales.

Customizing listening and response with cross-discipline teams in social media can help scale social media engagement. Meeting the different needs of consumers through all stages of the buying cycle can help businesses to achieve their marketing, advertising, public relations, sales, and overall business goals more effectively and efficiently.[33]

Yet increased mobile use has created an even more fragmented buyer's journey. Google calls these micro-moments. **Micro-moments** are the hundreds of real-time, goal-oriented, mobile actions that influence consumer decisions and preferences.[34] They occur frequently as we instinctively turn to mobile devices to act on a need, learn something, do something, discover something, watch something, or buy something. Decisions are made and preferences are shaped as people check their phones up to 150 times a day.[35] Google's research indicates that there are four mobile moments marketers should consider: "I want to know," "I want to go," "I want to do," and "I want to buy." A brand that creates the right social content in those moments could influence consumer decisions. In planning the social media

Figure 5.4. Working together in cross-discipline teams is needed for social media success.

© Scyther5 / iStock Photo

content calendar (discussed in chapter 14), ensure that the brand is regularly creating content that addresses each of these mobile micro-moments.

In "I want to know" moments, consumers are researching and exploring. Consider educational content that informs and inspires. For example, a company that sells outdoor gear could provide reviews of new equipment or tips and guides to enjoy the outdoors or tackle a tough mountain hike. A tax service could create content about retirement plans or itemized deductions. Let customers know you are there to help.

In "I want to go" moments, use geotargeting with unique location-based messages. The example outdoor brand could inform customers of local events such as group kayak tours or store locations that carry the brand. A tax service might highlight locations, workshops, and extended hours as the tax deadline approaches. Let customers know you are near.

With "I want to do" moments, customers are trying to figure something out and are looking for answers. This is where good how-to content can fill the gap. An outdoor brand could create a series on climbing knots or methods for purifying water while camping. The tax service might post quick answers to common tax questions such as tax brackets and standard deductions. Help customers and potential customers with what they are trying to do.

In "I want to buy" moments, consumers are ready to buy but may not know exactly what, how, or from whom. These moments are about more than promotions and sales messages. This may require getting customer service, B2C sales representatives, or B2B sales professionals involved. The example outdoor brand may sell group tours and have sales managers monitoring social media to provide answers to secure a booking. The tax service may have tax advisers monitoring social media, providing real-time answers, and building relationships that lead to a tax prep purchase.

Who has leveraged micro-moments? The credit repair company Progrexion found that customers in their "I want to know" moment needed education and began directing mobile traffic directly to their salespeople, resulting in a 221 percent increase in mobile sales. The car company Fiat made "I want to go" moments a part of an integrated marketing campaign by focusing mobile content on the nearest dealers to help grow unaided recall by 127 percent. The Home Depot has leveraged "I want to do" moments into 43 million views by expanding their "how-to" collection as more DIYers turn to their YouTube app while they work on home projects.[36]

Red Roof Inn leveraged a big "I want to" micro-moment when they uncovered research that said flight delays affect 90,000 people in the United States every day. The hotel chain began to track real-time flight delay and cancellation information from a flight schedules database. From that data, they sent out relevant geo-targeted ads near airports with stranded passengers, such as "Flight AA234 cancelled? Come stay with us!" The real-time relevance of the effort resulted in a 60 percent increase in revenue. Although executed with search ads, this same strategy could easily be supplemented with real-time, targeted social media content.[37]

Big Ideas and Being Interesting

T. S. Eliot wrote, "Distracted from distraction by distraction." This poetic reflection on the nature of time and order of the universe was written nearly fifty years before the internet existed and nearly seventy years before Web 2.0.[38] Yet the quote provides an astonishing observation on the current state of humans living in a continuously connected digital world. Todd Gitlin's review of *The Shallows: What the Internet Is Doing to Our Brains* adds another characterization. He appropriately sums up Nicholas Carr's book, saying that our information society has turned into the interruption society.[39]

The Pew Research Center has found that people see this distraction as a negative aspect of mobile connectivity. A quarter of US survey respondents said cell phones make it harder to give people attention and focus on single tasks.[40] Perhaps people are still operating under the myth that they are great multitaskers. However, there has been growing evidence that the ability to multitask is a myth. It can take up to 40 percent more time than single-tasking—especially for complex undertakings.[41]

As early as 2004, researchers in the *Journal of Advertising* sought to discover why people avoid ads on the internet. What they found was that prior negative experience, advertising clutter, and goal impediment were the most significant explanations. The authors note, "The unexpected appearance of advertising messages on the Internet disrupts user tasks or goals and causes consumers to extensively avoid the noise."[42] Remember Howard Gossage from chapter 2: "Nobody reads ads. People read what interests them."[43]

How do marketing messages not become the noise people want to avoid? Forget brand, product, and service for a moment and delve into the mind of the consumer. Become an account planner and dig deep for consumer insights that can turn into actionable strategy.

What Is Account Planning?

Account planning is designed to bring the consumer's perspective into the process of developing creative advertising and public relations messages and executions. While others worry about sales, clients, media placement, and creative awards, an account planner's job is to seek consumer truth and insight through primary and secondary research so advertising and public relations is relevant, entertaining, memorable, and effective.[a]

One of the most famous and successful examples of an account-planner–driven idea was the California Milk Processor Board's "Got Milk?" campaign. By now this campaign is so ubiquitous that every business from bath remodeling to used-car dealers has commandeered the slogan. But this great campaign started with an account planner's consumer research, which led to a "milk deprivation insight." This is the feeling people get when they run out of milk to go with a food that really needs milk.

How powerful was this consumer insight? It led to an integrated marketing communications campaign that reversed a twenty-year sales decline. The agency on the campaign, Goodby, Silverstein & Partners, used surveys and focus groups, but also collected research by placing video cameras in kitchens stocked with cereal, cake, and cookies and removed the milk to see how people genuinely reacted.[b]

Today account planning has evolved beyond consumer insights to being at the center of consumer engagement and brand experience across online and offline marketing channels. Carrie McCament, VP, Director of Client Engagement at creative agency Wray Ward, says account planning has evolved but remains at the core of strategic planning in a digital world. McCament says account planning "now sits squarely at the intersection of brand, consumer research, channel planning, UX/CX, data and analytics." No longer simply the starting point of inspired messages, account planning is a constant thread that connects all points across the brand experience.[c]

[a] "What Is Planning?" Apg.org.uk, accessed September 27, 2019, http://www. https://www.apg.org.uk/knowledge-whatisplanning.
[b] Jeff Manning and Kevin Keller, "Making Advertising Work: How GOT MILK? Marketing Stopped a 20 Year Sales Decline," *Marketing Management* (January/February 2003).
[c] Carrie McCament, "The Evolution of Agency Account Planning," WrayWard.com, May 22, 2019, https://www.wrayward.com/articles/evolution-agency-account-planning.

Account planning is a discipline imported from the United Kingdom to US advertising agencies in the 1990s that has since expanded to marketing departments, public relations firms, and digital and design agencies as an important method and discipline. The account planner finds consumer insight through research and ensures that the customer's perspective is represented in the marketing communications, advertising, and public relations strategic process.

If an organization doesn't have an official account planner, take on the mindset of one. Scour existing organizational research and research others have performed, and seek employees' knowledge of the target audience. Go on ride–alongs with salespeople, work with frontline employees, and interview customers directly. What kind of information should you be searching for? Actionable insight. **Actionable insight** is a true understanding of people in the target audience and situations related to the product or service that can be used to meet objectives of a marketing effort.[44]

Insight can be found anywhere. Goodby, Silverstein & Partners found insight with video cameras in kitchens. "Got Milk?" took that insight about people's reaction to a specific situation (such as chocolate cake and no milk) and made it a reason to keep refrigerators always stocked with milk. Search for an actionable insight that will lead to a big business-objective-exceeding idea.[45]

In a campaign for a regional airport, the insight came from an informal visit to the airport terminal. The integrated marketing communications team noticed the brief trip, close parking, and short lines compared to the big-city airports they normally drove hours to use on business trips. The consumer insight became actionable when it was linked to the marketing strategy and service benefits. The idea was a scavenger-hunt challenge in which two local radio celebrities raced each other to Chicago and back—one flying out of the regional airport and the other driving to the closest big-city airport. Live updates were reported on the radio and social media and culminated with a public relations event that evening with the local business association. The result was a campaign that not only announced the airport's new direct flight but also delivered the busiest month in the airport's history. Many times an insight is a common problem or solution to a problem. Sometimes it is simply a way of looking at a situation with empathy that acknowledges how the consumer feels.

In another successful campaign for a company that sold health insurance plans to businesses, the insight was found in the fact that the target audience, human resources managers, had gone through a lot emotionally. Human resources managers had nothing but bad news to deliver to their employees year after year for several years. The thought of holding yet another company meeting to inform employees that premiums were going up by double digits was downright depressing. Empathy, something the large competitor insurance company lacked, was the insight. It became actionable when linked to the smaller company's more flexible plans and account representatives who were empowered to deliver customized solutions that helped soften premium hikes. The campaign featured crying human resources managers in print and human resources managers singing the blues on the radio.[46]

A highly successful smoking-cessation campaign was inspired by research reported in an academic journal that linked quitting smoking with the same feeling people have in bad romantic relationships. The resulting campaign featured a woman trying to break up with a jerk boyfriend dressed as a cigarette.[47] Finding the right insight can make it easy to translate into media communication built around social interaction. Both the insurance and smoking-cessation campaigns would integrate nicely into social media content playing up the personal aspects of the cigarette and human resources manager.

Actionable insights can lead to big ideas. British brand-consulting firm Millward Brown defines a **big idea** as a driving, unifying force behind brand marketing efforts.[48] How does one know when they have a big idea? In three decades of working with companies, Chris Wirthwein, CEO of 5MetaCom, has found ten qualities that differentiate big ideas from "not so big ideas." See table 5.1 for an excerpt from his *Entrepreneur* article, "What's the Big Idea?"[49]

When selecting a big idea or big insight a main consideration should be making sure it is social. Social media is about personal interaction, and placing that at the heart of a

Table 5.1. Ten Qualities That Set Big Ideas Apart

1.	**Transformation:** Can it change attitudes, beliefs, and behaviors?
2.	**Ownability:** How closely can it be connected to your brand only?
3.	**Simplicity:** Do people get it without explanation?
4.	**Originality:** Is it unique enough to grab attention?
5.	**Surprise:** Will people see it as unexpected in a good way?
6.	**Magnetism:** Does it have a special allure or attraction?
7.	**Infectiousness:** How memorable is the idea?
8.	**Contagiousness:** Will it compel people to tell others?
9.	**Egocentricity:** Is it about people's self-interest?
10.	**Likability:** How much will people like it?

Source: Chris Wirthwein, "What's the Big Idea? 10 Qualities That Set Big Ideas Apart," Entrepreneur.com, October 20, 2014, http://www.entrepreneur.com/article/238441.

marketing, advertising, or public relations campaign is an excellent jumpstart. Think about the difference between traditional advertising and successful social media campaigns. A big idea in traditional advertising is not always a big idea in social media. Standard advertising practice places a corporate logo in the bottom right of a print ad. Yet in social media, it is hard to be personal with a corporate logo. Big ideas in social media should have personal interaction built in.

In the previous smoking-cessation example it is fairly easy to see how an abusive cigarette boyfriend could be dramatized in social media. Do not assume that this means a big idea must have a brand character. Without a character, social media big ideas can emphasize consumer-generated content or even employee-generated content. Imagine the "Got Milk?" campaign interacting with consumers by inviting them to share their own milk-deprivation stories. Consumers would become content generators for the effort. Zappos.com has built its brand on the insight that consumers love excellent customer service. So their big idea is having hundreds of employees posting on social media as themselves, providing that exceptional customer service experience.[50]

Perhaps what is needed is simply spending time watching the target audience. The academic term for this is "observational ethnographic research." Informally this can be accomplished by activities such as working the lunch hour at a convenience store, observing an operation at a hospital, informally asking questions of customers in a department store, or touring factories and talking to workers. This is what the team did with the regional airport to get their big idea. Even observing personal experiences with products, friends, family, and life in general can provide valuable insight. Never underestimate the power of instinct and don't hesitate to seek out the data and research to justify a gut feeling. The subconscious mind is often right.

To jumpstart the social media conversation, the big idea needs to be based on actionable consumer insight. This will make the marketing interesting, driving key factors needed to make a social media campaign successful. When you know the audience well, you deliver what the audience needs and desires. A great social media strategy can be brilliant on paper but a flop in the social world, like a job candidate who has an exceptional résumé but falls short in person.

Also, an idea is not big if it is not interesting. Advertising can buy attention, but social media must earn attention, engagement, and shares for additional views. In a world where we are constantly being "distracted from distraction by distraction," interruption is becoming less and less effective. Social media big ideas must be unifying but also interesting and engaging. Social media strategy is about creating relationships with consumers, not creating ads.

Big ideas must also have legs. **Having legs** means a campaign theme can be executed, or created for many different media, for a long period of time.[51] Having legs also refers to ideas big enough to take advantage of current events. How fast is the idea? Timing is another key to being interesting. Stand-up comics know this. So did the marketers at Oreo when they took advantage of a Super Bowl blackout by sending out a quick tweet: "Power Out? No problem," with an image of an Oreo cookie and the line, "You can still dunk in the dark." It was retweeted ten thousand times in one hour. The image released during the thirty-four-minute blackout was designed, captioned, and approved within minutes. What was the ROI on this tweet compared to a multimillion-dollar thirty-second Super Bowl TV spot?[52]

How do you know when you have the right big idea? A test comes from a popular format in creative briefs for IMC campaigns. A **creative brief** is a strategic document used to develop creative content for strategies and campaigns. Creative briefs vary but usually state the problem/opportunity, business objectives, target audience, current and future feelings, main message, support points, brand voice, and campaign requirements. It is useful to think of these as questions:

- Why are we communicating?
- What do we want people to do?
- Who do we want to do it?
- What does the target currently think?
- What would we like the target to think?
- What will move them from one to the other? (*Insight that leads to a big idea*)
- Why should they believe it?
- How will we communicate?
- Where will we communicate?

The right big idea will be the message that will move your target audience from their current state to a new mindset that will lead to meeting your objectives. Your big idea should break through the information clutter and connect with an audience. To do this you need content that "must relieve their anxieties and help them pursue their desires," say Kotler, Kartajaya, and Setiawan in *Marketing 4.0*, and it must have "stories that reflect the brand's characters and codes." Therefore an actionable insight or big idea produces content that moves people from one way of thinking to another and to action by connecting "the brand's stories to customers' anxieties and desires."[53] Seth Godin in *This is Marketing* simplifies this into three questions: What change are you trying to make? What promise are you making? Who are you seeking to change?[54] Here your big idea is the promise that you will make the change happen among the people you seek to change.

Figure 5.5. Corporate social responsibility can be an important social media message.

© Blue Cineman / iStock Photo

One consideration in determining the message that will move your target audience is that the message may not be directly about the product or service. As discussed in chapter 4, many consumers today are concerned about the "why" of a company. Consumers want the benefits that products and services provide but also care about the values of the company behind the products. Emphasizing those values could be a competitive advantage. **Corporate social responsibility (CSR)** is when companies consider the impact they have on all aspects of society including economic, social, and environmental. CSR can include philanthropy and volunteer efforts that not only can benefit society and help attract customers but can also help create stronger relationships between employees and companies, which boosts morale.[55]

Examples of CSR messaging in social media include brands such as Ben and Jerry's, which mixes ice cream messages with messages in support of climate change efforts. Patagonia mixes extreme sport messages with their support of environmental protection. TOMS shows its products, but also emphasizes its business model of giving back to improve lives. The hardware store chain Home Depot created separate social media accounts for the Home Depot Foundation to communicate the difference the company and their volunteer employees are making for veterans and communities impacted by natural disasters. Home Depot's competitor Lowe's supports the charity Habitat for Humanity, which builds houses for families in need. Lowe's helped create National Women Build Week with Habit for

Humanity and created a social media campaign promoting the effort with social media videos, images, and posts around the big idea of #BuildHer. The hashtag represents the company's effort to educate, inspire, and empower women to volunteer in their community to address the issue of affordable housing. The effort resulted in more than 18,000 women volunteering in more than three hundred communities.[56]

This talk of big idea is all well and good, but how do you actually come up with an idea? This was the question posed to James Webb Young, an advertising hall of fame copywriter. He didn't know at first, but through self-reflection he uncovered a five-step process for creating ideas first published in 1940 as *A Technique for Producing Ideas.*[57] Remarkably, aspects of this same process have been described by other creative people in vastly different fields of interest, from fine artists and writers to researchers and engineers. An idea is nothing more than two seemingly unrelated ideas coming together to form a new relationship and can be found following the creative process. **Creative process** is a method for developing ideas that follows the stages of gathering raw material, looking for relationships, letting the unconscious mind work, birth of the idea, and refinement. To come up with your own big ideas, follow the process below:

1. *Gather Raw Material:* Collect specific information about the product, service, and target audience. Always be collecting general knowledge about the world.
2. *Play Matchmaker:* Take different bits of raw information and view from all angles. Try all together, looking for a new relationship. Ask "why not?" Write it all down.
3. *Forget About It:* Make no direct effort to work on the problem. Play a game, run, see a film. Put it out of your conscious mind so your unconscious mind can get to work.
4. *Birth of the Idea:* If you follow the other stages, suddenly an unexpected idea will pop into mind from your subconscious. It can happen anywhere and anytime.
5. *Optimize the Idea:* Compare your subconscious "Eureka" ideas to the facts and conditions of the case. Get feedback from others. Refine ideas into practical usefulness.[58]

Telling a Story in Social Media

When working in marketing communications, many in advertising agencies and public relations firms are obsessed with finding the big idea. They are on the search for that great campaign and clever tagline that will get people talking, get people buying, and win them awards. This catchphrase even turned into the CNBC advertising executive talk show, *The Big Idea with Donny Deutsch.*[59]

However, in the Donny Deutsch show days, the big idea was more about running a six-month or annual advertising campaign with perhaps three print ads, a radio commercial, some banner ads, billboards, a press release, and a kick-off event. Big ideas were tidy mini-stories told in a small series of well-crafted and finely controlled media executions. Of course, this was before the explosion in social media use and increased influence of the consumer voice that this book is about. What then are social media professionals to do with this concept of the big idea?

In a way, big ideas today have to be bigger. Today's big idea is more than a clever tagline created by an advertising executive. Today's big idea is a big brand story. In social media, there are so many individual mini-brand communications created daily, by brands and their consumers. The big idea needs to be even bigger and more flexible to include trends and consumer comments and content. The big idea is a big brand story that doesn't end but evolves and is co-created over time through interaction with customers and even employees.[60]

If the big idea in social media is about story, what makes a good brand story? Research in the *Journal of Marketing Theory and Practice* analyzed two years of Super Bowl TV commercials—the one time all year people choose to watch advertisements for the enjoyment of the ads themselves. The researchers wanted to know which ads were the most liked, the ones that drew voluntary interest and the most votes in Super Bowl Ad ratings polls like *USA Today* Ad Meter and SpotBowl.com. Ratings indicated consumer likability but also valuable viral engagement and earned media coverage. They found commercials that told a complete story had significantly higher rates, finishing in the top of the polls. Commercials telling no story or less of a story had significantly lower ratings, finishing at the bottom of the polls.[61]

These findings were confirmed in a later study in the *Journal of Interactive Marketing* that looked at a large year-long study of viral advertising videos. Videos that told a more developed and full story had significantly higher shares and views on YouTube. Both studies coded their samples using Freytag's Pyramid, a theory that breaks a story down into five

Figure 5.6. What brand story will you tell in social media over time in each social platform?

© Siphotography/ iStock Photo

parts: introduction, rising action, climax, falling action, and resolve. Shakespeare used this story formula to draw mass audience for his five-act plays. Having all five parts creates a dramatic arc or plot of a fully developed story—the formula for being interesting. This is the same story formula you can apply to social media. But don't confuse brand storytelling as telling stories about the brand. Other research has found that the most engaging stories can include branding but not overt sales messages and should be built around characters relatable to the target audience and their life.[62]

Social media depends on producing frequent, consistent, quality content. Brand managers used to producing yearly advertising campaigns with a series of three to six ads are often left wondering what to post daily or weekly on their social networks. Establishing a bigger brand story can give you the content base you need. Then each social post or response can be a mini-chapter or character quote, expressing and advancing the overall story. To plan a larger brand story for social media, plan out the big idea, considering all five acts of storytelling as depicted in the Social Media Story Template (see table 5.2). Content in social media should be thought of as small story arcs that support the overall brand storyline and should be distributed across the entire social media customer cycle, delivering the right message and story at the right time.[63]

Act 1: Introduction. This story element is also called the exposition and provides the background details, setting, previous events, characters, etc. People buy brands for products

Table 5.2. Social Media Story Template

STORY ELEMENTS					
PLOT	**ACT 1** Introduction/ Exposition	**ACT 2** Conflict/ Rising Action	**ACT 3** Climax/ Turning Point	**ACT 4** Results/ Falling Action	**ACT 5** Resolve/ Release Tension
CHARACTERS POV: Brand/ Consumer					
SETTING Background/ Context					
CONFLICT Problem/ Solution					
THEME Moral/Lesson					

MINI CASE

Chipotle Scarecrow

Chipotle Mexican Grill has learned to talk about issues consumers care about in entertaining ways. Over the years, Chipotle has changed their product and operations to support sustainable farming, which is expressed in their "Food with Integrity" marketing campaign. In 2013, they created a mobile game and animated short film, *The Scarecrow*, telling the story of a scarecrow's fight against corporate food production.

The film reached 6.6 million YouTube views in less than two weeks.[a] Supported by a small online and mobile advertising campaign, plus public relations outreach, the campaign generated more than a half-billion media impressions and the game was downloaded more than five hundred thousand times in six weeks. The free iOS game delivered a sustainability message in a fun way, but also let players earn buy-one-get-one-free deals on Chipotle menu items, which drove traffic to the restaurant.[b]

In 2017, after brand reputation was damaged over multiple E. coli food poisoning outbreaks, they ran a traditional advertising campaign. "As real as it gets," featured celebrity comedians acting real inside a giant Chipotle burrito. The traditional effort was received with mixed results.[c]

[a] Jason Ankeny, "How These 10 Marketing Campaigns Became Viral Hits," Entrepreneur.com, April 23, 2014, http://www.entrepreneur.com/article/233207.

[b] Karlene Lukovitz, "Client of the Year: Chipotle Mexican Grill—The Content Marketing Master," Media Post.com, January 8, 2014, http://www.mediapost.com/publications/article/216937/client-of-the-year -chipotle-mexican-grill-the-c.html.

[c] Julie Jargon, "Chipotle Earnings Improve, But Customers Aren't Flocking Back," *Wall Street Journal*, July 25, 2017, https://www.wsj.com/articles/norovirus-outbreak-undoes-progress-at-chipotle-1500984001.

and service, but also for the backstory. Does your big idea have room for sharing the organization's history, people, and mission or vision through social media content?

Act 2: Rising Action. This part of the plot delivers a series of related incidents or events that build toward a point of greatest interest—the climax. When considering social media content, be careful of flat posts that simply contain the same information over and over in different ways. Think from a much broader and longer perspective of creating social media posts that build upon each other toward a big action, reveal, or turning point that consumers can look forward to, check in on, and keep coming back to see.

Act 3: Climax. This act of a brand story is the turning point that changes a main character's fate. The main character of a social media effort can be from the brand's perspective or the customer's point of view. In social media, consider presenting the brand or customer reaching a turning point and finding a solution or overcoming a challenge by drawing upon brand, product, or service strengths.

Act 4: Falling Action. During the falling action of the brand story element, the consequences of the turning point are revealed in greater detail and allowed to play out. If an obstacle was overcome, illustrate the results for the brand or consumer. If an opportunity was seized, detail the benefits and outcomes that point toward a final victory.

Act 5: Resolution. In this final phase of a complete story, all of the preceding events lead to an ending scene of the drama or narrative. Conflicts are resolved for the characters, which creates a release of tension and anxiety. Here social media content can show the brand or customer winning. Provide a glimpse at the goal of the brand and its customers—the happily ever after.[64]

Remember that in traditional marketing and advertising, brands interrupt the stories people want to see (TV shows, magazine articles, radio programs) with paid promotions. In social media, the brand must create the content people want to view and create a story that consumers want to be a part of themselves. Social media big ideas must inspire content that grabs people's attention, holds their interest, invites engagement, and elicits sharing. Storytelling expert Kathy Klotz has a unique approach to brand storytelling in social media. She draws from her experience as an improv comedian to recommend brands use collaborative storytelling to encourage target audiences to engage with and share content. Some tips include starting a story and then asking the audience to improve it or create a story with a beginning and middle (acts 1–3) and ask how they would end it (acts 4–5). Ask customers to write their own stories where they are the hero after using the product or service. Or begin with the brand story and ask the audience to make it their own. Finally, consider the "Yes, and" concept. Start your brand story and constantly integrate new aspects as customers add to the story and you encourage them with "yes, and. . . ."[65]

A great example of collaborative storytelling is when Toyota made a music video called "Swagger Wagon" where parents embraced driving a minivan in the form of a hip-hop video and made the song and graphic available to anyone. Thousands of families made their own version of the music video and uploaded it to YouTube, generating millions of additional views as Sienna customers literally became part of the brand story. Coming out of a recession when all car sales were down, and flat sales for Toyota because of bad publicity over a product recall crisis, Sienna experienced a sales increase of 18.5 percent—double the industry standard for minivans.[66]

As marketing communications professionals start to develop the big idea, strive to get out of a campaign mindset, and aim for a bigger brand story that leverages all five acts of storytelling that can be lived out in social media on a daily or weekly basis over a long time. This may also be a consideration whereas one of the fastest-growing areas in social media is stories. Daily active users of stories format in Instagram, Facebook, and WhatsApp all hit 500 million in 2019 in addition to Snapchat's 190 million daily users.[67] No matter what form, from a single YouTube video to a series of social posts or Instagram story, five-part story arcs take you on an emotional roller coaster where tension is created and then released, producing emotions you want to share with others.

Honda was trying to reach a younger demographic target audience for their certified pre-owned vehicles. Knowing that audience spent a lot of time on YouTube, the brand's advertising agency RPA came up with the big idea to create "pre-owned pre-roll." This idea combined insights from the target audiences' anxieties and desires concerning purchasing a pre-owned car, the humorous and entertaining videos they tended to watch, and Honda's casual yet confident brand voice. Instead of creating new ads, they went to other brands that aligned with their target audience and asked to buy their old ads. Brands like POM Wonderful, Del Taco, and Timbuk2 agreed and Honda added their own graphics, music, and voiceover. They indicated that Honda took over, which mimicked the process of buying certified pre-owned. The campaign resulted in over a half million video views with a 21 percent completion rate and a click-through rate four and a half times higher than previous campaigns. The big idea moved the audience from thinking that buying a used car is scary and no fun to feeling good about buying a Honda Certified Pre-Owned Vehicle.[68]

Theoretically Speaking: Ethnographic Observational Research

Ethnographic research has its roots in anthropology or the social sciences, but now marketing, advertising, and public relations have found this method to be useful in studying the culture of consumers. **Ethnography** is investigation of a group or culture based on immersion and/or participation to gain comprehensive understanding.[69] This type of investigation is often conducted via observational research. **Observation** is a form of qualitative research that involves the systematic collection of data where researchers use all of their senses to examine people in natural settings and situations.[70] Some researchers emphasize a distinction between observation and participant observation. As early as 1958, Raymond Gold described the roles a participant observer could play.[71] The following methods of observation could prove useful in various situations:

1. Direct or participant observation via handwritten or electronic field notes.
2. Self-reports via written and photographic journals kept by study participants.
3. Secondhand reports by people directly involved in the situation being studied.
4. Electronic observation via video or audio recorder, internet, or GPS.[72]

The "Got Milk?" campaign was discussed in this chapter as an example of a consumer insight discovered through observation. What other case studies reveal how this research method led to successful marketing communication strategies and campaigns?

Chapter 5 Checklist

Social media can change quickly. Visit Post Control Marketing (http://www.postcontrol marketing.com) for updates, but also use this chapter checklist to briefly check how social media statistics in this chapter have changed since publication.

✓ What are the latest developments in account planning? Is it still a separate discipline or has it become more a part of the way other communications professionals practice?
✓ Is silo syndrome still a problem? Is there evidence that marketing departments are working more closely with customer service, operations, and sales? If not, what are the barriers?
✓ Storytelling is a very powerful technique but is still often misunderstood. What is the difference in telling a story in a TV commercial, a news story, a YouTube video, and the story format in Snapchat or Instagram? Are there best practices for each? Can you tell a full story in a single non-video post with image and text?

SOCIAL PLAN PART 5

Repair Plan and Big Idea

In this part of the social media plan, go back to the social media audit to quantify and analyze negative versus positive social media content. In addition, social listening tools can be helpful in quantifying overall social media sentiment toward the brand. See appendix B: Social Media Tools and Resources for options. If negative commentary is significant, specifically identify customer service, product, operations, human resources, or marketing message problems that may be causing negative social media talk. Create an interdepartmental plan to fix the root cause of negative comments. Even if negative talk isn't significant, identify a plan to reduce the negative comments that are there. Next gather and conduct consumer research through various primary and secondary methods to discover a key actionable consumer insight that leads to a campaign big idea that is interesting and has legs. Report all research, findings, plans, and ideas in these areas:

1. Identify top brand social complaints and the root business-unit cause.
2. Devise an interdepartmental plan to fix issues and reduce negative talk.
3. Gather all research and uncover a key actionable consumer insight.
4. Create an interesting big idea that has legs across traditional and social media.

For a condensed version of the social plan see appendix A: Three-Part Social Plan.

KEY CONCEPTS

emotional cognition

customer service

operations

strategic business unit (SBU)

social media organization models

silo syndrome

purchase funnel

social media feedback cycle

AIDA model

social media marketing cycle

micro–moments

account planning

actionable insight

big idea

having legs

creative brief

corporate social responsibility (CSR)

creative process

ethnography

observation

QUESTIONS FOR DISCUSSION

1. If a company is used to planning out an advertising campaign with three print ads, two radio spots, and a TV commercial six months in advance, what challenges must they overcome in implementing a successful social media campaign?
2. If you are a marketer used to approving every brand message before it goes out, what best practices should be put in place to minimize concern?

3. Why is ethnographic observational research valuable? What are the potential differences in results or insight in observation versus traditional market-research surveys and focus groups?

4. Social media can put you in difficult ethical situations. You recently became the social media community manager for a brand. You have access to the company social media accounts on your phone. After a rough day with a difficult client you went home and complained about how awful the client is on your personal Facebook. One of your four hundred "friends" knows the client from their kid's soccer team and shares your post. What do you do?

ADDITIONAL EXERCISES

1. Do some silo smashing. Visit a customer service department and ask what the number one complaint is and how they deal with it. Visit operations and ask questions and listen. If the brand manufactures products, go on a factory tour. Talk to the managers and the employees on the front lines. Ask questions about their goals, accomplishments, and challenges. Don't forget to visit human resources and get their perspective. Do they have an employee social media policy in place? Students can perform this exercise by contacting the company they are working on, finding secondary research, or simply thinking from each perspective.

2. Get out of advertising-campaign thinking. Look at the social media stream of a brand that is currently excelling in social media. What do you notice about their messages? Are they contrived, fine-tuned, and overly clever? Or are they natural, in the moment, and more personal or human? Can you imagine your brand communicating like this? Devise a strategy that plans messages on a social media calendar but also allows for live, unscripted interactions. What guidelines are needed to allow social media that happens in the moment?

Notes

1. "Steve Jobs Quotes," BrainyQuote.com, accessed September 27, 2019, http://www.brainy quote.com/quotes/keywords/fault.html.

2. "What Can I Search for on Facebook?" Facebook.com, accessed September 27, 2019, https://www.facebook.com/help/400002116752060.

3. "Facebook Graph Search Makes Old Posts and Comments Searchable," SexySocial Media.com, accessed September 27, 2019, http://www.sexysocialmedia.com/facebook-graph-search-makes-old-posts-and-comments-searchable.

4. Sherrie Bourg, "High Octane Women," PsychologyToday.com, October 20, 2012, http://www.psychologytoday.com/blog/high-octane-women/201210/the-emotional-contagion-scale.

5. Tanya Lewis, "Emotions Can Be Contagious on Online Social Networks," ScientificAmerican.com, July 1, 2014, http://www.scientificamerican.com/article/facebook-emotions-are-contagious.

6. "Customer Service," Investopedia Dictionary, accessed September 27, 2019, http://www.investopedia.com/terms/c/customer-service.asp.

7. "Operations Management," Investopedia Dictionary, accessed September 27, 2019, http://www.investopedia.com/terms/o/operations-management.asp.

8. "Famous Quotes on Advertising & Copywriting," ZagStudios.com, accessed September 27, 2019, http://www.zagstudios.com/ZagStudios/famous_quotes_on_advertising.html.

9. James Carnrite, "Strategic Business Units: Examples, Definition & Quiz," Education-Portal .com, accessed September 27, 2019, http://education-portal.com/academy/lesson/strategic-business -units-examples-definition-quiz.html#lesson.

10. Charlene Li and Brian Solis, "The Evolution of Social Business: Six Stages of Social Business Transformation," Altimeter, March 6, 2013, https://www.slideshare.net/Altimeter/the -evolution-of-social-business-six-stages-of-social-media-transformation.

11. Priit Kallas, "(Report) Social Media Crises on Rise: The Social Business Hierarchy of Needs," Dreamgrow.com, September 28, 2011, http://www.dreamgrow.com/report-social-media -crises-on-the-social-business-hierarchy-of-needs.

12. Evan Rosen, "Smashing Silos," Businessweek.com, February 5, 2010, http://www.business week.com/managing/content/feb2010/ca2010025_358633.htm.

13. Philip Kotler, Hermawan Kartajaya, and Iwan Setiawan, *Marketing 4.0: Moving from Traditional to Digital* (Hoboken, NJ: Wiley, 2017), 149.

14. Jeff Howe, "How Hashtags and Social Media Can Bring Megacorporations to Their Knees," TheAtlantic.com, June 8, 2012, http://www.theatlantic.com/business/archive/2012/06/ the-rise-of-the-consumerate/258290.

15. "ABC Settles 'Pink Slime' Defamation Lawsuit," June 29, 2017, Fortune.com, http://fortune .com/2017/06/28/abcs-pink-slime-lawsuit-settled/.

16. "Purchase Funnel," Wikipedia, last modified August 23, 2019, https://en.wikipedia.org/ wiki/Purchase_funnel.

17. Dave Evans, *Social Media Marketing: An Hour a Day,* 2nd ed. (Indianapolis: Wiley, (2012).

18. "AIDA," OxfordReference.com, accessed September 27, 2019, https://www.oxford reference.com/view/10.1093/oi/authority.20110803095432783.

19. Annmarie Hanton, "The AIDA Model," SmarthInsights.com, September 6, 2019, https:// www.smartinsights.com/traffic-building-strategy/offer-and-message-development/aida-model/.

20. David Court, Dave Elizinga, Susan Mulder, and Ole Jørgen Vetvik, "The Consumer Deci- sion Journey," June 2009, https://www.mckinsey.com/business-functions/marketing-and-sales/ our-insights/the-consumer-decision-journey.

21. "How Search Enables People to Create a Unique Path to Purchase," ThinkWithGoogle .com, accessed September 26, 2019, https://www.thinkwithgoogle.com/feature/path-to-purchase -search-behavior/.

22. Derek Thompson, *Hit Makers: How to Succeed in an Age of Distraction* (New York: Penguin, 2017).

23. "Fifth Edition: State of Marketing," Salesforce Research, accessed September 26, 2019, https://c1.sfdcstatic.com/content/dam/web/en_us/www/assets/pdf/datasheets/salesforce-research -fifth-edition-state-of-marketing.pdf.

24. "Second Edition: State of the Connected Customer," Salesforce Research, accessed Septem- ber 26, 2019, https://www.salesforce.com/content/dam/web/en_us/www/documents/e-books/ state-of-the-connected-customer-report-second-edition2018.pdf.

25. "About Joseph Jaffe," JaffeJuice.com, accessed September 27, 2019, https://www.jaffejuice .com/about-joseph-jaffe.html; Jay Baer, Adam Brown, and Joseph Jaffe, "Are Social Networks Built to Suck?" SocialPros Podcast, ConvinceAndConvert.com, https://www.convinceandconvert.com/ podcasts/episodes/are-social-networks-built-to-suck/.

26. Mark Schaefer, *Marketing Rebellion: The Most Human Company Wins* (New Brunswick, NJ: Schaefer Marketing Solutions, 2019), 215.

27. Seth Godin, *This is Marketing: You Can't Be Seen Until You Learn How to See* (New York: Port- folio/Penguin, 2018).

28. "The Flywheel," HubSpot.com, accessed September 26, 2019, https://www.hubspot.com/flywheel.

29. "In Brands We Trust?" Trust Barometer Special Report, 2019, https://www.edelman.com/sites/g/files/aatuss191/files/2019-06/2019_edelman_trust_barometer_special_report_in_brands_we_trust.pdf.

30. "In Brands We Trust?" Trust Barometer Special Report.

31. Keith Quesenberry, "How to Create a Social Media Plan," SocialMediaExaminer.com, May 14, 2015, http://www.socialmediaexaminer.com/howtocreateasocialmediamarketingplan.

32. Rosalia Cefalu, "Can a People-Centric Social Media Strategy Scale?" HubSpot.com (blog), May 30, 2013, http://blog.hubspot.com/marketing/canapeoplecentricsocialmediastrategyscale.

33. Quesenberry, "How to Create a Social Media Plan."

34. "Micro-Moments: Learn More about This New Consumer Behavior, and What It Means for Brands," ThinkwithGoogle.com, accessed November 6, 2019, https://www.thinkwithgoogle.com/collections/micromoments.html.

35. "Micro-Moments," ThinkwithGoogle.com.

36. "Micro-Moments," ThinkwithGoogle.com.

37. Magnus Friberg, "Three Key Steps for Winning Mobile Moments," ThinkwithGoogle.com, October 2016, https://www.thinkwithgoogle.com/intl/en-154/insights-inspiration/industry-perspectives/three-key-steps-winning-mobile-moments/.

38. T. S. Eliot, "Four Quartets 1: Burnt Norton," *Poetry X*, edited by Jough Dempsey, July 13, 2003, http://poetry.poetryx.com/poems/755.

39. Todd Gitlin, "The Uses of Half-True Alarms," NewRepublic.com, June 7, 2010, http://www.newrepublic.com/book/review/the-uses-half-true-alarms.

40. Aaron Smith, "The Best (and Worst) of Mobile Connectivity," PewInternet.org, November 30, 2012, http://pewinternet.org/Reports/2012/Best-Worst-Mobile/Key-Findings/Overview.aspx.

41. Jim Taylor, "Technology: Myth of Multitasking," PsychologyToday.com, March 30, 2011, http://www.psychologytoday.com/blog/the-power-prime/201103/technology-myth-multitasking.

42. Chang-Hoan Cho and John Hongsik Cheon, "Why Do People Avoid Advertising on the Internet?" *Journal of Advertising* 33, no. 4 (2004): 89–97.

43. Howard Gossage, *The Book of Gossage* (Chicago: Copy Workshop, 2006), 20.

44. "Actionable Insight," Techopedia.com, accessed November 3, 2019, https://www.techopedia.com/definition/31721/actionable-insight.

45. Jeff Manning and Kevin Keller, "Making Advertising Work: How GOT MILK? Marketing Stopped a 20 Year Sales Decline," *Marketing Management* (January/February 2003).

46. "HealthAmerica: Get Relief from the Insurance Renewal Blues," Dawhois.com, accessed September 27, 2019, http://dawhois.com/www/healthamericachoice.com.html.

47. Kathleen Sampey, "Neiman Debuts Anti-Smoking Ads," *Adweek* 43, no. 46 (2002): 6.

48. Rob Hernandez, "Big Ideas: Research Can Make a Big Difference," MillwardBrown.com, accessed September 27, 2019, http://www.millwardbrown.com/docs/default-source/insight-documents/points-of-view/Millward_Brown_POV_Big_Ideas.pdf.

49. Chris Wirthwein, "What's the Big Idea? 10 Qualities That Set Big Ideas Apart," Entrepreneur.com, October 20, 2014, http://www.entrepreneur.com/article/238441.

50. Nicole Kelly, "What Zappos Insights Can Teach Us about Social Media Values," SocialMedia Explorer.com, November 17, 2011, http://www.socialmediaexplorer.com/social-media-marketing/what-zappos-insights-can-teach-us-about-social-media-values.

51. "Have Legs," Cambridge Dictionaries, accessed September 27, 2019, http://dictionary.cambridge.org/us/dictionary/british/have-legs.

52. Katherine Fung, "Oreo's Super Bowl Tweet: 'You Can Still Dunk in the Dark,'" Huffington Post.com, February 4, 2013, http://www.huffingtonpost.com/2013/02/04/oreos-super-bowl-tweet -dunk-dark_n_2615333.html.

53. Kotler, Kartajaya, and Setiawan, *Marketing 4.0*, 128–129.

54. Godin, *This is Marketing*, 25–28.

55. James Chen, "Corporate Social Responsibility (CSR)," Investopedia.com, November 27, 2019, https://www.investopedia.com/terms/c/corp-social-responsibility.asp.

56. "Habitat for Humanity, Lowe's and More than 18,000 Women Build with Families Nation-wide during National Women Build Week," Lowes Newsroom, May 3, 2018, https://www.multivu .com/players/English/8318351-lowes-habitat-for-humanity-national-women-build-week/.

57. James Webb Young, *A Technique for Producing Ideas* (New York: McGraw-Hill Education, 2003; first published 1940).

58. Young, *Technique for Producing Ideas*.

59. "The Big Idea: Donny Deutsch Questions People in Business, Entertainment and Poli-tics—CNBC," archived from the original on September 27, 2011, WebArchive.org, accessed Septem-ber 27, 2019, https://web.archive.org/web/20110927051404/http://www.cnbc.com/id/15838512/ site/14081545.

60. Keith Quesenberry, "Advertising Campaigns Are Dead: Brand Story Is the New Big Idea," March 24, 2014, PostControlMarketing.com (blog), https://www.postcontrolmarketing.com/ campaigns-are-dead-brand-story-is-the-big-idea/.

61. Keith A. Quesenberry and Michael K. Coolsen, "What Makes A Super Bowl Ad Super for Word-of-Mouth Buzz? Five-Act Dramatic Form Impacts Super Bowl Ad Ratings," *Journal of Market-ing Theory and Practice* 22, no. 4 (2014): 437–452.

62. Keith A. Quesenberry and Michael K. Coolsen, "Drama Goes Viral: Effects of Story Develop-ment on Shares and Views of Online Advertising Videos," *Journal of Interactive Marketing* 48 (2019): 1–16.

63. Kotler, Kartajaya, and Setiawan, *Marketing 4.0*, 128–129.

64. Keith A. Quesenberry, "The Power of Storytelling in Social Media Marketing," Social MediaToday.com (blog), April 8, 2015, http://www.socialmediatoday.com/marketing/2015-04-08/ power-storytelling-social-media-marketing.

65. Michael Stelzner, "How to Build Better Stories with Collaboration and Improv," Social MediaExaminer.com, August 31, 2018, https://www.socialmediaexaminer.com/storytelling -collaboration-improv-kathy-klotz-guest/.

66. Nick Bunkly, "Mocked as Uncool, the Minivan Rises Again," CNBC.com, January 4, 2011, https://www.cnbc.com/id/40909199.

67. Felix Richter, "Facebook's Snapchat Clones Have 500M Users Each," Digital image, April 25, 2019, accessed September 27, 2019, https://www.statista.com/chart/10558/daus -instagram-stories-whatsapp-status-snapchat/.

68. "Honda Certified Pre-Owned Vehicles: Pre-Owned Pre-Roll," ShortyAwards.com, accessed September 27, 2019, https://shortyawards.com/11th/honda-hcpv.

69. "Ethnography," Writing@CSU, accessed September 27, 2019, http://writing.colostate.edu/ guides/page.cfm?pageid=1345&guideid=63.

70. "Observation," Robert Wood Johnson Foundation, accessed September 27, 2019, http:// www.qualres.org/HomeObse-3594.html.

71. Raymond L. Gold, "Roles in Sociological Field Observation," *Social Forces* 36 (1958): 217–223.

72. University of Kansas, "Section 3. Data Collection: Designing an Observational System," Community Tool Box, accessed September 27, 2019, http://ctb.ku.edu/en/table-of-contents/ evaluate/evaluate-community-interventions/design-observational-system/main.

CHAPTER

6

Cross-Discipline Integration through Social Media

Welcome to convergence culture, where old and new media collide, where grassroots and corporate media intersect, where the power of the media producer and the power of the media consumer interact in unpredictable ways.[1]

—Henry Jenkins

PREVIEW

Have you heard of the term "information superhighway"? Perhaps you remember it and haven't used it or seen it in a while. Or maybe it is a term you've heard in older TV shows and movies. Today you may take for granted the enormous amount of information you have access to at the click of a button or the swipe of a finger. Questions like "Who invented the peanut butter and jelly sandwich?" don't have to go unanswered for even a moment. According to the National Peanut Board, PB&J sandwiches were invented in 1901 by Julia Davis Chandler, but became popular during World War II as a part of US military ration menus.[2]

What happened to the information superhighway? First appearing in 1983, the phrase **information superhighway** describes a telecommunications infrastructure used for widespread, rapid access to information.[3] It was a way for people to talk about the possibilities of new connections brought about with the development of the internet. In the mid-1990s enthusiasm for the internet as an amazing source of knowledge exploded and the term "information

135

superhighway" appeared in more than 4,500 major newspapers around the world. Yet a year later the term died down to half that number and by 1999 the news media played down information superhighway imagery to fewer than nine hundred mentions. Instead the term "e-commerce" rose in popularity and people began to talk more about the possibilities of electronic commerce. By 1999 major newspapers mentioned the term "e-commerce" more than 20,641 times.[4]

E-commerce describes activities related to the buying and selling of goods and services over the internet.[5] Why did the conversation shift so dramatically from information superhighway to e-commerce? People realized they could make money on the superhighway and then the emphasis became more on commerce than knowledge. Information was still shared, but the attention began to focus on building business in the new connected electronic marketplace. Marketers may be turning back to the original vision as they must now share valuable knowledge in social media to gain an audience to maintain and grow commerce. At the same time the social networks are more and more focused on revenue. The early years of social media focused on connecting people and building an audience, but once the major social networks went public, numbers like average revenue per user (ARPU) have become just as important as monthly active users (MAU).

The Real Convergence

Academic researchers and industry professionals have predicted convergence of media and technology for a long time, yet as renowned media scholar Henry Jenkins points out, the

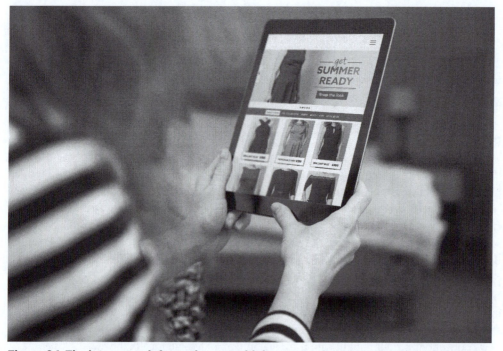

Figure 6.1. The internet as information superhighway soon became a road to e-commerce.

© Golibo / iStock Photo

actual convergence has happened in unpredictable ways. Within the concept of convergence there are two types of possibilities. One is convergence by the concentration of media. The other is convergence through the advance of technology. At first it was predicted that all devices would converge into one central machine that did everything for consumers. What scholars are actually noticing is that the technological hardware is diverging and it is the content that is converging.[6] The main vehicle for that converging content is the internet. Thus, a new term has emerged called **IP convergence,** which means using the Internet Protocol (IP) as the standard transport for transmitting all information such as video, data, music, and TV teleconferencing.[7]

What we are finding today is that the internet is the place for transmitting traditional communications media via devices like computers, tablets, smartphones, smart speakers, and smart TVs. Yet the internet is increasingly transmitting data from objects as well. This is called the **Internet of Things (IoT)**, or the network of physical objects with embedded technology that includes an IP address for internet connectivity to communicate with the external environment.[8] Now cars, thermostats, vending machines, lights, watches, doorbells, and even toasters and refrigerators are connected to the internet. Gartner research predicts over 20 billion connected things will be in use by 2020.[9]

Some possible marketing uses for IoT include real-time tracking of behavior such as use patterns to improve content delivery time or content.[10] This could be a running app letting you know it's time to get out and run based on the times and days you normally run, or it could be your refrigerator noticing that you are out of yogurt, recommending a specific brand, and putting it on a list for home delivery. Other marketing applications include improved segmenting of consumers based on actual behavior. An example given by Dr. Ari Lightman, professor of digital media and marketing at Carnegie Mellon University, is a car collecting driving habits of different users who may be in the same demographic target but vary in how they drive. The IoT data would enable the marketer to customize messaging to those who drive for performance versus those who drive for gas mileage and safety.[11] We are already seeing more car insurance companies offering different pricing based on customers' willingness to share their driving data.

IoT aside, what are some examples of converging content in terms of media communication? Newspapers and magazines have struggled in the transition to a more digital economy and many have gone out of business. Those still in business are still in print, but now they are also online and have added video, blogs, and social network content to their stories. In addition, newspapers and magazines have created mobile-optimized websites and have developed apps for tablets and smartphones. Some newspapers, like the *New York Times* or the *Wall Street Journal*, have ventured into audio and video podcasts.

Television shows are now multimedia spectacles as they scroll tweets across live programming and create rich interactive websites and apps that encourage the use of multiple media to enhance the content of the program. News, TV shows, music, and movies stream via the internet, and many customers are getting rid of their landline phone service entirely, using cell phones and video conferencing on the internet. People's phones are used more for messaging, social media, internet access, search, and apps streaming video or radio than for calling.

These trends have great implications for marketing, advertising, and public relations professionals. Organizations can no longer buy the attention of mass audiences as they could via traditional advertising. Instead, successful marketers are investing in multiple media buys filled with "converged content." As discussed in chapter 3, integrated marketing communication has developed into a primary strategy for marketers. This holistic approach leverages consistency of message and emphasizes complementary use of online and offline media for greater impact. Now it is evolving further to include the consumer conversation generated in social media.

As early as 2005, the *Wall Street Journal* reported that integrated marketing was the focus of most job searches for advertising agency executives.[12] Integration has been an important topic for marketers and advertisers who need to adjust strategies to fit with the new reality of converged media. When putting together a social media plan, marketers and communication professionals must not ignore the other communication activities in the organization. Whether social media is the lead or will support more traditional efforts, it must be integrated completely. Traditional efforts have not gone away, but they must be supplemented with cross-discipline efforts.

Today fewer people are talking about the coming media convergence because it is already here. Instead all communications professionals are focusing on **converged media**, which is the combining or blurring of paid (advertising), owned (brand channels), and earned media (public relations).[13] Brand-owned media can include brand websites, apps, text messages, events, blogs, social media pages, email newsletters, and other corporate publications. Brand-paid media is anything that the brand has to pay for distribution. This can include traditional advertising mediums such as TV ads, billboards, radio ads, direct mail, and print ads. Today paid also includes digital advertising in the form of display ads, paid search, mobile advertising, paid social media, affiliate marketing, and paid influencer marketing. Brand-earned media often comes from the efforts of public relations. This includes coverage by traditional and digital news media in print, TV, and online. Earned also includes blogger and social media influencer mentions and employee and customer advocates. Earned is also brand user–generated content distributed through social media as organic word of mouth.

For a converged media strategy Altimeter Group suggests using all these channels through a consistent story line, look, and feel. In order to accomplish this strategy, Altimeter emphasizes that execution of this strategy requires silo smashing for cross-channel integration.[14] The consumer does not see a difference in disciplines and is simply interacting in the new reality of media. Social media integration is an essential strategy as people consume more and more converged media.

With over 98 percent of customers switching between multiple devices in a day,[15] it is important for marketers to be able to use multiple channels to reach and interact with those customers. Different organizations are at various levels of integration and technology capabilities across the customer journey through these channels. At a base level, **multichannel marketing** uses multiple channels to communicate with customers, but each channel does not communicate with the others. At the top level, **omnichannel marketing** integrates multiple channels, exchanging information for a seamless and consistent customer experience.[16] Department store Macy's has been working on improving their omnichannel marketing strategy for years, breaking down the silos between their online and offline operations and merging their budgets and goals. They have found that their omnichannel customers are eight times more valuable than their single-channel customers.[17]

Figure 6.2. Omnichannel marketing is the ultimate goal for many businesses today.

© Chaay Tee / iStock Photo

Barbara Rentschler, CMO and senior vice president of global marketing for K'NEX Brands, agrees with a social integration strategy. Rentschler says, "Social media is another tool in the marketing toolbox. We seldom use a single tool when reaching out to our fans and look for ways to combine traditional and digital tools to super charge our communication efforts."[18] Converged media demands converged strategy.

K'NEX knows traditional marketing must be maintained to compete and drive sales in the toy industry, but they also know the value of leveraging social media. For example, K'NEX sent a personal thank-you and free product to an influential blogger who used the product name in a blog post. The gift in return spawned a full post on the brand, garnering further positive brand attention and awareness.[19]

Nike and its agency Wieden + Kennedy understood this when they planned an attempt to break the two-hour barrier for the marathon in the Breaking2 project. Eliud Kipchoge finished at 2:00:25, 2:32 faster than the world record. Even though he didn't break 2:00 hours, 5.2 million people watched the live stream on Facebook, and 6.5 million watched the short video of the finish. Additionally, it was broadcast live on Twitter and YouTube. The effort was covered by news media such as the *New York Times*, the *Guardian*, ESPN, and *Runner's World*.[20]

The global earned media was planned to lead up to the Nike Zoom Vaporfly Elite introduction. This global sports event was also an epic integrated marketing brand event. Competitor Adidas even congratulated Nike on the attempt via Twitter.[21] It also resulted in a full-length documentary produced in partnership with National Geographic.[22] Nike is not

The Attention Economy

The internet started with the promise of an information superhighway delivering all the wisdom of the world. Yet within a decade the discussion quickly shifted to the promise of sales through e-commerce. Nearly twenty years later, an ever-increasing number of technology companies are now battling for consumer attention. Once they get attention and build an audience, they resell that attention back to advertisers. In "The Distraction Economy: How Technology Downgraded Attention," Tomas Chamorro-Premuzic of the *Guardian* points out that when information has no limits, attention becomes rare and precious.[a] What is rare and precious becomes very valuable to those who obtain it.

As early as 1997 Michael H. Goldhaber wrote of this in *Wired* magazine. He proposed that we are not living in an information economy. On the contrary, he argues that the purpose of economics is to study how society uses scarce resources, and today information is not the resource that is scarce. Information is overflowing and available everywhere. Because of this, attention has become the scarce and desirable resource and thus society is now living in an attention economy.[b]

In relation to marketing, **attention economics** deals with the problem of getting consumers to consume brand messages. Since the cost to transmit brand messaging to consumers is now sufficiently low, more brand content can be delivered to a consumer than they can pay attention to and process. Thus, the consumer's attention becomes the scarce resource to be allocated.[c] What's more, brands no longer simply compete against competing products and services in their industry. They now also compete against anything that can draw a consumer's attention—from cute puppy videos to Netflix's latest binge-worthy series. As the entire economy shifts more toward attention, marketing, advertising, and public relations will grow in importance to play a more central role in business.

Perhaps as a sign that we have gone too far in creating content to capture the scarce attention of consumers, Netflix has added a new feature to speed up content consumption. It now lets viewers watch movies at up to 1.5 times the usual speed. The streaming entertainment service indicated that sped-up media viewing is already a norm with YouTube videos and in Apple's Podcast app that enable viewers to watch and listen at up to twice the normal rate.[d]

[a] Tomas Chamorro-Premuzic, "The Distraction Economy: How Technology Downgraded Attention," TheGuardian.com, December 15, 2014, http://www.theguardian.com/media-network/media-network-blog/2014/dec/15/distraction-economy-technology-downgraded-attention-facebook-tinder.
[b] Michael H. Goldhaber, "Attention Shoppers!" Wired.com, December 1997, http://archive.wired.com/wired/archive/5.12/es_attention.html.
[c] "Attention Economy," Encyclopedia.com, last updated October 6, 2019, https://www.encyclopedia.com/economics/encyclopedias-almanacs-transcripts-and-maps/attention-economy.
[d] Lucas Shaw, "Netflix Experiment Lets You Watch Movies at 1.5 Times the Speed," Bloomberg.com, October 28, 2019, https://www.bloomberg.com/news/articles/2019-10-28/netflix-experiment-lets-you-watch-movies-at-1-5-times-the-speed.

alone in knowing how valuable events can be. According to the Content Marketing Institute, 40 percent of B2C marketers and 61 percent of B2B marketers use in-person events to nurture their target audience.[23]

However, knowing that integration among communication channels is important is simply the beginning. Making it happen is something completely different. To get there, marketers and advertisers should comprehend the full context of why integration has not been an easy process. To understand this further, take a step back and look at the background and context of the silos that make up the traditional communications disciplines. Integrating these specific areas of advertising, public relations, digital (or interactive), and social media represents both challenges and opportunities.

Think Like an Expert in All Fields

Traditionally, marketers have hired advertising agencies, public relations firms, and digital companies to plan and promote marketing communication. Inside the agencies, the advertising copywriter and art director came up with the "big idea" for an advertising campaign. **Copywriters** are the writers of advertising or publicity copy[24] and **art directors** are the professionals who execute or coordinate the type, photos, and illustrations used in advertising design.[25] Both copywriters and art directors are usually employed at advertising agencies and are often called the creative team. In contrast, **public relations executives** are the professionals who focus on nonpaid forms of brand communication such as media relations, event planning, speeches, and crisis communication.[26] **Digital marketing specialists** are the professionals who handle online activities for a brand, such as web development, online advertising, search engine optimization (SEO), paid search (PPC or pay-per-click), and e-commerce.[27] Social media professionals who create social media campaigns and manage brand communities in social networks can come from any of these disciplines.

In the past, general advertising agencies would be the main driver of brand communication ideas as agency of record for major brands. The exceptions were campaigns or brands that didn't have an advertising agency of record or a large traditional advertising component. Then the publication relations and/or digital marketing firm would be hired to create a PR or digital focused effort from the beginning. With general agencies of record, the advertising creative team came up with the core campaign concept, then public relations and digital professionals were brought in to help execute that main strategic concept. These are two important viewpoints that were not represented in the creation of the core driving idea of the campaign. Public relations and digital marketing were left to retrofit their plans to something already created. The copywriter and art director may have considered public relations and interactive marketing, but their focus was on more traditional, high-profile advertising vehicles like TV and print. Right or wrong, this is how it worked in both large international advertising firms and small regional creative boutiques.

In the best cases, public relations and digital marketing are in separate departments inside the same company. But many times, advertising, public relations, and digital marketing are completely separate companies in different cities hired by the marketing client. Perhaps this makes sense in terms of hiring the best in each field, but it certainly is not the best

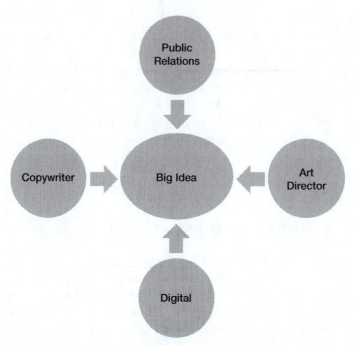

Figure 6.3. Brainstorm big ideas in multidisciplinary teams.

way to achieve integration. What further complicates integration is that many social media departments are found in-house with the marketing client. This makes sense for many reasons but represents a further segmenting and separation of discipline experts. Integration is much more effective when the creative process of idea generation goes beyond one person or team in one department or firm. In the best cases, real integration happens when an expanded cross-disciplinary team works together on the big idea from the beginning (see figure 6.3).

One example goes back to the regional airport case mentioned in chapter 5. Not only did the big idea come from observational research, but also a multidisciplinary team helped create it. An expanded team strategy was used to create the truly integrated effort. The advertising copywriter, art director, public relations executive, digital specialists, and social media expert drove to the airport and met in the terminal to come up with a "bigger" big idea. The idea was big because it was based on key consumer insights gained through observation. The idea was "bigger" because it truly drew from all disciplines, leveraging the strengths of each equally for a greater combined execution.[28]

Marketers and communications firms should strive to work in this type of expanded team whenever possible. If a marketer is creating a campaign by himself or herself, as within a small business or startup, or as a student, then it is possible to combine these skills individually. Study discipline-specific best practices and learn to think like an expert from each field. When brainstorming an idea, bring each discipline's perspective to bear in the formation of the integrated communications strategy.

One of the early advertising agencies to understand the concept of integrated disciplines was Crispin Porter + Bogusky. At an *Adweek* creativity conference, agency principal

Alex Bogusky said his agency always strived for "PR-able advertising." The public relations aspect meant more than traditional press releases and events. Crispin Porter + Bogusky saw the power of the internet and viral marketing before social media was big. In 2010, they were one of the first traditional advertising agencies to be named interactive agency of the year at the Cannes Lions International Advertising Festival.[29] The amazing part is that their early viral success with Subservient Chicken for Burger King happened before and without the power of social media.

In thinking about PR-able advertising that comprises advertising, public relations, digital marketing, and social media, marketers and advertisers may find it useful to visualize social media as the glue that holds the other disciplines together. Some organizations have even gone so far as to create new structures built upon this idea. On a tour of Target's Net-Base-powered social media command center, it was learned that the social media staff are located on the executive floor of the company and in their own department working with external advertising and public relations partners, and internal departments such as marketing, digital, corporate communication, and customer service. Target's CEO, Brian Cornell, takes social media listening seriously, seeing value in gaining crucial real-time consumer insights for action across business functions.[30]

Thinking of social media as an end-listening device to provide cross-discipline feedback is a good start, but in reality social media represents much more. True integration is about having public relations, advertising, and social media "baked" into the big idea from the beginning.[31] It is about not forgetting the other communications touchpoints. That is why social media strategies should never be planned in isolation. The base strategic approach for social media should work in owned, earned, and paid media.

When forming a big idea, start by looking for consumer insights that are actionable across all three communications disciplines. Marketers, advertisers, and public relations professionals must ask themselves, "What is the big campaign concept that will lead to engaging social media, newsworthy public relations, and motivating and inspiring advertising?" Ideally the insight will lend itself to powerful advertising, be unique enough to be picked up by the press, and be interesting enough to engage the target audience in social media. Also in thinking about public relations specifically, try to come up with an idea that goes beyond a single story or event. Look for an idea that can be sustained and will garner attention over a longer period.

Magic can happen when these disciplines work together. The magic comes from the increased attention and engagement that it can deliver. Marketing is now a two-way street, so a truly big idea should be big enough not only to integrate media but also to engage people to talk and spread the message. Organizations must join conversations consumers are already having, or get consumers to start brand conversations. Maintaining separate specializations and training is still valuable. Marketers need to have experts in all fields but should bring them together at the idea level. Adding customer service, human resources, research and development (R&D), and sales to the integration makes an even stronger strategic foundation and more compelling brand social media presence. Integration of these disciplines will be discussed in further detail in Part IV: Integrating Social Media across Organizations. Chapter 11 will discuss research, chapter 12 covers human resources, and chapter 13 covers customer service and sales integration.

The *International Journal of Integrated Marketing Communications* research study highlighted in chapter 3 demonstrated the importance of integration. In 421 Effie Award–winning marketing campaigns studied, it was proven that an increase in the number of marketing communication touchpoints was needed over time to achieve award-winning results. The level of integration increased from an average of two marketing consumer touchpoints in 1998 to an average of six in 2010 in campaigns awarded for meeting business objectives.[32]

While working on the big idea it is important to consider the concept of a brand. Brand has been mentioned many times so far in talking about brand communities, brand voice, and brand social media pages. But what is a brand? A **brand** is a name, design, or symbol that identifies one seller's product or services from others.[33] A brand is a combination of all representations in public from logos, taglines, and packages to TV ads, social media pages, and ratings and reviews. A brand's image is made up of a combination of what the brand presents about itself, what consumers say about the brand, and an individual's personal experience with the brand, its products, and its services. A brand tries to position itself favorably in the minds of consumers by having a clear and consistent positioning and authentic differentiation to support the positioning. **Brand positioning** is the way consumers view a brand compared to competitors.[34] Make sure as you work on the big idea and social strategy that you understand the brand's positioning and all brand standards they have set in place. A brand today is about overall customer experience and social media is a big part of this.

One technique that helps marketers determine brand positioning is called a perceptual map. A **perceptual map** is a marketing research technique that plots consumers' views about a brand, product, or service on a horizontal and vertical axis of different attributes (see figure 6.4).[35] The attributes are based on consumer perception and are usually ranked from

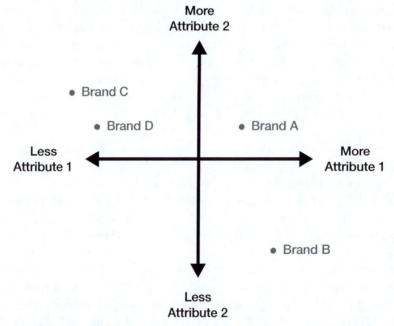

Figure 6.4. Perceptual maps can help determine brand positioning among competitors.

MINI CASE

Burger King Subservient Chicken

In April 2004, a chicken dressed in garters emerged on the internet responding to any command viewers typed. Subservient Chicken was the creation of Crispin Porter + Bogusky for marketing client Burger King. The viral campaign played off Burger King's "Have it your way" slogan and was created to help build awareness for the new TenderCrisp Chicken Sandwich. The agency and client decided to go with the more opt-in media of the web versus traditional TV advertising because that is where their target audience was spending more of their time. Agency employees first seeded the URL in a couple of chat rooms.

Within a year the microsite drew nearly 400 million hits, with visitors spending an average of six to seven minutes with the brand. This and the earned media coverage on major news outlets turned Subservient Chicken into a cultural icon. Further, sales of the sandwich increased 9 percent a week, with double-digit awareness, and total Burger King sales shot up 14 percent for the year after the campaign.[a] Bear in mind that the campaign managed to achieve these results before social media: Facebook was still limited to college students and Twitter wouldn't be created for another two years.[b]

In 2014 for the tenth anniversary, Burger King ran a campaign with advertising agency David that brought back Subservient Chicken to reconnect their viral marketing start with a younger audience. "Missing" posters in major newspaper print ads and brand social media read "Have you seen this chicken?" and indicated that he was "Last seen on subservientchicken.com." The website was relaunched with documentary-style short videos telling the story of the rise and fall of this internet star. It told the backstory of what the chicken had been up to after his fame faded and encouraged sharing on Twitter, Facebook, Google+, and Tumblr.[c]

[a] Mae Anderson, "Dissecting 'Subservient Chicken,'" Adweek.com, March 7, 2005, http://www.adweek.com/news/advertising/dissecting-subservient-chicken-78190f.
[b] Alex Alvarez, "Case Study: The Subservient Chicken," CMPMiami.com, August 31, 2012, http://www.cmpmiami.com/case-study-the-subservient-chicken.
[c] Dan Solomon, "10 Years Later, Burger King Brings Back the Subservient Chicken," FastCompany.com, April 28, 2014, https://www.fastcompany.com/3029775/10-years-later-burger-king-brings-back-the-subservient-chicken.

low to high along a Likert scale (1–5 or 1–7). Perceptual maps are great ways to quickly visualize the competitive landscape and understand how your brand uniquely meets customers' wants and needs. Most companies determine perceptual maps from traditional marketing research such as surveys and focus groups, but social media listening and monitoring can provide insight. Personal interviews such as were discussed in chapter 4 for creating buyer personas can provide information to create perceptual maps. Clients may already have perceptual maps.

Jim Joseph of global integrated communications agency BCW suggests using both function attributes or benefits and emotional attributes or benefits when creating a perceptual map. We know from psychology research that we make decisions based on both rational and emotional reasons (see chapter 15: Theoretically Speaking: Elaboration Likelihood

Model). If creating one perceptual map, use one axis for consumer needs or functional benefits and one for consumer wants or emotional benefits. Better yet, Joseph suggests creating two perceptual maps with one for the functional benefits of the product in the category and one for the emotional benefits of the brand in the industry.[36] Remember that a brand is more than a product or service and what it does for you. A brand is the feeling you get from that experience. BMW understood this in their "Story of Joy" branding campaign summed up by Jack Pitney, Vice President, Marketing, BMW North America: "All of our efforts in engineering and technology are about one thing, which is creating moments of joy."[37]

A consumer perception of a brand determines its value. Consumers who trust the brand and find it relevant will purchase it over competitors, often paying a premium, and will exhibit brand loyalty. Therefore brands can hold tremendous value often measured as brand equity. The world's most valuable brand today is Apple, valued at $214 billion. The top four most valuable brands are tech companies also, including Google, Amazon, and Microsoft. Yet the fifth most valuable brand in the world is Coca-Cola, valued at $66 billion.[38] **Brand equity** is a set of metrics used to measure the value of a brand.[39]

In the current social media environment customers are scrutinizing brands more than ever and have a powerful outlet to voice their displeasure. Transparency is important; brands can no longer overpromise and under deliver. A brand's identity must be communicated and positioned in a consistent and true manner across all marketing channels.[40] As you work on the big idea, social media strategy and then social media executions ensure you understand and properly convey the right brand positioning and follow all brand identity guidelines. If you are unsure, ask the marketing client; find your own standard if you work for the brand, and if you don't have any be sure to establish these before moving forward. Ensure that the brand positioning or promise matches the actual experience.

Social Media Advertising

There is another important reason to consider integration with traditional marketing methods—the amount of social media content is growing. Every minute it is estimated that there are 511,200 new tweets, 277,777 Instagram stories, 55,140 Instagram photos, and 4,500,000 YouTube and 1,000,000 Twitch videos watched.[41] That is new content every minute of every day, with much of it focused on brands. Social media consultant and author Mark Schaefer calls this "content shock" and it is only going to get worse.[42] In a Content Marketing Institute survey, 56 percent of B2C and B2B marketers expect to increase their spending on content creation in the next year.[43] Two terms that become important in this environment of content shock are reach and impressions. **Reach** is the number of unique people who see a piece of content. **Impressions** are the number of times a piece of content is displayed.[44] In social media an impression means your post showed up in someone's feed and every time they see it is an additional impression.

Because of this social media clutter, paying for social media reach has become a more important strategic consideration. Paid social media, also known as social advertising or

Figure 6.5. Paid social media has become an essential part of social media strategy.

© Good Life Studio / iStock Photo

native advertising, is simply paying for distribution or views in social media channels. This can take the form of promoted, sponsored, or boosted posts and other types of ads that appear in people's news feeds or other places in social media channels. Two general terms have emerged to describe paid social media. **Social media advertising** is advertising that relies on social information or networks in generating, targeting, and delivering paid marketing communications.[45] **Native advertising** is paid marketing that delivers useful, targeted content along with and in a form that looks like the social media site's or app's non-ad content.[46] Native ads can take the form of promoted tweets in Twitter, sponsored updates on LinkedIn, promoted Facebook posts, or articles on BuzzFeed. Some social networks offer other forms of paid social media such as display ads, text ads, pre-roll, or filters in the network.

The need for paid social advertising has increased as organic reach has decreased significantly. **Organic reach** is the number of unique people who saw a social media post through unpaid distribution. **Paid reach** is the number of unique people who saw a post as a result of paid distribution.[47] Organic reach is often calculated as a percentage by dividing the total number of users reached by the total number of posts. This is usually collected within a specific time frame such as thirty days. Then the average number of users reached per post is divided by the total number of followers, fans, or page "likes." Getting someone to "Follow us on Facebook" doesn't deliver nearly as much guaranteed exposure today as it did in the past.

With each social network becoming more flooded with content, reach is dropping. This is especially apparent in Facebook. By 2014 Facebook reported that the average person saw more than 1,500 stories in their news feed whenever they logged in to their account. This was too many to possibly read. Facebook responded by adjusting their algorithm to show only about three hundred stories.[48] This resulted in a drop of average organic reach to 3 percent for many business pages.[49] By 2016 average organic reach rates for top social channels included 2.27 percent for Facebook, 3.61 percent for Twitter, 20 percent for LinkedIn, and 20 percent for Instagram (before Instagram introduced the algorithm in 2018).[50]

Of course, the numbers reported here are averages and there are strategies to get above average organic reach. Some brands have managed to maintain impressive organic reach numbers with high engagement or other methods. A study found that some smaller Facebook pages can still see average organic reach of up to 11 percent.[51] Yet that is still low, and for most brands, paid social advertising is becoming a necessary part of the social media plan. The good news is that paid social reach can be one of the more effective forms of paid advertising. An *eMarketer* survey of US social media users reported that nine out of the top ten most effective marketing tactics included sponsored social media messages. TV commercials were the only nonsocial marketing tactics in the top ten.[52]

The reality is that paid social is an important part of any social media strategy today. In one survey, 68 percent of marketers are using paid methods to distribute their brand content.[53] Yet all this talk of paid social media does not mean that organic social media is ineffective. Organic is still very important. As Adobe points out in an article on their digital marketing blog titled "Stop Debating the Death of Organic Social Media," organic, or nonpaid, social media still has the benefit of branding without a budget. Even with lower organic reach rates, nonpaid social reach lowers marketing costs, builds brand-loyal communities (measured by engagement rates), and takes advantage of new social networks, early adopters, and niche audiences. Organic is great for brand community building and is a great testing ground for posts before spending money on them. Yet adding paid social media to organic posts helps extend your message by increasing reach. Paid social advertising also provides customized targeting, retargeting, and improved insights with advanced analytics and testing.[54] The bottom line is that paid and unpaid social media work best together.

Programmatic media buying is a growing method of purchasing advertising media globally. Programmatic trading accounts for over 85 percent of all online and mobile display spending in the United States and it is moving into other media such as online video and native and connected TV.[55] Programmatic advertising is a growing part of social media buying for platforms like Facebook,[56] Twitter,[57] Pinterest,[58] Instagram,[59] Snapchat,[60] and LinkedIn.[61]

What is it? **Programmatic advertising** is the automated buying and selling of advertising media targeting specific audiences and demographics placed through artificial intelligence (AI) and real-time bidding (RTB). Programmatic media buying is in online display, mobile display, online video, and social media advertising, and is expanding to digital outdoor, radio, and TV.[62]

Programmatic advertising has two distinct methods. First, **real-time bidding (RTB)** is auction-based ad transactions placed on real-time impressions in open and private marketplaces. Second, **programmatic direct** is ads purchased via a publisher-owned application program interface (API) like Facebook and Twitter or an existing demand-side platform (DSP) like DoubleClick (now part of Google Ads), SmartyAds, PubMatic, Simpli. fi, and MediaMath.[63] Programmatic social media buying offers more precise targeting and more efficient spending using online data (like browsing activity) and offline data (like loyalty card data) to laser-target the placement of ads. Data brokers match offline data with online data and license data-management platforms (DMP) to organize the data and use demand-side platforms (DSP) to automate the execution of media buys for more efficient spending.[64]

Social media marketers can run more effective campaigns through automated buying and by reaching a precise audience with highly relevant messages. One example is Red Bull targeting videos to Twitter feeds of people who have viewed extreme sports sites. Programmatic advertising enables buying ads and promoted posts on social media networks, but also placement of brand-sponsored articles and videos directly through publishers like BuzzFeed, the *New York Times*, and the *Wall Street Journal*.[65] These new forms of promotion bring up important issues of understanding the difference between information delivered in a traditional news article and an article written to promote a brand. Additionally, native programmatic budgets are going to native platforms such as Outbrain, Taboola, Sharethrough, Nativo, and Bidtellect that place sponsored content across the web. These platforms boost brand content, serving up links to sponsored articles with messages below publisher content such as "you may also be interested in . . ."[66]

Beyond social network ads and paid-content marketing, influencer marketing offers programmatic ad buying. **Influencer marketing** focuses on leveraging key leaders to advocate on behalf of a brand to reach the larger market.[67] For example, ROI Influencer Media (representing more than fifty thousand influencers from celebrities to social media all-stars) has partnered with programmatic platforms such as Rubicon Project, PubMatic, OpenX, MediaMath, and Google Ads. When buying programmatic ad packages, bundles of influencers appear as options where marketers pay for viewable impressions on influencers' social media sites and walls. Authenticity is preserved through influencers still having final approval and control over their feeds.[68] More measurement of impact is being put in place with companies like ROI Influencer touting The ROI Influencer Score™, which uses algorithms to measure and rank the most effective influencers across Facebook, Twitter, and Instagram. It combines reach, engagement, relevancy, and composition incorporating age, gender, interest, and location of audiences.[69]

Other companies like Fanbytes and Gnack offer programmatic buying of user-generated content from Snapchat and Instagram influencers and micro-influencers with fewer than ten thousand followers. Dashboards enable marketers, advertisers, and public relations professionals to bid on influencer ads programmatically, buying branded content on influencers' social media pages, blog pages, and websites. TapInfluence provides influencer marketing software, creating an easy-to-navigate marketplace for brands to find content creators and influencers.[70] Influencer marketing will be discussed further in chapter 12.

Another trend to consider is the rise of social commerce. **Social commerce** is the use of social networks for online buying and selling via e-commerce transactions.[71] As global retail e-commerce sales have increased four times since 2014, so has the number of social media users. Social commerce combines social media and commerce to streamline the buying process and increase the effectiveness of social advertising. Social media platforms are increasing social commerce features. Common social commerce features include buy buttons in social media posts, shoppable posts and stories, plus social commerce plug-ins and apps.[72]

Examples of social commerce include Kate Spade using shoppable links at the end of YouTube videos,[73] Lego using Buy Now buttons in Facebook Messenger,[74] and Gardener's Supply Company Buyable Pins on Pinterest.[75] Wish.com has used Snapchat's shoppable ads.[76] But social commerce doesn't always have to be about sales. It can drive other calls to action based on organizational objectives. For example, MoneyLion drove direct app installs of their finance app via Facebook video ads[77] and National Geographic has used Instagram Stories to educate and promote conservation efforts and then includes a Swipe Up call to action where people can pledge to reduce plastic usage.[78]

As established social channels became more crowded and move toward algorithms that further decrease organic reach like Facebook,[79] Instagram,[80] and Twitter,[81] the number of paid social opportunities are growing. The ways social ads are sold are maturing. Many of the social platforms are adding payment models that reflect the standards for buying ads in traditional media such as cost-per-thousand (CPM). For examples and definitions of social media advertising campaign objectives and buying models see table 6.1, Social Media Ad Objectives and Buying Terms. As you go through part III of the book, organic and paid opportunities will be presented with the social media platforms that offer them. Both organic and paid social ads should be considered when selecting social media channels for the plan. But no matter how much paid social media grows, it is important to note that paying for reach does not replace the need to create good engaging content. Paid social media may buy exposure but it does not buy engagement and action; that still requires quality content—the kind you create for organic social media posts. One strategy may be to take the best-performing organic content and then pay to boost the reach. Pay to increase reach on the content already proven to be a winner.

Table 6.1. Social Media Ad Objectives and Buying Terms

Social Media Ad Campaign Objectives	Social Media Ad Buying Options
Brand awareness	CPM/CPV—Cost per Mille (1,000 impressions) Cost per View
Website visits	CPC—Cost per Click
Website/direct sales	CPA/CPR—Cost per Action/Result
App downloads	CPI—Cost per Installed App
Community engagement	CPE—Cost per Engagement
Lead generation	CPL—Cost per Lead

Sources: Alfred Lua, "9 Social Media Goals You Can Set for Your Business (and How to Track Them)," Buffer.com, January 15, 2019, https://buffer.com/library/social-media-goals; Bartosz Bielecki, "What Is the Difference Between CPM, CPC, CPL, CPA, and Other Performance Marketing Pricing Models?" ZeroPark.com, October 19, 2019, https://zeropark.com/blog/difference-cpm-cpc-cpl-cpa-performance-marketing-pricing-models/.

Many marketers and advertisers have shifted from a focus on reach to engagement. Social media may become more important for engaging current and prospective customers than for generating awareness, for which traditional advertising and public relations in mass media are still effective tools. Facebook did announce more news feed changes and indicated they would emphasize more meaningful interactions. Posts with more engagement in the form of comments, likes, and shares from Facebook friends could be rewarded with more reach.[82] As the social media landscape becomes more crowded, marketers should not abandon traditional marketing communication methods. One method is not enough. Social media is more effective when you add advertising, paid media, and public relations earned media to help meet goals.[83]

Social Media Analytics

With the increase in social media marketing budgets and a greater emphasis on paid social advertising, there has become a greater need to prove ROI and continuously optimize efforts through analytics. **Analytics** is the process of discovering and communicating meaning from data.[84] One way to accomplish this is by having a social media measurement plan. A solid measurement plan ensures you start with your business objectives (what impacts the bottom line) first. From there you create strategies and tactics (current and new) to help meet those objectives. Then you determine how those outcomes will be measured through KPIs (metrics) tied to micro- and macro-conversions. This is how the social media strategy process has been designed; the social media measurement plan pulls it all together into a measurement framework.

To create a social media measurement plan, first start with your business objectives. What did you define in the beginning of the plan in chapter 4? You may know or may have been given specific business objectives or perhaps it is something you discovered in the situation analysis. The objective of most businesses is to increase sales, but each organization's situation is unique and requires a more nuanced definition. As discussed previously, there is usually a problem or opportunity that is the focus of marketing efforts and social media is to contribute to those efforts. The CMO Survey reports that most marketers view social media as a tool to help accomplish the following business objectives:

1. Brand awareness/brand building
2. Introducing new products/services
3. Acquiring new customers (conversion/sale)
4. Brand promotions (contest/coupons)
5. Retaining current customers
6. Improving customer service
7. Improving employee engagement
8. Marketing research
9. Identifying new customer groups
10. Identifying new product/service opportunities
11. Improving current products/services[85]

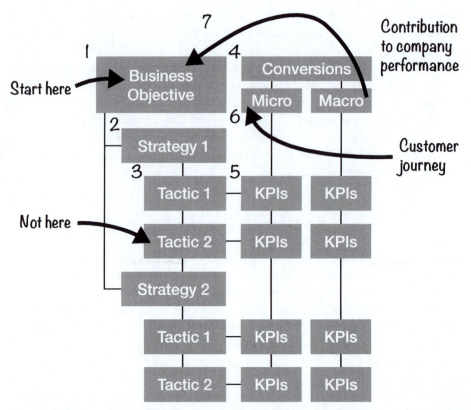

Figure 6.6. A social media plan connects business objectives to social media actions.

You may not know strategies and tactics yet, but this shows how they will be measured. To create a social media measurement plan first list all your strategies, such as an influencer marketing campaign, a special promotion, an employee advocacy effort, or branding social media ads. Then list the main tactics that support each strategy. For example, a business objective to increase sales to a new target market may have a brand awareness strategy supported by a tactic of targeted Facebook ads, a tactic of influencer marketing on Instagram, and a tactic of employee advocacy on LinkedIn.

Next list the measurable actions users take to fulfill your business objectives. They can take the form of macro-conversions and micro-conversions. Macro-conversions are the key actions closest to business objectives, such as an online sale through website data or an offline sale through CRM or point-of-sale (POS) data. Micro-conversions are the smaller actions that move a prospect closer, such as visiting webpages, signing up for a newsletter, downloading an app, or following a social media page. They can be tracked using various tools such as Google Analytics Tracking ID[86] and Facebook Pixel for social ads or organic posts.[87] Then link social media metric KPIs by tactic and strategy to macro- and micro-conversions. Linking social media metric KPIs will be covered more in chapter 14.

Creating a dashboard of the KPIs for macro-conversions by tactic and strategy can be a top line report of social media's contribution to company performance. Creating this in your digital measurement platform such as Google Analytics, Hootsuite, HubSpot, Salesforce, or Facebook Ads Manager gives you real-time access or the ability to schedule regular reports to share with management. Identifying and measuring micro-conversions on the way to macro-conversion can map out customer journeys. Micro-conversions help you understand human behavior, giving insight to optimize strategies and tactics. Analyze metrics by tactic KPI to determine how many people are completing the customer journey and where you are losing or retaining people.

Having a good measurement plan that includes both micro- and macro-conversions enables you to know which tactics and strategies are contributing the most to company performance. From there you can experiment with different tactics and strategies, replacing low-performing ones to optimize social media. The results of your regular social media audits can help identify which strategies and tactics to experiment with first. While no two customer journeys are alike, your micro-conversion and macro-conversion data can identify clusters of touchpoints versus outliers. Focus optimization efforts where many of your customers engage in the funnel stages on their unique journey. Also deliver custom messages through unique customer tracking such as Google Analytics User-ID.[88] Ultimately you want to lower your cost per result or conversion. Find things to improve, try new solutions, obtain results. Rinse and repeat. For more details on social marketing strategies to grow followers, engagement, and business results, see Hootsuite Academy's Social Marketing training and certification at https://education.hootsuite.com/courses/social-marketing-education. Another good resource for social marketing strategies is HubSpot Academy's Social Media training and certification at https://academy.hubspot.com/courses/social-media. **HubSpot Academy** is an online education site offering free and paid training courses and professional certifications.[89]

Social media agency Socialfly partnered with Girl Scouts of the USA to produce a public service announcement (PSA) to change perception from a traditional organization to a modern one that transforms lives. They created a video telling the story of real Girl Scouts taking action and addressing today's challenges. From this one-day shoot they created separate versions optimized for each social platform including Instagram, Instagram Stories, Facebook, YouTube, Hulu, Snapchat, and Spotify. The videos took the form of eight different lengths and formats for sixteen different videos plus twenty-seven additional creative assets of behind-the-scenes footage, interviews, and photos. The campaign was viewed over one million times, had over 107 thousand clicks, and received more than 382 thousand total engagements.[90] Girl Scouts utilized multiple strategies and tactics to meet their business objective.

Part III of this book will move into detail about selecting specific social media platforms or channels that fit the target audience and organization message, and that best execute the big idea. Before executing or creating the brand social media content, make sure the big idea is integrated and sustainable for the long term. As a marketer, advertiser, or public relations professional moves forward in the strategic process and focuses more directly on social media, it is important not to forget the traditional aspects of a marketing campaign.

Social Media Strategic Plan

Before moving on to explore each social media category and platform in part III, it is helpful to understand where you are headed. Chapter 14 is about writing and presenting a complete social media strategic plan. A **social media strategic plan** defines how an organization will use social media for communication to achieve measurable business objectives in conjunction with other marketing channels and the social platforms and tools it will use to achieve this.[a] Specific social media strategy elements will vary based on organization and situation, but the key elements of a plan include the following example social media plan format:

1. Brand, Industry, and Competitor Overview (SWOT, current marketing description)
2. Business Objectives and Target Audience (target social media use)
3. Social Media Audit (results and insights gained)
4. Social Strategy Big Idea (theme with digital marketing, advertising, and PR integration)
5. Recommended Social Platforms (add or remove with platform stats)
6. Creative Content and Calendar (persona, written/designed content, content calendar)
7. Policies, Guidelines, and Requirements (varies per organization needs but can include social media/privacy policy, crisis communication/event plan, influencer/advocate guidelines/disclosure requirements, or software/discipline integration recommendations)
8. Social Media Analytics (metrics by social platform and business objective, measurement and optimization plan including software tools and tracking methods)
9. Social Media Budget (cost estimate)

You can think of the categories above as significant subhead sections for a final social media plan report and significant components of a final social media plan presentation to key stakeholders. More direct guidance for what can specifically go in each of these sections with support tools and guides is provided in chapter 14 and the Three-Part Social Plan in appendix A. The Theoretically Speaking section in this chapter explains how a social media strategic plan uniquely brings together multiple disciplines, departments, and practices.

[a] James Gurd, "6 Reasons Why You Need A Social Media Strategy," SmartInsights.com, February 19, 2019, https://www.smartinsights.com/social-media-marketing/social-media-strategy/social-media-strategy-planning-essentials-6-reasons-need-social-media-strategy/.

Including traditional marketing communications media and campaigns will expand and leverage social media activity to achieve that magic integration. Many new social media efforts need traditional marketing and advertising to build awareness and jumpstart participation. Many social media efforts need traditional news coverage and events to bolster sharing and organic word-of-mouth reach. Once the big idea has been developed, move on to the next chapter and part III of the book to explore the best social media ways and places to bring that idea to life for the target audience.

Theoretically Speaking: Corporate and Marketing Communication, Public Relations, and Advertising

When discussing integration, it is first important to fully understand what is to be integrated. The above concepts are all interrelated yet sometimes can be confused in practice. **Corporate communications** involves managing internal and external communications aimed at corporate stakeholders.[91] **Marketing communications** coordinates promotional messages delivered through channels such as print, radio, television, and personal selling.[92] **Public relations** creates and maintains the goodwill of the public, such as customers, employees, and investors, through nonpaid forms of media.[93] **Advertising** is the placement of announcements and persuasive messages in time or space purchased in mass media,[94] while **integrated marketing communications** seeks to align and coordinate all marketing communications delivered to consumers to present a cohesive whole that persuades consumers to purchase.[95] Think of corporate communications as focusing on the enterprise in dealing with issue management, mergers, and litigation. Marketing communications deals with the products and services and with creating demand or positioning. From crisis management to media outreach, public relations can help meet both corporate and marketing goals. Advertising can be used for marketing and corporate communications when it is targeted to consumers and corporate stakeholders.

The BP oil spill in the Gulf of Mexico provides an example of how all these disciplines can work together. Following the spill, corporate communications focused on crisis management through both public relations and corporate TV advertising to inform stakeholders and consumers as to what BP was doing to clean up. The BP TV ad was also aimed at BP employees; **internal marketing** promotes the firm and its policies to employees as if they are customers of the firm.[96] The traditional definition of integrated marketing communications limits the practice to synergistic efforts to meet marketing objectives, but as seen with the BP example, it is possible to create a larger integrated plan that uses advertising, public relations, and internal efforts to meet both corporate stakeholder and marketing target market communication objectives.[97] Today BP has added social media such as LinkedIn, Twitter, Instagram, and YouTube as key channels to promote a message of producing energy with fewer emissions.[98] Have there been recent examples of where a brand fully integrated all these concepts into one cohesive effort?

Chapter 6 Checklist

Social media can change quickly. Visit Post Control Marketing (http://www.postcontrol marketing.com) for updates, but also use this chapter checklist to briefly check how social media statistics in this chapter have changed since publication.

- ✓ Has the Internet of Things (IoT) grown? Has IoT become more of a direct influence in social media strategy for marketing communications?
- ✓ What are the latest numbers in content marketing? Is content shock significantly disrupting social media marketing strategy and practice?

✓ What are the latest average organic reach statistics for the top social media channels? Are more social channels introducing algorithms to their feeds and offering more paid social media options? Have social commerce options increased?

 SOCIAL PLAN PART 6

Integrate Traditional Marketing with Social Strategy

In this part of the social media plan, focus on integration of traditional marketing, advertising, public relations, and digital marketing efforts with the new social media strategy. Collect and analyze information on all marketing efforts for the brand. What techniques are being used? What is the core message or promotion? Is there a common character, theme, or concept? Is there a brand or campaign tagline? Make note of current efforts and include what is being formed in the new social media plan, accounting for and explaining how current traditional efforts will be integrated into the new social effort. You may find that a new traditional marketing, advertising, and public relations effort or campaign is needed, and thus your plan should make those recommendations. Report all findings and ideas in these areas:

1. Identify all traditional brand marketing, public relations, advertising, and digital efforts.
2. Explain the current promotion, concept, character, theme, and tagline.
3. List ways in which the current marketing communications effort could be integrated with the new social media big idea.
4. If a new traditional marketing or advertising campaign and promotion are needed, explain what they should be.

For a condensed version of the social plan see appendix A: Three-Part Social Plan.

KEY CONCEPTS

information superhighway	digital marketing specialist
e-commerce	brand
IP convergence	brand positioning
Internet of Things (IoT)	perceptual map
converged media	brand equity
multichannel marketing	reach
omnichannel marketing	impression
attention economics	social media advertising
copywriter	native advertising
art director	organic reach
public relations executive	paid reach

programmatic advertising

real-time bidding (RTB)

programmatic direct

influencer marketing

social commerce

analytics

HubSpot Academy

social media strategic plan

corporate communications

marketing communications

public relations

advertising

internal marketing

QUESTIONS FOR DISCUSSION

1. With the increased importance of integration, should marketers continue to hire separate public relations, advertising, and digital firms? Or should every activity be brought in-house within the company? What are the advantages and disadvantages of each method?

2. Go back and look at the definitions and descriptions of integrated marketing communications and converged media strategy. What is the difference between these two models of thought? Which could be more effective and why?

3. Look more closely at the disciplines of public relations and advertising. What do the practices have in common? What is substantially different? What are ways public relations and advertising could work more closely together?

4. Ethics can get tough in social media where disciplines blur. You are a PR professional working on a campaign for a client to get earned media coverage. You contact a prominent contributor to a top publication. The author agrees to feature the brand's new product in an upcoming article but wants to be compensated for the mention. What should you do?

ADDITIONAL EXERCISES

1. Find evidence of the attention economy and answer the following questions: Explain which businesses are succeeding and why. Which tech companies are succeeding at gaining attention and what methods are they using? How are companies that produce physical products competing in the attention economy? What best practices from marketing communications, advertising, and public relations are organizations adapting into their business practices? Must every company now be interesting, or can attention still be bought?

2. Visit the American Association of Advertising Agencies website (https://www.aaaa.org). Look at the blogs and resources and note their emphasis and perspective. What is the purpose of advertising and what tools do advertising professionals have at their disposal? Now visit the Public Relations Society of America's website (https://www.prsa.org). Do the same, by visiting their resources, research, and articles. What are the goals of public relations and how do they achieve them? Finally, visit the American Marketing Association website (https://www.ma.org). Explore what they are talking about and are concerned with, and how they leverage social media to obtain their goals. Keep these professional perspectives in mind as you integrate and leverage each in the social media plan.

Notes

1. Henry Jenkins, *Convergence Culture: Where Old and New Media Collide* (New York: New York University Press, 2006).

2. "Who Invented the Peanut Butter and Jelly Sandwich?" NationalPeanutBoard.com, accessed October 1, 2019, http://nationalpeanutboard.org/news/who-invented-the-peanut-butter-and-jelly-sandwich.htm.

3. "Information Superhighway," Merriam-Webster.com, accessed October 1, 2019, http://www.merriam-webster.com/dictionary/information%20superhighway.

4. Norman Solomon, "Solomon: What Happened to the 'Information Superhighway'?" Alternet.org, April 25, 2000, http://www.alternet.org/story/587/solomon%3A_what_happened_to_the_%22information_superhighway%22.

5. "E-Commerce," Merriam-Webster.com, accessed October 1, 2019, http://www.merriam-webster.com/dictionary/e-commerce.

6. Cheskin Research, "Designing Digital Experiences for Youth," *Market Insights Series* (Fall 2002): 8–9.

7. "IP Convergence," *PC Magazine,* October 1, 2019, http://www.pcmag.com/encyclopedia/term/57267/ip-convergence.

8. Forrest Stroud, "IoT—Internet of Things," Webopedia.com, October 1, 2019, http://www.webopedia.com/TERM/I/internet_of_things.html.

9. Rob van der Meulen, "Gartner Says 8.4 Billion Connected 'Things' Will Be in Use in 2017, Up 31 Percent from 2016," Gartner, Inc., February 7, 2017, http://www.gartner.com/newsroom/id/3598917.

10. Nick Ismail, "3 Scenarios for Marketing with the Internet of Things," InformationAge.com, February 7, 2017, http://www.information-age.com/3-scenarios-marketing-internet-things-123464327/.

11. Mark Schaefer, "What Every Marketer Needs to Know about the Internet of Things," Marketing Companion Podcast, episode 93, December 27, 2016, https://www.businessesgrow.com/2016/12/27/internet-of-things-2/.

12. "Ad Agencies' Most Wanted: Integrated-Marketing Pros," *Wall Street Journal* online, January 22, 2008, http://online.wsj.com/article/C50330NEEDLEMAN.html.

13. Philip Kotler, Hermawan Kartajaya, and Iwan Setiawan, *Marketing 4.0: Moving from Traditional to Digital* (Hoboken, NJ: Wiley, 2017): 130–131.

14. Jeremiah Owyang, "Altimeter Report: Paid + Owned + Earned = Converged Media," Web-Strategist.com, July 19, 2012, http://www.web-strategist.com/blog/2012/07/19/altimeter-report-paid-owned-earned-converged-media.

15. Kerry Rivera, "Four Steps to Master Omnichannel Marketing," Forbes.com, October 27, 2017, https://www.forbes.com/sites/forbescommunicationscouncil/2017/10/27/four-steps-to-master-omnichannel-marketing/#766d07ea6d5d.

16. Nedra Hutton, "Let Me Explain: Multi-Channel vs. Cross-Channel vs. Omni-Channel Marketing," Blogs.Oracle.com, March 1, 2019, https://blogs.oracle.com/marketingcloud/let-me-explain:-multi-channel-vs-cross-channel-vs-omni-channel-marketing.

17. Kotler, Kartajaya, and Setiawan, *Marketing 4.0*, 87–140.

18. Rake Narang, "Barb Rentschler: Combine Traditional and Digital Tools to Super Charge Your Communication Efforts," PRWorldAwards.com, accessed October 1, 2019, http://www.prworldawards.com/people/Barb-Rentschler.html#.UknSdSTFYnU.

19. Trevor George, "K'NEX Lets Us Know 'We Are Being Heard,'" BlueWheelMedia.com (blog), January 25, 2012, http://bluewheelmedia.com/knex-lets-us-know-we-are-being-heard-2.

20. Angela Natividad, "The Story Behind Nike's Ambitious Effort to Run a Marathon in Less Than Two Hours," Adweek.com, May 8, 2017, http://www.adweek.com/brand-marketing/the-story-behind-nikes-ambitious-effort-to-run-a-marathon-in-less-than-2-hours/.

21. Jonny Collin, "Nike's Most Successful Failure Yet," Synergy.com (blog), May 8, 2017, http://synergy.global/nikes-most-successful-failure-yet/.

22. "Nike Celebrates Its Breaking2 Results," News.Nike.com, May, 6, 2017, https://news.nike.com/news/breaking2-results.

23. Lisa Murton Beets, "2019 B2B Content Marketing Research: It Pays to Put Audience First," ContentMarketingResearch.com, October 10, 2018, https://contentmarketinginstitute.com/2018/10/research-b2b-audience/.

24. "Copywriter," Merriam-Webster.com, accessed September 17, 2019, http://www.merriam-webster.com/dictionary/copywriter.

25. "Art Director," Merriam-Webster.com, accessed October 1, 2019, http://www.merriam-webster.com/dictionary/art%20director.

26. "Career Overview: Public Relations," WetFeet.com, November 30, 2012, https://www.wetfeet.com/articles/career-overview-public-relations.

27. "What Is a Digital Marketing Specialist?" Sokanu.com, accessed October 1, 2019, https://www.sokanu.com/careers/digital-marketing-specialist/.

28. Keith Quesenberry, "Three Is the Magic Number," PostControlMarketing.com (blog), March 18, 2011, http://www.postcontrolmarketing.com/?p=236.

29. "Crispin Porter + Bogusky Awarded Interactive Agency of the Year at the Cannes Lions International Advertising Festival," PRNewswire.com, accessed October 1, 2019, http://www.prnewswire.com/news-releases/crispin-porter—bogusky-awarded-interactive-agency-of-the-year-at-the-cannes-lions-international-advertising-festival-97067799.html.

30. Hope Nguyen, "Target Gets Serious about Social Data," NetBase.com (blog), January 10, 2016, https://www.netbase.com/blog/target-serious-social-data/.

31. Alex M. Bogusky and John Winsor, *Baked In: Creating Products and Businesses That Market Themselves* (Chicago: B2 Books, 2009).

32. Keith A. Quesenberry, Michael K. Coolsen, and Kristen Wilkerson, "IMC and the Effies: Use of Integrated Marketing Communications Touchpoints among Effie Award Winners," *International Journal of Integrated Marketing Communication* 4, no. 2 (2012): 60–72.

33. "Brand," MarketingDictionary.com, accessed September 30, 2019, https://marketing-dictionary.org/b/brand/.

34. "Brand Positioning," MarketingDictionary.com, accessed September 30, 2019, https://marketing-dictionary.org/b/brand-positioning/

35. "Perceptual Mapping," BusinessDictionary.com, accessed October 1, 2019, http://www.businessdictionary.com/definition/perceptual-mapping.html.

36. Jim Joseph, "Move Your Business Forward by Drawing a Perceptual Map," Entrepreneur.com, June 3, 2015, https://www.entrepreneur.com/article/246813.

37. Alina Dumitrache, "BMW Kicks-Off New 'Story of Joy' Campaign," AutoEvolution.com, February 15, 2010, https://www.autoevolution.com/news/bmw-kicks-off-new-story-of-joy-campaign-16782.html.

38. Thomas C. Frohlich and Michael B. Saunter, "What Are the World's Most Valuable Brands? Tech Companies like Apple, Google and Amazon," USAToday.com, October 9, 2018, https://www

.usatoday.com/story/money/business/2018/10/09/most-valuable-brands-apple-google-amazon/ 38061893/.

39. "Brand Equity," MarketingDictionary.com, accessed September 30, 2019, https:// marketing-dictionary.org/b/brand-equity/.

40. Kotler, Kartajaya, and Setiawan, *Marketing 4.0*, 48–49.

41. Andrew Hutchinson, "What Happens on the Internet Every Minute (2019 Version) [Infographic]," SocialMediaToday.com, July 16, 2019, https://www.socialmediatoday.com/news/ what-happens-on-the-internet-every-minute-2019-version-infographic/558793/.

42. Mark Schaefer, "Content Shock: Why Content Marketing Is Not a Sustainable Strategy," BusinessGrow.com (blog), January 6, 2014, https://www.businessesgrow.com/2014/01/06/ content-shock/.

43. Beets, "2019 B2B Content Marketing Research."

44. Alex York, "Reach vs Impressions: What's the Difference in Terms?" Sproutsocial.com, February 15, 2018, https://sproutsocial.com/insights/reach-vs-impressions/.

45. "Social Advertising," PCMag.com, accessed November 13, 2019, https://www.pcmag.com/ encyclopedia/term/58660/social-advertising.

46. Joe Pulizzi, "Hey WSJ—Content Marketing Is NOT Native Advertising," Content Marketing Institute (blog), November 6, 2014, http://contentmarketinginstitute.com/2014/11/ wsj-content-marketing-not-native.

47. "What's the Difference between Organic, Paid and Total Reach?" Facebook.com, accessed October 1, 2019, https://www.facebook.com/help/285625061456389/.

48. Brian Boland, "Organic Reach on Facebook: Your Questions Answered," Facebook.com (blog), June 5, 2014, https://www.facebook.com/business/news/Organic-Reach-on-Facebook.

49. Jamie Robinson, "Measuring Facebook Engagement," Wearesocial.com (blog), July 10, 2014, http://wearesocial.net/blog/2014/07/measuring-facebook-engagement.

50. Dan Virgillito, "Which Social Media Platforms Offer the Greatest Organic Reach?" Elegantthemes.com (blog), January 7, 2016, https://www.elegantthemes.com/blog/resources/ which-social-media-platforms-offer-the-greatest-organic-reach.

51. John Loomer, "Facebook Organic Reach Is Changing: Should Brands Share More Links?" JohnLoomer.com (blog), March 23, 2015, http://www.jonloomer.com/2015/03/23/ facebook-organic-reach-links/.

52. "Are Sponsored Social Posts the Most Effective Marketing Channel?" eMarketer.com, November 18, 2015, https://www.emarketer.com/Article/Sponsored-Social-Posts-Most-Effective -Marketing-Channel/1013242#sthash.JOBUzqW1.dpuf.

53. Lisa Murton Beets, "B2C Content Marketing: What a Difference Commitment Makes [2019 Research]," Content Marketing Institute, https://contentmarketinginstitute.com/2018/12/ b2c-research-commitment/.

54. Cici DeWaal, "Stop Debating the Death of Organic Social Media," Adobe.com (blog), July 15, 2016, https://blogs.adobe.com/digitalmarketing/social-media/stop-debating-death-organic -social-media/.

55. Lauren Fisher, "US Programmatic Ad Spending Forecast 2019," eMarketer.com, April 25, 2019, https://www.emarketer.com/content/us-programmatic-ad-spending-forecast-2019.

56. Garett Sloane, "Facebook Is Using Its Muscle to Remake the Ad Tech World," Digiday.com, May 31, 2016, https://digiday.com/media/facebooks-using-muscle-remake-ad-tech/.

57. Garett Sloane, "Twitter: Programmatic Pays More When It's 'Personal,'" Digiday.com (blog), August 11, 2015, https://digiday.com/media/twitter-shows-how-programmatic-pays-more -when-its-personal/.

58. Tim Peterson, "Pinterest Lets Brands Target Ads to People in Their Customer Data-bases," MarketingLand.com (blog), March 8, 2016, http://marketingland.com/pinterest-lets-brands-target-ads-to-people-in-their-customer-databases-167665.

59. Nisha Contractor, "Are Marketers Ready for Instagram's Open API?" Moxie.com (blog), August 21, 2015, https://moxieusa.com/Blog/2015/August/Instagram%20Open%20API.aspx.

60. Alison Weissbrot, "Snapchat Dips Its Toes in Programmatic, but Advertisers Want to See More," AdExchanger.com (blog), October 7, 2016, https://adexchanger.com/platforms/snapchat-dips-toes-programmatic/.

61. Marty Swant, "LinkedIn Is Launching Programmatic Advertising Display Ads," Adweek.com, June 28, 2016, http://www.adweek.com/digital/linkedin-launching-programmatic-advertising-display-ads-172275/.

62. "Automation and Programmatic," IAB.com, accessed October 1, 2019, https://www.iab.com/guidelines/programmatic-rtb/; "Programmatic Advertising & Media Buying," Marketing Land.com, accessed October 1, 2019, http://marketingland.com/library/display-advertising-news/display-advertising-programmatic-media-buying.

63. Monica Lay, "The Growth of Programmatic Advertising on Social," Adobe.com (blog), May 27, 2016, https://blogs.adobe.com/digitalmarketing/social-media/growth-programmatic-advertising-social/.

64. Dean Jayson, "How Programmatic Media Buying Is Saving the Banner Ad," HuffingtonPost.com (blog), November 26, 2016, http://www.huffingtonpost.com/dean-jayson/how-programmatic-media-bu_b_6225200.html.

65. Ben Plomion, "Going Programmatic to Get Your Content Seen," ConvinceAndConvert.com (blog), accessed October 1, 2019, http://www.convinceandconvert.com/content-marketing/going-programmatic-to-get-your-content-seen/.

66. Mike Shields, "Programmatic Native Ads Are Growing—But Banner Habit Is Hard to Break," WSJ.com, January 18, 2017, https://www.wsj.com/articles/programmatic-native-ads-are-growingbut-banner-habit-is-hard-to-break-1484737200; Frank Papsadore, "Native Advertising Optimism Gain Momentum," AdvertiserPerceptions.com (blog), November 7, 2016, https://www.advertiserperceptions.com/native-advertising-optimism-gain-momentum/.

67. "What Is Influencer Marketing?" TapInfluence.com (blog), accessed October 1, 2019, https://www.tapinfluence.com/blog-what-is-influencer-marketing/.

68. Sami Main, "Programmatic Ad-Buying Is Now Available for Social Influencers," Adweek.com, November 30, 2016, http://www.adweek.com/digital/programmatic-ad-buying-now-available-social-influencers-174811/.

69. "The Convergence of Top Influencers, Technology and Data," ROIInfluencer.com, accessed November 4, 2019, https://roiinfluencer.com/roi-influencer-score.

70. "Influencers," TapInfluence.com, accessed October 1, 2019, https://www.tapinfluence.com/influencers/.

71. "Social Commerce," Wikipedia.com, last modified September 26, 2019, https://en.wikipedia.org/wiki/Social_commerce.

72. Gavin Llewellyn, "Social Commerce Trends in 2019," SmartInsights.com, March 13, 2019, https://www.smartinsights.com/ecommerce/social-commerce-trends-2019/.

73. Llewellyn, "Social Commerce Trends in 2019."

74. Lise Pinnell, "Five Innovations in Social Commerce," Campaign.com, December 15, 2019, https://www.campaignlive.co.uk/article/five-innovations-social-commerce/1376901.

75. Megan Jones, "Pinterest Buyable Pins: Do They Actually Work? Plus How to Use Them," Revive.Social, March 18, 2018, https://revive.social/pinterest-buyable-pins/.

76. Tereza Litsa, "Eight Tips to Improve Your Snapchat Marketing Strategy," ClickZ.com, March 1, 2019, https://www.clickz.com/tips-improve-snapchat-marketing-strategy/226708/.

77. "MoneyLion: Increasing App Installs with a Simplified Facebook Ad Campaign Structure," Facebook.com, accessed October 1, 2019, https://www.facebook.com/business/success/money lion.

78. Christina Moravec, "9 Brands Crushing It with Instagram Stories," ConvinceAndConvert. com, accessed October 1, 2019, https://www.convinceandconvert.com/social-media-case-studies/crushing-it-with-instagram-stories/.

79. Will Oremus, "Who Controls Your Facebook Feed: A Small Team of Engineers in Menlo Park. A Panel of Anonymous Power Users around the World. And, Increasingly, You." Slate.com, January 2016, http://www.slate.com/articles/technology/cover_story/2016/01/how_facebook_s_news_feed_algorithm_works.html.

80. Elle Hunt, "New Algorithm-Driven Instagram Feed Rolled Out to the Dismay of Users: Say Farewell to Chronological Ordering of Posts—Users Are Now Seeing Their Feed as Organised by Instagram's Own Formula, and They're Not Happy," TheGuardian.com, June 7, 2016, https://www.theguardian.com/technology/2016/jun/07/new-algorithm-driven-instagram-feed-rolled-out-to-the-dismay-of-users.

81. Owen Williams, "Twitter Is Now Turning On Its New Algorithmic Timeline for Everyone," TheNextWeb.com, March 17, 2016, http://thenextweb.com/twitter/2016/03/17/twitter-quietly-turned-new-algorithmic-timeline-everyone/.

82. Keith Quesenberry, "Talk About Us on Facebook! How the News Feed Changes Should Change Your Social Media," PostControlMarketing.com (blog), January 21, 2018, http://www.postcontrolmarketing.com/talk-us-facebook-news-feed-changes-mean-social-media-strategy/.

83. Keith Quesenberry, "Can You Win the Content Marketing Arms Race?" SocialMedia Today.com (blog), May 1, 2015, http://www.socialmediatoday.com/social-business/2015-05-01/can-you-win-content-marketing-arms-race.

84. "Analytics," Techopedia.com, accessed December 4, 2019, https://www.techopedia.com/definition/30296/analytics.

85. "The CMO Survey Results February 2019," CMOSurvey.org, February 2019, https://cmo survey.org/results/february-2019/.

86. Jacinda Santora, "Google Analytics 101: How to Track Your Conversions (Step-by-Step)," Optimonster.com, September 16, 2019, https://optinmonster.com/google-analytics-101-how-to-track-your-conversions-step-by-step/.

87. Christina Newberry, "The Facebook Pixel: What It Is and How to Use It," Hootsuite.com, January 14, 2019, https://optinmonster.com/google-analytics-101-how-to-track-your-conversions-step-by-step/.

88. "About the User-ID Feature," Analytics Help, Support.Google.com, accessed November 6, 2019, https://support.google.com/analytics/answer/3123662?hl=en.

89. "All Courses & Certifications," Academy.HubSpot.com, accessed November 15, 2019, https://academy.hubspot.com/courses?page=1#certsOnly=true.

90. "Girl Scouts of the USA: All Girl Scout PSA," ShortyAwards.com, accessed October 1, 2019, https://shortyawards.com/11th/girl-scouts-of-the-usa-all-girl-scout-psa.

91. Cees van Riel and Charles Fombrun, *Essentials of Corporate Communication: Implementing Practices for Effective Reputation Management* (New York: Routledge, 2007).

92. "Marketing Communication," BusinessDictionary.com, accessed October 1, 2019, http://www.businessdictionary.com/definition/marketing-communications.html.

93. "Public Relations," BusinessDictionary.com, accessed October 1, 2019, http://www.businessdictionary.com/definition/public-relations.html.

94. "Advertising," BusinessDictionary.com, accessed October 1, 2019, http://www.business dictionary.com/definition/advertising.html.

95. "Integrated Marketing Communications," BusinessDictionary.com, accessed October 1, 2019, http://www.businessdictionary.com/definition/integrated-marketing-communications-IMC .html.

96. "Internal Marketing," BusinessDictionary.com, accessed October 1, 2019, http://www .businessdictionary.com/definition/internal-marketing.html.

97. Keith A. Quesenberry, "Corporate Communications, Marketing, IMC, PR and Advertising: What's the Difference?" PostControlMarketing.com (blog), March 21, 2011, http://www.post controlmarketing.com/?p=243.

98. "BP website," BP.com, accessed November 14, 2019, https://www.bp.com/.

PART

III

Choose Social Options for Target, Message, and Idea

CHAPTER

7

Social Networks, Blogs, and Forums

My best stories come from well-placed sources who point me in the right direction.[1]

—Wolf Blitzer

PREVIEW

What did your friends do last night and where did they do it? Where did your cousin's band play last weekend? What sights did your grandparents or parents see on their last trip? Is that girl or guy you met last week single or in a relationship? Where did they go to school? How do you know these things? Most likely you know a lot about what's going on in your family's and friends' lives because of Facebook. Yet Facebook wasn't always the social network.

Before Facebook there was a pioneering site called Friendster. **Friendster** was one of the original social network service websites allowing users to make contact with other members and share online content and media with them. Launched in 2002, Friendster reached more than three million users within months and was considered the top social networking site, eventually reaching 115 million users.[2] Friendster peaked around 2004 when Google wanted to buy it for $30 million, but it soon lost ground as Facebook grew. Friendster lost so many users that it became a gaming site in 2011 and shut down completely in 2015. Peter Pachal of *PC Magazine* says the main reason Friendster failed was its lack of a news feed. It never went beyond user profiles.[3]

Ten years after Facebook, Friendster's founder Jonathan Abrams told his side of the story in a Mashable article. Abrams explained that there were a lot of copycat social networks spamming Friendster and poaching users. The site planned to add Friendster College, a news feed, and music sharing, yet they faced technology issues and stability problems. The Friendster founder is now busy with Nuzzel, a social news aggregator launched in 2012.[4] As this anecdote points out, social networks can come and go. At the height of their popularity no one thought social giants like Friendster and MySpace would decline or close completely. When developing a social media strategy, focus on social media categories and characteristics while exploring the main social media channels. That way, individual social channels can come and go but a brand's core social strategy will continue.

Choosing Social Options

Part III of this book will cover key characteristics of the main types or categories of social media channels, and the major platforms in each. Each section describes the size of the channel, who is talking there, and what type of information they are sharing. This part of the book will also look at global use of each social channel, suggested strategies, and social media advertising options.

Entire books have been written on each of these social channels and by the time you read this, the statistics will have changed. The purpose is not to explain all of the details about specific platforms. A quick Google search will reveal the most recent usage numbers and guides such as Sprout Social's article "How the Facebook Algorithm Works and Ways to Outsmart It."[5] This section is an overview of each platform to choose the best by category for a specific social media strategy. Choose based on key characteristics that can be applied to any current social network or new one that emerges. In case today's Facebook becomes yesterday's Friendster, or Facebook decides to change its algorithm again, you still have a social strategy that works. Sometimes a platform can shut down unexpectedly like Vine after five years.[6] Or social platforms can rise quickly like Meerkat to go out just as quickly after only twenty months.[7] Yet a brand strategy based on short-form video or live video can continue on Instagram Live, Facebook Live, or Periscope.

Now that the business objectives, target audience, key consumer insight, and big idea are in place, it is time to select the optimal social channels to implement the social strategy. Like journalist Wolf Blitzer putting together a news story, think of each social channel as a well-placed source to launch a social media plan in the right direction.

What follows are descriptions of the central characteristics of key social channels (size, content, users, and ad options) in several categories. To gain a full appreciation of each, join the channel as a user and become a firsthand witness to the unique social experience delivered by each option. Think of each as a brand community and ask yourself some key questions. What benefit are they getting from being a part of a current brand community? What would be the benefits of joining a new brand community? How is it different on various social platforms?

In reading through each category and channel, keep the business objectives, target audience, and key insight with the big idea in the front of your mind. Look for the ideal vehicles to deliver brand messages and engage the target audience to deliver the right message to the right people in the right environment. This method will keep the social strategy focused and prevent wasted effort chasing every new social channel that makes headlines or assuming the biggest is always the best. This strategic approach allows adding new channels that make sense for the content and consumer as they emerge.

"Try on" each social platform, imagining the kind of content the social strategy idea could create from the organization, its employees, and consumers. Would this or is this a good opportunity for a brand community? Refer back to the creative brief questions from chapter 1: "What does the target audience currently think?"; "What would we like the target audience to think?"; and "What will move them from one to the other?" Then consider these additional questions when looking at each social platform:

- Is our target audience active on this platform?
- How do we communicate the big idea in this platform?
- What do we want them to do on this platform?

Notice that one of the questions is not "Is this platform the biggest?" A social platform is not the right choice simply because it has the most users. As discussed in chapter 1, social media has matured. Most people today have multiple social media accounts and different groups of people are active at various levels on different platforms for different reasons. It also depends on what you are trying to get people to do—your business objectives. Is the social platform environment right for the brand and message? For a summary of how to select social media channels for your social media strategic plan, see table 7.1.

The analytics company Parse.ly analyzed their own website and found that size of social platform did not predict the amount of referral traffic. When it came to overall referral traffic the largest social platform, Facebook, did send the most traffic. Yet the second and third highest platforms for referral traffic were Twitter and Pinterest, which are fourth and sixth in total users. In fact, Twitter, with only a third of Instagram's users, sent six times the traffic. When they looked more specifically at the social platforms sending the most returning visitors to their website, they found different results. Twitter was the highest-performing platform, followed by Facebook, Reddit, Pinterest, LinkedIn, and then Instagram.[8] The point here is not to select your social channels based on Parse.ly's results. You probably are

Table 7.1. Questions for Selecting Social Media Plan Channels

Users match target audience?	Yes/No	Demographics
Media type matches idea content?	Yes/No	Type
Existing brand account/page?	Yes/No	Changes
Existing brand community?	Yes/No	Opportunities
Competitor brand presence?	Yes/No	Strengths/Weaknesses
Paid social advertising options?	Yes/No	Options

not creating a social media strategy for a software analytics company with the same target audience and same business objectives. The point is to not assume that the largest social platform is the best for your plan and objectives.

Social Networks

Of all the types of social media, social networks seem to have drawn the most hype, and for good reason. Social channels such as Facebook and LinkedIn are big. Facebook may be known as "The Social Network" because of its enormous global reach and the movie about its founding, but it is not the only social network. A **social network** is any website where one connects with those sharing personal or professional interests.[9]

Social networks allow people to set up a profile and offer ways to join groups and interact with other users through updates or posts with media from links and text to photos and video. This is a good start for a definition, but today mobile access plays an ever-increasing role in social-network activity. Many social networks, which started on websites, are now mostly accessed via mobile devices in optimized websites and apps on smartphones and tablets.

Facebook

Founded in 2004, **Facebook** is an online social-networking service where users create profiles, connect to other users as "friends," and exchange messages, photos, and videos. Facebook has 2.27 billion global monthly active users and is by far the largest social media platform of any of the categories. For organizations, that number is hard to ignore. Facebook started as a social network for college students, but now its demographic makeup is much broader. Globally Facebook's ad audience is more male (57 percent) than female (43 percent) with the largest age groups twenty-five- to thirty-four-year-olds (32 percent) followed by eighteen- to twenty-seven-year-olds (27 percent). Facebook audience reach is highest in the United Arab Emirates (105 percent) and Philippines (98 percent) and lowest in Russia (11 percent) and China (0.2 percent). Facebook started as a website but now 96 percent of users access it via mobile smartphones and tablets in addition to laptops and desktops versus just 25 percent on their laptops and desktops only.[10]

Facebook use among people thirteen years and older in the United Kingdom and Canada is 71 percent, while use in Australia and the United States is 76 percent. Facebook users in the United States are more female (54 percent) than male (46 percent) and age groups skew older than global averages. The largest group is twenty-five- to thirty-four-year-olds (24 percent), but the second largest group is thirty-five- to forty-four-year-olds (19 percent). A sign of the maturing of Facebook is that there are now six times as many US Facebook users age sixty-five and older (12 percent) as thirteen- to seventeen-year-olds (2 percent).[11] Over two-thirds of Facebook users (71 percent) have at least some college education or a college degree while less than one-third (29 percent) have a high school degree or less. Facebook users are evenly divided among urban (35 percent), suburban (33 percent), and rural (31 percent) areas.[12]

Every person on Facebook has a profile page and a home page. The profile page is built on the timeline design, in which users' most recent activity is shown first and users can scroll down—and back in time—to birth. The home page is where they view the activity of friends or pages they have liked via the news feeds of recently posted updates. Facebook also allows users to create and join groups of common interests where photos and videos can be shared and discussions can take place. Pages or fan pages are where businesses and other entities exist on Facebook. Profiles are reserved for individual people. When an organization posts content on its page, some of it shows up in the news feeds of people who have liked or followed the page. A brand post may show up in a friend's news feed if someone liked, commented, or shared the content. In recent years, emoji reactions, 360 video, stories, and live video have been added, among other features. Moving forward, Facebook has indicated they will minimize the newsfeed and put more emphasis on events and groups.[13]

How are people using Facebook? The top social media activities on Facebook are viewing photos (65 percent), sharing content with everyone (57 percent), watching videos (46 percent), and sharing content one to one (43 percent).[14] The top reasons people use Facebook are to keep in contact with friends and family (51 and 45 percent), share things they find interesting (23 percent), and for looking at fun/entertaining content (23 percent).[15] While 74 percent of US adults eighteen years old and older visit Facebook daily, this statistic can be deceiving; it can vary by age group.[16] For example, among Generation Z (age thirteen- to twenty-one years old) only 34 percent visit Facebook daily compared to Instagram (65 percent), YouTube (63 percent), and Snapchat (51 percent).[17]

Not all friends or fans see all updates. Facebook organic reach is expressed in terms of a percentage of fans or followers who see a person's or organization's published content. This has been declining as Facebook has grown more crowded and adjusted the Facebook algorithm. An **algorithm** is a formula or set of steps used for solving a problem such as how to rank content to decide what is seen in social media feeds.[18] Increasingly Facebook is becoming the social platform of paid advertising for brands. Globally from 2018 to 2019 the percent of pages using paid media increased 26 percent and the average paid reach versus total reach increased 27 percent. This is due to declining organic reach on the platform, but organic reach can vary greatly by country and brand page size. Average organic reach in the United Kingdom and Australia is 6.9 percent, while it is 5.7 percent in the United States. Yet average organic reach can be much lower (3.5 percent) for larger brand pages (more than 10,000 fans) and higher (8.8 percent) for smaller brands (fewer than 10,000 fans).[19]

Marketing strategies for Facebook should include sharing information that fans of the brand would find interesting, entertaining, and shareable. Early strategies should focus on building a brand community. Established brand pages may need to refresh their content, ensure they are responding to fans and add or increase social ads to reach current fans and increase reach to new audiences. Contests and user-generated content can be effective, such as encouraging customers to upload photos of themselves using the product, and awarding prizes by voting on the best submission. Physical events build offline engagement and Facebook Events drive participation, promotion, and user-generated content. Facebook Groups are a way to tap into people interested in a subject that aligns with your target audience.

Figure 7.1. Facebook groups can increase organic reach and engagement.

© Bombus Creative / iStock Photo

Engagement can be much higher in groups with increased organic reach. Start your own or participate in an existing group—there are tens of millions of them. To many users, groups are most meaningful part of Facebook.[20]

Many have discovered that photos and video garner the most views and engagement. Besides the type of media, a recent study of the text in brand Facebook posts found that posts that contain "new" or "now" and time or date messages increase engagement through shares, likes, and comments. However, the same study found that posts with educational messages can decrease engagement.[21] The UNICEF Facebook page informs people about the organization and provides ways to help from a "Donate" button and an "Actions" tab, which lets users share an update with their friends and sign up for the nonprofit's newsletter.[22] UNICEF emphasized a new and date message following Hurricane Irma, letting people know they were helping children and mobilizing relief efforts to Florida.[23]

Hashtags can be used on Facebook but are more central to channels such as Twitter and Instagram. Straightforward promotions and product news can be shared on Facebook, but don't get too promotional or minimize promotional messages to a smaller percent of overall content. Use of Facebook stories has increased to 500 million users a day—the same as Instagram Stories and more than double Snapchat's 190 million users. As more Facebook users spend time in Stories, brands should follow.[24] With the Cambridge Analytica scandal, users have grown concerned about their privacy. A survey in spring of 2018 found that 67 percent thought Facebook had not done enough to safeguard personal data[25] and 54 percent considered deleting their Facebook profile.[26] Marketers should be up-front about what data they collect and take extra measures to protect users' privacy. This will be discussed further in chapter 15.

Facebook continues to tweak their algorithm toward engagement so that friends sharing, liking, or commenting on a brand post increases the chances it will be seen in another friend's post. Another option to boost reach is by Facebook tagging. Encourage fans to tag the brand page in their posts. This could extend reach to another page or person's followers. Also consider the organic post targeting tool. This allows you to customize content and then target posts to specific segments of brand page audiences based on unique interests. Similar to the way email segmentation boosts open and response rates, audience optimization in Facebook targets posts and messages to specific segments or groups of people who are most likely to be interested. A guaranteed way to ensure fans and followers see all your posts is to tell them to turn on Get Notifications and they will see up to five posts a day either in their news feed or see your posts first. Your most loyal fans may be glad to know this and do it. But ensure you only post quality content that they will value and that you are not posting too frequently cluttering up their feed.[27]

No matter what you do, a good overall strategy is to always post quality content. Buffer Social performed an experiment where they reduced their average Facebook posts from five or six a day to one or two. This resulted in a 330 percent increase in reach and engagement. The Buffer team found that a reduced schedule meant that they were not simply posting everything to Facebook. They posted only the best content right for Facebook, which they found was edu-tainment content.[28]

Most brands today are placing ads through Facebook Ads Manager or paying to boost posts through their Facebook page to gain more reach. When placing ads through Facebook Ads Manager, you first select your marketing goal from brand awareness and reach, app installs, traffic, lead generation, engagement, and video views—even conversions using Facebook pixel, store visits, and catalog sales. Facebook Business offers ads as boosted posts and ads that can appear as photo ads, video ads, stories ads, carousel ads, and slideshow ads. Playable ads allow an interactive preview before downloading an app. eCommerce brands can use collection ads that let people discover, browse, and buy what they offer. The Facebook Ads Manager enables specific audience-targeting by age, gender, education relationship status, job title, location, interests, behavior like prior purchases, device usage, and connections—customized audiences of people who have already completed certain actions from brand customer files and lookalike audiences to optimize ad buys. Dynamic ads enable brands to customize ads showing specific products or images to users based on their previous activity such as visiting the brand website or app making for efficient remarking campaigns.[29]

Most Facebook ads are purchased on an auction basis where you bid to reach your target audience for the lowest amount or on a consistent target amount. Larger advertisers with a higher budget can purchase ads based on reach and frequency where advertisers pay a fixed amount to reach the target audience. This is related to the way traditional advertisers are accustomed to buying print media. Certain bigger brands may also be able to buy video ads by target rating points similar to the way TV ads are bought. Most brands set campaign spending limits and account spending limits.[30]

Another consideration for this social network is Facebook Watch. **Facebook Watch** is a video-on-demand service built into Facebook that combines video-sharing with premium content. It can be found in the app or website in its own tab like Marketplace and Messenger. It is separate from newsfeeds, where video-only content can be found in categories such as Shows, Live, Food, News, Gaming, and Sports. The service allows creators to upload short- and long-form video, but also includes Facebook original comedy, drama, and news programming. Originals include the drama "Sorry for your Loss," starring Elizabeth Olsen, who portrayed Scarlet Witch in Marvel's Avenger movies and the reality show "Big Chicken Shaq," featuring basketball star Shaquille O'Neal opening his first chicken restaurant. There is no subscription cost, but viewers must have a Facebook account to access shows and videos. Videos can be found via Editor's picks, Top picks, search, and a user-created Watchlist.[31]

Facebook Watch is similar to YouTube and Instagram TV and doesn't include live television programming like cable replacement services such as Hulu + Live TV. It is an important consideration for marketers; videos that friends have liked or shared appear in the newsfeed and can be opened from Pages. Facebook reports 50 million viewers in the United States watching videos on the service for at least a minute the first year. Marketers are able to purchase ads in Showcase, which features Facebook's original programming shows. Advertisers can also place ads via options such as "In-Stream Reserve," which places brand messages in the most engagement-content creative videos, promising an average of 100 million viewers. Or marketers can get more targeting "contextually relevant" audiences.[32] For more details on marketing and advertising on Facebook, see Facebook Blueprint training and certification at https://www.facebook.com/business/learn. **Facebook Blueprint** features Facebook's free and paid online courses and certifications for marketing on Facebook, Instagram, Facebook Messenger, and WhatsApp.[33]

If a brand is a global organization, smaller social networks such as VKontakte, Qzone, and Sina Weibo may be more popular in specific countries.[34] This is simply an overview of Facebook. Best practices are a great place to start, but each brand and target audience is unique. Be sure to do your own Facebook research customized to your target audience, business objectives, and brand. Then experiment and discover what strategies and content work best. Be sure to visit the platform to discover what new features and updates have come out since publication.

LinkedIn

Launched in 2003, **LinkedIn** is a business-focused social-networking service that allows users to create professional profiles of work experience and form connections with other professionals. LinkedIn can be thought of as the professional side of social networking. After being acquired by Microsoft in 2016, it has grown to surpass 604 million users globally.[35] LinkedIn audience reach is highest in the Netherlands (60 percent), United States (59 percent), and Australia (56 percent) and lowest in China (4 percent), (Vietnam 4 percent), and Japan (2 percent). LinkedIn's audience penetration is 53 percent in Canada and 51 percent in the United Kingdom. LinkedIn promotes itself as the world's largest professional network. Global LinkedIn users are more male (56 percent) than female (44 percent) and the largest age group is twenty-five to thirty-four years old (38 percent) while the second-largest group is thirty-five to fifty-four years old (30 percent).[36]

In the United States, LinkedIn users skew more male (55 percent) than female (45 percent) and the largest group of users are older in mid-career (thirty to forty-nine years old) with the second-largest group younger in early career (eighteen to twenty-nine years old). Not surprisingly, LinkedIn users are highly educated, with 59 percent having a college degree, 30 percent with some college, and only 10 percent with high school or less. LinkedIn attracts its main users during or right after college graduation and is used by both men and women who are starting or are in the midst of their professional careers. Users tend to mostly live in urban (45 percent) and suburban (41 percent) areas rather than rural (14 percent).[37] Slightly more users are accessing LinkedIn via mobile (57 percent), but unlike Facebook a sizable number still access the network via desktop or laptop (43 percent).[38]

LinkedIn has always been a business-oriented social-networking site, and that remains the focus of its users' activities. Like other social networks, LinkedIn is built around profile pages, but here users list information such as job experience, education, and professional skills—the kind of information listed on a résumé. Instead of "friends," this community focuses on building a professional network through "connections." The emphasis here is on coworkers, bosses, former bosses, clients, business partners, and other professional contacts people have made over the years. However, LinkedIn has also become an important sales and recruiting tool where salespeople and recruiters also focus on connecting with prospective customers and clients or employees. One thing to keep in mind is that LinkedIn users are not as active as on other social networks. Of the more than 600 million members, only 303 million are active monthly (50 percent) and 121 million active daily (20 percent). This makes sense for the subject of the content and purpose of the network.[39] Marketers should factor this in when considering scheduling and timelines for campaigns and strategies.

Like Facebook, LinkedIn also offers groups, but here the subject is more professionally oriented. Groups are where professionals in the same field or with the same interests can share content, ask questions, or post and search for industry jobs. Job search is a major activity on the site, which has become a valuable tool for job searchers and recruiters alike whether with independent recruiting firms or in-house human resources personnel. Users can apply for positions through LinkedIn, and recommendations attached to users' profiles function much like letters of recommendation. LinkedIn is now the second leading job board by share of applicants in the United States behind Indeed and above Glassdoor and CareerBuilder.[40]

Similar to Facebook business pages, LinkedIn offers organizations the option to create a company page that can function like a corporate website with social-interaction features. Fresh content is delivered via status updates that appear under the activity feed of a user's profile or as discussion posts in groups. Like the rest of the site, the content shared favors industry or professional topics.[41] LinkedIn Publisher is an integrated publishing platform with basic blogging capabilities available via posts. Many users have had great success publishing their content directly into LinkedIn, instead of sharing it linked from external sites, thus expanding reach and increasing engagement through shares, likes, and comments.[42] New LinkedIn Pages add features such as associating LinkedIn Pages with hashtags and adding a customizable call-to-action button. Content Suggestions shows the type of content trending with your target audience to enable more targeted content creation and content curation. Post sharing is also now available for companies to easily share customer testimonials and product reviews. New mobile app updates enable easy sharing of images, photos, PowerPoint and SlideShare presentations, and PDF documents.[43]

LinkedIn app features include enabling users to submit job applications via mobile devices and geolocation check-in features to help recruiters keep track of job-candidate information during events and conventions.[44] LinkedIn has a redesigned desktop to be more like the mobile app, more engagement analytics, unified search capabilities, chat-like messaging, a calendar chatbot to set meeting times, and an easier blogging interface. The feed emphasizes more content and fewer status updates with new algorithms and editors.[45] LinkedIn has supplemented and enhanced multimedia capabilities like video, attaching multiple photos to posts, and tagging people using "@."[46] LinkedIn now also has hashtags to enable content discovery and has added LinkedIn Live, their new live video capability as another way to attract attention to your profile or page. These additional publishing and social engagement features have helped turn LinkedIn from an online résumé into a more professional news discovery engine that has increased time and engagement on the platform.[47]

Because of LinkedIn's professional focus, it can be especially beneficial for business-to-business (B2B) efforts, helping salespeople find leads, and sell trade-oriented products. Recruitment advertisers and marketers with an emphasis on personal sales should consider this an invaluable social media tool for their efforts. Paid access to LinkedIn Premium

Figure 7.2. LinkedIn is a great way to find and retain professional contacts.

© Pekic / iStock Photo

Professional provides additional features to help with prospecting through enhanced insights, search, and InMail capabilities.[48] To grow connections or followers, publish quality content in blog-like posts with graphics, photos, and video. In addition, consider influencer marketing with key organization employees such as presidents and CEOs to become thought leaders in their industry.

Through LinkedIn Marketing Solutions, paid social media options include sponsored content, sponsored InMail, display ads, text ads, carousel ads, dynamic ads, and autoplay video ads. Ads can be highly targeted by job title, company name, industry, profession, and personal interests. You can also place retargeting ads via customized targeting with matched audiences from website, contact, and account data. Advertisers control spending by setting a total budget, daily budget, and bids. Paying for ads also include cost-per-click (CPC), cost-per-1,000-impressions (CPM), and cost-per-send (CPS) for sponsored InMail. LinkedIn's Campaign Manager has added Facebook Ad Manager features. Set campaign objectives with impression-based awareness goals, consideration goals such as website visits, engagement, and video views, or conversion goals such as lead generation, website conversion, or job applicants.[49] LinkedIn Elevate is a new platform to enable and track employee advocacy programs.[50]

Like the Facebook section, this is an overview of LinkedIn. Each brand and target audience is unique. Ensure you do some of your own LinkedIn research for your target audience, business objectives, and brand. Visit the platform to discover what new features and updates have come out since publication. Experiment and discover what strategies and content work best.

Messaging Apps

Because of their personal and social nature, messaging apps will also be discussed under social networks. **Social messaging** is instant messaging or chat applications created around social networks for communication on mobile phones with fewer limits and more features than traditional texting.[51] Messaging apps are popular and have grown from just 616 million to 2.18 billion users worldwide.[52] Top apps have more than one billion users each, such as WhatsApp (1.5 billion) Facebook Messenger (1.3 billion), and WeChat (1 billion), with other popular messaging apps being QQ (803 million), Viber (260 million), and Line (194 million).[53]

WhatsApp is a free, cross-platform instant messaging service that allows encrypted multimedia communication through mobile cellular numbers. WhatsApp was founded in 2009 and bought by Facebook in 2014. **Facebook Messenger** is the instant messaging service application that enables sending multimedia content with optional encryption through Facebook accounts. It was first developed as Facebook Chat in 2008, but was relaunched as a stand-alone app in 2011.[54] WhatsApp is the dominant messaging app across much of the world, including Canada and the United Kingdom.[55] However, Facebook Messenger has grown significantly to become number one in the United States, Australia, and some western European countries.

In the United States the most used messaging apps are Facebook Messenger with 107 million monthly active users and then WhatsApp with 24 million.[56] The largest age groups on Facebook Messenger are twenty-five- to thirty-four-year-olds (89 percent), thirty-five- to forty-four-year-olds (85 percent) and then eighteen- to twenty-four-year-olds (81 percent).[57] Messenger users tend to be more female (55 percent) than male (45 percent).[58] WhatsApp usage in the United States is less and skews older with the largest group twenty-six to thirty-five year-olds (18 percent), but the second largest group is thirty-six to forty-five (16 percent), followed by forty-six to fifty-five (13 percent).[59] WhatsApp users are also more male (60 percent) than female (40 percent).[60]

People like social messaging for text chats, group chats, and notifications, and social features like status updates, media sharing, and stickers.[61] With advanced features, they can chat with friends, obtain customer service, make calls, play games, access content, and buy products.[62] A survey of users found messaging apps are seen to make communication simpler (69 percent), more ongoing (65 percent), easier for groups (65 percent), and more frequent (63 percent). People want to use messaging apps more for communicating one-to-one (50 percent), with groups (60 percent), and with businesses (67 percent). Fifty-three percent of Messenger users said they would more likely shop with a business that they could message directly.[63] Messaging apps can tell brand stories, demonstrate products, and create engaging quizzes, trivia contests, and games. Special offers, sales, promotions, and direct sales can occur in some messaging apps. The real-time nature and privacy of conversations makes messaging ideal for customer service.[64]

With social media networks getting more crowded, the growth of messaging apps, and people's desire to communicate one-on-one with businesses, some see conversation as the future of commerce. **Conversational commerce (c-commerce)** is when businesses chat with people via messaging to drive purchases. The top reasons c-commerce buyers say they chat with businesses are product and pricing information, instant responses at any time, easy way to shop, personalized advice, and negotiating prices or offers. What's more, 42 percent say they chat with the primary purpose to buy, online shoppers who chat with businesses report spending 7 percent more than those who don't, and 57 percent say they plan to increase their c-commerce spending in the future.[65] One of the ways that makes this one-on-one conversation with consumers scalable is chatbots. **Chatbots** are computer programs that simulate human conversation for customer service or information acquisition and distribution.[66]

As with other social media platforms, businesses and organizations should consider adding messaging apps to their marketing, advertising, and public relations strategies because their customers are there and are expecting brands to be there as well.[67] Messaging apps can provide access to direct sales and customer service, and they can extend the reach of brand content. Businesses should create a profile so potential customers know where to reach you, and you can provide customer care and send notifications. In Facebook Messenger you can enable transactions for direct purchase in the conversation. A good way to understand the possibilities for using messaging apps is to see what brands have done on various messaging platforms.

More brands are using messaging apps like Facebook Messenger. The fashion brand Michael Kors built an enhanced chatbot called Michael Kors Concierge for product discovery and aspirational storytelling to increase brand knowledge, provide personalized experiences, and drive purchase consideration. They also increased automation for frequently asked questions (FAQs) to provide a better customer care experience. The chatbot offers an inside look at New York Fashion Week, with behind-the-scenes, backstage content, and provides getaway tips via a travel quiz. Users could also discover new products and shop inside Messenger through guided-selling experiences including new arrivals, seasonal looks, tutorial videos, and user-generated content. Users could join the brand's loyalty program and get instant answers to more than one hundred FAQs. In a short time the brand grew to 370,000 active users with an average growth of 45,000 new users per month.[68]

Hellman's mayonnaise created a "WhatsCook" WhatsApp campaign in South America. Consumers sent a picture of what was in their refrigerator and chefs sent back custom recipes with pictures and videos. Average interactions lasted sixty-five minutes and the effort reached 5.5 million people.[69] Macy's partnered with Viber to offer in-chat shopping where users search and share Macy's products in the messenger app.[70] Adidas has used WhatsApp to build hyper-local brand communities in cities across the world offering members first notice of new releases, invites to events, and access to Adidas's ambassadors.[71]

Lego used Facebook Messenger to connect with its customers and drive real business results. To help customers find the right toy during the holidays, they built a chatbot named Ralph that served as a shopping assistant asking messenger users questions to help them find the perfect gift. Sales were so successful that the effort was expanded to Easter and is now a permanent part of the brand's account. The PR firm Edelman helped the toy brand create the bot that had the right brand voice of quirky, intelligent fun and efficiently drove

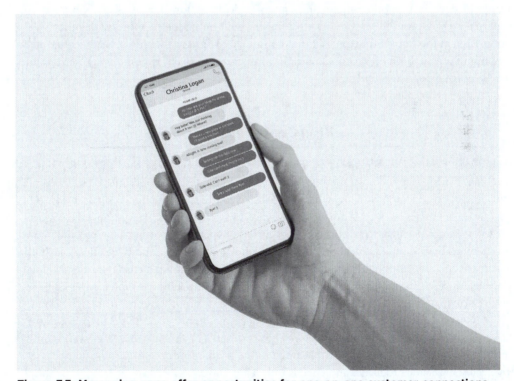

Figure 7.3. Messaging apps offer opportunities for one-on-one customer connections.

© Grinvalds / iStock Photo

customers to the point of purchase. Using a chatbot in a messaging app allowed the brand to scale one-on-one conversation to guide people through the customer journey.[72]

Advertising options are available through Facebook Ad Manager for Facebook Messenger but not WhatsApp. Messenger ads appear in the Chats tab in people's Messenger inbox. Clicking on the ad takes the user to a detailed view within Messenger with a call to action. Ads can be the same as you created for Facebook and Instagram.[73] With Facebook Messenger, Facebook Portal should be considered. **Facebook Portal** is a line of smart devices that enable video chat with Facebook friends through Facebook Messenger or WhatsApp and offers smart voice service.[74] Facebook Portal has its own "Hey, Portal" service but also partnered with Amazon Alexa. The camera automatically moves, zooms, and focuses, tracking user movement and offering a hands-free experience. It also offers augmented reality experiences available in Facebook Stories and Messenger. Privacy concerns have slowed early adoption of Portal and it is early to know how the company will connect its data and advertising products through the device. At the very least, data collected from Portal on users will be available for ad targeting purposes.[75]

Other messaging apps should be considered based on your specific brand, objectives, and target audience. WeChat is dominant in China and smaller messaging apps are popular in other regions like Line in Asia Pacific countries and Viber in eastern European countries. The messaging app Kik is unique in that it is popular with younger users aged thirteen to twenty-three. Messages by Google is growing in use but currently is only available on Android devices.[76] Another messaging app consideration for B2B is Slack, which is an internal communication tool for companies that will be discussed more with microblogging. Also, in the future some predict that consumers will have their own chatbots that will communicate with brand chatbots to gather information, make appointments, get quotes, or even make purchases for them.[77]

Blogs and Forums

Seth Godin's book *Poke the Box* says, "The cost of being wrong is less than the cost of doing nothing."[78] One way to "poke the box" is to test and get ideas by publishing a blog. **Blog** is an abbreviated version of weblog, which describes websites that contain a reverse chronological order of entries or posts featuring diary-type commentary or stories on specific subjects that range from personal to political.[79] Blogs include hyperlinks to other sites and also allow easy embedding of multimedia content such as photos, video, and audio. Readers can "talk back" to the author through comments under each post. The unique characteristics of blogs are that anyone can publish one easily on any topic and that blogs are interactive. The rise in popularity of blogs has helped remove the gatekeeper from professional media publishing.

However, a nonprofessional label for this social medium can be misleading. Top blogs have mass media appeal. The *Huffington Post* blog pulls in 110 million unique views a month and has secured a coveted seat in the White House briefing room.[80] To put this in perspective, *Time* magazine's total US audience is only 17 million.[81]

But a brand does not need to reach millions to be successful. A mommy blogger with twenty thousand monthly views can be worth a marketer's attention for the right product or

Figure 7.4. Blogs offer opportunities for individuals and brands to build an audience.

© Wonder Visuals / iStock Photo

service because her viewers are segmented and very focused.[82] Blogs often form active communities of common interests, and authors can be very influential in those areas. **Mommy blogger** is defined as a mother who blogs about her children, motherhood, parenting, and other related topics.[83] This term has become standard in marketing. However, it should be noted that many women find this term condescending, stating that they are moms but also writers, bloggers, business owners, website owners, and entrepreneurs. Critics argue that the term doesn't represent the professionalism of moms who own blogs, they don't call each other by this term, and not all moms blog about children. Others ask why there is no related term such as "daddy blogger."

How many blogs are there? In 2008 the Blog Herald reported roughly 200 million blogs.[84] By 2014, Technorati's Top 100 directory contained more than 1.3 billion blogs listed by category.[85] Unfortunately, Technorati shut down its blog ranking index in May 2014 to focus on its advertising platform. Of the blogs out there, Nielsen reports that 6.7 million people publish blogs on blogging websites and 12 million are writing blogs using social networks.[86]

We will first look at each of the major blogging platforms: WordPress, Blogger, and Tumblr. Each of these blogging platforms has unique users, content, and characteristics. Then we will explore forums. Similar to blogs, forums are online discussion sites that form around common needs or interests. There is usually a moderator, but no one person or group is responsible for creating content. Posts are like informal conversations versus more formal articles on blogs.

WordPress

WordPress is a free, open-source blogging and content-management system launched in 2003. WordPress averages roughly 600 million visitors a month.[87] WordPress is said to power 26 percent of the web, is the most popular content management system with 59 percent market share, and users make 41 million new posts and 60 million new comments each month.[88] WordPress reports they generate more than 42 million posts and 61 million comments a month.[89] WordPress.com is highly global, with 19 percent of visitor traffic coming from the United States. Top individual countries include Brazil (7 percent), Indonesia (6 percent), Mexico (4 percent), and France (4 percent).[90]

WordPress users are evenly split between male and female visitors who are likely to have a college or graduate degree and usually browse the blogging site from home versus work or school.[91] Most of WordPress traffic comes from search (roughly 60 percent), followed by direct (25 percent), referrals (7 percent), and social (6 percent). Interestingly, more than 50 percent of WordPress social traffic is generated by Facebook, compared to more than 52 percent of competitor Blogger's social traffic coming from YouTube.[92]

WordPress is known for its flexibility, with many different design themes and functional plug-ins to customize blogs.[93] WordPress.com offers free blogs with hosting and https:// WordPress.org allows free download of the software to install on other hosting services. Most large blogs are hosted on WordPress, so it is more of a platform for professional bloggers, media businesses, and companies than the simpler Blogger platform that will be discussed next.[94]

Some examples of the high-profile companies on WordPress include *People* magazine, *Harvard Business Review*, the *New York Times*, and Eddie Bauer. Eddie Bauer's blog features photos and stories about living an adventure lifestyle. Direct links send readers to the retail website.[95] Turkey Hill Dairy has been publishing their blog, the "Ice Cream Journal," since 2006, cultivating a community of ice cream. The blog receives high engagement, with posts reaching more than a hundred comments, and solicits feedback with an annual ultimate flavor tournament to determine the "Frosty Four" fan favorite new flavors. It also has been awarded top five ice cream blog.[96]

Blogger

Blogger is a blog-publishing service that allows free user accounts hosted at the subdomain of https://www.blogspot.com. This free blogging system is very clean, fast, and streamlined. It is the oldest of the three major blogging platforms. It started in 1999 and was acquired by Google in 2003.[97] It was the largest blogging platform but has lost ground to WordPress over the years. With roughly 70 million visitors a month, Blogger.com is highly global, with 18 percent of visitor traffic coming from the United States. Top individual countries include Brazil (10 percent), India (7 percent), and Indonesia (5 percent).[98]

Blogger users skew more male than female. They are more likely to have a college or graduate degree and to browse the blogging site from home versus work or school.[99] Overall, 58 percent of Blogger.com traffic comes from direct links, followed by 21 percent search,

MINI CASE

GM Fastlane Blog

At the turn of the century, General Motors was struggling to win back customers lost to foreign automakers. GM first fixed the product problem by hiring Bob Lutz, a rock star in product development. Yet the company felt the new cars were not getting a fair chance from the automotive press. So they launched the Fastlane blog to get the company's message directly to customers, enthusiasts, and media.[a]

Introduced in January 2005, the blog featured direct access to the candid thoughts of then vice chairman Bob Lutz and other GM executives. These higher-ups in the organization challenged the public to take a new look and test-drive their new cars and trucks. The effort helped GM overcome its dinosaur image, reach customers quickly, and attract web traffic through other sites and blogs linking to Fastlane. The results included millions of visitors and thousands of comments with more than five hundred other blogs linking to Fastlane. The blog was covered by mainstream press such as the *New York Times*, the *Wall Street Journal*, the *Financial Times*, and *Business Week*. The effort won a PRSA Bronze Anvil Award [b] and Forrester Research reported that the yearly value of the blog in consumer research insight alone was $180,000.[c]

Today GM has a general director of customer experience who leads up a global Social Media Center of Expertise (CoE). The CoE brings together social media practitioners from marketing, public relations, communications, and customer care teams. In the CoE marketing leads brand building and channel management, communications takes care of news and reputation management, and customer care focuses on resolving current and prospective customer issues and questions.

These functional areas integrate and collaborate in the Detroit headquarters, where there is a social media command center described as a "high-energy, state-of-the-art engagement environment featuring dozens of wireless work stations, multiple collaboration rooms and 18 HD monitors that display a wide variety of social feeds." GM has twenty-six full-time social media advisers who interact with social media users for in-market presale and customer care. The command center monitors 150 owned social channels for GM's car brands of Chevrolet, Buick, GMC, and Cadillac.[d]

[a] "GM Fastlane Blog: A Corporate Giant Fights Back," PRSA.org, accessed February 18, 2015, https://apps.prsa.org/SearchResults/view/6M-063005/0/GM_Fastlane_Blog_A_Corporate_Giant_Fights_Back#.XIU4qKhKg2w.

[b] Manning Selvage & Lee BlogWorks, "GM Fastlane Blog: A Corporate Giant Fights Back," PRFirms.com, accessed February 18, 2015, https://prcouncil.net/resources/gm-fastlane-blog-a-corporate-giant-fights-back/.

[c] Charlene Li, "New ROI of Blogging Report from Forrester," Empowered (blog), January 25, 2007, http://forrester.typepad.com/groundswell/2007/01/new_roi_of_blog.html.

[d] David Mingle, "Shhhh! Customer Listening in Progress," CIOReview.com, April 28, 2017, https://customer-experience-management.cioreview.com/cxoinsight/shhhh-customer-listening-in-progress-nid-24218-cid-118.html.

14 percent referrals, and 4 percent social. The ease of use and limited custom options also make it more the domain of casual bloggers.

With Blogger's ease of use come limitations in design choices, and it does not support plug-ins for advanced features and customization. Because Blogger is owned by Google, it provides easy integration with Google properties such as AdSense to earn income while posting and Google Analytics for stat tracking. For ease of use and integration with other Google accounts, Blogger may be the ideal tool to get an organization blog up quickly. Depending on target audience, it may also be a place to search for influential individual bloggers with sizable subscriber lists who appeal to a niche audience for the product or service.[100]

Tumblr

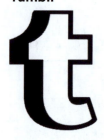

Tumblr is a blogging platform and social-networking website that allows users to post multimedia content in a short-form blog. Tumblr is a later blogging platform entry, beginning in 2007 and acquired by Yahoo in 2013.[101] By then the site had grown to roughly 600 million monthly visitors, but the site had become known for a lot of adult content. In December 2018, the platform banned pornography and adult content. Users dropped to 370 million in two months, but visits recovered to 381 million by July 2019.[102] In August 2019 WordPress's parent company Automattic purchased the blogging platform. Tumblr has more than 471 million registered blogs. Despite the drop in users, the new environment and new owner could make it an attractive option for marketers. Tumblr is global, yet roughly 46 percent of its visitors come from the United States. Other top countries include the United Kingdom (6 percent), Canada (5 percent), Australia (3 percent), and Germany (3 percent).[103]

Tumblr users are more men (65 percent) than women (35 percent)[104] and are overwhelmingly younger, with the largest percentage of users in the eighteen- to twenty-nine-year-old range (43 percent), with the next-largest group aged twenty-five to thirty-four (34 percent).[105] Users also tend to be more urban (60 percent) than rural (40 percent)[106] with many users (40 percent) having some college education, just under a third (31 percent) with high school or less, and just over a quarter (28 percent) with college or more.[107] Tumblr gets most of its traffic (66 percent) from direct traffic, followed by search (16 percent), and social traffic (13 percent). Most of Tumblr's social traffic comes from YouTube (35 percent), Pinterest (19 percent), and Twitter and Facebook (both 16 percent).[108]

Tumblr is unique in that its focus is on simple, quick posts that highlight images and videos. In fact, it could technically be considered a microblogging platform with social-networking features. For strategic purposes, Tumblr has been categorized as a highly visual, short-form blog. Yet this blogging platform emphasizes social media activities where users follow blogs, like posts, share content by reblogging it, and include "@" in posts to tag other users. Features also include links, quotes, chat, audio, and video.[109]

It should be no surprise that Tumblr's content focuses on multimedia such as photos and video, but it also engages users interested in games and internet memes.[110] Look for unique content such as infographics and comics. Tumblr is not ideal for text-heavy entries, and the emphasis on sharing means less original content. This environment lends itself to casual bloggers looking for something between Twitter and WordPress, and businesses that

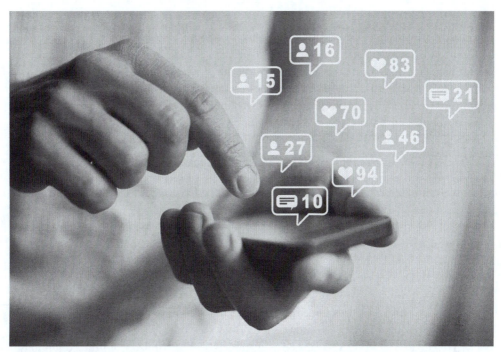

Figure 7.5. Tumblr is a short form blog with social media network features.

© Anyaberkut / iStock Photo

are more focused on visual content.[111] However, many media outlets have opened Tumblr accounts as another venue to share their program content.

Tumblr can be an ideal channel to feature high-quality graphics for users to share quickly. Tumblr is also a good network for blogger outreach if the target audience is in a niche fashion, graphic, craft, or design industry. For example, Electrolux created a unique Tumblr blog that reaches a foodie audience with artful photography and well-designed food recipe films.[112]

Tumblr does offer social ads through Tumblr Business. Brands can purchase sponsored posts, sponsored video posts, and a sponsored day. Sponsored days enable brands to pin their logos and taglines at the top of the Tumblr dashboard for twenty-four hours and link to exclusive brand content on an Explore page tab. Tumblr ads are targetable by gender, location, and interest.[113] Other blogging considerations are Medium and Typepad, and the website platforms Squarespace and Wix and the question-and-answer website Quora also support the creation of blogs.

Forums

Forums are online discussion sites where people hold conversations on related topics via posted messages. Forums differ from chat rooms in that the messages are usually longer and chat rooms happen in real time, more like a phone call, versus a forum discussion that functions more like an email conversation. Some estimate there are millions of internet forums. Forums are similar to blogs in that they provide digital meeting places for people interested in common subjects. Forums may also be called message boards, bulletin boards, discussion boards, threaded discussions, or discussion groups.[114]

On forums, people can create discussions by starting a new thread or subject and others respond with replies to those threads. Threads can be anything from simple statements and questions to longer opinions, stories, or how-tos. Unlike chat rooms, forums keep archives of discussions with many users linking to archived entries.[115]

One popular use for forums is learning how to repair items or troubleshoot computers and software. Forums have sprung up around products, services, and brands. On these forums, fans provide tech support to each other and discuss brand activities. They can be consumer-run forums like https://forums.tdiclub.com or brand-supported forums like https://discussions.apple.com. Marketers should find the forums relevant to their organization or industry.[116]

Forums have owners who administer them, build discussion categories, create moderators, and manage users. The moderators are assigned to monitor a certain category or categories and are given the power to delete messages or even ban individuals from the forum. Users are the individual members who have public access.[117]

Forums tend to have strict rules on behavior and policies on posting threads and replies. Participants can be scolded or banned for posting off-topic messages or for inappropriate activity such as personal attacks. On most forums, overt sales messages are especially not tolerated. Marketers do not want to be labeled as spammers and be banned from the community. This could especially be harmful on a forum centered on a brand. Try to be helpful, not pushy.

To find forums, try directories and search options including BoardReader (boardreader. com), ProBoards (proboards.com), or Omgili (Omgili.com). Perform searches around the brand, product, service, industry, and target audience. You probably found some during the social media audit. Now go back to those sites to look at their size, the kind of users the forum attracts, and the type of content they share. Is there potential for participation to help meet organizational objectives? Are the users in the target market? Does the content shared lend itself to the main message, key insight, or big idea? If so, those forums may need to be a part of the social media strategy. If no forums currently exist, could the brand benefit from starting one? Could a brand-sponsored forum help meet objectives or even help overcome some obstacles identified in the social media audit, such as poor product support?

Why engage bloggers or members of forums? Seth Godin has it right in his quote about poking the box. The emphasis should be presence over perfection. Failing to contribute to communities engaged in discussion about a brand, product, or industry costs organizations. As in any personal relationship between friends, spouses, or coworkers, silence is deadly. A well-meaning personal statement, if not perfect, goes a long way in the consumer's mind versus polished, push-marketing campaigns. Consider the **one percent rule (1% rule)** or the 90-9-1 principle, first coined by bloggers Ben McConnell and Jackie Hunt. It states that in collaborative sites such as blogs and forums, 90 percent of users view the content, 9 percent contribute infrequently, and only 1 percent actively create new content.[118] As a marketer, this is good news. If a brand can engage the 1 percent of bloggers or forum participants, they will spread the word to the other 99 percent.

Marketers, advertisers, and public relations professionals should know that people are out there talking about their organizations. Start reading, posting, and commenting on these blogs and forums, or start your own. The cost of not engaging in that conversation can be huge, such as a missed opportunity to stop an angry protest before it gets out of hand or an opportunity to fuel a viral campaign. Find the right fit for social media campaign objectives, target, and big idea.

Chapter 7 Checklist

Social media can change quickly. Visit Post Control Marketing (http://www.postcontrol marketing.com) for updates, but also use this chapter checklist to briefly check how social media statistics in this chapter have changed since publication.

✓ How have social networks, messaging apps, blogs, and forums changed? Are Facebook, LinkedIn, Messenger, WhatsApp, WordPress, Blogger, and Tumblr still the top platforms?

✓ Do a quick search to confirm key statistics for each of the social media channel options covered in this chapter. Update numbers for monthly and daily users, global and country use, user demographics such as gender, age, education, and income, plus new features. What type of content performs best on each?

✓ Check for new paid social media opportunities. Have any of the social media platforms covered in this chapter added new advertising options? Have the General Data Protection Regulation (see chapter 13), California Consumer Protection Act (see chapter 15), or other regulations changed the targeting and tracking capabilities of social media campaigns?

 SOCIAL PLAN PART 7

Select Social Networks, Blog Platforms, and Forums

In this part of the social media plan, explore all the major social media networks in consideration for the plan (ask questions in table 7.1). Research each, looking at the size and makeup of the users. Does the brand target audience match the main users of the social network? What kind of content is popular? What is the culture of the social network? Do these characteristics match brand, product, service, and big idea? Do the same exploration and comparison for blogs and forums. Could the brand benefit from a blog? Which platform would be best? What about a forum? Should the organization start its own or participate in existing forums? Report all findings and ideas in these areas:

1. Identify the top social networks where the target audience is active.
2. For each social network, describe the main type of content and culture.
3. Find existing brand, product, or service blogs and forums. How could the brand participate?
4. Is there a need for a customer-support forum or other type of forum?

For a condensed version of the social plan see appendix A: Three-Part Social Plan.

KEY CONCEPTS

Friendster

social network

Facebook

algorithm

Facebook Watch

Facebook Blueprint

LinkedIn

social messaging

WhatsApp

Facebook Messenger

conversational commerce (c-commerce)

chatbots

Facebook Portal

blog

mommy blogger

WordPress

Blogger

Tumblr

forums

one percent rule (1% rule)

QUESTIONS FOR DISCUSSION

1. Facebook is by far the largest and most dominant social media network. Do you feel all organizations must have a Facebook page? Can you think of an example where it wouldn't make sense?
2. How could a B2B (business to business) company use LinkedIn as a marketing tool? What strategies could be used on LinkedIn to build qualified leads and secure sales? Make this question specific, such as a local bank brand manager charged with growing business accounts. How could they leverage LinkedIn as an alternative to traditional cold calls?
3. The GM Fastlane corporate blog was a success. Find another company blog that has done well. What business objectives is the blog helping to meet? Can you find any ROI (return on investment) data to report? Alternatively, argue and find data that indicates brand blogs are no longer relevant.
4. Ethics in social media became big news in 2018 with the Facebook-Cambridge Analytica data scandal. Do you know what really happened, why it was controversial, and what changes have been made since then? Research some articles and/or documentaries, provide a summary, and weigh in on how it impacts your personal social use and use of social media for marketing.

ADDITIONAL EXERCISES

1. One of the best ways to learn about social-network options is to join them. This exercise challenges you to join these top social networks and others you feel may apply to the target audience of your brand. This doesn't mean launch an official business presence. Join them personally to get a firsthand look at the environment, how it works, and what content tends to be liked. Also, notice the posted and unposted community rules. Make note of them for later efforts. Have fun and think like a consumer, enjoying these social networks while observing them for strategic business insight. You probably have been on social networks like Facebook for years, but take notes and make observations from an outside perspective, noting what marketing seems to work and what doesn't.

2. As with social networks, one of the best ways to learn about blogs and forums is to join them. Do a search to find some of the most active forums in and around the brand, product, or service. Look for the most active contributors and identify them as possible influencers. Find some top blogs in your field and subscribe to them. Or perhaps start your own blog. Learn firsthand the characteristics and possibilities of this channel. Also, as with social networks, make a note of the community rules for your later efforts. Again, have fun and think like a consumer while observing for strategic business insight. Big social networks like Facebook and LinkedIn may get a lot of attention, but forums and blogs are active with an organization's most loyal fans and more influential people in industries.

Notes

1. "Wolf Blitzer Quotes," BrainyQuote.com, accessed October 5, 2019, https://www.brainy quote.com/search_results?q=Wolf+Blitzer.

2. Tania Dworjan, "History of Friendster," SocialNetworking.LoveToKnow.com, accessed November 15, 2019, https://socialnetworking.lovetoknow.com/history-friendster.

3. Peter Pachal, "Why Friendster Died: Social Media Isn't a Game," PCMagazine.com, April 28, 2011, http://www.pcmag.com/article2/0,2817,2384588,00.asp.

4. Seth Fiegerman, "Friendster Founder Tells His Side of the Story, 10 Years after Facebook," Mashable.com, February 3, 2014, http://mashable.com/2014/02/03/jonathan-abrams-friendster-facebook.

5. Brent Barnhart, "How the Facebook Algorithm Works and Ways to Outsmart It," Sprout social.com, May 31, 2019, https://sproutsocial.com/insights/facebook-algorithm/.

6. Tom Huddleston Jr., "Twitter Is Officially Shutting Down Vine Today," Fortune.com, January 17, 2017, http://fortune.com/2017/01/17/twitter-shut-down-vine-tuesday/.

7. Greg Kumparak, "Meerkat, Star App of 2015, Is Officially Dead," Techcrunch.com, September 30, 2016, https://techcrunch.com/2016/09/30/meerkat-star-of-2015-is-officially-dead/.

8. Kelsey Arendnt, "Outsized Influence: The Size of Social Media Platforms Has Little to Do with Their Referral Traffic," Blog.Parse.ly, August 22, 2019, https://blog.parse.ly/post/8921/outsized-influence-the-size-of-social-media-platforms-has-little-to-do-with-their-referral-traffic/.

9. "Social Network," Dictionary.com, accessed October 5, 2019, http://dictionary.reference.com/browse/social+network.

10. Simon Kemp, "Digital in 2019," wearesocial.com, 2019, https://wearesocial.com/global-digital-report-2019.

11. "Distribution of Facebook Users in the United States as of August 2019, by Age Group and Gender," Statista, September 9, 2019, https://www.statista.com/statistics/187041/us-user-age-distribution-on-facebook/.

12. "Social Media Fact Sheet," PewInternet.org, June 12, 2019, https://www.pewinternet.org/fact-sheet/social-media/.

13. Nick Statt, "Facebook is Redesigning Its Core App around the Two Parts People Actually Like to Use," TheVerge.com, April 30, 2019, https://www.theverge.com/2019/4/30/18523265/facebook-events-groups-redesign-news-feed-features-f8-2019.

14. "Social Media Activities on Select Social Networks by Social Media Users in the United States in February 2019," eMarketer, March 22, 2019, https://www.statista.com/statistics/200843/social-media-activities-by-platform-usa/.

15. "Which, if any, of the following reasons best describe what you use Facebook for?" YouGov, April 10, 2018, https://www.statista.com/statistics/856324/reasons-for-the-usage-of-facebook-usa/.

16. "Social Media Fact Sheet," PewInternet.org.

17. Lisa Eadicicco, "These Are the Social Media Platforms Teens Are Ditching in 2019," BusinessInsider.com, July 7, 2019, https://www.businessinsider.com/teens-ditching-facebook-for-youtube-2019-7.

18. Paul Ramondo, "The Facebook Algorithm Demystified: How to Optimize for News Feed Exposure," SocialMediaExaminer.com, May 31, 2017, http://www.socialmediaexaminer.com/facebook-algorithm-demystified-how-to-optimize-for-news-feed-exposure/.

19. Kemp, "Digital in 2019."

20. Statt, "Facebook is Redesigning Its Core App."

21. Keith A. Quesenberry and Michael K. Coolsen, "What Makes Facebook Brand Posts Engaging? A Content Analysis of Facebook Brand Post Text That Increase Shares, Likes and Comments to Influence Organic Viral Reach," *Journal of Current Issues & Research in Advertising* 39, no. 2 (2018).

22. Lindsay Kolowich, "The 16 Best Facebook Pages We've Seen This Year," HubSpot.com (blog), September 11, 2017, https://blog.hubspot.com/blog/tabid/6307/bid/28441/the-15-best-facebook-pages-you-ve-ever-seen.aspx.

23. UNICEF Facebook page, accessed September 11, 2017, https://www.facebook.com/unicef/.

24. Josh Constine, "You Might Hate It, but Facebook Stories Now Has 500M Users," TechCrunch.com, April 24, 2019, https://techcrunch.com/2019/04/24/facebook-stories-500-million/.

25. "In the past, do you think Facebook has or has not done enough to safeguard the personal data of people with Facebook profiles?" YouGov, April 10, 2018, https://www.statista.com/statistics/856374/opinion-facebook-safeguard-personal-data-profiles-usa/.

26. "Have you ever considered deleting your Facebook profile?" YouGov, April 10, 2018, https://www.statista.com/statistics/856418/facebook-users-considering-deleting-their-profiles-usa/.

27. Anja Skrba, "How to Use Facebook Audience Optimization for Better Organic Exposure," SocialMediaExaminer.com, September 21, 2017, https://www.socialmediaexaminer.com/facebook-audience-optimization-organic-exposure/.

28. Brian Peters, "The Simple Facebook Posting Strategy That Helped Us 3x Our Reach and Engagement," Buffer Social (blog), May 30, 2017, https://blog.bufferapp.com/facebook-posting-strategy.

29. "Reach Out to Future Customers and Fans," Facebook.com/Business, accessed October 3, 2019, https://www.facebook.com/business/ads.

30. "Reach Out," Facebook.com/Business.

31. Jeremy Laukkonen, "Facebook Watch: What It Is and How to Use It," Lifewire.com, November 8, 2019, https://www.lifewire.com/what-is-facebook-watch-4175805.

32. Sahail Ashraf, "Is Facebook Watch a Viable Option for Marketers?" Business2Community.com, April 15, 2019. Every month, more than fifty million people in the United States come to watch videos for at least a minute in Watch. Read more at https://www.business2community.com/facebook/is-facebook-watch-a-viable-option-for-marketers-02189990.

33. "Learning New Marketing Skills with Facebook Blueprint," Facebook.com, accessed November 15, 2019, https://www.facebook.com/business/learn.

34. Kemp, "Digital in 2019."

35. Sophia Bernazzani, "9 New LinkedIn Features You May Have Missed This Year," HubSpot.com (blog), April 6, 2017, https://blog.hubspot.com/marketing/new-linkedin-features.

36. Kemp, "Digital in 2019."

37. "Social Media Fact Sheet," PewInternet.org.

38. "Your Audience Is on LinkedIn," Business.LinkedIn.com, accessed October 4, 2019, https://business.linkedin.com/marketing-solutions/audience.

39. "46 Eye-Opening LinkedIn Statistics for 2019," 99Firms.com, May 9, 2019, https://99firms .com/blog/linkedin-statistics/.

40. "Leading Job Boards in the United States in 2017, by Share of Applicants," SlikRoad, June 15, 2018, https://www.statista.com/statistics/951382/job-boards-share-of-applicants-united-states/.

41. Stephanie Buck, "The Beginner's Guide to LinkedIn," Mashable.com, May 23, 2012, http:// mashable.com/2012/05/23/linkedin-beginners.

42. Michael Stelzner, "LinkedIn Publishing Platform: What Marketers Need to Know," SocialMediaExaminer.com, April 19, 2014, http://www.socialmediaexaminer.com/linkedin -publishing-platform-with-stephanie-sammons.

43. "LinkedIn Marketing in 2019: New Company Pages & Features You'll Want to Know," 360psg.com, accessed October 4, 2019, https://www.360psg.com/blog/linkedin-marketing-in -2019-new-company-pages-features-youll-want-to-know.

44. Lauren Mobertz, "Now You Can Apply to Jobs on LinkedIn Using Any Mobile Device," DashBurst.com, August 5, 2013, http://dashburst.com/linkedin-mobile-apply-jobs.

45. Bernazzani, "9 New LinkedIn Features."

46. Jessica Hilla, "Vende Buzz: New LinkedIn Features for 2017," VendeSocial.com (blog), September 13, 2017, https://vendesocial.com/blog/new-linkedin-features-2017/; Kurt Wagner, "LinkedIn Is Finally Selling Autoplay Video Ads," Recode.net (blog), October 12, 2017, https://www .recode.net/2017/10/12/16460338/linkedin-autoplay-video-ads-sell.

47. Keith A. Quesenberry, "How to Leverage Mobile Micro-Moments for Social Media Success," LinkedIn.com, March 15, 2017, https://www.linkedin.com/pulse/how-leverage-mobile -micro-moments-social-media-keith-a-quesenberry/.

48. "Unlock the Power of Your Network," Premium.LinkedIn.com, accessed August 2, 2017, https://premium.linkedin.com/professional.

49. "Your Audience Is on LinkedIn," Business.LinkedIn.com.

50. "LinkedIn Elevate," Business.LinkedIn.com, accessed October 4, 2019, https://business .linkedin.com/elevate.

51. Meghan Keaney Anderson, "Why We're Thinking About Messaging Apps All Wrong," Blog .HubSpot.com, February 1, 2017, https://blog.hubspot.com/marketing/messaging-apps.

52. "Number of Mobile Phone Messaging App Users Worldwide from 2016 to 2021 (in Billions)," eMarketer, July 21, 2017, https://www.statista.com/statistics/483255/number-of -mobile-messaging-users-worldwide/.

53. Kemp, "Digital in 2019."

54. Margaret Rouse, "Facebook Messenger," WhatItIs.TechTarget.com, September 2016, https:// whatis.techtarget.com/definition/Facebook-Messenger.

55. Vangie Beal, "WhatsApp," Webopedia.com, accessed November 15, 2019, https://www .webopedia.com/TERM/W/whatsapp.html.

56. "Most Popular Mobile Messaging Apps in the United States as of June 2019, by Monthly Active Users (in Millions)," Verto Analytics, September 9, 2019, https://www.statista.com/ statistics/350461/mobile-messenger-app-usage-usa/.

57. "Percentage of U.S. Internet Users Who Use Facebook Messenger as of January 2018, by Age Group," We are Flint, February 26, 2018, https://www.statista.com/statistics/814100/ share-of-us-internet-users-who-use-facebook-messenger-by-age/.

58. "Distribution of Facebook Messenger Users in the United States as of August 2019, by Gender," NapoleonCat, September 9, 2019, https://www.statista.com/statistics/951136/ facebook-messenger-user-share-in-usa-gender/.

59. "Percentage of U.S. Internet Users Who Use WhatsApp as of January 2018, by Age Group," We are Flint, February 26, 2018, https://www.statista.com/statistics/814649/whatsapp -users-in-the-united-states-by-age/.

60. "Percentage of U.S. Internet Users Who Use WhatsApp as of January 2018, by Gender," We are Flint, February 26, 2018, https://www.statista.com/statistics/814641/whatsapp-users-in-the-united-states-by-gender/.

61. Anderson, "Why We're Thinking About Messaging Apps All Wrong."

62. Clifford Chi, "The 5 Best Messaging Apps for Marketing in 2017," HubSpot.com (blog), September 29, 2017, https://blog.hubspot.com/marketing/best-messaging-apps-for-marketing.

63. "More Than a Message: The Evolution of Conversation," Facebook IQ (blog), August 4, 2016, https://www.facebook.com/iq/articles/more-than-a-message-the-evolution-of-conversation?ref=wpinsights_rd.

64. Christina Michelle Bailey, "Messaging App: The Wild West of Brand Marketing," Lifewire.com, March 22, 2017, https://www.lifewire.com/messaging-apps-brand-marketing-4059252.

65. "Why Conversation Is the Future of Commerce," Facebook.com/business, September 23, 2019, https://www.facebook.com/business/news/insights/conversational-commerce.

66. Jake Frankenfield, "Chatbot," Investopedia.com, accessed November 15, 2019, https://www.investopedia.com/terms/c/chatbot.asp.

67. Christina Newberry, "Messenger Apps for Business: How to Use Chat for Marketing," Hootsuite.com (blog), June 5, 2017, https://blog.hootsuite.com/messenger-apps/.

68. "Michael Kors: Facebook Messenger Chatbot (Michael Kors Concierge)," ShortyAwards.com, accessed October 5, 2019, https://shortyawards.com/11th/michael-kors-messenger.

69. "WhatsCook," cubo.cc, accessed September 29, 2017, http://cubo.cc/whatscook/.

70. Paul Sawers, "Chat App Viber to Launch In-App Shopping Feature with Brands Like Macy's and Rakuten.com," VentureBeat.com, February 23, 2017, https://venturebeat.com/2017/02/23/viber-to-launch-in-chat-shopping/.

71. Seb Joseph, "Adidas Spotlights 'Dark Social' to Be the 'Most Personal Brand,'" TheDrum.com, March 5, 2016, http://www.thedrum.com/news/2016/03/05/adidas-spotlights-dark-social-be-most-personal-brand.

72. "Cannes 2018: See How Lego Drives Sales on Messenger," Facebook.com/Business, June 19, 2019, https://www.facebook.com/business/news/cannes-2018-see-how-lego-drives-sales-on-messenger.

73. Reach Out," Facebook.com/Business.

74. Dale Smith, "Facebook Portal Refresh: 7 Things You Need to Know in 2019," CNet.com, September 18, 2019, https://www.cnet.com/news/facebook-portal-refresh-7-things-you-need-to-know-in-2019/.

75. Jonathan Crowl, "Here's What Facebook Portal Means for Marketers," Skyword.com, November 12, 2018, https://www.skyword.com/contentstandard/heres-what-facebook-portal-means-for-marketers/.

76. "Messages," Messages.Google.com, accessed October 9, 2019, https://messages.google.com/.

77. Daniel Sevitt, "The Most Popular Messaging Apps by Country," SimilarWeb.com (blog), February 27, 2017, https://www.similarweb.com/blog/popular-messaging-apps-by-country.

78. Seth Godin, *Poke the Box: When Was the Last Time You Did Something for the First Time?* (New York: Portfolio/Penguin, 2011).

79. "What Is a Blog?" WordPress, accessed October 5, 2019, http://codex.wordpress.org/Introduction_to_Blogging.

80. "Top 15 Most Popular Blogs," eBizMBA.com, last modified September 1, 2019, http://www.ebizmba.com/articles/blogs.

81. "Print Audience," TimeMediaKit.com, accessed October 4, 2019, https://www.timemediakit.com/audience/.

82. Larissa Faw, "Is Blogging Really a Way for Women to Earn a Living?" Forbes.com, April 25, 2012, http://www.forbes.com/sites/larissafaw/2012/04/25/is-blogging-really-a-way-for-women-to-earn-a-living-2.

83. "Mommy-Blogger," YourDictionary.com, accessed October 5, 2019, http://www.your dictionary.com/mommy-blogger.

84. Anne Helmond, "How Many Blogs Are There? Is Someone Still Counting?" Blog Herald.com, February 11, 2008, http://www.blogherald.com/2008/02/11/how-many-blogs-are-there-is-someone-still-counting.

85. Orun Bhuiyan, "Here's Technorati's Final List of Top Blogs Before It Disappeared," Seocial .com, June 16, 2014, http://www.seocial.com/technorati-blog-directory-deleted-may-29/.

86. "Buzz in the Blogosphere: Millions More Bloggers and Blog Readers," Nielsen.com, March 8, 2012, http://www.nielsen.com/us/en/newswire/2012/buzz-in-the-blogosphere-millions -more-bloggers-and-blog-readers.html.

87. "WordPress.com," SimilarWeb.com, accessed August 3, 2019, https://www.similarweb .com/website/wordpress.com#overview.

88. "21 Weird & Wonderful WordPress Statistics You'll Want to Tell Your Friends," Digital.com, November 12, 2018, https://digital.com/blog/wordpress-stats/.

89. "WordPress Stats," WordPress.com, accessed August 3, 2019, http://en.support.wordpress .com/stats.

90. "WordPress.com," SimilarWeb.com.

91. "Blogger.com Traffic Statistics," Alexa.com, accessed August 3, 2019, http://www.alexa .com/siteinfo/blogger.com.

92. "WordPress.com," SimilarWeb.com.

93. Marko Saric, "The Beginner's Guide to Building a Website," HowToMakeMyBlog.com, https://howtomakemyblog.com/blog/.

94. Kasia Mikoluk, "Best Blogging Platform: WordPress, Blogger, Tumblr, Squarespace, or Type-pad?" Udemy.com, June 20, 2013, https://blog.udemy.com/best-blogging-platform/.

95. "Live Your Adventure," EddieBauer.com (blog), accessed January 18, 2015, http://blog .eddiebauer.com.

96. "September Prize: What's Your Favorite Part of the Fall Season?" IceCreamJournal .TurkeyHill.com, September 8, 2017, https://icecreamjournal.turkeyhill.com/index.php/2017/09/08/september-prize-whats-your-favorite-part-of-the-fall-season/.

97. Dianna Gunn, "The History of Blogging: From 1997 Until Now (With Pictures)," ThemeIsle.com, June 3, 2019, https://themeisle.com/blog/history-of-blogging/.

98. "Blogger.com," Similarweb.com, accessed August 3, 2019, https://www.similarweb.com/website/blogger.com.

99. "Blogger.com Traffic Statistics," Alexa.com.

100. "Blogger," Blogger.com, accessed October 5, 2019, https://www.blogger.com/about.

101. "Tumblr," Wikipedia, last modified October 4, 2019, http://en.wikipedia.org/wiki/Tumblr.

102. "Combined Desktop and Mobile Visits to Tumblr.com from February 2018 to July 2019 (in Millions)," SimilarWeb.com, September 5, 2019, https://www.statista.com/statistics/261925/unique-visitors-to-tumblrcom/.

103. "Tumblr.com," SimilarWeb.com, accessed August 3, 2019, https://www.similarweb.com/website/tumblr.com.

104. "Share of U.S. Internet Users Who Use Tumblr as of January 2018, by Gender," Statista, February 26, 2018, https://www.statista.com/statistics/246213/share-of-us-internet-users -who-use-tumblr-by-gender/.

105. "Percentage of U.S. Internet Users Who Use Tumblr as of January 2018, by Age," We are Flint, February 26, 2018, https://www.statista.com/statistics/246214/share-of-us-internet-users-who-use-tumblr-by-age-group/.

106. "Percentage of U.S. Internet Users Who Use Tumblr as of January 2018, by Urbanity," We are Flint, https://www.statista.com/statistics/814686/share-of-us-internet-users-who-use-tumblr-by-urbanity/.

107. "Percentage of U.S. Internet Users Who Use Tumblr in April 2015, by Education Level," Pew Research Center, August 19, 2015, https://www.statista.com/statistics/246218/share-of-us-internet-users-who-use-tumblr-by-education-level/.

108. "Tumblr.com," SimilarWeb.com.

109. "What is Tumblr?" Tumblr.com, accessed October 4, 2019, https://www.tumblr.com/.

110. Mark Lindsey, "Round 2 of Tumblr vs. WordPress vs. Blogspot: Fight!" Compete.com, February 8, 2012, https://blog.compete.com/2012/02/08/round-2-of-tumblr-vs-wordpress-vs-blogger-fight.

111. Mikoluk, "Best Blogging Platform."

112. "Now You're Cooking," Electrolux (blog), accessed October 5, 2019, http://nowyourecooking.tumblr.com/; © Electrolux.

113. "Tumblr Business," Tumblr.com, accessed October 5, 2019, https://www.tumblr.com/business.

114. Institution of Engineering Technology, "What Is a 'Forum'?" accessed October 5, 2019, http://www.theiet.org/forums/blog/help/english/What_is_a_forum.htm.

115. Institution of Engineering Technology, "What Is a 'Forum'?"

116. TDI Club Internet Forum, accessed October 15, 2013, from http://forums.tdiclub.com.

117. Institution of Engineering Technology, "What Is a 'Forum'?"

118. Beverly Bird, "One Percent Rule," Investopedia, October 15, 2019, https://www.investopedia.com/terms/o/one-percent-rule.asp.

Microblogging and Media Sharing

Be sincere; be brief; be seated.[1]

—Franklin D. Roosevelt

PREVIEW

Have you ever looked forward to a three-hour lecture class? How about a client meeting you knew was going to last for hours or even a half or full day? Yet you may recall rejoicing when a class or meeting let you out earlier than expected. There is something in our minds that drives us to believe shorter is better.

As an illustration, the following words were spoken at a historical event: "Standing beneath this serene sky, overlooking these broad fields now reposing . . ."[2] Do you remember what speech these words are from? On the other hand, these words began another speech that day: "Four score and seven years ago our fathers brought forth . . . " Many people probably don't know the first quote, yet remember the second quote as the beginning of the Gettysburg Address given by Abraham Lincoln on November 19, 1863.[3]

The first quote was from the main Gettysburg Address given by Edward Everett. Everett's speech was a two-hour, nearly fourteen-thousand-word oration on the event of the US Civil War. Right after Everett's speech, Lincoln spoke just ten sentences in two minutes and accomplished much more than Everett.[4]

When *Time* magazine published a Top 10 List of greatest speeches, Abraham Lincoln's Gettysburg Address was included among those of other greats such as Socrates, Martin Luther King Jr., and Winston Churchill. It is also interesting to note that Winston Churchill's famous "Blood, Toil, Tears and Sweat" speech of 1940 lasted a mere five minutes.[5] The lesson here is that clear and concise communication is often the most powerful and memorable.

Microblogging

In the Franklin D. Roosevelt quote that started this chapter, he may have been giving his son instructions for making a speech, but this way of thinking is behind some of the most influential social media channels. Even as we spend more and more time engaging with social media, placing limits on those individual interactions has spawned three of the most popular social media icons: Twitter, Pinterest, and TikTok.

Microblogging is a form of traditional blogging where the content is smaller in both file size and length. Microblogs limit exchange to smaller bits of information such as short sentences, single images, or video that can be called microposts. Like traditional blogs, users post on topics from what they are doing and seeing right now to motorcycles or chocolate or television programs like *The Voice*.[6] The difference may seem small, but microblogs are used in very different ways from traditional blogs or other social media channels.

Another key characteristic of microblogging is the real-time reporting that has emerged from the short nature of updates that allows users to post items quickly. Twitter has developed into a source of news for crises such as the Mumbai terror attacks, the Boston Marathon bombing, the George Floyd protests, and the Paris attacks. Citizens have become sources of information outside formal journalism to influence or even cause mass media coverage. Microblogging also creates an enormous amount of data that can then be analyzed for trends with services such as Trendsmap.[7]

Additionally, microblogging has become an increasingly mainstream customer support channel. When a customer has a problem with a product or service, they often turn to microblogs like Twitter first, not only to voice their discontent but also with the expectation of a timely response. There is also potential for collaborative work in organizations where email has become slow and inefficient. There are many free and open-source software services that act as hosted microblogging platforms for private organizational use. A popular microblog for organizational use is Slack. **Slack** provides a quick employee communication platform for messaging, sharing files, searches, and apps and is used by companies such as Samsung, Ogilvy, Time, Pinterest, eBay, and Ticketmaster.[8]

Why do people microblog? The findings of a study by Emily Pronin and Daniel Wegner suggest a link between short bursts of activity and feelings of elation, power, and creativity.[9] Is there some connection between these feelings or the live news feel and the organization's brand, product, or service? Can microblogging be leveraged in the social media plan? Does one of these microblogging social media platforms connect specifically with your unique target audience? Find out by looking at the three main microblogging platforms, Twitter, Pinterest, and TikTok in further detail.

Twitter

Twitter is an online social-networking service that enables users to send short, character-count-limited messages. Launched in 2006, this microblogging platform defines itself as "what's happening in the world and what people are talking about right now."[10] Twitter has 326 million global monthly active users[11] and 139 million active daily.[12] Globally Twitter's ad audience is mostly male (65 percent) and skews older with twenty-five- to thirty-four-year-olds as the largest age group (31 percent) followed by thirty-five- to forty-nine-year-olds (21 percent). Twitter's highest reach is in Saudi Arabia (43 percent), Japan (34 percent), and Ireland (31 percent) and lowest in Vietnam (1 percent), India (1 percent), and China (0.1 percent).[13] Twitter started as a website before developing its app, but from the beginning Twitter's inspiration was short message service (SMS) short codes of mobile networks. Today 80 percent of Twitter users access the platform from mobile versus desktop or laptop,[14] and in 2019 Twitter redesigned its website interface to look more like its mobile interface.[15] Twitter is more of a niche audience with use among people thirteen years and older in the United Kingdom at 19 percent, the United States and Canada at 17 percent, and Australia at 12 percent.[16]

Twitter users in the United States are more evenly divided between men (52 percent) and women (47 percent) and age groups skew older, with the largest age groups being twenty-five- to thirty-four-year-olds and fifty-four- to sixty-four-year-olds (both 21 percent), followed by thirty-five- to forty-four-year-olds (19 percent) and forty-five- to fifty-four-year-olds (16 percent). Like Facebook, Twitter is maturing; there are seven times as many US Twitter users age sixty-five and older (7 percent) as (thirteen to seventeen-year-olds (1 percent).[17] Along with the older age group, close to half of Twitter users have a college degree (46 percent) with more than a third on their way to earning one with some college experience (35 percent). Twitter users are more urban than Facebook users, with nearly half coming from urban areas (43 percent), more than a third from suburban regions (36 percent), and about a fifth from rural areas (21 percent).[18]

What do these users share? They share thoughts, news, information, jokes, pictures, and links in 280 characters or less. These message updates are called tweets and 42 percent of US users are tweeting or reading tweets daily.[19] After ten years of having a 140-character count limit, in 2017 Twitter officially expanded to a new 280-character limit.[20] No matter the character count, Mashable says Twitter "makes global communication cheap and measurable." Like the social networks, users have profiles, but on Twitter most are public for anyone to see. In addition to a profile, each user is assigned a handle, which is their username. Usernames vary from real names and abbreviations to nicknames or organizations. Organizations can open Twitter accounts with profiles. They are not restricted to separate pages as they are on Facebook.[21]

Users follow other users who interest them so that their tweets appear in the other user's feed, or stream of tweets (updates), on their home page. The more people following, the more people see the updates. That is why early marketing efforts on Twitter should concentrate on building followers. If a user sees a tweet they like in their feed, they can "retweet" (RT), or reshare, the message, giving credit to the original author, but then having it appear in the feed of everyone following them. Yet tweets move by quickly. Unlike some other social platforms, it is suggested to post the same tweets multiple times to increase the chances they will be seen.

Another way to acknowledge another user and separate specific tweets from all conversation is with a mention (using the @ symbol). For example, adding @Kquesen to a tweet notifies the author of this book, initiating a discussion in this public space. Twitter users can also direct-message (DM) another user to conduct private messages back and forth with the same character limit. Yet users can only DM a user who follows them. Twitter has added curated feeds based on an algorithm known as "Show the best Tweets first," which included popular tweets from people users did not follow. After a user backlash in 2018, it restored the ability to turn this feature off with a switch to only see tweets from people they follow in chronological order.[22]

The top social media activities on Twitter are news (56 percent) viewing photos (42 percent), and watching videos and sharing content with everyone (both 32 percent).[23] Yet only 10 percent of Twitter users send 80 percent of tweets, which means the platform is good for influencer outreach. Getting the 10 percent to tweet for you can help you reach the other 90 percent.[24]

Many brands have found that including photos and videos improves user engagement. **Twitter Cards** can be a useful tool in this regard because they enable users to attach rich photos, videos, and media experiences to tweets and drive traffic to websites. Twitter Cards work by creating special pages on the brand's website and then sharing that URL. Users who tweet the link to that content will have a "card" added to the tweet that's visible to followers. There are four Twitter card types including summary cards with a title description and thumbnail image and a summary card with a large image. An app card has a direct download to a mobile app and a player card provides video and audio media.[25]

Another popular strategy on Twitter is to host and participate in Twitter Chats. **Twitter Chats** are when an organization or individual talks live with others about a topic during a preplanned time using a hashtag. To start a Twitter Chat, use a tweet chat directory to find hashtags that are already being used, then create your own, set a time and topic, and promote it to followers. Sites such as Twubs.com and TweetChat.com can help you set up and participate in Twitter Chats. Example Twitter Chats include #HootChat, #SproutChat, #ViralChat, #SmallBizChat, #PRChat, and #MillennialChat.[26] Brands could host Twitter Chats to establish thought leadership, become influencers, share content, and increase awareness. Twitter Chats build engagement, followers, and brand community while providing insights into what customers need, which can lead to valuable and engaging content development. They also offer an opportunity to connect with customers and leads. Brands can do this through their own Twitter Chat or brand influencers and salespeople can participate in other relevant and popular Twitter Chats.[27]

Companies such as Verizon provide customer service via Twitter. These companies try to get angry customers off the public feed by encouraging them to follow and then send a direct message. Other companies such as airlines have opened separate Twitter accounts dedicated to customer service. With some 500 million tweets a day, users find related messages by including a hashtag (#) to designate a topic of conversation such as #TheVoice or #startup.[28] Hashtags are the main search tool for Twitter that allows users to find all tweets

Figure 8.1. Holding Twitter chats has been a valuable strategy for many brands.

© Hocus-Focus / iStock Photo

about a given subject—even from users they don't follow. Twitter also owned the social media app Vine, which emphasized short video content in the form of six-second looping clips, but shut down that platform in January 2017. Twitter also owns the Periscope app, which streams live video, and has integrated it into Twitter, thus adding live video broadcasting capabilities to Twitter.[29]

One of the main attractions of Twitter is its real-time reporting. Marketers like HGTV use the channel to share interesting content, but also to promote their shows in real time.[30] With 81 percent of Americans owning a smartphone and just over 50 percent owning a tablet, they are now accessing Twitter while watching television at the same time, which has made TV programming a more interactive experience.[31] *The Bachelor* generates an average of 596,000 Twitter interactions per episode, followed by *WWE Monday Night Raw* (330,000 Twitter interactions), and *America's Got Talent* (308,000 Twitter interactions).[32]

Social advertising is an option for Twitter. Like many other platforms, Twitter Business has marketing focus on setting goals based on awareness, engagement, website traffic, app installs, and follower growth. Marketers set daily budgets and Twitter ads are bought by bidding in an auction where you pay per interaction, such as new follower or website click, or automatic bidding determines the best bid based on budget and goals.

Audiences for Twitter ads can be targeted by language, gender, interests, followers, device, geographic, keyword, and behavior targeting such as shopping and spending patterns. Also take advantage of remarketing via using a company's CRM list to target existing customers on Twitter or people who have visited a website but not performed certain actions.

Twitter Promote Mode automatically boosts the reach of organic posts to selected target audience for a flat-rate subscription. Twitter social ads can track impressions, engagement rate, results, and cost-per-result for each campaign objective. In Twitter ads it is actually recommended that you don't use #hashtags or @mentions so the audience does not click from the ad before completing your interaction goal.[33] For more details on Twitter advertising, see Twitter Flight School training at https://www.twitterflightschool.com/. **Twitter Flight School** is Twitter's free online training for marketing on Twitter.

Journalists are the largest, most active verified group worldwide on Twitter, making up nearly a quarter (24.6 percent) of authenticated users, followed by sports teams and athletes (17.9 percent) and actors and entertainers (13.6 percent).[34] Of full-time journalists, editorial writers, bloggers, and full-time freelance journalists, 70 percent see Twitter as a valuable social media tool with 27 percent indicating that it is their primary news resource.[35] With these statistics Twitter could especially apply to public relations efforts to garner earned media coverage.

Pinterest

Pinterest is a web and mobile social network that enables visual discovery, collection, and sharing and serves as a storage tool. A newer platform than Twitter, Pinterest began in 2010 and has grown to more than 300 million global monthly active users.[36] Globally Pinterest's ad audience is overwhelmingly female (70 percent) versus male (20 percent).[37] Top countries include the United States (76.3 million users), Germany (11.2 million users), and the United Kingdom (10.2 million users). Canada has 8.1 million Pinterest users and Australia has 5 million.[38]

In the United States, Pinterest users skew even more female with nearly three-quarters female (74 percent) versus male (26 percent).[39] Pinterest users are fairly evenly split across age groups, with the largest being twenty- to twenty-nine-year-olds (23 percent) and forty- to forty-nine-year-olds (22 percent) and then ten- to nineteen-year-olds (20 percent) with the remaining groups just under at thirty- to thirty-nine-year-olds (18 percent) and fifty years and older (17 percent).[40] Most Pinterest users have a college degree (43 percent), followed by some college (32 percent), and the lowest number (21 percent) has a high school or less education. Like Twitter, use tends to be more urban (43 percent) and suburban (36 percent) with rural use (21 percent) less than Facebook.[41] Over 17 percent of US Pinterest users are active on the platform daily[42] and 85 percent access this microblogging platform from a mobile device versus desktop or laptop.[43]

The two most popular activities on this platform are sharing photos (59 percent) plus finding and shopping for products (47 percent).[44] This online pin board has a high amount of business activity with one of the highest percentages of business accounts, which may help explain why only about one-fifth of Pinterest images contain faces. This channel is focused on products, designs, and ideas. It is not a family-photo-sharing service. Pinterest has an impressive influence on purchases with 87 percent of users purchasing a product because of Pinterest and 93 percent using Pinterest to plan a future purchase.[45]

Pinterest may be thought of more as a highly visual search engine where images that users like can be collected in categories for later reference. Some describe its main activity

Figure 8.2. Florist takes photo for Pinterest holiday decorating pin board.

https://ico© Sol Stock / iStock Photonmonstr.com/pinterest-1-png/

as "virtual scrapbooking," but this scrapbook enables users to collect and share photos, videos, and articles of their interests. Like other social sites, this channel starts with a profile where users place their name, bio, and photo. The main action is to pin. A pin is a post or update that is shared on the public network. Each pin added is automatically linked back to the website from which it came. A collection of pins is linked by a topic and collected on a board. A board of "Famous Chili" could have pictures of different chilis with links to the recipes.[46]

Campbell's food leverages the recipe and themed boards well for their Campbell's Kitchen recipe content.[47] The content on Pinterest tends to favor topics like fashion, food, DIY, and crafts. Despite being photo-centric, images with faces are not popular on this site. Pinterest and Instagram expert Alisa Meredith says that images with people tend to not feature faces so the viewer can envision themselves wearing the clothes or creating the craft. Images with faces perform better on Instagram. She also indicates that warmer colors tend to perform better on Pinterest versus cooler colors on Instagram.[48]

Like other social channels, users select other users to follow. Being a follower means the person can follow all of another user's pins or just certain boards. When following, those pins show up on the Pinterest home page under the following board. This activity functions like a Facebook or Twitter stream. Similar to a retweet on Twitter, users can repin an image they like and add it to their own board, but it still gives credit to the original author and maintains the source link. Authors can add captions to their images but are limited to five hundred characters and are not allowed to include hyperlinks in the text.[49]

Pinterest also enables users to like pins that they approve of, but this will not place it on that user's board the way a repin does. Similar to Twitter hashtags, Pinterest's pins and boards can be tagged by category, such as "Food & Drinks" or "Gifts." Gifts may be categorized with price tags and users can search for gifts by price range. The site has added price alerts that automatically send an email when the price of a pinned product drops.[50]

Social advertising is available on Pinterest. Like other social platforms, marketers set their goals first from building awareness, driving consideration, or getting conversions. The easiest way to advertise on Pinterest is to promote from existing pins. For more sophisticated efforts use Ads Manager to build full campaigns. Advertising formats include promoted pins, promoted video pins, promoted carousels (swipe through up to five images), and promoted app pins (download apps inside Pinterest). Promoted pins can be targeted based on keywords to appear in search results as related pins that can be targeted by match types or negative keywords and use a search term report to optimize ads.

Brands can target interests to reach people based on the types of boards they've created and the pins they have engaged with. There are more than 3,400 possible interest types from muscle cars and surfer girl fashion to shellfish recipes and Christmas sweaters. Targeting is also available by demographics such as location, language, device, or gender. Retargeting is available to website visitors, CMR database, or to people who have already engaged with the brand on Pinterest. There is also an "actalike" option similar to Facebook's lookalike audiences to target people with similar interests and behaviors.[51]

Pinterest Analytics measures campaign performance. The Pinterest tag tracks website conversions and how Pinterest users interact with the brand website. Third-party tools can also help measure foot traffic, app installs, and multi-touch attribution. The Pinterest Ads Manager tracks metrics such as cost per acquisition and return on ad spend. Ad partners can track ad viewability, impressions, and click delivery.

Like other social media platforms, Pinterest ads are purchased based on bidding for a certain action like click or engagement. Brands set maximum bids and set total budgets for a campaign period or set a daily budget. Pinterest social ads are unique by increasing views of already-published organic pins so they look and feel natural. Promoted pins can be targeted by category interests, keyword targeting, demographics, and behavioral audience targeting. Businesses are charged per performance as cost-per-click versus merely views.[52] For more details about marketing on Pinterest, see Pinterest Academy training at https://business.pinterest.com/pinterest-academy.

TikTok

TikTok is a social media short-form video app for creating and sharing lip-sync, comedy, and talent videos. This app was first created in China in 2016 as Douyin by ByteDance, a Chinese internet technology company. In 2017 it was launched as TikTok for markets outside China. TikTok first grew in popularity in Asia and then the app's parent company bought the social media video platform Musical.ly in late 2017. At the time Musical.ly had 200 million monthly active users.[53] In 2018 the two apps were merged under the TikTok name.[54]

Since the Musical.ly merger TikTok has quickly grown to 800 million global monthly users.[55] Unlike previous social networks that relied on organic growth of their platforms, Tik-Tok has invested in advertising its app on competing social platforms. Some have described the social platform as an "enormous meme factory,"[56] and "Vine (RIP) on steroids,"[57] while Tik-Tok's own tagline promises to "Make your day." Globally TikTok users are younger than most other social platforms with 41 percent aged sixteen to twenty-four years old and 60 percent are under thirty years old[58] with slightly more males (56 percent) than females (44 percent).[59] TikTok has 26.5 million users in the United States and 3.7 million in the United Kingdom.[60]

In the United States, TikTok is the second most popular mobile social networking app behind Facebook. Facebook users spend an average of thirteen hours per month on the app; TikTok users have risen to six hours per month in comparison to three hours per month for Snapchat.[61] Average session length is at the top, with nearly ten minutes per session compared to Pinterest's and Facebook's five minutes average and just two minutes for Snapchat.[62] TikTok is one of the first mobile-first platforms to use artificial intelligence and machine learning to show users more of what they like with advanced interest behavioral targeting.[63] Yet despite the growth and active engagement, TikTok is a niche audience with just roughly 2 percent reach among US mobile users, placing it sixteenth behind Facebook with 91 percent reach and Snapchat's 26 percent reach.[64] Even among gen Z (thirteen- to twenty-one-year-olds) Instagram (65 percent), YouTube (63 percent), and Snapchat (51 percent) are still the most popular social networks based on daily use compared to TikTok (11 percent).[65]

Like other social networks, TikTok users have a profile that includes a photo, username, and bio. Users follow other accounts to see their videos. Popular videos are liked with a heart counter appearing over the video and organized by hashtags that appear as trending on a Discover Page. Examples of trending hashtags include #whywebrokeup, #rocktober, and #facetrackingchallenge.[66] TikTok enables users to create short music and lip-sync videos of three to fifteen seconds and short looping videos of three to sixty seconds. Videos can be sped up, slowed down, and edited with filters and background music from music genres. Users can also create short lip-sync videos to popular songs. The react feature allows users to film their reactions in a small window over the video. The duet feature enables filming two videos alongside each other for duets. Unlike Facebook, videos by default have the sound turned on. Therefore, subtitles are not as important.[67]

Interactions occur through comments and messages. Users can create private accounts and set specific videos to public, friends only, or private similar to Facebook settings. The For You page provides a feed of recommended videos based on previous actions. There is a saved section for videos, hashtags, and sounds users want to keep. Videos created on TikTok can be easily shared on other social networks such as Instagram, Facebook, Twitter, and YouTube. The social platform has also become a new way for musicians to be discovered, launching unknown artists into stardom and record deals. Users can also search by song to find videos and challenges created around specific songs.[68]

The For You page is TikTok's front page, the landing page when users first open the app. The For You page is based on an algorithm designed to show you more content similar to what you have liked in the past from people you do not follow. At the bottom of the page users can find content outside the For You algorithm through the Search and Explore page.

This is the opposite of Instagram, where upon opening the app you first see content from users you follow; then you can switch to the Explore tab.

Thus, getting on this page is important to going viral and is a goal of many users to grow their followers, much like a brand trying to get into the newsfeed of Facebook users. TikTok has not released information on how to get a video onto the For You pages, but many speculate that it has to do with engagement such as likes and more people watching the entire video (retention rate). Hashtags users have indicated they like also most likely matter, but many also include #foryou, #foryoupage, or #fyp trying to get on this page, gain more exposure, and become TikTok famous.[69]

Organizations can participate by creating a brand channel and uploading and sharing relevant content. For a list of popular TikTok video trends, see table 8.1. Brands can work with influencers to spread messages to a broader audience.[70] TikTok also offers social ads including standard native in-feed video, Hashtag Challenges that encourage user-generated content, brand takeovers that run full screen, and branded lenses using AR face filters and 3D objects similar to Snapchat and Instagram. Ads can be targeted by age, gender, state-level geotargeting, and custom audiences from CRM lists. The platform boasts advanced interest targeting based on AI and ML technology.

Based on campaign goals, marketers set TikTok ad time periods and budgets and can be charged on a cost per thousand (CPM), cost per click (CPC), or cost per view (CPV) basis. TikTok's managed service platform offering fully self-serve biddable ads is under development and should be available soon. Early advertisers have included Grubhub to drive app downloads and the NFL to court younger viewers.[71] TV stars such as Jimmy Fallon have embraced the new platform. His #TumbleweedChallenge created eight thousand videos with more than nine million views in just seven days on the social app.[72]

This fast-growing social platform is not without controversy. The US government opened investigations into TikTok owner ByteDance, alleging the Chinese company may be censoring politically sensitive content and questioning how it stores personal data.[73] Users have also complained that their videos are being used in TikTok ads on other social platforms such as Snapchat and Instagram without being asked or paid. Yet everyone who signs up for TikTok agrees to the terms of service that allows this use.[74] These terms are similar to what other apps and social platforms have included in their small print, but perhaps they have been noticed more with the high profile of TikTok's ad campaign. These issues will be discussed further in chapter 15 along with California's new data privacy law (CCPA) that offers similar privacy protection and disclosure requirements to Europe's General Data

Table 8.1. Popular TikTok Video Trends

Hashtag challenges	Duets
Brand advertising	Slow-Mo
For You Page	Celebs
Memes	Cosplay
Influencer Sponsorships	Twins

Source: "10 Top TikTok Trends in 2019," MediaKix.com, September 27, 2019, https://mediakix.com/blog/tik-tok-trends/.

MINI CASE

Pharrell's "Happy"

The song "Happy" by Pharrell was originally produced for the animated hit *Despicable Me 2*, but the artist and producers wanted to broaden its appeal. The world's first twenty-four-hour video was created and launched at 24hoursofhappy.com. The song played and replayed for twenty-four hours while viewers could tune in at any time to see people going about their jobs dancing to "Happy."[a] The music video featured an interactive sequence showing Pharrell and three hundred people, some famous and some not, dancing around Los Angeles over the course of a day.

The viral video took the top prize, a Grand Prix in Cyber Craft, at Cannes Lions.[b] The idea spawned imitations, some of which became viral hits of their own. Clips of the video and these imitations spread via social sites like YouTube. After the viral release, sales of the single rose sharply by 14,000 percent. This promotion was one of the biggest hits of all time, drawing close to 10 million visitors from around the world. The United Nations even named March 20 as Happiness Day, sponsored by Pharrell.[c]

Today Pharrell still embraces viral content from everyday people. When visiting pharrellwilliams .com the viewer is invited to "Discover Pharrell's World Through His Fans." Clicking Enter brings you to an infinity scroll of cards representing individual fan favorite projects in music, tv, film, social good, art, design, and fashion. The site also invites anyone to "Create Your Card" to tell the world what inspires you. When viewers like a project they are invited to share it via Facebook, Twitter, or Pinterest.[d]

[a] Ed Owen, "24 Hours of Happy Wins Cannes Cyber Grand Prix," Global Academy of Digital Marketing, June 24, 2014, http://www.gogadm.com/24-hours-of-happy-wins-cannes-cyber-grand-prix.

[b] Ann-Christine Diaz, "Pharrell's 24-Hour 'Happy' Video, Chipotle's 'The Scarecrow' and Volvo's 'Live Tests' Take Cyber Grand Prix at Cannes," AdAge.com, June 18, 2014, http://adage.com/article/special-report-cannes-lions/pharrell-happy-chipotle-volvo-cannes-cyber-grand-prix/293773.

[c] Owen, "24 Hours of Happy Wins Cannes."

[d] "Welcome to PharrellWilliams.com," accessed November 4, 2019, https://pharrellwilliams.com/.

Protection Regulation (GDPR) and may change the way companies disclose and what they do with people's data.

Despite these concerns, brands have moved forward on the platform to reach its young user base. To promote the movie *Jumanji: The Next Level*, Sony Pictures launched a multichannel social campaign including #JumanjiChallenge on TikTok, gaining 1.4 billion worldwide video views in just one week. Celebrities Dwayne "The Rock" Johnson, Kevin Hart, and Nick Jonas helped promote the challenge, which featured a custom-branded effect with motion-activated technology that pulls users into the video game to the *Jumanji* soundtrack with body swapping and outfit and location changes. The campaign also featured augmented reality experiences on YouTube and Snapchat.[75]

The size of content and the user base of the leaders in microblogging are both smaller than in the big social networks. But the type of content, type of users, and channel capabilities might be perfect for the right big idea, target audience, and business objective. As FDR told his son, being brief can be much more powerful than being long. Also remember the lesson learned from Everett's and Lincoln's Gettysburg addresses. Short can be impactful. Be sure to explore the top microblogging platforms as social strategy options.

Media Sharing

Virginia Woolf said in *The Common Reader*, "For pleasure has no relish unless we share it." She tells us that her intention is for her essays to be read by the "common reader" who reads books for personal enjoyment.[76] Perhaps that is why social media sharing has become so popular on the internet and through apps on mobile devices. It is a common desire for people to share and read for enjoyment. When asked, 70 percent of internet users say they have shared some type of content on social media in the previous month. With the growing popularity of visually focused sites such as Instagram, it is no surprise that pictures are the most popular type of content, followed by people's opinions, status updates, links to articles, and recommendations.[77] The top reasons people post content are to share interesting things (61 percent), important things (43 percent), and funny things (43 percent). People also want to let others know what they believe in (39 percent), want to recommend a product or service (30 percent), and want to provide support to a cause or organization (30 percent) that they believe in.[78]

Video is also a rising form of sharing and viewing online. Cisco reports that by 2022, 82 percent of all the world's internet traffic will be online video—a rise from 64 percent in 2014. Social media video is growing in popularity in terms of views and power in terms of message.[79] Online video will continue to rise in importance; recent studies indicate younger audiences are watching less and less traditional live TV. For example, time spent watching live TV among eighteen- to twenty-four-year-olds in the United States plunged 30 percent in four years from 17 hours a week in 2014 to just 9.5 hours by 2018.[80]

These survey results give organizations an idea of the type of content to create that will most likely be shared through social media word-of-mouth. Another important point is to make sure sharing is easy by adding social media share buttons to all content. Take a look at the top media-sharing sites online and on mobile apps to see how YouTube, Instagram, and Snapchat could possibly fit with the organizational business objectives, target audience, and campaign idea.

YouTube

YouTube is a video-sharing website that enables users to upload, view, and share user-generated and corporate-media video. YouTube is the top video-sharing website, with more than two billion users or one-third of all people on the internet globally. Founded in 2005 and bought by Google in 2006, the video-sharing site has grown enormously from just six hours of video uploaded every minute to the platform in 2007 to more than 500 hours every minute in 2019.[81] YouTube is the second-largest social media platform with two billion global monthly active users[82] and 99 million active daily.[83] It is also important to note that YouTube is the world's second-largest search engine and third-most-visited website after Google and Facebook.[84]

In the United Kingdom, YouTube is the second-most-used social platform, close to Facebook with 37.1 million users.[85] It is reported that Canadians watch more YouTube than anyone in the world with 17.6 million people or 71 percent of all Canadian internet users.[86] In Australia YouTube is also the second-most-popular social platform with roughly the same number of users per month as Facebook with 15 million users of both per month and 50 percent of Australians on YouTube.[87]

In the United States there are 197 million YouTube viewers[88] and 51 percent are active daily.[89] US users are fairly evenly split between male (53 percent) and female (47 percent) and age groups skew slightly younger, with the largest group being eighteen- to twenty-nine-year-olds (32 percent), followed by thirty- to forty-four-year-olds (30 percent) and fifty-to sixty-four-year-olds (24 percent). Education levels are evenly spread with slightly more holding a college degree (36 percent) and having some college (35 percent) than a high school degree (29 percent), and users are roughly evenly divided between urban (36 percent), suburban (34 percent), and rural areas (30 percent).[90]

The introduction of YouTube in 2005, and later Vimeo, drove video use up from 33 percent to 72 percent in less than ten years. Some have dubbed this incredible increase the "YouTube Effect."[91] Viewing of YouTube videos has shifted to mobile (62 percent), but still nearly a quarter is viewed on desktop (24 percent), and now 14 percent is viewed through over-the-top media services displayed on TV.[92] **Over-the-top media services (OTT)** are streaming media TV services offered directly to viewers over the internet, bypassing cable, broadcast, and satellite platforms.[93] As more consumers cut the cord, streaming TV through devices like Apple TV, Fire TV, gaming consoles, and Smart TVs, YouTube viewing on TV should grow—especially with YouTube Live providing access to traditional cable and broadcast TV channels. Marketers should keep this in mind as a way to get back on consumers' TV sets after years of declining TV ads.

More than a video-hosting site, YouTube has features and characteristics of a social network. Users have profiles listing occupation and hobbies and upload a picture. They upload videos and mark them as public or private. Videos are separated by content that is organized into channels, from brand channels to channels on interests such as comedy videos, how-to videos, or business videos. Channels also follow other channels with mutual interests. Each video allows users to enter a title, description, and category. Popular categories include home improvement, fitness, sketch comedy, travel, beauty, and cooking.[94] The Dove brand has used its YouTube channel to distribute Dove Films for years. These videos draw viewers in and provide positive messages to consumers that are transferred to the beauty brand.[95]

What makes a popular brand video one that will go viral? In a study published in the *Journal of Interactive Marketing*, researchers analyzed brand-advertising videos collected by viral video firm Unruly. Content analysis of the top-performing videos found that average shares and views were higher for videos that told a story following a five-act dramatic form—stories that have a plot with an introduction, rising action, climax, falling action, and wrap up in a conclusion.[96] For further insight, see the "Social Media Story Template" introduced in chapter 5.

The top reasons people in the United States say they use YouTube are to be entertained (82 percent), to get news (23 percent), and to follow brands (18 percent).[97] Another survey reveals people use YouTube to follow celebrities (31 percent), follow brands (31 percent), and stay up to date on societal issues (26 percent).[98] Video content on YouTube is longer than videos on other social channels that limit length or don't perform well. The average length of a YouTube video is twelve minutes, with time varying based on video category from twenty-five minutes for gaming videos to seven minutes for music videos.[99] When creating a brand channel and videos on YouTube it is important to optimize content for search. Be sure to include searchable titles and descriptions using the right keywords. Also be sure to include calls to action telling viewers what you want them to do. Tell them to leave a comment or share the video, or give them a challenge, asking a question or inviting their own video. Information cards are also a YouTube feature that enables brands to make key moments of videos actionable where you can invite them to "learn more," "download the app," "buy now," or "watch more."[100]

Viewers can like or dislike a video as a general rating, enter comments, and offer video shout-outs. People can also reply to commenters directly or add to the general conversation. Videos get positive and negative comments, but may also get extremely negative, callous, anonymous remarks. These negative commenters enjoy bullying and are called trolls. **Trolls** intentionally post inflammatory, extraneous messages in online communities to provoke emotional responses.[101] Brands can engage trolls with witty remarks, block their accounts, or simply ignore them and let other commenters defend them.[102] Note that trolls are not a problem limited only to YouTube. Brands should also watch out for them in forums and in the comments sections of blogs, online articles, and on social network accounts.

A popular video version of blogging occurs on YouTube. A **video blog,** or vlog, is a combination of video, images, and text that can be thought of as a form of web television.[103]

Figure 8.3. Vloggers can amass millions of subscribers.

© Skynesher / iStock Photo

Vloggers talk about anything from politics to pop culture. Some are personal thoughts and chronicles of their lives. Others are comedy sketches or fictional dramas. Many have amassed millions of views and subscribers by doing product and service reviews. It may be worth a marketer's time to find the top reviewers in their category or industry and seek a positive review through outreach.[104] Just make sure to follow the FTC disclosure rules as discussed in chapter 15.

YouTube provides a variety of social ad and more traditional online ad options. Advertising on YouTube offers TrueView in-stream ads, which are the skippable or non-skippable video ads that appear before the main video. Brands can also place TrueView discovery ads that show up in YouTube search results, on the YouTube homepage, and alongside related videos. Bumper ads are short, six-second videos that work well on mobile. YouTube Masthead ads are also a consideration for the right campaign.[105] Like other social advertising, placing ads is set up around a campaign where you first select your goals, which can be leads, website traffic, brand awareness and reach, or product and brand consideration.

Targeting capabilities on YouTube are available via demographics such as age, gender, parental status, household income, college student, location, homeowner, and new parents. You can also target by device and interests through audience targeting, which is based on people's online behavior by topic, keywords, and life events. Video remarketing targets viewers based on previous YouTube actions such as viewing certain videos or channels.[106] YouTube ads are usually placed by setting up a daily budget. YouTube suggests at least $10.00 per day and for TrueView ads you pay only for engagement—when someone watches for at least thirty seconds or clicks on the ad.

Performance is measured with video analytics via metrics such as views, view rate, audience retention, earned actions such as clicks or likes, and percent of views and percent of cost. For each video you can also see total views, view rate, average cost per view, watch time, and average watch time. For more details on YouTube advertising, see Google Ads Video training and certification at https://skillshop.exceedlms.com/student/path/18216-google-ads-video-certification. **Google Ads Certification** provides free online training and certifications in Google Ads search, display, video, and shopping ads.[107]

Instagram

Instagram is an online mobile social-networking service that enables users to take photos and videos and share them on a variety of social networking platforms. Instagram launched in 2010, but this photo- and video-sharing social-networking service has grown tremendously via its mobile app. Facebook acquired Instagram in 2013, and integration with the popular social network has occurred for users and businesses. Instagram has more than one billion global monthly active users[108] and 500 million daily active users with most access occurring via mobile phone or tablet versus desktop or laptop.[109] Globally Instagram users are evenly split between male (50 percent) and female (50 percent) with many users skewing younger with the top age groups twenty-five to thirty-four (33 percent) and eighteen to twenty-four (32 percent). Instagram audience reach is highest in Turkey (58 percent) and Sweden (58 percent) and lowest in Nigeria (5 percent) and China

(0.3 percent). Instagram use of people thirteen years and older in the United Kingdom is 42 percent, 40 percent in Canada, and 30 percent in Australia. In the United States, 44 percent of people are on Instagram.[110]

In the United States, Instagram users skew more female (57 percent) than male (43 percent)[111] with the majority in younger age groups of twenty-five- to thirty-four-year-olds (36 percent) and eighteen- to twenty-four-year-olds (22 percent), followed by thirty-five- to forty-four-year-olds (19 percent).[112] For comparison, 64 percent of Instagram users are thirty-four years old and under whereas 60 percent of Facebook users are thirty-five years old and older.[113] Instagram users tend to have higher education, with 36 percent having a college degree, 35 percent with some college, and 29 percent with a high school degree or less. Users are slightly more in urban (36 percent) and suburban (34 percent) areas than rural (30 percent). Of all users in the United States, 63 percent access the social platform daily.[114]

Instagram is unique in that it enables users to take pictures and videos, apply digital filters, and share directly on other social sites, such as Facebook, Twitter, and Tumblr. Instagram is all about quality photos. Initially, these were distinctive in that they were square in shape, similar to the old-time Kodak Instamatic camera. Later the platform released this restriction, allowing differently shaped photos. The service also supports video by allowing up to fifteen-second short clips. This feature was originally added to compete with Twitter's Vine, which has now shut down. In 2018 IGTV was launched for long-form video distribution more like YouTube. Videos are vertical or horizontal full screen content up to an hour long divided into three categories: "For You," "Following," and "Popular," feeds.[115]

Figure 8.4. Instagram offers opportunities for photos, stories, and video brand content.

© Anatolly Sizov / iStock Photo

Users can create a social media profile with recently shared photos and a biography. Instagram users follow other users, like and comment on their photos, and share them. Instagram also uses hashtags to categorize photos and videos like Twitter and added "direct," which allows users to send photos only to a specific user or group, to compete with other popular services such as Snapchat.[116]

As the popularity and ad revenue of Snapchat grew, Instagram became more aggressive in pursuing younger users by adding Snapchat-like features including stories, slideshows, overlaid creative tools, disappearing DMs (direct messages), and face filters.[117] Besides reaching a younger audience, Instagram is also known for its high engagement rates and user-generated brand content. The popularity and growth of the social platform made news feeds too crowded and was switched to a timeline of users' photos based on an algorithm versus chronological order, reducing organic reach.[118] In a short time, Instagram grew to 500 million daily stories users[119] quickly outgrowing Snapchat's 203 million daily users.[120] The most popular social media activities on Instagram are viewing photos (77 percent), watching videos (51 percent), sharing content with everyone (45 percent) and sharing content one-to-one (31 percent).[121]

The most popular categories of posts on Instagram are sports teams, fashion, health and beauty, retail, influencers, home décor, media, hotels and resorts, and higher ed.[122] Look for a match in content type and quality. Also remember that Instagram is a visual-first platform so your content should be highly visual and you should work on creating a unique brand visual identity—whether photos or videos—that matches your brand voice. Think of specific fonts, colors, and layouts that will stand out, not just in a signal image but also in your Instagram account grid. Plan your posts for specific times when you will get the most engagement.

Consider Instagram-specific contests, such as asking fans to repost images and use branded hashtags. Be sure to reward people making branded posts by "regramming," giving credit and thanking your fans. In Instagram this is not as easy as a retweet or share. You have to screen shot and repost or use a third-party tool such as Later (https://later.com). Remember that most images on Instagram involve people versus images on other platforms like Pinterest that are mainly objects. Consider telling stories beyond a single post across your account and with hashtags.

Outside of Instagram try to create "Instagrammable" moments through live events, physical store, or fan challenges. What event, store display, or user challenge would create scenes that would make everyone stop and snap a picture or video and share? Be sure to include a call to action to call out your brand account and use a brand hashtag. **Instagrammable** is an object, scene, or moment deemed worthy of sharing, usually as a photo or video.[123] Instagram shopping is a great way to integrate purchase of products into the kind of lifestyle photos that work well on Instagram. Brands can create shopping posts and stories on their organic posts and stories. Customers can see and tap a product tag and be taken to a product description page where they see a photo, description, and price of the product with a link to the brand website where they can purchase it.[124]

Instagram can be used to post photos of products, employees, store environment, or events. Mobile-only Instagram serves as a great channel for engaging photo or video contests to gain user-generated content. If you are creating your own brand video for mobile, you may want to consider square video. Buffer Social points out that square video (1:1 aspect ratio) takes up to 78 percent more space in mobile news feeds than landscape video (16:9 aspect ratio). In content experiments across Instagram, Facebook, and Twitter, Buffer Social found that square video outperformed landscape video in likes, comments, and shares with 30 to 35 percent higher views and 80 to 100 percent increased engagement.[125] The platform does not allow links in post text. One link only is allowed in account bios. Brands must get creative in organic posts when driving actions by campaigns. That is why many focus on engagement for organic posts.

Hashtags matter in Instagram. Trending hashtags relevant to the brand can be used to participate in discussion to build brand community. Posts with at least one hashtag average over 12 percent more engagement and 75 percent of users take action, like visiting a website after viewing an Instagram advertising post. Instagram expert Sue B. Zimmerman says that the key to success is moving beyond the most popular hashtags and focusing on the niches that are relevant to your target audience. She also suggests adding five to twelve hashtags following the acronym CLEEP, which stands for category, location, emotion, event, and product. Good lighting, composition, and consistent design are important and the biggest mistake is leaving consumer questions unanswered.[126] Creating authentic brand stories in Instagram has also become an important strategy. Benefit Cosmetics UK follows best practices, creating custom photos for Instagram to attract followers and engagement.[127]

Social ads are available for Instagram within the app, through Facebook Ads Manager or an Instagram partner agency. The simplest way is to promote organic posts that are already doing well to reach new audiences. For more considered campaigns start by selecting an objective. Choose whether you want to drive awareness, consideration, or conversion. This will determine creating ads with reach, reach and frequency, brand awareness, local awareness, website clicks, website conversions, videos views, mobile app installs, or mobile app engagement objectives.

Instagram for Business offers photos ads, videos ads (up to sixty seconds), carousel ads (swipe through multiple photos), and stories ads—including interactive stories. In addition, collection ads allow direct purchase of products while browsing options through video, images, or both and Ads in Explore reach a broader audience. You can also create custom audiences for remarking to lists from brand CRM databases and lookalike audiences, which finds new people similar to existing brand customers.[128]

Targeting capabilities include by demographics such as age, gender, language, and location down to the city. Brands can also target by interests such as apps people use, ads they click, and accounts they follow, along with behavioral targeting based on what they do on and off Instagram and Facebook. Instagram ads are bought by setting a budget based on a campaign with a start and end date. Since Instagram ads are purchased through Facebook Ads Manager, they follow similar price options with bidding and reach and frequency. For more details on marketing and advertising on Instagram, see Facebook Blueprint training and certification at https://www.facebook.com/business/learn.[129]

Currently, sponsored content is mostly posts (66 percent) versus stories (34 percent), which represents an opportunity for more brands to stand out with stories content.[130] One example of a company that took advantage is Hydro Flask. To increase awareness and increase sales of new promotions, colors, and limited-edition designs, the brand worked with social marketing agency SocialWithin to create visual, branded vertical videos in Instagram Stories ads telling a short story in a creative way. Ads targeted lookalike audiences based on existing most valuable customers plus interest-based audience targeting that aligned with the brand and ideal audience. In just four months the brand captured 12,000 purchases for an 80 percent increase in revenue and a return sixteen times their advertising spend.[131]

Snapchat

Snapchat is a photo- and video-sharing messaging service in which media and messages are only available for a short time before disappearing. This mobile app was launched in 2011, but grew quickly in popularity among younger high school– and college-aged users due to the anonymity of messages being deleted after ten seconds.[132] Globally Snapchat has more than 287 million monthly active users[133] with 203 million active daily.[134] Snapchat's ad audience globally is more female (60 percent) than male (40 percent) and overwhelmingly younger with the larger age groups twenty-one- to thirty-four-year-olds (41 percent) and thirteen- to twenty-year-olds (38 percent). Only 18 percent of users are more than thirty-five years old. Snapchat's audience reach is highest in Saudi Arabia (52 percent) and Denmark (43 percent) and lowest in Thailand (0.9 percent) and Kenya (0.9 percent). Being a social platform built for mobile from the beginning, most access is from mobile versus desktop or laptop. Snapchat use among people thirteen years old and older in Canada is 24 percent, in the United Kingdom and Australia it is 30 percent, and in the United States it is 34 percent.[135]

In the United States, Snapchat users are more evenly split between male (53 percent) and female (47 percent) users but also skew younger with fifteen- to twenty-five-year-olds being the largest group (53 percent) and twenty-six- to thirty-five-year-olds the second (34 percent).[136] This means that 87 percent of Snapchat's users in the United States are under thirty-four years old compared to 64 percent of Instagram users and just 34 percent of Facebook users.[137] Among teens in the United States, the most popular social network is Snapchat (41 percent) closely followed by Instagram (35 percent) with Twitter and Facebook in a distant third (6 percent).[138] The top activities people report on Snapchat are viewing photos (64 percent), watching videos (50 percent), sharing content with everyone (46 percent), and sharing content one-to-one (45 percent),[139] with 61 percent doing these activities daily.[140]

The motivation for Snapchat came early on from CEO Evan Spiegel: "We're building a photo app that doesn't conform to unrealistic notions of beauty or perfection but rather creates a space to be funny, honest or whatever else you might feel like at the moment you take and share a Snap." The intention was to create a fun alternative to Facebook where obsession over perfect selfies, competition for friends and likes, and embarrassing tagged photos become permanent records. Snapchat's interface is different from other social platforms and dubbed by *Wall Street Journal* tech reporter Joanna Stern as "the most confusing social network." This difference may be one of the reasons older users stayed away from the platform early on, which was probably fine with younger users who didn't want their parents and grandparents there anyway.[141]

Figure 8.5. Snapchat is a social platform with high daily use by younger target audiences.

© Nikada / iStock Photo

Snaps are vertical photos and ten-second videos sent to one or many friends that disappear after viewing. Stories collect a series of pictures or videos that stay on the app for twenty-four hours, shared with friends or public. Lenses from augmented reality effects or lenses can be added and matched to facial movements such as "dog with tongue." 3D World Lenses add augmented reality animation over objects from the facing-out camera.

Text and art can also be added to snaps with emojis, graphics, and hand-drawn doodles for unique, personalized creations. Multiple filters can be applied to snaps including add time, temp stamp, or a location theme. Geofilters are overlays tied to a specific location or event only available when a user enters that area. Keep swiping to add multiple filters and effects. Users can also chat through messaging in the app and save snaps or screenshots in Memories. Snap Map allows users to share their location with friends or followers and Bit-mojis are integrated avatars of users. Discover is content from publishers and brands such as Cosmopolitan, ESPN, CNN and BuzzFeed.[142]

To add friends in Snapchat, the user must know a person's Snapchat username or already have them in their contacts. However, snapcodes (QR codes) offer a way to promote Snapchat accounts and add friends and are shared on other social channels or in print to be scanned on the phone.[143] A **QR code** (quick response code) is a two-dimensional bar code that provides quick and easy access to online information through a smartphone camera.[144] In 2018 Snapchat tried to redesign the interface, switching to a more algorithmic feed from chronological, mixing in more advertising and to make it easier for older users. The result was a backlash from its core younger users.[145] The latest version of the app divides Discover into three sections of tiles. Friends is where friends' stories appear, while Subscriptions shows Stories you have subscribed to. And the For You section is where recommended Shows and Stories, Sponsored Stories, and publisher Stories appear.

One way for brands to succeed on Snapchat is to grow friends organically and create valuable daily content. This does take a lot of effort but may be worth it for the unique engagement and demographic reach that other social media channels don't deliver. Also be sure to promote the Snapchat account on other brand marketing materials. Brands must post often due to the twenty-four-hour expiration on posts and stories. Brands can also screen shot or save content created in Snapchat and post on other channels to be repurposed beyond the twenty-four-hour story expiration. Influencer takeovers can increase followers and engagement, along with user-generated content, discounts and promocodes, exclusive content, and promoted events.[146]

Snapchat for Business offers a variety of advertising options. Through the ad manager you set up campaigns by selecting objectives such as other social platforms for awareness, consideration, and conversions through branding, app installs, traffic and conversions, website traffic and conversions, engagement, video views, lead generation, and catalog sales. Brands can run Snap Ads that appear with Stories and drive action with a swipe, Collection Ads that showcase of series of products to shop for and buy, and Story Ads with a series of Snaps with a sponsored Discover tile. Sponsored AR Lenses are engaging augmented reality experiences users can create and send to friends. Sponsored Filters are branded overlays of graphics and type users can add to their photo and video messages. Commercials are six-second non-skippable videos that run within premium Snapchat content.[147]

Snapchat audiences can be targeted with demographics such as age, gender, income, and parental status plus locations by country and location category like universities or radiuses around specific addresses. Target by behaviors and interests, add custom audiences to retarget customers from previous actions and CRM data, and target lookalike audiences similar to existing customers. The Ads Manager provides real-time reporting to test, learn, and optimize campaigns based on metrics like impressions, swipes, app installs, viewability, reach, resonance, reaction, and web conversions across devices with Snap Pixel.[148] Papa John's is an example of a brand that used a Snapchat AR lens that overlaid heart-shaped pizzas over selfie Snaps to share with loved ones. The effort resulted in an increase in orders of 25 percent and a boost in awareness of 6 percent.[149] For more details on how to grow business on Snapchat, see Snapchat Explore training at https://snapchatexplore.exceedlms .com. **Snapchat Explore** is Snapchat's free training for how to use Snapchat's advertising solutions to meet business objectives.[150]

Virginia Woolf wanted to reach the "common reader" with her writing. Never since the invention of the printing press has such an explosion in technology enabled more reading and sharing of stories and information. Which of the top three media-sharing channels is right for your audience, message, and big idea? Other social media–sharing channels to consider are Imgur, Flickr, Vimeo, and SlideShare. Live-streaming video apps like Periscope and Facebook or Instagram Live will be covered in chapter 9.

Chapter 8 Checklist

Social media can change quickly. Visit Post Control Marketing (http://www.postcontrol marketing.com) for updates, but also use this chapter checklist to briefly check how social media statistics in this chapter have changed since publication.

✓ How have microblogs and media–sharing social media changed? Are Twitter, Pinterest, TikTok, YouTube, Instagram, and Snapchat still the top platforms?

✓ Do a quick search to confirm key statistics for each of the social media channel options covered in this chapter. Update numbers for monthly and daily users, global and country use, user demographics such as gender, age, education, and income, plus new features. What type of content performs best on each?

✓ Check for new paid social media opportunities. Have any of the social media platforms covered in this chapter added new advertising options? Has the General Data Protection Regulation (see chapter 13), California Consumer Protection Act (see chapter 15), or other regulations changed the targeting and tracking capabilities of social media campaigns?

 SOCIAL PLAN PART 8

Choose Most Strategic Content Sharing

Explore and choose content-sharing channels that best fit your social media plan. Consider all the top social media–sharing platforms (ask questions in table 7.1). Research each, looking at the number and makeup of the users to ensure a match with your target audience. Do the brand, product, or service and the big idea fit the type of content that is shared on the channel? How can the organization leverage the real-time, seasonal, and topical characteristics of microblogging? What type of content is ideal for sharing—text, photo, video, AR? Report all findings and ideas in these areas:

1. Identify microblogs where the target audience is active.
2. Describe the type of content that is shared and popular on each.
3. Find photo- and video-sharing platforms that match the target audience.
4. Explain what content the brand could create.

For a condensed version of the social plan see appendix A: Three-Part Social Plan.

KEY CONCEPTS

microblogging
Slack
Twitter
Twitter Cards

Twitter Chats
Twitter Flight School
Pinterest
TikTok

YouTube

over-the-top media service (OTT)

trolls

video blog

Google Ads Certification

Instagram

Instagrammable

Snapchat

QR code

Snapchat Explore

QUESTIONS FOR DISCUSSION

1. "Tweets per minute" is a measure of total activity on Twitter. It is known to spike during large events, such as the Super Bowl blackout. How could a brand take advantage of these spikes in Twitter activity?
2. Pinterest is unique in its user base and content. Make a list of brands that would work well on the microblog and a list of brands for which Pinterest is not a good fit. Explain your answers.
3. Look at the difference between TikTok posts, Instagram posts, and Snapchat posts. Do some research and explain how a brand should adjust their content to be popular on each platform.
4. Social media can get amateurs and pros into sticky situations. Nobody is perfect, but all should be responsible and respectful on social media. If someone makes an inappropriate tweet, what should they do? What should employers do? When does an inappropriate tweet rise to the level of termination or resignation? When should there be forgiveness?

ADDITIONAL EXERCISES

1. For this exercise, join the top microblogs and get an idea of what is happening in this social space. Follow some industry leaders on Twitter, follow your competition, and search for some trending topics. What are people doing and saying on the site? Is content mostly text or pictures or are they sharing video? Do they provide links? Do the same for Pinterest. Who knows? You may discover a brilliant business idea, or simply a great new BBQ recipe. Have fun, but also look for strategic business opportunities. How could your business engage consumers, influencers, and the media through microblogging?
2. Jump into the content-sharing sites and look for characteristics your brand, product, or service can leverage. Start with YouTube. You have probably viewed hundreds of videos here, but ask yourself, "What makes a video popular or of interest to me?" Also, consider what type of consumer-oriented video your organization could produce to help meet your plan objectives. Do the same on Instagram, TikTok, Pinterest, and Snapchat. You are simply exploring here. If these sites are not right for your plan, then don't include them. You want to try them all, but cannot and should not implement them all.

Notes

1. "'Be sincere. Be brief. Be seated.' Public Speaking's Best Advice?" GingerPublicSpeaking .com, accessed October 14, 2019, http://www.gingerpublicspeaking.com/be-sincere-be-brief-be -seated-public-speakings-best-advice.

2. "Edward Everett, 'Gettysburg Address,'" VoicesofDemocracy.com, accessed October 14, 2019, http://voicesofdemocracy.umd.edu/everett-gettysburg-address-speech-text.

3. "The Gettysburg Address," AbrahamLincolnOnline.com, accessed October 14, 2019, http://www.abrahamlincolnonline.org/lincoln/speeches/gettysburg.htm.

4. "The Gettysburg Address," History.com, September 26, 2019, https://www.history.com/topics/american-civil-war/gettysburg-address.

5. "Top 10 Greatest Speeches," Time.com, accessed October 14, 2019, http://content.time.com/time/specials/packages/completelist/0,29569,1841228,00.html.

6. "Microblogging," TechTerms.com, March 12, 2014, https://techterms.com/definition/microblogging.

7. "Trendsmap," Trendsmap.com, accessed October 14, 2019, http://trendsmap.com.

8. "About Slack," Slack.com, accessed October 14, 2019, https://slack.com/.

9. Emily Pronin and Daniel Wegner, "Manic Thinking: Independent Effects of Thought Speed and Thought Content on Mood," *Psychological Science* 17, no. 9 (2006): 807–813.

10. "About Twitter," Twitter.com, accessed October 14, 2019, https://about.twitter.com/en_us.html.

11. Simon Kemp, "Digital in 2019," wearesocial.com, 2019, https://wearesocial.com/global-digital-report-2019.

12. Ingrid Lunden, "Twitter Q2 Beats on Sales of $841M and EPS of $0.20, New Metric of mDAUs up to 139M," TechCrunch.com, July 26, 2019, https://techcrunch.com/2019/07/26/twitter-q2-earnings/.

13. Kemp, "Digital in 2019."

14. "Twitter by the Numbers: Stats, Demographics & Fun Facts," OmincoreAgency.com, September 5, 2019, https://www.omnicoreagency.com/twitter-statistics/.

15. Michael Kan, "Like It or Not, You're Getting Twitter's Redesigned Website Soon," PCMag.com, July 15, 2019, https://www.pcmag.com/news/369546/twitters-redesigned-desktop-website-will-replace-the-old-la.

16. Kemp, "Digital in 2019."

17. "Distribution of Twitter Users in the United States as of September 2018, by Age Group," Video Advertising Bureau, December 10, 2018, https://www.statista.com/statistics/192703/age-distribution-of-users-on-twitter-in-the-united-states/.

18. "Social Media Fact Sheet," PewInternet.org, June 12, 2019, https://www.pewinternet.org/fact-sheet/social-media/.

19. "Social Media Fact Sheet," PewInternet.org.

20. Aliza Rosen, "Tweeting Made Easier," Twitter.com (blog), November 7, 2017, https://blog.twitter.com/official/en_us/topics/product/2017/tweetingmadeeasier.html.

21. Brandon Smith, "The Beginner's Guide to Twitter," Mashable.com, June 5, 2012, http://mashable.com/2012/06/05/twitter-for-beginners.

22. Aja Romano, "At Long Last, Twitter Brought Back Chronological Timelines. Here's Why They're So Beloved," Vox.com, September 20, 2018, https://www.vox.com/culture/2018/9/20/17876098/twitter-chronological-timeline-back-finally.

23. "Social Media Activities on Select Social Networks by Social Media Users in the United States in February 2019," eMarketer, March 22, 2019, https://www.statista.com/statistics/200843/social-media-activities-by-platform-usa/.

24. "Distribution of Tweets Sent by Twitter Users in the United States as of December 2018, by Engagement," Pew Research Center, April 24, https://www.statista.com/statistics/1018825/share-of-us-adult-tweets/.

25. "Optimize Tweets with Cards," Twitter.com, accessed October 14, 2019, https://developer.twitter.com/en/docs/tweets/optimize-with-cards/guides/getting-started.

26. Rob Mathison with files from Matt Diederichs, "A Step-by-Step Guide to Hosting a Successful Twitter Chat," Hootsuite.com (blog), May 22, 2019, https://blog.hootsuite.com/a-step-by-step-guide-to-twitter-chats/.

27. Ruby Rusine, "10 Benefits of Twitter Chats for Your Business," SocialSuccessMarketing.com (blog), March 29, 2016, http://socialsuccessmarketing.com/benefits-of-twitter-chats-for-business/.

28. "Twitter Usage Statistics," InternetLiveStats.com, accessed October 9, 2019, http://www.internetlivestats.com/twitter-statistics.

29. Casey Newton, "You Can Now Broadcast Live Video from the Twitter App," The Verge.com, December 14, 2016, https://www.theverge.com/2016/12/14/13942840/twitter-live-video-periscope-integration.

30. "HGTV Twitter Account," accessed October 14, 2019, https://twitter.com/hgtv.

31. "Mobile Fact Sheet," PewInternet.org, January 12, 2019, http://www.pewinternet.org/fact-sheet/mobile/.

32. "Most Popular Television Series in the United States in 2018, Sorted by Average Number of Twitter Interactions (in 1,000s)," Nielsen, December 20, 2018, https://www.statista.com/statistics/304363/us-twitter-tv-series-audience-buzz/.

33. "Twitter Ads Campaigns," Business.Twitter.com, accessed October 8, 2019, https://business.twitter.com/en/twitter-ads.html.

34. Benjamin Mullin, "Report: Journalists Are Largest, Most Active Verified Group on Twitter," Poynter.org, May 26, 2015, https://www.poynter.org/2015/report-journalists-are-largest-most-active-group-on-twitter/346957/.

35. "Shareability, Credibility, & Objectivity: The State of Journalism in 2018," Muck Rack & Zeno Group, accessed October 8, 2019, https://info.muckrack.com/journalistsurvey.

36. Kemp, "Digital in 2019."

37. "Distribution of Pinterest Users Worldwide as of July 2019, by Gender," DataReportal, Hootsuite, and We Are Social, July 18, 2019, https://www.statista.com/statistics/248168/gender-distribution-of-pinterest-users/.

38. "Leading Countries Based on Number of Pinterest Users as of July 2019 (in Millions)," DataReportal, Hootsuite, and We Are Social, July 18, 2019, https://www.statista.com/statistics/328106/pinterest-penetration-markets/.

39. "Distribution of Pinterest App Users in the United States as of July 2019, by Gender," App Ape, August 21, 2019, https://www.statista.com/statistics/408225/us-pinterest-reach-penetration/.

40. "Distribution of Pinterest App Users in the United States as of July 2019, by Age Group," App Ape, August 21, 2019, https://www.statista.com/statistics/248165/age-distribution-of-us-pinterest-users-mobile/.

41. "Mobile Fact Sheet," PewInternet.org.

42. "Share of Active Pinterest App Users in the United States as of July 2019," App Ape, August 21, 2019, https://www.statista.com/statistics/318823/pinterest-use-usa/.

43. "Your Inspiring Ideas Belong Here," Pinterest for Business, accessed October 8, 2019, https://business.pinterest.com/en.

44. "Social Media Activities," eMarketer.

45. Emma Dunbar, "10 Reasons Why Your Business Needs to Be on Pinterest," Business.Pinterest.com, September 16, 2015, https://business.pinterest.com/en/blog/10-reasons-why-your-business-needs-to-be-on-pinterest.

46. Rebekah Radice, "How to Use Pinterest for Business: 'Getting Started' Guide for Beginners," PostPlanner.com (blog), accessed October 14, 2019, https://www.postplanner.com/how-to-use-pinterest-for-business-beginner-guide/.

47. Campbell's Kitchen Pinterest Account, accessed October 14, 2019, http://www.pinterest.com/campbellkitchen.

48. Alisa Meredith, Jay Baer, and Adam Brown, "Why Pinterest Hates Faces and Instagram Loves Them," Social Pros Podcast, ConvinceAndConvert.com, accessed October 14, 2019, http://www.convinceandconvert.com/podcasts/episodes/why-pinterest-hates-faces-and-instagram-loves-them/.

49. Radice, "How to Use Pinterest for Business."

50. Donna Tam, "Pinterest, Now with Price Alerts, Panders to Shoppers," CNET.com, August 1, 2013, http://news.cnet.com/8301-1023_3-57596521-93/pinterest-now-with-price-alerts-panders-to-shoppers.

51. "How to Advertise on Pinterest," Business.Pinterest.com, accessed October 8, 2018, https://business.pinterest.com/en.

52. "How to Advertise on Pinterest," Business.Pinterest.com.

53. Dan Rys, "Musical.ly, Apple Music Ink New Partnership, With More to Come," Billboard.com, April 28, 2017, https://www.billboard.com/articles/business/7776302/musically-apple-music-partnership.

54. Rebecca Jennings, "TikTok, Explained," Vox.com, July 12, 2019, https://www.vox.com/culture/2018/12/10/18129126/tiktok-app-musically-meme-cringe.

55. Kemp, "Digital in 2019."

56. Jim Tolentino, "How TikTok Holds Our Attention," NewYorker.com, September 23, 2019, https://www.newyorker.com/magazine/2019/09/30/how-tiktok-holds-our-attention.

57. Brian Feldman, "Unraveling the Mystery of the TikTok 'For You' Page," NYMag.com, November 12, 2019, http://nymag.com/intelligencer/2019/11/how-to-get-on-the-tiktok-for-you-page.html.

58. Chris Beer, "Is TikTok Setting the Scene for Music on Social Media?" Blog.GlobalIndex.com, January 3, 2019, https://blog.globalwebindex.com/trends/tiktok-music-social-media/.

59. Maryam Mohsin, "10 TikTok Statistics That You Need to Know in 2019 [Infographic]," Oberlo.com, July 23, 2019. https://www.oberlo.com/blog/tiktok-statistics.

60. Ellie Zolfagharifard, "The Incredible Rise of TikTok in the West Raises Questions for Regulators," *The Telegraph*, April 17, 2019, https://www.telegraph.co.uk/technology/2019/04/03/incredible-rise-tiktok-west-raises-questions-regulators/; "13 TikTok Statistics Marketers Need to Know: TikTok Demographics & Key Data," Mediakix.com, accessed October 9, 2019, https://mediakix.com/blog/top-tik-tok-statistics-demographics/.

61. "Most Popular Mobile Social Networking Apps in the United States as of June 2019, by User Engagement (in Minutes per Month),"Verto Analytics, September 9, 2019, https://www.statista.com/statistics/579358/most-popular-us-social-networking-apps-ranked-by-engagement/.

62. "Most Popular Mobile Social Networking Apps in the United States as of June 2019, by Average Session Duration (in Minutes)," Verto Analytics, September 9, 2019, https://www.statista.com/statistics/579411/top-us-social-networking-apps-ranked-by-session-length/.

63. "TikTok Ads," TikTok.com, accessed October 9, 2019, https://ads.tiktok.com/i18n/?redirect_uri=%2F%3Frefer%3Dtiktok_web.

64. "Most Popular Mobile Social Networking Apps in the United States as of June 2019, by Reach," Verto Analytics, September 9, 2019, https://www.statista.com/statistics/579334/most-popular-us-social-networking-apps-ranked-by-reach/.

65. "Most Popular Social Networks and Apps According to Gen Z Social Media Users in the United States as of January 2019, Based on Daily Usage," eMarketer, August 16, 2019, https://www.statista.com/statistics/306947/us-teens-social-media-apps-dau/.

66. "Trending," TikTok.com, accessed October 9, 2019, https://www.tiktok.com/tag/mosaiczoom?langCountry=en.

67. Tolentino, "How TikTok Holds Our Attention."

68. Jennings, "TikTok, explained."

69. Julia Alexander, "Your Guide to Using TikTok: Beyond the App's 'For You' Page," April 2, 2019, https://www.theverge.com/2019/4/2/18201898/tiktok-guide-for-you-challenge-creator -trend-algorithm-privacy; Feldman, "Unraveling the Mystery."

70. "TikTok Marketing for Beginners," InfluencerMarketingHub.com, accessed October 9, 2019, https://influencermarketinghub.com/tiktok-marketing-for-beginners-a-marketers-guide-to -advertising-on-tiktok/.

71. Mikey Dunn, "What You Need to Know About Advertising on TickTok," SocialMedia Today.com, August 20, 2019, https://www.socialmediatoday.com/news/what-you-need-to-know -about-advertising-on-tiktok/561235/; "TikTok Ads," TikTok.com; Dani Lee, "The NFL is Now on TikTok to Court Younger Viewers," TheVerge.com, September 3, 2019, https://www.theverge .com/2019/9/3/20847461/tiktok-nfl-partnership-football-weready-challenge.

72. "13 TikTok Statistics Marketers Need to Know," Mediakix.com.

73. Greg Roumeliotis, Yingzhi Yang, Echo Wang, and Alexandra Alper, "Exclusive: U.S. Open National Security Investigation into TikTok—Sources," Reuters.com, November 1, 2019, https://www.reuters.com/article/us-tiktok-cfius-exclusive/exclusive-u-s-opens-national-security -investigation-into-tiktok-sources-idUSKBN1XB4IL.

74. Garett Sloane, "TikTok Users Are Surprised to Find Themselves in Ads for the App," AdAge.com, October 7, 2019, https://adage.com/article/digital/tiktok-users-are-surprised -find-themselves-ads-app/2204996.

75. "Sony Pictures Digital Marketing Raises the Stakes on Augmented Reality with 'Jumanji: The Next Level' Campaign," APNews.com, December 12, 2019, https://apnews.com/ PRNewswire/8063781fcdfa37f5e29d2733b4ca9495.

76. Virginia Woolf, *The Common Reader* (New York: Harcourt, 1984).

77. "What Internet Users Like to Share on Social Media Sites," MarketingCharts.com, September 19, 2013, http://www.marketingcharts.com/wp/online/what-internet-users-like-to -share-on-social-media-sites-36804.

78. Ayaz Nanji, "Why People Share on Social Media," MarketingProfs.com, http://www .marketingprofs.com/charts/2013/11564/why-people-share-on-social-media.

79. "Cisco Predicts More IP Traffic in the Next Five Years Than in the History of the Internet," Cisco.com, November 27, 2018, https://newsroom.cisco.com/press-release-content ?type=webcontent&articleId=1955935.

80. "Average Weekly Time Spent Watching Live TV among 18-to-24 Year-Olds in the United States from 2nd Quarter 2014 to 2nd Quarter 2018 (in Hours)," ScreenMedia, January 2, 2018, https://www.statista.com/statistics/800215/time-spent-live-tv-millennials/.

81. "Hours of Video Uploaded to YouTube Every Minute as of May 2019," YouTube and Tubefilter, May 7, 2019, https://www.statista.com/statistics/259477/hours-of-video-uploaded -to-youtube-every-minute/.

82. "Number of Monthly Logged-In YouTube Viewers Worldwide as of May 2019 (in Billions)," CNET, May 2, 2019, https://www.statista.com/statistics/859829/logged-in-youtube -viewers-worldwide/.

83. Amy Gesenhues, "Mary Meeker: Social Media Usage Is Flat Globally, Mobile Ad Spend Continues to Climb," MarketingLand.com, June 12, 2019, https://marketingland.com/ mary-meeker-social-media-usage-is-flat-globally-mobile-ad-spend-continues-to-climb-262403.

84. Kit Smith, "36 Fascinating and Incredible YouTube Statistics," Brandwatch.com (blog), June 8, 2016, https://www.brandwatch.com/blog/36-youtube-stats-2016/.

85. Alison Battisby, "The Latest UK Social Media Statistics for 2019," AvocadoSocial .com February 12, 2019, https://www.avocadosocial.com/latest-social-media-statistics-and -demographics-for-the-uk-in-2019/.

86. "YouTube Stats," AlgonquinCollege.org, accessed October 10, 2019, https://www.algonquincollege.com/ac-social-media/youtube-stats/.

87. David Cowling, "Social Media Statistics Australia—January 2019," SociaMediaNews.com.au, https://www.socialmedianews.com.au/social-media-statistics-australia-january-2019/.

88. "Number of YouTube Viewers in the United States from 2018 to 2022 (in Millions)," eMarketer, April 10, 2019, https://www.statista.com/statistics/469152/number-youtube-viewers-united-states/.

89. "How Often Do You Use YouTube?" Statista, May 21, 2019, https://www.statista.com/forecasts/1011631/frequency-of-using-youtube-in-the-us.

90. "Social Media Fact Sheet," PewInternet.org.

91. Jeff Bullas, "35 Mind Numbing YouTube Facts, Figures and Statistics—Infographic," Jeffbullas.com (blog), May 23, 2012, http://www.jeffbullas.com/2012/05/23/35-mind-numbing-youtube-facts-figures-and-statistics-infographic.

92. "Distribution of YouTube Video Views in the United States as of 1st Quarter 2018, by Platform," Pixability, April 30, 2018, https://www.statista.com/statistics/727572/youtube-video-audience-distribution-platform-usa/.

93. Clay Halton, "Over-the-Top (OTT)," Investopedia.com, July 17, 2019, https://www.investopedia.com/terms/o/over-top.asp.

94. Eric Larson, "The Beginner's Guide to YouTube," Mashable.com, October 5, 2013, http://mashable.com/2013/10/05/youtube-beginner-guide.

95. "Dove United States YouTube Channel," YouTube.com, accessed October 14, 2019, https://www.youtube.com/user/doveunitedstates.

96. Keith A. Quesenberry and Michael K. Coolsen, "Drama Goes Viral: Effects of Story Development on Shares and Views of Online Advertising Videos," *Journal of Interactive Marketing* 48 (November 2019): 1–16.

97. "Leading YouTube Usage Reasons According to Users in the United States as of 3rd Quarter 2019," AudienceProject, October 3, 2019, https://www.statista.com/statistics/187007/youtube-usage-reasons-usa/.

98. "What Do You Use YouTube for?" Statista, May 21, 2019, https://www.statista.com/forecasts/1011656/drivers-for-youtube-usage-in-the-us.

99. "Average YouTube Video Length as of December 2018, by Category (in Minutes)," Pex, and Rain News, June 10, 2019, https://www.statista.com/statistics/1026923/youtube-video-category-average-length/.

100. "YouTube Playbook for Small Business," Services.Google.com, accessed October 10, 2019, https://services.google.com/fh/files/misc/youtube_playbook_for_small_businesses_en.pdf.

101. "Troll," Merriam-Webster.com, accessed November 4, 2019, https://www.merriam-webster.com/dictionary/troll.

102. Larson, "Beginner's Guide to YouTube."

103. "Vlog," Merriam-Webster.com, accessed November 4, 2019, https://www.merriam-webster.com/dictionary/vlog.

104. "YouTube Advertising: How It Works," YouTube.com, accessed October 10, 2019, https://www.youtube.com/ads/how-it-works/.

105. "YouTube Advertising: How It Works," YouTube.com.

106. "About Targeting for Video Campaigns," Support.Google.com, accessed October 10, 2019, https://support.google.com/google-ads/answer/2454017.

107. "About the Google Ads Certification," Support.Google.com, accessed November 15, 2019, https://support.google.com/google-ads/answer/9029201?hl=en.

108. Kemp, "Digital in 2019."

109. Gesenhues, "Mary Meeker."

110. Kemp, "Digital in 2019."

111. "Distribution of Instagram Users in the United States as of August 2019, by Gender," NapoleonCat, September 9, 2019, https://www.statista.com/statistics/530498/instagram-users-in-the-us-by-gender/.

112. "Distribution of Instagram Users in the United States as of August 2019, by Age Group," NapoleonCat, September 9, 2019, https://www.statista.com/statistics/398166/us-instagram-user-age-distribution/.

113. "Distribution of Facebook Users in the United States as of August 2019, by Age Group," NapoleonCat, September 9, 2019, https://www.statista.com/statistics/187549/facebook-distribution-of-users-age-group-usa/.

114. "Social Media Fact Sheet," PewInternet.org.

115. Taylor Loren, "IGTV: The Ultimate Guide to Instagram's New Video Platform," Later.com, August 29, 2019, https://later.com/blog/igtv/.

116. Josh Constine, "Instagram Launches Selfie Filters, Copying the Last Big Snapchat Feature," Techcrunch.com, May 16, 2017, https://techcrunch.com/2017/05/16/instagram-face-filters/.

117. Ed Oswald, "While Everyone Freaked Out about Instagram's New Logo, A Bigger Change Took Place," DigitalTrends.com, May 16, 2016, https://www.digitaltrends.com/social-media/instagram-algorithm/.

118. Constine, "Instagram Launches Selfie Filters."

119. "Number of Daily Active Instagram Stories Users from October 2016 to January 2019 (in Millions)," Facebook, January 30, 2019, https://www.statista.com/statistics/730315/instagram-stories-dau/.

120. Matt Southern, "Daily Users—Now at 203 Million in Total," SearchEngineJournal.com, July 23, 2019, https://www.searchenginejournal.com/snapchat-gains-13-million-daily-users-now-at-203-million-in-total/317983/.

121. "Social Media Activities," eMarketer.

122. "Average Number of Daily Brand Posts on Instagram in 2018, by Vertical," Rival IQ, February 15, 2019, https://www.statista.com/statistics/873935/daily-instagram-brand-posts-by-vertical/.

123. Katy Steinmetz, "'Instagram' Is Officially a Verb, According to Merriam-Webster," Time.com, September 4, 2018, https://time.com/5386603/instagram-verb-merriam-webster/.

124. "Shopping on Instagram," Facebook.com, accessed October 10, 2019, https://www.facebook.com/business/help/582645198813984.

125. Brian Peters, "Square vs. Landscape Video—$2.5K Worth of Experiments: Here's How They Compare," Buffer.com, May 2, 2019, https://buffer.com/resources/square-video-vs-landscape-video.

126. Sue B. Zimmerman, Jay Baer, and Adam Brown, "Why Stories Is the Key to Company Instagram Success Today," Social Pros Podcast, ConvinceAndConvert.com, accessed October 14, 2019, http://www.convinceandconvert.com/podcasts/episodes/stories-key-company-instagram-success-today/.

127. "Benefit Cosmetics UK Instagram Post," Instagram.com, accessed October 14, 2019, https://instagram.com/benefitcosmetics/?hl=en.

128. "Build Your Business on Instagram," Business.Instagram.com, accessed October 14, 2019, https://business.instagram.com/advertising/.

129. "Build Your Business on Instagram," Business.Instagram.com/.

130. "Distribution of Sponsored Content on Instagram Worldwide in 2018, by Type," eMarketer, February 14, 2019. Statista. Accessed October 10, 2019, https://www.statista.com/statistics/986026/instagram-sponsored-content-by-type/.

131. "Colder. Hotter. Longer," Business.Instagram.com, accessed October 10, 2019, https://business.instagram.com/success/hydro-flask.

132. "Estimated Number of Monthly Active Snapchat Users from 2013 to 2016 (in Millions)," Statista, August 4, 2017, https://www.statista.com/statistics/626835/number-of-monthly-active-snapchat-users/.

133. Kemp, "Digital in 2019."

134. "Number of Daily Active Snapchat Users from 1st Quarter 2014 to 2nd Quarter 2019 (in Millions)," Snap Inc., July 23, 2019, https://www.statista.com/statistics/545967/snapchat-app-dau/.

135. Kemp, "Digital in 2019."

136. "Percentage of U.S. Internet Users Who Use Snapchat as of 3rd Quarter 2019, by Age Group," AudienceProject, October 3, 2019, https://www.statista.com/statistics/814300/snapchat-users-in-the-united-states-by-age/.

137. "Distribution of Facebook Users in the United States as of August 2019, by Age Group," NapoleonCat, September 9, 2019, https://www.statista.com/statistics/187549/facebook-distribution-of-users-age-group-usa/.

138. "Most Popular Social Networks of Teenagers in the United States from Fall 2012 to Spring 2019," Piper Jaffray and Business Wire, April 8, 2019, https://www.statista.com/statistics/250172/social-network-usage-of-us-teens-and-young-adults/.

139. "Social Media Activities," eMarketer.

140. "Social Media Fact Sheet," PewInternet.org.

141. Joanna Stern, "How to Use Snapchat," WSJ.com, January 12, 2016, https://www.wsj.com/articles/snapchat-101-learn-to-love-the-worlds-most-confusing-social-network-1452628322.

142. Maggie Tillman, "How Does Snapchat Work and What's the Point?" Pocket-lint.com, June 11, 2019, https://www.pocket-lint.com/apps/news/snapchat/131313-what-is-snapchat-how-does-it-work-and-what-is-it-used-for.

143. Margaret Rouse, "QR Code (Quick Response Code)," WhatIs.TechTarget.com, accessed October 14, 2019, http://whatis.techtarget.com/definition/QR-code-quick-response-code.

144. "About Search," Support.Snapchat.com, accessed October 14, 2019, https://support.snapchat.com/en-US/a/search.

145. Harrison Weber, "Older Users Seem to Like the New Snapchat, and That's About the Only Good News Snap Shared Today," Gizmodo.com, May 1, 2018, https://gizmodo.com/older-users-seem-to-like-the-new-snapchat-and-that-s-a-1825697373.

146. "15 Ways to Use Snapchat for Your Business," QuickSprout.com, April 19, 2019, https://www.quicksprout.com/snapchat/.

147. "Snapchat for Business Advertising," ForBusiness.Snapchat.com, accessed October 11, 2019, https://forbusiness.snapchat.com/advertising.

148. "Snapchat for Business Advertising," ForBusiness.Snapchat.com.

149. Robert Williams, "Papa John's Snapchat Lens Boosted Pizza Orders 25% for Valentine's Day," MobileMarketer.com, September 17, 2019, https://www.mobilemarketer.com/news/papa-johns-snapchat-lens-boosted-pizza-orders-25-for-valentines-day/563040/.

150. Andrew Hutchinson, "Snapchat Launches Updated Snap Ads Education Courses for Marketers," SocialMediaToday.com, February 27, 2019, https://www.socialmediatoday.com/news/snapchat-launches-updated-snap-ads-education-courses-for-marketers/549255/.

CHAPTER

9

Geosocial, Live Video, Ratings, and Reviews

Not all those who wander are lost.[1]

—J. R. R. Tolkien

PREVIEW

How transparent has your life become? Do you share your location in social media posts? Do you leave ratings and reviews for products you've bought or restaurants you have been to? Have you gone "live" by video streaming your last birthday party, performance, or workout? Whether you're watching and commenting on other people's lives or sharing your own geolocation, ratings, reviews, and live video, these interactive media features have made everyone's lives more social and more open.

Many people like "checking in" online and giving reviews and ratings. How much of a difference can they make? Business professor Michael Luca set out to measure this in his research, "Reviews, Reputation and Revenue." In a study of Seattle Yelp restaurant reviews, the researcher found that a one-star increase in Yelp rating led to a 5 to 9 percent increase in revenue. However, the increase was only found with independent restaurants, not chain restaurants. In fact, the study found that chain-restaurant market share declined as Yelp penetration increased.[2]

A negative result of this powerful influence on business is that it has created an intense incentive to post fake reviews. Michael Luca teamed up with Georgios Zervas in a follow-up Yelp

223

study. They found that businesses without many existing reviews and those that face intense competition are more likely to engage in review fraud. How big is the overall problem? In a site-wide measurement of suspicious reviews, the researchers found that roughly 16 percent of all reviews are filtered or removed by Yelp for being fake.[3] These findings are important to keep in mind. Where there is money to be made, some will try to cheat the system. Yet marketers, advertisers, and public relations professionals must always consider the ethical consequences. In the end, getting caught is far worse than the initial economic gain.

Geosocial

J. R. R. Tolkien is best known for his fantasy books *The Hobbit* and the *Lord of the Rings* trilogy, which have been made into a very successful Hollywood film series. His quote can be applied to social location networks where users discover new adventures and earn rewards for wandering to new locations.

As smartphones have grown in popularity, so has the use of real-time location data, which has enabled sharing a user's location with friends or the public in the form of a check-in. **Check-in** is defined as self-reported positioning to share one's physical location through a social-networking service.[4] A related activity is **geotagging**, where geographical identification information is added to media such as a picture, video, or social media post.[5] Foursquare is the innovator in this category that built a social community around checking in to locations and earning points and badges for doing so. Not to be outdone, many social media services such as Facebook, Instagram, Twitter, Snapchat, and Yelp have added or included location layers to their platforms (see table 9.1).

Roughly 38 percent of all US smartphone owners share their location with social media apps, often called geosocial. **Geosocial** is a type of social networking in which user-submitted location data allow social networks to connect and coordinate users with local people, businesses, or events. Social "checking in" has increased from only 12 percent in 2013.[6] Geosocial networking is also an important part of ratings and reviews, with 90 percent of smartphone owners looking for recommendations based on location. Apps offering more of a direct benefit for location sharing such as driving directions, ordering a pizza for delivery, or finding a restaurant have a higher percentage of owners enabling location services.[7] Younger age groups tend to be more comfortable granting mobile app location access, with 40 percent of eighteen- to thirty-four-year-olds being most comfortable (4 and 5 out of 5) versus just a quarter of thirty-five-year-olds and older (26–27 percent—4 and 5 out of 5).[8]

Table 9.1. Major Social Platforms That Include Location Layers

Facebook	Reddit
Foursquare/Swarm	Snapchat
Google My Business	Twitter
Instagram	TripAdvisor
Periscope	Yelp

Geosocial networking still offers many opportunities for businesses to further engage target consumers and drive participation at physical locations. Foursquare may have been the innovator in checking in, but other social services have taken much of this activity from it.[9] The top location-based social services covered in this chapter include Foursquare (Swarm), location layers on Facebook, Instagram, and Snapchat, plus Google My Business. These could be the optimal fit for an organization's objectives, target audience, and big idea.

Foursquare

Foursquare, founded in 2009, is a personalized local search-and-discovery-service mobile app that enables users to find friends and read recommendations. Foursquare is comprised of the Foursquare City Guide app and Foursquare Swarm app. Like Instagram and Snapchat, Foursquare is a social-networking service first developed for mobile devices.[10] Foursquare has 50 million users, with some 9 million check-ins per day.[11] The location service has global participation by users and has more than 105 million venues mapped around the world.[12] Foursquare has accumulated over 13 billion check-ins worldwide.[13]

In the United Kingdom and Canada, 2 percent of people indicated that they use Foursquare regularly, below more popular social networks such as Facebook, YouTube, Instagram, Pinterest, and Twitter. However, in the United Kingdom, regular Foursquare use is above Yelp at 1 percent.[14] In Australia the drop-off rate of Foursquare has been low compared to other social networks such as Twitter, Instagram, and Snapchat, which means the app is maintaining a loyal base of users.[15]

In the United States, 3 percent indicated they use Foursquare regularly, below more popular social networks.[16] Foursquare's apps have significantly more male (69 percent) than female (31 percent) users.[17] The social media platform is most popular with younger age groups, with half of users under thirty-five years old. Specifically, eighteen- to twenty-four-year-olds (26 percent) followed by twenty-five- to thirty-four-year-olds (24 percent) make up the largest age groups.[18] Foursquare users tend to be more in urban areas (61 percent) than rural areas (39 percent).[19] Forty-three percent of Foursquare app users have some college education and 40 percent have no college education.[20]

In 2014 Foursquare made a bold move by dividing its social network into two apps based on its two most popular functions: a new version of Foursquare and Swarm. Foursquare Swarm is the more personal app for locating friends and checking in to venues. With the update, Foursquare became Foursquare City Guide, more focused on mobile local searches and activity recommendations. People check in through the Swarm app, but tips, photos, and location information are based in Foursquare City Guide, so businesses are still able to see a list of active customers.[21] People use Swarm as the personal side of Foursquare to "keep up and meet up" with friends, but can check in to let friends know they are at a business. Businesses show up as a check-in option if a user is nearby.[22]

Foursquare City Guide enables users to search for restaurants, shops points of interest, and attractions under categories of breakfast, lunch, dinner, coffee and tea, nightlife, and things to do. The app allows users to define their "tastes" in food, atmosphere, etc., which is added to their profile to provide more customized recommendations. The app gives personalized recommendations near the user's current location based on previous check-ins, venue ratings, and "tastes." The geosocial platform also highlights user-written tips for locations written as reviews. Ratings consist of emojis of a heart, smiley face, or broken heart. Tips are limited to two hundred words, but can include a photo and links and can easily share on Facebook and Twitter. Users who leave quality tips can earn an "expertise" designation for a location such as a neighborhood or category such as Chinese restaurants.[23]

Swarm is described as a lifelogging community with social networking features to keep track of places users have been. Users can search statistics of their journeys, share where they have been with their friends, and see pins on a map to track their adventures. The app explains that you'll never have to ask "What's the name of that place?" again. Check-ins to locations earn points or virtual coins and friends can challenge each other with check-ins on weekly leaderboards. There are different categories to check in at different venues to unlock virtual stickers. Users try to visit different categories such as museums, parks, and gyms.[24]

Both Foursquare City Guide and Swarm have push notifications what will send messages of local venues when users enter those areas. Foursquare City Guide and Swarm have a small but engaged user base that on average spends nearly an hour per month with the app in thirty-three sessions, gathering valuable location-based data to advertisers, developers, and retailers as part of its business model.[25] Foursquare for Business overs free and paid social media options. First, businesses should claim their listing, ensure it is accurate, upload quality photos, and provide updated information on address, hours, menus, and phone numbers. Businesses should also regularly monitor activity, thanking and responding to people checking in and leavings tips and ratings.[26]

Foursquare for Business offers ads to promote listings to be seen first by targeting people in the local area searching for what the business offers or who have visited similar businesses. Targeting can be narrowed to location-based keyword search or people who have visited competitors. Brands can also target users with custom messages based on location, time, or action like a check-in. Or a business can take a great customer tip about their brand and turn it into a targeted ad. Campaigns are created based on monthly budgets and can start and end at any time. Businesses only pay per action such as tapping for business information or visiting the brand's website. The ad manager dashboard keeps track of metrics and performance. Foursquare can be a powerful option for brands with physical locations, considering research that has found 78 percent of people who search locally on their phone make a purchase.[27]

Social App Locations

Many of the top social network and social sharing platforms have added location-service features over the years. It is useful to focus on these functions in this section and consider broader geosocial strategies that can be applied to the platforms that offer them, including Facebook, Instagram, Snapchat, and Reddit.

Facebook Places started as a mobile app but location-tagging is now integrated into Facebook. This feature enables users to tag or check in to a specific place or business, which shows up as a status update, image, or video post in the user's news feed. Facebook users can tag friends in specific locations within an update or post, which then appears in the friends' news feeds. These features were added to emulate the features first available in Foursquare.[28]

Another important feature is that when users click on "check-in," businesses and organizations nearest to their current location appear as options for the post. Organizations should make sure that the physical location of their business is in their Facebook page description to automatically be included in the Facebook Places directory and show up in search results. A post tagged with the business location will lead those who click it to the business's Facebook page. Location tagging on Facebook adds another way for organizations to appear in news feeds, but also allows businesses to publish promotions and discounts on the Facebook page after users click on the tag in a news feed.[29]

In 2018 Facebook updated their business pages, making it easier to connect and interact with local businesses. The five-star ratings system was simplified and made more prominent with a new binary system asking, "Do you recommend this business?" The new recommendation score is based on the number of people who recommend or don't recommend the business page, plus previous ratings. Users can add text, tags, and photos to recommendations. Tags appear at the bottom of a business recommendation page to show what a business is known for.[30] The "Nearby" tab on the Facebook mobile app can help users find businesses.[31] With 1.6 billion people connecting to small businesses on Facebook, location features can increase reach and awareness through search and news feeds.[32] Brands should ensure all location, contact, and business hours information is correct.[33] Plus, one in three people on Facebook use the platform to look specifically for recommendations and reviews so be sure to monitor on a regular basis.[34]

Instagram also has locations features integrated through Facebook Places. Both are ways to increase exposure for businesses and events for search by location versus hashtag. To create a place in Instagram, you create it in Facebook Places through the Facebook mobile app. Instagram is a popular app to use during events. If the brand is involved with an event, be sure to create a location tag. For example, the band U2 created a location tag for each city on their Joshua Tree Tour that appeared as an option every time someone went to post from the concert. A story ring at the top of Explore is filled with stories happening near them. Stories come from people or brands with location stickers on stories.

Instagram expert Jenn Herman explains that customers who click on a geotag location see all other posts to the geotag, which can showcase brand products and services and help reach new customers through location search. Geotagged posts also allow brands to source user-generated content (UGC). Reposting publicly shared brand experiences shows customers the brand is listening, appreciates their contributions, and presents a more believable perspective. Just ensure you get permission first before sharing. Permissions will be covered in chapter 15.[35]

Two other considerations for geosocial are geocaching and geofencing. **Geocaching** is an outdoor game where people use GPS on a mobile device to hide and then seek containers called geocaches at locations marked by coordinates.[36] Doubleday used geocaching and Facebook to launch John Grisham's book *The Racketeer*. Five thousand golden Grisham Geocoins were distributed in geocaches across the United States. People who found the coins re-hid them in new locations. People who found the coins uploaded pictures to Facebook with their coin for a chance to win a real gold bar. Facebook fans voted for the winner

Figure 9.1. The Pokémon GO app was a hit leveraging geosocial and augmented reality.

© Wachlwit / iStock Photo

and helped increase reach of the campaign 220 percent and boost overall sales 23 percent.[37] Another version of geocaching used virtual caches and virtual reality. Pokémon GO was a location-based augmented reality game that became a global craze in the summer of 2016, becoming one of the most used and profitable mobile apps.[38]

Geofencing is setting up a virtual perimeter for a real-world geographic area and using a smartphone's GPS to trigger a message or customize content.[39] Geofencing must be used via a mobile app with location services turned on or triggered by an event like a geotagged post on social platforms such as Facebook, Instagram, Twitter, and Foursquare. Geofences can also be used to trigger mobile ads on popular apps that sell them.[40] The benefits of geofencing include increasing local sales by pushing notifications to customers in the area, improving analytics by measuring location-based sales, time, and frequency metrics, and adding personalization to highlight offers and messages to local preferences.[41]

Best practices include not making the geofence too large by keeping it to within a five-minute travel time.[42] Be sure to have a call to action that is concise and locally relevant, and that requires prompt response. Be transparent about privacy, letting customers know what location information is being used. Also target messaging by context (relief from downtown crowds), time of day (lunchtime specials), and retargeting (customers who haven't visited in a while).[43]

Other geofence strategies may include building geofences around competitor locations to attract new customers with special offers or using a geofence around an airport to attract tourists. Or think about using geofences near arenas and events to attract attendees.[44]

Advanced geofilter strategies include adding data to make geo messages more relevant. A retailer could use browsing data from an app or website to target a customer who had viewed formal dresses on her phone. When she enters the store, she would receive a formal dress message instead of a general sales or promotion message. In addition, consider more helpful messages that could help increase loyalty. For example, a hotel, shuttle, or rental car app might remind a person to check in online, book their shuttle, or rent a car via the app before leaving an airport.[45]

A final consideration is that when offers or promotions are used, they should be significant and not too frequent. Getting interrupted by a mobile notification to save fifty cents may be more annoying than motivating. Also keep track of frequency so that you do not disturb people. Both of these actions could lead to the customer turning off location services, which prevents further location-based notifications.[46]

Snapchat leverages geofencing with geofilters. This opportunity offers organizations the opportunity to get creative with people's selfies for stores, brands, restaurants, and events. As discussed in chapter 8, Snapchat Geofilters are paid social media ad opportunities. However, small businesses can purchase custom-branded geofilters for as little as five dollars.[47] Brand Snapchat geofilters are purchased for specific dates, times, and locations—established by drawing a geofence around a location. The exception is Snapchat Geofilters for community events, cities, neighborhoods, schools, and landmarks. If Snapchat reaches the right target audience, paid geofilters can be valuable for creatively driving awareness and engagement.[48]

Google My Business

Google My Business is a listing that ensures that businesses show up in searches and includes social media features such as updates, comments, photo sharing, ratings, and reviews. Google My Business gets businesses added to Google location search and Google Maps and includes consumer ratings and reviews. The platform also provides analytics on how customers are finding the business.[49] For brands with locations, this is a very important consideration.

How should brands include Google My Business in their social media strategy? The first step is to verify the business by signing up. Verification happens by mailing a verification code to a physical address, which can take up to a week to process. Next, verify that all of the information in the brand listing is accurate, from address, phone, and website to hours and driving directions. Brands should then monitor the five-star ratings, customer reviews, and consumer photos. Businesses can add their own photos and updates and respond to customers' comments.[50]

In 2018, Google My Business added Questions and Answers where consumers can ask questions and other users of the business can answer. Be sure to activate notifications to get a notice when someone asks a question and respond in a timely manner. Some may be asking if the business is open and the lack of a timely response could result in a loss of business. Also monitor for other users providing incorrect answers, which should be corrected in a polite way.[51] Google reviews appear next to a business's listing in Maps, Search, and other Google services. Ratings and reviews will be covered more in the next section, but Google My Business reviews can have a great impact on search, so brands should follow up positive customer interactions with requests to leave reviews and try to address the causes of negative reviews.

Local paid search ads can appear in Google My Business as Promoted Pins. Brands can bid on keywords to pay to appear as purple pins among red pins on Google Map searches for business types and products. Coupon-based deals can also be promoted. Promoted Pins are sold on a cost-per-click (CPC) basis on clicks such as get location details, get directions, website clicks, and click to call.[52] The most popular businesses on Google My Business by number of photos posted include hotels, restaurants, car dealerships, bars, tourism and entertainment, weddings and events, caterers, and photographers.[53] Other geosocial channels to consider include Nextdoor, a private, location-based social network with more than 204,000 neighborhoods. It offers business pages, recommendations, and paid social media–sponsored post options.[54]

Social Live Video

Live streaming video became big when the Meerkat app was launched in spring 2015 at SXSW (South by Southwest) followed by Periscope a week later. Then in late summer 2015, Blab was introduced, followed by the launch of Facebook Live in spring 2016. Within a short time Meerkat and Blab live video platforms came and went, shutting down in less than two years.[55] No matter which social platform offers it, **live streaming video** is compressed video content sent over the internet and displayed in real time.[56]

Figure 9.2. Live streaming video is a high engagement strategy across multiple platforms.

© Twinster Photo / iStock Photo

Yet streaming video had already been around for nearly a decade. Live video streaming websites like Livestream and Ustream (now IBM CloudVideo) both launched in 2007. Why the sudden, more recent interest in live streaming video? The newer apps were designed for mobile phones and smartphone use has increased dramatically. From 2011 to 2016, smartphone ownership in the United States alone more than doubled from 35 percent to 72 percent.[57] Live video apps have also grown dramatically—more quickly than previous social media apps. Instagram Live reached 10 million users in one year while Periscope grew much faster, reaching 10 million users in just five months. Despite this enormous growth, live streaming use is still relatively limited compared to established social activity, yet there is real opportunity for brands to use live video.[58]

After years of declining viewership (ratings), the TV industry has learned the value of live programming combined with social commenting. Nielsen finds that live TV shows leveraging Twitter boosts TV ratings.[59] There is something about the word "live" that makes consumers want to join in and not miss out. Live combined with social media means participation in consumption of content within a community—a community brands can join. Live breaks down geographical barriers and geosocial networking localizes social interaction to build community. Live social media through live tweeting or live video streaming brings everyone to that event and location. Consumers are all participating in a local event from hundreds of miles away. Live also builds in a sense of urgency. Some can't resist tuning in for fear of missing out; they crave the community, shared experience, and direct interaction live video offers.[60]

Live video can also build awareness. Live streaming content is getting preference over other content, with Twitter, Facebook, and Instagram highlighting and even alerting their current social media users that live content is available. Facebook, Instagram, and Periscope send out notices so friends, fans, or followers know a connection is live. Periscope has added apps on services like Apple TV. Social media expert Kim Garst says people watch her "scopes" like a morning TV show. Facebook sends followers a notification of live broadcasts and live videos are given preference in the news feed. These notices reach your audience, driving up organic reach.[61]

Live video can also help drive conversion. What better way to build rapport than live interaction with a real person? Seeing it in video makes it real. From product demonstration to sharing valuable content and answering questions, live video speeds up the know, like, and trust process and can quicken time to conversion. Live video could be a key tool to bring the full power of personal sales to social media. Seeing and interacting live with a real person is powerful. Research has indicated that the impact of communication is determined 7 percent by words, 38 percent by voice, and 55 percent by nonverbal communication. Not using live video could mean missing out on up to 93 percent of communication effectiveness.[62]

Live video also allows brands to adjust messages on the fly based on the number of people coming and going, hearts or likes the speaker is receiving, and questions being asked. Of course, not everyone is trained or even comfortable to be in front of a live camera and a lot can go wrong on the fly. Getting the right people, providing the right training, and simply getting comfortable with the idea is a big hurdle for many brands. Public relations professionals may relate it to media training in news media interview situations.

Table 9.2. Advantages and Disadvantages of Social Live Video

Advantages	Disadvantages
Sense of urgency	No retakes
More exposure/reach	Practice is live
Unique customer interaction	
Real-time interaction	
Building trust	
No time restrictions	
Repurposing content	
Cost-efficiency	

Source: "The Advantages (and Disadvantages) of Live Streaming for Brands and Businesses," ManyCam.com, accessed December 9, 2019, http://blog.manycam.com/live-streaming-for-brands/#.Xe68Qb9OkWo.

Now that social live video has been out for a couple of years, the landscape of platforms has changed. Early innovators such as Meerkat and Blab have shut down. The main platforms offering live video include Periscope, Facebook Live, Instagram Live, and YouTube Live. We will also look at the social platform Twitch, which has grown around live streaming of gamers and built a gamer social community. For a list of advantages and disadvantages of live video for any platform, see table 9.2.

Periscope is a live video streaming mobile app integrated into the microblogging social media service Twitter. Twitter acquired this live video platform in the development phase before it was publicly launched in 2015, a week after Meerkat. Periscope is also about the broadcast of the individual, but close integration with Twitter is a bonus with Periscope streams viewable live in a person's Twitter stream, the ability to go live from Twitter, and a red live button alerting Twitter users when someone they follow is broadcasting live. Originally all videos disappeared after twenty-four hours, but now users can choose to keep broadcasts on the platform and save the videos. Periscope also added an app for streaming TV devices and Smart TVs to expand broadcasts from mobile devices.[63]

In an attempt to leverage Twitter's news content strength and leverage the growth of podcasts, Periscope added audio-only broadcasts to the live-steaming app in 2018 and in 2019 added the ability to invite guests onto a live recording. This allows streamers to bring in audience members and then broadcast audio from that person to everyone else in the live stream with up to three guests in addition to the host. The last available Periscope statistics indicate 10 million users, 1.9 million daily active users, and more than 200 million broadcasts.[64]

Facebook Live is a live video streaming feature added to the Facebook mobile app for any user to broadcast live video. Six months after the launch of Meerkat and five months after the launch of Periscope in 2015, Facebook Live was first available for celebrities through the Facebook Mentions app. By 2016 broadcasting live video was rolled out to any Facebook user integrated into the Facebook mobile app. In 2017 live video streaming capabilities were extended to the Facebook website through desktops and laptops. The big news here is that any of the more than 2.5 billion Facebook users can share a live video stream as easily as making a status update. Like Periscope, Facebook Live videos can be saved for later use on other platforms.[65]

Facebook Live includes 2 billion viewers with more than 3.5 billion live broadcasts. Facebook Live videos create six times as many interactions and ten times more comments as regular videos. One out of every five Facebook videos is a live broadcast and users watch Facebook Live videos three times longer than pre-uploaded videos.[66] The service had its first viral video star when Candace Payne decided to broadcast live on Facebook sharing her excitement after buying a Chewbacca mask at Kohl's department store. The live video attracted more than 166 million views and was then reposted on other social networks like YouTube. Kohl's was listening and the department store brand launched several initiatives to take advantage of the exposure. Airbnb leveraged live video for the 100th Anniversary of North America's National Parks. A Facebook Live stream was started from Airbnb houses with beautiful backyards in National Parks. The effort gained more than 2.5 million total impressions in twelve hours with 98 percent positive comment sentiment that led to more than 260,000 people considering a vacation with Airbnb.[67]

Instagram Live is a live video streaming feature added to the Instagram mobile app for any user to broadcast live video. This feature was added in late 2016. Unlike Periscope and Facebook Live, Instagram videos disappear in the stream after the live broadcast, creating a greater sense of urgency to watch so users don't miss out. However, a feature has been added allowing the broadcaster to save the stream to their camera roll after the broadcast has ended. TechCrunch described Instagram Live as combining the best of Snapchat and Periscope.[68] Users can stream video in real time, save a replay of the video to Instagram Stories, engage with followers as they send likes or comments, and pin follower comments to the top of the video.[69] Live video can be found by browsing the Explore page of Instagram Live videos. Users can send live video via direct message. Users can also save live videos to Stories so they are available to watch for twenty-four hours before they disappear. Snapchat-like features are also available; users can add text and draw overlays.[70]

YouTube Live is a live video streaming feature added to the YouTube website and mobile app to broadcast live video. YouTube live streams were made available through the website in 2013 and the feature was added to the YouTube mobile app in 2017. Any user can stream live video from a webcam on desktop or laptop, but live streaming through the YouTube app is limited to users with one hundred subscribers or more. Live streaming of 360-degree video up to 4K resolution is supported.[71] Many brands are adding multiple platforms to their live streaming to increase audience. In 2019 Apple streamed its iPhone 11 event on the Apple website, Twitter, and YouTube Live.[72]

Twitch is a live video streaming platform focused on live video game streaming. Launched as a website in 2011 and purchased by Amazon in 2014,[73] the social media platform has grown to 100 million monthly active users, with 15 million active daily.[74] The Twitch mobile app was made available in 2017, with the ability to live stream from the app, participate in chat communities, and organize content by Live, Pulse for curated content, and Browse to discover new content.[75] Twitch users skew heavily male (82 percent) and younger (55 percent eighteen- to thirty-four years old). While still mainly a gaming platform to watch people play games, Twitch has expanded its content base to include other areas of interest such as comics, food, music, art, DIY, travel, and sports through streaming shows and chat.[76]

Twitch offers advertising opportunities through both native and display options. Bounty Boards are a form of influencer marketing where Twitch influencers select from a market-place brand campaigns to go live with based on their audience's interests. Homepage Carou-sel, Headliner, Rectangle, and Leaderboard ads promote brand live stream channel content. Twitch video ads can be integrated into live streams on desktop and mobile.[77]

Other brands have leveraged popular online games such as Fortnite to build their brand community on Twitch. Wendy's hosted a live stream of Fortnite on Twitch built around the game's "Food Fight" mission. After ten hours of live streaming the brand increased from zero followers to 7,400 on Twitch. The engagement resulted in 43,500 comments during the stream compared to the average of 3,000 Wendy's mentions that occur on Twitter each day. Wendy's senior director of media and social, Jimmy Bennett, said, "What we did wasn't down to a paid relationship with either Twitch or Fortnite. We didn't have to do so much heavy lifting and put so much money to support it because we were able to organically lean into the experience."[78]

How can brands use live streaming video in social media? There are many possibilities for brands. Consider strategies including broadcasting live organization events, making live announcements, holding live interviews, starting a live video blog, and moderating live panel chats.[79] Also consider promoting other brand content, live streaming a discussion about a brand report, white paper, or eBook, or creating a live Q&A session.[80] Other social media

Figure 9.3. Some brands are creatively engaging with gamers through Fortnite and Twitch.

© JJ Farquitectos / iStock Photo

live video opportunities include supplementing customer research with real-time feedback, broadcasting live about trending topics and developing stories, or product demonstrations.[81] The MTV Video Music Awards promoted their live event with additional engagement opportunities for fans through live video streaming in Facebook Live, YouTube Live, and on Twitter. The live streams not only showed live coverage of the event, but also provided exclusive content. A Backstage Pass on Facebook Live included interactive polls and embedded cameras that followed celebrity entourages and YouTube Live showed a Fashion Detail camera for the red carpet. The result was the most streamed award show in MTV history with more than 285 million streams—a 70 percent increase from the previous year.[82]

There are legal aspects to all social media strategy, but live streaming video brings up even more concerns. Before broadcasting live on one of these live streaming channels, consider the legal implications. In response to this new need, social media law expert Kerry O'Shea Gorgone produced a live streaming legal checklist that includes areas such as considerations in location, privacy, intellectual property, likeness, and contingency plans.[83] Of course, before publishing or broadcasting any social media effort, brands should consult with their own lawyers; individual organization, industry, and country standards vary greatly. More topics for social media law and ethics will be considered in chapter 15.

As Foursquare says, geosocial services are all about trying to "keep up & meet up with friends on-the-go." This also applies to broadcasting live video where friends, family, fans, and followers can experience a live event no matter where they are in the world. These services really bridge the gap between fantasy digital worlds and real physical places. J. R. R. Tolkien would probably have been inspired by this combination. What kind of brand story can the brand tell to engage and encourage participation from the target audience? If driving consumers to a location or broadcasting live video supports the organization's goals, geosocial and social live video may be ideal options in the social media plan.

Ratings and Reviews

Mark Twain once said, "The public is the only critic whose opinion is worth anything at all."[84] Mark Twain wrote *The Adventures of Huckleberry Finn*, which has been called the great American novel. His quote may be truer today than ever before. As seen in the early chapters of this book, social media has turned every individual into a publisher with the potential influence and reach of a professional. An organization may get a rave review in the *New York Times*, but consumers publishing negative comments through ratings and reviews can stagnate sales.

Reviews are reports that give someone's opinion about the quality of a product, service, or performance.[85] **Ratings** are also a measurement of how good or bad something is, but expressed specifically on a scale that is a relative estimate or evaluation.[86] Five-point rating scales are popular and can be expressed as straight numbers, stars, or even spoons. Reviews are longer descriptions of a critic's opinion of a product or experience with a service. Back in Mark Twain's day, most critics were professional and only a few were published. Here we are talking about social media–powered ratings and reviews where any amateur critic can voice his or her opinion on numerous social channels.[87]

MINI CASE

McDonald's Q&A

In early 2012 McDonald's US had a PR crisis in social media with #McDStories where consumers were to share positive stories about the restaurant, but instead many negative stories were shared and that became a news story. Within hours the brand stopped promoting the hashtag.[a] **Hashtag hijacking** is when the original positive intent of a hashtag is hijacked to promote negatives of the brand.[b] This is different from newsjacking, which is a positive use of trending topics including hashtags and is a part of real-time marketing strategy. Both of these topics will be covered in chapter 11 as a part of crowdsourcing.

After the hashtag hijack in the United States, McDonald's Canada made a bold move, taking a different approach with a Q&A social media campaign that truly embraced transparency. The company knew that consumers were active with ratings and reviews of the restaurant and were asking tough questions online about how the company made its food. Instead of the previous campaign that had the brand's true consumer perception wrong, they launched a website to answer user-submitted questions head-on about ingredients, prep, food sourcing, and advertising. Answers appeared via text, photos, and video, allowing the brand to address rumors, misinformation, and myths. The campaign was a success, attracting global media attention fielding more than fourteen thousand questions within months and spawning an integrated traditional advertising campaign of TV, digital, and outdoor ads.[c]

In 2014 McDonald's expanded the Q&A campaign to the United States with the help of *Myth-Busters* TV show cohost Grant Imahara. The "Our Food. Your Questions" campaign used TV commercials showing real people's questions and inviting consumers to pose more via social media. The effort also used webisode videos (short online-only TV shows) by Imahara addressing consumers' main doubts and questions about McDonald's food. The brand said this was their first big effort into two-way dialogue with consumers, giving them a behind-the-scenes view of the restaurant chain.[d]

[a] Erik Sherman, "How McDonald's Twitter Campaign Fell into the Fire," CBSNews.com, January 27, 2012, https://www.cbsnews.com/news/how-mcdonalds-twitter-campaign-fell-into-the-fire/.

[b] Conor Denton, "Understanding Hashtag Hijacking and How It Can Work for You," Internet MarketingTeam.com, March 14, 2015, https://internetmarketingteam.com/understanding-hashtag-hijacking-and-how-it-can-work-for-you/.

[c] Paula Bernstein, "Would You Like to See How We Make Our Fries with That? Behind McDonald's Big Transparency Play," FastCompany.com, November 6, 2012, http://www.fastcocreate.com/1681832/would-you-like-to-see-how-we-make-our-fries-with-that-behind-mcdonalds-big-transparency-play.

[d] "McDonald's, 'MythBuster' Launch Food Q&A," HuffingtonPost.com, October 13, 2014, http://www.huffingtonpost.com/burgerbusiness/mcdonalds-mythbuster-laun_b_5976250.html.

How important are social ratings and reviews? According to a survey by Dimensional Research, 90 percent of respondents who remembered reading online reviews said positive online reviews influenced buying decisions and 86 percent said negative reviews influenced their buying. One consumer survey found that reading reviews, comments, and feedback in social media is more influential to online buying than receiving promotional offerings and viewing ads. If the majority of a marketer's time and budget is spent on promotions and ads while ignoring ratings and reviews, it may be time to adjust strategy.[88] Where do these reviews happen? Reviews can be found on online review sites, retail sites, company sites, and in searches.

Ratings and reviews are a key factor that builds trust in a business[89] and a key factor that erodes trust in a business.[90] Shoppers indicate that ratings and reviews increase their purchasing confidence (73 percent), improve customer feedback (71 percent), create a more authentic shopping experience (67 percent), and are more interesting than brand content (65 percent).[91] When it comes to online shopping, ratings, and reviews (53 percent) are the second most important attribute after easy search and navigation (61 percent) and ahead of fast and convenient check-out process (50 percent).[92]

In a survey conducted during the holiday shopping season, consumers indicated that online ratings and reviews influenced both their online (48 percent) and in-store (37 percent) purchases more than other factors, such as email (35 percent online, 27 percent in-store) and Google search (31 percent online, 20 percent in-store). Display advertising only influenced purchase by 16 percent online and 15 percent in-store. Additionally, respondents indicated mobile advertising only influenced 11 percent of online and 9 percent of in-store purchases.[93] Social ratings and reviews can be very influential in purchase decisions. While organizations cannot and should not directly create reviews and ratings, they need to be monitored, influenced, and optimized to help meet organization goals.

Brands should not be afraid of negative reviews. Digital marketing consultant Shane Barker points out how bad reviews can be good for your business. Negative reviews highlight positive reviews, lead to more informed purchase decisions, help build trust, provide opportunities to engage with customers, and help brands learn from their mistakes.[94] Philip Kotler, Hermawan Kartajaya, and Iwan Setiawan point out in *Marketing 4.0* that even the biggest, most successful businesses have brand lovers and brand haters. YouGov BrandIndex reveals that Starbucks has 30 percent lovers and 23 percent haters. Kotler argues that the haters activate the lovers to defend the brand. Both positive and negative advocacy makes brand conversation more interesting and engaging.[95] General ratings and review strategies can apply anywhere, but this section will look at an overview of three of the most influential ratings-and-reviews services: Yelp, TripAdvisor, and Amazon. Consider how these channels could fit into a social media plan, depending upon target audience and big idea.

Yelp

Yelp is a website and mobile app that publishes crowdsourced ratings and reviews about local businesses. Yelp is an early innovator in social recommendations, first founded in 2004. Yelp has grown to 176 million unique visitors per month with more than 192 million user-generated reviews.[96] Because Yelp is location-specific, it has expanded city by city, first starting in the United States but now in thirty-two countries. This ratings and review site with geosocial features can be very influential on sales for many businesses. Top categories include restaurants, home services, shopping, beauty, fitness, health, and auto. Yelp has also become very mobile with 79 percent of searches and 72 percent of reviews done on a mobile device.[97] Yelp gets most of its traffic from the United States, Canada, and the United Kingdom.[98] In Australia there are 1.5 million monthly active Yelp users.[99]

Figure 9.4. Customers posting ratings and reviews highly influence purchase decisions.

© Shafbdn / iStock Photo

Yelp users in the United States have been more female (54 percent) than male (46 per-cent). Are fairly evenly split across age groups of thirty-five- to fifty-four (36 percent), eigh-teen to thirty-four (33 percent) and fifty-five and older (31 percent). They are also highly educated, with 61 percent having a college degree and 19 percent a graduate degree.[100] The number of reviews submitted to the ratings and review social platform continues to grow 15 to 20 percent each year in recent years.[101]

Yelp encourages users to review and rate businesses using their five-star rating system. The system filters these ratings and reviews to remove unhelpful, biased, or fraudulent reviews.[102] To encourage and reward good reviews, the service offers a Yelp Elite Squad des-ignation to those who contribute well-written reviews, offer great tips, have a full profile, and communicate nicely with other Yelp users. Yelp emphasizes to businesses that people love to talk about the things they love. Statistics show that 69 percent of all reviews on Yelp are four stars or higher.[103]

Depending on the type of business, Yelp ratings can significantly impact performance. Yelp restaurants in Seattle were found to increase revenue 5 to 9 percent per one-star increase in Yelp rating.[104] Yelp users can review any local business, service, or place, such as restaurants, shops, bars, salons, spas, dentists, mechanics, parks, and museums. Yet despite this enormous impact, only one out of nine Yelp reviews gets a response from the brand. Marketers of any business need to remember that they don't choose their marketing chan-nels. The customer chooses the channel they prefer to communicate to the business and the brand must respond. This doesn't just apply to customer service responding to negative reviews, but also responding to the positive reviews to build brand community and further marketing through digital word-of-mouth.[105]

In addition to reviews, Yelp allows users to find local events, from music fests and parties to dance lessons and networking opportunities. Users also submit lists such as top diners, favorite places, wedding venues, or fitness hot spots. Yelp enables a location-sharing check-in feature that includes badges with rankings and can earn users special offers from businesses.[106] Businesses can use Yelp's check-in feature for promotions and events, and it can be a great way to jumpstart traffic through public relations. In addition, Yelp has restaurant reservations as a feature through Yelp Reservations. Yelp also offers local city discussion forums where users can talk about local interests under various categories. To participate, a user must register and create a user profile similar to other social networking sites.

A business can set up a free account with a profile containing information such as hours, phone number, and website. Businesses can post offers and photos and directly message customers. Business pages can also enable customers to get quotes, make appointments, and ask questions. Yelp offers robust analytics with an alert system so business owners can respond right away to negative or positive comments. The platform keeps track of response rate and response time—so businesses should keep on top of requests and comments. Yelp tracks real-time metrics such as clicks, calls, page visits, and analytics that help identify where customers are coming from, and the most vocal fans and critics for outreach.[107]

Yelp does have paid social media options for business. Yelp for Business enables brands to purchase ads to feature businesses first in relevant searches and competitor business pages. Full-service Yelp advertising includes targeted location advertising, competitor ad removal, call-to-action buttons, slideshows, videos, reservation management, plus engagement and lead analytics.[108] Yelp offers businesses ways to entice regular and new customers to purchase with Yelp Deals and Gift Certificates.[109] Another feature for businesses is Yelp WiFi, which is a new way to track offline attribution through location analytics. Customers who view Yelp ads are tracked by using business Wi-Fi and email. During a one-month test for Canadian restaurant chain Jack Astor's Bar & Grill, the business saw $110 in revenue for every $1 spent on Yelp ads and 30 percent of customers were new to the restaurant.[110]

TripAdvisor

TripAdvisor is an online travel company providing hotel booking and reviews of travel-related content with travel forums. Founded in 2000 as more of a travel guide in the form of professional published guidebooks, newspapers, and magazines, the site included a "Visitors add your own review" button and soon consumer-generated reviews surpassed the official ones, turning the service into a user-generated social media platform. Today this ratings and review site averages 375 million unique visitors a month with more than 250 million reviews covering 5.2 million accommodations, restaurants, and attractions around the world in forty-five countries and in twenty-eight languages. There are 61.4 million TripAdvisor users in the United States, 11 million in the United Kingdom, 7.1 million in Canada, and 4 million in Australia.[111]

TripAdvisor users are slightly more female (58 percent) than male (42 percent), nearly a third (32 percent) have completed college, many are married (43 percent) and married with children in the household (40 percent). TripAdvisor users take three to four personal domestic trips a year, spending $2,500 to $7,499 in online travel. Top vacation activities include outdoor activities, cultural and history sites, dining, shopping, and the beach. Roughly 52 percent of TripAdvisor traffic comes from mobile in North America and 49 percent in the United Kingdom.[112]

If you are a marketer, advertiser, or public relations professional working on or for a travel and tourism–related brand, TripAdvisor is an important social media platform. Unless it is a very new location, chances are the business already appears in TripAdvisor. The first step is to claim that listing and take advantage of free tools. Optimize the listing with the latest business description and add photos of key features. Monitor reviews to obtain fast feedback and participate in the conversations with management responses. Brands receive valuable engagement analytics ranked with competitors and can offer private surveys for confidential feedback on hotel stays.[113]

Additional strategies include encouraging more reviews by adding TripAdvisor widgets to websites and adding TripAdvisor reviews to Facebook. TripAdvisor stickers, business cards, magnets, stamps, inserts, and envelopes can also be used at physical locations. Premium accounts like Business Advantage offer enhanced photo tools such as storyboard and slideshow, plus instant contact details to influence booking decisions in real time with special offers, announcements, favorite reviews, and mobile click-to-call. Businesses can also upgrade to add a "Book on TripAdvisor" button for instant booking.[114]

TripAdvisor offers traditional display and native advertising options. TripAdvisor sells sponsored custom content, pages, sweepstakes, advertorials, maps, and forums. The social platform also offers standard display, rich media, and mobile and video ads.[115] Does social media marketing on TripAdvisor work? The platform reports that nearly 90 percent of travelers say reviews are influential in choosing where to book, more than 60 percent say management responses make them more likely to book, and properties adding at least one photo to their listings see 138 percent more engagement than properties without a photo.[116]

Amazon

For any brand with significant e-commerce products or a brand in the retail industry, Amazon is hard to ignore. Launched in 1994, Amazon.com was originally an online book retailer but has grown enormously to offer everything from music and electronics to clothing and groceries.[117] Amazon attracts 197 million monthly visitors offering more than 12 million products. Amazon has 49 percent of the US e-commerce market compared to the top three competitors, eBay (6.6 percent), Apple (3.9 percent), and Wal-Mart (3.7 percent).[118] Amazon is used by nearly 90 percent of consumers in the United Kingdom,[119] and in Canada Amazon gets roughly 120 million visits a month.[120] In Australia, Amazon has grown dramatically, but still remains a small proportion of the online retail market.[121] Amazon has the third most monthly active users for all apps in the United States.[122]

Amazon Reviews is a feature on Amazon.com that allows users to submit reviews and ratings to the web page of each product sold on the e-commerce site. Amazon reviewers rate each product on a rating scale of one to five stars. Anyone with an Amazon account can review and rate a product whether or not they purchased it from Amazon. In addition, users may comment and vote on the reviews, indicating whether the review was helpful. Reviews with the most helpful votes appear on the front page of the product. Reviews are attributed to the real name of the reviewer based on confirmation of their credit card account. A machine-learning system analyzes which reviews are most helpful, giving more weight to newer reviews and reviews from verified Amazon purchasers, in addition to the customer vote for being helpful reviews. With the system, the five-star rating is not a pure average of all reviews to a weighted average, but instead based on those three criteria, so that ratings may change more often.[123]

There have been reports of a large market for incentivized positive reviews with free products and services and, in some cases, direct payment. Direct payment for positive reviews has never been allowed, but in 2017 Amazon updated its community guidelines to also disallow incentivized reviews.[124] Previously, vendors could send a free product to a reviewer in exchange for a review as long as this was disclosed. Now this can only still be done for books.[125] Amazon has also fought fake reviews by suing fake review websites.[126]

With the end of incentivized reviews, marketing strategies have changed. Some Amazon marketing experts suggest adding marketing inserts to packages. Such inserts might emphasize the value of the product to the customer and then ask for a review, making it easy by providing a shortened URL directly to the Amazon product review page. (If you have found this book to be valuable in better understanding how to create strategic social media plans, please leave a review at http://bit.ly/3EdSMS.)

Brands can also create an email follow-up sequence that includes a purchase confirmation right away, a purchase follow-up within days, and then an email asking for a product review in a couple of weeks. Amazon also offers a paid option where incentivized reviews can still be offered but brands must pay to access the Amazon Vine program.[127] Other expert practices include publicly responding to negative reviews, but ensure that you do not get defensive or emotional. It is best to sympathize with the customer and demonstrate that you really want to address or solve their issue or concern.[128] Amazon does offer advertising opportunities unrelated to reviews with sponsored products and sponsored brands that appear in search results. They also offer sponsored display ads and brand stores.[129]

Other rating and review social channels to consider include Angie's List and Home-Advisor. The Better Business Bureau and online Yellow Pages also have consumer ratings and reviews that may be influential to your target audience. Brands should not forget the ratings and reviews on Google My Business, Facebook, and Foursquare, and consider adding ratings and reviews to their own website. If a marketer's, advertiser's, or public relations professional's product is sold on their own website or other top online retailer websites such as Wal-Mart, Macy's, Best Buy, or Home Depot, ratings and reviews should be monitored there as well.

Kindra Hall, author of *Stories that Stick*, encourages businesses to take a slightly different approach to ratings and reviews. She encourages brands to not to simply say, "Give us a review." Instead encourage customers to tell a story because stories are so much more powerful than a rating and simple review. Instead ask questions such as "What were you struggling with before purchasing the product?" Or ask, "What happened once you started using the product?" This leads to stories that don't just rate but engage and encourage others to share their stories of struggle and how the product helped them. Then brands have more than a review on a single platform; they have a user-generated brand story that can be shared across multiple social media platforms and brand owned assets.[130] These brand stories become even more powerful when you remember that the Edelman Trust Barometer research found that a majority of consumers (63 percent) are more trusting of influencers than a brand's advertising.[131]

Mark Twain may have been right more than he knew. The power of public opinion (amateur critics) is undeniable in today's social media environment. Depending on the type of organization, product, and service, ratings-and-reviews social channels should be considered. Where is the brand target audience expressing their opinions about the brand and its competitors? Has the organization optimized its brand presence in that channel, and are they monitoring it, ready to engage both the positive and negative ratings and reviews? Or perhaps the brand doesn't have much of a presence but needs to encourage comments and content from the most loyal fans. In what ways can happy customers be encouraged to share their opinions? The reputation management software ReviewTrackers suggests asking for reviews via email, text message, landing pages, point of sale, in-person tablets, and kiosks.[132] Consider leveraging reviews by displaying them on the brand's website, including them in digital marketing campaigns, and adding them to traditional advertising and displays in-store.

Chapter 9 Checklist

Social media can change quickly. Visit Post Control Marketing (http://www.postcontrol marketing.com) for updates, but also use this chapter checklist to briefly check how social media statistics in this chapter have changed since publication.

- ✓ How have geosocial networking, live video, and ratings and reviews in social media changed? Are Foursquare, Google My Business, Facebook Places, Instagram Locations, Snapchat Geofilters, Periscope, Facebook Live, Instagram Live, Yelp, TripAdvisor, and Amazon still the top platforms?
- ✓ Do a quick search to confirm key statistics for each of the social media channel options covered in this chapter. Update numbers for monthly and daily users, global and country use, user demographics such as gender, age, education, and income, plus new features. What type of content performs best on each?
- ✓ Check for new paid social media opportunities. Have any of the social media platforms covered in this chapter added new advertising options? Has the General Data Protection Regulation (see chapter 13), California Consumer Protection Act (see chapter 15), or other regulations changed the targeting and tracking capabilities of social media campaigns?

SOCIAL PLAN PART 9

Strategic Use of Location, Ratings, and Reviews

Take an in-depth look at geosocial plus live video channels and features in social networking sites. Also analyze ratings and review sites and features on social networks in consideration for the plan (ask questions in table 7.1). How can these features benefit the brand and social media plan? Where is the target audience? Are they checking in or looking up ratings and reviews about the products and services? Where are they doing it? What can the brand do to leverage these features and influence conversation and discovery? What type of content (text, photo, video, live video) is needed to best take advantage of these social services? Report all findings and ideas in these areas:

1. Identify geosocial and live video channels or social networks where the target audience is participating.
2. Describe the type of activity and content that is popular on each.
3. Find the rating and review networks where the target audience is most active. In what social networks or retail websites are they discovering ratings and reviews?
4. Discover and explain how the organization can best leverage this information about the brand to help meet business objectives.

For a condensed version of the social plan see appendix A: Three-Part Social Plan.

KEY CONCEPTS

check-in

geotagging

geosocial

Foursquare

Swarm

geocaching

geofencing

Google My Business

live streaming video

Periscope

Facebook Live

Instagram Live

YouTube Live

Twitch

reviews

ratings

hashtag hijacking

Yelp

TripAdvisor

Amazon Reviews

QUESTIONS FOR DISCUSSION

1. Facebook has geosocial features such as checking in and local business features. How many Facebook users are actually using these features? Is Facebook where people are discovering and interacting with local business or are some of the other platforms more popular?

2. Live video use is expanding. Dig deeper into all aspects of social live video. What are some best practices for organizations to leverage live video? What are some of the negative aspects of live video, considering past highly publicized violence, murders, and suicides that have been broadcast on Facebook Live?

3. Amazon's dominance in online retail can be hard to ignore. What are the ways a brand can market on the platform? What are current best practices for ratings and reviews? How can a brand get its products more exposure on the ecommerce platform?

4. Ratings and reviews present ethical challenges for marketers and business owners. Yelp can make or break a local business. How accurate are ratings and reviews on the website and app? What are the ethical standards for leaving fair and accurate ratings and reviews and how does Yelp monitor and police them? What can a business do ethically to boost its ratings, gain more positive reviews, and challenge unfair ones?

ADDITIONAL EXERCISES

1. Go onto Facebook and Instagram and explore their check-in features. Whether you are comfortable checking in yourself or not, see the rich information location-sharing offers. Also, go into Snapchat and start noticing the available geofilters as you travel around to different locations. If your organization has a physical location, location-based social media could be a key part of your strategy. Perhaps the business is already on Facebook and Instagram but has not completely taken advantage of location-based features. Is the target audience right for taking advantage of Snapchat geofilters? Take some time and brainstorm ways the brand could use location information for a business advantage.

2. Reviews are powerful. Have you taken the time to read them? Find all the ratings and reviews written about your organization, brand, product, or service. Start with key ratings-and-reviews sites in the industry and then move into the social media channels highlighted here. What did you discover? If there are few reviews, what do you need to do to get people writing? Are the reviews negative? What do you need to fix? Are reviews positive? How do you leverage them in other social channels and encourage more?

Notes

1. "Lost," BrainyQuote.com, accessed October 16, 2019, http://www.brainyquote.com/quotes/keywords/lost.html.

2. Cited in Brad Plumer, "How Yelp Is Killing Chain Restaurants," WashingtonPost.com, October 3, 2011, http://www.washingtonpost.com/blogs/wonkblog/post/how-yelp-is-killing-chain-restaurants/2011/10/03/gIQAokJvHL_blog.html.

3. Cited in Kevin Li, "Research: Underdog Businesses Are More Likely to Post Fake Yelp Reviews," *Harvard Business Review*, August 30, 2013, https://hbr.org/2013/08/research-underdog-businesses-a.

4. Paige Worthy, "All the Social Media Definitions You Need to Know," Hootsuite.com, February 11, 2019, https://blog.hootsuite.com/social-media-glossary-definitions/#C.

5. "Geotagging," Techopedia.com, accessed November 15, 2019, https://www.techopedia.com/definition/86/geotagging.

6. Kathryn Zickuhr, "Location-Based Services," PewInternet.org, September 12, 2013, http://pewinternet.org/Reports/2013/Location/Main-Report/LocationBased-Services.aspx.

7. David Kaplan, "Overwhelming Number of Smartphone Users Keep Location Services Open," GeoMarketing.com, April 22, 2016, http://www.geomarketing.com/overwhelming-number-of-smartphone-users-keep-location-services-open.

8. "How comfortable are you with a mobile app having access to the device's precise location?" MediaPro, April 30, 2019, https://www.statista.com/statistics/1050277/us-perception-on-granting-smartphones-location-access-age/.

9. Zickuhr, "Location-Based Services."

10. "What is Foursquare City Guide?" Support.Foursquare.com, accessed November 15, 2019, https://support.foursquare.com/hc/en-us/articles/201015194-What-is-Foursquare-City-Guide.

11. "30 Foursquare Statistics to Help You Optimize the Platform in 2019," 99Firms.com, April 7, 2019, https://99firms.com/blog/foursquare-statistics/.

12. "About Us," Foursquare.com, accessed October 15, 2019, https://foursquare.com/about.

13. "About Us," Foursquare.com.

14. "Which social networks do you use regularly?" Statista, April 23, 2019, https://www.statista.com/forecasts/997886/social-network-usage-by-brand-in-the-uk; "Which social networks do you use regularly?" Statista, April 23, 2019, https://www.statista.com/forecasts/998543/social-network-usage-by-brand-in-canada.

15. "Social Networking Sites Consumers Have Stopped Using in Australia from 2014 to 2018," Yellow, June 25, 2018, https://www.statista.com/statistics/648850/australia-social-networking-sites-drop-off-rate/.

16. "Which social networks do you use regularly?" Statista, April 23, 2019, https://www.statista.com/forecasts/997135/social-network-usage-by-brand-in-the-us.

17. "Percentage of U.S. Internet Users Who Use Foursquare as of January 2018, by Gender," We are Flint, February 26, 2018, https://www.statista.com/statistics/814722/share-of-us-internet-users-who-use-foursquare-by-gender/.

18. "Percentage of U.S. Internet Users Who Use Foursquare as of January 2018, by Age Group," We are Flint, February 26, 2018, https://www.statista.com/statistics/814726/share-of-us-internet-users-who-use-foursquare-by-age/.

19. "Percentage of U.S. Internet Users Who Use Foursquare as of January 2018, by Urbanity," We are Flint, February 26, 2018, https://www.statista.com/statistics/814715/share-of-us-internet-users-who-use-foursquare-by-urbanity/.

20. Brandon Gaille, "26 Great Foursquare Demographics," BrandonGaille.com, January 13, 2015, http://brandongaille.com/26-great-foursquare-demographics/.

21. Evan Lepage, "Foursquare vs. the Swarm App: What's the Difference?" Hootsuite.com, accessed October 16, 2019, http://blog.hootsuite.com/foursquare-vs-the-swarm-app-whats-the-difference.

22. "Swarm for Business," Foursquare Help Center, accessed October 16, 2019, https://support.foursquare.com/hc/en-us/articles/202005800-Swarm-for-Merchants.

23. "What is Foursquare City Guide?" Support.Foursquare.com.

24. "What is Foursquare City Guide?" Support.Foursquare.com.

25. Connie Hwong, "Chart of the Week: The Return of Foursquare," VertoAnalytics.com, October 11, 2108, https://www.vertoanalytics.com/chart-of-the-week-the-return-of-foursquare/.

26. "Foursquare for Business," Business.Foursquare.com, accessed October 15, 2019, http://business.foursquare.com/ads/.

27. "Foursquare for Business," Business.Foursquare.com.

28. Wilson Alvarez, "Foursquare versus Facebook Places," WilsonAlvarez.com (blog), February 14, 2013, http://www.wilsonalvarez.com/foursquare-versus-facebook-places/.

29. "Find Places Nearby and Check In," Facebook Help Center, accessed October 10, 2014, https://www.facebook.com/help/461075590584469.

30. Nikola Bojkiv, "[Guide] New Facebook Recommendations and Reviews System," EmbedSocial.com, October 14, 2019, https://embedsocial.com/blog/facebook-recommendations/.

31. Brittany Darwell, "Facebook Lets Users Rate Any Place and Change Their Ratings from Desktop Pages," InsideFacebook.com, May 5, 2013, http://www.insidefacebook.com/2013/05/15/facebook-lets-users-rate-any-place-and-change-their-ratings-from-desktop-pages/.

32. "Introducing Location and Hashtag Stories on Explore," Instagram-Press.com (blog), May 23, 2017, accessed October 15, 2019, https://instagram-press.com/blog/2017/05/23/introducing-location-and-hashtag-stories-on-explore/.

33. "Connect to Your Customers with Facebook WiFi," Facebook Business, accessed September 18, 2017, https://www.facebook.com/business/facebook-wifi.

34. Bojkiv, "[Guide] New Facebook Recommendations."

35. Jenn Herman, "How to Use Geotags on Instagram for Your Business," Jenn'sTrends.com, March 2, 2015, http://www.jennstrends.com/geotags-on-instagram/.

36. "Geocaching 101," Geocaching.com, accessed November 15, 2019, https://www.geocaching.com/guide/.

37. Courtney Eckerle, "Social Media Marketing: Doubleday Combines Geocaching and Facebook to Boost Sales 23% for John Grisham Book," MarketingSherpa.com, May 9, 2013, https://www.marketingsherpa.com/article/case-study/geocaching-facebook-boost-sales.

38. Ryan Mac, "The Inside Story of 'Pokémon GO's' Evolution from Google Castoff to Global Phenomenon," Forbes.com, July, 26, 2016, https://www.forbes.com/sites/ryanmac/2016/07/26/monster-game/#6d505529356a.

39. Margaret Rouse, "Geo-fencing (geofencing)," WhatIsIt.Techtarget.com, December 2016, https://whatis.techtarget.com/definition/geofencing.

40. Aaron Strout, "Location-Based Marketing: Where Is It Today, and Where Is It Headed?" MarketingLand.com, November 21, 2016, https://marketingland.com/location-based-marketing-going-195732.

41. "The Power of Geofencing and How to Add It to Your Marketing," Salesforce.com, accessed October 16, 2019, https://www.salesforce.com/products/marketing-cloud/best-practices/geofencing-marketing/.

42. Emily Basileo, "7 Tips to Map Out Your Next Geo-Fencing Strategy," Inmobi.com, September 30, 2014, http://www.inmobi.com/blog/2014/09/30/7-tips-to-map-out-your-next-geo-fencing-strategy.

43. "Power of Geofencing," Salesforce.com.

44. Rip Gerber, "6 Secrets of Successful Geofence Campaigns," MobileMarketer.com, accessed October 16, 2019, http://www.mobilemarketer.com/ex/mobilemarketer/cms/opinion/columns/14036.html.

45. Ross Hamer, "Geofence Marketing: 3 Case Studies," Business2Community.com, June 5, 2017, http://www.business2community.com/marketing/geofence-marketing-3-case-studies-01853594#2ksh6hYytlDCjGVT.97.

46. Gerber, "6 Secrets of Successful Geofence Campaigns."

47. Lauryn Chamberlain, "Snapchat Now Offers Custom, On-Demand Geofilters—Starting At $5," Geomarketing.com, February 22, 2016, http://www.geomarketing.com/snapchat-now-offers-custom-on-demand-geofilters-starting-at-5.

48. "Geofilters," Snapchat.com, accessed October 16, 2019, https://www.snapchat.com/geofilters.

49. Jana Haecherl, "How To Get More Google My Business Reviews Without Having to Nag Customers," StorEdge.com, January 6, 2017, https://www.storedge.com/how-to-get-more-google-my-business-reviews.

50. Haecherl, "How To Get More Google My Business Reviews."

51. Joy Hawkins, "Google Questions and Answers: Everything You Need to Know," Search EngineLand.com, January 25, 2019, https://searchengineland.com/google-questions-answers-everything-need-know-290120.

52. Cydney Hatch, "Bring on the Traffic! How to Use Google Maps Promoted Pins," DisruptiveAdvertising.com, February 13, 2019, https://www.disruptiveadvertising.com/google-ads/google-maps-promoted-pins/.

53. BrightLocal, "Average Number of Images per Business on its Google My Business (GMB) Listing as of June 2019, by Industry [Chart]," July 15, 2019, Statista, accessed October 15, 2019, https://www.statista.com/statistics/1041481/number-of-gmb-photos-per-industry/.

54. "Nextdoor Business," Alignable.com, accessed October 16, 2019, https://us.nextdoor.com/business.

55. Tom Meisfjord, "The Not-So-Ancient History of Live Streaming," Swtichboard.Live, April 23, 2018, https://switchboard.live/blog/live-streaming-history.

56. Margaret Rouse, "Streaming Video," TechTarget.com, March 2008, http://searchunified communications.techtarget.com/definition/streaming-video.

57. "Mobile Fact Sheet," PewInternet.org, February 12, 2017, http://www.pewinternet.org/fact-sheet/mobile/.

58. Bernadette Johnson, "How Twitter Periscope Works," Computer.HowStuffWorks.com, accessed November 15, 2019, https://computer.howstuffworks.com/internet/social-networking/information/twitter-periscope1.html.

59. Mike Snider, "Twitter Can Boost TV Ratings," USAToday.com, August 6, 2013, https://www.usatoday.com/story/tech/personal/2013/08/06/nielsen-twitter-affects-tv-ratings/2613267/.

60. Michael Stelzner, "Periscope: How Your Business Can Benefit from Live Video," Social MediaExaminer.com, March 18, 2016, http://www.socialmediaexaminer.com/periscope-how-your-business-can-benefit-from-live-video-with-kim-garst/.

61. Kim Garst, "How Live-Steaming Is Changing the Face of Social Media," SalesForce.com, October 14, 2015, https://www.salesforce.com/ca/blog/2015/10/live-streaming-and-social-media.htm.

62. Jeff Thompson, "Is Nonverbal Communication a Numbers Game?" PsychologyToday.com, September 30, 2011, https://www.psychologytoday.com/blog/beyond-words/201109/is-nonverbal-communication-numbers-game.

63. Salman Aslam, "Periscope by the Numbers: Stats, Demographics & Fun Facts," Omnicore Agency.com, January 6, 2019, https://www.omnicoreagency.com/periscope-statistics/.

64. Nick Staff, "Twitter Now Lets You Invite Guests into Periscope Live Streams," The Verge.com, February 4, 2019, https://www.theverge.com/2019/2/4/18210750/twitter-periscope-invite-guests-live-streams-new-feature.

65. "Facebook Live," Facebook.com, accessed November 15, 2019, https://www.facebook.com/facebookmedia/solutions/facebook-live.

66. "28 Facebook Live Stats to Know in 2019," 99Firms.com, May 13, 2019, https://99firms.com/blog/facebook-live-stats/.

67. Christine Austin, "9 Facebook Live for Business Examples You've Got to See," Impactbnd.com, January 17, 2017, https://www.impactbnd.com/blog/facebook-live-business-examples.

68. Josh Constine, "Instagram Stories Hits 250M Daily Users, Adds Live Video Replays," Techcrunch.com, June 20, 2017, https://techcrunch.com/2017/06/20/instagram-live-video-replays/.

69. "Instagram Live," SproutSocial.com, accessed October 15, 2019, https://sproutsocial.com/glossary/instagram-live/.

70. Rachel Parker, "5 Ways Live Video Can Rock Your Content Marketing," Business2Community.com, July 19, 2015, http://www.business2community.com/content-marketing/5-ways-live-video-can-rock-your-content-marketing-01275553#boT3lWOUTXoFGH6W.99.

71. Alex X, "History of YouTube," Engadget.com, November 10, 2016, https://www.engadget.com/2016/11/10/the-history-of-youtube/; "Introduction to Live Streaming," YouTube Help, accessed October 15, 2019, https://support.google.com/youtube/answer/2474026?hl=en.

72. Tom Warren, "Apple Will Live Stream Its iPhone 11 Event on YouTube for the First Time," TheVerge.com, September 7, 2019, https://www.theverge.com/2019/9/7/20854050/apple-iphone-11-event-youtube-stream.

73. Darren Geeter, "Twitch Created a Business around Watching Video Games," February 26, 2019, https://www.cnbc.com/2019/02/26/history-of-twitch-gaming-livestreaming-and-youtube.html.

74. Michael Stelzner, "Twitch: What Marketers Need to Know," SocialMediaExaminer.com, June 29, 2018, https://www.socialmediaexaminer.com/twitch-what-marketers-need-to-know-luria-petrucci/.

75. "New Twitch Mobile App Available Now," Blog.Twitch.tv, July 5, 2017, https://blog.twitch.tv/en/2017/07/05/new-twitch-mobile-app-available-now-aa527264091b/.

76. Stelzner, "Twitch"; "About Twitch," Twitch.tv, accessed October 15, 2019, https://www.twitch.tv/p/en/about/?utm_referrer=https://www.google.com/.

77. "Twitch Advertising," TwitchAdvertising.tv, accessed October 15, 2019, https://twitchadvertising.tv/.

78. Seb Joseph, "How Brands Like Wendy's and the NFL are Marketing on Fortnite," Digiday.com, February 18, 2019, https://digiday.com/marketing/brands-wendys-nfl-marketing-fortnite/.

79. Ann Handley, "3 Ways to Integrate Video into Your Marketing Strategy," Entrepreneur.com, September 28, 2015, https://www.entrepreneur.com/article/250138.

80. Emily Bacheller, "Live Streaming Showdown: Meerkat versus Periscope," TopRankBlog.com, April 2015, http://www.toprankblog.com/2015/04/meerkat-vs-periscope/.

81. Kerry O'Shea Gorgone, "Live Streaming with Meerkat & Periscope: A Marketer's Legal Checklist," KerryGorgone.com, http://www.kerrygorgone.com/meerkat-periscope-checklist/.

82. "2018 MTV Video Music Awards," ShortyAwards.com, accessed October 21, 2019, https://shortyawards.com/11th/2018-mtv-video-music-awards.

83. Gorgone, "Live Streaming with Meerkat & Periscope."

84. "Critic," BrainyQuote.com, accessed September 18, 2019, http://www.brainyquote.com/quotes/keywords/critic.html.

85. "Review," Merriam-Webster.com, accessed October 16, 2019, http://www.merriam-webster.com/dictionary/review.

86. "Rating," Merriam-Webster.com, accessed October 16, 2019, http://www.merriam-webster.com/dictionary/rating.

87. "How Social Media Influences Shopping Behavior: Social Commerce Has Also Evolved," eMarketer.com, March 17, 2016, https://www.emarketer.com/Article/How-Social-Media-Influences-Shopping-Behavior/1013718.

88. Cited in Amy Gesenhues, "Survey: 90% of Customers Say Buying Decisions Are Influenced by Online Reviews," MarketingLand.com, April 9, 2013, https://marketingland.com/survey-customers-more-frustrated-by-how-long-it-takes-to-resolve-a-customer-service-issue-than-the-resolution-38756.

89. "Factors that Help U.S. Consumers Trust a Business as of 2017," Furniture Today, March 12, 2018, https://www.statista.com/statistics/860389/factors-that-help-consumers-trust-a-business-us/.

90. "Factors that Cause U.S. Consumers to Lose Trust in a Business as of 2017," Furniture Today, March 12, 2018, https://www.statista.com/statistics/885237/factors-that-cause-consumers-to-lose-trust-in-a-business-us/.

91. "Impact on User-Generated Content Such as Customer Reviews and Ratings According to Online Shoppers in the United States as of March 2017," June 19, 2017, https://www.statista.com/statistics/253371/ways-online-customer-reviews-affect-opinion-of-local-businesses/.

92. "Most Important Attributes of the Online Shopping Experience According to Shoppers in the United States as of November 2018," 451 Research, November 20, 2018, https://www.statista.com/statistics/973413/most-important-attributes-online-shopping-shoppers-usa/.

93. "Ratings and Reviews a Top Shopping Influencer during the Holiday Season," Marketing Charts.com, January 9, 2014, http://www.marketingcharts.com/wp/online/ratings-and-reviews-a-top-shopping-influencer-during-the-holiday-season-39087/?utm_campaign=rssfeed&utm_source=mc&utm_medium=textlink.

94. Shane Barker, "5 Ways Bad Reviews Can Actually Be Good for Your Business," Inc.com, March 9, 2017, https://www.inc.com/shane-barker/5-ways-bad-reviews-can-actually-be-good-for-your-business.html.

95. Philip Kotler, Hermawan Kartajaya, and Iwan Setiawan, *Marketing 4.0: Moving from Traditional to Digital* (Hoboken, NJ: Wiley, 2017), 109.

96. "An Introduction to Yelp Metrics as of June 30, 2019," (Yelp Factsheet), Yelp.com, accessed October 16, 2019, https://www.yelp.com/factsheet.

97. "Audience: Who's On Yelp," Yelp.com, accessed June 26, 2015, http://www.yelp.com/advertise/agency/audience.

98. "Yelp.com," SimilarWeb.com, accessed October 16, 2019, https://www.similarweb.com/website/yelp.com.

99. David Cowling, "Social Media Statistics Australia—January 2019," SocialMediaNews.com.au, https://www.socialmedianews.com.au/social-media-statistics-australia-january-2019/.

100. "Yelp Factsheet," Yelp.com.

101. "Cumulative Number of Reviews Submitted to Yelp from 2009 to 2018 (in Millions)," Yelp, February 27, 2019, https://www.statista.com/statistics/278032/cumulative-number-of-reviews-submitted-to-yelp/.

102. "Yelp Common Questions," Yelp.com, accessed October 16, 2019, https://biz.yelp.com/support/common_questions.

103. "Yelp Factsheet," Yelp.com.

104. "Yelp Common Questions," Yelp.com.

105. Jay Baer, Adam Brown, John Carroll, "The Right Way to Handle Reviews in 2019 According to Yelp," SocialPros Podcast, ConvinceAndConvert.com, August 23, 2019, https://www.convinceandconvert.com/podcasts/episodes/the-right-way-to-handle-reviews-in-2019-according-to-yelp/.

106. "Introduction to Ratings and Review Sites," SocialQuickstarter.com, accessed October 16, 2019, http://www.socialquickstarter.com/content/78-introduction_to_ratings_and_review_sites.

107. "Full Service Advertising," Biz.Yelp.com, accessed October 16, 2019, https://biz.yelp.com/.

108. "Yelp Factsheet," Yelp.com.

109. Morgan Remmers, "Get Ready for Holiday Shoppers with Yelp Deals and Gift Certificates!" Yelp Blog for Business Owners (blog), October 31, 2014, https://biz.yelp.com/blog/get-ready-for-holiday-shoppers-with-yelp-deals-and-gift-certificates.

110. Greg Sterling, "Yelp Tests Offline Attribution Using Guest WiFi and Email Matching," SearchEngineLand.com, February 20, 2018, https://searchengineland.com/yelp-tests-offline-attribution-using-guest-wifi-email-matching-292522.

111. "Why TripAdvisor," TripAdvisor.com, accessed October 16, 2019, https://static.tacdn.com/img2/adops/why_tripadvisor.pdf.

112. "Why TripAdvisor," TripAdvisor.com.

113. "Free or Premium? A Guide to Marketing on TripAdvisor," TripAdvisor.com, January 10, 2018, https://www.tripadvisor.com/TripAdvisorInsights/n2423/free-or-premium-guide-marketing-tripadvisor.

114. "Why TripAdvisor," TripAdvisor.com.

115. "Free or Premium?" TripAdvisor.com.

116. "TripAdvisor Study Reveals 42% of Travelers Worldwide Use Smartphones to Plan or Book Their Trips," Globe Newswire, CNBC.com, June 30, 2015, https://www.cnbc.com/2015/06/30/globe-newswire-tripadvisor-study-reveals-42-of-travelers-worldwide-use-smartphones-to-plan-or-book-their-trips.html.

117. Lauren Gensler, "The World's Largest Retailers 2016: Wal-Mart Dominates but Amazon Is Catching Up," Forbes.com, May 27, 2017, https://www.forbes.com/sites/laurengensler/2016/05/27/global-2000-worlds-largest-retailers/#57b6ffaebbb0.

118. Emily Dayton, "Amazon Statistics You Should Know: Opportunities to Make the Most of America's Top Online Marketplace," accessed October 16, 2019, https://www.bigcommerce.com/blog/amazon-statistics/.

119. Tyrone Stewart, "Amazon Is Used by Almost 90 Percent of UK Consumers—Report," MobileMarketing.com, July 3, 2019, https://mobilemarketingmagazine.com/amazon-uk-user-base-prime-mintel.

120. "Amazon.ca," SimilarWeb.com, accessed October 16, 2019, https://www.similarweb.com/website/amazon.ca#overview.

121. Dominic Powell, "Amazon Australia Grows Revenue More than 1500% but Remains a "Small Proportion" of the Retail Market," Smartcompany.com, April 2, 2019, https://www.smartcompany.com.au/industries/retail/amazon-australia-revenue/.

122. April Berthene, "Mobile Shopping Trends in 2018 for Amazon," DigitalCommerce 360.com, March 25, 2019, https://www.digitalcommerce360.com/2019/03/25/analyzing-amazons-mobile-users-in-2018/.

123. Ben Fox Rubin, "Amazon Looks to Improve Customer-Reviews System with Machine Learning," CNet.com, June 19, 2015, https://www.cnet.com/news/amazon-updates-customer-reviews-with-new-machine-learning-platform/.

124. Yuyu Chen, "Confessions of a Paid Amazon Review Writer," Digiday.com, March 20, 2017, https://digiday.com/marketing/vendors-ask-go-around-policy-confessions-top-ranked-amazon-review-writer/.

125. Rubin, "Amazon Looks to Improve."

126. Greg Mercer, "How to Get Amazon Reviews without Incentivizing Customers," January 5, 2017, JumpSend.com (blog), https://www.jumpsend.com/blog/how-to-get-amazon-reviews-without-incentivizing/.

127. Tara Johnson, "Experts Reveal 5 Best Practices for Increasing Amazon Product Reviews," CPCStrategy.com (blog), September 16, 2015, http://www.cpcstrategy.com/blog/2015/09/increase-amazon-product-reviews/.

128. Heidi Abramyk, "Top 10 Review Websites to Get More Customer Reviews On," Vendasta .com (blog), February 27, 2017, https://www.vendasta.com/blog/top-10-customer-review-websites.

129. "Advertise with Intent," Amazon Advertising, Advertising.Amazon.com, accessed October 21, 2019, https://advertising.amazon.com/?ref_=sspa_us_g_ext_ppc_ggl_mt_e_kw_amazon%20advertising_ct_303150274962_ex_.

130. Jay Baer, Adam Brown, and Kindra Hall, "How to Maximize the Storytelling Impact of Your Social Media," SocialPros Podcast, ConvinceAndConvert.com, accessed October 16, 2019, https://www.convinceandconvert.com/podcasts/episodes/how-to-maximize-the-storytelling-impact-of-your-social-media/.

131. "Only One-Third of Consumers Trust Most of the Brand They Buy," Edelman.com, June 18, 2019, https://www.edelman.com/news-awards/only-one-third-of-consumers-trust-most-of-the-brands-they-buy.

132. "How to Ask Customers for Reviews," ReviewTrackers.com, accessed October 21, 2019, https://www.reviewtrackers.com/guides/ask-customers-review/.

CHAPTER

10

Social Bookmarking and Social Knowledge

Organizing is what you do before you do something, so that when you do it, it is not all mixed up.[1]

—A. A. Milne

PREVIEW

Do you have a favorite topic or hobby that you are very interested in? Is it something you are very familiar with, keep up to date on the latest developments, and love to talk about? Do your friends know you as the _____ person? Perhaps you even belong to a group of people who all care about that same topic as much as you do. You and the other people interested in that topic may be referred to as being "in the know."

What value is there in being perceived as being "in the know"? In chapter 1 social capital theory was defined as the power of an individual to exert influence on a group or individual to mobilize resources.[2] The concept can also be applied to more group benefits where **social capital** is actual or virtual resources collected by an individual or group by mutual association and recognition.[3] Social capital benefits people because they can draw upon resources shared by other members of the social network, such as information and connections for personal and career networking. Belonging to a social network and sharing knowledge benefits both the receiver and giver. As individuals and a group build up social capital, everyone in the network benefits.[4] Perhaps that can partially explain the rise of social bookmarking and social-knowledge sites.

Another reason people like to share knowledge is that it simply makes them feel better. Psychology researchers have found that forms of social capital have been related to well-being, such as increased self-esteem and satisfaction with life.[5] Why do people share information and answer questions online for free? It benefits them personally as well as professionally, and simply makes them feel good.

Social Bookmarking

No one really knows how many web pages make up the internet, but Kevin Kelly, founder of *Wired* magazine, estimates that there are more individual web pages than our brain has individual neurons. In his 2010 book *What Technology Wants,* he wrote, "The Web holds about a trillion pages. The human brain holds about 100 billion neurons."[6] Keeping track of all that information is difficult, to say the least. A. A. Milne, most famous for his *Winnie-the-Pooh* series, understood the importance of organization. A main feature in Pooh books is the map of the Hundred Acre Wood. Without it one might get mixed up in the story. The same can be applied to the internet. The information age can become useless if we have no way of saving and organizing all that data. Bookmarking management systems were developed for this reason.

Social bookmarking is an online service where users can save, comment on, and share bookmarks of web documents or links.[7] These types of services have been around since 1996, but the founding of Del.icio.us in 2003 helped the words "social bookmarking" and "tagging" catch on. **Tagging** is the way social-bookmarking programs organize links to resources.[8] Tagging in social-bookmarking systems has also created **folksonomy**, which refers to a simple form of shared vocabularies.[9] **Collaborative tagging** can be used to analyze trends and determine popularity of content over time as different sources converge.[10] Examining different social-bookmarking tags can also reveal correlations to identify community or shared vocabularies as a form of crowdsourcing.[11]

Social-bookmarking systems enable users to save links to web pages to access later or share with others. Bookmarks can be viewed via searches, tags (categories), or chronologically. Web feeds enable users to become aware when new bookmark links are saved under specific tags. This activity allows users with similar interests to network and collaborate. Over the years these bookmarking management systems have added comments, ratings, web annotation (layered web-page comments), and groups with social networking features.[12]

For individual users, social bookmarking is useful for collecting bookmarks from various computers, organizing them, and enabling access from anywhere with easy sharing to others. Organizations can use social bookmarking to increase information-sharing between members. Social bookmarking can also benefit organizations in terms of search engine optimization (SEO). When the editor of TheAtlantic.com, Adrienne LaFrance, tried to discover how many websites publish the trillions of individual web pages on the internet, she found estimates around one billion. Despite these vast options, the average person only visits around

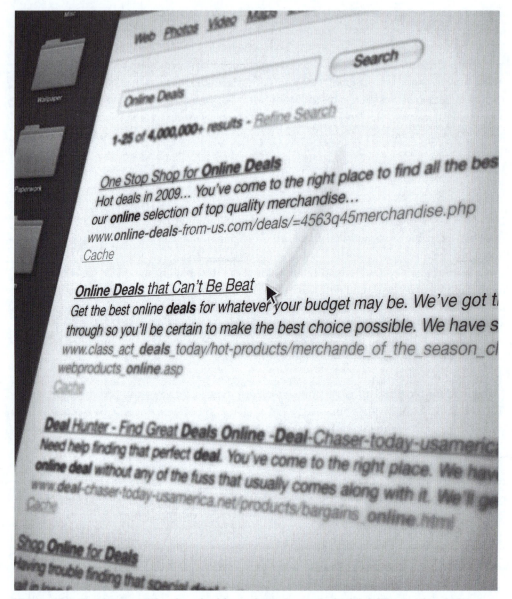

Figure 10.1. Content curation is valuable and much needed with trillions of websites.

© SpiffyJ / iStock Photo

a hundred (96) separate sites a month.[13] How do people get from one billion possibilities to the one hundred websites they end up visiting? Content curation is one way.

Content curation is a process of gathering information relevant to a specific topic or area of interest to present to others.[14] An organization or social platform can be seen as a resource for valuable information by bookmarking and sharing the top developments on a specific topic. This is different from **news aggregation**, which uses software to collect all new syndicated web content from many newspapers, magazines, and blogs into one page.[15]

Considering the trillions of web pages and billions of websites, sorting through millions of possibilities and serving up relevant content is a valuable service.

The three most popular social-bookmarking platforms by number of users are Reddit and Digg. We will also look at BuzzFeed as a content aggregation platform with social networking features under this category.[16] We will look at these three platforms as possible key channels for brand social media strategy. Other early social bookmarking platforms have shut down with Del.icio.us shutting down in 2017 and StumbleUpon shutting down in 2018. A key to success in social bookmarking is joining a community and being active. As an organization or an individual, begin by submitting links, writing reviews, rating other stories, and starting to network with others who share the same interests. The more active a user is, the better their reputation and the more trusted their links will become.[17]

Reddit

Reddit is a social news and entertainment company founded in 2005 and acquired by Condé Nast Publications in 2006.[18] Reddit has 330 million active users globally, making it the top social-bookmarking site and surpassing other social platforms like Twitter and Snapchat.[19] Nearly half of Reddit's traffic comes from the United States (almost 50 percent). The next-largest countries include the United Kingdom (8 percent), Canada (8 percent), and Australia (4 percent).[20] Globally Reddit users are young, with the largest age groups being sixteen to twenty-four years old (32 percent) and twenty-five to thirty-four years old (32 percent), and over two-thirds under thirty-five years old.[21]

In the United States, Reddit users tend to be more male (65 percent) than female (35 percent), and are younger with top age groups of eighteen- to twenty-four-year-olds (32 percent), thirty- to forty-five-year-olds (31 percent), fifty-to sixty-four-year-olds (24 percent) and sixty-five years old and older (13 percent). Reddit users have above-average college or graduate school degrees (71 percent) and most users live in urban or suburban areas (70 percent).[22] Reddit is the seventh most popular social networking mobile app in the United States just behind Snapchat and above WhatsApp.[23] Reddit users are also engaged with average session lengths of nearly five minutes, the fourth longest of mobile apps behind TikTok (10 minutes), Pinterest (5 minutes), and Facebook (5 minutes).[24] Top reasons people use Reddit include entertainment (72 percent), news (43 percent), to follow brands/companies (17 percent) and to strengthen professional networks (8 percent).[25]

Reddit is often referred to as "the front page of the internet." To be effective on Reddit, organizations must get involved with the community of users called Redditors. This social site is about bookmarking web links, but the most important part is sharing. Users post things they find interesting, cool, horrible, and strange. Then they comment on the posts and upvote or downvote them, which moves items up or down in ranking. Ranking is also based on age of the submission, feedback ratio, and total vote count. From the front page, shared content is organized by Subreddits, which are communities centered on a topic, from Mobile to Minecraft. Brands can create their own Subreddit or participate in others and keep track of updates by subscribing.[26] A newer feature is integration with Snapchat, where Redditors can easily share their favorite Reddit posts with friends in a snap.[27]

Like many communities, Reddit has its own language. OP refers to an original poster. TIL means "today I learned," which is a common abbreviation. Many posts are TIL observations and realizations. Among the most popular abbreviations are IAmA and AMA, referring to an Ask Me Anything thread. Well-known people have done AMAs, including former US president Barack Obama, Canadian astronaut Chris Hadfield, Madonna, and Bill Gates. Obama's AMA was so popular the increased traffic brought down many parts of the website.[28]

As on other social channels, each Reddit user creates a profile, but here numbers indicate how much Karma a user has earned. Redditors get Karma points for posts and comments that have been upvoted by other users. Increased link and comment Karma points help boost a user's influence. For a small fee, users can purchase a premium gold membership to get access to secret Subreddits and other features.[29] In 2017, Reddit added more social network features to go with user profile pages, including the ability to follow other users and location tagging by partnering with Foursquare.[30] Organizations should be aware of the Reddit or Slashdot Effect, when a smaller website suddenly gets a huge influx of traffic due to Reddit. Be prepared so that this immense traffic doesn't crash an organization's website.[31]

Social Media Examiner suggests several ways organizations can use Reddit to grow their businesses. First, find brand enthusiasts through Subreddits or create new ones related to the product or service. Next, encourage user submissions such as pictures. Finally, feature the best submission that week. Reddit is also a place to monitor customer questions, suggestions, and complaints. Be sure to get these customers to the right internal channels for customer service.[32] Richard Edelman of public relations firm Edelman adds that Reddit can help identify leading stories of the day, serve as an early warning for potential brand crises, and help uncover significant consumer insights. For example, insights found in discussion during an AMA led to a new Ben and Jerry's flavor.[33] It is important for brands to approach this social channel from the right perspective. Reddit cannot be seen simply as another marketing promotion channel. Reddit offers guidelines for successful marketing on Reddit called "brandiquette." Their advice focuses on transparency, genuine engagement, and honest offers (see table 10.1).[34]

Table 10.1. "Brandiquette" for Advertisers on Reddit

- Respond to comments.
- Keep it real!
- Include a thumbnail.
- Offer promo codes or special deals for Redditors.
- Customize a splash page.
- Research your brand on Reddit.
- Avoid ad fatigue.
- Share your promotion.
- Have fun!

Source: "Brandiquette," Reddit.com, June 2015, https://www.reddit.com/wiki/brandiquette; © Reddit Inc.

Brands can also use Subreddits to keep fans updated with organization news and events. The Philadelphia Phillies major league baseball team uses the sidebar to feature an updated team schedule and league ranking board. Brands can also leverage the popularity of AMAs to hold interviews with key employees or supporters of the organization, brand, product, or service.[35] What type of content works? Reddit posts with external links receive the most upvotes, with video and photo links generating more upvotes than website links; top posts tend to be between 20 and 120 characters.[36]

Reddit has paid social media options such as promoted posts that include text, website, image, and video links. Like other social platforms, these native social ads start with selecting objectives from brand awareness and reach, website traffic, website conversions, app installs, or video views. Call-to-action buttons in ads match objectives such as download, install, show now, and view more.

Ads are purchased on a bidding system that varies by campaign objective from cost-per-thousand impressions (CPM), cost-per-click (CPC) and cost-per-view (CPV). Brands set up daily budgets or lifetime budgets based on start and end dates for each campaign, which are called ad groups. Brands can target audiences by device, location, interest category or subcategory, and Subreddit. There are thousands of different topics, so aim to find the group that is most passionate about areas in which your brand is most relevant.[37]

Metrics are measured via "Click Trackers" and are reported in a central dashboard to analyze results and optimize performance. Brands can boost organic content already shared by fans with promoted posts and mobile-specific ads. There are low daily budget minimums and campaigns are tracked with analytics reporting tools.[38] L'Oréal had success with Reddit advertising promoting a new La Roche-Posay Effaclar product line to enthusiasts in Reddit's passionate beauty and skincare communities. The effort increased awareness but also had high engagement because the brand used an AMA with a board-certified dermatologist for users to ask their questions. Campaign results included a 20 percent lift in brand awareness, a 10 percent brand favorability lift, and 9 percent purchase intent lift.[39]

Digg

Digg is a social news website that aggregates news and publishers' streams via peer evaluation of voting up content, and also supports easy sharing of content to other social platforms such as Twitter and Facebook.[40] The social channel was founded in 2004 and has roughly 7.5 million visitors a month. Forty-three percent of Digg users come from the United States, followed by India (26 percent) and Japan (7 percent).[41] Digg users tend to be more men than women, with above-average college or graduate school degrees. Top Digg user interests include news and media, computer electronics and technology, and arts and entertainment.[42]

This social channel lets users discover, share, and recommend website content, describing itself as "What the Internet is talking about right now." Digg members submit a web page on Digg.com and then other members vote the page up to Digg It. Users can easily save stories and share via Twitter or Facebook. Voting also takes place across the web through Digg button widgets added to other websites that allow visitors to vote as they browse.[43] Additional features include categories such as science, business, entertainment, and technology, plus an editorially driven front page. Digg also has enhanced mobile features.[44]

Digg has had a bumpy road from being an early innovator to losing traffic to competitor Reddit. As a result, Digg was torn apart in 2012 when it had only 3.8 million users. The site recreated itself with a new staff, design, and interface. Since the relaunch, Digg steadily regained users to 18 million in 2017, but dropped again to less than 8 million by 2019. Stories with the most "Diggs" make their way to the home page, but the Digg Score also factors in Facebook shares and tweets. Digg moderators also add a human factor that consists of Digg Editors who decide what and where stories should appear.[45] The home page has big photos and minimal text, and comments were eliminated.[46] The focus of Digg is on quality content that users want to read, with a goal of highlighting sixty to seventy posts a day. Digg wants the home page to be a calm and clear place that is not noisy.[47]

For organizations Digg represents a way to spot trends, collect and distribute content, and build awareness. Digg is a great way to fuel public relations campaigns by spreading earned media coverage. Publishers like Digg because it drives traffic to their stories. Digg could also drive traffic spikes to organization websites. Open an account and submit links every time an organization creates a new piece of content or is featured in an article from another news source. In 2016 Digg entered into a partnership with the media company Gannett and in 2018 Digg was bought by advertising company BuySellAds. Digg Reader, its RSS Reader, was shut down in 2018.[48]

The Digg widget button should also be added to business websites and blogs to enable easy Digg voting. Another strategy is to monitor Digg and write blogs and posts, or create content about the topics that have made it to the front page. This can generate search activity from what may be a hot topic but also will provide links to direct traffic and improve SEO. Getting popular within the site will boost search engine rankings and referral traffic.[49]

Paid social media is an option for Digg. Brands can purchase native advertising by working with brand partners to display and co-create content to be featured on the platform. They offer both promoted native content and multiple display advertising formats purchased on a CPM basis. Ad campaigns are targeted by audience interest groups and geotargeting by country, state, or metro area. Ads can run for specific dates or ongoing renewal every thirty days. Campaigns are data driven and measured for performance, but the social-bookmarking platform makes it clear they are looking for valuable content, describing its paid options as "Digg makes suck-free ads that work."[50]

BuzzFeed

BuzzFeed, founded in 2006, is a social news and entertainment company that collects and creates viral content from around the web.[51] BuzzFeed is more on the content-discovery side of this category but has attracted a lot of attention, with roughly 150 million global monthly visitors to the social platform on mobile and desktop. Top countries include the United States with 50 percent of traffic followed by Japan (9 percent), the United Kingdom (7 percent), Canada (6 percent), and Australia

Figure 10.2. Brands like Home Depot have partnered with BuzzFeed to create DIY content.

© Mapodile / iStock Photo

(4 percent).[52] BuzzFeed users skew younger with the platform indicating it reaches 60 percent of millennials aged twenty-four to thirty-eight years old. In recent years BuzzFeed has also started creating native content inside social media networks and platforms such as Facebook and YouTube, generating more than nine billion monthly content views and reaching an audience of more than 650 million.[53] In fact, 80 percent of BuzzFeed's audience discovers its content on other websites such as Facebook, Snapchat, YouTube, WeChat, and Apple News.[54]

BuzzFeed has become a top destination for news, with people in the United States listing it as the sixth online news source behind the *New York Times* and just as popular as MSNBC, the *Washington Post*, and MSN online.[55] In the United Kingdom, BuzzFeed is also the sixth most popular online news source with MSN News and just below the *Sun* and *Mirror* online.[56] In Australia, BuzzFeed is the seventh most popular online news source below the *Sydney Morning Herald* and just as popular as the *Daily Telegraph* and the *Herald Sun*.[57] Among English-speaking Canadians, BuzzFeed is the ninth most popular online news site just below *Globe and Mail* online and just as popular as the *Toronto Star*.[58] In 2016 the platform separated its news and entertainment content with BuzzFeed News focused on serious investigative journalism.[59]

BuzzFeed originally started as an algorithm created to track stories around the web that showed signs of becoming viral. Over the years the company added content curators, editors, and staff reporters delivering breaking news and in-depth reporting. BuzzFeed is most known for its aggregated listicles, of which it creates hundreds daily.[60] A **listicle** is short-form writing based on an often numerical theme structure with added copy to be

MINI CASE

Behr Paints BuzzFeed

In 2013 Behr Paints decided to go after a younger crowd by partnering with the social news-content site BuzzFeed. Behr sponsored the new DIY BuzzFeed content vertical to offer household solutions and share ideas. Instead of buying traditional advertising, which millennials are known to be more skeptical of, Behr partnered with BuzzFeed to offer value-added content. Brand-sponsored BuzzFeed articles included "35 Money-Saving Home Décor Knock-offs," and "The 24 Most Colorful Cities in the World."[a]

Behr partnered with public relations firm Burson-Marsteller to create eighteen custom editorial posts about painting and decorating tips and tricks from Behr's director of color marketing, Erika Woelfel. The native advertising effort kicked off with Behr giving the BuzzFeed office a DIY make-over that generated more custom posts. The five-month campaign resulted in nearly 60 million impressions.[b]

Five years later the toy brand Hot Wheels partnered with BuzzFeed to reach younger parents skeptical of ads. The native advertising format worked well as parents first needed to understand the benefits of play versus more "educational" toys. A series of custom posts and videos provided news-worthy research that highlighted the benefits of children playing with Hot Wheels in a relevant and engaging way. The campaign resulted in a higher share rate that was four times and an engagement rate two times greater BuzzFeed's normal rate.[c]

[a] Karl Greenberg, "Behr Paints BuzzFeed," MediaPost.com, April 9, 2013, http://www.mediapost.com/publications/article/197671/behr-paints-buzzfeed.html.

[b] "Case Study: Behr's BuzzFeed Campaign," Burson-Marsteller.com, accessed February 18, 2015, http://www.burson-marsteller.com/case-studies/behrs-buzzfeed-campaign.

[c] "Hot Wheels Success Story," BuzzFeed.com, August 21, 2018, https://www.buzzfeed.com/buzzfeedmarketing/hot-wheels-success-story.

published as an article.[61] One example of a trending BuzzFeed listicle is "21 Feel–Good Tweets That Will Make You Feel Better About Everything: Featuring Cute Family Members and Even *Cuter* Pets."[62]

BuzzFeed is also known for its online quizzes, which were created out of the viral success of listicles. Results of identity quizzes such as "Which '00s Indie Band Are You?" gives readers the perfect content to want to share with others. They have become so popular that other news publications write about them, such as in a *Slate* article by Heather Schwedel questioning whether the quizzes may have become too weird now that they have evolved to build quizzes such as "Build a Bowl of Mac 'n' Cheese and We'll Accurately Guess Your Height."[63]

Content is divided into news, videos, quizzes, tasty (recipes), and thirty additional topic areas. There are a variety of feeds from LOL, win to fail, and trending within which users can vote on stories for each category. Many stories are a collection of social media posts curated by BuzzFeed staff and posts have comments like a blog.[64] Anyone can sign up for a Buzz-Feed Community account and create their own BuzzFeed posts. It is against community guidelines for businesses to create brand content or any content that is promotional. Buzz-Feed also does not sell traditional online advertising such as banner ads.

However, there are paid social media options to reach this social platform's large audience. The big opportunity for marketing with BuzzFeed is native advertising. BuzzFeed focuses on advertising partners who help create "custom content worth sharing." Brands can work with BuzzFeed's creative and video teams to create original content, then distribute audience-targeted, brand-sponsored content across BuzzFeed's website and social accounts. Brands track content performance via a real-time social dashboard. Content options include custom social posts, original video, promotion, and story units to promote the brand content. BuzzFeed's Social Discovery (SoDisco) team also promotes branded content with native ads on social networks like Facebook.[65]

An example of branded content on BuzzFeed is the Macy's-sponsored listicle, "11 Back-To-School Outfits That'll Crush It on Social Media: Get Ready to Have a Fashionable Feed This Fall, Only with Macy's."[66] BuzzFeed has also worked with brands like Staples to create YouTube videos like "6 School Hacks You're Going to Need This Year Presented by BuzzFeed & Staples."[67] In 2019 BuzzFeed introduced new commerce-based advertising options that included more options to drive clicks and direct sales. BuzzFeed will create custom posts for brands and drive purchase through affiliate links. They are also offering a shoppable ad unit that appears across relevant shopping posts.[68]

The Hundred Acre Wood was a big place, and readers of *Winnie-the-Pooh* needed a map to get around. A. A. Milne knew a little organization can go a long way. That is the goal of bookmarking sites and news aggregators for dealing with the vast amount of information found on the web. They can help narrow the billions to the fewer than one hundred websites that consumers visit each month. Marketing communications professionals can leverage them for brand social media strategies. Public attention is hard to garner with so much clutter, but a cohesive social-bookmarking strategy could be a way for brands, products, and services to direct that attention their way. In addition to the social channels presented here, also consider Slashdot.org as a niche social-bookmarking site and NowThis for brand marketing video partnerships that create video news to distribute on social network feeds.[69]

Social Knowledge

Brian Eno said, "Every collaboration helps you grow."[70] Brian Eno is an innovator in ambient music, but what most of the public is probably more familiar with is Eno's collaborative efforts with well-known artists such as David Bowie, Talking Heads, U2, Coldplay, and Paul Simon.[71] Collaboration can improve organizations and their social media through wikis and social-knowledge channels that make it easier than ever.

Writing is normally the solo act of a single person collecting knowledge and then individually sharing it with others. This is true for interpersonal communication, articles, books, and even encyclopedias. Yet wikis helped change this. A **wiki** is simply a website that allows collaborative editing by multiple contributors. The word "wiki" comes from **WikiWiki-Web**, which was the first website to use a wiki style of programming in 1995.[72]

Encyclopedia salesmen used to go house-to-house selling parents the key to knowledge for their children to succeed in life. Today, this type of knowledge is no longer held by a few. No matter a person's opinion of the quality and accuracy of Wikipedia, most cannot argue with its influence. Before discussing Wikipedia, it is important to first consider private wikis. Internal communications can improve organization performance through integrated employee communication. Most businesses are separated into silos that make up the company's collective knowledge. This institutional memory or knowledge can get locked up with specific employees, on individual hard drives, or lost completely when an employee leaves.[73]

Private wikis provide access to a business's most up-to-date collective knowledge. **Company wikis** can bring together global divisions and partners who may not be in the same building, city, or country.[74] The main reasons an organization would use a wiki include documentation (19 percent), knowledge base (19 percent), project management (17 percent), tacit knowledge (17 percent), meeting management (14 percent), and encyclopedia (12 percent).[75]

Employee-only wikis can be run on a company's own servers or outsourced to an online wiki provider. The key to success is defining the goal of the wiki. Goals would be to provide or house anything from supply orders and entertainment spots for clients to ways to operate specialized equipment and valuable marketing knowledge about key competitors. Aggregate questions and answers to the public wiki to cut down on answering the same question repeatedly. The level of transparency and collaboration helps make efforts much more efficient and timely. Competitive advantage may come from the shared knowledge gained from a corporate wiki. It is working for IBM, which runs 56,000 internal wikis that have more than a million page views a day.[76]

Beyond private wikis, public **social knowledge platforms** or networks are internet-based information exchanges where users can ask questions and get answers from real people. These services have become social as they base answers on the wisdom of the crowd, user ratings, followers, commenting, and sharing. Users of these services see themselves as influencers making a difference in their areas of expertise.

Here we will look at the top public wiki, Wikipedia, and how it can influence organizations and businesses. Then we will discuss Yahoo! Answers and Quora, two of the top social-knowledge channels. Question-and-answer sites can be an effective way for organizations to connect with a target audience, build a brand, and improve SEO.

Wikipedia

Wikipedia is a collaboratively edited, free, internet encyclopedia supported by the nonprofit Wikimedia Foundation. Founded in 2001, Wikipedia attracts nearly 500 million unique monthly visitors and has more than 70,000 active contributors.[77] There are nearly six million English-language articles and more than 40 million articles total on Wikipedia. Many of these articles are centered on businesses and organizations.[78] How should brands interact with Wikipedia? If they do not already have an article about their brand, should they create one?

First, find out if the business or organization qualifies. Anyone can make a Wikipedia article, but if it does not meet the social site's guidelines, a moderator will delete it. Wikipedia is not a directory, and its guidelines state that businesses must meet certain requirements. The main qualification is reputation. If an organization is a startup or small business, it may not be eligible.[79] High-level media exposure is the main hurdle to having a Wikipedia page, and that requires coverage in large media outlets.

For businesses that do meet the guidelines, a Wikipedia article can help add legitimacy to the organization. Users know the site is not marketing- or advertising-driven and is more factually based. Wikipedia is social media–driven, yet still an encyclopedia. Opinions are not allowed, and a Wikipedia article offers a place to present the facts about an organization. It is also great for exposure, since nearly all Google searches return Wikipedia's listings in the top links.[80]

There are negative aspects to being on Wikipedia. Moderators do not like employees or business owners making updates. Organizations normally need to find someone unassociated with the business to update content and be active on the Talk page.[81] That said, there is little control once an article is up. Anyone, from disgruntled customers to competitors, can go in and update a business page. This means the page needs to be monitored constantly. A Wikipedia entry can significantly boost the reputation of a business but can also seriously hurt it through a piece of misinformation.

Yahoo! Answers

Yahoo! Answers is a community question-and-answer website or social-knowledge platform started by Yahoo! in 2005.[82] The site attracts roughly 150 million visits a month worldwide. The platform is very global, with the site available in twelve different languages. Top countries of users include the United States (31 percent), Taiwan (19 percent), Brazil (12 percent), Mexico (5 percent), and Italy (5 percent). Top audience interests include games, video games, computer electronics and technology, science, and education.[83]

Yahoo! Answers users can ask any question, as long as they do not violate the community guidelines. Contents of answers are owned by users, but Yahoo! has a royalty-free right to publish the information. Misuse or misinformation is monitored by users, who report abuses. Some subject areas are based more on personal opinion, but most answers must be based on fact, and users are required to mention their sources. Posts are removed if a significant number of trusted abuse reports are received. To ask and answer questions, users must have a Yahoo! ID. Questions are assigned to a category and remain open for four to eight days.[84]

Social points encourage users to answer questions and help limit spam. They can receive ten points for giving the Best Answer designated by the asker of the question or voted by the community. Points are divided from Level 1 (1–249 points) to Level 7 (25,000+ points), which designate how active a user has been and provide more access to the site. Badges are used to designate Yahoo! Answers contributors with Top Contributor, Staff, and Official, which is used for celebrities or government departments. Knowledge Partners badges designate organizations that share their personal knowledge and experience.[85]

Features of the Yahoo! Answers website include a personalized home page, content activity streams, and the ability to add photos and video. The Yahoo! Answers website is designed to be mobile-friendly, but the question-and-answer website launched a mobile app

Figure 10.3. The importance of Q&A content and platforms will increase with voice search.

© Antonio Guillem / iStock Photo

in 2016. The Yahoo! Answers Now mobile app includes features such as notifications and questions sent to experts in categories for better answers.[86]

It is important to note that Yahoo! Answers has been criticized for its answers not always being factual or very deep. Some claim this stems from a reward system based on activity and not quality. However, the community guidelines do require factual information with sources and users monitor answers that can be removed.[87]

Celebrities have appeared on Yahoo! Answers to promote causes and organizations. During the 2008 US presidential campaign, Hillary Clinton, John McCain, Barack Obama, and Mitt Romney posted questions. For a nonprofit awareness campaign, UNICEF ambassadors asked questions to garner support.[88]

Ideas for brand social media strategy include having an employee or multiple key employees open accounts and fill in the user profile with a website link and bio that emphasizes expertise in a specific area. Find a niche by answering questions that can be answered well to build authority and drive traffic. Including a website link in every answer could be labeled as spam. Deliver real value and users will find the organization via the account bio.[89] Contribute to the community. Don't just add content. The individual must also engage with other users. Vote on other contributors' answers and make helpful comments. Take off the "marketing, advertising, or PR hat" to start connecting, leading, and influencing. Contributing highly valued answers builds credibility and boosts image as an industry leader.

Participation in Yahoo! Answers can help organizations drive traffic, generate awareness, or establish a brand reputation. Providing helpful, significant answers can help generate qualified leads. Monitoring questions in key categories is also a great consumer-research tool. Knowing what people are looking for can help improve business offerings. Search engines try to find the best answer to questions typed in the search box. Even Google returns a high number of Yahoo! Answers pages. This can lead to high visibility for an organization to build brand awareness and traffic. Paid social media options for Yahoo! Answers are not available.[90]

Quora

Quora is a question-and-answer website where questions are submitted and answered by its community of users. This social-knowledge channel was founded in 2009 and today has more than 300 million global unique visitors a month.[91] More than a third (35 percent) of Quora's user traffic comes from the United States, with other top countries including India (21 percent), the United Kingdom (6 percent), Canada (5 percent), and Australia (3 percent). Top audience interests include computers, electronics, technology, news, and media.[92] In the United States, Quora users tend to be highly educated.[93]

Quora was started by two former Facebook employees to build a better question-and-answer site. Promoted as "Your best source for knowledge," this social site collects user-submitted questions and answers. Content is organized into more than 400,000 topics for information discovery and easier navigation. Users collaborate by editing questions and suggesting edits to other users' answers, as they do on Wikipedia. Users can also upvote or downvote answers. Quora includes full-text search and a blogging platform to create and follow blogs.[94] Quora also has a Stats feature described as a dashboard for authors. The Quora question-and-answer site and blogging platform was built to enable anyone sharing great content to gain a big audience.[95]

Quora's home page highlights content from across the service rather than just people users follow. As TechCrunch says, "You don't have to be a celebrity or have built up a personal following to make a splash." Quora Stats helps track that traffic through views on questions, answers, and blog posts over time. It also tracks upvotes and shares.[96]

Quora requires users to register with their real name versus a screen name. Quora attracts a higher quality of experts than other question-and-answer sites. Big-name CEOs, Hollywood producers, and well-known journalists answer questions. High-profile users such as Jimmy Wales, Michael Dell, Steve Case, Marc Andreessen, and Ashton Kutcher were early adopters.[97] Yet people don't need to be famous to get big exposure on Quora. Users vote for quality answers. Make sure contributions are thoughtful, intelligent, and interesting.

For success on Quora, company representatives should start by establishing credibility by announcing who they are, what their background is, and their job titles. Instead of giving a predictable, straightforward response, try to take answers in a unique yet related direction. People love stories. Stats are great, but support an opinion with a story that brings it to life, is entertaining to read, and makes the answer memorable.[98]

Quora offers an opportunity to build a brand as an expert or thought leader in an industry. Set up an account for a key employee and fill out the bio section that also connects the account to jobs the individual had, educational institutions attended, and cities where he or she has lived. Include a link to the company website or blog.[99]

Answering questions increases links and SEO. By keying in on relevant topics, an organization can reach its target audiences and engage them where they are looking for solutions. Helpful, informed answers can generate qualified leads. Yet don't be pushy, or contributions could be labeled as spam.[100]

Added features include editors to create more visible and organized answers and Writing Sessions, which are live Q&A sessions with experts in different fields. This was seen as a way to create high-profile events much like Reddit's AMAs. Some Writing Sessions have featured entrepreneur "angel" investor David Rose, president of Planned Parenthood Cecile Richards, and Facebook COO Sheryl Sandberg.[101] Quora also added Knowledge Prizes as incentives for experts to answer important questions in different areas or industries. Answers benefit a lot of people and cash prizes can be kept by experts or donated to charity.[102]

Paid Quora social media advertising options are also available through Quora Ads Manager. Brands should start with their campaign objectives such as website traffic, website conversions, app downloads, or brand awareness. Set your budget and schedule with campaign start and end dates with daily or lifetime campaign budgets. Quora ads are bought on a real-time bidding auction system. Metrics are tracked via Quora Pixel to measure conversion data and optimize campaigns. Quora ad formats include native Text, Image, and Promoted Answers.[103]

Then select from contextual, audience, behavioral, and broad targeting options. Contextual targeting includes showing ads by topics, keywords, or specific questions relevant to your product or service. Audience targeting via website traffic, lookalike, and list match options show ads to Quora users who match your brand's website visitors, an audience that looks like an audience you have already created, or an audience based on an uploaded email list from CRM data. Behavioral targeting shows ads to users based on their interest engagement and history. Interest, Keyword and Question targeting shows ads to people who have engaged with certain topics, keywords they have viewed, or questions they have visited. Finally, broad targeting shows ads widely across the Quota audience based on location and device.[104]

An example of Quora ads is a campaign run by *The Economist* that chose Quora for their highly educated readers. The goals included reaching new audiences to drive subscriptions and engaging existing subscribers around the publication's content to gather insight into their questions and interests. They used Quora Sessions for its experts to write about topics the brand was less known for, such as science and technology. This broadened people's view of the publication's expertise. *The Economist's* journalists and editors also created personal accounts as thought leaders and to join conversations responding to questions to interact with current and prospective subscribers. Results of the effort include a regular monthly Economist Session, individual content views of up to five million views, and more than nine thousand followers.[105]

There are numerous social-knowledge platforms and networks from Wikipedia to question-and-answer websites. In addition to the websites covered here, also consider Answers.com, ChaCha, Ask.com, and WikiAnswers (now part of Answers.com). A new experiment in Q&A services is Alexa Answers. Amazon opened its smart assistant to user-submitted answers to "teach Alexa." Contributors are rewarded with points and badges. Early performance of the smart speaker Q&A platform were not promising; answers were being delivered, as Jack Morse of Mashable indicates, "ranging from unintentionally inaccurate, to deliberate trolling, to calculated misinformation."[106] Despite Amazon's experiment, voice search on mobile phones is increasing and Q&A content is important for voice search SEO. As with other social media channels, no marketer, advertiser, or public relations professional can do it all. The key to success is to choose the right social knowledge platform for brand, target audience, and message. Then invest in the platform by contributing quality content and building real engagement.

Another consideration in social knowledge is RSS feeds. **RSS (rich site summary)** is a convenient way for people to listen to and read what others are saying and writing. RSS, also known as "really simple syndication," uses standard web feed formats to publish frequently updated information including blog entries, news, audio, and video. RSS allows authors to syndicate or publish content automatically to subscribers who want to receive current updates from favorite websites on their computers or mobile devices. This makes it easier for users and it enables news aggregation. Users subscribe by entering their feed's URL into their RSS reader or by clicking the feed icon. The important consideration for business use of RSS is to make sure organization of content is easy to share and easier to collect.[107]

Brand websites and blogs should offer an RSS feed to ensure updated content is delivered automatically via email or a feed reader. A feed reader is also a convenient way to keep up to date on competitor activity and industry developments. With the shutdown of the popular Google Reader in 2013, millions of RSS users had to switch to alternatives. Readers are available to use on computers and mobile apps. Top RSS readers include Feedly, News-Blur, Inoreader, G2Reader, and Feeder.[108] RSS feeds are also needed for podcast distribution. The next section will cover a topic related to social knowledge. Podcasts enable social knowledge to be sent automatically to subscribers via audio or video content.

Podcasts

George Carlin said, "The reason I talk to myself is that I'm the only one whose answers I accept."[109] Yet podcasts have grown immensely based on the truth that we do like to hear answers, insights, and stories from others. Whether it is delivering comedy sketches, newscasts, poetry, or business tips, a **podcast** is a series of episodes of audio or video content delivered digitally. Podcasts are subscribed to and downloaded through web syndication or streamed online through a computer or mobile device.[110]

The term "podcast" is a combination of *broadcast* and *pod,* referring to the iPod as the main delivery device of audio podcasts. Files are user-selected and downloaded onto the device, and then can be taken anywhere for listening or viewing later offline.[111] This has provided more listening opportunities to consumer podcast content with top places including doing housework or cooking at home, in the car while driving, while walking outside, running or working out at the gym, and while using public transportation. In fact, the number one reason people feel podcasts are enjoyable is that you can do other things while listening.[112]

Podcasting follows the main characteristic of social media in that it bypasses the traditional gatekeepers in broadcast media such as radio stations. No one owns the technology and it is free to create and listen to content. Considering the broad array of devices that can use the medium, another generic term that can be used is netcasting. Podcasting was around before, but gained its big start in 2005 when Apple released iTunes 4.9 with native support for podcasts. A version of podcasts is a **video podcast**, which is a series of video clips or web television series delivered digitally that are often subscribed to and downloaded or streamed online through a computer or mobile device. Sometimes video podcasting is called vodcasting.[113] Video podcasts are now delivered via iTunes but can also refer to video distributed through the internet on websites or social channels such as YouTube.[114]

In 2013, Apple announced that it had surpassed one billion subscriptions for podcasts via its iTunes app, and today one thousand new podcasts are premiered in iTunes each week. *USA Today* has reported a resurgence in podcast contributors and listeners and *Marketing News* has announced that the age of the podcast has arrived.[115] The mainstream is heading to podcasting, with actors and comedians such as Alec Baldwin, Ice-T, and Tom Green starting shows along with CBS, NBC, ABC, Fox, and NPR, which are now offering audio versions of their TV news shows. Top podcasts are attracting millions of listeners, but organizations can be successful with a smaller number by attracting the right niche.[116]

Edison Research reports 51 percent of people in the United States have listened to podcasts, nearly a third (32 percent) are monthly podcast listeners, and 22 percent listen to podcasts weekly. The number of people who have listened to a podcast has grown steadily since 2013 (see figure 10.4). Marketing on podcasts can be highly effective with 54 percent of consumers saying they are more likely to consider brands if they have heard about it on a podcast. In terms of time spent listening to audio sources, podcasts have surpassed (28 percent) traditional AM/FM radio (24 percent).[117]

There are slightly more men (55 percent) than women (45 percent) listeners of podcasts. Podcasts are most popular with younger age groups, reaching 40 percent of twelve- to twenty-four-year-olds and twenty-five- to forty-four-year-olds compared to just 17 percent of people over fifty-five years old.[118] The most popular topics for podcasts include music (39

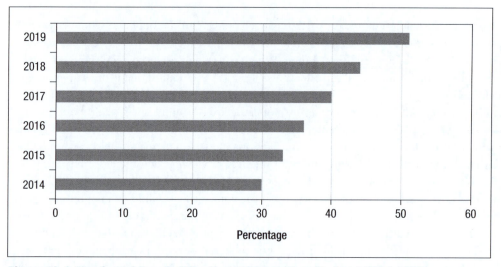

Figure 10.4. Number of People Who Have Listened to a Podcast 2014–2019

Source: "The Podcast Consumer 2019," EdisonResearch.com, 2019, https://www.edisonresearch.com/the-podcast-consumer-2019/.

percent), news (36 percent), entertainment (32 percent), history (31 percent), sports (31 percent), and food (30 percent). Podcast listening occurs mostly on mobile devices (65 percent) compared to desktop and laptops (25 percent), but smart speaker listening has increased to 10 percent.[119]

Podcasting has also grown past its iTunes roots to reach new audiences on apps such as SoundCloud, Stitcher, SoundCloud, TuneIn Radio, iHeartRadio, Google Podcasts, Audible, and Spotify. Anyone can produce a hit show and the outlets for distribution are growing. Stitcher has 250 million monthly active users and allows users to "stitch" together their favorite radio shows and podcasts from more than 65,000 options into custom playlists for everything from workouts to weekends. Stitcher also has editors who create lists such as Top 20 Comedy or Top 20 News & Politics shows.[120] SoundCloud boasts 175 million unique monthly listeners and podcasts can play anywhere on the web, on Sonos, Google Chromecast, and Xbox One podcast apps.[121] Another option is TuneIn, which has 60 million users and 5.7 million podcasts.[122]

With the growth of smartphones and Bluetooth in cars, audiences for all podcasts should continue to grow and podcasts could be a serious threat to traditional broadcast radio. Clear Channel, the largest radio broadcaster in the United States, responded by allowing consumers to record their own podcasts and submit them to iHeartRadio alongside professional shows from ABC, NPR, and Ryan Seacrest. Amazon-owned Audible is known for audio books but also has podcast content.

In 2019 Spotify invested heavily in podcasts, acquiring Gimlet, Parcast, and Anchor along with funding exclusive and original shows. The streaming music platform now offers hundreds of thousands of podcasts that users can add to playlists[123] and offers self-serve audio advertising through Spotify Ad Studio.[124] The cooler company Yeti has become a successful lifestyle brand and their Spotify playlists extend that experience. They have partnered with popular artists such as the Lumineers, Jack Jonson, the Highwaywomen, and Robert Plant to curate exclusive playlists for the Yeti nation that are "Built for the wild."[125] Podcasts can be a great engagement tool and distribution channel for content marketing efforts. Brands should consider creating their own podcasts. There is still room for growth; 65 percent of consumers say they would listen more if there were more podcasts on topics in which they are interested.[126]

iTunes

iTunes is the Apple media player used to play, download, and organize digital audio and video on computers in the macOS and Microsoft Windows operating systems and mobile devices, including iPhone, iPod touch, and iPad. First released in 2001, iTunes has grown to more than 800 million iTunes accounts.[127] Podcasts through iTunes are now available in more than 150 countries, making iTunes the top podcast distributor in the United States and the world.[128] iTunes hosts more than 550,000 active podcasts and has surpassed 50 billion episode downloads.[129]

If producing a podcast, there are some best practices to follow. Beyond using a quality microphone and recording and editing equipment, a good podcast has "intros" and "outros," with music and voice-overs announcing the show title, host, organization, and call to action to drive traffic to other social channels or corporate websites and blogs. In the beginning, podcasts should tell the audience what they can expect in terms of content, frequency, and format. Consider having guest interviews of employees or industry experts to keep content fresh and interesting.[130]

In each episode, enter the title, artist, and album information, including keywords as relevant tags to be found in searches. The iTunes format divides podcasts into sixteen categories, from business and health to government and technology. List podcasts in the right categories to be discovered by the target audience. Social features of iTunes include ratings and reviews, so it is a good idea to regularly ask listeners to rate and review the podcast to help new listener discovery.[131]

Podcasting can be a useful channel for a business to connect with target audience members on a personal level in their car, in the gym, or in the office while they are performing other activities. Podcasting is really a one-on-one medium that can build engagement with existing clients and draw in potential consumers. Because of the unique intimacy of podcasts, where the social media personality talks in listeners' ears in any environment, strong connections can be formed. "You have to remember that there's no fourth wall. When you're talking to someone, you're whispering in their ear. You're in the shower with them. You're on their commute to work," says Gina Delvac, producer of the friendship podcast "Call Your Girlfriend," hosted by Ann Friedman and Aminatou Sow.[132]

Sociologists developed the concept of parasocial relationship in the 1950s to describe the connection between TV viewers and celebrities. Today a **parasocial relationship** can be the emotional bond or feeling of real friendship felt by one person but not the other through the intimacy of social media. Social media publishers can form these one-sided

Figure 10.5. Podcasts enable brands to connect with an audience anywhere.

© Monkey Business Images / iStock Photo

relationships with fans and followers. These relationships can be powerful. Studies show that the followers form feelings of affection, gratitude, and encouragement that lead to loyalty.[133]

Measurement can be a challenge with podcasts, but Apple does have a podcast analytics tool that is available through the Podcasts Connect website. Metrics include number of devices, total time listened, time per device, percent of subscribed versus not subscribed, and countries by device. Podcasters can break these insights down by episode to provide insights into what type of content is performing better for optimization.[134] Another consideration is Podtrac, which is a podcast measurement system approved by the Interactive Advertising Bureau (IAB).

To grow a podcast's audience, use other social channels to encourage sharing, such as Twitter and Facebook. Deliver relevant, helpful content to a niche group of consumers.[135] A podcast does not need a large subscriber base to be successful; it just needs the right subscribers—a relevant target audience. One way to ensure the podcast delivers relevant, engaging content is to review the main question-and-answer social channels to see what questions users are asking in an organization's category.

Social native advertising also applies to podcasting. Many top podcasters sell sponsored ads inside the shows. These can be highly influential because they can be seen as endorsements. Most ads in podcasts are read by the host, with talking points provided by the advertiser. Most hosts will only accept ads from products and services they believe in, which adds to the credibility of the message. Podcast advertising is on the rise, with revenue at $479 million in 2018 with forecasts to exceed one billion by 2021. The most common ad unit for podcast is host-read, embedded, mid-roll ads, typically around sixty seconds, but many hosts exceed that. Experts suggest providing bulleted talking points that the host can use to keep the organic and conversational nature of the ad.[136]

Despite George Carlin's quote earlier in the chapter, people like to hear others talk and do accept their answers. In fact, comedians now use podcasting as a marketing tool. Podcasting is growing and could be an important part of an organization's social media strategy. Take a look again at target audience, objectives, and social media big idea. Could podcasting be the ideal channel to implement the social strategy for the business or organization?

As we conclude the social channel section of this book (part III), many may feel overwhelmed. That is okay and not cause for worry. The number of social channels and platforms covered in this section may have been eye-opening. Don't let the sheer number of options cause a paralysis of analysis. **Analysis paralysis** is when a decision is never made because there are too many options or it is thought of as overcomplicated.[137] Social media marketing is not complicated with a strategic planning process. The key to success is realizing that a brand or organization does not have to be in every social media channel to see real results—just the right ones.

Keep focused on the strategic framework developed in part II and select a few choice social media channels to deliver that strategy based on business objectives, target audience, insight, and big idea. Start small or optimize the social presence the organization already has by closing unproductive social channels and adding promising channels that support existing activity.

Yet remember that social media goes beyond marketing communications to impact many other areas of business operation. Social media has significantly changed the practice of product development, customer service, human resources, and more. Part IV of this book takes a deeper look at how marketing needs to integrate with other important areas of business function.[138]

One last consideration for this part of the book is that there are social media channels that are more popular in specific countries. This collection was based on global traffic and considered popularity in the United States, Canada, United Kingdom, and Australia, but if a brand is active in other specific countries, conduct additional research on usage in those specific countries. As noted in chapter 7, consider social media with more country-specific platforms such as Qzone, WeChat, VKontakte, Odnoklassniki, and others.

Chapter 10 Checklist

Social media can change quickly. Visit Post Control Marketing (http://www.postcontrol marketing.com) for updates, but also use this chapter checklist to briefly check how social media statistics in this chapter have changed since publication.

✓ How has social bookmarking and social knowledge changed? Are Reddit, Digg, BuzzFeed, Wikipedia, Yahoo Answers!, Quora, and iTunes still the top platforms?

SOCIAL PLAN PART 10

Buzz Building and Knowledge Sharing

People love to share knowledge. Look at the major social-bookmarking and social-knowledge channels (ask questions in table 7.1). What valuable information or partnerships can the brand form? What questions can the organization answer? How does knowledge sharing fit with the social media insight and big idea? Which users of social-bookmarking and knowledge channels match most closely with the target audience? Also take an in-depth look at podcasts. Is there an opportunity to start a brand podcast or partner with an existing program? Is the target audience actively listening to podcasts and looking for the type of insight and information the brand can deliver? Report all findings and ideas in these areas:

1. Identify the major social-bookmarking and knowledge-sharing sites where the target audience is active.
2. Describe the type of activity and content that is popular on each, and list the type of content the brand could provide that matches the social media plan's big idea.
3. Find the top podcasts to which the target audience is listening, and on which platform they are most active.
4. List and explain possible new podcast shows the brand could create or current shows the brand could contribute to and sponsor.

For a condensed version of the social plan see appendix A: Three-Part Social Plan.

✓ Do a quick search to confirm key statistics for each of the social media channel options covered in this chapter. Update numbers for monthly and daily users, global and country use, user demographics such as gender, age, education, and income, plus new features. What type of content performs best on each?

✓ Check for new paid social media opportunities. Have any of the social media platforms covered in this chapter added new advertising options? Has the General Data Protection Regulation (see chapter 13), California Consumer Protection Act (see chapter 15), or other regulations changed the targeting and tracking capabilities of social media campaigns?

KEY CONCEPTS

social capital

social bookmarking

tagging

folksonomy

collaborative tagging

content curation

news aggregation

Reddit

Digg

BuzzFeed

listicle

wiki

WikiWikiWeb

private wiki

company wiki

social knowledge platforms

Wikipedia

Yahoo! Answers

Quora

RSS (rich site summary)

podcast

video podcast

iTunes

parasocial relationship

analysis paralysis

QUESTIONS FOR DISCUSSION

1. Find a story that has gone viral on one of the social-bookmarking sites. Analyze characteristics such as topic, timing, copy, pictures, and headline. Try to determine what made the story go viral versus other stories. A fun example is Mr. Splashy Pants on Reddit.

2. Question-and-answer sites are all about delivering value to others by answering their questions. Which of the Q&A social websites are most appropriate for your brand and target audience?

3. Research the top viral posts on BuzzFeed. Identify the structure, characteristics, and topics. Are there common threads? Based on what you found, pick a brand and write a sponsor BuzzFeed listicle or quiz.

4. Part of the ethics of social media is that posts can last forever. Citizens in the European Union have the "right to be forgotten." They can request any organization to erase links to pages or posts with personal data. What are the pros and cons of this rule? Should it also apply to organizations that find false information that is damaging to their brand?

ADDITIONAL EXERCISES

1. Social bookmarking is all about contributing and building into a community before taking out. The goal of this exercise is to join and explore the three social-bookmarking sites and then meaningfully contribute to one and earn a reputation as a value creator. This will pay off down the road when you start sharing your own more promotion-oriented content. What happens if you don't invest the time up front? You could be banned from the community for sharing too many promotional links or messages. In which social-bookmarking community do you see the most potential? Become a valued member and it could provide an enormous amount of traffic and awareness.

2. You may not have checked out a podcast in a while. Now is the time. In this exercise go to iTunes or another podcasting service and explore all the podcasts. Don't just look at the top overall shows. Explore the different topic categories such as marketing and management, society and culture, and technology. Is there a show that is related to your brand and targets your customers? Can you envision starting a new show for a brand or organization? Be sure to explore both audio and video podcasts. Some marketers are now creating limited podcast series for new product or service introductions. Whether you see a place for podcasts in your strategy or not, you may find some useful podcasts that will help optimize your time and keep you up to date on the latest developments in the industry.

Notes

1. "Organizing," BrainyQuote.com, accessed October 19, 2019, http://www.brainyquote.com/quotes/keywords/organizing.html.

2. Tristan Claridge, "Bourdieu on Social Capital—Theory of Capital," SocialCapitalResearch.com, April 22, 2015, https://www.socialcapitalresearch.com/bourdieu-on-social-capital-theory-of-capital/.

3. Pierre Bourdieu and Loic J. D. Wacquant, *An Invitation to Reflexive Sociology* (Chicago: University of Chicago Press, 1992), 14.

4. Nicole B. Ellison, Charles Steinfield, and Cliff Lampe, "The Benefits of Facebook 'Friends': Social Capital and College Students' Use of Online Social Network Sites," *Journal of Computer Mediated Communication* 12, no. 4 (2007): 1,143–1,168.

5. John A. Bargh and Katelyn Y. A. McKenna, "The Internet and Social Life," *Annual Review of Psychology* 55, no. 1 (2004): 573–590.

6. John D. Sutter, "How Many Pages Are on the Internet?" CNN.com, September 12, 2011, http://www.cnn.com/2011/TECH/web/09/12/web.index.

7. Margaret Rouse, "Social Bookmarking," WhatIsIt.TechTarget.com, June 2006, https://whatis.techtarget.com/definition/social-bookmarking.

8. "Tagging," Webopedia.com, accessed November 4, 2019, https://www.webopedia.com/TERM/T/tagging.html.

9. "Folksonomy," Techopedia.com, accessed November 4, 2019, https://www.techopedia.com/definition/30196/folksonomy.

10. "What is Collaborative Tagging?" IGI-Global.com, accessed November 15, 2019, https://www.igi-global.com/dictionary/collaborative-tagging-for-collective-intelligence/4432.

11. Rouse, "Social Bookmarking."

12. Rouse, "Social Bookmarking."

13. Adrienne LaFrance, "How Many Websites Are There? So, So, So Many," TheAtlantic .com, September 30, 2015, https://www.theatlantic.com/technology/archive/2015/09/how-many -websites-are-there/408151/.

14. Kim Majali, "Content Curation," EuropeITOutsourcing, August 9, 2017, https://www .europeitoutsourcing.com/blog/content-creation/content-creation-definition/.

15. William A. Hanff, "News Aggregator," Britannica.com, October 10, 2019, https://www .britannica.com/topic/news-aggregator; https://en.wikipedia.org/wiki/News_aggregator.

16. Rouse, "Social Bookmarking."

17. Lou Dubois, "How to Use Social Bookmarking for Business," Inc.com, September 16, 2010, https://www.inc.com/guides/2010/09/how-to-use-social-bookmarking-for-business.html.

18. Simon Kemp, "Digital in 2019," wearesocial.com, 2019, https://wearesocial.com/ global-digital-report-2019.

19. "Join the Conversation," About.Reddit.com, accessed October 19, 2019, https://about .reddit.com/advertise/.

20. "Reddit.com," SimilarWeb.com, accessed October 19, 2019, https://www.similarweb.com/ website/reddit.com.

21. "Reach of Active Reddit Users as of 2nd Quarter 2015, by Age Group," GlobalWebIndex, October 13, 2015, https://www.statista.com/statistics/472986/reddit-global-active-user-reach-age/.

22. "Social Media Fact Sheet," PewInternet.org, June 12, 2019, https://www.pewinternet.org/ fact-sheet/social-media/.

23. "Most Popular Mobile Social Networking Apps in the United States as of June 2019, by Monthly Users (in Millions)," Verto Analytics, September 9, 2019, https://www.statista.com/ statistics/248074/most-popular-us-social-networking-apps-ranked-by-audience/.

24. "Most Popular Mobile Social Networking Apps in the United States as of June 2019, by Average Session Duration (in Minutes)," Verto Analytics, September 9, 2019, https://www.statista .com/statistics/579411/top-us-social-networking-apps-ranked-by-session-length/.

25. "Leading Reddit Usage Reasons According to Users in the United States as of 3rd Quarter 2019," AudienceProject, October 3, 2019, https://www.statista.com/statistics/262331/digital -communication-platforms-of-us-internet-users/.

26. Jacob O'Gara, "Reddit 101: A Beginner's Guide to the Front Page of the Internet," Digi-talTrends.com, December 20, 2013, http://www.digitaltrends.com/social-media/reddit-101.

27. Andrew Hutchinson, "Reddit Launches New Content Sharing Integration with Snap-chat," SocialMediaToday.com, October 15, 2019, https://www.socialmediatoday.com/news/ reddit-launches-new-content-sharing-integration-with-snapchat/564986/.

28. Seth Fiegerman, "Aliens in the Valley: The Complete History of Reddit, the Internet's Front Page," Mashable.com, December 3, 2014, https://mashable.com/2014/12/03/history-of-reddit/.

29. O'Gara, "Reddit 101."

30. Jon Russell, "Reddit's New Location Tagging Feature Continues Its Push to Become a Social Network," Techcrunch.com (blog), May 31, 2017, https://techcrunch.com/2017/05/31/ reddit-foursquare-location-tagging/.

31. Fiegerman, "Aliens in the Valley."

32. Ben Beck, "6 Ways to Use Reddit to Grow Your Business," SocialMediaExaminer.com, September 20, 2012, http://www.socialmediaexaminer.com/reddit.

33. Richard Edelman, "A PR Pro's Guide for Reddit," Edelman.com (blog), May 14, 2015, https://www.edelman.com/p/6-a-m/a-pr-pros-guide-for-reddit/.

34. "SXSWi 2014: You're Doing Reddit Wrong," Reddit.com, accessed October 19, 2019, http://www.reddit.com/r/sxswdoingredditwrong.

35. Beck, "6 Ways to Use Reddit."

36. Maggie Archibald, "31 Jaw-Dropping Reddit Statistics for Marketers in 2019," Foundation-Inc.co, July 15, 2019, https://foundationinc.co/lab/reddit-statistics/.

37. "Reddit Help Advertising," RedditHelp.com, accessed October 19, 2019. https://www.reddithelp.com/en/categories/advertising/creating-ads/create-campaign-objective.

38. "Reddit Help Advertising," RedditHelp.com.

39. L'Oréal Builds Love in Reddit Communities," RedditInc.com, accessed October 19, 2019, https://www.redditinc.com/assets/case-studies/LOreal_Case_Study.pdf.

40. KeriLynn Engel, "Digg: Its Rise and Fall and Rebirth," WhoIsHostingThis.com, November 12, 2018, https://www.whoishostingthis.com/blog/2016/08/22/digg-rise-fall/.

41. "Digg.com," Alexa.com, accessed October 18, 2019, http://www.alexa.com/siteinfo/digg.com.

42. Engel, "Digg."

43. "Digg.com," SimilarWeb.com, October 18, 2019, https://www.similarweb.com/website/digg.com#overview.

44. "Digg Homepage," Digg.com, accessed October 19, 2019, http://digg.com.

45. Om Malik, "Will the Digg Effect Make a Comeback?" Gigaom.com, August 18, 2013, http://gigaom.com/2013/08/18/will-the-digg-effect-make-a-comeback.

46. Don Gilbert, "Using Digg to Build Traffic and Links," MastersOfSEO.com, accessed October 10, 2014, http://www.mastersofseo.com/using-digg-and-putting-up-a-digg-this-button.

47. Engel, "Digg."

48. Engel, "Digg."

49. Gilbert, "Using Digg to Build Traffic and Links."

50. "Digg Advertising," Digg.com, accessed October 19, 2019, http://digg.com/advertising.

51. Alyson Shontell, "How BuzzFeed CEO Jonah Peretti Took an Instant Messaging Bot and Turned It into a $1.5 Billion Media Empire," BusinessInsider.com, June 1, 2007, https://www.businessinsider.com/buzzfeed-jonah-peretti-startup-success-how-i-did-it-interview-podcast-2017-5.

52. "BuzzFeed.com," SimilarWeb.com, accessed October 19, 2019, https://www.similarweb.com/website/buzzfeed.com#overview.

53. "BuzzFeed Advertise," BuzzFeed.com, accessed October 19, 2019, https://advertise.buzzfeed.com/.

54. Derek Thompson, *Hit Makers: How to Succeed in an Age of Distraction* (New York: Penguin, 2017), 300.

55. "Share of Consumers Who Have Used Selected Global Online News Brands to Access News in the Last Week in the United States as of February 2019," Reuters Institute for the Study of Journalism, June 11, 2019, https://www.statista.com/statistics/262520/leading-online-news-brands-in-the-us/.

56. "Leading Online News Brands Accessed in the United Kingdom (UK) as of February 2019," Reuters Institute for the Study of Journalism, June 17, 2019, https://www.statista.com/statistics/262514/leading-online-news-brands-accessed-in-the-uk/.

57. "Main News Brands Accessed Online by Consumers in Australia as of February 2019," APO, und University of Canberra, June 18, 2019, https://www.statista.com/statistics/588545/australia-online-news-brands/.

58. "Main Online News Sources Used by Anglophone News Consumers in Canada as of February 2019," Reuters Institute for the Study of Journalism, June 11, 2019, https://www.statista.com/statistics/563500/online-news-sources-anglophone-in-canada/.

59. Shontell, "BuzzFeed CEO Jonah Peretti."

60. Shontell, "BuzzFeed CEO Jonah Peretti."

61. "Listicle," Merriam-Webster.com, accessed November 15, 2019, https://www.merriam-webster.com/dictionary/listicle.

62. Remee Patel, "21 Feel-Good Tweets That Will Make You Feel Better About Everything: Featuring Cute Family Members and Even *Cuter* Pets," BuzzFeed.com, June 13, 2017, https://www.buzzfeed.com/remeepatel/wholesome-tweets-that-will-make-you-feel-good-about-the?utm_term=.ngEAb3w9l#.xuOmkvAy8.

63. Heather Schwedel, "BuzzFeed Keeps Trying to Guess My Height. What's With the Site's Weird New Quizzes?" Slate.com, May 16, 2017, http://www.slate.com/blogs/browbeat/2017/05/16/buzzfeed_s_weird_quizzes_that_try_to_guess_your_height_age_and_other_things.html.

64. "BuzzFeed Advertise," BuzzFeed.com.

65. "BuzzFeed Advertise," BuzzFeed.com.

66. Macy's Brand Publisher, "11 Back-To-School Outfits That'll Crush It on Social Media: Get Ready to Have a Fashionable Feed This Fall, Only with Macy's," BuzzFeed.com, August 7, 2017, https://www.buzzfeed.com/macys/back-to-school-outfits-that-were-totally-made-for-social?utm_term=.klA8nwOzd#.dvXl3AM97.

67. "6 School Hacks You're Going to Need This Year Presented by BuzzFeed & Staples," BuzzFeed Blue, YouTube.com, August 14, 2015, https://youtu.be/-gViYXQ9zc8.

68. Sahil Patel, "Buzzfeed Looks to Bring More Advertisers to Its Commerce Business," DigiDay.com, March 7, 2019, https://digiday.com/media/buzzfeed-looks-to-bring-more-brands-to-its-commerce-business/.

69. Maciej Ceglowski, "Pinboard Acquires Delicious," Pinboard.in (blog), June 1, 2017, https://blog.pinboard.in/2017/06/pinboard_acquires_delicious/.

70. Jason Ankeny, "Brian Eno," AllMusic.com, accessed November 15, 2019, https://www.allmusic.com/artist/brian-eno-mn0000617196/biography.

71. Ankeny, "Brian Eno."

72. "Wiki," Merriam-Webster.com, accessed October 19, 2019, http://www.merriam-webster.com/dictionary/wiki.

73. Dan Misener, "Why You Should Set Up a Company Wiki," TheGlobeAndMail.com, February 20, 2012, http://www.theglobeandmail.com/report-on-business/small-business/sb-digital/web-strategy/why-you-should-set-up-a-company-wiki/article547626.

74. Rebecca Shakespeare, "Wikis for Innovative Work," Innovation Series, December 12, 2012, http://www.innovation-series.com/2012/12/17/wikis-for-innovative-work.

75. Misener, "Why You Should Set Up a Company Wiki."

76. Misener, "Why You Should Set Up a Company Wiki."

77. "Wikipedia," Wikipedia, last modified October 19, 2019, http://en.wikipedia.org/wiki/Wikipedia.

78. Nicole Harrison, "Wikipedia: Is It a 'Go' or 'No Go' for Your Business?" Socialnicole.com, accessed October 19, 2019, http://socialnicole.com/wikipedia-for-business.

79. Harrison, "Wikipedia."

80. "Talk: IBM," Wikipedia, accessed October 19, 2019, http://en.wikipedia.org/wiki/Talk:IBM.

81. Harrison, "Wikipedia."

82. James Zygmont, "Yahoo! Answers," KnowYourMeme.com, accessed November 15, 2019, https://knowyourmeme.com/memes/sites/yahoo-answers.

83. "Yahoo.com," SimilarWeb.com, accessed October 19, 2019, https://www.similarweb.com/website/answers.yahoo.com#overview.

84. "About Yahoo! Answers," Yahoo! Answers.

85. "About Yahoo! Answers," Yahoo! Answers.

86. Tin Su, "Introducing Yahoo Answers Now—A New App for the Q&A Community," Yahoo.Tumblr.com, December 8, 2016, https://yahoo.tumblr.com/post/154215434969/introducing-yahoo-answers-now-a-new-app-for-the.

87. Zygmont, "Yahoo! Answers."

88. "Introducing the New Yahoo Answers!," Yahoo! Answers, September 12, 2013, http://yahooanswers.tumblr.com/post/61040172053/introducing-the-new-yahoo-answers.

89. Helen Vozna, "How to Get Traffic to Your Website with the Help of Q&A Sites," Webceo.com (blog), October 29, 2013, http://www.webceo.com/blog/how-to-get-traffi-to-your-website-with-the-help-of-qa-sites.

90. Vozna, "How to Get Traffic to Your Website."

91. Martin Luenendonk, "Using Quora for Business Purposes," Cleverism.com, November 13, 2014, https://www.cleverism.com/using-quora-business-purposes/.

92. "Quora.com," SimilarWeb.com, accessed October 19, 2019, https://www.similarweb.com/website/quora.com#overview.

93. "Quora for Business," QuoraForBusiness.com, accessed October 19, 2019, https://go.quoraforbusiness.com/.

94. Luenendonk, "Using Quora for Business Purposes."

95. "Quora for Business," QuoraForBusiness.com.

96. Josh Constine, "Quora Signals It's Favoring Search Ads for Eventual Monetization, Launches Author Stats Tool," Techcrunch.com (blog), November 12, 2013, https://techcrunch.com/2013/11/12/quora-confirms-its-favoring-search-ads-for-eventual-monetization-launches-author-stats-tool/.

97. Lisa B. Marshall, "How to Use Quora to Build Your Brand (Part 1)," QuickAndDirtyTips.com, June 13, 2013, http://www.quickanddirtytips.com/business-career/public-speaking/how-to-use-quora-to-build-your-brand-part-1.

98. Marshall, "How to Use Quora."

99. Krista Bunskoek, "Blog Traffic: How to Use Q&A Sites and Niche Forums to Increase Blog Visitors," Wishpond.com, accessed October 19, 2019, http://blog.wishpond.com/post/65245501112/blog-traffic-how-to-use-q-a-sites-and-niche-forums-to.

100. Luenendonk, "Using Quora for Business Purposes."

101. Ashley Carman, "Quora Launches Writing Sessions as Challenge to Reddit's Ask Me Anything," TheVerge.com, November 20, 2015, https://www.theverge.com/2015/11/20/9771850/quora-writing-sessions-reddit-ama.

102. Richard Henry, "Knowledge Prizes: Unlock Answers to Important Questions," Quora.com (blog), January 27, 2016, https://blog.quora.com/Knowledge-Prizes-Unlock-answers-to-important-questions.

103. "Quora for Business," QuoraForBusiness.com.

104. "Quora for Business," QuoraForBusiness.com.

105. "The Economist Connects with New and Existing Readers through Writing Sessions on Quora," QuoraForBusiness.com, accessed October 19, 2019, https://go.quoraforbusiness.com/rs/384-CMP-465/images/The_Economist_Case_Study_Sessions.pdf.

106. Jack Morse, "Amazon's 'Alexa Answers' is a Hot Mess, Surprising Exactly Not One," Mashable.com, November 2, 2019, https://mashable.com/article/amazon-alexa-answers-hot-mess/.

107. Tyler Lacoma, "What Is an RSS feed?" DigitalTrends.com, August 21, 2019, https://www.digitaltrends.com/computing/what-is-an-rss-feed/.

108. Daniel Nations, "Top 7 Free Online RSS Readers," Lifewire.com, July 7, 2017, https://www.lifewire.com/top-free-online-rss-readers-3486649.

109. "Talk," BrainyQuote.com, accessed September 14, 2019, http://www.brainyquote.com/quotes/keywords/talk.html.

110. "Podcast," Merriam-Webster.com, accessed October 19, 2019, http://www.merriam-webster.com/dictionary/podcast.

111. Stephanie Watson, "How Podcasting Works," Computer.HowStuffWorks.com, accessed November 15, 2019, https://computer.howstuffworks.com/internet/basics/podcasting1.htm.

112. "The Podcast Consumer 2019," EdisonResearch.com, 2019, https://www.edisonresearch.com/the-podcast-consumer-2019/.

113. "Vodcasting," TheFreeDictionary.com, accessed November 4, 2019, https://www.thefreedictionary.com/Video+podcast.

114. Zach Brooke, "Podcasts Offer Cheap Advertising to a Growing Affluent Audience," American Marketing Association, October 1, 2017, https://www.ama.org/publications/MarketingNews/Pages/the-rise-of-the-podcast.aspx.

115. Jefferson Graham, "Remember Podcasting? It's Back—and Booming," USAToday.com, August 15, 2013, http://www.usatoday.com/story/tech/columnist/talkingtech/2013/08/15/podcast-explosion/2647963.

116. "Podcast Consumer 2019," EdisonResearch.com.

117. "Podcast Consumer 2019," EdisonResearch.com.

118. Ginny Marvin, "U.S. Podcast Audiences Keep Growing, 62 Million Listening Weekly," MarketingLand.com, March 7, 2019, https://marketingland.com/u-s-podcast-audiences-keep-growing-62-million-listening-weekly-258179.

119. "Podcast Consumer 2019," EdisonResearch.com.

120. "Welcome to the Spoken World: Podcasts, News, & Public Radio On-Demand," Stitcher.com, accessed October 19, 2019, https://www.stitcher.com/learn-more.

121. "Podcasting on SoundCloud," SoundCloud.com, accessed October 19, 2019, https://soundcloud.com/for/podcasting.

122. "About TuneIn," TuneIn.com, accessed October 19, 2019, https://tunein.com/about/.

123. Sarah Parez, "Spotify Now Lets You Add Podcasts to Playlists," Techcrunch.com, September 30, 2019, https://techcrunch.com/2019/09/30/spotify-now-lets-you-add-podcasts-to-playlists/.

124. "Be heard," Spotify Ad Studio, AdStudio.spotify.com, accessed October 21, 2019, https://adstudio.spotify.com/.

125. "Yeticoolers," Spotify.com, accessed October 29, 2019, https://open.spotify.com/user/yeticoolers.

126. "Podcast Consumer 2019," EdisonResearch.com.

127. Dan Graziano, "Apple Now Adding Half a Million New iTunes Accounts Each Day," BGR.com, June 14, 2013, http://bgr.com/2013/06/14/apple-itunes-accounts.

128. Josh Morgan, "How Podcasts Have Changed in Ten Years: By the Numbers: Podcasting Is Booming, and Podcasts Are Getting Longer and More Diverse," Medium.com, September 2, 2015, https://medium.com/@monarchjogs/how-podcasts-have-changed-in-ten-years-by-the-numbers-720a6e984e4e.

129. Roger Fingas, "iTunes Hosts over 550,000 Active Podcasts, Surpasses 50 Billion Episode Downloads," AppleInsider.com, June 5, 2018, https://appleinsider.com/articles/18/06/05/itunes-hosts-over-550000-active-podcasts-surpasses-50-billion-episode-downloads.

130. Brooke, "Podcasts Offer Cheap Advertising."

131. John Lee Dumas, "How to Start a Business Podcast," SocialMediaExaminer.com, July 10, 2013, http://www.socialmediaexaminer.com/how-to-start-a-business-podcast.

132. Cited in Jamie Lauren Keiles, "Even Nobodies Have Fans Now (For Better or Worse)," *New York Times Magazine*, November 13, 2019, https://www.nytimes.com/interactive/2019/11/13/magazine/internet-fandom-podcast.html.

133. Nomi-Kaie Bennett, Amy Rossmeisl, Karisma Turner, Billy D. Holcombe, Robin Young, Tiffany Brown, and Heather Key, "Parasocial Relationships: The Nature of Celebrity Fascinations," FindAPsychologist.com, accessed December 10, 2019, https://www.findapsychologist.org/parasocial-relationships-the-nature-of-celebrity-fascinations/.

134. Travis Albritton, "Apple Podcast Analytics: How to Find & Use These Podcast Statistics," BuzzSprout.com, November 20, 2018, https://www.buzzsprout.com/blog/apple-podcasts-analytics.

135. Brooke, "Podcasts Offer Cheap Advertising."

136. Krystina Rubino and Lindsay Shaw, "Cracking the Code on Podcast Advertising for Customer Acquisition," TechCrunch.com, September 27, 2019, https://techcrunch.com/2019/09/27/cracking-the-code-on-podcast-advertising-for-customer-acquisition/.

137. James Chen, "Analysis Paralysis," Investopedia.com, August 19, 2019, https://www.investopedia.com/terms/a/analysisparalysis.asp.

138. Keith A. Quesenberry and Michael K. Coolsen, "Research Reports: How to Integrate Social Media into Your Marketing Strategy: Best Practices for Social Media Management," AdAge.com, May 20, 2013, http://adage.com/trend-reports/report.php?id=74.

PART

IV

**Integrating
Social Media across
Organizations**

CHAPTER

11

Social Media Insights and Crowdsourcing

Money won't buy happiness, but it will pay the salaries of a large research staff to study the problem.[1]

—Bill Vaughan

PREVIEW

When facing a decision, do you ever ask your friends for advice? You could ask one, but then you might want a second opinion and then another. Eventually you may seek advice from a group of friends to see what the majority thinks. Perhaps you have done this with what clothes to wear to a job interview or special occasion. Perhaps you have sought advice from several friends on what color to paint a room. Do you feel your friends have always given the right advice?

Another way to seek advice is to seek the wisdom of the crowd. In *Science* magazine, Ralph Hertwig tells us that since the late nineteenth century, psychology research has associated the group or crowd with unparalleled wisdom and magical creativity or inferior decision-making and disastrous outcomes. Yet, Hertwig says, "the key to benefiting from other minds is to know when to rely on the group and when to walk alone."[2] Leveraging the wisdom of the crowd has been the focus of research for many years.

As early as 1907 researcher Francis Galton published "Vox Populi (The Wisdom of Crowds)" in the magazine *Nature*. Galton found evidence that the median estimate of a group can be more accurate than estimates of experts.[3] This **wisdom-of-the-crowd** effect has been supported more recently in experiments involving areas from stock markets and political elections to quiz shows. Thus wisdom of the crowd is the collective opinion of a group rather than a single expert.[4]

Yet researchers Jan Lorenz, Heiko Rauhut, Frank Schweitzer, and Dirk Helbing found that social influence can undermine the wisdom of a crowd. In their experiment, subjects reconsidered responses to factual questions after receiving the average or full information of the responses of others. Groups were initially "wise," but knowledge about estimates of others narrowed the diversity of opinions, creating a "social influence effect."[5] Other studies indicate that the accuracy of the wisdom of a crowd can diminish when more confident members in a group dominate decisions.[6] These findings should be kept in mind when exploring social research and crowdsourcing as sources of market intelligence.

Leveraging Social Media Insights

Bill Vaughan was an American columnist and author known for his folksy approach and no-nonsense opinions. His quote at the beginning of this chapter is especially relevant for those who have ever had to pay for consumer research studies. Traditional research is expensive. Fortunately, today marketers have a vibrant research alternative that is inexpensive, efficient, and responsive. Social media can be a way to collect data-driven consumers' insights for business, marketing, and communications challenges of large corporations, startups, and small businesses alike. Traditional research can also be slow. It can take three to six months to develop, field, and obtain results. On the other hand, social media listening can capture real-time consumer insight for continuous brand, product, and service optimization. This is not to say that organizations should eliminate traditional research altogether. It is a valuable tool and provides much information and accuracy that social research cannot.

Despite all the hype over social media, gathering social media insight from social media research has been slow to catch on. Wharton Customer Analytics still reported a social media research imbalance. US companies spent more than $10 billion a year on consumer research yet were using traditional methods more than three decades old. Many organizations rely predominantly on focus groups and customer surveys, despite declining customer participation and long turnaround times.[7] There are signs that organizations are coming around and indications that social research is growing. One report shows the global social media analytics market growing from $1.6 billion in 2015 to $5.4 billion in 2020. That is an annual growth rate of 28 percent.[8]

Traditional market research involves face-to-face or traditional media methods, such as focus groups, in-depth interviews, shop-alongs, ethnographic observation, intercepts, and telephone and mail surveys. **Digital market research** involves using new digital media to collect results through methods such as online surveys, online focus groups, online communities, bulletin boards, and social media sites.[9] Organizations can benefit from adding digital market-research methods to more traditional research, thereby gaining valuable cross-discipline insight from the real-time intelligence that social media can provide. **Social media research** involves using various tools and techniques to collect and analyze data from social media networks or platforms.[10]

Figure 11.1. Traditional research like surveys can be supplemented with social research.

© Kasayizgi / iStock Photo

Think about all the information that is generated online every day about brands, products, services, competitors, and industry. Research today should be about leveraging that constant flow of real-time data generated from website analytics, individual-level customer data, and social media conversations. Consumer data can come in many forms, such as polls on organization websites, questions on Facebook pages, or tests of advertising and product ideas on corporate blogs. It can be about collecting large datasets (big data) and analyzing for optimization. The idea is to use any digital tool available to leverage research insight from the enormous amount of social data. Misia Tramp, Vice President of Customer Experience Strategy and Insight at Metia digital marketing group in London, describes social data as "just simply the world's best ethnography." She goes on to argue that marketers shouldn't think in terms of traditional versus social. Research should instead be "data-agnostic."[11]

A simple example of leveraging social insights is when Barclays bank launched the first person-to-person mobile payments app in the United Kingdom, called Pingit. A traditional new product development approach would follow a process of creating prototypes, conducting a series of focus groups, and then fielding test markets before fully introducing the new product into the market. This process can take up to eighteen months, which is an eternity when trying to launch a new, competitive tech product, service, or feature.[12]

Instead, Barclays released the app sooner and then used real-time social media analysis to significantly improve the product. Through sentiment analysis, they saw that the app was received well, but there was still a small percentage of negative mentions. Zeroing in on those comments led to an insight that teens and their parents were upset that the new money-transfer app did not give access to account owners under eighteen.[13]

For example, one tweet said, "Pingit disappointment—sent money to both kids, but it didn't work because they are under 18 (even though they are both Barclays customers)." Barclays was responsive, adjusting access requirements quickly. This helped public relations efforts by avoiding news stories picking up the negative feature and making it a significant part of the earned media coverage of the launch.[14] Today the app is a success, receiving more than fifteen thousand reviews in the Android Apps store and with an average rating of four out of five stars.[15]

As seen in the Barclays example, the real power of this research is that it occurs in real time. Data can be collected by monitoring social channels for product issues or brand perception, or it can be collected in closed brand communities. Getting this close to the consumer experience provides rich insight. Companies such as SurveyMonkey make social research easy by offering a free app to embed polls, surveys, and questionnaires into Facebook. Marketers can leverage a large group of social media fans to improve marketing efforts, product features, and service delivery. This is an attractive tool versus email surveys, considering the difficulty of obtaining email lists and the potential of a network of friends or fans sharing the survey on their respective networks for more and faster response.[16] There are many options across numerous social media channels including Twitter polls and interactive poll stickers for Instagram Stories.[17]

Another product development example is when Heinz social listening found that Heinz Mayochup was trending on Twitter in the United Kingdom despite it only being available in the Middle East. The brand created a Twitter poll asking if it should release Heinz Mayochup in the United States, promising to launch the product if they received 500,000 yes votes. Through listening again, the brand discovered people also were chiming in with alternative product names. The brand designed images of the bottles with people's alternative names such as "Ketcho" and "Mayup!" and offered them as limited editions. The Twitter poll helped @HeinzKetchup_US earn one billion impressions in forty-eight hours. The poll received nearly one million votes with 55 percent voting "Yes" and the brand launched the product in the United States. As a result Heinz Mayonnaise saw a 28 percent lift in brand awareness.[18] The product launch from social media insights was such a success that it produced a whole product line with new additions of Mayomust and Mayocue.[19]

Jim Tobin, president of Ignite Social Media, explains how they use social insight for content optimization: "We create 100, 150, 200 pieces of content around a brand and a product, put it out on the social web, see which 15, 20 pieces do really well and then syndicate it."[20] The global social listening platform Synthesio summarizes the areas in which research can gain insights from social analytics: audience segmentation and profiling, traditional research validation, new product development, marketing optimization, trend tracking, and competitive intelligence.[21]

New social media research companies have also emerged as social analytics specialists to help brands optimize their social media strategies working with top marketers, advertising agencies, and public relations firms. Many collect and look for insights in the trillions of posts that create the vast amounts of unstructured social media data. This data and

Figure 11.2. Why guess what your customers want when you can ask them in social media?

© Martin-DM / iStock Photo

benchmarking help deliver marketing insights to improve social media content and performance. Brandwatch and NetBase are some of these social analytics firms.[22] Other companies specialize in more specific areas. For example, Unmetric collects brand social media data from tens of thousands of leading brands across platforms and analyzes it with artificial intelligence.[23] Another company, Unruly, specializes in viral advertising video insights collected across social platforms.[24]

Even one social channel can provide valuable insight with not much effort. Instead of simply monitoring for positive and negative comments like Barclays, the marketers at Nabisco took a more direct approach. The Oreo brand engaged its Facebook fans by asking, "How would you describe Oreo cookies to someone who never tasted them?" In response, the brand page received more than 3,600 replies in just six days.[25] Powerful insight was obtained quickly from loyal consumers. In just a few days the marketer and its advertising and public relations partners had obtained a valuable outside perspective from their target audience into the most important aspects of its product and brand.

Dove used social media for research by analyzing more than five million social media mentions on Twitter. This led to the shocking consumer insight that 80 percent of women online had experienced negative body shaming comments.[26] Dove uncovered that of the five million negative tweets about beauty and body image, four out of every five were from women talking about themselves. Dove realized that with all the ideas and opinions about beauty constantly shared through social media feeds, people are crowdsourcing a definition of beauty. Dove wanted to change that definition to something positive. With this social

Social Media Research Process

Social media research should not just be a series of random questions or polls. To achieve optimum results, conduct a social search with the same formal conventions and processes as traditional consumer marketing research. Yean Cheong, head of digital at Mediabrands, suggests using these steps:[a]

- Identify the target audience.
- Post open-ended information-gathering questions.
- Engage in social conversations.
- Categorize and analyze threads.
- Determine feedback patterns.
- Connect trends to develop insights.

Marianne Hynd, director of Social Media Research Association (SMRA Global) indicates that social research is different from more general social media listening and monitoring. Hynd suggests that the goals of social research include:

- Use social media content to answer specific questions related to a marketing initiative.
- Obtain metrics to test hypotheses and dive deeper into understanding consumer behavior.
- Collect consumer content outside direct brand sharing for general consumer insight.[b]

[a] "Insight: Media Debate-Planning—Social Media's Role in Real-Time Research," *Campaign Asia-Pacific* 56 (2012).
[b] Marianne Hynd, "Will Social Research Replace Traditional Marek Research?" NealSchaffer .com, accessed October 21, 2019, https://nealschaffer.com/will-social-research-replace-traditional -market-research/.

media insight Dove partnered with Twitter to launch a campaign encouraging women to #SpeakBeautiful. Women didn't completely realize the power of their posts.[27]

The Dove campaign launched with a big event that tends to focus on women's beauty and is discussed on Twitter—the Oscars. A TV commercial during the awards broadcast drove awareness with tweets from real women showing the problem. The ad called for women to join Dove and Twitter and turn the negative tweets into positive ones. The brand used Twitter Analytics tools to measure use of #SpeakBeautiful and real-time data visualizations of positive and negative beauty words women used most on Oscar night. The campaign sparked user-generated content of real women and even celebrities who picked up the cause, sharing their own messages and videos of beauty positivity that extended to other events like the MTV Video Music Awards (VMAs). Twitter research also revealed that there are peak times when beauty confidence is the lowest—mornings, Mondays, and weekends. Dove monitored the conversation live, responding one-on-one to women and providing encouragement in these challenging moments.[28]

Dove's #SpeakBeautiful effort exceeded their expectations leading to positive behavior change in social media and positive attention for the brand. The year after the campaign negative tweets about beauty or body image sent by women overall dropped 37 percent. Change also occurred during the two key events. During the Oscars women posted 30 percent fewer negative tweets and 69 percent more positive tweets from the previous year. During the VMAs the beauty conversation was 76 percent positive as #SpeakBeautiful was a trending topic both nights. The one-on-one personal encouragement with women resulted in shifting sentiment in 85 percent of conversations. Finally, the campaign drove affinity for Dove, increasing brand sentiment 17 percent. As can be seen in this case, social media is a powerful tool for research insight, crowdsourcing, brand messaging, behavioral change, and brand results.[29]

No matter what process brands use to conduct social media research, it is essential to collect data beyond the narrow scope of the company or organization. Also gather information about competitors and the overall industry. Looking at the broader context adds valuable background and perspective that can make the difference in real insight. Yet no matter how powerful it may be, social media research cannot and should not completely replace traditional research. Traditional research methods are still valid and provide valuable information social media research cannot collect. View social research as a way to augment traditional research data and methodologies.

How else can social data be used? Another example involves the hotel industry. The Synthesis agency set up global, regional, and hotel-specific dashboards for Accor hotels to monitor its properties and key competitors. Measurement was based on many factors, from open-ended comments in social media to rating scores on ratings-and-reviews sites such as TripAdvisor. The system allowed Accor to identify underperforming locations in real time and act on negative comments quickly. Traditional research may take months or up to a year to report these findings and could result in a large number of lost bookings. Accor management said that the social media–monitoring research system resulted in a rise in brand equity, satisfaction, and bookings.[30]

These examples demonstrate that social research is good for business-to-consumer (B2C) relationships, but is social media research also effective for business-to-business (B2B) organizations? Research does indicate that there are enough social conversations about B2B firms to monitor for brand, product, and service optimization. A study in the *World Journal of Social Sciences* reported robust social conversation about two B2B manufacturing companies in Europe. Using social media–monitoring software, these B2B manufacturers found they generated more than sixty mentions a day. This was a large and significant number in terms of total buzz for the industry sector.[31] Conducting social research for organization-to-organization selling also provides valuable insight that can help meet business objectives.

Social analytics company Crimson Hexagon says that social data analysis can be used for brand management, corporate communications, product development, consumer insights, customer care, and digital marketing (see table 11.1). One example is a social analysis Crimson Hexagon performed for the Nespresso coffee maker to uncover brand-specific audience interests. In a comparison of Nespresso and competitor Keurig's social media audience data, they discovered that Nespresso's audience had a strong interest in hotels and resorts. The brand leveraged this information into a placement strategy of forming partnerships with

Table 11.1. Organizational Uses for Social Data Analysis

Brand management	Consumer insights
Corporate communications	Customer care
Product development	Digital marketing

Source: "Social Media Analytics throughout the Enterprise: How Different Departments Can Leverage Social Analytics," Crimsonhexagon .com, accessed October 21, 2019, http://pages.crimsonhexagon.com/ WC2016-06-28-GU-SocialAnalyticsThroughouttheEnterprise_Regis tration.html.

multiple hotels. Resulting social listening revealed that consumers loved the brand's new hotel collaborations upon discovering the machines in their rooms.[32]

Some have taken this method of research further to form a new discipline combining the more academic study of conversation analysis and ethnomethodology with new software in online text analysis. **Social conversation analysis** is the study of the group talk produced in ordinary human interactions collected from the vast amounts of social media conversation data.[33] The Conversation Research Institute (CRI) was founded to promote and advance this type of research that goes beyond what can be found in simple social media listening algorithms. Here, human analysis is employed to examine the data more thoroughly, beyond simple keywords, to determine all the phrases used in natural conversation about a topic and to focus on the most relevant conversations. From there, those conversations are further parsed out into subcategories that may be actionable across many business units from marketing to product development, operations, human resources, and customer service.[34]

CRI co-founder and chief instigator Jason Falls suggests that social conversation analysis research needs to go beyond just tracking what consumers are saying about a brand and its competitors. It also needs to look at the broader, nonbrand-specific conversations happening in the category. This can lead to new ideas but is also especially important in categories where brands may not be as relevant in the conversation. It can help discover unmet needs, laser focus content strategy, and understand consumer nuances. For example, in the senior care industry, where customers tend to not mention specific brands, CRI was able to analyze more than 1,200 relevant conversations to map out the senior care buyer's journey.[35]

Once an organization has implemented a continuous monitoring program, consider expanding what is being tracked. In addition to following opinions, complaints, and questions that could influence product design, customer service, marketing messaging, and social media outreach, use trend analysis to track perception and sentiment over time. Look for rises in positive or negative comments to learn what should be repeated or avoided.[36] Don't forget to track competitor actions through social data. Real-time social media research can improve lead generation, new products, and new product launches, and provide insight into potential customers and their decision processes.

Marianne Hynd, director of Social Media Research Association (SMRA Global), indicates that some of the benefits of social media research include larger pools of data and content, cost and time efficiencies, and removal of observer effects. Social media research can also complement traditional methodologies by making study design more efficient; it can investigate "rabbit holes" quickly and corroborate and evaluate other study outcomes. Hynd says, "While social media research is still in its infancy . . . researchers should better understand what social media is and how it can work simultaneously and concurrently with traditional research methodologies. It's important to remember that social content influences the masses."[37]

Crowdsourcing the Wisdom of the Crowd

Elvis Presley said, "A live concert to me is exciting because of all the electricity that is generated in the crowd and on stage. It's my favorite part of the business, live concerts."[38] Marketers, advertisers, and public relations professionals may not consider themselves to be rock stars, but there is something that can be learned from Elvis's observation. Except for personal sales and events, much of business, marketing, advertising, and public relations happens away from the action and results are delayed. Think of a musician spending weeks in a recording studio and waiting months to release a record before getting fan feedback and interaction. Social media can bring a level of real-time crowd interaction to a marketer like a live concert to a musician. Interacting with an organization's target audience at this level of engagement is called crowdsourcing.

Crowdsourcing takes a job normally performed by a professional, such as an employee, and outsources it to a large group of people through an open call.[39] What makes crowdsourcing so influential today is that it is empowered through social media—especially in the areas of product development or improvement. It can make these business functions more efficient and effective. Crowdsourcing has also been used in other areas, such as developing taglines and logos and even advertising materials like television commercials. Which industries are most likely to use crowdsourcing competitions? In a global survey online, crowdsourcing and co-creation platform eYeka (see figure 11.3) found that food companies are the most likely to use crowdsourcing competitions followed by household, electronics, finance, beauty, and beverage companies.[40] Crowdsourcing is different yet related to crowdfunding. **Crowdfunding**, discussed further below, is using small amounts of capital from a larger group of people to finance a new business venture. Crowdfunding utilizes social media networks and crowdfunding websites such as Kickstarter to expand the pool of investors beyond traditional owner, relatives, and venture capitalists.[41]

Carl Esposti, founder of Crowdsourcing.org, says the benefit of crowdsourcing is that it enables companies to bypass restrictions, such as limited resources. This is an especially useful tool for startups and small businesses to obtain low-cost feedback. For larger corporations, crowdsourcing jumpstarts thinking outside the box of a confining corporate structure or culture. It can drive innovation and gratify a consumer's desire to be heard.[42] Instead of fighting negative social media comments, brands can leverage them to make a better product or service. Better product or service delivery, in turn, creates more positive social media buzz. *Marketing Week* called this a move from firefighting to co-creation, where an organization leverages the crowd for everything from consumer-goods ideas to advertising concepts and executions.[43] Thus social media can become a part of traditional **research and development (R&D),** which is the process where often departments of engineers or scientists are charged with new product development and design.[44]

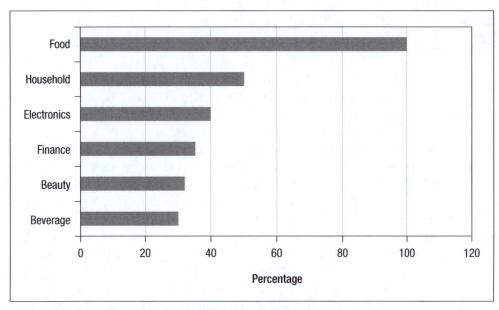

Figure 11.3. Crowdsourcing Competitions by Industry

Source: François Pétavy, "The Age of Ideation Crowdsourcing Report 2017" eYeka, 2017, https://en.eyeka.com/resources/reports?download=cs_report_2017.pdf.

Crowdsourcing can also be much more cost effective. Innovation can occur at a lower cost than with traditional research or development process methods. Research by Thomas Malone, Robert Laubacher, and Tammy Johns found that design competitions run by Top-Coder often provided clients with development work previously obtained by traditional means for as little as 25 percent of the cost.[45] Not only can crowdsourcing deliver lower costs, but it often provides a unique outside perspective that is hard to maintain working from within an organization.

Crowdsourcing has been used to design everything from cars to gaming tablets. Fiat engaged the crowd beyond its team of designers and engineers to crowdsource the design of the Fiat Mio. Fiat received more than seventeen thousand suggestions via Twitter and Facebook from people in more than 160 countries to help create a concept car that was met with rave reviews.[46] Fiat also leveraged the crowd by asking Facebook users to vote on a logo design for the American launch of the 500.[47] The company continues crowdsourcing efforts to this day, where Facebook and other social media insights fuel features and design decisions on new models.

In another crowdsourcing example, two hundred artists (editors, artists, DJs, musicians, and audiophiles) designed the V-MODA Crossfade M-100 headphones, and then more than ten thousand music fans voted on the final design. Razer designed the "Razer Edge" Windows 8 gaming tablet by asking gamers to tweet or post on Facebook specs they would want in a gaming tablet. Again, more than ten thousand responded with suggestions on options such as the game chipset, weight, thickness, and price they would be willing to pay.[48]

Yet crowdsourcing is not only for consumer crowds and consumer products. Mobile tech firm Psion has created an online forum called Ingenuity Working. This community of

MINI CASE

Fiat Mio

In 2009 Fiat Brazil wanted to create a new product and engage consumers. Their idea was to co-create a car with internet users. To emphasize that the product belonged to consumers, they named it *Fiat Mio* or "My Fiat." Designing an entire car is complicated and takes expertise, so this crowdsourcing project was not created as a competition to find the best idea and award a winner. Instead, consumers were invited to share their firsthand experience with cars to bring novel ideas that may never have occurred to design and production experts.[a]

In twelve months, Fiat's online platform received suggestions from more than seventeen thousand people across 160 countries. Suggestions covered various areas including internal and external design, gadget integration, electronic security, and economy. Ideas were screened by the Fiat research and development design team and then decisions were communicated through the online platform. The result was the world's first crowdsourced car, launched at the Sao Paulo Automotive Show. The company achieved strong brand engagement.[b] Today the company continues to include its consumers by soliciting ideas for new features on all its cars via its website and social media channels. They engage with the brand community on Instagram, Twitter, Facebook, YouTube, and Pinterest encouraging people to post pictures to #myfiatpic.[c]

[a] Fabio Prado Saldanha, Patrick Cohendet, and Marlei Pozzebon, "Challenging the Stage-Gate Model in Crowdsourcing: The Case of Fiat Mio in Brazil," *Technological Innovation Management Review* (September 2014), http://timreview.ca/article/829.

[b] "Creation of the Fiat Mio Concept Car," Aegis Group, accessed January 18, 2015, http://files.investis.com/aegis/annualreport2010/business_review/case_studies/case_study_01.html.

[c] "Fiat USA," FiatUSA.com, accessed November 15, 2015, https://www.fiatusa.com/.

more than fifteen thousand customers, partners, employers, and resellers visit the site more than six thousand times a month to exchange ideas, support each other, design product and feature solutions, and evaluate choices.[49] Imagine the value of getting everyone in the supply chain offering suggestions for improvement in a continuous feedback cycle.

Crowdsourcing does not always have to be a formal competition with a winner. Dell turned years of negative social media comments into a product design community called IdeaStorm. Within a year, nine of its laptops and desktops featured innovations generated from consumers in the community.[50] Dell captured more than ten thousand ideas, ultimately implementing more than four hundred of them.[51] This helped Dell greatly improve their product and customers' perception of the company in the marketplace. IdeaStorm is still co-creating with brand fans today. By 2017 more than sixteen thousand ideas had been submitted with more than five hundred implemented.[52]

Lay's potato chips came up with a clever crowdsourcing campaign that drove not only new product flavor ideas but also fan engagement and a viral spread of awareness. Lay's "Do Us A Flavor" contest asked consumers to submit ideas for the next potato chip flavor. The third year of the campaign tapped local interests and tastes, generating ideas such as Philly Cheesesteak, Buffalo Chicken Wing, and Chicago Deep Dish. Four finalists were made and sold across the United States and votes were collected to name the winner. Southern Biscuits and Gravy beat out New York Reuben, Greektown Gyro, and West Coast Truffle Fries.[53] The first year of the campaign, Lay's estimated they would receive one million votes. By the third year they were up to 14 million votes cast in the campaign.[54]

On a grander scale, the Unilever Foundry is the company's platform for partnering with startups to accelerate innovation through collaboration. The goal is to combine creativity and expertise to unleash disruptive innovation on a global scale. The platform crowdsources procurement and marketing, partnerships, brand licensing, new product development, joint ventures, and startup investment. The effort has resulted in more than two hundred pilots with $20 million invested and more than 10,000 startups profiled.[55] As you can see with the Unilever Foundry, crowdsourcing can be used to fund startups, which is often called crowdfunding. Crowdfunding is using small amounts of capital from a large number of people to finance a new business venture.[56] Crowdfunding makes use of access to vast networks of people through popular social media crowdfunding platforms. Examples include Kickstarter, which focuses on business, inventions, and creative works. GoFundMe is a platform more for funding individuals' personal needs, projects, and trips. And Crowdrise is a platform that focuses on socially conscious objectives such as funding for nonprofits and charities.[57]

Why continue to guess what features and products consumers want when marketers can simply ask? Start working with customers to develop better goods and services to fit their needs. David Bratvold, the founder of Dailycrowdsource.com, sums it up by saying, "Your actual customers are telling you how to sell to them and what they like."[58] Perhaps it is time to start treating customers more like coauthors of the brand and less like targets.

Figure 11.4. Crowdfunding through social media has helped create more new businesses.

© Svetikd / iStock Photo

There are many other uses of crowdsourcing beyond marketing and product development. For example, Facebook faced the enormous challenge of translating its website into seventy languages, so it created a website to mobilize the crowd into helping. The crowd responded by translating Facebook's French site in a day using three hundred thousand volunteers.[59]

The bottom line is that businesses can benefit from seeking their customers' wisdom and not just what's in their wallets. A summary of reasons organizations should crowdsource via social media includes customer input can improve products, it wins customer loyalty and positive word-of-mouth, it's less expensive, and customers can create content for you.

The outdoor retailer REI took advantage of this last reason with their 1440 Project. Tasked with generating engaging messages and images to promote the store in social media, they crowdsourced brand content.[60] REI asked fans to upload photos of themselves enjoying the outdoors to social media sites such as Instagram tagged with #REI1440Project. A website was created to represent all 1,440 minutes in a day based on the time stamps of consumer-generated photos. Within months REI collected more than ten thousand photos and five hundred thousand website visitors.[61] Now REI crowdsources local outdoor adventures for customers to #OptOutside on their website, pulling in consumer-created, -suggested, and -rated hikes, mountain bike routes, climbs, trail runs, and ski/board locations.[62]

Kellogg's used a combination of reasons in the launch of White Chocolate Coco Pops. Customer social media comments provided inspiration for the flavor, but by the time the product was created and brought to market it was years later. They were still able to leverage user-generated content through paid social media. To reignite interest the brand resurfaced a 2016 tweet requesting the flavor with a paid social media budget promoting the tweet. The brand started retweeting other older posts, mentioning white chocolate Coco Pops as far back as 2012. This became a news story in and of itself and turned into a full influencer, ad and PR effort that also expanded to Instagram. It was Kellogg's biggest product launch in the United Kingdom. Other brands that have leveraged the crowd by paying to promote those consumers' tweets include a Carlsberg beer brand campaign and KFC's launch of their new fries.[63] For another popular approach to crowdsourcing social media brand content, see the box "Crowdsourcing Surprise and Delight."

A form of crowdsourcing leverages the real-time data that comes from social media monitoring to promote a brand with popular live events and trending topics. Taking marketing action based on this live data is often called real-time marketing. **Real-time marketing** is systematically responding to consumers with dynamic, personalized content across channels that is relevant in the moment.[64] Other ways to think about real-time marketing are delivering the right message at the right time or creating "on-the-fly" content that is relevant to your target audience. Real-time marketing is leveraged through access to data, such as social media monitoring, with an understanding of the brand's target audience and competitors. Real-time marketing gained attention with the Oreo "You can still dunk in the dark," Super Bowl tweet mentioned in chapter 5. It can take the form of live response during big events such as the Super Bowl or the Oscars. Real-time marketing can also occur in response to relevant, trending topics and news or by engaging with competitor brands through friendly banter as the fast-food chain Wendy's has been known to do.[65] Real-time marketing is also simply responding to individual consumers one at a time, delivering the right message in the right buying stage or at the right mobile micro-moment.

Crowdsourcing Surprise and Delight

Surprise and delight is a form of marketing to attract and nurture customers through unexpected rewards.[a] The hotel brand Hilton uses a form of surprise and delight. Their unique service Hilton Suggests strives to be that friend you know who has traveled everywhere and can recommend the best local restaurants, attractions, and shops that an internet search would not reveal. Hilton Suggests empowers Hilton employees in 115 cities around the world to give their best local advice to surprise and delight anyone on Twitter. They use Lithium Social Web for social listening to find travelers who would not expect to hear from Hilton, not just customer tweeting to @HiltonSuggest or using the Hilton hashtag.

How does Hilton find surprise and delight moments? After years of social listening they have developed a list of "travel excitement" keywords based on past tweets that indicate a person is sharing excitement and anticipation about an upcoming trip. Sabrina Callahan, director of social media planning and integration at Hilton, trains and works with more than 120 social media brand representatives worldwide to implement the program. In an interview with Samantha Word for a Social Media Today article Callahan shared the following lessons learned from running the Hilton Suggest program:

1. *Any Tweet or Social Response Can Make an Impact.* Surprise and delight isn't about carefully crafted or scheduled posts. It is simply looking for opportunities to use your knowledge to help make someone's experience better.
2. *The Program Isn't For Everyone.* Hilton Suggests is voluntary for employees. It works because it leverages everyday employees at specific locations who know the local area. It is not executed by social media professionals in the social media command center at corporate headquarters. Employees volunteer but are only selected for the program after training and when they demonstrate they can provide a personal touch and good recommendations.
3. *Internal Branding and Marketing are Important.* Creating an employee program doesn't mean employees will participate. Hilton has had to focus on internal marketing to recruit representatives across the company. They use new employee onboarding and storytelling for training. The program also includes incentives such as their Global Guide Awards.[b]

Hilton Suggest is refreshing because they will help anyone, even people they know are staying at a competing hotel brand. These employee engagements are also genuine and sincere. These are not overt sales messages and promotional advertising. It is simply Hilton employees genuinely interested in helping someone have a better experience. For those they help it creates an emotional connection with the brand that will be hard to forget next time they book a trip.

Hilton is not the only brand using surprise and delight in social media. Kleenex's "Feel Good" campaign monitored Facebook looking for people posting a status they were not feeling well. Kleenex contacted friends to surprise the person with a Kleenex Kit filled with get-well items. Mastercard executes their "Priceless Surprises" campaign by finding customers in social media and giving them surprising rewards such as free concerts and getaways.[c] And sometimes surprise and delight is part of customer care. Southwest Airlines flight attendants discovered that a couple on their flight were nervous because they were flying to pick up a baby girl they were adopting. The attendants got other passengers to write well wishes on napkins and the employees on the ground at their destination rallied for them a celebration once they landed. Photos and videos of the encounter became user-generated content shared on behalf of the brand.[d]

[a] Ivy Wigmore, "Surprise and delight, WhatIs.TechTarget.com, October 2017, https://whatis .techtarget.com/definition/surprise-and-delight.

[b] Kaya Ismail, "5 Successful Surprise and Delight Marketing Campaigns," CMSWire.com, March 29, 2019, https://www.cmswire.com/digital-marketing/5-successful-surprise-and-delight -marketing-campaigns/.

[c] Ismail, "5 Successful Surprise and Delight Marketing Campaigns."

[d] Caroline Patrickis, "Southwest Airlines surprises couple on the way to meet their adopted newborn," WJLA.com, August 2, 2019, https://wjla.com/news/local/southwest-airline s-surprises-couple-on-the-way-to-meet-their-new-baby-through-adoption.

A form of real-time marketing that in essence crowdsources interest is newsjacking. **Newsjacking** is the strategy of injecting a brand into breaking news through social media or content marketing to get the brand noticed. Newsjacking has been a public relations strategy for years but has gained new relevance with the increased use of social media and the twenty-four-hour news cycle.[66] Newsjacking in this new context was first introduced by marketing and public relations expert David Meerman Scott in his book *Newsjacking: How To Inject Your Ideas Into a Breaking News Story and Generate Tons of Media Coverage*. Scott explains that news gathering happens in real time today as journalists quickly look for credible information on breaking news through searches and social media. Journalists tend to easily find the "who, what, when, and where" of the story, but the "why" is harder to find. To take advantage of newsjacking, brands should focus on quickly creating this "why" content and distributing it through social media, such as tweets and blog posts, with the trending keyword or hashtag of the story.[67] As part of a social media strategy, brands should constantly be monitoring breaking news and trending hashtags and be prepared to create "on-the-fly" content to take advantage of these real-time marketing opportunities. Yet, be careful not to come across as opportunistic in "trendjacking" sensitive situations.

Another consideration related to crowdsourcing is diversity. Society has become more diverse and it is important to consider and be inclusive of diverse people and perspectives in brand social media. According to the US Census, nearly a quarter of the American population is made up of multicultural groups that will be the source of all growth in the country's youth and working age population, and much of the growth in its consumers.[68] **Diversity marketing** strives to target audiences with marketing communication that is sensitive to individual attitudes and practices.[69] Ensure you are sourcing from the diverse makeup of the crowd of varied races, bodies, genders, and socioeconomic classes. Ronald Dod, CMO and co-founder of Visiture, suggests some best practices. This includes first hiring diverse employees to lead projects and using market research and social media listening to better understand the concerns and motivations of people from different cultures and how they relate to the brand. It also includes crowdsourcing user-generated brand content and product and service ideas from diverse groups and ensuring brand social media influencers include people from varied groups for diverse perspectives and messages.[70]

Figure 11.5. Diversity in social media content begins with hiring diverse employees.

© Raw Pixel / iStock Photo

Be sure to create media that is inclusive of people of color, with disabilities, and with gender identities; follow best practices for using language and avoid harmful stereotypes. Mistakes to avoid in brand social media diversity include using people as token representatives, using social issues out of your brand's depth for attention and sales, getting defensive in responses to criticism, using victim/hero language, and not aligning message with practice.[71] Several studies have found that diversity and inclusion make better marketing. A Shutterstock study found that most marketers believe diverse images in ads help a brand's reputation.[72] Sixty-one percent of gen Z consumers and 60 percent of millennials say they prefer seeing ads with diverse types of families.[73]

At the end of the day Dod's first advice is probably the most beneficial not only for creating diverse social media marketing, but also for having a diversity of ideas for new products and services, and improved ways to run your business. Warren Moss, CEO of Demographica sums it up well in *Chief Marketer:* "Audiences all across the globe are diverse, so in order to reach and resonate with those diverse audiences, you need a diverse output. And that's impossible if you don't diversify the creative and strategic team that comes up with the campaign in the first place."[74]

Theoretically Speaking: Local Search Constrains R&D

In 1996, Toby Stuart and Joel Podolny looked at the evolutionary changes occurring in corporate research due to technological advances. Research into industry innovation found that "local search" constricts the direction of corporate research and development.[75] Organizations that initiate R&D projects with the same technological content and outcomes of their prior searches limit possibilities. Using the same technologies and relying on previous thinking may hold back innovative solutions. For true innovation, organizations need a method outside their current processes and previous solutions.

Mary Tripsas and Giovanni Gavetti furthered this line of thought in their research, indicating that existing technological capabilities, set in routines and procedures, limit adaptive intelligence. In other words, Tripsas and Gavetti say, "A firm's prior history inhibits its future behavior in that learning tends to be premised on local processes of search."[76] When firms need to innovate, they can fall into traps where core competencies actually become limitations.[77] A **competency trap** is repeating what was successful in the past and overlooking important opportunities for future success.[78] Whether organizations are researching and developing a new product or a new marketing, advertising, or public relations campaign, social media research and crowdsourcing offer new ways to avoid these competency traps. Firms constrained to their traditional research methods may be limiting possibilities when opening processes to outsiders through social media could increase innovation.

Recent examples of competency traps include Blockbuster, Tower Records, and Apple Music. Blockbuster became so good at video rental it couldn't imagine DVD rental through the mail and eventually streaming video as a small rival called Netflix could. While Tower Records was really good at music retail, Apple made the leap from being a computer company to a digital music distributor. But Apple became so good at selling digital music that they fell behind in innovation as startup Spotify created subscription streaming to a 36 percent market share worldwide over Apple's 19 percent.[79] What examples can you think of today of organizations that have run into competency traps? Who has become so good at what they do that they can't learn to do anything new? How could social media crowdsourcing get them out of local search for innovation? How many failed social networks fell to local search and competency traps by failing to add unique features and services?

Chapter 11 Checklist

Social media can change quickly. Visit Post Control Marketing (http://www.postcontrol marketing.com) for updates, but also use this chapter checklist to briefly check how social media statistics in this chapter have changed since publication.

✓ How have social media research and crowdsourcing changed? Are more organizations leveraging the insights from social media data or analytics? Does traditional research still claim the majority of research budgets?

✓ Do a quick search to find the top data analytics firms. What are the latest types of research they are finding for their clients? What are some recent examples or case studies of brands leveraging social media insight including social conversation analysis or even crowdfunding platforms?

✓ Check for new crowdsourcing opportunities. What are the latest examples like Fiat and REI? How are brands leveraging the crowd for their brands today? How are brands leveraging real-time marketing and newsjacking to reach their objectives?

SOCIAL PLAN PART 11

Adding Crowdsourcing into a Campaign

Take the social media plan beyond marketing promotion and communication to other aspects of the Four Ps or Four Cs. What social media data does the organization need or could it benefit from? Are they launching a new product? Perhaps the brand could use social media insight into existing products or services for improvement. Or maybe the brand could use additional insight from consumers to create advertising, public relations, or social media content. What specific project could create a crowdsourcing campaign? Report all thoughts, plans, and ideas in these areas:

1. Identify needs traditional research is currently serving at the organization, and list how social media research could support those efforts.
2. Does the brand have an ongoing social media–monitoring system in place? What formal social research plan could be put in place?
3. List marketing projects, such as product design and advertising creation, or brand-content creation currently done in-house.
4. Of the list above, identify the top projects that could benefit from crowdsourcing. Explain how and why.

For a condensed version of the social plan see appendix A: Three-Part Social Plan.

KEY CONCEPTS

wisdom of the crowd

traditional market research

digital market research

social media research

social conversation analysis

crowdsourcing

crowdfunding

research and development (R&D)

real-time marketing

surprise and delight

newsjacking

diversity marketing

competency trap

QUESTIONS FOR DISCUSSION

1. What is your point of view on the concept of the wisdom of the crowd? Is the collective opinion of a crowd always right or better than individual ideas or thoughts? Find examples or research to support your opinion.
2. The real advantage of social media monitoring is real-time insight and intelligence. Find an example of a brand that, through real-time social media monitoring, either took advantage of an opportunity or avoided a public relations crisis with quick action.
3. What role does traditional research play, such as focus groups and surveys? What cannot be accomplished or gained solely through social media research?

4. Social research may be easier, less expensive, and quicker than traditional research but there are still ethical lines that can be crossed. What is "informed consent" and how does it apply to social research? Look up reports on Facebook's emotion manipulation or emotion cognition study of its users. Did it breach ethical guidelines?

ADDITIONAL EXERCISES

1. Plan a crowdsourcing effort for your brand. What does the organization need done that traditionally is handled by a small group of people inside the organization? To ensure a successful crowdsourcing effort, James Euchner, of *Research Technology Management*, suggests starting with a well-defined problem, a large population of experienced problem-solvers, feedback to the crowd for ideas to evolve, a policy for intellectual property, and a person or group to filter ideas.[80] The last action should especially be considered. Some aspects of social media are free, like media costs, but the real cost to an organization is time. Before launching crowdsourcing content or a campaign, allocate dedicated resources for analysis and implementation of hundreds or even thousands of ideas.
2. In this exercise, explore the topic of diversity in social media marketing further. Is there additional research that indicates diversity is preferred by consumers and makes a difference in marketing results? What are best practices for including diversity in opinion, message, and imagery? Then find an example of a brand that you believe is following these standards in their social media posts. Compare and contrast those posts with a brand that you believe is behind in their integration of diversity. Take screen grabs of example posts and then make recommendations for adjustments you feel would be a better effort.

Notes

1. "Research," BrainyQuote.com, accessed October 21, 2019, https://www.brainyquote.com/authors/bill-vaughan-quotes.

2. Ralph Hertwig, "Tapping into the Wisdom of the Crowd—with Confidence." *Science* 336, no. 6079 (2012): 303–304.

3. Francis Galton, "Vox Populi (The Wisdom of Crowds)," *Nature* 1949, no. 75 (1907): 450–451.

4. Clay Halton, "Wisdom of the Crowds," Investopedia.com, July 23, 2019, https://www.investopedia.com/terms/w/wisdom-crowds.asp.

5. Jan Lorenz, Heiko Rauhut, Frank Schweitzer, and Dirk Helbing, "How Social Influence Can Undermine the Wisdom of the Crowd Effect," *Proceedings of the National Academy of Sciences of the United States of America* 108, no. 22 (2010): 9,020–9,025.

6. Asher Koriat, "When Are Two Heads Better than One and Why?" *Science* 336, no. 6,079 (2012): 360–362.

7. "Listening to the Online Voice of the Consumer," Wharton Customer Analytics Initiative, accessed February 20, 2015, www.wharton.upenn.edu/wcai/files/Insights_Netzer_WCAI.pdf.

8. Bailey Roy, "Social vs. Traditional Media: Has the Battle Already Ended?" PRSA.org (blog), April 1, 2016, http://apps.prsa.org/Intelligence/Tactics/Articles/view/11445/1124/Social_vs_Traditional_Media_Has_the_Battle_Already#.WYn7CIpGmV4.

9. "Traditional vs. Digital Market Research Methods: Does 'New' Mean Better?" Marketing Directors, February 23, 2012, https://themarketingdirectors.wordpress.com/2012/02/23/traditional-vs-digital-market-research-methods-does-new-mean-better.

10. "Social Media Research," FoodRisc.org, accessed October 21, 2019, http://resourcecentre.foodrisc.org/social-media-research_35.html.

11. Cited in Natalie Meehan, "Let's Debate: Traditional Market Research versus Social Insights," Brandwatch.com, July 13, 2016, https://www.brandwatch.com/blog/lets-debate-traditional-market-research-versus-social-insights/.

12. Jeremy Taylor, "How to Use Social Media Monitoring for a Product Launch," Our SocialTimes.com, November 1, 2013, http://oursocialtimes.com/how-to-use-social-media-monitoring-for-a-product-launch.

13. Taylor, "How to Use Social Media Monitoring."

14. Taylor, "How to Use Social Media Monitoring."

15. "Barclays Pingit," Google Play Android Apps, accessed October 21, 2019, https://play.google.com/store/apps/details?id=com.barclays.apps.pingit&hl=en.

16. "Facebook Polls & Surveys," SurveyMonkey.com, accessed October 21, 2019, https://www.surveymonkey.com/mp/facebook.

17. "Introducing Polls in Instagram Stories," Instagram.com, October 21, 2019, http://blog.instagram.com/post/166007640367/171003-polling-sticker.

18. How Heinz Harnessed the Power of Twitter and Got 1 Billion Impressions in 48 Hours," Marketing.Twitter.com, accessed October 21, 2019, https://marketing.twitter.com/na/en/success-stories/how-heinz-harnessed-the-power-of-twitter-and-got-one-billion-impressions.

19. Gwen Ihnat, "Success of Mayochup Has Now Spawned Mayomust and Mayocue," TheTakeOut.com, March 5, 2019, https://thetakeout.com/heinz-releasing-mayomust-mayocue-mayochup-condiments-1833064875.

20. Meehan, "Let's Debate."

21. Premanjali Gupta, "6 Ways Researchers Can Use Social Analytics," Synthesio.com (blog), November 11, 2015, http://www.synthesio.com/blog/6-ways-researchers-can-use-social-analytics/.

22. Jeff Engel, "After Social Analytics Sector Shakeout, Crimson Hexagon Grabs $20M," Economy.com, March 8, 2016, http://www.xconomy.com/boston/2016/03/08/after-social-analytics-sector-shakeout-crimson-hexagon-grabs-20m/; "Machine Learning," Crimsonhexagon.com, accessed October 21, 2019, https://www.crimsonhexagon.com/machine-learning/.

23. "Unmetric," Unmetric.com, accessed October 21, 2019, https://unmetric.com/.

24. "Unruly Whitepapers," Unruly.co, accessed October 21, 2019, https://unruly.co/insight/.

25. Ray Poynter, "Chatter Matters: Social Media Research Is Reaching Its Tipping Point," *Marketing Research* 23, no. 3 (2011): 22–28.

26. Adam Coombs, "7 Tips on How to Use Social Media for Market Research," Unamo.com, 2017, https://unamo.com/blog/social/7-tips-on-how-to-use-social-media-for-market-research.

27. "Dove and Twitter #SpeakBeautiful," ShortyAwards.com, accessed November 20, 2019, https://shortyawards.com/8th/dove-and-twitter-speakbeautiful-2.

28. "Dove and Twitter," ShortyAwards.com.

29. "Dove and Twitter," ShortyAwards.com.

30. Poynter, "Chatter Matters."

31. Aarne Tollinen, Joel Jarvinen, and Heikki Karjaluoto, "Social Media Monitoring in the industrial Business to Business Sector," *World Journal of Social Sciences* 2, no. 4 (2012): 65–76.

32. "Social Media Analytics throughout the Enterprise: How Different Departments Can Leverage Social Analytics," Crimsonhexagon.com, accessed October 21, 2019, http://pages.crimsonhexagon.com/WC2016-06-28-GU-SocialAnalyticsThroughouttheEnterprise_Registration.html.

33. Richard Nordquist, "Conversation Analysis (CA)," ThoughtCo.com, April 3, 2017, https://www.thoughtco.com/what-is-conversation-analysis-ca-1689923; Ashley Crossman, "The Definition and Function of Ethnomethodology," ThoughtCo.com (blog), March 13, 2017, https://www.thoughtco.com/ethnomethodology-definition-3026314.

34. Conversation Research Institute web page, ConversationResearchInstitute.com, accessed October 21, 2019, http://www.conversationresearchinstitute.com/.

35. Jason Falls, "Transform Your Market Research with Social Conversation Analysis," Social Pros Podcast, August 11, 2017, http://socialpros.libsyn.com/transform-your-market-research-with-social-conversation-analysis.

36. Maria Ogneva, "How Companies Can Use Sentiment Analysis to Improve Their Business," Mashable.com, April 19, 2010, http://mashable.com/2010/04/19/sentiment-analysis.

37. Marianne Hynd, "Will Social Research Replace Traditional Marek Research?" Neal Schaffer.com, accessed October 21, 2019, https://nealschaffer.com/will-social-research-replace-traditional-market-research/.

38. "Elvis Presley Quotes," BrainyQuote.com, accessed October 21, 2019, https://www.brainyquote.com/quotes/elvis_presley_400394.

39. "Crowdsourcing Definition/Examples," Crowdsourcing.org, accessed October 21, 2019, http://www.crowdsourcing.org/document/crowdsourcing-definitionexamples/1363.

40. François Pétavy, "The Age of Ideation: The State of Crowdsourcing in 2017," eYeka, https://en.eyeka.com/resources/reports?download=cs_report_2017.pdf.

41. Tim Smith, "Crowdfunding," Investopedia.com, June 26, 2019, https://www.investopedia.com/terms/c/crowdfunding.asp.

42. Mary Brandel, "Crowdsourcing: Are You Ready to Ask the World for Answers?" *Computerworld* 42, no. 10 (2008): 24–26.

43. Michael Nutley, "There's a Lot More to Social Media than Fire-fighting a Wall of Gripes," *Marketing Week* 35, no. 15 (2012): 12.

44. "Research and Development (R&D)," Investopedial.com, June 25, 2019, https://www.investopedia.com/terms/r/randd.asp.

45. Thomas W. Malone, Robert Laubacher, and Tammy Johns, "The Big Idea: The Age of Hyperspecialization," *Harvard Business Review*, July–August 2011, https://hbr.org/2011/07/the-big-idea-the-age-of-hyperspecialization/ar/1.

46. Eric Markowitz, "The Case for Letting Your Customers Design Your Products," Inc.com, September 20, 2011, http://www.inc.com/guides/201109/how-to-crowdsource-your-research-and-development.html.

47. Jake Holmes, "Fiat Asks Facebook Users to Pick Logo for American 500," CarAndDriver.com, May 24, 2010, http://blog.caranddriver.com/fiat-asks-facebook-users-to-pick-logo-for-american-500/.

48. Julie Bort, "6 Great Products Designed by the Internet: Crowdsourced Product Design," SAP Business Innovation (blog), March 1, 2013, http://blogs.sap.com/innovation/innovation/crowdsourced-product-design-027607.

49. Maeve Hosea, "Why Social Brands Follow the Crowd," *Marketing Week* 35, no. 17 (2012): 27.

50. Anthony Malakian, "Harnessing the Power of the Crowd," *Bank Technology News* 21, no. 12 (2008): 20.

51. Laurence Ang, "Community Relationship Management and Social Media," *Journal of Database Marketing & Customer Strategy Management* 18, no. 1 (2011): 31–38.

52. "About IdeaStorm," IdeaStorm.com, accessed August 21, 2019, http://www.ideastorm.com/idea2AboutIdeaStorm?v=1351322692099.

53. Kim Speier, "4 Examples of Clever Crowdsourcing Campaigns," Mainstreethost.com (blog), January 7, 2016, https://www.mainstreethost.com/blog/four-examples-of-clever-crowdsourcing-campaigns/.

54. "Cheesy Garlic Bread Chips: Lay's Lesson in Marketing and Brand Awareness," Knowledge@Wharton High School, May 13, 2015, http://kwhs.wharton.upenn.edu/2015/05/lays-lesson-in-brand-awareness/.

55. "Unilever's Platform for Partnering with Start-Ups to Accelerate Innovation on a Global Scale," TheUnileverFoundry.com, accessed October 21, 2019, https://www.theunileverfoundry.com/.

56. Smith, "Crowdfunding."

57. Larry Kim, "Top Crowdfunding Platforms of 2018," Marketing and Entrepreneurship, October 11, 2018, https://medium.com/marketing-and-entrepreneurship/top-10-crowdfunding-platforms-of-2018-45513d6be48d.

58. Cited in Hosea, "Why Social Brands Follow the Crowd."

59. Hosea, "Why Social Brands Follow the Crowd."

60. Keith Quesenberry, "Treat Customers as Co-authors, Not Targets, and Hit a Marketing Bullseye," Entrepreneur.com, November 12, 2015, https://www.entrepreneur.com/article/252209.

61. Andy Sernovitz, "Andy's Answers: How REI Created a Sustainable, User-Generated Content Resource," SmartBrief.com (blog), January 29, 2015, http://www.smartbrief.com/original/2015/01/andys-answers-how-rei-created-sustainable-user-generated-content-resource.

62. "How Do You Want to #OptOutside?" REI website, accessed October 5, 2017, https://www.rei.com/opt-outside.

63. Seb Joseph, "Kellogg's Social-Driven Strategy to Launch New Products," DigiDay.com, June 20, 2019, https://digiday.com/marketing/inside-kelloggs-social-driven-strategy-to-launch-new-products/.

64. "The Marketer's Guide to the Right Message at the Right Time: Real-Time Marketing 101," Signal, cdn2.hubspot.net, accessed August 21, 2019, https://cdn2.hubspot.net/hubfs/370829/Marketing_101_eBook_Series/Real-Time_Marketing_101_by_Signal.pdf; Lianna Turchin, "Wait—What Is Real-Time Marketing?" OnlineMarketingInstitute.com, November 9, 2015, https://www.onlinemarketinginstitute.org/blog/2015/11/wait-what-is-real-time-marketing/.

65. Tom Ward, "Inside Wendy's Social Media Secret Sauce," SocialMediaToday.com, June 9, 2017, http://www.socialmediatoday.com/social-networks/inside-wendys-social-media-secret-sauce.

66. Mark Sherbin, "Newsjacking: 6 Tips to Help Your Branded Content Use the News," ContentMarketingInstitute.com, January 9, 2013, http://contentmarketinginstitute.com/2013/01/help-branded-content-use-news/.

67. David Meerman Scott, "What Is Newsjacking?" Newsjacking.com, accessed August 21, 2019, http://www.newsjacking.com/what-is-newsjacking-newsjacking.

68. William H. Frey, "The US Will Become 'Minority White' 2045, Census Projects," Brookings.edu, March 14, 2018, https://www.brookings.edu/blog/the-avenue/2018/03/14/the-us-will-become-minority-white-in-2045-census-projects/.

69. Bridgette Austin, "Importance of Diversity in Marketing," SmallBusiness.chron.com, accessed October 21, 2019, https://www.brookings.edu/blog/the-avenue/2018/03/14/the-us-will-become-minority-white-in-2045-census-projects/.

70. Ronald Dod, "Here's Why the Demand for Diversity Is Driving Digital Marketing Success," MarketingLand.com, August 9, 2019, https://marketingland.com/heres-why-the-demand-for-diversity-is-driving-digital-marketing-success-265221.

71. Dod, "Here's Why."

72. Erik Oster, "Most Marketers Agree Diverse Images in Ads Help a Brand's Reputation, According to New Report: Shutterstock Study Surveyed 1,500 Marketers," December 5, 2017, https://www.adweek.com/brand-marketing/most-marketers-agree-diverse-images-in-ads-help-a-brands-reputation-according-to-new-report/.

73. "Do Ads with a Possible Liberal Spin Pose Too Much Risk?" eMarketer.com, February 7, 2017, https://www.emarketer.com/Article/Do-Ads-with-Possible-Liberal-Spin-Pose-too-Much-Risk/.

74. Warren Moss, "The Importance of Diversity in Marketing Strategy," ChiefMarketer.com, March 12, 2018, https://www.chiefmarketer.com/importance-diversity-marketing-strategy/.

75. Toby E. Stuart and Joel M. Podolny, "Local Search and the Evolution of Technological Capabilities," *Strategic Management Journal* 17 (1996): 21–38.

76. Mary Tripsas and Giovanni Gavetti, "Capabilities, Cognitions, and Inertia: Evidence from Digital Imaging," *Strategic Management Journal* 21, no. 10/11 (2000): 1,147.

77. Dorothy Leonard-Barton, "Core Capabilities and Core Rigidities: A Paradox in Managing New Product Development," *Strategic Management Journal* 13 (1992): 111–126.

78. Charlotte Ren, "Why Firms Should Be Wary of Sticking with What They Know," MackInstitute.Wharton.UPenn.edu, 2015, https://mackinstitute.wharton.upenn.edu/2015/competency-trap-why-firms-should-be-wary-of-sticking-with-what-they-know/.

79. "Share of Music Streaming Subscribers Worldwide as of the First Half of 2018, by Company," Music Industry Blog, September 13, 2018, https://www.statista.com/statistics/653926/music-streaming-service-subscriber-share/.

80. James A. Euchner, "The Limits of the Crowds," *Research Technology Management* 53, no. 5 (2010): 7–8.

CHAPTER

12

Content Marketing and Influencer Marketing

Engaging with the audience lets them know I'm approachable.[1]

—Sheila E.

PREVIEW

What's your favorite meme? Evil Kermit, Caveman SpongeBob, Damn Daniel, Harambe, Ken Bone? Or perhaps you like old-school memes such as Rebecca Black's Friday, Grumpy Cat, Gangnam Style, ALS Ice Bucket Challenge, The Dress? Maybe you have another. Whatever comes to mind for you, these moments in cultural history are shared memories that touched off worldwide sensations. Would your organization love to become a popular meme like the Ice Bucket Challenge or Kony 2012, discussed in chapter 1?

In 2013 Abigail Posner, head of Google's Agency Strategic Planning team, started the Engagement Project to find meaning in memes. **Memes** are ideas expressed as visuals, words, and/or videos that spread on the internet from person to person. To study memes and how they spread, Posner partnered with cultural anthropologists, psychologists, and creators of digital content to determine what motivates creating, curating, and connecting across the web. What makes one particular idea or concept more likely to be picked up and shared on a mass scale than other pieces of content?

People are attracted to the fascinating familiar. On the web, everyday moments that are framed in a different way or juxtaposed for a new perspective elevate those regular moments by tapping into imagination and discovery. Our brains love synaptic play. We also love the freedom of the visual web where different, unrelated images and clips can come together in a childlike way. Online, cats play keyboards and babies ride roller skates easily, connecting random components in our brains to form synapses. This is the basis of creative joy. We love the energy of exchange with other humans. Sharing is caring, but also amplifies our own pleasure. Sharing a picture or video on the web is really about sharing the emotional response to the object. The sharing of the object becomes a gift or movement of pleasure that bonds us.[2]

Derek Thomas in the book *Hit Makers: How to Succeed in an Age of Distraction* explains hits such as memes in a similar way, saying that hit makers are architects of familiar surprises. People are curious to discover new things but afraid of anything too new. The right combination places an audience in a moment between the anxiety of confronting something new and the satisfaction of understanding it. When they do finally put it together and see a relationship to create meaning they get a rewarding feeling of "aha." Thomas says, "Great storytellers excel in creating tension followed by a cathartic release—aha."[3]

Facebook has also conducted research into memes. Their data scientists found that adding the words "please post this" or "copy and paste" makes a meme twice as likely to go viral. In addition, researchers found phrases that are easy to agree or identify with, such as "if you love your" or "share if you agree," drive content sharing. Brands that understand these factors can increase their chances for social media marketing success.[4] Can brands create memes? Heinz created a meme campaign by tapping into the timeless debate on whether tomatoes are a fruit or a vegetable. The brand posted questions and graphics asking "If you had to decide right now if a tomato is a fruit or a vegetable, which would you choose?" then asked people to take sides with hashtags #TeamFruit or #TeamVegetable. The result was four million impressions, or four times the goal, and more than 80,000 total engagements across Facebook and Instagram, placing Heinz top of mind for the Millennial target audience. The strategy was for the brand to become a part of the stories or conversations their audience was already having in social media.[5]

Personas and User-Generated Content

Many marketing, advertising, and public relations professionals create a customer profile or buyer persona that provides an in-depth description of the target, not only to define who may respond to their marketing communications but also why.[6] This provides a deeper understanding into the types of content and messages that will most resonate with your target audience. Therefore, before discussing the various types of engagement through content marketing, we will first consider personas. We will also consider user-generated content and how brands can better engage and share the brand content consumers are already creating about their products and services in social media.

A **buyer persona** is a semifictional portrayal of the ideal customer based on real data.[7] Think of a buyer persona as the historical fiction story of a single person in the target audience that fills in a real life around research statistics. Remember the target audience example given in chapter 4? "Twenty-five- to thirty-four-year-old married women professionals with young children living in urban and suburban areas interested in staying fit and active." The buyer persona would dig deeper into developing a greater understanding of what it is like to be a specific woman in that target audience on a typical day juggling the demands of home and work while wanting to still devote time to her own health and well-being.

John Jantsch of Duct Tape Marketing interviewed Adele Revella, president of the Buyer Persona Institute, to discover the important components of creating a customer persona for your ideal customer. Revella says there are five areas of insight that are important to personas:

1. Priority initiatives—What is important to your customers now?
2. Success factors—What does success look like to them?
3. Perceived barrier—What holds them back from buying?
4. Buying process—How do they collect information and purchase?
5. Decision criteria—What factors do they consider?[8]

HubSpot suggests identifying your current ideal customers and prospects and then interviewing them to uncover these insights. Also interview people who don't know your company or may be with a key competitor to gather their insights.[9] Aim for at least three to five interviews for each category. While you interview people who know your brand and people who don't, it may be helpful to add some questions to get their thoughts about your brand and competitor brands based on key benefits or criteria. This could be helpful in creating a perceptual map and determining brand positioning as was discussed in chapter 6.

Another concept that adds context to personas is the jobs to be done theory by Harvard business professor Clayton Christensen. **Jobs to be done theory** shifts the focus of marketing from demographics and product attributes to the functional, social, and emotional reasons customers buy products to get a "job" done or make progress to a larger goal. As Christensen says, "People don't simply buy products or services, they 'hire' them to make progress in specific circumstances." Understanding this can add additional valuable insight into crafting engaging content that grabs the consumer's attention because it is conveying the real underlying reason they would want the product and service.[10] Adding a job to be done insight to a buyer persona could be key to achieving greater success.

A classic example of jobs to be done theory is when McDonald's was looking to improve their milkshake recipe to improve milkshake sales. Researchers asking questions about the milkshake's taste didn't produce significant enough insights to improve sales. Then two consultants tried a different approach. They went to a restaurant and observed milkshake sales over the course of a day. They noticed that a lot of milkshakes were unexpectantly being sold in the morning. For further inquiry they conducted interviews asking people what "job" the milkshake served. What they found was that people were buying them as easy-to-eat breakfast alternatives for their long commutes. Once the marketers understood this, they made changes that made a difference in increased sales.[11] To engage consumers with brand content you need to understand their perspective. Create a buyer persona, then add these jobs to be done questions:

1. What "jobs" are people trying to do by buying the product or service?
2. What functional, emotional, and social component is the "job" fulfilling?
3. What messages convey the story of getting the job done?[12]

Create the buyer persona to ensure you understand the person but also understand how your product or service helps them get closer to achieving their goals by way of a job to be done.[13] With these two strategic tools you will have a more complete understanding to craft multifaceted content to attract attention, gain engagement, and move customers to action in achieving business, marketing, and organizational objectives. To gain insight into the jobs to be done, add the jobs to be done questions to interviews you conduct for creating buyer personas or conduct observational research as explained in chapter 4 and described in the McDonald's milkshake example.

Finally, organizations should consider the value of brand content created and shared by consumers in social media. **User-generated content** is any photo, video, post, or comment published through a social media platform by an unpaid contributor.[14] User-generated content (UGC) can be a powerful tool for brands in social media. Garmin Fitness was able to grow their Instagram account from one thousand to two hundred fifty thousand with a core strategy of UGC. Through social media listening, they discovered a lot of runners who are passionate about the Garmin brand sharing photos of the stats on their watches after runs. Carla Meyer, Global Digital Advertising and Social Media Manager at Garmin, said many agree for the brand to share their photos, called "wristies," and UGC has become an

Figure 12.1. User-generated content is an important part of any social media plan.

© Leo Patrizi / iStock Photo

important addition to brand-created content. In part, they grew the community by sharing the community's own content.[15]

UGC can be powerful. A Mavrck analysis of user-generated Facebook posts found that user-generated content featuring a brand achieved 6.9 times higher engagement than brand-generated content.[16] Outdoor clothing and equipment retailer REI has run a Black Friday campaign that promotes UGC by closing its stores and encouraging its employees and customers to opt to spend time outside instead of braving the crowds at shopping malls. In two years, nearly eight million people posted photos to the hashtag #OptOutside. The brand has created an "experiential search engine" at https://www.REI.com/opt-outside that shows user-generated #OptOutside images from Instagram and adds real-time information such as the hiking trail name, difficulty rating, trailhead directions, and user reviews.[17]

Implementing and managing a UCG strategy can be challenging, but software tools are emerging to automate tasks and improve efficiency. For example, the visual content marketing software CrowdRiff uses artificial intelligence to curate relevant images, secure rights, and distribute and optimize user-generated photos.[18] And Olapic aggregates user social media images from across social media channels such as Twitter, Instagram, Pinterest, and Facebook and uses an algorithm to identify the best suited for brand content. The software then can be used to easily request rights, tag to products, and organize to publish across web, social, and mobile to curate at scale. Olapic also tracks signals to determine which UGC photos drive the highest engagement and conversion rates.[19]

Are consumers really willing to share their photos for brand use? Olapic has found that 70 percent of consumers say yes when asked for permission to user their photos.[20] Whether organizations monitor for existing brand UGC and seek permission to share it like Garmin or create a specific campaign calling for it like REI, UGC should be a consideration for any social media strategy.

Engagement through Content Marketing

Sheila E. is a Grammy-nominated singer and drummer with a long, successful music career on her own and in collaboration with other famous artists such as Lionel Richie, Prince, Jennifer Lopez, Beyoncé, and Kanye West. Sheila E. and many other artists know that one secret to success is engaging with their audience. Organizations must ask themselves if their organization is engaging their target audience. Traditional paid advertising and promotional sales messages are not engaging. Remember that in social media, the audience has to choose to spend time with the brand; the brand cannot buy their attention. Even paid social media advertising only buys a view, not a like, comment, share, or click. If you gain their attention with something they find interesting, they will share it with friends for increased organic reach. Remember Howard Gossage from chapter 2? People don't read ads. They read what interests them.

How can brands gain the attention of their audience in social media? Create valuable content that the target audience will find entertaining or useful. The Content Marketing Institute defines **content marketing** as "a strategic marketing approach focused on creating and distributing valuable, relevant, and consistent content to attract and retain a clearly defined audience—and, ultimately, to drive profitable customer action."[21] Often content marketing seeks to create content that drives target audiences to a brand-owned property such as a company website. A significant part of that strategy is search engine optimization. **Search engine optimization (SEO)** is improving the visibility of a website in unpaid (organic) web search engine results.[22] In addition, many companies also use search engine marketing for that same purpose. **Search engine marketing (SEM)** is improving the visibility of a website in search engine results pages through paid advertising such as pay-per-click ads (PPC).[23]

BMW was an early innovator in content marketing. In 2001, they took $25 million normally spent on Super Bowl commercials and produced online short films with Hollywood directors and actors. The films were excellent stories that happened to take place around the brand's cars. These brand films were a great example of telling a story as discussed in chapter 5 and mastering tension-filled moments of new and familiar to produce the rewarding "aha" moments of memes. The car manufacturer's busy target audience no longer had time for or interest in traditional media. Within a year, more than 21 million people downloaded the first film, and the effort delivered the most successful sales year in BMW's history. In 2002, three more films were added, with a download total of 100 million. One million customers even bought a DVD of all eight of the BMW marketing films.[24] For the fifteenth anniversary of this effort, the brand brought back BMW Films in late 2016 with the original actor Clive Owen starring in "The Escape." In addition to BMWFilms.com, this time the film was also distributed on YouTube.[25]

Today, we call this type of strategy content marketing or branded content. A more recent star in content marketing has been Red Bull. Red Bull was the original energy drink but has managed to maintain its dominance despite many competitors entering the market. Red Bull is still the top brand, controlling 38 percent of market share.[26] Red Bull has done little traditional advertising over the years. Instead they created Red Bull Media House (RBMH) with more than 135 employees, which produces extreme-lifestyle content in print, online, on TV, and in feature films.

Red Bull's sports magazine *Red Bulletin* has a circulation equal to *Sports Illustrated*. Red Bull has distributed thousands of videos and photos free of charge, and they show up in the news on MSNBC and ESPN and in TV shows. Red Bull TV is distributed through their website but also on mobile phones, Amazon Fire TV, Apple TV, Chromecast, Kindle Fire, Xbox 360, and Smart TVs. Rebecca Lieb, analyst at Altimeter Group, observes, "Nobody is going to go to a website and spend 45 minutes looking at video about a drink. But Red Bull has aligned its brand . . . with extreme sports and action." It is working. They are selling nearly five billion cans a year doing it.[27]

Content marketing is powerful, even in the business-to-business (B2B) context. Research by the Content Marketing Institute reports that 55 percent of the most successful B2B marketers plan to increase their spending on content marketing. Why? B2B marketers indicate the top goals they achieve with content marketing include creating brand awareness, educating audiences, building credibility and trust, generating leads, nurturing subscribers, and building loyalty with current customers. And social media is an increasingly important part of content strategy; 61 percent of B2B marketers increased their use of social media for content marketing in 2019 and paid social media was the top type of paid content above PPC ads. But the type of content and message matters. Don't forget buyer personas

Figure 12.2. Content marketing is key to business-to-business marketing success.

© Anyaberkut / iStock Photo

and jobs to be done insights. Research indicates that 90 percent of top-performing B2B content marketers put their audience's information needs ahead of their company's sales and promotional messages. Nearly three-quarters (73 percent) of B2B marketers indicated they use or plan to use personas for their content marketing.[28]

In the travel industry, Google research found the average person dreaming about a trip has hundreds of micro-moments researching details for one destination and then going back and reconsidering all options across various desktop and mobile devices. And 72 percent indicate they are looking for the most relevant information regardless of who provides it. They key is creating content in all the channels they are looking at and being useful with content they want. How do you know what they want? Google says to ask, "What is the traveler's need that you're solving for?" In other words, uncover the job to be done. The more relevant branded content a company publishes across social media channels, the more likely it is that people planning trips will come across it.[29]

Branded content using SEO tags on social platforms such as Facebook, Twitter, You-Tube, and Instagram can deliver multiple hits per search versus a single hit for a brand website. Creating content around a related subject ultimately can help drive more customers to an organization's website for conversion. Google found that 67 percent of travelers are more likely to book with a travel brand that has relevant information on the travel destinations they are interested in. Marriott Hotels leveraged this insight by appointing a VP of content creation, creating an in-house content creation studio, and publishing *Marriott Traveler* online magazine. In addition, they are creating vlogs of documentary-style videos and partner with YouTube influencers to cover cities around the world.[30]

Remember that native advertising is different from content marketing in that it is paid media. However, sponsored posts or articles on sites like *Forbes*, BuzzFeed, and the *Huffington Post* are growing in popularity as a way to reach a larger audience more quickly. As discussed in part III of this book, many of the social platforms have added paid social media options where brand content can either be created for the platform or boosted for additional exposure as sponsored posts. Another option for native advertising is to boost reach of content through content recommendation engines that appear at the ends of articles, such as "From the Web" listings on media sites like Fast Company.

With the growing demand for branded content, some organizations are outsourcing to content marketing agencies and others are hiring their own in-house departments. A survey of the members of the Association of National Advertisers found that 78 percent have developed some form of in-house agency, up from just 58 percent five years ago. Another trend is brands buying popular blogs to jumpstart their content marketing strategy, such as Microsoft purchasing GitHub as a way to gain access to a software engineer audience.[31]

Unfortunately, some organizations get into content marketing as a result of high-profile failures. In 2007, an *MSN Money* journalist wrote a column criticizing Home Depot for horrible customer service. More than seven thousand people agreed and posted mostly negative comments. Boldly, Frank Blake, Home Depot's CEO, responded with his own comment to the blog post offering an apology and a promise to change. Social media became a key component in that change.[32] Today, Home Depot uses store associates to produce valuable social media content with how-to videos on a branded YouTube channel. Store associates also provide home improvement advice and tips on Home Depot's Facebook and Twitter accounts. Home Depot's strategy has expanded beyond orange-aproned sales associates and DIY content. Senior Director, Agile Marketing (and previously Senior Director of Social Media) Melanie Babcock says they also work with the public relations department to create a variety of stories about Home Depot's history, inspiring happenings around each store and corporate communication.[33]

How do brands create content? In *EContent*, Ahava Leibtag suggests marketers first consider the format.[34] Popular social channels for B2B are LinkedIn, Twitter, YouTube, and SlideShare. But B2B marketers are also finding success on Facebook, Instagram, and Quora.[35] For business to consumer (B2C), an organization should study the target audience's social media patterns and create content to engage consumers where they are talking about the brand, product, or service. Are they asking questions? Create articles, videos, and tips that answer them. Plan when and where to distribute brand content with a content calendar, which will be discussed in chapter 14.

Finally, don't forget about brand mobile apps as another content marketing channel for increased engagement with customers including live chat and notifications that can be trigger with beacon, NFC, or RFID technologies. Brand mobile apps can be used as media, self-service channels, and as core parts of the product or service. L'Oréal brought these various aspects together in their app Makeup Genius. It uses augmented reality for customers to see what the makeup looks like on them and enables them to create personalized content and then share the pictures on social media.[36]

MINI CASE

Dove Real Beauty Sketches

Dove originally launched the Campaign for Real Beauty in 2004 in reaction to a study that found the definition of beauty had become limiting and unattainable, with overly thin models setting an impossible standard. Dove released the short film *Evolution* on YouTube in 2006, and it became a viral success. Thus, Dove films started a global conversation.[a]

Nearly ten years after the campaign began, the brand kept it fresh with *Dove Real Beauty Sketches*. This short film documented a social experiment where an FBI-trained sketch artist drew women's portraits, one according to her own self-description and another according to a stranger's description of her. The contrast struck an emotional chord, resulting in the most viewed online video ad of all time with more than 163 million global views. Additionally, the campaign generated more than 4.6 billion public relations and blogger media impressions and more than one million likes on the Dove Facebook page, reaching one out of every ten Facebook users. The campaign was awarded a Titanium Grand Prix at the Cannes Lions Festival.[b]

The promotion continues today with campaigns for multiple issues including hashtags for #ConfidentGirl, #BeautyBias, and #WomenGetTold.[c] In 2019, PRWeek awarded the Dove Campaign for Real Beauty by Unilever and Edelman as the best US campaign of the past twenty years.[d]

[a] Kiley Skene, "A PR Case Study: Dove Real Beauty Campaign," Tuning In (blog), April 11, 2014, http://www.newsgeneration.com/2014/04/11/pr-case-study-dove-real-beauty.

[b] "Real Beauty Shines Through: Dove Wins Titanium Grand Prix, 163 Million Views on YouTube," ThinkwithGoogle.com, June 2013, https://www.thinkwithgoogle.com/case-studies/dove-real-beauty-sketches.html.

[c] "Dove Campaigns," Dove.com, accessed November 3, 2019, https://www.dove.com/us/en/stories/campaigns.html.

[d] "Dove Campaign for Real Beauty wins Best U.S. Campaign of the Past 20 Years," PRWeek.com, March 21, 2019, https://www.prweek.com/article/1579871/dove-campaign-real-beauty-wins-best-us-campaign-past-20-years.

Enterprise software company SAP has found success with content marketing in the B2B space. SAP has managed to create a customized content marketing strategy for nineteen customer segments in twelve industries across the globe. The brand maintains a consistent look and feel while delivering valuable content around popular topics in each industry relevant to customer segments. Content is distributed among traditional marketing channels and social media including blog posts, tweets, LinkedIn updates, and posts in the SAP Community Network. The effort has created more than 3.6 million marketing-generated opportunities.[37] What is most remarkable is that SAP started this effort with a minimal budget and volunteer contributors writing articles to answer their customers' top questions.[38]

In content marketing, treat the customer or potential customer as a friend rather than a target. Magazines and newspaper publications have readers, not target audiences. They deliver valuable information to a community with shared interests. In content marketing, brands must do the same to succeed. Joe Pulizzi, founder of the Content Marketing Institute, says that marketers need to take off their sales hats and put on publisher hats.[39] As discussed in chapter 3 under careers in social media, this has led to increased demand by organizations for people to fulfill hybrid journalist social media content developer roles. As Sheila E. says, being approachable is the only way to be engaging. Look for collaboration opportunities with content providers and consumers or start a new brand or organization content delivery vehicle. For more details and strategies for content marketing see HubSpot Academy's Inbound training and certification at https://academy.hubspot.com/courses/inbound. Also consider HubSpot Academy's Content Marketing training and certification at HubSpot Academy's Content Marketing training and certification at https://academy.hubspot.com/courses/content-marketing.

Advocates and Brand Ambassadors

Facebook founder Mark Zuckerberg says, "But it's really all about how people are spreading Facebook around the world in all these different countries. And that's what's so amazing about the scale that it's at today."[40] Zuckerberg may have built a new and unique online network, but the really amazing part is how Facebook simply spread via people to more than two and a half billion users around the world. That is the power of Web 2.0 customer evangelism. This process doesn't have to happen all on its own. Organizations can deliberately recruit and equip loyal fans to be word-of-mouth brand ambassadors.

Evangelism marketing is a form of word-of-mouth marketing in which marketers develop relationships with customers who strongly believe in a product or service and who voluntarily advocate for the brand.[41] This is also sometimes called advocate marketing. **Advocates** are super-fans and brand loyalists who engage with a brand because they love it and may not have a large sphere of influence. **Brand ambassadors** are influencers who are rewarded or hired by the brand for long-term relationships. This is different from influencers who may be paid for shorter-term campaigns or even individual posts. **Influencers** bring expertise to a specific area, have a sizable group of engaged followers, and usually share brand messages for compensation.[42] Influencer marketing will be covered in the next section.

Social media, such as Facebook, turns fans into media vehicles for companies, especially considering that the average Facebook user has 338 friends.[43] In addition, research finds that consumers trust other people more than advertising. Brand evangelists have enormous potential to greatly impact the demand and perception of a product or service. Knowing how to tap into these consumers presents an opportunity to tap into enormous marketing potential. A Salesforce survey of US internet users found that the most-trusted sources of accurate product information were online reviewers (31 percent) and friends, family, and colleagues (23 percent), ahead of the brand itself (20 percent). These numbers skew higher when limited to the millennial generation, which trusts online reviewers first (40 percent), followed by friends, family, and colleagues at nearly a quarter (24 percent), and the brand itself at only 19 percent.[44]

Procter & Gamble (P&G) knows how to supercharge word-of-mouth. They set up a website community called Vocalpoint for influential mothers in 2009. These mothers share

Figure 12.3. Brand ambassador and advocate strategies differ from influencer marketing.

© Designer 491 / iStock Photo

their experiences with new P&G products, and they often reach out to social networks outside of Vocalpoint with remarkable results. P&G found markets, or cities, with active Vocalpoint online community influencers produced twice the revenue of that in markets without Vocalpoint.[45] Word-of-mouth supercharged P&G's traditional marketing, advertising, and public relations efforts.

Vocalpoint continues today and has expanded beyond the website to Facebook, Twitter, Instagram, Pinterest, and Facebook Live shows. A survey of Vocalpoint members reveals what makes these brand advocates great: 77 percent like to be the first in their group to share a new product or trend; 72 percent often snap and post pics or video of restaurants, new products, vacations, and funny stuff; 85 percent like to see their favorite product or brands succeed and put energy into recommending them; and 88 percent won't recommend products until they have used them and are sure they work.[46] P&G has added additional online communities including Empty Nesters, Home Made Simple, My Black is Beautiful, and Pampers Village.[47]

Yet a business doesn't have to be a big corporation to benefit from social media evangelism. For example, Kurt Walchle launched Survival Straps through social media. In six years of business, his company found that nearly 50 percent of its sales came from word-of-mouth social media efforts. This helped him grow from a home-based business into a thriving company with more than fifty employees.[48] Survival Straps continues to be a success with a 10,000-square-foot facility; the company connects with its brand advocates on Facebook, Twitter, Pinterest, and Instagram.[49]

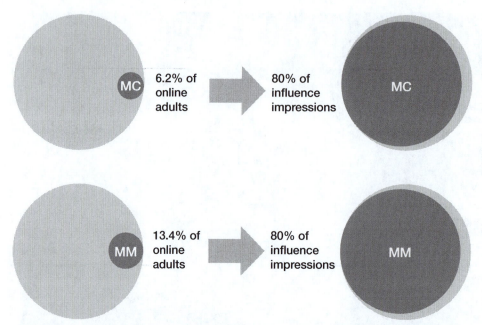

Figure 12.4. Mass influencers such as Mass Connectors (MC) and Mass Mavens (MM) create 80 percent of the product and service impressions each year.

Source: Josh Bernoff, "Spotting the Creators of Peer Influence," AdAge.com, April 20, 2010, http://adage.com/article/digitalnext/marketing-spotting-creators-peer-influence/143372/.

In *The Tipping Point*, Malcolm Gladwell advises that marketers should find "connectors"—the people who seem to know everyone and have the ability to reach and influence a variety of consumers. When influenced by a "market maven," someone Gladwell depicts as knowing a lot about products, a connector follows trends in specific areas and shares this information with others, joining consumers and brands.[50] Figure 12.4 shows how this small group of mass influencers is responsible for 80 percent of the more than 500 billion online impressions made about products and services every year.[51]

Gladwell's concepts are related to similar ideas proposed by Seth Godin in his book *Unleashing the Ideavirus*. In fact, Gladwell wrote the foreword. Godin explains that in order for an idea to spread you must identify the "sneezers" in the appropriate "hive."[52] Interestingly, *Unleashing the Ideavirus* followed its own advice and became an ideavirus by first distributing the book online for free with the message "Steal This Idea!" and spread the word about the book, which is still available today on Seth's blog at https://seths.blog/wp-content/uploads/2008/12/2000Ideavirus.pdf.

One way to organize an evangelism program for advocates and brand ambassadors is to drive desired behavior through gamification. **Gamification** is the application of elements of games to marketing, such as point scoring and competition, to encourage brand loyalty and engagement.[53] Gamification has been applied to marketing for many years in the form of loyalty programs, such as airlines awarding frequent-flyer miles and other perks to customers for repeat purchases. Customers are motivated with ever-increasing rewards tied to tiers of higher status and privileges. Gamification can also be applied to online communities to incentivize brand engagement, user-generated content, and advocacy. Community members can be ranked and awarded badges for higher levels of contributions, given early access to insider information, and rewarded with special offers.[54]

Brand evangelism through gamification also provides the opportunity to collect data to identify your best customers. Since rewards are given only to customers who perform specific actions such as referrals or increased purchases, more expensive rewards can be reserved for only the most valuable customers. Behavioral data can also be collected on these customers for customization, personalization, and targeting. For example, lookalike audiences could be created based on the highest-tier customers for a highly targeted Facebook or Instagram social ad campaign.[55] In Pat Flynn's book *Superfans*, he recommends a system to move customers along this path. Flynn suggests a system that creates intentional magic movements that turn followers into fans. The pyramid of fandom is way to view audience relationships to nurture them moving up levels from casual members to active participants, then connected community members, and finally super-fan brand supporters.[56]

A great example of brand leveraging advocates and brand ambassadors is Pura Vida. This jewelry brand has grown from a startup in 2010 to a $68 million business mostly through word of mouth and social media.[57] The brand has nearly two million followers on Instagram and is a must have for VSCO girls as part of the latest teen trend.[58] Their brand ambassador program called #PuraVidaCrew invites fans to apply. Those who are selected are encouraged to tell their friends, family, and followers about their unique ambassador code to get 20 percent off purchases. Ambassadors earn commission and free products plus have access to sneak peaks, exclusive content, VIP giveaways, and other rewards. Pura Vida also promotes them on their content brand ambassador social channels.[59] The result is an army of Pura Vida marketers sharing authentic lifestyle images across the world promoting the brand's products in ways and in volume they could never create on their own.[60]

In *Return on Influence*, Mark Schaefer explains that influence has become the new currency of the social media age. Brands can identify and quantify social media influencers who can drive demand for products and services.[61] Many brands today are looking for people with influence in a specific field or with a specific group versus mass influence across many channels. An influencer who has built their influence on one social platform or in one industry may have less mass appeal but has high engagement with a specific community that trusts their suggestions and views, which can be powerful for a brand. Don't just consider the celebrities with mass appeal and the huge follower counts. Look for influencers on individual social platforms and look for high engagement rates with smaller communities for more authentic influence.

Another example of a consumer evangelist program built around passionate product enthusiasts is Lego Ambassadors. Lego drives word-of-mouth by placing the company's most enthusiastic adult fans into an exclusive club. Members get previews about upcoming products, which they in turn share with their personal networks. Not everyone gets in. Enthusiasts must vie with one another to be chosen. The competition for limited membership energizes fans to become brand spokespeople.[62]

In 2014 Lego expanded the ambassador program into the Lego Ambassador Network (LAN), which has grown into LAN Ambassadors representing three hundred communities divided into Lego user groups and fan media. Lego describes the network as a place where

How to Find a Brand Evangelist

In the book *Evangelist Marketing*, Alex Goldfayn suggests that you should find the average consumer who is a "hyper-repeat customer."[a] In order to turn these customers into advocates and brand ambassadors, marketers, advertisers, and public relations professionals have to leverage the organization's strengths. The blog Scripted explains how to find brand evangelists through these five steps:[b]

1. *Excel at service.* When someone has a great experience they want to tell everyone about it.
2. *Show appreciation for repeating customers.* Give them special deals or offers.
3. *Listen and respond to complaints.* Admitting a mistake and fixing it also gives customers something to talk about.
4. *Leverage employees.* Train and reward employees who spread the brand message.
5. *Focus on quality, not quantity.* Relationships take time, so concentrate efforts on a smaller group of influential customers or clients to make the effort more manageable.

To take your evangelism marketing to the next level, add a gamification layer. Philip Kotler, Hermawan Kartajaya, and Iwan Setiawan in *Marketing 4.0* suggest the following steps:

1. Define gamification objectives based on the customer actions you want triggered.
2. Define how customers enroll in the program and how they move up and down tiers.
3. Decide on rewards and recognition incentive classes for customers to move up tiers.[c]

[a] Alex Goldfayn, *Evangelist Marketing: What Apple, Amazon, and Netflix Understand About Their Customers (That Your Company Probably Doesn't)* (Dallas: BenBella Books, 2012).
[b] Alan K., "How to Find Evangelists in Your Audience," Scripted (blog), November 18, 2013, http://scripted.com/content-marketing-2/how-to-find-evangelists.
[c] Philip Kotler, Hermawan Kartajaya and Iwan Setiawan, *Marketing 4.0: Moving from Traditional to Digital* (Hoboken, NJ: Wiley, 2017).

"LAN Ambassadors engage in joint activities and discussions, help each other, and share information. They build relationships that enable them to learn from each other to the benefit of their role as LAN Ambassadors and the community they represent."[63]

Another form of brand evangelism with advocates and brand ambassadors is employee advocacy. **Employee advocacy** is the promotion of a business by its workforce usually through social media.[64] For a list of employee advocacy benefits see table 12.1. LinkedIn Marketing Solutions recommends that employee advocacy programs need to be strategic, sustainable, and organic to succeed. First, you need to establish objectives of the program and ensure metrics are in place to measure progress. Next, ensure the program is designed for the long term with upper management support and promotion. Finally, participation needs to be voluntary and out of interest. Forced participation is not authentic and therefore will not be effective.[65] Once an employee advocacy program is developed, there are software tools that can make the execution of the program easier. For example, Hootsuite offers a solution

Table 12.1. Top Benefits of Employee Advocacy Programs

Increase brand visibility	Build brand loyalty
Attract new business	Amplify thought leadership
Humanize the brand	Share customer stories
Raise employee profiles	Highlight workplace culture
Strengthen employee engagement	Recruit and retain talent

Source: G. I. Sanders, "Top 10 Employee Advocacy Benefits," DynamicSignal.com, accessed December 9, 2019, https://dynamicsignal.com/2019/04/30/benefits-of-employee-advocacy/.

called Amplify that creates an easy to share and track platform to boost social reach through employee advocacy. The mobile first environment enables on-the-go content sharing in a format employees are used to using.[66]

An employee advocacy program can be used in multiple ways. Employees amplifying brand content can boost visibility to prospective customers and attract new business. Employees talking about and sharing their experiences working for the company can be a great way to promote company culture for recruitment efforts to attract new talent.[67] This second form of employee advocacy can be part of a larger employer branding effort. **Employer branding** focuses on attracting, engaging, and retaining talent.[68] Employer branding is often created by human resource managers working with marketing and applying brand concepts to recruitment and employee relations. Social media can be a powerful tool for employer branding.

The international IT company Cisco has an award-winning employer branding and employee engagement program based on #WeAreCisco. More than 95 percent of their content is employee-generated on the Life at Cisco Blog, Twitter, Facebook, LinkedIn, Instagram, YouTube, and Snapchat. The effort has resulted in a 6 percent increase in traffic to the Cisco Careers website, has led to direct hires, and has helped change the perception of company culture.[69]

Other brand advocacy and ambassador examples include Sephora's Beauty Talk, the SAP Community Network, PlayStation Community, and Harley Owners Group.[70] Think of ways an organization can motivate and excite its most active fans, perhaps even on an amazing scale such as Mark Zuckerberg described. That is the unlimited power of social media–powered word-of-mouth marketing.

Influencer Marketing

A related form of word-of-mouth or evangelism marketing focuses on people with a high level of influence and persuasion and relies more on payment for specific campaigns. As first defined in chapter 6, **influencer marketing** focuses on leveraging key leaders to advocate on behalf of a brand to reach the larger market.[71] Influencer marketing software company TapInfluence explains that influencer campaigns either have the influencer create content for the brand or the brand creates the content for the influencer to share via their social channels.[72] Influencers can simply be people with a large social following in specific areas of interest or industries or they could be celebrities such as sports stars, musicians, or

Hollywood actors. Influencer marketing is the fastest-growing part of the marketing mix estimated to be a $10 billion industry in 2019. Why are so many brands investing in influencers? Research from Edelman's Trust Barometer indicates 63 percent of consumers trust what influencers say about brands more than they trust the brands themselves.[73]

This type of social media word-of-mouth can take the form of earned influencer marketing, in which existing relationships are leveraged to promote the brand or paid influencer marketing campaigns that pay influencers to promote the brand.[74] The type of brand message can vary from full-blown testimonials to subtle mentions. Either way, influencer marketing is a growing strategy with 93 percent of global marketing, communications, and public relations professionals indicating they use influencer marketing and 60 percent plan to increase their influencer marketing budgets.[75]

To create an influencer marketing campaign, brands can leverage existing sponsorship deals with influencers, find influencers themselves and negotiate a campaign, or use one of the influencer marketing agencies and automated systems that can find, deliver, and pay dozens or even hundreds of influencers for the brand. Influencer marketing can work for any brand, but the fashion and beauty industry has especially taken advantage of these types of campaigns with high-profile celebrities such as Kylie Jenner.

However, don't think that a brand needs a high-profile celebrity to succeed. Research has revealed that noncelebrity influencers may be ten times more likely to drive in-store purchases. Collective Bias conducted a survey of US online consumers and found that 30 percent were more likely to purchase a product endorsed by a noncelebrity blogger than by a celebrity. Of that number, 70 percent of eighteen- to thirty-four-year-olds had the highest preference for "peer" endorsement.[76] And Edelman's research found that only 18 percent of their respondents indicated they were attracted to influencers for their larger following. Relatability was nearly two times as important as popularity as a quality that attracts people to influencers.[77] Based on these results, a micro form of influencer marketing has arisen. **Micro-influencer marketing** is when brands partner with people who have smaller followings on social media to promote products in an authentic way versus sponsored ads. Micro-influencers may have smaller groups of followers numbering in the thousands, but they have super-engaged audiences.[78]

To put together an effective influencer marketing program, first identify your objectives, message, and target audience. If you have created a social media plan following the method outlined in this book, you already know these answers. Your target audience or audiences will determine your influencers. List the social platforms on which your target audiences are most active. List the message you are trying to convey or the interest area you are trying to influence. Are you trying to get your makeup brand discovered by a teen audience on Instagram or to get your software considered by a small business audience on LinkedIn? Then, identify the influencers who are active on those social platforms discussing those interest areas. If you have multiple target audiences you will need separate messages, social platforms, and influencers.[79] Some marketing tools can be used to find influencers and brand advocates including Awario, Followerwonk, Klear, BuzzSumo, BuzzStream, Traackr, and Upfluence.[80]

Also consider the level of influencer. Are you looking for a celebrity (famous in traditional media), a social media star (known for or because of social media), or a thought leader

Figure 12.5. Influencer marketing is one of the fastest-growing brand strategies.

© Jacob Lund / iStock Photo

(known for industry knowledge)? Celebrities can have a lot of advantages, including their mass reach and appeal. Yet film, music, or sports celebrities can be expensive and people may question the authenticity of their product endorsements. Social media stars may have fewer followers, but those followers could be more engaged and endorsements could be seen as more believable. Thought leaders are a good choice for certain product or service categories in B2B. A mention or recommendation by an industry leader can carry a lot of weight.[81]

Influencers can also be categorized in terms of follower numbers. Many marketers now divide influencers into four categories. **Mega-influencers** have more than one million followers and are often considered celebrities who may be more famous than influential. **Macro-influencers** have between 100,000 and one million followers and usually gained their fame through the internet. **Micro-influencers** include people with 1,000 to 100,000 followers and focus on a specific niche as industry experts or topic specialists. **Nano-influencers** have fewer than 1,000 followers and have influence within their community. Nano-influencers can often be advocates engaged through user-generated content and as part of brand ambassador programs.[82]

It may be tempting to only go for the mega- or macro-influencers because of their massive reach, but micro-influencers are often more effective.[83] *Adweek* reports micro-influencer engagement rates can be 60 percent higher, their buys are 6.7 times more efficient, and they can drive 22 times more conversions.[84] According to the Association of National Advertisers, in the United States more than half of brands use mid-level (66 percent) or micro-influencers (59 percent) while less than half are using macro-influencers (44 percent).[85] No matter what type of influencer you use, a growing concern is influencer fraud.

Influencer marketing software companies are working on ways to detect fraud and make it more obvious for brands to identify while creating industry standards.[86]

Influencer marketing can be structured in several ways. Small organizations with a minimal number of influencers or big companies with larger internal resources may want to create and manage their own influencer program. For more help, brands can work with influencer platforms or networks that streamline processes and payments and make it easier to find influencers. Fees are charged for the convenience and you may be limited only to influencers in their network. A third option is hiring an influencer agency. These agencies provide the most options, customization, services, and access to influencers, but will also cost the most in fees.

Another increasingly popular option for influencer marketing is affiliate programs. Affiliate marketing has been around for many years, but in the past it focused on building websites to draw an audience and send traffic to product links for sales. The retailer rewards the affiliate for each visitor or customer. Today more affiliates are using social media to attract audiences and insert links in social media posts. Instead of paying per post or sending free product, brands pay a commission per sale, which could motivate affiliates to send traffic for a longer period. Options include building and managing a brand affiliate program, working with an affiliate platform and network, or hiring an affiliate agency. Amazon has launched the Amazon Influencer Program, which is an extension of their Amazon Associates affiliate program for social media influencers. Members get their own page on Amazon with a vanity URL to showcase recommended products. Amazon Influencers earn money from purchases in a similar way to Amazon Associates.[87]

Once you have your influencers, decide how content will be created and spread. You may think it is best to have the most control, but content created by the brand and merely shared could come across as not genuine. Certain influencers or influencer networks may also have their own standards for what they will or will not do. Consider the pros and cons for each option, such as influencer-shared brand content, influencer-created brand content, or product and service reviews and mentions. Or get creative with options such as influencer brand account takeovers, brand guest content contributions, or collaboration on a contest or giveaway. Another consideration is to repurpose influencer content in other channels and in other forms, such as sharing on brand social media or incorporating into digital and offline ads.[88]

Not everyone is effectively measuring influencer marketing, but according to the State of Influencer Marketing report, 70 percent are measuring ROI and those firms average an earned media value of $5.20 per dollar spent on influencer marketing.[89] Kim Kardashian famously charges $250,000 for a single Instagram post, but many have found that influencer marketing works better with less mass appeal influencers.[90] Influencer rates drop with number of followers. Average rates for influencers with more than 500,000 followers is $2,085 per post, 30,000 to 500,000 followers is $507 per post, 5,000 to 30,000 followers is $172 per post, and 500 to 5,000 followers is $100 per post.[91] Other research has found rates average $10 per 1,000 followers on Instagram, $20 per 1,000 subscribers on YouTube, and $0.10 to $0.35 per view on Snapchat.[92]

Sports brands have also had success with their sponsored athletes promoting products in their social media channels. In fact, the average athlete has a 6 percent engagement rate on social media compared to the average sports team that has an engagement rate of only

0.3 percent.[93] Opendorse is an influencer platform that specializes in athletes to automate communication, approvals, and distribution. The platform helped the National Hockey League (NHL) team the New Jersey Devils leverage their players' influence as advocates for the team brand. They lead all NHL teams in total player engagement and engagement rate, adding more than 130,000 followers during the season and Stanley Cup Playoffs.[94]

No matter which influencer campaign a brand runs, from earned to paid or celebrity to micro-influencer, the law requires influencers to disclose their financial relationship with the brand. This will be discussed further in chapter 15. Another consideration is risk versus reward. Carefully research the content and perspective of influencers to ensure that their views match the values of the brand. High-profile celebrity sponsorships get executive-level consideration and considerable vetting. Yet a micro-influencer may simply pass through a media buyer and not get much thought. A high-profile example was when a Disney affiliate, Maker Studios, terminated a joint venture with YouTube star Felix Kjellberg, known as PewDiePie, over anti-Semitic content.[95]

Theoretically Speaking: Consumer-Brand Relationships

Can a person have a relationship with a product? This is a question researchers have been asking themselves for decades. As early as 1959, Sidney Levy proposed that products and brands can go beyond their utilitarian value and can be used as symbols with social meaning.[96] When a consumer displays or uses a product, the brand meaning is transferred to the consumer.[97] Branded products contribute to and communicate a consumer's self-image and personality, thus creating product attachment. A close relationship with the brand is formed because repeated usage satisfies the consumer's needs. **Consumer-brand relationship** is a line of theoretical research that proposes repeated interactions between a brand and customers can begin to reflect characteristics of relationships between people.[98]

Kurt Matzler, Elisabeth Pichler, Johann Füller, and Todd Mooradian took this theory one step further to brand communities. Consumers identify with other consumers who use the same products and brands. In their study, they found that both attachment to the product and ties to a brand community led to greater brand trust and loyalty.[99] Other researchers, Hyejune Park and Young-Kyung Kim, proved this theory with a study on Facebook published in the *Journal of Retailing & Consumer Services*. They found that a brand's social network can positively influence a consumer's perception of the investment the brand has made in the consumer relationship. This contributes to both brand relationship quality and the willingness to spread good words about the brand through social networks, further advancing the consumer-brand relationship.[100]

Investing in social media strengthens a consumer attachment to a product and builds stronger ties with the brand community, leading to the consumer sharing brand social content and increasing brand trust and loyalty. It seems that consumers can have a relationship with a brand and that social media is enabling this to happen even more. Visit Pura Vida's Instagram account. What specific evidence do you see of consumer-brand relationships? How has this company turned selling bracelets into a community? How has social media like Instagram enabled this?

Chapter 12 Checklist

Social media can change quickly. Visit Post Control Marketing (http://www.postcontrol marketing.com) for updates, but also use this chapter checklist to briefly check how social media statistics in this chapter have changed since publication.

✓ How has content marketing changed? Are brands continuing to increase the amount of brand content they are creating? What are the latest statistics? Are brands getting better results or are results decreasing because of content clutter? Have the General Data Protection Regulation, California Consumer Protection Act (see chapter 15), or other regulations changed the targeting and tracking capabilities of content marketing?

✓ How has influencer marketing changed? Are there new terms for this strategy besides evangelist, advocate, ambassador, and influencer? Are brands increasing their use of both "mass" and "micro" influencers? What are the top influencer marketing firms?

✓ Check for the latest way to curate, distribute, and measure user-generated content. Are there new platforms or software tools? Are more brands using consumer-generated content? What is the latest example of a brand success with UGC?

 SOCIAL PLAN PART 12

Creating Brand Content and Motivating Brand Evangelists

Take the social media strategy, consumer insight, and big idea to the next level with branded content and brand evangelism. What content is the target audience looking for? What type of content do they tend to view and share? Develop ideas for educational and entertaining text, photo, and video content. Will the content be brand-generated or co-created? Where will it be distributed? Also, devise a strategy and policy to engage and reward brand evangelists. What information, products, promotional trips, or events can the organization offer the most loyal and outspoken fans? Set guidelines in terms of scale and scope for the evangelists and the reward program. Finally, also consider influencer campaigns—sometimes motivation is payment. Would influencer marketing help in the plan effort? Report all thoughts, plans, and ideas in these areas:

1. Identify the information and entertainment needs of the target audience. List the main types of content they view and share.
2. Explain the types of content the brand can create to match target audience interests. Plan content to be brand-generated, consumer-generated, or co-created.
3. Research and identify the organization's most active customers in social media.
4. Create a brand evangelist program to both engage and reward the brand advocates. Spell out specific policies, promotions, and events. Alternatively, or in addition, detail an influencer campaign for social media promotion.

For a condensed version of the social plan see appendix A: Three-Part Social Plan.

KEY CONCEPTS

meme	gamification
buyer persona	employee advocacy
jobs to be done theory	employer branding
user-generated content	influencer marketing
content marketing	micro-influencer marketing
search engine optimization (SEO)	mega-influencers
search engine marketing (SEM)	macro-influencers
evangelism marketing	micro-influencers
advocates	nano-influencers
brand ambassadors	consumer-brand relationship
influencers	

QUESTIONS FOR DISCUSSION

1. Pura Vida has grown into a powerhouse brand in a short time through content marketing, social media, and brand evangelism. Visit the brand's Instagram page and website. What are best practices do you see for brand content, user-generated content, customer engagement, eCommerce, ratings and reviews, nurturing advocates, and creating brand ambassadors?

2. The Dove Real Beauty campaign is more than ten years old. What could the brand do next to sustain attention and drive further viral success? How do you know when it's time to quit a campaign and start something new?

3. Tom Webster from the Marketing Companion podcast with Mark Schaefer suggests searching #spon to find sponsored content on social media. Do this for Twitter or Instagram. What do you find? What is the quality of the content? Are brands getting what they pay for? Are there best practices you would suggest?[101]

4. Branded content has the potential to cross ethical boundaries. Find some sponsored articles on news websites and social channels. How do you know that it is sponsored? Is the content biased or valuable? Is the small disclaimer enough? Can you find an example of branded content that you feel may cross ethical boundaries?

ADDITIONAL EXERCISES

1. For this exercise, remove your marketing hat and put on your publisher hat. Make a list of possible content you could create for your brand's customers, potential customers, or influencers. What common problems does your customer face? Can you provide tips, advice, or solutions? Do you have existing content somewhere that is not being accessed or used to its full potential? Also consider delivering value in other ways. An entertaining video or story can be just as engaging to a consumer audience. After you generate a list of ideas, go back and look for real opportunities to generate real value for your customers while meeting social media strategy objectives.

2. For this exercise, think about ways you can energize your brand evangelists. Customer evangelism doesn't always require big programs. Tap the power of evangelists simply by creating opportunities for customers to participate in the brand. Think about creating experiences they will in turn share with their social networks. Parties, openings, product launches, and cause-related events are ways to include brand enthusiasts and generate shareable content including videos, pictures, blog posts, and evites. Sponsoring an event or cause that a target audience cares about can really motivate evangelists to participate and spread the word. What is possible with your product or service?

Notes

1. "Engaging," BrainyQuote.com, accessed November 3, 2018, https://www.brainyquote.com/quotes/sheila_e_537345.

2. Abigail Posner, "The Engagement Project: Finding the Meaning in Memes," *Think with Google* Newsletter, June 2013, https://www.thinkwithgoogle.com/articles/memes-with-meaning.html.

3. Derek Thompson, *Hit Makers: How to Succeed in an Age of Distraction* (New York: Penguin, 2017), 57.

4. Lada Adamic, Thomas Lento, Eytan Adar, and Pauline Ng, "The Evolution of Memes on Facebook," Facebook.com, January 8, 2014, https://www.facebook.com/notes/facebook-data-science/the-evolution-of-memes-on-facebook/10151988334203859.

5. Aidan Cole, "More Than a Trend: Meme Marketing Is Here to Stay," Forbes.com, July 19, 2018, https://www.forbes.com/sites/forbesagencycouncil/2018/07/19/more-than-a-trend-meme-marketing-is-here-to-stay/#6a7af4732487.

6. Adrianne Glowski, "5 Critical Tips for Identifying Your Target Audience," Technori.com, accessed September 23, 2019, http://technori.com/2013/02/3122-5-critical-tips-for-identifying-your-target-audience.

7. Sam Kusinitz, "The Definition of a Buyer Persona [in Under 100 Words]," HubSpot, March 8, 2014, http://blog.hubspot.com/marketing/buyer-persona-definition-under-100-sr.

8. John Jantsch, "What If Your Customers Were Actually People?" Marketing Podcast with Adele Rvella, DuctTapeMarketing.com, accessed October 1, 2019, https://ducttapemarketing.com/customer-personas/.

9. Pamela Vaughan, "How to Create Detailed Buyer Personas for Your Businesses [Free Persona Template]," HubSpot.com, October 1, 2019, https://blog.hubspot.com/marketing/buyer-persona-research.

10. Clayton Christensen, "Jobs to Be Done," ChristensenInstitute.com, accessed October 12, 2019, https://www.christenseninstitute.org/jobs-to-be-done/.

11. Christensen, "Jobs to Be Done."

12. Tony Ulwick, "The Fundamentals of Jobs-to-be-Done Theory," CustomerThink.com, December 1, 2017, http://customerthink.com/the-fundamentals-of-jobs-to-be-done-theory/.

13. Loren Bornstein, "Buyer Personas vs. Job to Be Done," Blog.MarketMuse.com, October 4, 2018, https://blog.marketmuse.com/buyer-personas-vs-jobs-to-be-done/.

14. Margaret Rouse, "User-Generated Content (UGC)," Techtarget.com, March 2013, http://searchcio.techtarget.com/definition/user-generated-content-UGC.

15. Carla Meyer, Jay Baer, and Adam Brown, "How Garmin Integrates Social Media and Product Design," Social Pros Podcast, ConvinceAndConvert.com, February 28, 2017, http://www.convinceandconvert.com/podcasts/episodes/how-garmin-integrates-social-media-and-product-design/.

16. "The 2017 Facebook User-Generated Content Benchmark Report," Mavrck.co, accessed November 20, 2017, http://info.mavrck.co/facebook-user-generated-content-benchmark-report-q1-2017.

17. "REI to Repeat Black Friday #OptOutside Campaign," BicycleRetailer.com, October 30, 2017, http://www.bicycleretailer.com/retail-news/2017/10/30/rei-repeat-black-friday-optoutside-campaign#.WhLRXoZryRs.

18. "The Smartest Way to Work with Visuals," CrowdRiff.com, accessed November 2, 2019, https://crowdriff.com/.

19. "Amplify Every Touchpoint with Engaging Content," Olapic.com, accessed November 2, 2019, https://www.olapic.com/product/.

20. Christine Magee, "Olapic Will Replace Brands' Stock Photos with Your Instagram Pics," TechCrunch.com, June 23, 2015, http://techcrunch.com/2015/06/23/with-15-million-in-funding-olapic-will-replace-stock-photos-with-your-instagram-pics/.

21. "What Is Content Marketing?" Content Marketing Institute, accessed November 3, 2019, http://contentmarketinginstitute.com/what-is-content-marketing.

22. Vangie Beal, "SEO—Search Engine Optimization," Webopedia.com, accessed September 27, 2019, https://www.interaction-design.org/literature/topics/search-engine-optimization.

23. Vangie Beal, "SEM—Search Engine Marketing," Webopedia.com, accessed September 24, 2019, https://www.webopedia.com/TERM/S/SEM.html.

24. Gail Edmondson, "Online Extra: The Secret of BMW's Success," *Bloomberg Businessweek*, October 15, 2006, https://www.bloomberg.com/news/articles/2006-10-15/online-extra-the-secret-of-bmws-success.

25. E. J. Schultz, "BMW Films Is Coming Back—But Does It Matter?" AdAge.com, October 19, 2016, http://adage.com/article/cmo-strategy/bmw-films-coming-back-matter/306309/.

26. "2019 State of the Beverage Industry: Energy Drinks Maintain Competitive Edge," Beverage Industry, July 15, 2019, https://www-bevindustry-com/articles/92242-2019-state-of-the-beverage-industry-energy-drinks-maintain-competitive-edge/.

27. James O'Brien, "How Red Bull Takes Content Marketing to the Extreme," Mashable.com, December 19, 2012, https://mashable.com/2012/12/19/red-bull-content-marketing/.

28. Lisa Murton Beets, "2019 B2B Content Marketing Research: It Pays to Put Audience First," ContentMarketingInstitute.com, October 10, 2018, https://contentmarketinginstitute.com/2018/10/research-b2b-audience/.

29. "How Micro-Moments Are Reshaping the Travel Customer Journey," ThinkWith Google.com, July 2016, https://www.thinkwithgoogle.com/marketing-resources/micro-moments/micro-moments-travel-customer-journey/.

30. "I-Want-to-Get-Away Moments: What They Mean for Travel Marketing," ThinkWith Google.com, July 2016, https://www.thinkwithgoogle.com/marketing-resources/micro-moments/get-away-moments-travel-marketing/.

31. Robert Rose, "Say No to the Rise of Internal Content Agencies—and Other 2019 Trends," ContentMarketingInstitute.com, January 1, 2019, https://contentmarketinginstitute.com/2019/01/content-trends-2019/.

32. Emily Cardin, "Home Depot CEO Explains Business Philosophy," Technique, February 11, 2011, http://nique.net/news/2011/02/18/home-depot-ceo-explains-business-philosophy/.

33. "How the Home Depot Manages a Balanced Social Media Content Calendar," Social-Media.org, August 11, 2015, https://socialmedia.org/blog/how-the-home-depot-manages-a-balanced-social-media-content-calendar/.

34. Ahava Leibtag, "Is a Mobile-First Mentality Right for Your Organization?" *EContent* 35, no. 8 (2012): 12.

35. Dom Nicastro, "Where B2B Marketers Are Winning in Social Media," CMSWire.com, March 6, 2019, https://www.cmswire.com/digital-marketing/where-b2b-marketers-are-winning -in-social-media/.

36. Philip Kotler, Hermawan Kartajaya, and Iwan Setiawan, *Marketing 4.0: Moving from Traditional to Digital* (Hoboken, NJ: Wiley, 2017), 156, 42.

37. Michael Brenner, "How SAP Used Subscribers to Fuel Content Marketing Success," ContentMarketingInstitute.com (blog), June 8, 2015, http://contentmarketinginstitute.com/2015/06/ subscribers-content-marketing-success/.

38. Nancy Davis Kho, "Content Connects People with Products," *EContent* 33, no. 6 (2010): 30–34.

39. Joe Pullizzi, "How to Build a Million-Dollar Baby without a Big Ad Budget," Linked In.com, October 30, 2013, https://www.linkedin.com/pulse/20131030101713-5853751-how-to -build-a-million-dollar-baby-without-a-big-ad-budget.

40. "Spreading," BrainyQuote.com, accessed November 3, 2019, http://www.brainyquote.com/ quotes/keywords/spreading.html.

41. "Evangelism Marketing," Influitive.com, accessed September 1, https://influitive.com/ dictionary/evangelist-marketing/.

42. Bill Sussman, "Influencers vs. Ambassadors vs. Advocates: Stop the Confusion!" Entrepreneur. com, October 20, 2015, https://www.entrepreneur.com/article/249947.

43. Aaron Smith, "What People Like and Dislike about Facebook," PewResearch.org, February 3, 2014, https://www.pewresearch.org/fact-tank/2014/02/03/what-people-like-dislike-about -facebook/.

44. Jeremy Kressman, "Consumer Trust Is Evolving in the Digital Age," *eMarketer.com,* January 3, 2017, https://www.emarketer.com/Article/Consumer-Trust-Evolving-Digital-Age/1014959.

45. Karen Russo, "Debate: Does Social Media Deliver Results for Small Business?" *Wall Street Journal,* February 12, 2012, http://online.wsj.com/article/SB10001424052970204883304577221664 033429788.html?mod=googlenews_wsj.

46. "Get to Know Us," VocalPoint.com, accessed November 2, 2019, https://www.vocalpoint .com/about-18.

47. "P&G Everyday All Communities," PGEveryday.com, accessed November 2, 2019, https:// www.pgeveryday.com/all-communities.

48. Alex Goldfayn, *Evangelist Marketing: What Apple, Amazon, and Netflix Understand About Their Customers (That Your Company Probably Doesn't)* (Dallas: BenBella Books, 2012).

49. "Our Amazing Company," SurvivalStraps.com, accessed November 2, 2019, https://www .survivalstraps.com/our-company-and-beliefs/.

50. Malcolm Gladwell, *The Tipping Point: How Little Things Can Make a Big Difference* (Boston: Little, Brown, 2000).

51. Mark Josh Bernoff, "Spotting the Creators of Peer Influence," AdAge.com, April 20, 2010, http://adage.com/article/digitalnext/marketing-spotting-creators-peer-influence/143372.

52. Seth Godin, *Unleashing the Ideavirus.* Do You Zoom, Inc, August 17, 2000, https://seths.blog/ wp-content/uploads/2008/12/2000Ideavirus.pdf.

53. "Gamification," Lexico.com, accessed November 2, 2019, https://www.lexico.com/en/ definition/gamification.

54. Kotler, Kartajaya, and Setiawan, *Marketing 4.0,* 160–161.

55. Kotler, Kartajaya, and Setiawan, *Marketing 4.0.*

56. Superfans: The Easy Way to Stand Out, Grow Your Tribe, and Build a Successful Business," PatFlynn.com, accessed November 2, 2019, https://patflynn.com/superfans/.

57. Jasmine Wu, "Vera Bradley Acquires a Majority Stake in Online Jewelry Store Pura Vida Bracelets," CNBC.com, June 20, 2019, https://www.cnbc.com/2019/06/20/vera-bradley-acquires -a-majority-stake-in-pura-vida-bracelets.html.

58. Courtney Thompson, "What's a VSCO Girl? Shop the Latest Teen Trend," CNN.com, October 17, 2019, https://www.cnn.com/2019/10/14/cnn-underscored/what-is-a-vsco-girl/index.html.

59. "Become a Brand Ambassador," PuraVidaBracelets.com, accessed November 2, 2019, https:// www.puravidabracelets.com/pages/brand-ambassadors.

60. Griffin Thall, Jay Baer, and Adam Brown, "Is This the Best Business on Instagram?" Social-Pros Podcast, ConvinceAndConvert.com, September 13, 2019, https://www.puravidabracelets.com/ pages/brand-ambassadors.

61. Mark Schaefer, *Return on Influence*, BusinessGrow.com, accessed November 2, 2019, https:// businessesgrow.com/social-media-marketing-books/return-on-influence/.

62. "Lego Ambassador Network: About Us," Lan.Lego.com, accessed November 3, 2019, https:// lan.lego.com/aboutus/overview/.

63. "Lego Ambassador Network: About Us," Lan.Lego.com.

64. Margaret Rouse, "Employee Advocacy," WhatIsIt.TechTarget.com, October 2014, https:// whatis.techtarget.com/definition/employee-advocacy.

65. Katie Levinson, "What Is Employee Advocacy and How Do Marketers Win with It?" LinkedIn Marketing Solutions Blog, Business.LinkedIn.com, March 13, 2018, https://business .linkedin.com/marketing-solutions/blog/linkedin-elevate/2017/what-is-employee-advocacy--what -is-it-for--why-does-it-matter-.

66. "Amplify," Hootsuite.com, accessed November 2, 2019, https://hootsuite.com/products/ amplify.

67. Levinson, "What Is Employee Advocacy?"

68. Sarah Lybrand, "What Is Employer Branding and How Can It Grow Your Business," Business.LinkedIn.com, March 1, 2018, https://business.linkedin.com/talent-solutions/blog/ employer-brand/2018/employer-branding.

69. "WeAreCisco Employee-Generated Content for Employer Branding," ShortyAwards.com, accessed November 2, 2019, https://shortyawards.com/9th/wearecisco-employee-engagement-for -talent-bran.

70. Pat Hong, "10 Exceptional Examples of Brand Communities," Linkdex.com, January 15, 2015, https://www.linkdex.com/en-us/inked/10-exceptional-examples-of-brand-communities/.

71. Gerardo A. Dada, "What Is Influencer Marketing and How Can Marketers Use It Effectively?" Forbes.com, March 14, 2017, https://www.forbes.com/sites/forbescommunicationscouncil/ 2017/11/14/what-is-influencer-marketing-and-how-can-marketers-use-it-effectively/#54bbdf9623d1.

72. "What Is Influencer Marketing?" TapInfluence.com, February 6, 2015, https://www.tap influence.com/blog-what-is-influencer-marketing/.

73. Richard Edelman, "In Brands We Trust? 2019 Edelman Trust Barometer Special Report," 2019, Edelman.com, https://www.edelman.com/sites/g/files/aatuss191/files/2019-07/2019 _edelman_trust_barometer_special_report_in_brands_we_trust_executive_summary.pdf.

74. "Marketers Pair Up with Influencers—and It Works," eMarketer.com, July 9, 2015, https://www .emarketer.com/Article/Marketers-Pair-Up-with-Influencersand-Works/1012709?ecid=MX1086.

75. "Report: 60% of Marketers Will Increase Their Influencer Marketing Budgets in 2019," Mobile Marketer.com, February 4, 2019, https://www.mobilemarketer.com/press-release/20190204 -report-60-of-marketers-will-increase-their-influencer-marketing-budgets-i-1/.

76. Colleen Vaughan, "Influencer Marketing Update: Non-Celebrity Influencers 10 Times More Likely to Drive In-Store Purchases," CollectiveBias.com, March 29, 2016, http://collective

bias.com/blog/2016/03/influencer-marketing-update-non-celebrity-influencers-10-times-likely
-drive-store-purchases/.

77. Edelman, "In Brands We Trust?"

78. Sophia Bernazzani, "Micro-Influencer Marketing: A Comprehensive Guide," HubSpot.com
(blog), October 16, 2019, https://blog.hubspot.com/marketing/micro-influencer-marketing.

79. Keith Quesenberry, "A Simple Guide to Influencer Marketing in Social Media," Post
ControlMarketing.com, August 23, 2018, https://www.postcontrolmarketing.com/simple-guide
-influencer-marketing/.

80. Aleh Barysevich, "Seven Best Tools to Find Influencers on Social Media," SearchEngine
Watch.com, March 4, 2019, https://www.searchenginewatch.com/2019/03/04/best-tools-to
-find-social-media-influencers/.

81. Quesenberry, "Simple Guide."

82. Kaya Ismail, "Social Media Influencers: Mega, Macro, Micro or Nano," CMSWire
.com, December 10, 2018, https://www.cmswire.com/digital-marketing/social-media-influencers
-mega-macro-micro-or-nano/.

83. Quesenberry, "Simple Guide."

84. Sami Main, "Micro-Influencers Are More Effective with Marketing Campaigns Than
Highly Popular Accounts," Adweek.com, March 30, 2017, https://www.adweek.com/digital/micro
-influencers-are-more-effective-with-marketing-campaigns-than-highly-popular-accounts/.

85. "Advertisers Love Influencer Marketing: ANA Study," ANA.net, April 3, 2018, https://
www.ana.net/content/show/id/48437.

86. Kerry Flynn, "Influencer Marketing Platforms Are Making Fraud 'Very Obvious' for
Brands to Identify," DigiDay.com, July 30, 2018, https://digiday.com/marketing/influencer
-marketing-platforms-making-fraud-obvious-brands-identify/.

87. "Introducing Amazon Influencer Program," Afflilliate-Programs.Amazon.com, accessed
November 2, 2019, https://affiliate-program.amazon.com/influencers.

88. Josephine Hardy, "6 Ways to Repurpose Influencer Content," AcornInfluence.com, June 21,
2018, https://acorninfluence.com/blog/6-ways-to-repurpose-influencer-content/.

89. "The State of Influencer Marketing 2019: Benchmark Report [+Infographic]," Influencer
MarketingHub.com, May 28, 2019, https://influencermarketinghub.com/influencer-marketing
-2019-benchmark-report/.

90. Stacy Jones, "How Much Kim Kardashian Charges for an Instagram Post," Holly-
woodBranded.com, November 27, 2018, https://blog.hollywoodbranded.com/how-much-kim
-kardashian-charges-for-an-instagram-post.

91. Matt Southern, "New Data Reveals How Much Brands Are Paying Influencers,"
SearchEngineJournal.com, July 16, 2019, https://www.searchenginejournal.com/new-data-reveals
-how-much-brands-are-paying-influencers/316963/#close.

92. John E. Lincoln, "How Much Does Social Media Influencer Marketing Cost?" Ignite
Visibility.com, accessed November 2, 2019, https://ignitevisibility.com/much-social-media
-influencer-marketing-cost/.

93. Blake Lawrence, Adi Kunalic, Jay Baer, and Adam Brown, "How opendorse Rev-
olutionized Athlete Marketing in Social Media," SocialPros Podcast, ConvinceAndConvert
.com, July 5, 2019, https://www.convinceandconvert.com/podcasts/episodes/how-opendorse
-revolutionized-athlete-marketing-in-social-media/.

94. How the New Jersey Devils Help Players Build Brands and Engage Fans," opendorse.com,
accessed November 2, 2019, https://opendorse.com/blog/nj-devils-case-study-2/.

95. Olivia Solon, "Disney Severs Ties with YouTube Star PewDiePie over Anti-Semitic Videos," February 13, 2017, https://www.theguardian.com/technology/2017/feb/13/pewdiepie -youtube-star-disney-antisemitic-videos.

96. Sidney J. Levy, "Symbols for Sale," *Harvard Business Review* 37 (1959): 117–124.

97. Kelly Tepper Tian, William O. Bearden, and Gary L. Hunter, "Consumers' Need for Uniqueness: Scale Development and Validation," *Journal of Consumer Research* 28 (2001): 50–66.

98. "Brand Relationship," Knowledge@Wharton, accessed December 4, 2019, https://kwh s.wharton.upenn.edu/term/brand-relationship/.

99. Kurt Matzler, Elisabeth Pichler, Johann Füller, and Todd A. Mooradian, "Personality, Person-Brand Fit, and Brand Community: An Investigation of Individuals, Brands, and Brand Communities," *Journal of Marketing Management* 27, no. 9/10 (2011): 874–890.

100. Hyejune Park and Young-Kyung Kim, "The Role of Social Network Websites in the Consumer-Brand Relationship," *Journal of Retailing & Consumer Services* 21, no. 4 (2014): 460–467.

101. Mark Schaefer, "New Media, New Culture and How It's Confounding Brands," Schaefer Marketing Solutions: Mark Schaefer, March 3, 2017, https://www.businessesgrow.com/2017/03/07/ pewdiepie/.

Social Care and Social Selling

Right or wrong, the customer is always right.[1]

—Marshall Field

PREVIEW

When was the last time you had a customer service issue with a product or service you purchased? How did you handle it? Where did you go first? What were your expectations? If you are like many people today, your first instinct when you have a problem is not to call the customer service number. You may complain on social media, or contact the brand on their social media account, or chat or message the company. In a similar fashion, if you have more of a business-related issue or decision to make, your first step is probably not picking up the phone to call a sales rep. Chances are you avoid calls from sales reps. Customer service and sales have changed significantly in a short time. Both have become more social.

Providing customer service has a lot to do with the systems it uses. A **customer service system** is a combination of technological structure and organizational networks designed to provide services that satisfy customers.[2] This term is used in and by service management, operations, marketing, engineering, and design. Service systems provide value that can improve customer service and create competitive advantage, especially within industries where there is much parity in products. How did we get to today's current state of customer service operations?

In the beginning, customer service was limited. If a person had a problem with a product, they either fixed it themselves or physically returned it to the store owner. With the invention of the telephone in the late 1800s came direct ways to contact stores and companies from home or office. However, early telephone switchboards and rotary-dial technology still made it challenging to contact companies and thus limited customer complaints. As technology improved through touch-tone dialing and the introduction of the 1-800 number, more customers began to call companies. This increase in demand led to the creation of the call center, and call centers evolved into customer service departments.

In the 1970s and 1980s, customer support departments began using interactive voice response technology to improve efficiency and created automated responses that led customers through complex phone trees. At the end of the 1980s, formal customer service strategies emerged, and outsourcing customer service functions to other countries became a mainstream practice to help meet increased demand from customers in more cost-effective ways.[3]

In the 1990s and early 2000s, customer service changed dramatically with the introduction of the internet as a new channel of contact, leading to the development of customer service email, instant messaging, and live chat as well as integrated customer service management systems. Thus the story of customer service is tied directly to the development of technology. Now organizations are faced with the new communications technology of social media. When a new avenue opens to contact companies, customers will use it, customer service expectations will change, and customer service systems must evolve to follow suit.

Yet this evolution is not only occurring in the customer service department. Customer access to social media means direct and immediate access to brands, other consumers, and journalists, which can cause social media crises that need a new approach to crisis communication plans and have spawned the need for ongoing online reputation management strategies. Similar changes are happening in sales departments as business-to-business (B2B) customers' preferred methods of contacting sales representatives and the type of information they are seeking has changed with increased adoption of social media for business use.

The Customer Is Always Right

Marshall Field of Chicago department store fame is credited with the saying, "The customer is always right." If this saying applied in the 1800s before digital media, it certainly applies even more today. Now even "wrong" customers, with the power of social media, can turn a single complaint into a movement against a company.

Molly Katchpole, discussed in chapter 2, provides just one example. Through a social media campaign using Facebook, Twitter, and Change.org, she was able to get Bank of America to revoke a $5.00 debit-card fee.[4] In chapter 4, Dave Carroll demonstrated how he indirectly used his voice, YouTube, and Twitter to cause United Airlines' stock to drop 10 percent.[5] A similar incident happed ten years later with Dr. David Dao and United Flight 3411.[6] The consumer voice is more powerful today than it has ever been, and customer demands on customer service quality and delivery are increasing.

Whether an organization is big or small, customer service is at the heart of keeping current customers happy and attracting new ones. Business is built on reputation and relationships through care, honesty, and trust that can be nurtured through social media.[7] In 2008, Frank Eliason of Comcast figured this out and went on to become the most famous customer service manager in the United States. Eliason grew tired of all the negative talk that was occurring on social media about his cable company. Instead of sitting back and letting it occur, Eliason got the idea to use Twitter to interact with those Comcast cable customers. Instead of making the customer come to him, he decided to engage the customers where they were having the conversations.[8]

Eliason's idea was so effective that it became Comcast Cares, providing real-time customer service on Twitter and Facebook with a full-time dedicated social media staff. Cable customers love the immediate online results, compared to fruitless hours spent on the phone. Comcast's Social Care team worked on improving their company's J. D. Power Overall Satisfaction score.[9] The beginning of this improvement was based on the simple idea of delivering service on the customer's terms, not the corporation's.

Today Comcast Cares has evolved into a Digital Care team assisting customers across social platforms such as Twitter, Facebook, Instagram, and Facebook Messenger 24/7, 365 days a year. According to Lisa Blackshere, Comcast's senior vice president, communications digital media strategy and operations, the Digital Care team has four hundred members located across the country to handle 5.8 million customer interactions a year in various time zones and languages. This has improved their J. D. Power scores and Net Promoter Score to one of the highest in the country. Over the years they have developed best practices such as hiring diverse agents from multiple stages of life to match the maturing social media user, adapting to their customers' tone to interact on a more personal level, and communicating real-time customer reactions and issues to communications, PR, and branding teams.[10]

Much of the latest research indicates that the 1–800 number may be in decline as new forms of social media, messaging, and chat are preferred by customers. A survey by BI Intelligence and Aspect software indicate that customer service via email and phone have fallen 7 percent and have decreased customer service talking to a live agent by 10 percent in two years. Nearly 60 percent would rather go through other channels than use their voice for customer service.[11]

Social media through social networks and messaging apps is an important part of this shift. As customer service activity moves to social media, companies must be prepared. To be effective, marketing and its advertising and public relations partners must work with customer service. The customer doesn't distinguish between company departments and business disciplines and will seek engagement with all in the same channel. As early as 2012, customer service was the second-most-used business activity in social media behind marketing (see figure 13.1).[12] Today, smart organizations are using social media to manage customer relationships. Social media can help increase customer retention by finding complaints early and making the service personal. It can also uncover mismatches in advertising promises and product or service delivery and serve as an early warning system for public relations crisis communication.

Social media customer relationship management can also reduce operational costs because providing online customer service is generally less expensive than providing service over the phone.[13] Businesses spend $1.3 trillion on customer service calls a year.[14] In *Groundswell*, Charlene Li and Josh Bernoff estimated that the average call to a company's call center costs $6.00 or $7.00 and technical support calls can cost as much as $10.00 to

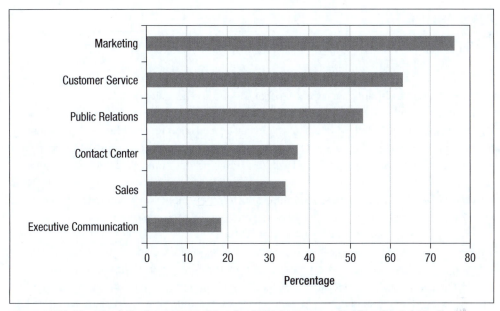

Figure 13.1. Types of Business Activities for Which Companies Use Social Media

Source: Donna Fluss, "Using Social Media for Customer Service," *CRM Magazine* 16, no. 4 (2012): 10.

$20.00.[15] In contrast, Incite reports that a social media interaction costs only $1.00.[16] Social media support can cost less because representatives are able to handle several customers at once and take advantage of automated tasks and standardized information. When you factor in the potential of AI and chatbots providing service via messaging services, costs can be reduced another 30 percent while speeding up response times.[17]

On the flip side, improving customer service in social media can generate additional revenue. Research from Applied Marketing Science and Twitter found that resolving a negative airline customer issue in Twitter increased brand value with the customer willing to pay $6.00 more for a ticket in the future. For wireless carriers, customers who had their issues resolved through Twitter would be willing to pay $8.00 more per month. Responding to a positive airline customer comment generated $28.00 more for a future ticket and $12.00 more per month for a wireless plan.[18]

Resolving issues in public view has other advantages as well. Solving one customer's problem or answering a question in the public social media stream enables everyone to benefit from the response. Often people can solve their problems on their own before contacting customer service. Solving a problem in a real-time stream within public view can also stop negative conversation before it spreads to more permanent links such as blogs, forums, an article, or even a book.[19] This happened with airline JetBlue when a customer started numerous complaints on social media about their new $50.00 fee for checking small bikes. Before it got out of hand, they changed the policy and dropped the fee for all customers. Then JetBlue's manager of corporate communications and social media strategy, Morgan Johnston, said, "We fixed the policy, and in fact, fixed it before the negative story gained [a] larger audience from customer advocacy sites, turning it into a positive one."[20]

MINI CASE

Hertz 24/7 Social Care

In 2014 Hertz Rent-a-Car announced 24/7 global social customer care. Hertz's director of service excellence, Laura Smith, said the company was shifting from a marketing-oriented view of social media to a customer-oriented view. Prior to this initiative, marketing was the owner of social media and customer complaints. Because of this former structure, customer complaints in social media were filtered through marketing staff, who would in turn email the complaints to customer service agents. The customer service agents would then often take days to respond. The new Hertz 24/7 social care system includes customer service in its social media monitoring for improved efficiency and quicker response. Now the cross-discipline departments work together.[a]

When only Hertz marketing was monitoring social media, service was limited to Monday through Friday. Marketing would forward social media posts, customer service would reply via email, and then marketing would post the responses on social media. For the new system, Hertz partnered with software vendor Conversocial to give customer service a seat at the social media–monitoring table. The company reports that responding to customer service issues in real time via social media has influenced other users and is increasing customer loyalty, which contributes to customer lifetime value.[b] The new Hertz cross-departmental social care system has enabled the company to exceed expectations.

Today Hertz ranks highest as the most engaged, responsive, and fastest car rental brand to respond to customers on Twitter. A survey by HelpHandles over twelve weeks found the average response time of sixteen minutes for @Hertz compared to competitors @EnterpriseCares and @Avis with averages over two hours and three hours respectively. This places Hertz in the top 10 percent of all brands on Twitter. The social audit also found Hertz had a 58 percent public response rate with 90 percent of responses coming under thirty minutes compared to Enterprise's 52 percent and Avis's 25 percent response under thirty minutes. The social audit found the Hertz team effectively uses empathy and attentiveness to turn negative experiences into more positive interactions. The brand also experiences high levels of brand advocacy and higher levels of positive versus negative sentiment.[c]

[a] Lloyd Waldo, "Hertz Hands the Social Media Keys over from Marketing, to Customer Care," *Future Care Today*, October 31, 2014, http://futurecare.today/news/hertz-hands-the-social-media-keys-over-from-marketing-to-customer-care.

[b] "Video: How Hertz Provides 24/7 Social Customer Service Globally," WhySatisfy.com, October 10, 2014, http://whysatisfy.com/video-how-hertz-provides-247-social-customer-service-globally.

[c] Dean McCann, "How Hertz Became the No.1 Car Rental Brand for Customer Service on Twitter," Medium.com/Help-Handles-Insight-Series, June 27, 2017, https://medium.com/help-handles-insight-series/how-hertz-became-the-1-car-rental-brand-for-customer-service-on-twitter-fbf3eb1b5588.

Social Care Is No Longer a Choice

Organizations may no longer have a choice on whether to provide social media customer service. Customer expectations for service and response in this new medium are rising. A Sprout Social survey of Facebook, Twitter, and Instagram users found 90 percent had used social media to directly communicate with a brand and that social media was the first place they turned when they had a problem, instead of phone or email. A study conducted by Edison Research for Jay Baer's book *Hug Your Haters* found that customers only get a response on social platforms roughly half the time.[21] Would you only answer half your customer service calls and emails or ignore half the customers seeking help in a store?

The Sprout Social survey found that brands are increasing messages sent but they are mostly promotional—sending an average of twenty-three promotional messages for every one response. The survey found that people expect a four-hour response, yet average brand response time is ten hours.[22] This gap represents a real opportunity for competitive advantage to the companies who take the time to respond. A simple response can make a happy customer who, in social media, can easily share that happiness with others and can influence their future purchase decisions.

Jay Baer's research found that failing to respond on social media can result in a 43 percent decrease in customers' advocacy, whereas a reply can increase advocacy 20 percent.[23] Applied Marketing Science research indicates that timely responses can increase revenue. When customers tweet a business and receive a response, they're willing to spend from 3 to 20 percent more on a future product or service from that business. What's more, they are also 44 percent more likely to share their experience online and offline, 30 percent more likely to recommend the business, and they rate the business a point higher on customer satisfaction surveys.[24] Providing excellent customer service on social media becomes a marketing activity that contributes directly to marketing, public relations, and business objectives.

Customers have high expectations for engagement online. In the past, businesses have had to make adjustments by offering customer service via telephone service, email, and live

Figure 13.2. Customer service turns into marketing with happy customers on social media.

© Fizkes / iStock Photo

chat. Now demand for that customer service is shifting to social media networks, and organizations must follow. The impact of social media is why companies such as Comcast, Dell, Best Buy, and United Airlines monitor Twitter, Facebook, and other social platforms to find mentions of their brands and to resolve customer issues with social care teams. **Social care** refers to the efforts employees make through social media to care for customers.[25] Many companies now have dedicated social care employees.

Southwest Airlines now has nearly forty employees dedicated to social care stationed in the Listening Center at their headquarters in Dallas with a large screen showing weather, news, and social media updates. With 2,300 tweets and 1,900 Facebook posts a day, they manage to maintain a fifteen-minute response time. Their social media tool Lithium keeps track of previous interactions with customers and pulls in their social media accounts to identify influencers with a large following.[26] Brand voice is important for more than marketing, advertising, and PR communication. Southwest social care employees are trained in the same "Southwest Voice" used by flight attendants: "Instructions are always relayed clearly, sometimes with a hint of sass when the situation calls for it." However, sass is different from a brand voice that roasts its followers. The Wendy's brand voice would not be appropriate for a brand whose logo is shaped like a heart and that promotes itself as having a heart.[27]

Social media is also fully integrated into Southwest's operations with a seat on the bridge along with representatives from many departments. Next to ground operations, the chief pilot and meteorologist is a social media employee who monitors customer response in real time, and large monitors show a live look at the airline's social media feeds for all to see. Brooks Thomas, a social business senior advisor for the airline, says, "Our goal is to essentially fully integrate social as a way of life throughout Southwest Airlines, whether you are on the front lines, or a communicator, or a marketer, or somebody hiring, or doing training."[28]

In the definition of social care and the Southwest example, notice that social care is not limited to traditional contact center agents working in customer service departments. Many

---

 Types of Social Information Impacting Customer Service

Customer service provided via social media can deal with multiple issues in many areas. What are those possibilities? According to DMG Consulting, five out of the top six types of information gained from social media engagement directly impact customer service:[a]

1. Positive or negative sentiment
2. Issues with products
3. Complaints or follow-ups for previous customer service interactions
4. Issues with procedures
5. Crisis identification

[a] "Social Media: Guide for Building a Customer Support Strategy," DMG Consulting, July 7, 2010, http://www.dmgconsult.com/publications/whitepapers.asp.

companies are empowering customer service representatives, engineers, product managers, and executives to provide positive customer service on social media.[29] Another airline, JetBlue, staffs their @JetBlue account with team members from marketing, corporate communications, and customer service.[30] Good customer service can also help meet marketing, advertising, public relations, and sales goals. A good social care team requires cross–business unit integration. This is yet another reason to do some silo smashing in an organization.

In a white paper on social care, TELUS International authors Kim Keating and Dave Evans suggest many strategies for forming a successful social care program. One of the best practices is to start by defining the vision and objectives of the social care effort. Once vision and objectives are in place, recruit a cross-functional team that includes employees from all departments. It is important to ensure the team is working toward a common goal and that all departments are represented, but it is equally important to be sure that each individual has a defined role. Following a strategic structure from the beginning will more likely lead to a successful social care program. See table 13.1 for an example of cross-functional social care team organization and responsibilities.[31] Even with a common vision, core objectives, and defined roles, frequently one of the biggest social care challenges is getting everyone on the same system. Each department may be working with different social media software and have their own legacy CRM systems that do not integrate well.

Bianca Buckridee, vice president of social media operations for JPMorgan Chase, says that an advantage she sees in social customer service is that customers can go to Chase's Twitter page and see the person they are chatting with. This restores some of the intimacy and comfort lost in a phone conversation. She has seen Chase customers returning to social media saying, "Hey, let me know when Theo gets in" or "I want to talk to Danni; she knows exactly where I'm at and what I'm going through." Social media can help bring back that personal connection once found in the small-town marketplace described in *The Cluetrain Manifesto* mentioned in chapter 4.

Table 13.1. Cross-Functional Social Care Team Organization and Responsibilities

Department	Responsibility
Customer Service	Set up to be the main point of contact for service-related issues.
Marketing	Promote social support and provide brand briefing on communication style.
Corporate Communication/PR	Develop crisis and stakeholder communication plans.
Legal	Define social media policies that govern agent responses.
Human Resources	Define hiring profiles and set training standards for social agents.

Source: Kim Keating and Dave Evans, "Benchmarking Social Media Customer Service: Uncovering Opportunities & Best Practices for Social Care," TELUS International, accessed February 20, 2015, https://www.yumpu.com/en/document/read/34428333/to-access-the-white-paper-telus-international.

The Chase customer service team also crosses lines of business so that customers can tweet one handle and get help for a retail account, credit card, mortgage, auto loan, student loan, or investment.[32] This is an excellent example of the transition in thinking from the Four Ps of product, price, promotion, and place to the Four Cs of consumer, cost, convenience, and communication. Rather than social media being a burden, it simplifies the process for companies and customers alike. It is also a good example of social media tearing down silos and cutting down on phone transfers to other departments that simply waste everyone's time. There is also the employee perspective. Frustrated customers can be testy over the phone, which can contribute to high call center turnover rates. Yet frontline customer service employees report that customers mellow out when they communicate through text, making customer care a more pleasant job.[33]

The marketing department can and should take the lead in social media monitoring, brand content development, and brand voice while striving to remove functional silos, but marketing professionals must also remember there is still value in discipline-specific expertise. Jonathan Salem Baskin reminds marketers of this in his *Ad Age* article "Customer Service Belongs to Operations, Not Marketing: How Apple Turned Problem-Fixing into a Promotional Tool." He explains that the core capability of fixing customer product or service problems is not a communications solution that marketers or their advertising and public relations partners can provide. Marketers, advertisers, and public relations professionals cannot reboot routers, install software patches, send replacement parts, or answer billing problems. Providing service belongs to operations. Social monitoring can reveal how bad operations issues may be and how the public is reacting to them, but operations people are the ones who actually need to fix the problems. On the other hand, when operations provides excellent service, the service can be a driver of the brand and enable marketing.[34]

The gourmet burger chain Five Guys leverages a cross-functional social care team with corporate marketers running the main brand account but also utilizes frontline employees to market local promotions and events on specific location accounts. These local employees also provide customer service where it makes more sense to respond at the local level for an issue with a particular store. Not only does this make brand engagement more personal and sincere; it also enables quicker response by dividing the task among more than 1,200 individual franchisees.[35]

Hewlett-Packard (HP) divided the task of customer care a different way in creating HP Support Forums where HP customers can ask questions and get help from other customers. This branded, managed community enabled HP to quickly scale social care. Kriti Kapoor, global director of HP social customer care, says that each accepted solution on the forum is viewed forty times on average compared to a phone interaction that only solves one customer problem at a time. Kapoor works with cross-functional teams from marketing, product research and development, and information technology to meet common HP goals. One important consideration when setting up a customer support forum is to ensure that there are community guidelines in place. Hewlett-Packard does this with a rules page titled "HP Support Forum: Rules of Participation."[36]

Many companies run consumer customer support forums such as the Apple Support Communities, Oracle Community, and H&R Block "Get Answers."[37] As discussed in the beginning of the chapter, support forums allow customers to help themselves by answering common questions and resolving issues, making customer service more efficient. Taking the idea of support forums one step further, the social customer service provider Conversocial has a capability called Crowds that extends this peer-to-peer resolution to social networks. Social conversations can be routed to brand experts across multiple community channels. Experts are also rewarded and recognized, earning points and appearing on a leader board.[38]

As discussed in chapter 7, another important consideration is the move to messenger apps. For example, 67 percent of people expect to be using social messaging like Facebook Messenger for communicating with businesses.[39] As consumers make this shift, brands should also consider following with a customer service presence in top messaging apps like Facebook Messenger, WhatsApp, and WeChat. In messenger apps and social care there is great opportunity to provide better customer service and increase efficiencies with the use of artificial intelligence. High-performing service organizations are twice as likely to be using AI-powered chatbots as a way to augment human skills that can then focus more on solving complex problems.[40] The potential is enormous; one study indicates 80 percent of customers' inquiries can be resolved without human supervision and those chatbots are scalable no matter the volume 24/7, 365 days a year.[41] The benefits and opportunities of artificial intelligence in all areas of social media will be discussed further in chapter 14.

KLM Royal Dutch Airlines has used messenger apps to improve their social media customer service. They have a Facebook Messenger chatbot that streamlines sending boarding passes, flight information, and updates along with customer support and travel directions. Customer service is also provided through WeChat. KLM's social media efforts have been credited with helping to improve their Net Promoter Score from 35 to 43.[42] **Net promoter score (NPS)** is a measure of customer experience to determine the presence of brand promoters, passives, and detractors. In response to the question, "How likely is it that you would recommend _____ to a friend or colleague?" using a 1–10 scale, scores of 9–10 are considered promoters who are loyal enthusiasts. Scores of 7–8 are considered satisfied but unenthusiastic. And scores of 0–6 are considered unhappy customers. Subtracting the percentage of detractors from the percentage of promoters produces the net promoter score, which can range from a low of −100 to a high of 100. Many companies use NPS to evaluate their customer experience management programs and chances are you have received this question from a company after a transaction or interaction.

Research indicates that consumers find the phone to be the most frustrating customer service experience—five times more frustrating than Twitter or messaging apps.[43] Knowing this and that willingness to promote a brand is the new standard of customer satisfaction, why would you continue to rely on traditional customer service systems? If your organization has not adjusted its approach to customer care, it is time to reconsider the channels and methods that are best for the business and customer.

Before we leave the subject of customer care, we must make a point that not all customers are created equal. The **Pareto principle (80/20 rule)** states the roughly 80 percent of sales come from 20 percent of customers.[44] Perry Marshall, author of *80/20 Sales and Marketing*, took this further and found that the 20 percent of your top customers, or the top 4 percent overall, represent 64 percent of your sales.[45] The truth is that some customers cost your company money, some make your company money, and others make your company a lot of money. Your exact percentages may vary, but if you have a CRM system you know this is true. If you know this is true and you have integrated your CRM system into your customer service system and social media software, then you should empower customer care employees to act on it. Seth Godin in *This Is Marketing* says that we should always ask the question "What is the purpose of this interaction?" When one of your most valuable customers reaches out—one who has been a long-term customer, advocates for your brand online, and generates eight times the revenue of an average customer—what is that interaction for? Godin asks is the goal "to get it over with . . . deny responsibility, read the script, use words like 'as stated' and 'our policy'?" Or is the goal to be human and delight an extraordinary customer by going the extra mile?[46]

But also remember that someone is watching an organization's every tweet, post, and update. The 80/20 rule does not give you permission to be rude to everyone other than your 20 percent. Marshall Field understood this on a smaller scale. Field's department store employees were always instructed not to push products on uninterested customers and to know that even when the customer was wrong, they were right. Perhaps brands could benefit from that nineteenth-century personal sales wisdom in this twenty-first-century social interaction technology. For more details on CRM systems, see Salesforce's Trailhead training and credentials at https://trailhead.salesforce.com/en/home. **Salesforce Trailhead** is an online education site offering free training and professional credentials.[47]

Crisis Communication and Reputation Management

Fixing customer service problems or appeasing disgruntled customers in social media is one consideration, but sometimes a negative comment can turn into a big public relations disaster. Social media crisis communication is now a large part of public relations practice. Crises can occur for many reasons but traditionally have involved threat to an organization, its stakeholders, and its industry. A crisis can disrupt operations, create a loss of market share, and decrease an organization's reputation or even its stock price, as seen with the United Breaks Guitars example in chapter 4.[48]

Public relations professionals are an integral part of crisis management to protect an organization from threats and reduce their impact. There are many interpretations of what crisis communications means, but SHIFT Communications, innovator of the social media press release, summarizes them well. **Crisis communication** is attempting to reduce the damage to a company or individual reputation by third party sources due to an unexpected event.[49] This is the reverse of traditional PR. Instead of trying to increase positive earned media by increased attention, you are trying to reduce negative earned media to "put the fire out."[50]

An important distinction to consider is the difference between traditional crisis and social media crisis. Karen Freberg in *Social Media for Strategic Communication* makes this point well, saying a social media crisis is caused by messages, situations, or responses that occur on social media platforms themselves. On the other hand, traditional crises happen offline and are discussed in social media. Think inappropriate tweet by a CEO or professional team athlete versus a natural disaster or product recall.[51] How should an organization handle a complaint or issue that could quickly get out of control? Digital specialist Rob Stokes suggests a few rules:[52]

Figure 13.3. Crisis communication is a necessary part of social media strategy.

© Antonio Guillem / iStock Photo

- *Be humble.* Listen before acting. Get an understanding of the scale and scope of the problem and how consumer complaints evolved.
- *Act right away.* Responding quickly by acknowledging a wrong and promising to correct it can wipe out a brand attack before it gets started.
- *Keep negative pages out of search engines.* Add positive content and links to drive negative links off the first page of search results.
- *Respond via blogs.* This will help to present the organization's side of the story.
- *Care about the customer.* Show them the organization truly cares about their concerns. Treat them with kindness and respect.

Remember that when a business enters social media, it must act like an individual. Practice good personal skills, the same that would be used in a face-to-face conversation. Encourage social media employees to think of the customer first and try to treat them the way they would want to be treated. These simple practices can go a long way. No one expects perfection, but they do expect empathy, apology, and corrective action. The last thing a brand wants to get into is a flame war. A **flame war** is a series of angry, disparaging comments exchanged by two or more people in an online argument.[53] Take a breath before responding and be strategic about response.

These are good short-term tips, but any social media plan should include a written crisis communication plan that thinks through potential risks and plans for specific responses, when and by whom. Steve Goldstein and Ann Marie van den Hurk suggest ways to integrate social media into every crisis scenario. First, remember to not censor criticism on social media channels. Removing a negative comment leads to worse comments. Remember that tone matters. Leave the corporate tone for other outlets. Social media responses should be personal and polite and not dismissive. Quick response is important, but be sure to take time to really understand what the person wants. Then respond directly and publicly. Customize messages for each channel. Social media platforms have unique tones and messages need to be customized to fit the environment.[54]

Consistency in crisis response is important, but the official statement on the website should not simply be pasted on every channel repeatedly. All channels need to be updated 24/7. During a crisis, customers will turn to all channels for current information. Finally, don't be afraid to professionally present the brand's side of the story. Address real concerns but also don't allow the brand to be bullied if the accusations are unfounded.[55]

Once you have a crisis management plan in place, continually monitor and listen. Also, try to anticipate potential situations that may lead to a crisis. Be mindful of potential unfortunate situations in social media. Karen Freyberg and HubSpot Academy identify potential hot spots:

- Employees/former employees going rogue
- Cyber-attacks or hacking of social media accounts
- Outrage over something that has been shared or posted
- Trendjacking during a sensitive situation
- Not thinking through the impact of a hashtag
- Fake news and rumors
- Unpredictable actions in live video
- Advocates calling for boycotts[56]

Bruce Kennedy, social media manager at Cision, says that social media crisis communication plans have to be a lot more specific than traditional crisis communication plans of the past. With an official statement in a press release you don't get immediate feedback and questions as you do on social platforms. He suggests coming up with crisis messaging and then have team members role play to try and poke holes in the message to come up with responses. Think of it as an internal FAQ team members can reference during a crisis.[57]

Kennedy also recommends using the analytics of social monitoring to decide when and when not to respond. Look at the metrics to know in real time if the issues or post is gaining traction and requires response. Some things are best left to die out on their own. Also, don't come out with a "fauxpology." A **fauxpology** is an apology that seems to express remorse but doesn't acknowledge any wrongdoing.[58] If it is a serious issue that demands attention, give it sincere and immediate attention from a high-level employee. For complete transparency, consider making the response on Facebook Live and let customers ask questions.[59] Many brands try to avoid politically sensitive issues, but with the growing protests following the tragic killing of George Floyd, many decided that silence was not an option. Big brands delivered messages of support, denounced wrongs, and responded with actions. For more on social media communication during an extended national crisis, see the box "How Does COVID-19 Impact Social Media Strategy?"

An example of a social media crisis communication case study and proof that brand issues can emerge suddenly from anywhere is what happened to Crock-Pot. Imagine waking up to a social media firestorm of people questioning the safety of your product, afraid that it will burn their houses down and kill their families. Was there a real product defect and fire risk? No. The night before, the popular prime time NBC show *This Is Us* aired an episode where one of the main characters, Jack Pearson, died as a result of a house fire caused by a short-circuit in an old 1970s Crock-Pot. This was a fictional story not based on a real safety crisis. Yet customers were throwing away real products, feeling real emotions against the brand for killing one of their favorite characters, and damaging the reputation of the company. One person on Twitter wrote, "I just threw my Crock-Pot out the window."[60]

Fortunately, Crock-Pot had a crisis plan in place. Crisis management strategist Melissa Agnes pointed out that instead of writing this off as an irrational overreaction that would die down, they saw it as an emotional reaction producing real action and threatening the brand. They reacted quickly, compassionately, and with facts in the communication channels where consumers were reacting. An official statement in a traditional press release would not do. Instead of suing the network, the communication team at Edelman PR decided to engage the consumer and change the conversation.[61]

Before this, Crock-Pot didn't even have a Twitter account. They quickly opened @CrockPotCares to reach customers and journalists where they were already communicating, using the trending #Crockpot hashtag to get their voice in the conversation.[62] A Crock-Pot spokesperson said the company launched its first-ever Twitter account "so we could comfort fans over the loss of Jack and at the same time share facts about safety." On Facebook, some of Crock-Pot's followers created a trending hashtag #CrockPotIsInnocent, which the brand then turned into a message for a TV commercial that ran just before the Super Bowl. Partnering with NBC, the ad showed Jack Pearson ladling a bowl of chili out of a Crock-Pot saying, "find the ability to forgive."[63] Instead of a disaster, a month later it was reported that Crock-Pot sales actually increased from the brand exposure.[64]

 How Does COVID-19 Impact Social Media Strategy?

Coronavirus changed our world unlike anything we have experienced in our lifetimes. Personal lives, businesses, and organizations were devastated. In an extended global crisis, brands still need to communicate with the public in social media. Yet, traditional crisis communications plans don't usually account for the scale and scope of a pandemic. How do you reset a social media plan put in place before an extended global health and economic crisis?

Examine how social media use has changed. In the months following stay-at-home orders, active users of social media increased.[a] Where, when, and how people engaged with social media changed.[b] With an event as disruptive as coronavirus, your target audience may be engaging in different places, at different times, and with different topics than a couple months ago.

Separate the uncontrollable crisis from controllable. COVID-19 was a traditional offline crisis that impacted everyone. The way a brand responds online could create a second social media crisis. No brand could avoid the first crisis, but all brands can ensure they adjust plans for appropriate communication to try to avoid the second. Messages of support can be met with criticism if they are too vague with no concrete actions.

Act like an individual. Practice good personal skills as in a face-to-face conversation. Be polite, never dismissive, and don't be tone deaf. Brand voice is discussed in chapter 14 with social media content creation. But keep in mind that brand voice needs to adjust tone for the situation. A playful brand voice might need a different tone, language, and purpose for a period of time as people adjust to a new normal.

Respond promptly but properly. Listen to gauge the mood before jumping into the conversation. Consider how different platforms call for variations of message and tone. Customize message, language, and purpose for each social media platform. For COVID-19 some social platforms called for health and safety messages, others called for encouragement and celebration of frontline workers, and some needed a business, jobs, and economy message.

Consider the new context. With every message ask if it is right in the situation and location. A post for New Mexico with fewer restrictions may be insensitive in New York. Stock images of large happy gatherings may not be received well. Caribou Coffee discovered their pre-pandemic drink sleeve message, "Fight the urge to remain indoors. Life is short. Stay awake for it," was not quarantine appropriate after a TikTok post and *BuzzFeed* article went viral.[c] Show you care, but don't come across as opportunistic in trendjacking a sensitive situation.

Pull back on scheduling. Brands may need to operate more on a day-to-day or weekly basis for a while. Do more listening and live posting. Evergreen posts and chatbot scripts may need adjustments. During an extended crisis it is hard to predict the news on a daily basis. Brands may need to pivot to meet changing needs or communicate with new customers.

ROI could look different. If direct-sell CTAs feel inappropriate in the days, weeks, or months following a big crisis, social media metrics and objectives might need adjusting. Click-based sales' KPIs may need to shift to engagement metrics and long-term ROI based on customer lifetime value. Perhaps focus on building brand community that can lead to revenue rewards down the road. Engage the brand community. If they are not in the mood or able to buy at the time, ask what they need to solve the problems you are facing together.

Think about how you can be helpful. Look for moments of need and ways to contribute. Someday life will feel more normal and the people a brand helps during the crisis will remember what they did during their time of need. The best way to send the right message is to do the right thing. Be relevant to current needs with products and services and communicate that relevancy.

A crisis the size of COVID-19 doesn't mean business communication must stop. People have needs and businesses can help. Some may need to shift what they offer and to whom they offer it. That needs to be communicated. During an extended crisis is not the time to be forgotten as a brand; yet, communicating in a national event does require adjustments. If you are starting a new social media strategy months or years after COVID-19, then all the information you gather through the strategic process will include the impact of this unprecedented event.

[a] Kasia Majewska, "Stats on Social Media Use in COVID-19 Hotspots: February vs. March 2020," NapoleanCat.com, April 7, 2020, https://napoleoncat.com/blog/stats-on-social-media-use-covid-19-hotspots.

[b] Elizabeth Arens, "How COVID-19 Has Changed Social Media Engagement," SproutSocial.com, April 27, 2020, https://sproutsocial.com/insights/covid19-social-media-changes.

[c] Julia Reinstein, "Pour One Out for Caribou Coffee, Whose Drink Sleeves Are Hilariously Inappropriate for the Pandemic," May 20, 2020, https://www.buzzfeednews.com/article/juliareinstein/coronavirus-caribou-coffee-sleeve-indoors-tiktok.

Figure 13.4. A significant part of online reputation management involves social media.

© Martin Prescott / iStock Photo

A related topic to crisis communication that must be considered with social media is reputation management. This is another concept rooted in traditional public relations practice that has evolved with the advent of new technologies of online and social media. Traditional reputation management is a practice that has to do with influencing or controlling the reputation of an individual or organization.[65] If crisis communication can be compared to putting a fire out, reputation management aims to keep the fire danger low so wildfires don't erupt. With the growth of the internet and social media, reputation management evolved to focusing on managing search results where negative brand mentions can be easily found by consumers.

Online reputation management (ORM) refers to strategies to influence public opinion of an individual's or organization's reputation online through digital and social media. A core strategy of ORM is to minimize negative content by creating more positive content that pushes the negative mentions down in search engine results pages (SERPs) and in social media newsfeeds.[66] There are companies and software that specialize in online reputation management to complement offline reputation management. Most use multiple channel strategies to influence public opinion about a brand, product, service, or individual.

Online reputation management uses a combination of PR tactics and search engine optimization strategies. Jonas Sickler of ReputationManagement.com recommends a multifaceted approach including:

- Creating and optimizing websites
- Building high quality links

- Publishing thought leadership articles
- Managing social media
- Managing reviews
- Increasing content production

What's at stake? Negative articles and bad reviews showing up in search results can drive away potential customers. Research has found that just four negative search results could cost a business 70 percent of potential business. Also, a negative online reputation could impact employee recruitment efforts; 69 percent of job seekers won't apply to companies with negative reputations. Therefore, ensure that online reputation management strategies are considered as part of an overall social media strategy. Be sure to monitor for online reputation, searching key brand-related terms. Regularly perform a search audit in addition to regular social media audits.[67]

Leverage social media channels to share positive brand content from the brand and third parties such as customers and media. Expand digital presence with keyword optimized brand and product websites and corporate blogs. Earn positive reviews with exceptional service; ask for and make it easy to leave reviews. Strive to become an expert in your field by publishing credible articles, white papers, and reports. These longer pieces of content can then be great resources to repurpose into smaller pieces of social media content scheduled over time and customized per social channel environment and audience.[68]

Nissan's Social Media Command Center is at the heart of online reputation management. Operating as a separate unit not housed under public relations or marketing has given social media a unique position in the company. The structure is informed by their customer experience approach. Instead of a viewing social media as another channel to publish brand content, Nissan's senior manager of social media and customer strategy says they listen for everyone in the company.[69] That has enabled them to cross departmental silos to bring social media data to the overall organization. Even the physical design of the command center is an open layout that representatives from other areas of the company see and walk through when getting off the elevator at company headquarters.[70]

Because not one department controls social media listening they ensure data and insights get distributed across the organization through a dashboard easily shared to departments, units, brands, and countries. Sharing information is critical to crisis communication and online reputation management, especially with a brand that has a diverse online presence from brand websites, ads, and social media to dealer websites and social media. Their main goals are to increase revenue, decrease risk to brand reputation, and reduce costs. Ultimately Nissan's social media department wants to listen to the customer and share that social feedback internally to preserve the brand message across the customer experience—advertising, native websites, consumer affairs, dealer websites, and the dealership lot.[71]

Social Selling and B2B Sales Strategy

Social media has caused major disruptions in strategy and practice for advertising and public relations firms and marketing and customer service departments. The sales department has not been immune to these changes either. Statistics indicate traditional sales processes are becoming less effective. Sales prospects are taking control of their path to purchase, seeking information on their own. Gartner has found that the average business-to-business (B2B) buyer is now more than halfway (57 percent) through the purchase decision before engaging a supplier sales representative.[72] Traditional sales strategies like cold calls and cold emails are becoming less effective. Other research reveals that it takes eighteen calls to connect with a single buyer, callback rates are under 1 percent, and less than a quarter (24 percent) of sales emails are ever opened.[73]

Yet more than 62 percent of B2B buyers say they respond to salespeople who connect with them in social media to share insights and opportunities relevant to their businesses.[74] What's more, 92 percent of B2B buyers are willing to engage with a sales professional who is known as an industry thought leader[75]—an identity that Hootsuite's Christina Newberry explains can be established by posting consistently valuable and relevant content in social media.[76] Buyers are seeking solutions, yet many salespeople are stuck in a sales-only mentality. Successful sales professionals are leveraging what is called social selling.[77]

Social selling is a process of developing relationships through social media as part of the sales process.[78] One of the key challenges for salespeople in adopting a social selling strategy is that it often takes longer to see results. Social selling is about building long-term relationships with prospective customers in social media. Finding prospects, connecting with them, creating and sharing valuable content, and answering their questions can take a longer investment of time.[79] Yet the longer sales process is worth the wait because ultimately it pays off. For example, a LinkedIn survey found that 90 percent of top salespeople use social selling compared to only 71 percent of all salespeople. Sales professionals who use social selling tools such as LinkedIn, Twitter, and Facebook view them as having the highest impact on revenue. They generate more sales opportunities and ultimately are 51 percent more likely to meet their quotas[80] and 78 percent of social sellers outsell peers who don't use social media.[81]

B2B buyers have changed the way they make purchase decisions, altering the sales process and thus requiring new sales strategies. An International Data Corporation survey found that 75 percent of B2B buyers and 84 percent of C-level/VP executives use social media to make purchase decisions. Professional social media networks are the top place to seek information in the final stage of the buying process and social media is seen as helping to provide greater confidence in their decisions.[82] Social selling and B2B content marketing will grow in importance with the new European Union (EU) **General Data Protection Regulation (GDPR)**, which set legal protection guidelines for any company that collects and processes the personal data of EU citizens.[83] What's more, many states in the United States are moving to implement similar restrictions with the California Consumer Protection Act (CCPA) the first to take effect in 2020. CCPA will be discussed more in chapter 15.

The GDPR impacts any business that has customers in the EU. Among other things, the GDPR sets higher standards for opt-ins and makes it easier for consumers to opt out of receiving electronic communication. This puts a greater emphasis on providing more value in content. It also limits the ability to buy direct marketing lists, creating a greater need for businesses to build their own lists through value creation and opt-ins through permission marketing.[84] **Permission marketing** is when sales prospects must first explicitly agree to

Figure 13.5. Social selling is an important part of personal sales and B2B marketing.

© Prykhodov / iStock Photo

receive marketing communication.[85] This concept was first introduced in 1999 by business author Seth Godin in his book *Permission Marketing.* Then it applied to opt-in email, but the concept has since become applicable to social media as well.[86]

How can sales departments integrate social media into their sales strategies and processes? One of the keys is integration into other social media activities of the brand. Marketing and sales should collaborate on social media content, techniques, and best practices by joining advertising, public relations, and customer service as part of the social care team. Marketing can help train salespeople in social media. All departments should set common goals and metrics and meet regularly to have a common social media vision.[87] Other best practices include integrating software systems and creating a content portal. This can help make selling more efficient; 39 percent of B2B professionals say they are able to reduce account and contact research time with social selling tools.[88]

B2B firm BMC Software integrated social media into sales and marketing when they set up a portal with Sprinklr called BMC BeSocial. On this hub timely, brand-relevant social media content and brand social media guides were housed for social media managers, salespeople, and employees.[89] Mack Trucks built a similar resource hub where they publish company videos and aggregate all brand social channels and posts where salespeople can easily access them. The content is segmented by product and easy to share on sales professionals' social channels.[90] Another example is Bryan E. Jones, vice president of commercial marketing in North America for Dell Technologies. He requires all staff to go through internal social media training to become Social Media and Community University or SMaC U certified. Since starting the program in 2010, Dell has graduated and certified more than fifteen thousand SMaC U team members who are leveraging social media best practices to increase sales, improve customer service, and bolster talent acquisition.[91]

For salespeople looking to leverage social media, Hootsuite suggests several best practices. First, salespeople must be present on the social channels and engage in an authentic personal way to build relationships. They should also use social media to identify prospect needs by listening. Prospective buyers in social media are asking questions, sharing their struggles, and seeking solutions. Resist launching into a sales script right away. Take time to listen and really understand their true needs.

Next, provide value. Help prospects with their questions and needs. Give them the insights they need when they need them. Start with solutions over features. Bring the specific product or service up later after proving its value. Finally, salespeople should not forget their prospects over time. Monitor contacts' social media activities and keep in touch with them by looking for opportunities to like and comment on content. Congratulate contacts on promotions or job changes. Continue to be of value so that the next time they are ready to purchase, they will think of contacting the salesperson who has already been helping them.[92]

Salesforce provides additional insights for B2B social sales such as setting up alters for terms and social streams for hashtags related to competitor brand names, products, and key people while following customers, prospects, and thought leaders. Join key customers' groups in LinkedIn or even Facebook to begin monitoring what they are saying and monitor SlideShare for new presentations and documents created by competitors, partners, and leading industry events. Also look for additional industry and customer prospect insights on Q&A sites such as Quora. Finally, don't forget current customer follow-up. Social selling isn't just for prospecting, approach, presentation, and close. Social can also be a valuable sales tool for follow-up.[93] Be sure to monitor current customers in social media; look for potential issues to address proactively and avoid costly lost business.[94]

Tim Washer, creative director at Cisco, has taken a different approach to B2B sales in social media by creating comedy videos. He says that as more content marketing clutter fills the digital space, enterprise brands need to stand out and grab attention. Comedy also has the power of getting people to let their guard down and open up to messages. He suggests targeting clients' pain points and heightening that situation to see the humor in it. This shows empathy for their situation. Also try putting the business situation into another context such as comparing product attributes to a dating app like Tinder.[95] Another comedy tool is to juxtapose two seemingly unrelated objects, as he did for an award-winning IBM video that compared a million-dollar mainframe to a barn.[96] When Cisco sees influencers and thought leaders in their target industries sharing the videos, they know they are working. For details on social selling, see HubSpot Academy's Inbound Sales training and certification at https://academy.hubspot.com/courses/inbound-sales. Another good resource is Hootsuite Academy's Social Selling training and certification at https://education.hootsuite.com/courses/social-selling-exam.

Mack Trucks is a good example of a B2B brand leveraging B2C strategies in social media in the United States and Canada. John Walsh, Mack Trucks' vice president of global marketing, says the brand uses a funnel of awareness, interest, consideration, purchase, and repurchase to map the customer journey. Customers are already in the consideration stage when then go to a dealer; most are self-educating online. The brand social strategy is closely aligned with a multichannel marketing strategy to track results. Social drives to landing pages to capture sales leads in their Oracle Eloqua customer database, which sends those leads to dealers who turn them into sales.[97]

Clicks and likes are nice but with an integrated effort Walsh is focused on tracking a sales pipeline. He admits it was a challenge to get buy-in through the 120-year-old organization and they are still working on getting salespeople used to the CRM system. Having an integrated digital marketing sales funnel and CRM system behind Mack Trucks' social media enables them to not only track engagement but also personalize the social and digital content with messages relevant to where the prospect is in the sales funnel. Based on the content they consume, they self-identify as sales-ready and those leads are sent to the dealers, which accounts for 90 percent of the brand's truck sales.[98]

Mack Trucks' strategy includes multiple stakeholders. Their primary audience is truck purchase decision makers and influencers in their company. But a third audience is truck drivers because there is currently a shortage of drivers in the industry. Mack integrates efforts to reach various audiences across multiple tradition, digital and social channels including print ads, trade shows, email, and a Mack Blog that focuses on customer stories. The goal is to create a fully integrated customer experience consistent across service, product, marketing, sales, and PR.[99]

Mack's content marketing strategy includes a documentary series, RoadLife, featuring Discovery Channel–like episodes that focus on people who spend a lot of time on the road, such as truck drivers, sanitation workers, musicians, and race car drivers. BullDog Studios produces and releases the series through Roadlife.tv. But RoadLife isn't just a content marketing strategy. It is also distributed on the brand's YouTube channel alongside truck model and technology videos. Season 2 of RoadLife featured the Alaska Department of Transportation and what it takes to keep roads clear in one of the snowiest places in North America.[100] The video series became social with #RoadLife on Instagram, where customers' lives and Mack Trucks are celebrated. Each RoadLife episode is also published on IGTV.[101]

On Twitter the brand brings a highly visual approach to engagement, sharing images and videos of truck owners, events, news, and causes leveraging product, brand, and customer life hashtags such as #MackTruck, #Anthem, #truckerlife, #Mactastic, and #MackLovin.[102] The Mack Facebook page celebrates things like #VeteransDay with camo Mack Anthem diecast toy trucks donated to a charity to support military families. They also engage fans, answering questions and responding to reviews.[103] LinkedIn is where they share product and event news, but also emphasize the employer brand for recruitment.[104] Mack also has an influencer marketing strategy with two big trucking social influencers that have Anthem trucks. Both documented their fuel savings and shared their experiences for a year with the hashtag #Mackonomics.[105]

For B2B social sales, the obvious social channel choices are platforms like LinkedIn, Twitter, and SlideShare, but many organizations have had success on other channels such as Facebook, YouTube, and Instagram. As can be seen with Mack Trucks, B2B and B2C can merge in social media to become more B2P or business to people. No matter what type of social selling content is developed, from thought leadership eBooks and customer story blogs to news/event coverage and entertaining video, ensure that it is valuable to the prospect. Salesforce research indicates that sales reps' time connecting with customers virtually has increased three times more than time meeting with customers in person in the last couple of years, but there is still a lot of room for improvement.[106] As you conclude the social media plan, consider what role personal sales has in the business or organization and what type of social sales is appropriate for the target audience, big idea, and social channel selections.

Theoretically Speaking:
Word-of-Mouth in a Service Context

Most agree that word-of-mouth marketing is powerful, but few have delved deeper into why that is. Researchers focusing on word-of-mouth (WOM) have contended that it is one of the most powerful forms of marketing because consumers rely on personal communication sources in making purchase decisions over organizational sources such as advertising campaigns. The sender of the information generally has nothing to gain from the receiver's actions, so the opinion is seen as unbiased and more credible.[107] WOM in a service context is unique because it offers special solutions to the problem of intangibility of services. Before service consumption, a consumer might seek WOM information from an experienced source.[108] Thus, WOM is also important in shaping expectations of service and becomes especially important within the purchase decision.

How can organizations improve WOM? Researchers Harvir Bansal and Peter Voyer conducted a study that found marketers should initiate WOM messages that try to focus on ties between the sender and the receiver in their target audience.[109] In other words, company communications should not only emphasize the attributes of the product or service but also suggest consumers seek information from other people in the target audience who they consider "friends." This is called tie-strength. The closer the relationship or the more a person can relate to the person offering the WOM communication, the more impact it has in the decision-making process. Brands should encourage happy customers to share their positive experiences through social media WOM so that others can discover the company.[110]

This is important in both B2C and B2B contexts. Ratings and reviews are one of the first places to which consumers turn when making a purchase decision. But research also indicates that word-of-mouth recommendations from peers influence more than 90 percent of all B2B buying decisions. To put this in practical context look up the net promoter score for top brands on a site such as https://customer.guru/net-promoter-score/top-brands. Compare brands with high and low NPS scores and then take a quick look at the WOM communication about the brand in ratings and reviews. Is there a correlation?

Chapter 13 Checklist

Social media can change quickly. Visit Post Control Marketing (http://www.postcontrol marketing.com) for updates, but also use this chapter checklist to briefly check how social media statistics in this chapter have changed since publication.

✓ How has customer service in social media changed? Are more brands providing customer service in social media and what percentage are using social messaging apps? Has progress been made in integration of cross-discipline social care teams? How have consumer expectations changed and are brands keeping pace?

✓ How has social media crisis communication changed? Are there new best practices, tools, and strategies? What are the latest social media crisis examples? Are there new learnings from the way those brands did or did not handle the situation well? What was learned from brand response to the extended and extensive health, economic, and social crisis of COVID-19 and the protests in response to George Floyd's death?

✓ How have social sales changed? Are more salespeople using social media as a sales tool? What are the latest statistics? Are there new best practices for social sales techniques and integration?

SOCIAL PLAN PART 13

Creating Cross-Functional Social Care and Social Sales

If the organization does not have an active social care program, now is the time to plan it. First investigate and analyze the existing system that is in place. Is there a customer service department? How do they currently find out about customer needs? What systems are they using? Is customer service limited by delivery method or hours? Is the organization conducting social media monitoring? If so, who is doing it? Are other departments involved? Is there a social media crisis communication plan in place? What about sales? Are salespeople using social selling? How can the sales department be integrated into the overall social strategy and social care team? Table 13.1 describes a plan for a cross-functional social care team. Report all thoughts, plans, and ideas in these areas:

1. Identify the current system. Explain what kind of social media monitoring is occurring. Is it 24/7 or intermittent? What systems are being used?
2. Identify the employees responsible for social media monitoring. What department are they from? Is the team cross-functional?
3. Plan a structure for a new cross-functional social care team that can address all areas of social information efficiently and effectively. What systems are needed?
4. Plan the marketing, advertising, and public relations responsibility in a cross-functional social care team by explaining how each will provide social support. Also provide a briefing on the brand communication style and big idea for the social media plan.
5. Update or create a crisis communications plan to account for a social media crisis. Plan strategies for the sales department's use of social media for a social selling strategy.

For a condensed version of the social plan see appendix A: Three-Part Social Plan.

KEY CONCEPTS

customer service system	net promoter score (NPS)
social care	Pareto principle (80/20 rule)

Salesforce Trailhead
crisis communication
flame war
fauxpology

online reputation management (ORM)
social selling
General Data Protection Regulation (GDPR)
permission marketing

QUESTIONS FOR DISCUSSION

1. Hertz Rent-a-Car's 24/7 social care response is impressive, but what can a small business or startup do with fewer resources? Is there a software system or employee response that can help? Should expectations be lowered or not given at all?

2. Most of the discussion around social media crisis communication is on the brand doing something by responding to the brand reputation threat. Can you find an example of where a brand ignored a potential threat by not responding and it died down? Had they responded, would it have brought more attention to the issue and turned it into a crisis?

3. Social sales is a new strategy for sales professionals to leverage social media as one of their key sales tools. What software tools or systems exist to help make social selling more efficient and automate some processes?

4. Ethical considerations can arise when it comes to reputation management. As a social media professional you may be asked to create positive content for a client to push down negative content in search results. What if, in researching the organization, you find that you are personally troubled with the actions they have taken that generated the negative mentions?

ADDITIONAL EXERCISES

1. For this exercise, go on Twitter and make comments and requests to the handles or hashtags of several companies. Note how long it takes to get a response, who responds, and how they respond. Compare the different company actions. From what you observe, try to determine what type of social care plan the organization is running. Do they have a plan? Is one department, such as marketing, obviously running it without the other departments being involved? Or is there truly a cross-functional social care system in place? Pick one of the companies and ask the same question or try to solve the same issue via another communication channel, such as the telephone or email. Do you notice a difference in response time, quality, and content?

2. For this exercise, think about worst-case scenarios. In social media, brand attacks can spring up instantly for reasons you can't always predict. What should an organization do? Make a list of some of the bad situations in which the organization could find itself. Think of horrible customer service experiences, product failures and recalls, environmental disasters, scandals, and accidents. What about extended global health, economic, or social crises? How should a company react when social media is lighting up with activity? How should these social media crisis strategies integrate with overall crisis communication plans? Create your own internal FAQ through role playing as Bruce Kennedy, social media manager at Cision suggests.

Notes

1. "Marshall Field," BrainyQuote.com, accessed November 6, 2019, http://www.brainyquote.com/quotes/quotes/m/marshallfi379060.html.

2. Jamie Edwards, "The History of Customer Service: Ticket Troubleshooting to Proactive and Personal," Kayako.com, October 13, 2016, https://www.kayako.com/blog/history-of-customer-service/.

3. Marc Herschberger, "The Complete History of Customer Service Operations," Eventus Contact Center Solutions, March 31, 2014, from http://www.eventusg.com/blog/the-complete-history-of-customer-service-operations.

4. Jeff Howe, "How Hashtags and Social Media Can Bring Megacorporations to Their Knees," TheAtlantic.com, June 8, 2012, http://www.theatlantic.com/business/archive/2012/06/the-rise-of-the-consumerate/258290.

5. Ravi Sawhney, "Broken Guitar Has United Playing the Blues to the Tune of $180 Million," FastCompany.com, July 7, 2009, http://www.fastcompany.com/blog/ravi-sawhney/design-reach/youtube-serves-180-million-heartbreak.

6. John Beckett, "United Airlines PR Disaster: What You Can Learn from Their #FAIL," Devumi.com, April 21, 2017, https://devumi.com/2017/04/united-airlines-pr-disaster-what-you-can-learn-from-their-fail/.

7. John George and Phil Simon, "Connecting with Customers," *Baylor Business Review* 30, no. 1 (2011): 22–25.

8. Donna Fluss, "Using Social Media for Customer Service," *CRM Magazine* 16, no. 4 (2012): 10.

9. Bill Gerth, "Lithys 2014: Comcast—Excellence in Customer Satisfaction," Lithium.com, April 1, 2014, http://community.lithium.com/t5/Social-Customer-Excellence/Lithys-2014-Comcast-Excellence-in-Customer-Satisfaction/idi-p/140812.

10. Lisa Blackshear, Jay Baer, and Adam Brown, "How Comcast Interacts with Customers on Social Media 6 Million Times Each Year," ConvinceandConvert.com, July 6, 2019, https://www.convinceandconvert.com/podcasts/episodes/how-comcast-interacts-with-customers-on-social-media-6-million-times-each-year/.

11. Rayna Hollander, "Customers Are Abandoning Traditional Customer Service Channels," BusinessInsider.com, January 24, 2018, https://www.businessinsider.com/consumers-are-abandoning-traditional-customer-service-channels-2018-1.

12. Fluss, "Using Social Media for Customer Service."

13. Nichole Kelly, "How to Measure Social Media's Impact on Customer Retention," SocialMediaExaminer.com, September 8, 2010, http://www.socialmediaexaminer.com/how-to-measure-social-media%E2%80%99s-impact-on-customer-retention.

14. Trips Reddy, "How Chatbots Can Help Reduce Customer Service Costs by 30%," IBM.com, October 17, 2017, https://www.ibm.com/blogs/watson/2017/10/how-chatbots-reduce-customer-service-costs-by-30-percent/.

15. Charlene Li and Josh Bernoff, *Groundswell, Expanded and Revised Edition: Winning in a World Transformed by Social Technologies* (Boston: Harvard Business Review Press, 2011).

16. Sofie De Beule, "7 Can't-Miss Social Customer Service Stats for 2017," CXSocial.Clarabridge.com, January 5, 2017, http://cxsocial.clarabridge.com/7-cant-miss-social-customer-service-stats-2017/.

17. Reddy, "How Chatbots Can Help."

18. Wayne Huang, John Mitchell, Carmel Dibner, Andrea Ruttenberg, and Audrey Tripp, "How Customer Service Can Turn Angry Customers into Loyal Ones," *Harvard Business Review,*

January 16, 2018, https://hbr.org/2018/01/how-customer-service-can-turn-angry-customers-into -loyal-ones.

19. Dave Evans, *Social Media Marketing an Hour a Day,* 2nd ed. (Indianapolis: Wiley, 2012).

20. David Gianatasio, "JetBlue Knows How to Communicate with Customers in Social, and When to Shut Up," Adweek.com, September 9, 2013, http://www.adweek.com/brand-marketing/ jetblue-knows-how-communicate-customers-social-and-when-shut-152246/.

21. Jay Baer, "How to Respond When Customers Get Sour on Social Media," Marketing Land.com, February 9, 2019, https://www.reputationmanagement.com/blog/online-reputation -management-guide/.

22. "Shunning Your Customers on Social?" SproutSocial.com, accessed August 11, 2017, https:// sproutsocial.com/insights/data/q2-2016/.

23. Baer, "How to Respond When Customers Get Sour."

24. Wayne Huang, "Study: Twitter Customer Care Increases Willingness to Pay," Twitter .com, October 5, 2016, https://blog.twitter.com/marketing/en_us/topics/research/2016/study -twitter-customer-care-increases-willingness-to-pay-across-industries.html.

25. "Why Social Media Is Important Customer Service Channel," TELUS International, accessed January 20, 2015, http://telusinternational-europe.com/why-social-care-is-important-customer -service-channel.

26. Evan Hoopfer, "Social media LUV: How Southwest Airlines connects with customers online," Dallas Business Journal, March 3, 2019, https://www.bizjournals.com/dallas/news/2019/03/03/ southwest-airlines-social-media.html.

27. Hoopfer, "Social media LUV."

28. Hoopfer, "Social media LUV."

29. "Why Social Media Is Important," TELUS International.

30. Lindsay Kolowich, "Delighting People in 140 Characters: An Inside Look at JetBlue's Customer Service Success," HubSpot.com, August 20, 2017, https://blog.hubspot.com/marketing/ jetblue-customer-service-twitter.

31. Kim Keating and Dave Evans, "Benchmarking Social Media Customer Service: Uncovering Opportunities & Best Practices for Social Care," TELUS International, accessed February 20, 2015, https://www.yumpu.com/en/document/read/34428333/to-access-the-white-paper-telus -international.

32. "The Ignored Side of Social Media: Customer Service," Knowledge@Wharton, January 2, 2014, http://knowledge.wharton.upenn.edu/article/ignored-side-social-media-customer-service.

33. Geoffrey A. Fowler, "Want Better Customer Service? Don't Call. Text," WashingtonPost .com, August 9, 2018, https://www.washingtonpost.com/technology/2018/08/09/want-better -customer-service-dont-call-text/.

34. Jonathan Salem Baskin, "Customer Service Belongs to Operations, Not Marketing: How Apple Turned Problem-Fixing into a Promotional Tool," AdAge.com, June 27, 2011, http://adage .com/article/cmo-strategy/customer-service-belongs-operations-marketing/228447.

35. "Five Guys: See How Five Guys Keeps Its Family-Owned Personality—While Letting Over 1,200 Franchisees Join the Conversation on Social," Hootsuite.com, accessed November 5, 2019, https://hootsuite.com/resources/case-study/five-guys-case-study.

36. Francisca Fanucchi, "5 Things You Should Do to Scale Social Care (An Inside Look at HP)," Adweek.com, October 5, 2016, http://www.adweek.com/digital/francisca -fanucchi-lithium-technologies-interview-hp-kriti-kapoor/.

37. Pat Hong, "10 Exceptional Examples of Brand Communities," Linkdex.com, January 15, 2015, https://www.linkdex.com/en-us/inked/10-exceptional-examples-of-brand-communities/.

38. "Crowds," Conversocial.com, accessed November 16, 2019, http://www.conversocial.com/crowds.

39. "More Than a Message: The Evolution of Conversation," Facebook IQ, August 4, 2016, https://www.facebook.com/iq/articles/more-than-a-message-the-evolution-of-conversation?ref=wpinsights_rd.

40. Natalie Petouhoff, "What Is a Chatbot and How Is It Changing Customer Experience?" Salesforce.com, April 25, 2019, https://www.salesforce.com/blog/2019/04/what-is-a-chatbot.html.

41. Laduram Vishnoi, "Chatbot vs. Live Chat: Which is Winning the Customer Service Game and Why?" Acquire.io, September 19, 2019, https://acquire.io/blog/chatbot-vs-live-chat/.

42. Alfred Lua, "Why I Think Social Media Is for Branding and Engagement, Not Traffic or Revenue," BufferSocial.com, July 20, 2017, https://blog.bufferapp.com/social-media-is-for-branding.

43. "Customer Service Channels That Frustrate Customers," eMarketer.com, February 26, 2016, https://www.emarketer.com/Article/Customer-Service-Channels-That-Frustrate-Consumers/1013637.

44. Jim Chappelow, "Pareto principle," Investopedia.com, August 29, 2019, https://www.investopedia.com/terms/p/paretoprinciple.asp; Dave Lavinsky, "Pareto Principle: How to Use It to Dramatically Grow Your Business," Forbes.com, January 20, 2019, https://www.forbes.com/sites/davelavinsky/2014/01/20/pareto-principle-how-to-use-it-to-dramatically-grow-your-business/#3643c88e3901.

45. Perry Marshall, *80/20 Sales and Marketing*, accessed November 7, 2019, https://www.perrymarshall.com/8020-book/.

46. Seth Godin, *This is Marketing: You Can't Be Seen Until You Learn How to See* (New York: Portfolio/Penguin, 2018).

47. "Welcome to Trailhead, the Fun Way to Learn," Salesforce.com, accessed November 15, 2019, https://www.salesforce.com/services/learn/overview/.

48. "Crisis Management and Communications," InstituteForPR.org, October 30, 2007, https://instituteforpr.org/crisis-management-and-communications/.

49. "Crisis communication," BusinessDictionary.com, accessed November 5, 2019, http://www.businessdictionary.com/definition/crisis-communication.html.

50. "What Is Crisis Communication?" ShiftCommunications.com, December 20, 2019, https://www.shiftcomm.com/blog/what-is-crisis-communications/.

51. Karen Freberg, *Social Media for Strategic Communication: Creative Strategies and Research-Based Applications* (Thousand Oaks, CA: Sage, 2019), 234.

52. Rob Stokes, *eMarketing: The Essential Guide to Online Marketing, v. 1.0* (Irvington, NY: Flatworld Knowledge, 2010).

53. "Flame war," Dictionary.com, accessed November 5, 2019, https://www.dictionary.com/browse/flame-war.

54. Steve Goldstein, "Social Media Checklist for Your Crisis Communications Plan," PRNewsOnline.com, February 14, 2017, http://www.prnewsonline.com/water-cooler/how-to-integrate-social-media-into-your-crisis-plan; "The Book of Crisis Management Strategies & Tactics," PRNewsOnline.com, accessed November 6, 2019, http://www.prnewsonline.com/crisis-management-guidebook-vol-9/.

55. Goldstein, "Social Media Checklist"; "Book of Crisis Management," PRNewsOnline.com.

56. Karen Freberg, "Transcript: Essentials for Continued Success with Social Media," HubSpot Academy, https://academy.hubspot.com/lessons/essentials-for-continued-success-with-social-media; Freberg, *Social Media for Strategic Communication*.

57. Bruce Kennedy, Jay Baer, and Adam Brown, "Why Social Media Crisis Management Has Changed Forever," SociaPros Podcast, ConvinceAndConvert.com, July 7, 2019, https://www.convince andconvert.com/podcasts/episodes/why-social-media-crisis-management-has-changed-forever/.

58. "Fauxpology," YourDictionary.com, accessed December 4, 2019, https://www.your dictionary.com/fauxpology.

59. Kennedy, Baer, and Brown, "Why Social Media Crisis Management Has Changed Forever."

60. Priya Krishna, "How 'This Is Us' Unwittingly Reinvented the Humble Crock-Pot," NewYorker.com, February 21, 2018, https://www.newyorker.com/culture/annals-of-gastronomy/ how-this-is-us-unwittingly-reinvented-the-humble-crock-pot.

61. Nicole Lyn Pesce, "How That Devastating 'This Is Us' Fire Actually Boosted Crock-Pot Sales," MarketWatch.com, May 10, 2018, https://www.marketwatch.com/story/how-that -devastating-this-is-us-fire-actually-boosted-crock-pot-sales-2018-05-10.

62. Melissa Agnes, "Baffling Proof That Issues Can Strangely Emerge from Anywhere," MelissaAgnes.com, February 1, 2019, https://melissaagnes.com/baffling-proof-issues-can-strangely -emerge-anywhere/.

63. Krishna, "How 'This Is Us' Unwittingly Reinvented The Humble Crock-Pot."

64. Pesce, "How That Devastating 'This Is Us' Fire Actually Boosted Crock-Pot Sales."

65. "Reputation management," BusinessDictionary.com, accessed November 2, 2019, http:// www.businessdictionary.com/definition/reputation-management.html.

66. "Online Reputation Management (ORM)," Techopedia.com, accessed November 5, 2019, https://www.techopedia.com/definition/29591/online-reputation-management-orm.

67. Jonas Sickler, "The Expert's Guide to Online Reputation Management," Reputation Management.com, May 9, 2019, https://www.reputationmanagement.com/blog/online-reputation -management-guide/.

68. Sickler, "Expert's Guide to Online Reputation Management."

69. Bryan Long, "Nissan: The State of Social Media: A Customer Experience Approach, Presented by Bryan Long," Vimeo.com, SocialMedial.org, April 15, 2016, https://vimeo.com/162972670.

70. Bridgette Cude, "Inside Nissan's Social Media Command Center," Ragan.com, July 20, 2016, https://www.ragan.com/inside-nissans-social-media-command-center/.

71. Cude, "Inside Nissan's Social Media Command Center"; William Comcowich, "Nissan's Alternative Road to Social Media Listening Success," Glean.info, March 15, 2017, https://glean.info/ blog/page/42/?source=post_page.

72. "The Digital Evolution in B2B Marketing: Driving Marketing Performance with Multi-Channel Content, Communications and Analytics," CEBGlobal.com, accessed November 6, 2019, https://www.cebglobal.com/marketing-communications/digital-evolution.html.

73. Bryan Gonzalez, "Sales Development Technology: The Stack Emerges," TopoBlog.com, accessed November 6, 2019, http://blog.topohq.com/sales-development-technology-the-stack -emerges/.

74. Regis Crawford, "What Is Social Selling and How Does It Work?" Salesforce.com, April 2, 2019, https://www.salesforce.com/blog/2017/08/guide-to-social-selling.html.

75. "Establish Your Professional Brand: LinkedIn Sales Solutions," SlideShare.net, September 17, 2015, https://www.slideshare.net/linkedin-sales-solutions/establish-your-professional-brand.

76. Christina Newberry, "Social Selling: What It Is, Why You Should Care, and How to Do It Right," Hootsuite.com, June 19, 2017, https://blog.hootsuite.com/what-is-social-selling/.

77. Laurence Minsky and Keith Quesenberry, "How B2B Sales Can Benefit from Social Selling," Harvard Business Review, November 8, 2016, https://hbr.org/2016/11/84-of-b2b-sales -start-with-a-referral-not-a-salesperson.

78. Crawford, "What Is Social Selling?"

79. Steven MacDonald, "29 Social Selling Statistics: How to Master the Art of Social Selling," SuperOffice.com, accessed November 6, 2019, https://www.superoffice.com/blog/social-selling-statistics/.

80. "State of Sales in 2016," Business.LinkedIn.com, accessed November 6, 2019, https://business.linkedin.com/content/dam/me/business/en-us/sales-solutions/resources/pdfs/linkedin-state-of-sales-2016-report.pdf.

81. Crawford, "What Is Social Selling?"

82. Kathleen Schaub, "Social Buying Meets Social Selling: How Trusted Networks Improve the Purchase Experience," IDC white paper, Business.LinkedIn.com, April 2014, https://business.linkedin.com/content/dam/business/sales-solutions/global/en_US/c/pdfs/idc-wp-247829.pdf.

83. "General Data Protection Regulation (GDPR)," Investopedia.com, accessed November 6, 2019, https://www.investopedia.com/terms/g/general-data-protection-regulation-gdpr.asp.

84. "What Will the GDPR Mean for B2B Marketing Professionals?" Kingpin, May 2017, http://kingpincomms.com/wp-content/uploads/2017/04/Kingpin_GDPR-eBook-20172-002.pdf.

85. Margaret Rouse, "Permission Marketing," TechTarget.com, accessed November 6, 2019, http://searchcrm.techtarget.com/definition/permission-marketing.

86. Kayla Carmichael, "What Is Permission Marketing & How Does It Work?" Blog.HubSpot.com, August 14, 2019, https://blog.hubspot.com/marketing/permission-marketing-automation.

87. Minsky and Quesenberry, "How B2B Sales Can Benefit from Social Selling."

88. Crawford, "What Is Social Selling?"

89. Carlos Gil, "Employee Advocacy for B2B," SlideShare.net, March 22, 2016, https://www.slideshare.net/MarTechConf/employee-advocacy-for-b2b-by-carlos-gil.

90. Neil Tolbert, Jay Baer, and Adam Brown, "How to Grow a Facebook Page from 6,000 to 175,000 Fans," Social Pros Podcast, ConvinceAndConvert.com, October 20, 2017, http://www.convinceandconvert.com/podcasts/episodes/grow-facebook-page-6000-175000-fans/.

91. Amy H., "5 Years of Making Social Superheroes," Dell.com, August 25, 2015, https://blog.dell.com/en-us/5-years-of-making-social-superheroes/.

92. "Inbound Marketing Case Study: Fisher Tank Company," Weidert.com, September 2013, https://www.weidert.com/case-studies/inbound-marketing-for-specialty-manufacturers-a-case-study.

93. Roger A. Kerin and Steven W. Hartley, *Marketing: The Core*, 8th ed. (New York: McGraw-Hill Education, 2020): 496.

94. Crawford, "What Is Social Selling?"

95. "Mainframe: The Art of the Sale, Lesson One," 360comedy, YouTube.com, August 18, 2006, https://youtu.be/MSqXKp-00hM.

96. Leon G. Schiffman and Leslie Lazar Kanuk, *Consumer Behavior*, 6th ed. (Upper Saddle River, NJ: Prentice Hall, 1997).

97. Ginger Conlon, "'Digital Is Marketing Nirvana': Mack Trucks' Marketing Chief Blurs B2B and B2C Strategies," TheDrum.com, May 3, 2019, https://www.thedrum.com/news/2019/05/03/digital-marketing-nirvana-mack-trucks-marketing-chief-blurs-b2b-and-b2c-strategies.

98. Conlon, "'Digital Is Marketing Nirvana.'"

99. Conlon, "'Digital Is Marketing Nirvana.'"

100. "RoadLife 2.0—Alaska DOT," Mack Trucks, YouTube.com, June 20, 2019, https://www.youtube.com/watch?v=XlFm0ddw5q8.

101. "Mack Trucks," Instagram.com, accessed November 6, 2019, https://www.instagram.com/macktrucks/.

102. "Mack Trucks," Twitter.com, accessed November 6, 2019, https://twitter.com/MackTrucks.

103. "Mack Trucks," Facebook.com, accessed November 6, 2019, https://www.facebook.com/MackTrucks.

104. "Mack Trucks, Inc.," LinkedIn.com, accessed November 6, 2019, https://www.linkedin.com/company/mack-trucks.

105. Conlon, "'Digital Is Marketing Nirvana.'"

106. Crawford, "What Is Social Selling?"

107. Julia M. Bristor, "Enhanced Explanations of Word of Mouth Communications: The Power of Relationships," *Research in Consumer Behavior* 4 (1990): 51–83.

108. Valarie A. Zeithaml and Mary Jo Bitner, *Services Marketing* (New York: McGraw-Hill, 1996).

109. Harvir S. Bansal and Peter A. Voyer, "Word-of-Mouth Processes within a Services Purchase Decision Context," *Journal of Service Research* 3, no. 2 (2000): 166.

110. "Use Cases," Influitive.com, accessed November 6, 2019, https://influitive.com/use.

PART

V

**Pulling It
All Together**

Write Your Plan,
Plan Your Sell

Even when you have gone as far as you can, and everything hurts, and you are staring at the specter of self-doubt, you can find a bit more strength deep inside you, if you look closely enough.[1]

—Hal Higdon

PREVIEW

Do you sometimes have trouble seeing the big picture? Perhaps you get so caught up in today's deadlines or due dates that you can't see tomorrow. Then tomorrow comes with its own set of tasks. So you end up just taking on each day's "to do" list, reacting to what is immediately in front of you. Yet those daily lists never end, and you spend little time looking and planning ahead to the next week, next month, or next year.

"Being unable to see the forest for the trees" is a phrase familiar to many. It was first recorded in John Heywood's 1546 collection of proverbs. It means getting so caught up in the small details that a person fails to understand the bigger picture. Yet the ability to discern an overall pattern from a mass of details is a valuable skill.[2] This skill is at the heart of strategies that plan and marshal organizational resources to meet and exceed business goals. This ability is seen as very valuable.

Management Research Group (MRG) conducted a global study of more than sixty thousand managers that accessed more than twenty leadership practices and twenty measures of effectiveness. Practices included innovation, persuasion, communication, and results orientation. Effectiveness measures included future potential, credibility, business aptitude, and people skills. Results of the study found that having a strategic approach was ten times more important to effectiveness than other leadership behaviors, and almost fifty times more important than tactical behaviors. In a follow-up study, ten thousand senior executives were asked to select the leadership behaviors most critical to an organization's success. *Strategic* was chosen 97 percent of the time.[3]

Strategic thinking means taking a broad, long-range approach and thinking systematically. Most people may agree that this skill is very important, yet thinking strategically is not easy. Strategic thinking is especially hard when immediate demands are often rewarded over long-term vision and planning. When faced with more than eight hundred social media sites, apps, and services with hundreds of possible tactics and tools, being able to focus on a long-term approach and systematic thinking is necessary for action. Seeing the forest for the trees is more than a mindset. It is a leadership quality that is a necessity for success.[4]

Slow and Steady Wins the Race

Hal Higdon is a famous marathon runner, and the longest-contributing writer to *Runner's World* magazine (more than forty years), who has written more than thirty marathon-training books. Yet what he says about training for a marathon can easily be applied to social media strategy and planning. Training for a marathon is long. Most marathon-training programs last four months and only begin after months of setting a solid base of twenty to thirty miles a week.[5]

The marathon itself is long. The beginning is exciting with the crowd, the newness, and the scenery. Then somewhere after the halfway point, away from the spectators, the novelty wears off. The excitement is gone and is simply replaced with grueling mile after mile. This is when doubt sets in for many runners. "Why am I doing this?" "I can't do this!" "What was I thinking?" Then around mile twenty, runners hit "the wall." At the wall, all energy is used up and it feels as if one cannot continue. Yet if they pop some energy gels and will themselves to the end, most runners discover running the marathon is more than worth it. The *Baltimore Sun* captured that feeling appropriately in an article following the Baltimore Marathon. The article described a runner who crossed the marathon finish line, vomited, and then said, "That was the best time of my life!"

Social media can be like this. Not necessarily the vomiting part, but more the day-to-day posting, monitoring, content generation, and curation. The grueling post after post and comment after comment can be draining. Despite all the talk about ROI and immediate measurement, most social media strategies don't give immediate significant return like traditional mass media ad and PR campaigns that can spike retail sales the weekend the marketer launches it. Viral hits are the exception, and overnight successes are rare. Behind most overnight success stories is a long journey that simply is not told or forgotten. Many are

Figure 14.1. A social media plan needs well-executed content creation.

© Flippo Bacci / iStock Photo

jumping into the social media race, but they must be in for the long haul to see real results.[6] Take a step back to see the forest of the hundreds of social media trees.

Social media expert Jay Baer captured this mindset well in his blog post "Are You Slow Enough to Succeed in Social Media?" He observes that social media adoption is quick, but interacting and engaging with customers and prospects happens on a one-to-one or one-to-few basis, and that takes time. Social media is also built on trust, and building trust is a longer process. Baer likens this process to recruiting a volunteer marketing army, one soldier at a time. This doesn't happen overnight.[7] If marketers, advertisers, and public relations professionals are accustomed to mass audience attention through traditional methods, the slow burn of social media could require some adjustment time. It also could require explanation to organization management to set up realistic expectations.

Reading the trade press, case studies, and white papers on social media efforts can be deceiving. From these accounts, you may think social growth and success can happen overnight if they simply find the right formula. We read about social media stars, but many of those articles tend to skip over the backstory and the years of groundwork. The Dove Real Beauty campaign is one example. Before Dove turned to social media with its online films, the campaign started as a traditional advertising campaign. They proved success in small steps at first and built trust with company management before the campaign became the viral-success case study we see now. This type of example happens in the music industry all the time. A band will be positioned in the press as an overnight success, but upon further inspection, readers may find that the band is actually on its fifth or sixth album release and has been playing small venues for a decade.

Seth Godin is a great example of this long-term thinking. He has been publishing a blog post every day since 2002. For more than eighteen years, he has faithfully put out daily social media content. Highly successful now, his blog did not always have a mass audience. Godin's first post, "Death of a Myth?" to this day only has one tweet and four likes. Yet a more recent post, "Trading Favors," received 1,162 tweets and 568 likes.[8] Keep this long-term perspective in mind as you complete a social media strategy and start to execute the plan. Success may not take fifteen years, but it also may not happen in fifteen days. Once the social media plan is finished, the real race and real work have just begun.

Yet for those who have patience and daily persistence, social media does deliver results. It may not take years, but it may take longer than some expect. NASCAR is a good example of social media strategic thinking on the right time scale. David Higdon was NASCAR's IMC managing director at a time when the brand needed to attract younger fans. At an integrated marketing communications conference, he spoke about the brand's remarkable overhaul that came from a focus on a younger audience and a commitment to reach them in the social channels where they participate.

NASCAR's social media effort can be seen as successful. After the new strategy was implemented, sponsorship deals rose 8 percent and 23 percent of Fortune 500 brands became a part of NASCAR, an increase of 20 percent.[9] A consumer survey also found that 61 percent of eighteen- to thirty-four-year-old avid fans were more interested in NASCAR than the previous year, and 65 percent of those had been fans for fewer than five years. This increase in fan interest was attributed to NASCAR's social media engagement efforts.[10] However, the real insight into NASCAR's success is that these results came after an eighteen-month review and then a three- to five-year integrated marketing communications plan to achieve those successful results.

How does a three- to five-year timeline work in a business culture where the average CMO is ousted every two to three years? Culture simply must change. Trying to apply old strategies and expectations in this new social media–empowered consumer environment does not work. Social media marketing is a different game with different rules. Push marketing and all its perceptions and expectations do not apply.[11] Perhaps David Higdon of NASCAR learned the new rules from his father, Hal Higdon of marathon fame. Did the father's marathon strategy influence the son's social media strategy? Shortsighted sales results are slowly giving way to consumer lifetime value, and the increasing importance of social media consumer engagement may be helping to drive that change. **Customer lifetime value** is a concept that shifts focus from short-term profit to long-term profit from the continuing relationship with a customer.[12]

Tom Martin from Converse Digital polled digital marketers and asked how long it takes to see results from social media marketing. Most respondents felt six months was a fair average if you were doing it right. Others thought time frames of nine to eighteen months were more appropriate.[13] Why do social media results take so long? Some answer that question with another question. How long does it take to create a loyal following? Social media is about engagement, relationships, and listening. It can take months to curate a community by targeting them with articles, pictures, videos, and other content to foster engagement.[14]

Social Media Content Creation

A survey of social media professionals investigated in which areas they spent most of their time. The results revealed that only 12 percent of social media staff's time was spent on strategy development, and most of their time (60 percent) was devoted to content creation. In social media, content development takes up nearly six times the amount of time as strategy development, posting content, listening and monitoring, measuring, responding to fans and followers, and reporting results to leadership (see figure 14.2).[15] After putting the social media plan together and completing the social media strategy process, be prepared to spend the majority of time on content development, followed by engagement, measurement, and reporting.

While individual results will vary based on target audience, brand voice, campaign message, and social platform, there are some best practices to consider when writing and designing social media posts. Most experts agree active voice helps create more engaging social media copy. It will produce clear, concise, action-oriented sentences. **Active voice** is a sentence where a subject performs an action directly, using a verb to show the action.[16] **Passive voice** is a sentence where the action verb or object of a sentence is emphasized over its subject.[17] For example, you can see that the second active voice version of the following sentences would be better at grabbing audience attention and interest while keeping copy shorter and to the point. "The two-hour marathon barrier was broken by team Nike!" "Team Nike broke the two-hour marathon barrier!"[18]

Also put your audience first by writing from their point of view and conveying a clear benefit to them. **Point of view** is the angle of considering things, as in writing from a first-,

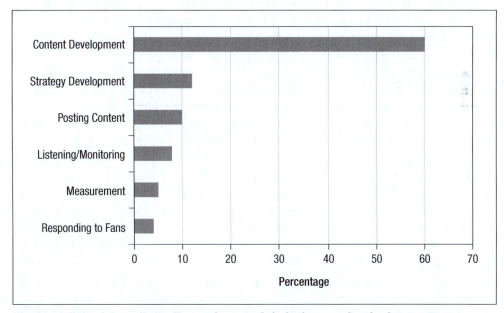

Figure 14.2. Social media staff spend most of their time on developing content.

Source: "Social Media Marketing's Main Expense is Staff. How Do They Spend Their Time?" MarketingCharts.com, May 2014, http://www.marketingcharts.com/online/social-media-marketings-main-expense-is-staff-how-do-they -spend-their-time-42651/attachment/smmu-top-areas-social-media-time-investment-may2014/.

second-, or third-person view of a story. First person is the point of view that uses pronouns "I" or "we," second person uses "you," and third person uses "he," "she," "it," "they," or a name.[19] In social media writing, focus on second person, saying "you" more than "us." Using second person helps to draw audience attention, focusing the message on them. Conveying the message as a benefit makes the post more interesting and more likely to be shared. This can be seen in the following examples of first, second, and third person points of view with and without a clear benefit. "We made the Vaporfly shoes that broke the two-hour marathon." "You can run in the Vaporfly shoes that broke the two-hour marathon." "Vaporfly shoes broke the two-hour marathon."

Social media posts should encourage tagging and sharing. This can come from writing messages the audience will want to share because they know it is something their friends will like, it expresses appreciation of them, or it expresses beliefs and causes they care about. Also ensure a clear match between the post message and link destination. Sending an audience to a general homepage or unrelated page will cause confusion and lost leads. The destination page must deliver on the message promised in the post and remain focused on the action you want the audience to take. The best practice is to create an optimized landing page. A **landing page** is a specially designed page with a main goal to generate sales or capture leads from a campaign.[20]

Social media writing should be clear and concise, written in a conversational tone; avoid pushy overt sales messages and invite curiosity. Highlight rational and emotional benefits and include a call to action based on strategy and campaign objectives. Include brand keywords, taglines, and hashtags optimized per social platform and follow the brand voice. Brand voice was described in chapter 4, but how do you write in a brand voice? Hootsuite suggests thinking of a few celebrity and/or popular TV/movie characters that capture the essence of the brand attitude and perspective. Is the brand more of an Ellen DeGeneres, Alicia Keys, Wonder Woman or a Will Smith, Dwayne Johnson, Iron Man?[21]

Next find your adjectives (see table 14.1). Try to narrow down a list three or four that best describe the brand. Also, write the way you talk, as if the brand were a person talking out loud to another person. Don't write the way you would a blog article or business report. Avoid jargon that will make posts sound less personal and drop boastful claims such as "top," "best," or "only." Be genuine, telling fun, helpful, and exciting stories. And remember that this is a two-sided conversation. Listen for cues from each person and respond in an appropriate tone. A brand voice should stay consistent, but tone should change with the situation, specific customer, and platform. Even a fun, casual brand should take a more serious tone with a truly upset customer.[22] And brands such as JetBlue and Wendy's will vary their brand voice to different audiences across various platforms.

Make posts more powerful by creating text and images that work together. Creatively connect the two in a way that invites the viewer to fill a gap, creating an "aha" moment. As discussed in chapter 12, that feeling of creative joy is something they will want to share. It is tempting to quickly grab generic stock imagery, but a unique image that complements the copy draws interest; it looks more professional and less like spam. Invest in the right image to complement your message and make it more engaging. Change individual messages but be consistent in overall campaign message, brand voice, and design. Follow brand standards for colors, logos, and fonts to ensure brand consistency across social, digital, and traditional media.

Table 14.1. List of Example Adjectives to Describe Brand Voice

Adorable, Adventurous, Appealing, Artistic, Athletic, Attractive, Bold, Breathtaking, Bright, Busy, Calm, Capable, Caring, Casual, Charming, Cheerful, Chic, Classic, Clever, Cocky, Collaborative, Colorful, Comfortable, Conservative, Contemporary, Convenient, Cool, Creative, Daring, Dashing, Dazzling, Delicate, Delightful, Detailed, Dramatic, Dry, Earthy, Easy, Eccentric, Efficient, Elegant, Elevated, Enchanting, Endearing, Energetic,	Ethereal, Exciting, Exuberant, Fabulous, Familiar, Fancy, Fantastic, Fashionable, Festive, Fierce, Flirty, Formal, Fresh, Friendly, Fun, Functional, Futuristic, Glamorous, Graceful, Hip, Historic, Honorable, Impressive, Industrial, Informal, Innovative, Inspiring, Intense, Inviting, Lively, Low Maintenance, Lush, Majestic, Modern, Natural, Nautical, Nifty, Noisy, No-nonsense, Nostalgic, Novel, Old, Organic, Playful, Pleasant, Powerful,	Predictable, Professional, Quaint, Quirky, Radiant, Rebellious, Relaxing, Reliable, Retro, Revolutionary, Ritzy, Romantic, Royal, Rustic, Savvy, Scholarly, Secure, Serious, Silly, Sleek, Smart, Soothing, Sophisticated, Stable, Stimulating, Striking, Strong, Stunning, Stylish, Swanky, Tasteful, Thoughtful, Tranquil, Trustworthy, Unconventional, Unique, Upbeat, Urban, Versatile, Vintage, Whimsical, Wild, Wistful, Witty, Youthful

Source: Todd Clarke, "How to Establish Your Brand 'Voice' on Social Media," Hootsuite.com, February 21, 2019, https://blog.hootsuite.com/how-to-build-an-authentic-voice-on-social/.

Good social media design keeps text to a minimum, ensuring that it is easy to read. Make sure text is large enough, keeping in mind that most social media is viewed on mobile devices. A unique font can be used for emphasis, but limit the number of fonts used in a single post. Ensure you have good contrast when placing text or graphics over images or colors so they can be seen.[23] Good design does not overcrowd the layout or image with too much text. This can feel overwhelming and busy. Leave room for white space.

White space (negative space) is the area found between design elements that enables them to stand out. Keep in mind that white space does not have to be white. It can be any color, texture, pattern, or image. Having negative space around other design elements such as text, images, logos, and call-to-action buttons enhances communication. It is tempting to pack as much text and images into available space to communicate more, but you'll probably end up communicating less or nothing. Use of white space helps focus a message to stand out and grab an audience's attention. It also helps establish a hierarchy of communication, guiding the reader on a path or flow through primary and secondary messages.[24]

Good images and layouts also tend to follow the rule of thirds. The **rule of thirds** is a principle that divides an image or layout into thirds horizontally and vertically to place elements in a more appealing, balanced way. This creates a grid of nine boxes and four lines. Research shows that people's eyes tend to focus on one of the intersection points rather than the center, where most amateurs tend to place the subject of their image or design. Instead, place the subject of the image in one of the intersecting points or "sweet spots" to create more dynamic, natural, and interesting layouts and images.[25] See figure 14.3 for the rule of thirds grid.

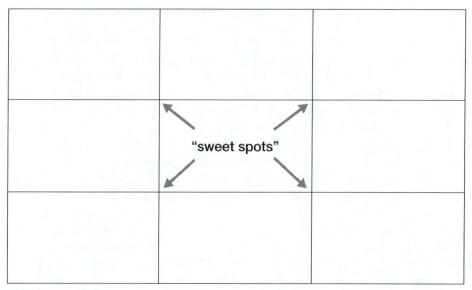

Figure 14.3. The rule of thirds creates more appealing and balanced images and layouts.

Also keep in mind that each platform is different in design standards and requirements. For specifics you can refer to each platform; most provide requirements such as sizing by pixels on their advertising/business webpages. In addition, many design tools created for social media posts include templates for the most popular platforms. Software tools that specialize in content creation vary but include Canva,[26] Adobe Spark,[27] and built-in platform-specific tools such as Facebook Creative Hub[28] and Snapchat Instant Create.[29] For additional details on using Adobe Spark for image, video, and design creation see LinkedIn Learning Adobe Spark Training and Tutorials at https://www.linkedin.com/learning/topics/adobe-spark-3 and Adobe Education Exchange Courses and Workshops at https://edex.adobe.com. For additional details on using Canva and design best practices, see Canva Design School at https://designschool.canva.com/courses. **LinkedIn Learning** is an online education site offering paid training courses and certifications for software, creative, and business skills.[30] LinkedIn Learning features content from Lynda.com and offers a monthly subscription, purchase of individual courses, and a free one-month trial. **Adobe Education Exchange** is an online site offering free courses, workshops, and teaching materials for Adobe Creative Suite.[31] **Canva Design School** is an online education site offering free training courses in design and using their software.[32]

Another consideration for content development is video and live broadcasts. Hootsuite suggests overall best practices for video. Try to record in HD for the best quality or if recording from a smartphone, use a tripod. Sound quality is important; it is suggested that you invest in an external microphone with windscreen and pop filter. Good lighting can make a big difference; video requires more light than still images. Invest in a couple of lights, placing two in front and two on the side of your subject to make lighting even and bright. Be sure to record for the platform, checking optimum dimensions, landscape, vertical, square, and file size.[33]

When recording, capture extra footage including close-ups and various angles to provide options for editing. Free editing programs such as iMovie and Windows Movie Makers will work, but paid options such as Final Cut Pro or Adobe Premiere provide more options and effects. Many people watch social video with the sound off, so be sure to add subtitles. Short videos tend to work better overall and some social platforms limit video to specific lengths, but longer videos can work on YouTube or with Live content.[34] **YouTube Creator Academy** is an online education site offering free training courses on creating and optimizing YouTube videos and channels.[35] For more details on creating YouTube videos plus optimizing YouTube channels, see YouTube Creator Academy at https://creatoracademy .youtube.com/page/home. If you're a YouTube partner manager or have access to Content ID, you can become YouTube Certified by learning more at https://support.google.com/ youtube/answer/7380223.

Live video is different in that you don't have time for additional footage and editing. Live can show authenticity and provide real-time engagement with brand communities but requires more preparation upfront. Live videos should be longer to allow time for more viewers to join in. Facebook suggests ten minutes to a couple of hours. A live broadcast will require extra people to use the camera, monitor sound, and manage comments. The presenter should make it a point to respond to audience questions and comment live. Test everything in private mode before going public. Live video also needs to be promoted ahead of time. Use the host social channel and other social channels to create buzz a couple of days before the broadcast. If your strategy is to create a series or show, be sure to set up a consistent weekly time and day.[36]

Best practices are a great place to start, but keep in mind that the best content is created to be unique to each platform customized to the environment and brand community. A one-size-fits-all post does not work across all social channels. People use different social platforms for different reasons with different expectations. You want to stand out within the environment, but not stand out as if your post were made for another platform and shared across all channels. Remember that what worked for one marketer will not necessarily work for your brand. Test variations in designs and copy to optimize as you go. This will keep posts fresh and avoid ad fatigue.

Sometimes you can't predict what will improve results. Will a green or red call-to-action button perform better? From the psychology of color, you may say red because it induces a feeling of excitement. But you may also argue for green because it could convey a feeling of confidence.[37] The only true way to know is to create both versions and test them with split testing or A/B testing. **A/B testing** is where two or more variants of a piece of content are shown to users at random and statistical analysis determines which performs better.[38]

Social Media Content Calendar

When and where should you distribute all of this brand social content? A main tool for content creation is a social media content calendar. A **content calendar** is a way to plan and visualize how content will be distributed during a specified period.[39] Note that many content calendars are built into social media software tools for easy auto scheduling and integration with cross-discipline team members. Shared online spreadsheets are also a good way to create content calendars.

The social media content calendar template in table 14.2 is good for strategic purposes and can be integrated into a social media plan as a table showing an example week of posting. The left side of the calendar template is where you place the social media channel and list the target audience or persona. If the social media strategy calls for multiple target audiences, the calendar should list each one individually and include all social channels being used to communicate with that target audience. Also note that one social channel may be used to communicate with multiple target audiences. For example, a college may use Facebook to communicate with both prospective students and their parents, so it may want to plan different content accordingly.

Next on the calendar, indicate which content will be distributed on which day, at what time, and identify the title or theme of the effort, such as Saucony's "Find Your Strong," Dove's "Real Beauty," or REI's "1440 Project." Assets specify what is needed for the post, including which images, videos, or links go with each post. Finally, indicate the hashtags and keywords that need to be included, from campaign and brand hashtags to trending topics. By researching best practices and by tracking brand results for days, times, themes, assets, hashtags/keywords, and repetition, content should be optimized for the greatest response.

You also must determine posting times and posting frequency by social platform. Perform a Google search on phrases such as "How often to post on _____ (insert each social media platform)?" or "When is the best time to post on _____ (insert each social media platform)?" to start with a research-informed schedule. As you execute the social media plan and measure results over time, you will discover your own best frequencies and times customized to your industry, target audience, and brand.[40]

The example content calendar is set for one week, but content calendars can be easily replicated to cover longer periods from a month or quarter up to an entire year. When developing a content calendar for the social media strategy, there are key questions to consider. What content is the target audience looking for in each platform? When are they most likely looking for it? What questions are they asking that the brand can answer? Consider educational and entertaining text, photo, and video content that delivers value. Which content will be brand-generated versus consumer-generated? Where will it be best delivered and how often? All decisions should be optimized by target and platform. Craft different versions of content, matching the proper format for each social platform.

Plan messages ahead of time, but also be flexible to fit in live, unscripted interactions with individual customers and to address emerging topics. Aim for a mix of real-time relevant content and longer-term evergreen content. **Evergreen content** is content that doesn't go out of date. It involves a topic that will always be relevant to your audience regardless of current topics, news, or season. Evergreen content is important because it can draw traffic to brand pages over a long period versus shorter spikes for time-specific topics.[41] One final consideration is to integrate your larger content marketing and digital marketing activities into the social media content calendar. Indicate when key pieces of other content are being published for promotion, including blog posts, articles, research, case studies, white papers/reports, eBooks, presentations, webinars, and email newsletters.[42] Content calendars can also become automated through various social media software that will select best days

Table 14.2. Social Media Content Calendar

Social Media Channel Target/Persona:	Mon. (time) Title/Theme: Assets: Tags/Keywords:	Tue. (time) Title/Theme: Assets: Tags/Keywords:	Wed. (time) Title/Theme: Assets: Tags/Keywords:	Thu. (time) Title/Theme: Assets: Tags/Keywords:	Fri. (time) Title/Theme: Assets: Tags/Keywords:	Sat. (time) Title/Theme: Assets: Tags/Keywords:	Sun. (time) Title/Theme: Assets: Tags/Keywords:

and times for you. For a list of content-scheduling software, see appendix B: Social Media Tools and Resources.

Remember that brands don't have to and shouldn't create all social media content on their own. Curation and user-generated content are important components of content creation. Women's and men's clothing company Betabrand keeps this in mind when creating and optimizing their ads for Facebook. They monitor their ads and posts, looking for comments that get the most likes and replies. When social media representatives notice that a user's comment receives a lot of likes or comments, they quickly publish related entertaining and useful information relevant to the conversation. The brand comments then drive users following the conversation to their website to generate sales leads.[43]

Social Media Metrics and Analytics

Now that you have a social media strategy and content schedule, ensure you have a plan to measure success based on social media metrics through analytics. **Metrics** are standards of measurement by which efficiency, performance, or progress can be assessed.[44] The metrics behind social media efforts are very important to gain approval and to prove ROI in order to acquire funding to implement and continue social media plans. Yet the sheer amount of data and the options of what can be collected and where may be overwhelming. The key to understanding social media metrics is knowing how to collect data, track metrics, and identify key performance indicators (KPIs) to link social media actions to business objectives for measurement and optimization.

The first place to look for social media metrics is the social media platforms. Top social channels each offer their own analytics, and certain metrics are the most important.[45] As examples, the specific metrics available from Facebook, Twitter, LinkedIn, Pinterest, Instagram, and YouTube will be explained. Engagement rate is a popular metric for social media professionals that is often used across social platforms. **Engagement rate** measures the amount of interaction social content earns relative to other audience figures such as reach. Engagement rate can be calculated against reach, post, or impressions. Other social media managers calculate daily engagement rates and cost per engagement. Cost per engagement is the total amount spent divided by total engagements. The metrics that are right for your plan depend on your unique objectives and what management considers to be valuable.[46]

Facebook Insights is the tool to track organic and paid performance on Facebook pages. This tool offers metrics on page posts such as likes (unlikes, organic likes, paid likes), reach, engagement, engagement rate, impressions, and demographic information for fans, plus additional people with whom brands have engaged. There are also detailed video stats including number of views.[47] **LinkedIn Analytics** is the tool that provides insights into company page performance for organic and paid brand actions. For updates, it provides insights on post performance with metrics such as impressions, clicks, likes, comments, and shares. Followers can be tracked by total number or broken down by organic (gained without advertising) and acquired (gained through sponsored content and ads). Visitors can be tracked by page views, unique visits, and separate career-page clicks with visitor demographics on business-focused variables such as seniority, industry, company size, and function.[48]

Twitter Analytics is the tool that measures organic and paid impact for brand account performance. It offers metrics including total tweets, tweet impressions, profile visits, mentions, followers, tweets linking to you, engagement rate, link clicks, retweets, likes, and replies. It also provides demographic, lifestyle, consumer behavior, and mobile information about followers. Twitter Analytics also measures the effectiveness of Twitter Cards. **Pinterest Analytics** is the tool that provides data on organic and paid pin performance. It delivers metrics as a daily average or for specific periods organized by impressions, repins, and clicks. It also provides demographic information for the people you reach by average monthly viewers and average monthly engaged by country, language, metro area, and gender. It shows interests, boards, and businesses that audiences are interested in. Pinterest Analytics can also provide brand website content metrics, including impressions, saves, clicks, and original (first-time) pins.[49]

Instagram Insights is the tool that details metrics on how people are viewing brand Instagram organic and paid content. It tracks overall metrics such as impressions, reach, website clicks, and profile views along with follower gender, age, and location information. It also reports post-specific metrics including likes, comments, saved, impressions, reach, engagement, and video views. With Instagram Stories, Insights also provides story impressions, reach, replies, and exits.[50] **YouTube Analytics** provides data on YouTube brand channel organic and paid video performance. It delivers data in different reports such as subscribers, subscriber status, traffic, traffic sources, views, watch time, earnings, likes, dislikes, comments, shares, favorites, devices, audience retention, and organic versus paid traffic. YouTube also offers demographic information on viewers such as location, age, and gender.[51]

These are just six of the top social media channels. Other social channels offer their own version. Metrics for social media platforms can often be obtained through third-party software tools, and metrics from various channels can also be collected in unified dashboards and reports within software tools. Once you understand the metric possibilities for each channel, the key to make it actionable is linking the specific metrics for each channel as KPIs to specific business objectives. Use a social media metrics template (see table 14.3) to help organize and visualize how specific social media channel data and business objectives come together to measure the success of social media marketing efforts. Place your business objective or objectives across the top. The number of columns you use depends on the number of objectives. In the left column, place each social media platform. Each platform should be in a separate row. Therefore, the number of rows you have is dependent on the number of social platforms in your plan.

Identify the broader business objectives, making sure they are quantified and time bound—expressed as business objectives that follow SMART guidelines. This was discussed in chapter 4 and should have been established at the beginning of the social media strategy plan. A startup or business with a new product or service may be focused on building awareness among a certain target audience (views, reach, impressions, demographic data, etc.). Another company or organization may have issues with reputation and be looking to change perception (negative to positive sentiment). Or perhaps the business needs to drive leads or online sales (traffic sources, conversion pages, etc.). Maybe a brand needs to focus on retention of existing customers for continued sales or recruiting of new customers via word-of-mouth (likes, comments, shares, etc.). An organization may also have all of these

Table 14.3. Social Media Metrics Template

Social Media Channel	Business Objective 1:*	Business Objective 2:*	Business Objective 3:*	Business Objective 4:*
	KPI:	KPI:	KPI:	KPI:
	KPI:	KPI:	KPI:	KPI:
	KPI:	KPI:	KPI:	KPI:
	KPI:	KPI:	KPI:	KPI:

*Ensure objectives follow SMART guidelines (specific, measureable, achievable, relevant, and time bound) and refer to business objectives to connect social media activity to organization mission and goals to measure ROI.

objectives and more, as long as they are quantified and assigned unique KPIs for each social channel.

The Sprout Social research highlighted in chapter 4 found that marketers' top business goals for social media are to increase brand awareness, increase sales, increase leads, increase community engagement, grow brand audience, and increase web traffic. Whichever goals you choose, now you are connecting specific metrics. Sprout Social suggests the following metric KPIs for each business goal category:

- Brand Awareness: followers, impressions, traffic, share of voice, reach
- Sales/Leads: sales revenue, lead conversion, non-revenue conversions, email sign-ups
- Community Engagement: clicks, likes, shares, comments, mentions
- Brand Audience: mentions, followers, share of voice, engagement rate
- Web Traffic: traffic, link clicks, conversions, email sign-up, product trials[52]

Your plan should be unique in connecting your specific social platform metrics to your business objectives, but this gives you an idea of where to start. Also remember that you will not be measuring these once at the beginning of the plan and once at the end, six months or

Figure 14.4. Software tools can collect social metrics from data analytics dashboards.

© Nico ElNino / iStock Photo

a year later. The idea is to identify what KPI metrics you will measure and track in real time to optimize efforts as you go. Overall strategies and plans should be set and revaluated yearly, but individual campaigns, promotions, and tactics should be measured and optimized continuously throughout the year. Managers may require reports quarterly, monthly, or weekly. Many software tools make it easy to set up dashboards of KPI metrics and schedule analytics reports generated and automatically sent to specific team members on a regular basis. You should track the effectiveness of different strategies and tactics as shown in figure 6.6.

An additional tool to help link social activity to business goals to prove ROI is integrating Google Analytics on websites with social media. Google Analytics Social Reports break down social traffic to let businesses know how and which social media efforts are working. The Social Conversions report shows which social networks lead to website conversions. Conversions can be anything from a direct sale to a download, an email subscription, an event registration, a quote request, or more. Setting up Google Analytics goals with specific dollar values per conversion will show dollar values per social channel. This helps determine where to focus time and money beyond followers and engagement and connects social media to the bottom line.[53] Using social media monitoring, publishing, and analytics tools such as Hootsuite, HubSpot, Salesforce, Sysomos, and NUVI, or other tools like Social Mention, True Social Metrics, Sprout, and Buffer can also help track and organize social metrics. For a more complete list of options, see appendix B: Social Media Tools and Resources.

Another way to make sense of social media metrics is to organize the data by key social media metrics categories. Social media expert Jay Baer of Convince & Convert suggests four

Dark Social

Mark Zuckerberg opened a more recent Facebook F8 keynote saying, "The Future is Private." He explained that Facebook was created to be a digital town square to share thoughts, opinions, and beliefs. Yet today people don't want to be that public anymore and conversations are shifting from the town square to the living room. Social networks have become so big many people no longer feel comfortable sharing openly and are shifting their interaction to private messaging apps.[a] What type of content is being shared via dark social? GlobalWebIndex research has found people share personal photos (72 percent), entertaining photos or videos (70 percent), links to websites (50 percent), good deals or discounts (49 percent), links to social media posts (48 percent), and links to pictures of a product (45 percent).[b]

Dark social is web traffic with no referral data because the link was shared through unmeasurable social media.[c] This can happen when direct URLs are copied and pasted to be shared through email, texting, secure browsing, direct messages (DMs), or messaging apps such as WhatsApp, WeChat, and Facebook Messenger. Why is it dark? In analytics programs like Google Analytics, this traffic appears to be direct traffic as if the exact URL was manually typed into the browser. Yet that is highly unlikely when you have complicated, long URLs. Links shared this way are missing referral tags, which makes them hard to track. GetSocial has found that 69 percent of social shares are dark social and that 71 percent of shares are made by copying and pasting a link. They also found that 63 percent of people prefer to share via private messaging apps versus social media (54 percent), SMS/texting (48 percent), and email (37 percent).[d]

Once a brand is aware of dark social traffic, there are steps to start measuring its impact including (1) using shortened URLs to share unique links in social networks and emails or on websites to track clicks; (2) adding social share buttons on websites for visitors to use instead of copying and pasting the direct URL to track referral traffic;[e] (3) using Google Analytics to narrow direct traffic to referrals that are most likely dark social using advanced audience segments by behavior filtering to remove easy-to-remember web pages;[f] (4) tracking dark social traffic with share buttons and HTML codes that find copy-and-paste shares of page content or URLs.[g] These tools include GetSocial.io, SiteCTRL, AddThis, ShareThis, Bitly, and Po.st.[h]

Another approach is to interact directly with consumers in these dark social channels, creating more relevant and shareable content in the private environments. Dark social shouldn't be thought of as something that is bad. It simply represents opportunities to provide one-to-one customer service and interactions with customers. These types of strategies were discussed in chapter 7 with messaging apps including conversational commerce (c-commerce). At the end of this chapter artificial intelligence will be discussed, including how AI-powered chatbots can help scale one-on-one interactions with customers in messaging apps.

[a] João Romão, "'The End of Likes': The Last Meaningless Proxy for Social Media Success?" Blog .GetSocial.com, May 9, 2019, https://blog.getsocial.io/the-end-of-likes/.

[b] Olivia Valentine, "How Brands Can Capitalize on the Rise of Dark Social," Blog.Global WebIndex.com, April 8, 2019, https://blog.globalwebindex.com/chart-of-the-week/brands -capitalizing-on-the-rise-of-dark-social/.

[c] Alexis C. Madrigal, "Dark Social: We Have the Whole History of the Web Wrong," The Atlantic.com, October 12, 2012, https://www.theatlantic.com/technology/archive/2012/10/ dark-social-we-have-the-whole-history-of-the-web-wrong/263523/.

ᵈ Andreia Loureiro, "Dark Social: An Expert Guide to Answer All of Your Questions," Blog.Get Social.com, May 2, 2019, https://blog.getsocial.io/dark-social/.

ᵉ "The Dark Side of Mobile Sharing," RadiumOne.com, June 7, 2016, https://radiumone.com/wp-content/uploads/2016/08/radiumone-the-dark-side-of-mobile-sharing-June-7-2016.pdf.

ᶠ Rachel Moore, "How to Track Dark Social Traffic in Google Analytics," SocialMedia Examiner.com, July 26, 2017, http://www.socialmediaexaminer.com/how-to-track-dark-social-traffic-in-google-analytics/.

ᵍ "The Dark Side of Mobile Sharing," RadiumOne.com.

ʰ Keith Quesenberry, "Shedding Light on Dark Social Media," SocialMediaToday.com, August 4, 2017, https://www.socialmediatoday.com/social-networks/shedding-light-dark-social-media.

categories of social media metrics to measure success of content marketing efforts, including (1) consumption metrics, which are how many people viewed, downloaded, or listened to social media content; (2) sharing metrics, which measure how relevant the social content is and how often is it shared with others; (3) lead-generation metrics, which measure how often social media content consumption results in a lead; and (4) sales metrics, which measure whether money was made from social media content.

The last category of sales metrics is often the most important, but marketers have known for decades that not all marketing action can be directly attributable to sales. For example, traditional media advertising such as TV, radio, billboards, or magazine and newspaper ads are seen as valuable contributors to metrics such as awareness, opinion, or recall, but don't always lead to a direct, traceable sales action. These contributions are often expressed in traditional marketing with the sales or purchase funnel as discussed in chapter 5. Think of each social media metric category in a similar way—each is important and leads to the others. The related social media journey can be thought of as consumption, then sharing, and finally lead generation and sales.

The number of social media channels, each channel's unique metrics, and social media monitoring and analytics options can be overwhelming. Yet it becomes more manageable by taking a step back and connecting specific KPI metrics to each business objective, and then finding the right tools to collect and monitor that data. But be careful not to place too much emphasis only on last-touch attribution. Tools like Google Analytics are great but may only report on the last visited digital location before a conversion. Looking only at the end of the buyer's journey could discount the important role of other social media and brand content. Be sure to include metrics that track performance at each stage of the buyer cycle (pre-purchase, purchase, post-purchase) and purchase funnel (awareness, interest, desire, action). See figure 5.3 for more perspective.

Link management is one way to ensure measurement across all purchase stages and multiple digital channels. A link management tool like Bit.ly can improve visibility of every touch point, control where consumers are sent, and show results for insights. Bit.ly can create branded customized shortened links and unique customer-specific links that integrate with CRM systems such as Salesforce and HubSpot for easy measurement and optimization. Companies like TrendKite are advancing public relations analytics to measure and report earned media's contributions to the bottom line. And location-based platforms such as HYP3R are emphasizing the value of location-based engagement with high-value customers. For more detail on social analytics, see Google Analytics Academy Google Analytics training and certification at https://skillshop.exceedlms.com/student/path/2938-google-analytics-individual-qualification. **Google Analytics Academy** is an online education site offering free training and professional certifications for Google Analytics.[54]

Social Media Budget

You have worked hard on researching and developing a social media strategy, schedule, and metrics, but how much will it cost? Budgeting is an important part of social strategy and most likely will be necessary if you want your strategy executed. Few managers or business owners will approve any effort without first knowing the cost. Understanding expense is also an important step to calculating ROI. This can be easier if you follow a budgeting process. See table 14.4 for an example social media budget template.

In the budget template, costs are broken down into five expense categories and each category is divided into in-house costs (to be performed by employees) and outsource costs (to be hired out). Also calculate the percentage of each line item under a category and the percentage of each category out of the total budget to understand where the most money is being spent.

Table 14.4. Social Media Budget Template

Budget Category Type/Description	In-House Expense Fixed/Percentage	Outsource Expense Fixed/Percentage	Total Category Fixed/Percentage
Content Creation	($ per hour x hours per month)	(# pieces content x $ per piece/project)	<u>$ %</u>
Writing			$ %
Graphics			$ %
Video			$ %
Social Advertising	(N/A)	($ per day x days per month)	<u>$ %</u>
(social channel 1)			$ %
(social channel 2)			$ %
(social channel 3)			$ %
Social Engagement	($ per hour x hours per month)	($ per hour x hours per month)	<u>$ %</u>
(social channel 1)			$ %
(social channel 2)			$ %
(social channel 3)			$ %
Software/Tools	(N/A)	($ per month)	<u>$ %</u>
Monitoring			$ %
Scheduling			$ %
Analytics			$ %
Promotions/Contests	($ per campaign)	($ per campaign)	<u>$ %</u>
(social channel 1)			$ %
(social channel 2)			$ %
(social channel 3)			$ %
Total	$ %	$ %	$

After understanding how each category is contributing more or less to overall success, consider adjusting budget category percentages to match contribution level. Each item and category is calculated as a monthly expense and percentage of the total per the five categories of content creation, social advertising, social engagement, software/tools, and promotions/contests.

"Content Creation" covers in-house or outsourced time to write and design social media plus any fixed costs such as stock photos or video production. Estimate time to create the content needed for the strategy in a month. Brands can get an idea of how much content is needed from the previously discussed content calendar. For in-house employees, divide salary into an hourly rate. For outsourced help, calculate by their hourly rate or their cost per piece or project.

"Social Advertising" is paid, outsourced costs for reach per social channel such as Facebook, LinkedIn, Twitter, Pinterest, Instagram, and Snapchat. Start with the content calendar and estimate how many posts will be paid/sponsored native ads or promoted/boosted posts. Then calculate costs based on current rates per social media network. Because much of social advertising works on a bidding process, many brands set per-day limits. Thus, this category is estimated based on spending per day, per network, multiplied by the number of days a brand expects to be running social ads in a month.

"Social Engagement" is the cost for employees or contractors to listen and respond to brand talk per channel. Listening and engagement are important activities in social media. They cannot be planned ahead of time but, based on current activity and planned strategies, this cost can be estimated. An idea of the level of customer activity on brand social media channels can be gauged from a social media audit. Are there hundreds or even thousands of posts every day or a few dozen? From there, estimate hours per day needed to engage all or a percentage of those customers per channel. Multiply the number of hours by employee or outsourced rates.

"Software/Tools" covers monthly costs for social media monitoring and other automation services. These can help save time and money in other categories such as content creation and engagement. There are many free tools, but to get access to advanced features and enterprise-level service you must pay. This budget category is broken down into monitoring, scheduling, and analytics as a first step. Depending on what software you find, it may be useful to add categories such as consumer research, customer service, automation, or scheduling software. A software solution may also cover multiple categories, thus eliminating the need for categories. Or a software solution may provide services outside the scope of social media, such as Salesforce and CRM. In that case, divide a percentage of the cost for the integrated systems by social media–only services. Some tools may have one-time costs, but most are billed as monthly access fees.

"Promotions/Contests" are costs for prizes, discounts, and coupons. Besides buying reach through social ads, many businesses build audience and engagement through special offers and contests. Whether they are executed through a Facebook app, hashtag, or unique offer code, sales promotions have hard costs associated with them. In this category, estimate those expenses per campaign. For example, a brand may offer a summer campaign and a holiday campaign, or campaigns that coincide with specific holidays that include promotions and contests. A brand may also have a social campaign built around a live event that includes promotions and contests that have costs that need to be included.

Finally, add totals per month, per line item, and per category. Also calculate the percentage of each category and the category percentage of the total budget. As a general guideline, one survey found that top social media costs were internal employee compensation (37 percent), followed by social media advertising (18 percent), external staff compensation (10 percent), and content costs (7 percent).[55] These percentages are a good way to estimate how much a social media strategy will cost to execute.[56]

A way to put total social media budgets into context is to compare them to those of competitors. The social media audit may have uncovered insight that a main competitor is much more active in social media and seeing business success as a result. A brand's strategy may then be to increase social activity to compete and the budget becomes an estimate of what it costs to match the competitor's level of social media engagement or social media voice. Another way to put social media budgets into context is to compare them to industry standards by looking at typical percentages of overall marketing spending and social spending. Take the existing marketing budget and estimate social media spending based on current standards. The CMO Survey indicates that businesses now spend an average of 11 percent of their marketing budget on social media and this number is expected to increase to 20 percent by 2024.[57]

How do you know if the total is too much or too little overall? A general guideline would be to take the brand's existing marketing budget as a percentage of revenue (businesses spend an average of 10 percent of revenue on marketing, but this varies by industry),[58] and then calculate a percentage of the marketing budget (such as 11 percent) dedicated to social media. If the estimated budget from the social media budget template is significantly off from this general number, then the social media plan and/or the business objectives may need to be adjusted to fit available resources. Another option is to start with the general estimate and then complete the budget template to see what level of social engagement the brand can afford. If a brand is budgeting against a social media strategic plan tied to real business objectives and the right metrics are in place, then ROI can be justified. Hootsuite has reported that small businesses in Canada (fewer than twenty employees) spend an average of $30,000 on social media marketing. Mid-sized companies (Twenty to forty-nine employees) spend $60,000 on average, and companies with more than fifty employees spend more than $100,000 annually.[59] Since most marketing budgets, business objectives, and reports are set on a yearly basis, you can see how it is useful to set your social media plan, objectives, and budget on the same time frame.

Artificial Intelligence

Artificial intelligence (AI) is a buzzword that can be confusing and even scary. Some predict AI robots will replace humans, but here we will focus on what AI exists now and how it can help improve your social media strategy and make it more efficient. AI-empowered social media can assist in many areas such as content optimization and generation, 24/7 engagement, automated bidding and placement of social ads, enhanced audience targeting, automated analytics, personalization, and social listening.[60] **Artificial intelligence** is computer systems performing tasks that normally require human intelligence.[61]

Simpler forms of technology used to improve social media efforts include automation of functions and activities. **Automation** is software that does tasks without human intervention.[62] Examples include Amazon tracking shopping history to suggest similar items to automate cross-selling. Automated testing pulls data to generate scheduled reports. And automated reminders help employees and customers through alerts and notifications.[63] **Drip marketing** automates sending a series of communications on a schedule or by consumer trigger actions.[64] Drip marketing has used email for years but also now uses chatbots in Facebook messenger.[65]

More advanced AI methods include machine learning, natural language processing and generation, plus image recognition. **Machine learning** is when computers learn from experience by modifying processes from new input.[66] Machine learning can use algorithms to try random variables to learn which work best to achieve a goal such as lowest cost per impression or acquisition. Programmatic advertising uses machine learning and automated bidding and placement for social media ad buying.[67] **Natural language processing (NLP)** finds linguistic patterns to analyze and synthesize speech.[68] NLP is how Hootsuite Insights determines sentiment of brand social media conversations[69] and software solutions like Dataminr monitor real-time social conversations for crisis communication and real-time marketing.[70] **Natural language generation (NLG)** takes non-language inputs and generates spoken language.[71] Phrasee uses NLG to help organizations generate AI-powered copywriting, creating data-driven, human-sounding brand copy for Facebook and Instagram.[72]

Image recognition or computer vision is software that can recognize people, animals, and other objects.[73] Brandwatch has an image detection and analysis tool that finds images containing a brand to report how, when, and where consumers are seeing it.[74] CrowdRiff uses image recognition to discover user-generated content (UGC).[75] They combine this with brand-owned images and performance data for content optimization. Pinterest has AI-powered visual search called Pinterest Lens[76] and brands can purchase search ads to appear in that search and use Shop the Look pins.[77]

Other AI tools include predictive and prescriptive analytics, plus virtual assistants. **Predictive analytics** helps understand future performance based on current and historical data.[78] **Prescriptive analytics** helps determine the best solution among various choices.[79] Salesforce's Einstein uses AI for customer and lead predictions and recommendations. Einstein analyzes sentiment and intent to route social conversations to the right person, streamlining workflow.[80] IBM's Watson uses AI for campaign automation and marketing personalization.[81] **Intelligent virtual assistants** add a human interface to software to answer questions and respond to commands.[82] Watson Assistant replaces tedious queries and spreadsheets with simple questions such as "How did social media perform this month?"[83]

AI-empowered chatbots can be used for drip marketing automation, lead nurturing, onboarding, renewals, confirmations, and engagement. Chatbots can also help lead customers through the sales funnel. For awareness, bots can initiate conversation at scale, communicating one-to-one with five or five hundred people. At the interest stage, bots provide 24/7 engagement at the moment of interest. In the decision stage, bots supply information, answer questions, and send content. For the action stage, the bot can complete smaller purchases or hand off more complex ones to a human.[84] AI-powered support can improve customer service via social media. ManyChat's Facebook Messenger chatbots give customers

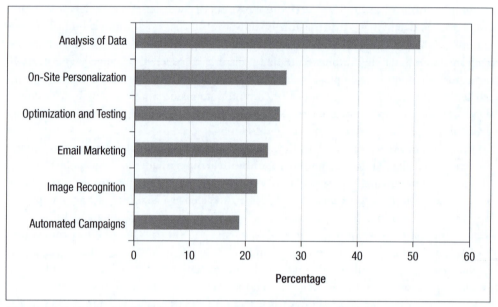

Figure 14.5. Marketing-Related Use of Artificial Intelligence (AI)

Source: "Marketing-related use of artificial intelligence (AI) according to industry professionals worldwide as of January 2018, by region," Adobe, November 07, 2019, https://www.statista.com/statistics/915372/marketing-related -use-artificial-intelligence-world/

convenience and speed. Simple chatbots spot keywords and respond with predetermined answers. AI-powered chatbots use NLP to create conversations like human agents. When problems get too complex, chatbots can recognize this and hand off the conversation to a real agent. Some report chatbots could save businesses $11 billion in support costs by 2025.[85]

Pattern89 uses AI to analyze billions of data points daily to discover what social ad dimensions drive customer behavior. Their AI analyzes every combination of placement, device, interests, age ranges, behaviors, and demographics for custom optimization insights.[86] Clinch provides personalized programmatic social media content across the customer journey. AI enables them to generate unlimited personalized ad versions with real-time optimization for text, image, and video.[87] Motiva AI works with Oracle's Eloqua marketing platform to scan campaigns and make performance recommendations, optimize time and frequency suggestions, run auto multivariate messaging experiments, and automatically discover new audience segments.[88] See figure 14.5 for the top marketing-related uses of artificial intelligence.[89]

Theoretically Speaking: Uses and Gratification

Why do people find media valuable? Uses and gratifications has been a core theory in communications since the early 1970s. Researchers such as Jay Blumler, Elihu Katz, Michael Gurevitch, and Alan Rubin first developed this theory. To them it represented a dramatic shift from previous mass-communications research. It flipped the perspective from studying what mass media does to people to what people do to mass media.[90] **Uses and gratifications**

theory proposes that audiences are active in media consumption and that they consciously select media content to satisfy their various needs. This theory also shifted perspective in another way by suspending judgments about the cultural value of content. Uses and gratifications assume all content has a potential functional value.[91] Today this even applies to funny cat videos or any meme. Some people value them simply for the entertainment.

With the current increased use of interactive and social media, uses and gratifications theory has taken on new dimensions. Shyam Sundar and Anthony Limperos write about this transition in "Uses and Grats 2.0: New Gratifications for New Media." The authors argue that with the development of interactive, two-way media, more and different gratifications are being sought and obtained from media. Understanding how consumers use various media and the different gratifications they seek can help brands tailor traditional and social media content to be more effective. Some of the proposed new gratifications sought by consumers from media technology include modality, agency, interactivity, and navigability. Modality or forms include realism, coolness, novelty, and "being there." Agency or ability to act independently includes agency-enhancement, community building, bandwagon, filtering/tailoring, and ownness, which is being unique to oneself. Interactivity includes interaction, activity, responsiveness, and dynamic control. Navigability includes browsing/variety-seeking, scaffolds/navigation aids, and play/fun.

Social media professionals can look at these media technology gratifications and consider how knowing the gratification sought by a target audience could influence the content produced in a social media plan.[92] A good example of uses and grats in practice is the Lay's "Do Us A Flavor" campaign discussed in chapter 11. Instead of posting ads in social media to get people to try the brand's new potato chip flavor, Lays let customers determine that flavor. The brand turned it into a game with interactivity and navigability with variety seeking. The modality played up novelty, and agency included ownness and community building.

Leap of Faith?

It is one thing to create a smart social media strategy; it is another to sell it to management and implement it in the real world. The *Guardian* looked at this issue when reporting results of a poll of global senior marketers. The survey found that only half of all boardrooms were convinced about social media's value.[93] Why don't executives believe in the business power of social media? It's hard to see the value of social media if a person is not actively using it. According to another survey, fewer than half of CEOs of top companies in the United States and United Kingdom have a social media presence.[94] Thus, many marketing, advertising, and public relations professionals may face roadblocks when presenting social media plans and pitches to the executive level.

It is easier to understand the influence of a TV commercial on purchasing decisions when one has the personal experience of watching TV. It is harder to see how Facebook or Instagram could influence a purchase decision when one does not personally use the social media networks. However, the bottom line is that social media marketing works, not because executives are using it but because the customer is using it to acquire purchasing-decision information. And this reality will impact the organization's bottom line as social engagement becomes an increasingly influential factor in consumers' purchasing decisions.

Figure 14.6. Social media professionals must make presentations to get executive buy-in.

© Jacob Lund / iStock Photo

Because of this reality, social media strategists must not only understand social media and how to complete and execute plans, but they must also play another role. In addition to being a social media strategist, a social media professional must also be willing to be a social media educator. It is the social media manager's job to help executive decision makers understand that the world is embracing social media and it is influencing business results. Explain that customers are making purchasing decisions in social media about consumer products and services and about business-to-business products and services. Show the data that proves more and more consumers are relying on social media to help them determine what products and services to buy.

Be sure to build a solid social media strategic plan, but also plan to build a solid case for social media acceptance. For a social media plan to be successful, it must first be approved. Build the case for organizational use of social media and be prepared to combat corporate-suite skepticism. It may be helpful to follow other brand examples, like Dove, which built social media efforts slowly over time. Complete the full plan, but gain approval for smaller-scale efforts that can be supplemented as success is proven.

Chapter 14 Checklist

Social media can change quickly. Visit Post Control Marketing (http://www.postcontrol marketing.com) for updates, but also use this chapter checklist to briefly check how social media statistics in this chapter have changed since publication.

MINI CASE

Saucony Find Your Strong

Saucony is a brand of shoes and apparel that focuses on the sport of running. The company is unique from other brands that manufacture products for multiple sports. To emphasize this difference, the brand wanted to create a campaign that really connected with their exclusive target audience of runners.

The result was the "Find Your Strong Project." Find Your Strong was described on the Saucony microsite as: "This Site Is Dedicated to You, The Runner. You are our inspiration and the reason we do what we do. Rather than tell you how we feel about running, we'd rather hear from you." Emphasizing interactivity and leveraging two-way social media, the campaign was based on an ever-changing Running Manifesto of user-generated social media content. The brand community website featured live aggregated content of sayings and photos from real runners sharing their passion for running and the brand. User-generated brand content was shared on Twitter sent to @Saucony or posted with #findyourstrong.[a] The campaign also integrated traditional print and banner ads in publications like *Runner's World*, but most of the effort was delivered through social media such as Twitter, Facebook, blogs, and YouTube videos.

The campaign increased social media followers from ten thousand to one million in just three years. Chris Lindner, CMO of Saucony, said, "The message was whether you run to get physically stronger or for other reasons, people were finding strength from running. . . . We didn't say, 'Be like Saucony.' We said, 'Find your strong.' People really internalized that and shared their stories with us."[b] During those three years, the Find Your Strong campaign helped to propel Saucony into becoming the fastest-growing brand in the running channel.[c] The brand found a way to translate product features into customer benefits and express them using social media in a way that invited participation. Saucony also created a campaign that helps lessen the pressure and workload of generating all social media content themselves.

Today the brand has the "Run for Good Saucon Community" and Shop Social that aggregates user-generated content around the hashtag #RunForGood and @Saucony and then pairs what the runner is wearing with suggested related shoes to purchase on their website.[d] Along with the effort the brand launched the world's first Instagram relay race around the world on Global Running Day to raise money for health-related charities. For each mile run they donate money to charities for those who post selfies on Instagram and tag #RunForGood and @Saucony. The goal is to raise $50,000 over the 24,901 miles.[e]

[a] "The Find Your Strong Project," Saucony.com, accessed January 20, 2015, http://community.saucony.com/findyourstrongproject/.

[b] Amy Gesenhues, "Get to Know: CMO & SVP of Business Development for Sperry Top-Sider Chris Linder," MarketingLand.com, July 16, 2014, http://marketingland.com/get-know-cmo-svp-sperry-top-sider-chris-lindner-90798.

[c] Meredith Derby Berg, "Saucony Finishes Strong With Its 'Find Your Strong' Strategy," AdAge.com, January 27, 2014, http://adage.com/article/news/saucony-finishes-strong-find-strong-strategy/291329.

[d] "Shop Social Gallery," Saucony.com, accessed November 8, 2019, https://www.saucony.com/en/shopsocial/.

[e] Victoria Pallien, "Run for Good: Saucony Launches Instagram Relay Race," DigitalMediaSolutions.com, June 24, 2019, https://insights.digitalmediasolutions.com/articles/saucony-instagram-relay-race.

✓ How has social media content creation changed? What are the best practices for marketers, advertisers, and public relations professionals to follow? What types of text, images, and video are garnering the most engagement? How does it vary by social media platform? Is there a new social platform where the best practices don't apply? Has AI taken over social media content writing, image, and post creation?

✓ How has social media measurement changed? What are the key social media metrics that marketers, advertisers, and public relations professionals use to measure performance today? Which platforms have new analytics capabilities and what metrics have been added to the social media platform analytics described here? Are there new cross-platform metrics tools?

✓ How has social media budgeting changed? Are there new categories of social media expenses? Have social media budgets in general increased? Is the average marketing spending on social media still around 11 percent or has it increased to 20 percent or more?

SOCIAL PLAN PART 14

Compile the Parts and Sell the Story

For this final part of the plan, collect all other social plan parts, 1 through 13, that have been completed throughout the book. Pull these sections together into one cohesive social media marketing story. Strategically this is a plan to follow, but also a story to sell. Even though most leaders know social media is important and want to do something with it, most are still skeptical of social media methods. This plan will serve as a reference to follow, but also to show and present to organization decision makers in order to get social media efforts approved, funded, and running.

Begin by pulling out the main sections from each part of the plan completed from chapters 1 to 13. Compile the sections into a single report that tells the overall social media story, from research, target audience, and insight to big idea, selected social channels, content, schedule, metrics, and budget. As you tell the social media plan story, remember to support and quantify everything with outside references and data to build a strong and convincing argument. Don't forget to define social media terms for full context and understanding. Most executives may not be familiar with social media terminology. Also, remember that a picture is worth a thousand words. Use screen grabs and charts and graphs when appropriate to provide a more complete and convincing vision of the proposed effort.

Finally, put the pieces together in an order that makes sense. Start with a big picture of the current situation, objectives, and background leading up to the brilliant-solution big idea and executions in the selected ideal social media channels. Explain why you chose those channels and help people see what the campaign will look like with example content posts. Show at least one "mock up" post per social media channel, visually set in screen grabs of the environment to make each post look as real as possible. Use Canva, Adobe Spark, or social platform tools like Facebook Creative Hub to design these. Provide an example content schedule to preview weekly activity. Ensure that metrics are explained to show how success will be measured, and finally, estimate costs to secure final approval. While structure of the final plan document and presentation can vary, below is an example social media plan format and order to follow:

1. Provide an overview of the brand, main competitor, and current marketing communication activities including a SWOT graphic summary (see figure 4.1).
2. Identify overall business objectives, define the target audience (demographics and psychographics), and describe their social media use.
3. Include the social media audit results in a table and describe insights gained (see table 4.2).
4. Explain social media strategy big idea with theme/hashtag and how it integrates with traditional media including digital marketing, advertising, and PR.
5. Provide the social media platforms added and removed with selection rationale considering user statistics, culture, and content.
6. Create a buyer persona (see chapter 12), write and design content in appropriate formats for each social platform, and include a content calendar with optimal posting dates/times, keywords, calls to action, and links (see table 14.2).
7. Include other sections important to the individual organization such as a social media and privacy policy, crisis communication and event plan, influencer/advocate guidelines and discloser requirements, or software and discipline integration recommendations.
8. Identify metrics by social platform and business objective using the metrics template (see table 14.3) to show how success will be measured and efforts optimized while considering specific analytics software tools and methods for tracking.
9. Estimate costs with a budget using a method described in chapter 14 following the social media budget template (see table 14.4). Indicate which social media platforms (e.g., Facebook) and programs (e.g., Influencers) will require/include ad spending.
10. Provide an overall introduction and conclusion or executive summary.

Once the formal written report is complete, create a presentation to sell the plan in person to organization management and decision makers. Keep slides simple, using them for visual support, and tell the audience the social media story. Once you have obtained approval, be sure to take social media law, ethics, and etiquette into consideration as you move toward implementation (see chapter 15).

For a condensed version of the social plan see appendix A: Three-Part Social Plan. Also refer to the key elements (subhead section outline) of a social media plan provided in the Social Media Strategic Plan box in chapter 6 and again provided in appendix A: Three-Part Social Plan.

KEY CONCEPTS

strategic thinking
customer lifetime value
active voice
passive voice
point of view
landing page
white space (negative space)
rule of thirds
LinkedIn Learning

Adobe Education Exchange
Canva Design School
YouTube Creator Academy
A/B testing
content calendar
evergreen content
metrics
engagement rate
Facebook Insights

LinkedIn Analytics

Twitter Analytics

Pinterest Analytics

Instagram Insights

YouTube Analytics

dark social

Google Analytics Academy

artificial intelligence

automation

drip marketing

machine learning

natural language processing (NLP)

natural language generation (NLG)

image recognition

predictive analytics

prescriptive analytics

intelligent virtual assistants

uses and gratifications theory

QUESTIONS FOR DISCUSSION

1. The Saucony "Find Your Strong" and "Run for Good" campaigns rely heavily on user-generated content. Find another example of a brand that uses fan content as a main component of its social media efforts and explain how they motivate or reward participation.

2. Conduct a brief content analysis of NASCAR's social media presence. What strategy are they following and what kind of content are they producing? How has their strategy evolved and how does it compare to other professional sports such as the NHL or FIFA?

3. Measurement, metrics, budgeting, and ROI are very important. Do some research and determine what experts agree to be the top social media metrics that prove real ROI.

4. Ethics in social media is an important consideration with metrics, analytics, and ROI. How confident can you be in the numbers that social media platforms report? Is there any wiggle room in the way numbers could be reported to clients? Do some research into fake and over-inflated metrics in social media. How big is the problem and what should be done?

ADDITIONAL EXERCISES

1. For this exercise, go to Seth Godin's blog (https://seths.blog) and read through some of the thousands of posts he has made over the years. Be sure to cover earlier and later periods. What do you notice about the posts? Are they all of equal quality? If each is not an earth-shattering insight, then what is consistent that has drawn hundreds of thousands of readers over time? What specifically can you learn from Seth Godin's persistence and consistency that you can apply to your social media strategy? List at least three qualities.

2. For this exercise, go back to the uses and gratifications theory. Look at the proposed new gratifications consumers seek from media technology by Shyam Sundar and Anthony Limperos. Select the gratifications that most apply to social media. Next, select five different social media categories or channels (that is, social networks and media sharing or Facebook and YouTube) and list the types of gratifications each social channel or category could possibly satisfy. Finally, brainstorm and explain examples of the type of brand content that would be created for each type of gratification within each social channel or category.

Notes

1. "Hal Higdon Quotes," GoodReads.com, accessed November 6, 2019, http://www.good reads.com/author/quotes/69749.Hal_Higdon.

2. Wiktionary, "See the forest for the trees," accessed November 6, 2019, http://en.m .wiktionary.org/wiki/see_the_forest_for_the_trees.

3. Robert Kabacoff, "Develop Strategic Thinkers throughout Your Organization," *Harvard Business Review*, February 7, 2014, https://hbr.org/2014/02/develop-strategic-thinkers-throughout -your-organization.

4. Craig Smith, "How Many People Use 800+ of the Top Social Media, Apps and Digital Services?" DMR Digital Marketing Ramblings, January 23, 2015, http://expandedramblings.com/index .php/resource-how-many-people-use-the-top-social-media.

5. "Hal Higdon Biography," HalHigdon.com, accessed November 6, 2019, http://www.hal higdon.com/biography.

6. Keith A. Quesenberry, "Social Media Is Like Running a Marathon," PostControlMarketing .com, July 31, 2014, http://www.postcontrolmarketing.com/?p=1938.

7. Jay Baer, "Are You Slow Enough to Succeed in Social Media?" ConvinceAndConvert .com, accessed November 6, 2019, http://www.convinceandconvert.com/social-media-strategy/ are-you-slow-enough-to-succeed-in-social-media/.

8. Seth Godin, "Trading Favors," SethGodin.typepad.com, July 31, 2014, http://sethgodin .typepad.com/seths_blog/2014/07/trading-favors.html.

9. Matthew Rocco, "Fortune 500 Brands Ride Shotgun as NASCAR Grows," Fox Business.com, July 30, 2013, http://www.foxbusiness.com/industries/2013/07/30/fortune-500 -brands-ride-shotgun-as-nascar-grows.

10. Alicia Jessop, "NASCAR's Innovative Social Media Approach Leads to Significant Growth in Fan Base," Forbes.com, November 17, 2012, http://www.forbes.com/sites/aliciajessop/2012/11/17/ nascars-innovative-social-media-approach-leads-to-significant-growth-in-fan-base.

11. Quesenberry, "Social Media Is Like Running a Marathon."

12. Margaret Rouse, "Customer Lifetime Value (CLV)," SearchCustomerExperience .Techtarget.com, July 2015, https://searchcustomerexperience.techtarget.com/definition/customer -lifetime-value-CLV.

13. Tom Martin, "How Long Before a Social Media Campaign Shows Results," Converse Digital.com, January 17, 2012, http://www.conversedigital.com/social-media-marketing-strategy/ how-long-before-a-social-media-campaign-shows-results.

14. Keith Quesenberry, "FoMO: Why Fear of Missing Out Could Hurt Your Social Media Efforts," SocialMediaToday.com, May 19, 2015, http://www.socialmediatoday.com/ social-business/2015-05-19/fomo-why-fear-missing-out-could-hurt-your-social-media-efforts.

15. "Social Media Marketing's Main Expense Is Staff. How Do They Spend Their Time?" MarketingCharts.com, May 21, 2014, https://www.marketingcharts.com/digital-42651.

16. "Definition of Active Voice," LiteraryDevices.net, accessed November 8, 2019, https:// literarydevices.net/active-voice/.

17. "Definition of Passive Voice," LiteraryDevices.net, accessed November 8, 2019, https:// literarydevices.net/passive-voice/.

18. Ben Sailer, "This Is How to Write for Social Media to Create the Best Posts," April 19, 2019, CoSchedule.com, https://coschedule.com/blog/how-to-write-for-social-media/.

19. "Definition of Point of View," LiteraryDevices.net, accessed November 8, 2019, https:// literarydevices.net/point-of-view/.

20. "Landing Page Optimization," Optimisely.com, Optipedia, accessed November 9, 2019, https://www.optimizely.com/optimization-glossary/landing-page-optimization/.

21. Todd Clarke, "How to Establish Your Brand 'Voice' on Social Media," Hootsuite.com, February 21, 2019, https://blog.hootsuite.com/how-to-build-an-authentic-voice-on-social/.

22. Clarke, "How to Establish Your Brand 'Voice.'"

23. Keran Smith, "10 Creative Graphic Design Tips for Social Media," LyfeMarketing.com, September 30, 2019, https://www.lyfemarketing.com/blog/graphic-design-tips/.

24. Mads Soegaard, "The Power of White Space," Interaction-Design.org, February 2019, https://www.interaction-design.org/literature/article/the-power-of-white-space.

25. Darren Rose, "Rule of Thirds," Digital-Photography-School.com, accessed November 9, 2019, https://digital-photography-school.com/rule-of-thirds/.

26. "Design Anything. Publish Anywhere," Canva.com, accessed November 8, 2019, https://www.canva.com/.

27. "Transform Your Ideas into Stunning Visual Stories," Spark.Adobe.com, accessed November 8, 2019, https://spark.adobe.com/.

28. "Bring Your Creative Ideas to Life," Creative Hub, Facebook.com, accessed November 8, 2019, https://www.facebook.com/ads/creativehub.

29. "Create a Snap Ad in a Few Minutes," ForBusiness.Snapchat.com, accessed November 8, 2019, https://forbusiness.snapchat.com/ads.

30. "Keep Learning in the Moments that Matter," LinkedIn Learning with Lynda.com Content, accessed November 22, 2019, https://www.linkedin.com/learning/.

31. "Adobe Education Exchange," Edex.Adobe.com, accessed December 5, 2019, https://edex.adobe.com/browse.

32. "Design School," Canva Design School, accessed November 22, 2019, https://designschool.canva.com/.

33. "Best Practices for Creating Social Videos," Hootsuite.com, accessed November 9, 2019, https://hootsuite.com/education/courses/social-marketing/content/social-video.

34. "Best Practices for Creating Social Videos," Hootsuite.com.

35. "Welcome to the Creator Academy," YouTube, accessed November 22, 2019, https://creatoracademy.youtube.com/page/home.

36. "Best Practices for Creating Live Social Videos," Hootsuite.com, accessed November 9, 2019, https://hootsuite.com/education/courses/social-marketing/content/live-social-video.

37. Gregory Ciotti, "The Psychology of Color in Marketing and Branding," HelpScout.com, accessed November 9, 2019, https://www.helpscout.com/blog/psychology-of-color/.

38. "A/B Testing," Optimizely.com, Optipedia, accessed November 9, 2019, https://blog.hootsuite.com/calculate-engagement-rate/.

39. Jamie Griffiths, "How to Build a Content Calendar (Plus a Free Template)," ConvinceAndConvert.com, January 7, 2014, http://www.convinceandconvert.com/social-media-strategy/how-to-build-a-content-calendar-plus-a-free-template-for-2014/.

40. Ben Sailer, "The Best Time to Post on Social Media in 2019 According to 25 Studies," CoSchedule.com, accessed November 9, 2019, https://coschedule.com/blog/best-times-to-post-on-social-media/; Kole Riggs, "What Is the Lifespan of Social Media Posts?" Epipheo.com, accessed November 9, 2019, https://epipheo.com/learn/what-is-the-lifespan-of-social-media-posts/.

41. Si Quan Ong, "Evergreen Content: What It Is, Why You Need It and How to Create It," Ahrefs.com, May 7, 2019, https://ahrefs.com/blog/evergreen-content/.

42. Sharon Hurley, "15 Content Formats Proven to Boost Audience Engagement," Optinmonster.com, September 27, 2019, https://optinmonster.com/types-of-content-formats/.

43. Mark Schaefer and Brooke Sellas, "Video Everywhere: Exploring Marketing Ubiquity," BusinessGrow.com, accessed November 10, 2019, https://businessesgrow.com/2019/08/08/video-everywhere/.

44. "Metrics," BusinessDictionary.com, accessed November 6, 2019, http://www.businessdictionary.com/definition/metrics.html#ixzz4EyMdcmWd.

45. Dominique Jackson, "All of the Social Media Metrics that Matter," SproutSocial.com, October 24, 2016, https://sproutsocial.com/insights/social-media-metrics-that-matter/.

46. Katie Sehl, "All the Different Ways to Calculate Engagement Rate," Hootsuite.com, April 10, 2019, https://blog.hootsuite.com/calculate-engagement-rate/.

47. "Insights," Facebook.com, accessed November 6, 2019, https://www.facebook.com/help/794890670645072.

48. Kaylynn Chong, "LinkedIn Analytics: A Guide for Marketers," Hootsuite.com, December 17, 2018, https://blog.hootsuite.com/linkedin-analytics/.

49. "Pinterest Analytics," Help.Pinterest.com (blog), accessed November 6, 2019, https://help.pinterest.com/en/articles/pinterest-analytics.

50. "About Instagram Insights," Facebook.com, accessed November 6, 2019, https://www.facebook.com/business/help/788388387972460?helpref=faq_content.

51. "YouTube Analytics Basics," Support.Google.com, accessed November 6, 2019, https://support.google.com/youtube/answer/1714323?hl=en.

52. Brent Barnhart, "How to Set (and Achieve) Meaningful Social Media Goals," SproutSocial.com, October 10, 2019, https://sproutsocial.com/insights/social-media-goals/.

53. Lars Lofgren, "The Ultimate Guide to the New Google Analytics Social Reports," Kissmetrics.com, accessed November 6, 2019, https://blog.kissmetrics.com/google-analytics-social-reports/.

54. "Learn Analytics with Free Online Courses," Analytics.google.com, accessed November 15, 2019, https://analytics.google.com/analytics/academy/.

55. Ty Mays Kelly, "Social Media Spending on the Rise for Most Companies," SocialMediaImpact.com, May 12, 2014, http://www.socialmediaimpact.com/social-media-spending/#.

56. Megan Conley, "How to Manage Your Entire Marketing Budget [Free Budget Planner Templates]," HubSpot.com, January 30, 2018, https://blog.hubspot.com/marketing/how-to-manage-marketing-budget-free-budget-templates.

57. "CMO Survey: Results February 2019," CMOSurvey.org, February 2019, https://cmosurvey.org/results/february-2019/.

58. Nick Rojas, "How to Determine Your Social Media Marketing Budget," TheNextWeb.com (blog), May 12, 2016, https://thenextweb.com/insider/2016/05/12/how-to-determine-your-social-media-marketing-budget/#gref.

59. Katie Sehl, "A Social Media Budget Breakdown for Every Size Business," Blog.Hootsuite.com, July 17, 2019, https://blog.hootsuite.com/the-7-components-of-every-social-media-budget/.

60. Vijay Mandeep, "The Future of AI-Assisted Social Media Marketing," Hackernoon.com, February 19, 2019, https://hackernoon.com/the-future-of-ai-assisted-social-media-marketing-7f8e91afbec1.

61. "Artificial intelligence," Lexico.com, accessed November 7, 2019, https://hackernoon.com/the-future-of-ai-assisted-social-media-marketing-7f8e91afbec1.

62. Kamila Hankiewicz, "What Is the Real Difference Between Automation And AI?" Becoming Human.com, August 8, 2019, https://becominghuman.ai/what-is-the-real-difference-between-automation-and-ai-366513e0c910.

63. Andrew Moore, Roy Solomon, and Matt Barney, "Understanding AI and Automation," ComputerScienceOnline.com, accessed November 7, 2019, https://www.computerscienceonline.org/learn-automation-ai/.

64. Joe Stych, "What is Drip Marketing? The Complete Guide to Drip Campaigns, Lifecycle Email, and More," Zapier.com, February 16, 2015, https://zapier.com/learn/email-marketing/drip-marketing-campaign/.

65. Larry Kim, "Facebook Messenger Chatbot Marketing: The Definitive Guide (2018)," Marketing and Entrepreneurship Medium.com, accessed November 7, 2019, https://medium.com/marketing-and-entrepreneurship/facebook-messenger-chatbot-marketing-the-definitive-guide-2018-e839e2888e62.

66. Mike Kaput, "The Marketer's Guide to Artificial Intelligence Terminology," November 1, 2016, https://www.marketingaiinstitute.com/blog/the-marketers-guide-to-artificial-intelligence-terminology.

67. Keith Quesenberry, "Programmatic: A Growing Part of Social Media Strategy," Social MediaToday.com, January 24, 2017, https://www.socialmediatoday.com/social-business/programmatic-growing-part-social-media-strategy.

68. "Natural language processing," Lexico.com, accessed November 7, 2019, https://www.lexico.com/en/definition/natural_language_processing.

69. "How Does Hootsuite Analytics Determine Sentiment?" Hootsuite, accessed November 7, 2019, https://help.hootsuite.com/hc/en-us/articles/360017491214-How-does-Hootsuite-Analytics-determine-sentiment-.

70. "Corporate risk," Dataminr.com, accessed November 7, 2019, https://www.dataminr.com/corporate-risk.

71. "Natural Language Generation (NLG)," Techopedia.com, accessed November 7, 2019, https://www.techopedia.com/definition/33012/natural-language-generation-nlg.

72. "Want to Know How Phrasee Works?" Phrasee.co, accessed November 7, 2019, https://phrasee.co/how-it-works/.

73. "Image recognition," Techopedia.com, accessed November 7, 2019, https://www.techopedia.com/definition/33499/image-recognition.

74. "Image Insights: World Leading Image Detection and Analysis," BrandWatch.com, accessed November 7, 2019, https://www.brandwatch.com/image-insights/.

75. "Product Overview," CrowdRiff.com, accessed November 7, 2019, https://crowdriff.com/platform/.

76. Clark Boyd, "Pinterest Visual Search: Statistics, Advertising, and How to Get Started with Pinterest Lens," Data Driven Investor, Medium.com, January 14, 2019, https://medium.com/datadriveninvestor/pinterest-visual-search-statistics-advertising-and-how-to-get-started-with-pinterest-lens-c9750328b2b3.

77. "Shop the Look Pins," Business.Pinterest.com, accessed November 7, 2019, https://business.pinterest.com/en/shop-the-look-pins.

78. "Predictive Analytics," Investopedia.com, accessed November 7, 2019, https://www.investopedia.com/terms/p/predictive-analytics.asp.

79. Margaret Rouse, "Prescriptive Analytics," SearchCIO.TechTarget.com, accessed November 7, 2019, https://searchcio.techtarget.com/definition/Prescriptive-analytics.

80. "Quickly Build AI-Powered Apps for Employees and Customers on a Complete Artificial Intelligence Platform," Salesforce.com, accessed November 7, 2019, https://www.salesforce.com/products/einstein/features/?d=cta-body-promo-9.

81. "Explore the New Watson Campaign Automation Navigation Experience," IBM.com, accessed November 7, 2019, https://www.ibm.com/watson/marketing-automation.

82. "Intelligent virtual assistant," Techopedia.com, accessed November 7, 2019, https://www.techopedia.com/definition/31383/intelligent-virtual-assistant.

83. "IBM Watson Campaign Automation," IBM.com, accessed November 7, 2019, https://www.ibm.com/us-en/marketplace/digital-marketing-and-lead-management/details.

84. Nathan Sykes, "How a Chatbot Can Help Lead Customers Through the Sales Funnel," Lead-Fuze.com, accessed November 7, 2019, https://www.leadfuze.com/chatbot-for-sales/.

85. "Chatbots for Customer Service: Why You Need AI Customer Support in 2019," ManyChat.com, March 29, 2019, https://manychat.com/blog/chatbots-for-customer-service/.

86. "AI Explained: How Algorithms Optimize Facebook Ads," Pattern89.com, June 4, 2019, https://www.pattern89.com/blog/ai-explained-how-algorithms-optimize-facebook-ads/.

87. "Personalized Video Ads," Clinch.co, accessed November 7, 2019, https://clinch.co/.

88. "Motiva AI Cloud for Oracle Eloqua," Motiva.com, accessed November 7, 2019, https://www.motiva.ai/eloqua/.

89. "Marketing-Related Use of Artificial Intelligence (AI) According to Industry Professionals Worldwide as of January 2018, by Region," Adobe, February 12, 2018, https://www.statista.com/statistics/915372/marketing-related-use-artificial-intelligence-world/

90. Elizabeth Perse, "Uses and Gratifications," Oxford Bibliographies, accessed November 7, 2019, 2017, http://www.oxfordbibliographies.com/view/document/obo-9780199756841/obo-9780199756841-0132.xml.

91. Elihu Katz, Jay G. Blumler, and Michael Gurevitch, "Uses and Gratifications Research," *Public Opinion Quarterly* 37, no. 4 (1973): 509.

92. Shyam S. Sundar and Anthony M. Limperos, "Uses and Grats 2.0: New Gratifications for New Media," *Journal of Broadcasting & Electronic Media* 57, no. 4 (2013): 504–525.

93. Sharon Flaherty, "Why the C-suite Don't 'Get' Social Media Marketing—And How to Change That," The *Guardian.com*, August 4, 2014, https://www.theguardian.com/media/2014/aug/04/c-suite-social-media-marketing-adoption-boardroom.

94. Chloe Taylor, "These CEOs Have the Strongest Social Media Presence, Survey Shows—Here's Why That Matters," CNBC.com, June 17, 2019, https://www.cnbc.com/2019/06/17/these-ceos-have-the-strongest-social-media-presence-survey-shows.html.

Social Media Law, Ethics, and Etiquette

All of us who professionally use the mass media are the shapers of society. We can vulgarize that society. We can brutalize it. Or we can help lift it onto a higher level.[1]

—Bill Bernbach

PREVIEW

When was the last time you looked forward to watching or reading an ad? You most likely don't turn on the TV to watch your favorite television commercial. You probably have never searched Google for the latest banner ads. Yet, you may look forward to seeing some good ads during the Super Bowl, World Cup, or Olympics and you probably don't mind when you see a good ad that is interesting, funny, or provides valuable information. You may even seek out the entertaining ones on YouTube. Other times you intentionally leave the room during commercials, skip them, or even block them when they get annoying. Our acceptance and rejection of ads has been an ongoing battle in both traditional and online media.

When marketers, advertisers, and public relations professionals abuse their professions by not following the law, by being unethical, or simply by not following good etiquette, they can suffer a decrease in credibility as an individual, brand, or entire industry. Once you lose credibility, it becomes harder to get others to listen to you. In recent years, the demand for ad-blocking software has increased as a way to avoid marketing scams, bait and switch offers, publicity stunts, PR spin, overly distracting on-screen ads, annoying pop-ups, and unwanted auto-playing videos. Typical online magazine or news articles, once clicked, now download ten KB to five MB of marketing data around the content readers want. This "bloat" slows computers, crashes browsers, and places codes on users' computers to track their actions across the internet, raising privacy concerns. It is no wonder that the use of ad-blocking software such as AdBlock Plus and Adguard is on the increase.[2]

An **ad blocker** is a program that removes online ads from a website user's desktop and mobile experience.[3] Globally, ad-blocking software users have risen from just 54 million in 2013 to 615 million by 2017.[4] Today 40 to 50 percent of consumers worldwide use ad-blocking software from 40 percent in Europe to 45 percent in North America to 50 percent in Asia Pacific.[5] This is a significant problem for publishers who rely on advertising to fund the free content they provide because ad blocking decreases revenue. Publications such as *Forbes* depend on up to 80 percent of their total revenue from online advertising. Yet consumers use ad blockers to decrease clutter and distractions, and to speed up loading times. They want to protect their privacy, protect themselves from malware, and save bandwidth and battery on mobile devices. This has led to a somewhat combative relationship between publishers and their readers.[6]

Instead of altering the environment that led to the use of ad blockers and seeking alternative means to generate income, many publishers have increased their war on ad-blocking software and users. Some publishers have fought back with their own blocking, creating ad-block walls that users cannot get around.[7] In the end, this tactic may not work to increase ad revenue; 74 percent of ad-block users say they simply leave websites with ad-block walls. However, ad-block users indicate they are willing to view some forms of ad formats.

Other publications have had success taking a different approach, such as shifting to more acceptable forms of advertising and increasing revenue through online subscriptions. The *New York Times* has created content paywalls to increase subscriptions and has created alternative forms of online advertising such as social media–branded content.[8] In 2018, the *New York Times* digital subscriptions grew 27 percent. During that same period, digital ad revenue grew 23 percent, surpassing print advertising for the first time.[9] The *Guardian* has taken another approach by asking readers directly to make one-time contributions to avoid the publication putting up a paywall.[10] Whatever the solution, a more user-centric approach may help negotiate a truce in this battle between readers and publishers where advertising is used as the weapon between sides. Perhaps social media can be a bridge to a more acceptable future.

Social Media Laws and Regulations

Bill Bernbach was an advertising creative director who helped launch the famous international advertising agency Doyle Dane Bernbach (DDB). He was also seen as integral to helping launch the "Creative Revolution of Advertising" in the 1960s, when advertising moved away from more rational, homogenous appeals, proving that creativity could attract attention and increase sales. Bernbach and his techniques and agency are referenced many times in the popular AMC show *Mad Men*, featuring a fictional ad agency from the early 1960s.[11] Bernbach's quote at the beginning of this chapter is especially meaningful with regard to the subject of social media marketing communications law and ethics. What are the professional responsibilities of using social media?

Like any marketing, advertising, public relations, or business practices, actions taken are subject to laws and regulations by government and industry organizations. This also applies to social media action. The **Federal Trade Commission (FTC)** is responsible for protecting consumers in the United States from unfair trade practices including deceptive advertising and the use of social media for marketing communication. Businesses within highly regulated industries such as pharmaceuticals, medical devices, financial, gambling, tobacco, alcohol, and firearms have additional restrictions and are further monitored for compliance by agencies such as the Federal Communications Commission (FCC), the US Food and Drug Administration (FDA), US Securities and Exchange Commission (SEC), and the Bureau of Alcohol, Tobacco, Firearms, and Explosives (ATF). The US Department of Labor also has specific requirements for employers that may require or prohibit specific actions in relation to employees and social media.

The European Union and other countries around the world have their own social media laws and regulatory agencies. In the United Kingdom, the Competition and Markets Authority (CMA) regulates competition and ensures consumer protection. In Canada, the Competition Bureau ensures that businesses and consumers prosper under fair competitive conditions, and in Australia, the Australian Competition and Consumer Commission (ACCC) protects fair trade to benefit consumers and businesses.

With the great increase in global commerce, social media laws and regulations are taking on a global perspective. The **International Consumer Protection and Enforcement Network (ICPEN)** is an organization composed of consumer protection authorities from more than sixty countries. With the aim to protect cross-border commercial activities, the ICPEN has released a series of guidelines: "ICPEN Guidelines for Review Administrators," "ICPEN Guidelines for Traders and Marketing Professionals," and "ICPEN Guidelines for Digital Influencers." These guides can be found on their website at ICPEN.org.[12] See table 15.1 for a summary list of main government organizations that regulate social media. When it comes to social media laws, there are too many details to include them all. What will be covered in this chapter are general overall guidelines to be followed and guidance on where to look for the details. What is provided is not intended to be legal advice or to address every situation. Each business and organization should consult their own attorneys to apply current law to specific circumstances and jurisdictions.

A good foundation to start with is the US FTC's truth-in-advertising standards, which are based on Section 5 of the FTC Act. The FTC's Business Center publishes an "Advertising FAQs: Guide for Small Business," which is a valuable resource for any size business or organization. Any brand claim made in social media must first meet these general standards. The FTC's "Deception Policy Statement" declares that an ad is deceptive if it contains a statement or omits information that (1) is likely to mislead consumers acting reasonably under the circumstances; and (2) is "material"—that is, important, to a consumer's decision to buy or use the product. The FTC looks at the context of the ad for a consumer acting reasonably on information important to their purchase decision and considers both express and implied claims that must be based on objective evidence. In addition, there are specific requirements for alcohol, tobacco, drug, dietary supplement, environmental, food,

**Table 15.1. Main Government Organizations that
Regulate Social Media**

United States
Federal Trade Commission (FTC)
Canada
Competition Bureau
United Kingdom
Competition and Markets Authority (CMA)
Australia
Australian Competition and Consumer Commission (ACCC)
European Union
European Commission
Global
International Consumer Protection and Enforcement Network (ICPEN)

and children's ads, as well as rules regarding bait and switch, comparative ads, contests and sweepstakes, endorsements, testimonials, free claims, rebate offers, guarantees, new claims, pricing, and sales.[13]

It is useful to note that the business or marketer and any communications firm they hire, such as advertising agencies and public relations firms, are all held accountable for any misleading claims. Marketing communications partners should make independent checks to ensure that claims are substantiated. If a company violates the law, penalties from the FTC or courts can include cease-and-desist orders, per-day fines, civil penalties ranging from thousands to millions of dollars, and required corrective advertising.[14]

In 2009, the FTC came out with additional endorsement guidelines because of the growth of bloggers being compensated with free products, money, or advertising revenue for writing product reviews that consumers used as unbiased opinions to inform their purchase decisions. Those endorsement guidelines have been expanded to include social media networks where influencers are posting on behalf of brands. Due to the large increase in this type of activity, the FTC issued a press release in 2017 reminding influencers and brands of their responsibility to clearly disclose relationships and an additional document "The FTC's Endorsement Guides: What People Are Asking." The **FTC Endorsement Guides** explain that marketers, advertisers, public relations professionals, and influencers promoting or endorsing products are responsible for clearly and conspicuously disclosing material connections that affect the weight or credibility consumers give to an endorsement in social media. Influencers can be consumers, celebrities, spokespersons, and employees. Material connections could include monetary payment, free product gifts, or a business and family relationship.[15]

The FTC does not require specific wording but suggests wording such as "Company X gave me this product to try" or "Some of the products I'm going to use in this video were sent to me by their manufacturers." It also matters where and when these disclosures are given. The FTC advises that it is not enough to have a general disclosure on the home page of a website or blog, in the description of a video, or even at the end of an Instagram post. Disclosures must be given clearly and prominently at the beginning of the actual post, video, or podcast, close to the claims to which they relate, and not hidden behind hyperlinks. Special consideration is given for microblogs like Twitter due to the character limit. The FTC advises starting tweets with the words "#sponsored," "#promotion," or "#ad." If a brand and endorser are using a live video steam or video game stream, the FTC suggests a continuous, clear, and conspicuous disclosure.[16]

Additional considerations include barring endorsers from talking about products if they haven't tried them and from saying that products are great if they actually think they are awful. If a brand is running a contest or sweepstakes in social media, this should be disclosed with wording such as "#contest" or "#sweepstakes." Asking for honest opinions and reviews is okay, but if the person receives some form of value in return, like a free product or a discount, this must be disclosed. Keep in mind that ratings and review sites such as Amazon or Yelp will have their own standards that brands must follow. Brands that use bloggers and social media influencers to promote their products have a responsibility to provide reasonable training about claims and disclosure requirements and to regularly monitor them to ensure compliance. If employees post about employers' products and services, they must disclose that relationship. This also applies to any advertising agency or public relations firm employees who are endorsing a client's product or service. Responsibility for compliance rests with the company and any communications firms that may be hired to implement plans and programs.[17]

It is recommended that you view these guidelines for yourself, including "Advertising FAQ's: A Guide for Small Business" and "The FTC's Endorsement Guides: What People Are Asking" at FTC.gov. In 2019, the FTC issued additional materials for guidance, "Disclosures 101 for Social Media Influencers" at FTC.gov. Two other areas should be considered that apply to social media professionals. With an increase in use of native advertising, the FTC issued an Enforcement Policy Statement on Deceptively Formatted Advertisements and with the increase in ratings and reviews the FTC issued the Consumer Review Fairness Act (CRFA).

With the Enforcement Policy Statement on Deceptively Formatted Advertisements, the FTC addressed increasingly innovative digital forms of native content presenting advertising and promotional messages integrated into and presented as non-commercial content whether described as native advertising, sponsored content, or some other term.[18] To avoid deceptive native ads the FTC recommends transparency, stating that "An advertisement or promotional message shouldn't suggest or imply to consumers that it's anything other than an ad." How? Some native ads may be so clearly an ad that specific disclosure may not be required, but in other instances a disclosure should be added to ensure consumers know the content is advertising.

These FTC guidelines apply to native ad content that appears next to non-advertising content, including news or content aggregator sites, social media platforms, or messaging apps. It could also apply to native ad content embedded in professionally produced or user-generated videos in social media, infographics, images, animations, and video games. Another consideration is to avoid using "deceptive door openers." Ensure native ads are identified as ads before consumers click on a link to advertising content. If a disclosure is required it must be clear and prominent and guidelines for adding clear and prominent disclosures to native ads are similar to those discussed above for endorsements.[19]

The FTC Consumer Review Fairness Act protects consumers' ability to share honest opinions about a business's products, services, and conduct in any form, which includes online ratings and reviews, social media posts, photos, and videos. Specifically, businesses are not allowed to create contracts or online terms and conditions that prohibit honest reviews and threaten legal action for posting negative reviews by customers. The law doesn't apply to employment contracts or agreements with independent contractors. The law also allows businesses to prohibit or remove a review that contains confidential or private information, is unrelated to its products and services, is clearly false or misleading, and is libelous, harassing, abusive, obscene, vulgar, sexually explicit, or inappropriate in relation to race, gender, sexuality, and ethnicity. But the law does protect consumers, giving them the ability to honestly speak about products, services, and their experience with a company.

To comply with the law, the FTC suggests reviewing contracts and online terms and conditions (the small print) and "remove any provision that restricts people from sharing their honest reviews, penalizes those who do, or claims copyright over people's reviews (even if you've never tried to enforce it or have no intention of enforcing it)."[20] It is recommended that you view these guidelines, including "Native Advertising: A Guide for Business" and "Consumer Review Fairness Act: What Businesses Need to Know" for yourself at FTC.gov.

For brands operating in the United Kingdom, the Competition and Markets Authority (CMA) has a guidance publication similar to the FTC's, which can be found on the website

Figure 15.1. Do you read all the terms and conditions you agree to in social media?

© Anyaberkut / iStock Photo

The FTC Takes Action

The Federal Trade Commission creates acts to protect consumers and sets standards for businesses to act within the law, but do they enforce these acts and standards? In 2019, the FTC enforced the Consumer Review Fairness Act for a vacation rental company that allegedly included a paragraph under disclaimers in rental contracts stating, "by signing below, you agree not to defame or leave negative reviews (includes any review or comment deemed to be negative . . . as well as any review less than a '5 star' or 'absolute best' rating) about this property and/or business in any print form or on any website." According to the complaint the contract also stated that violations would "immediately result in minimum liquidated damages of $25,000."[a]

The FTC also took action against a website that allegedly sold fake followers, subscribers, views, and likes on social platforms to influencers who wanted to increase their appeal as online influencers and companies that wanted to boost their credibility to potential clients. According to the complaint, the company sold tens of thousands of sales of fake influence on platforms including Twitter, LinkedIn, YouTube, and Pinterest. Clients included individuals such as actors, athletes, musicians, writers, speakers, law firm partners, and investment professionals. Company clients included software companies; banking investment, financial, and human resources firms; plus marketing, advertising, and public relations firms.[b]

The FTC has also policed the Consumer Review Fairness Act for a company posting fake reviews. The FTC alleged that a skincare company had managers post fake reviews on the brand website using fake accounts and requested other employees to do the same. The FTC alleges the company used a VPN (virtual private network) account to hide IP addresses when reviews were written. The FTC complaint quotes from an email directing staff to set up three accounts and included step-by-step instructions for setting up new personas and using a VPN to hide their identities, and directed employees to "always leave 5 stars" and to "dislike" negative reviews.[c]

[a] Mitchell J. Katz and Carl H. Settlemyer, "FTC Announces Two Actions Enforcing the Consumer Review Fairness Act," FTC.gov, June 3, 2019, https://www.ftc.gov/news-events/press-releases/2019/06/ftc-announces-two-actions-enforcing-consumer-review-fairness-act.

[b] Michell J. Katz and Michael Ostheimer, "Devumi, Owner and CEO Settle FTC Charges They Sold Fake Indicators of Social Media Influence; Cosmetics Firm Sunday Riley, CEO Settle FTC Charges That Employees Posted Fake Online Reviews at CEO's Direction," FTC.org, October 21, 2019, https://www.ftc.gov/news-events/press-releases/2019/10/devumi-owner-ceo-settle-ftc-charges-they-sold-fake-indicators.

[c] Katz and Ostheimer, "Devumi, Owner and CEO Settle FTC Charges."

GOV.uk. Entitled "Online Reviews and Endorsements: Advice for Businesses," it details the requirements for social media reviews and endorsements.[21] In Canada, the Competition Bureau offers a guidance document, "The Deceptive Marketing Practices Digest," covering online advertising and disclosure issues that can be found on CompetitionBureau.gc.ca.[22] In Australia, the Australian Competition and Consumer Commission (ACCC) offers advice on avoiding misleading claims in social media. This can be found under the business section of their website at ACCC.gov.au.[23] In addition, remember that the ICPEN offers overall global guidance at ICPEN.org.

Despite these government guides and resources, there has been a rise in undisclosed promotional posts. The *Guardian* reports that complaints about content on social networks in the United Kingdom have risen 193 percent since 2012. Many social influencers are failing to inform readers that they have been paid to publicize products.[24] In the United States, the FTC sent warning letters to twenty-one influencers including Naomi Campbell and Lindsay Lohan to remind them of their disclosure obligations in 2017.[25] Despite the FTC efforts, a year after major actions, just a quarter (25 percent) of celebrities and YouTube and Instagram influencers were following the FTC disclosure guidelines. A report looking at Instagram accounts in the United States, United Kingdom, and Canada found that 72 percent disclosed monetary partnerships, but only 25 percent did so in a way that was FTC compliant.[26]

For any organization or company today, it is important to have a social media policy that sets standards for employees, vendors, partners, and the brand. A **social media policy** is an organization's standards for conduct regarding the way its employees post content in social media as part of their jobs or as private individuals.[27] The Forbes Human Resources Council suggests that a social media policy should be a comprehensive document including guidelines across many categories, and best practices with training tips for employees.[28] Jylian Russell on the Hootsuite blog indicates social media policies can vary greatly depending on the organization and can be more of a condensed document presenting straightforward guidelines.[29]

General Motors' Social Media Policy includes a summarized version on the website with eight key points and a link to the full policy. GM's example can be viewed on their website.[30] The Mayo Clinic has guidelines for employees and students that apply whether posting on their own sites or commenting on other sites including personal blogs and social media sites. The policy for sharing Mayo Clinic stories includes ten guidelines with links to other applicable organization policies that can be viewed on their website.[31] Depending on your organization, it may be appropriate to create different social media policies with different standards for key stakeholders. The New York City Department of Education has one social media policy for students (over thirteen),[32] and one for school staff published on their websites.[33]

A good policy will consider standards for official brand accounts and standards for employees on their own accounts. Russell suggests that a social media policy include rules and regulations for behavior and conduct including brand guidelines, etiquette, engagement, and confidentiality. Roles and responsibilities should be specified from message approval to service and security. Legal risks should be addressed, such as crediting sources, confidentiality, and disclosure. A security risks section can educate on best practices about secure passwords, attacks, or scams, and accountability should be addressed to remind employees of their responsibility.[34]

The Forbes Human Resources Council takes a different approach, explaining that a social media policy should include important categories of information to help keep a brand safe. They indicate that a policy should first educate about social media, including specific platforms' terms of use, conditions, and limitations. Then remind employees about blurred personal and professional lives and how personal social media actions can have professional implications. Finally, they should be reminded to think carefully before posting about controversial issues and to follow conventions as a representative for the brand. Standards for respecting professional boundaries of coworkers should be set, including guidelines for addressing workplace issues and conflicts inside the company and not on a public social forum. Employees should know to clarify and assert their opinions as their own, indicating that they do not represent the company, and they need to ensure that they do not disclose confidential or proprietary information.[35]

Another important legal consideration in social media is the use of user-generated content or UGC. UGC is an important part of any effective social media effort. Fans often share content to the brand hashtag or handle, and brands may run contests, events, and promotions to elicit this content. Social media professionals should take care to follow best practices and ensure good policies when it comes to sharing, repurposing, and eliciting user-generated brand social media content. One important practice is attribution. **Attribution** is giving original authors credit for their content.[36] The fan-based marketing company Tradable Bits offers suggestions on how to repurpose UGC from social media. The way to attribute UGC varies per platform, but a general standard is to include the original network's official log, author's username, profile picture, and a live link to the original content. On Sprout Social's blog, Alex York suggests adding the words "credit," "photo," "cc," or "by" for attribution.[37]

In addition, brands should explicitly and transparently request permission for the rights to use fan photos and post content. This can be as simple as replying to fan posts offering praise and asking that they grant the brand rights with a response. To go with rights requests, ensure that the organization has a publicly published rights-granted policy that spells out the details of how the brand will utilize UGC. That way fans know exactly what rights they are granting.[38] Having a published user-generated content policy is another best practice to go along with an employee or brand social media policy.

A **user-generated content policy** is an organization's standards for rights granted to use consumer-created content in brand marketing. The website TermsFeed suggests that such policies include clauses addressing intellectual property, liability, privacy, and acceptable use.[39] Macy's has a "User Generated Content Policy" published on their website that covers brand social media channels and hashtags.[40] Pier1 also has a "User Content Policy" on their website.[41] While these general guidelines may be helpful, brands should consult their own companies' general counsel before implementing any UGC campaign. When it comes to user-generated content such as photos or comments, some UGC software tools can help automate aspects of obtaining rights including Curalate, Olapic, TINT, ShortStack, and CrowdRiff.[42]

Social media also includes content curation on social networks and writing of new content such as blog posts pulled from many sources. It is important that brands take into consideration how to properly cite internet sources. Craig Silverman of the American Press Institute indicates that the starting point for curation or aggregation of social media content is attribution. Beyond that, be careful not to extract all the value of an original post or include so many quotes that there is nothing more for the reader to gain from visiting the original source.[43] Pawan Deshpande on the Content Curation Marketing blog adds that brands should strive to only reproduce the portion of a headline or article that is required to make the point and provide context and commentary for the material used.[44]

Corey Wainwright on the HubSpot blog recommends that when quoting someone else's online content, use direct quotes, include their name and company, and link to the source. Also check the website's or blog's content usage guidelines to ensure you follow them. Statistics or data used should give credit to the company and link directly to the page where the data was published. If an idea was originated or a story was first broken by someone else, indicate that in the copy as well with name, company, and link. Wainwright suggests citing sources in social media by using "via@username" in Twitter or Instagram. On Facebook, find the person and link to their timeline, and in LinkedIn, share the content and mention the person and company name. Other considerations include "photo by @ username" or "content by @username."[45]

Photos and videos are different. If you took the photo or created the video yourself, or if the brand bought stock photos or rights from a photographer, you don't need attribution if it is used under the rights provided. But be careful not to assume ownership or rights. Just because you found a photo or video in a brand folder, don't assume the company has bought it and has the right to use it forever in all circumstances. Before using any photo, be sure you have the rights and that you are using the photo within those rights in terms of the acceptable media and within the specified period. Alternatives include free stock photo resources and Creative Commons copyright licenses.

Creative Commons provides licenses as an alternative way for creators to retain copyright while allowing others to copy, distribute, and make some use of their work. There are multiple levels of licenses available, from attribution commercial use to noncommercial attribution.[46] Be sure to check the license level of any work found. Do not simply perform a Google images search and use what you find. The fact that it is on the internet doesn't mean that it is free. Be sure to check each photo's individual copyright notice and seek permission from the owner.

As mentioned previously, different industries will have even more specific guidelines and standards that need to be addressed and followed; failure to comply can result in significant actions by employers and government agencies. In the healthcare industry, social media presents a challenge when it comes to the US HIPAA (Health Insurance Portability and Accountability Act) guidelines. The *HIPAA Journal* reports violations have included nursing assistants being fired and serving jail time for sharing a video of a patient in their underwear on Snapchat.[47] Tesla CEO Elon Musk was fined $20 million by the US Securities and Exchange Commission for a tweet with information about taking Tesla private.[48] A US Federal Court of Appeals ordered that president Donald Trump could not block comments of critics on his Twitter account as a violation of the First Amendment. This was similar to a decision by another appeals court over the Facebook page of a Virginia politician. Others say that these are personal accounts or a privately owned digital platform, not a public forum. It is unclear whether the US Supreme Court will eventually take up how the First Amendment applies to digital spaces for public debate.[49]

Again, these are simply general guidelines and do not imply legal advice. Brands should consult their own lawyers and directly reference the law. Many requirements came out of the Digital Millennium Copyright Act. The **Digital Millennium Copyright Act (DMCA)** updated US copyright law to apply to the development of electronic commerce, distribution of digital works, and protection of copyright owners' rights.[50] Brands from other countries or global brands operating in multiple countries should check with each applicable governing authority regulating commerce, competition, and consumer protection

Figure 15.2. Industries such as healthcare have unique social media policy requirements.

© Tempura / iStock Photo

such as the Competition and Markets Authority in the United Kingdom, the Competition Bureau in Canada, the Australian Competition and Consumer Commission, and the International Consumer Protection and Enforcement Network for overall global perspective.

Social Media Ethics

In addition to the social media laws and regulations already discussed, each organization and marketing communications group should consider its own industry's code of ethics. These codes of ethics vary on the unique situation, but some overall considerations are the American Marketing Association (AMA), the American Association of Advertising Agencies (AAAA), the American Advertising Federation (AAF), the Institute for Advertising Ethics (IAE), and the Public Relations Society of America (PRSA). Other country-associated professional groups and individual company industry groups vary from the American Medical Association (AMA) to SNAC International (formerly the Snack Food Association). In the United Kingdom, look for industry associations such as the Marketing Agencies Association (MAA), the Advertising Association (AA), and the Public Relations and Communications Association (PRCA). In Canada, consider the Canadian Association of Marketing Professionals (CAMP), the Association of Canadian Advertisers (ACA), and the Canadian Public Relations Society (CPRS). Australia has the Australian Association of National Advertisers (AANA), the Australian Marketing Institute (AMI), and the Public Relations Institute of Australia (PRIA).

MINI CASE

Wal-Marting Across America

In 2006 a blog appeared online published by a couple named Jim and Laura who were chronicling their journey across the United States in an RV traveling from Las Vegas to Georgia. As they drove across the country, they stayed for free in Wal-Mart store parking lots. Along the way the couple wrote about how great the stores were and interviewed Wal-Mart employees who all loved their jobs. This was a public relations professionals' and marketers' dream. However, this amazing earned media wasn't earned; it was completely orchestrated and paid for by Wal-Mart through their public relations agency, Edelman. What was the problem?

The fact that the bloggers were paid was never disclosed. People felt deceived when they found out that the trip and the blog were just a PR stunt. Consumers were misled into thinking that the couple and tour did not have a connection to Wal-Mart.[a] Even before the specific social media disclosure rules were written by the FTC, this fell under the category of deceptive advertising.

BusinessWeek.com finally revealed that "Wal-Marting Across America" was a fake blog supported through a corporate-funded organization called Working Families for Wal-Mart. An *Advertising Age* article noted that Edelman Worldwide helped to write the WOMMA code of ethics, which states, "Honesty of identity: You never obscure your identity." It was also against the Public Relations Society of America (PRSA) code of ethics. The incident was an embarrassment for the agency, industry, and company.[b] It also led to a new term called flog. **Flog** is a paid-for, fake blog. CEO Richard Edelman apologized for failing to be transparent about the identity of the bloggers and reconfirmed the agency's commitment to openness and trust.[c] Many companies that are good at social media today first learned from mistakes early on, such as we've already discussed—Dell (chapter 11), Home Depot (chapter 12), and Comcast (chapter 13).

Today Wal-Mart is focusing on using user-generated content to change the brand's perception. And Edelman publishes the industry-respected Trust Barometer that helps monitor consumer trust in business, governments, NGOs, and media across the world.[d]

[a] Kiley Skene, "A PR Case Study: Wal-Marting Across America," NewsGeneration.com (blog), April 4, 2014, http://www.newsgeneration.com/2014/04/04/pr-case-study-walmarting-across-america/.

[b] Mya Frazier, "Edelman Eats Humble Pie: Unmasked as Force Behind Wal-Mart Blog, PR Giant Does Damage Control," AdAge.com, October 19, 2006, http://adage.com/article/news/edelman-eats-humble-pie/112588/.

[c] "Edelman Company Profile," CorporateWatch.org, March 30, 2012, https://corporatewatch.org/edelman-company-profile/.

[d] "2019 Edelman Trust Barometer," Edelman.com, January 20, 2019, https://www.edelman.com/trust-barometer.

The Public Relations Society of America issued an ethical standards advisory as additional insight into the Member Code of Ethics indicating speed, frequency, and open accessibility of communication via social media has the ability to quickly amplify ethical mistakes. The recommended best practices in social media include full disclosure, safeguarding confidences, conflicts of interest, free flow of information, and enhancing the profession.

For further details visit prsa.org.[51] For a look at an early blog campaign from a national brand and public relations firm that didn't follow some of these standards, see "Mini Case: Wal-Marting Across America."

Other ethical considerations in social media include paying for reviews and buying followers. Brands should always be transparent and truthful in social media. It may be very tempting to jumpstart a campaign by purchasing followers and positive reviews, but these practices ultimately have negative consequences. David Hagenbuch of Mindful Marketing found that five thousand followers can be bought for as little as $29.00 or fifty thousand followers for $119.00. In addition, social media account owners can buy "likes." Prices for likes start at $14.00 for five hundred worldwide likes and up to $1,325.00 for twenty thousand US likes. He says this type of marketing is deceptive. Consumers make purchase decisions based on the numbers of followers and likes. If their followers and likes are fake, there is no basis for this social proof. Hagenbuch also points out that it is unjust. A company can work hard for months to obtain a legitimate ten thousand followers, yet a competitor may simply pay $39.00 and get them overnight. In the end, it is simply mindless marketing and eventually consumers will uncover the fake facade.[52]

Many retailers, websites, and social media platforms with ratings and reviews are stepping up enforcement of rules and removing companies with fake ratings and reviews. Other social platforms are cracking down on fake followers; this is an important measurement for paid social media and impacts the overall credibility of a platform. AdEspresso did an experiment where they grew an Instagram account the regular way and by buying fake followers using bots. Over the long term, the regular method beat out the bot for total followers, engagement, and sales.[53] Moreover, consumers often find out about such deceptive practices on their own, which can blow up into a public relations crisis as stories are shared in social media and picked up by the news media. In January 2018, the *New York Times* published an article on the social media black market that exposed companies that sell fake followers and revealed that numerous celebrities, athletes, and politicians had purchased fake followers. In the box early in this chapter "The FTC Takes Action" we saw how they filed actions against a company in 2019 for selling fake social influencers; that company has since shut down.

Not only are these practices unethical, but they can also cost organizations. In Canada, Bell Mobile was forced to pay a $1.25 million penalty by Canada's Competition Bureau for having employees write online reviews in the Apple AppStore and Google Play store without disclosing their ties.[54] In the United Kingdom, the Competition and Markets Authority has worked with the International Consumer Protection and Enforcement Network to prevent a US firm from using deceptive online reviews posted by employees and to ensure compliance by Norwegian online newspapers to clearly distinguish marketing messages from editorial content.

In another case, the ICPEN sought to stop an Australian property management company from blocking guests the company feels may leave negative TripAdvisor reviews from receiving emails inviting their feedback.[55] Amazon has been suing companies that sell fake reviews along with individuals offering to write fake reviews. In one year the online retail giant went after more than one thousand defendants for posting false reviews.[56] Crys Wiltshire from digital marketing firm gShift says that buying fake followers decreases engagement rates and can get accounts flagged or suspended. A brand may also be wasting money investing in influencers without large numbers of real fans, which can hurt social media metrics and ROI.[57]

One other ethical consideration is the use of social media automation or bots. Automation can be a great time saver for an organization and there are many tools and options. Yet automation must be used carefully in social media in the right ways in the right channels. Early attempts often got brands into trouble. Auto-responder programs help scale engagement, but they don't understand sarcasm and nuance. They are only based on simple keywords and commands, so a lot could go wrong if no human is watching.[58] A **social bot** is a computer program used in social media networks to automatically generate messages simulating conversation.[59] Social bots are also used in the unethical practices discussed above to generate fake followers and engagement such as likes and shares.

During the Occupy movement in the United States, Bank of America's automated Twitter bot had some unfortunate responses. After @OccupyLA posted "you can help by stop stealing people's houses!!!!" @BofA_Help responded with "We'd be happy to review your account with you to discuss any concerns. Please let us know if you need assistance." The account kept repeating the same four or five prewritten responses promising that they were there to help, listen, and learn from their customers while directly responding to outright criticisms of the bank. To one person who tweeted that they were chased away from Bank of America headquarters by New York City police, the brand responded, "Thank you for following up. Have a great weekend!"[60]

Be sure to understand that a social bot is different from an AI-powered chat bot discussed in chapter 14. If the customer is looking for engagement on brand social media pages, they are probably expecting real human engagement. But if they are seeking help with customer service issues in designated customer care pages and messenger platforms, they may be fine with bots to get their needs met quickly and efficiently. AI technologies have improved; in certain circumstances consumers could prefer speaking with a bot, and many brands are no longer trying to hide the fact that they are using bots. KLM Airlines uses "Blue Bot" on Facebook Messenger and Google Home to assist customers. Beauty retailer Sephora has created Sephora Reservation Assistant to help clients quickly identify locations and make appointments. Capital One has developed a chatbot named Eno to communicate with customers via text message to carry out bank transactions.[61] Jenn Chen on the Sprout Social blog suggests bots should not automate comments, likes, retweets, favorites, follows, or auto-posting from one network to another. Brand accounts should also always be monitored by people—automated responses are not a substitute for real human listening and response.[62]

Sometimes ethical best practices and standards become law as was the case in 2019 with a state law in the United States. The **California Bot Disclosure Law** requires a bot to be disclosed when it is used to incentivize a purchase or sale of goods or services in a commercial transaction or to influence a vote in an election.[63] Legal writer Robert Bateman says that the requirement probably doesn't apply to standard customer support, but this could get blurred in certain circumstances such as a bot that helps you find and book a restaurant or a bot that handles processing returns and refunds but then suggests an alternative item. He suggests that when in doubt it is better to disclose. Disclosures should be clear and conspicuous at the beginning of communication and should explain what a bot is for customers who may not be aware of the term. You should also teach the bot to respond with the right answer if asked directly whether it is a bot.[64] If a company has national or international operations, chances are it has customers in California and should comply and seek professional legal advice on specific ways to comply.

Social Media Etiquette

Beyond brand considerations, social media brings together our personal, professional, and working lives in a way no other medium has before. With 3.5 billion active social media users in the world,[65] 92 percent of Fortune 500 companies active on LinkedIn, 90 percent on Facebook, 79 percent on Twitter, and 49 percent on Instagram[66] and 92 percent of recruiters using social media to find candidates, it is too important not to carefully consider your actions.[67] How should someone navigate this social landscape where worlds collide and brands communicate like people in one-on-one conversations with consumers?

Ethics studies ideas about good and bad behavior.[68] **Etiquette** is the proper way to behave.[69] Both combine into **professionalism**, which is the skill, good judgment, and polite behavior expected from a person trained to do a job such as social media marketing.[70] Because social media often blurs the lines between personal and professional lives, it is useful to look at actions in social media from three perspectives: personal (as an individual), professional (as an employee or prospective employee), and brand (as an organization). Because personal, professional, and brand posts are often compressed through the same public social medium to reach personal friends, professional contacts, and brand fans, care should be taken when posting (see figure 15.3). From these perspectives certain questions should be considered before posting content in social media. Many people have also began managing their careers as if they were a brand.

Most reading this book have experienced social media via personal social use. Yet it shouldn't be assumed that what is done on personal social media accounts only applies to personal life. A CareerBuilder survey found that 70 percent of employers use social sites to research job candidates; 54 percent have decided not to hire a candidate based on their social media profiles. Even if someone tries to keep their social profiles completely private, 57 percent of employers say they are less likely to interview someone if they find no information about that person online. Half of employers check current employees' social media profiles and more than a third have reprimanded or fired an employee for inappropriate content.[71] It should be noted that these insights are based on responses to surveys. Employers and human resources professionals should consult their own policies, lawyers, and the latest regulations concerning employment laws. This can especially vary across industries, such as in healthcare where HIPAA laws apply, or from country to country where stricter protection for employees in social media may be enforced.

The top types of social media content that concern employers include inappropriate photographs and videos, drinking and using drugs, discriminatory comments, denigrating a previous company or fellow employee, and poor communication skills. However, employers also find information in social media that may cause them to consider hiring a candidate, including a background that supports job qualifications, a professional image, a personality that fits company culture, a well-rounded range of interests, and great communication

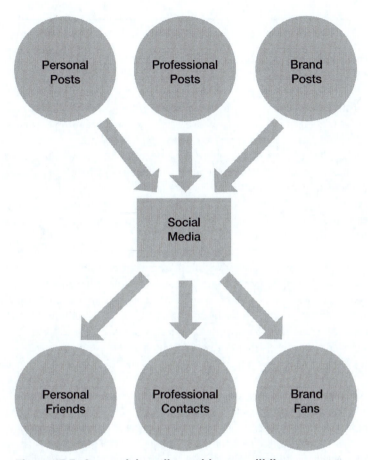

Figure 15.3. Our social media worlds are colliding.

skills.[72] What about ranting? Rants seem to be a popular activity in social media, and many may feel that ranting can help blow off steam and make you feel better. But research has found that people's moods actually decline after reading rants, and after writing rants, they became more angry, not less.[73] Forum moderator Bill Horne describes ranting as watching "others being burned at the electronic stake as they abandon logic, courtesy, common sense and self-respect."[74] In the end no one feels better.

Recruitment professional Kate Croucher says about candidates and social media, "If they are sharing lots of interesting things, and making insightful comments or forming strong opinions, and interacting with others in a positive way, it shows their ability to rally people behind them and develop effective relationships."[75] The following is a list of questions to consider before posting on social media from a personal, professional, and brand perspective. For a summary of these questions and considerations, see table 15.2.

From a personal etiquette perspective, consider the following questions before posting or commenting. *Is it all about me?* No one likes someone who only talks about themselves. The same applies in social media. Balance boasting with complimenting. *Am I stalking someone?* It is good to be driven and persistent, but be careful not to cross the line into creepy.

Personal Branding

Considering that so much of our lives is impacted by online presence, many have started managing their careers online by treating themselves as a brand. **Personal branding** is a practice where people market themselves and their careers like brands.[a] Personal branding includes marketing in terms of creating a brand, advertising by promoting oneself, and public relations for reputation management and press coverage. Personal branding can also be thought of as an ongoing process of establishing a desired image to obtain career opportunities.

The social media strategic process outlined in this text can be easily applied for your own personal brand. Follow a modified social strategy process applying the main concepts to promote your personal brand:

1. Identify your personal brand business objective. What is that dream job, position, or service opportunity you are ultimately seeking? List specific titles and/or companies/organizations.
2. Identify your target audience. Who who would be the decision maker to put you in that position? Develop a "buyer persona" for the hiring manager.
3. Perform your own personal situation analysis. Add results of a social media audit of your personal social media channels. Summarize in a SWOT graphic.
4. Formulate your message. See chapter 5 to identify what the hiring managers currently think and what you want them to think. What message will move them from one to the next? Be sure to establish a brand voice and set some focused topic guidelines.
5. Now identify the social channels you need to deliver that message. What needs to change in your current social media platforms and which do you need to add to deliver your message?
6. Make these adjustments and start creating your content to establish your personal brand.
7. Search job descriptions and ads. Make a list of skills employers are seeking. Emphasize those skills with keyword optimization of your social media content, profiles, cover letters, and résumés. In cover letters research to mention something specific and recent about the brand.
8. Are you missing any important skills? Find courses, certifications, and/or internships to earn those qualifications.
9. Finally, keep your online personal brand, but also don't underestimate the importance of in-person connections. Seek out professional networking opportunities and attend all you can.

[a] "What is Personal Branding: An Influencer Guide," InfluencerMarketingHub.com, last modified May 16, 2019, https://influencermarketinghub.com/what-is-personal-branding/.

Don't be too aggressive in outreach. *Am I spamming them?* Not everything or even the majority of what you post should ask for something. Don't make everything self-serving. *Am I venting or ranting?* Venting and ranting may feel good, but research says it doesn't help and no matter how justified you feel, it never presents you in a positive light. Do not post negative comments or gossip. *Did I ask before I tagged?* You had a great time and want to share those memories, but your friends, family, or employer may have different standards. Check before you tag people in posts.

Figure 15.4. Don't forget the importance of in-person networking for personal branding.

© AzmanL / iStock Photo

Also be careful with what you comment on or post to ensure that it actually reflects your personal beliefs. Did I read before commenting or sharing? Don't make yourself look foolish by not fully reviewing something you are commenting on or sharing with others. Don't jump to conclusions. *Am I grateful and respectful?* Don't take people for granted. Respond and thank those who engage with you. *Is this the right medium for the message?* Not everything should be said in social media. Consider the feelings of the other person. Some messages should be given in person, by phone, or in email. *Am I logged in to the right account?* There are too many corporate examples of embarrassing posts meant for personal jokes that went out on official brand accounts. Always double-check which account you are on. Don't post personal information on brand accounts.

When it comes to professional social media use as an employee or contractor, consider how social impacts careers and employers. This impact could occur on professional social networks such as LinkedIn, in a professional group on Facebook, or in separate social media accounts or on a blog with a more professional or career purpose. Once hired, always refer to the company's social media policy, but there are also useful general guidelines to consider. Not only should social media activity not hurt the company, but many companies today also see active personal social media use as a medium of advocacy for their brand. Consider that anything that is posted may impact professional image as a potential employee at another company or organization.

Before posting a comment as a professional, consider the following questions. *Does it meet the social media policy?* Most organizations have official social media policies that

Table 15.2. Social Media Etiquette and Ethics Template

Personal Social Action (As an Individual)	Professional Social Action (As a Current/Prospective Employee)	Brand Social Action (As an Organization)
Is it all about me? (Compliment, don't just boast)	**Does it meet Social Media Policy?** (Follow employer/client requirements)	**Does it speak to target market?** (Meets their wants/needs, not yours)
Am I stalking someone? (Don't be too aggressive in outreach)	**Does it hurt company reputation?** (Personal posts represent your employer)	**Does it add value?** (Make it educational, insightful, fun)
Am I spamming them? (Don't make everything self-serving)	**Does it help company marketing?** (Be an advocate for your brand)	**Does it fit the social channel?** (Environment, policies, standards)
Am I venting or ranting? (Don't post negative comments/gossip)	**Would my boss be happy seeing it?** (Private posts aren't fully private)	**Is it authentic and transparent?** (Don't hide/exclude anything relevant)
Did I ask before I tagged? (Check before you tag people in photos)	**Am I open about who I work for?** (Reveal financial connections)	**Is it real and unique?** (Don't use auto-responses or spam)
Did I read before commenting or sharing? (Don't jump to conclusions)	**Am I being fair and accurate?** (Constructive criticism with evidence)	**Is it positive and respectful?** (Don't bad-mouth competition/customers)
Am I grateful and respectful? (Respond and thank those who engage)	**Am I respectful, not malicious?** (Don't post what you wouldn't say in person)	**Does it meet codes of conduct?** (See WOMMA Code of Ethics, etc.)
Is it the right place for the message? (Some messages are appropriate elsewhere)	**Does it respect intellectual property?** (Get permission to post content)	**Does it meet laws and regulations?** (See FTC Social Guidelines, etc.)
Am I in the right account? (No personal posts on brand accounts)	**Is this confidential information?** (Don't disclose nonpublic info)	**Does it meet the Social Media Policy?** (Follow your own organization's standards)

Am I listening twice as much as I am talking?

you probably received when hired. Don't assume you know what the policy says. Many employees have been fired for not following company social media regulations. Make sure you know and follow employer or client requirements. *Does it hurt my company's reputation?* No matter how many disclaimers you put on your accounts, such as "views are my own," certain content and behavior will negatively impact your employer. If your bio states where you work, your personal account represents your employer. *Does it help my company's marketing?* Employee advocacy is an important strategy. Have a positive impact on your company's image and when you can advocate for your brand in social. *Would my boss/client be happy to see it?* You may not have "friended" your boss or client, but a coworker may have, and your post is only a share or screen grab away. Even private accounts are never fully private.

As a social media professional also consider questions such as A*m I being open about who I work for?* It is good to post positive content about your employer and it is nice to receive gifts, but if you are trying to pass it off as unbiased opinion, that is wrong. Be transparent about your financial connections. *Am I being fair and accurate?* Everyone is entitled to his or her personal opinion, but if your opinion tends to always be unfounded and seems to have an agenda, it will reflect negatively upon you. Criticism is welcome when it is constructive and opinion when backed by evidence. *Am I being respectful and not malicious?* People can get very insensitive, judgmental, and angry in social media posts. That does not convey a professional image. Don't post what you wouldn't say in person. Even an outburst in person fades in memory, but a malicious post is there forever. *Does it respect intellectual property?* Not everything on the internet is free. Check for or get permission to post company or client brand assets and content. *Is this confidential information?* As an employee or contractor, you are granted access to privileged and confidential information. Don't assume it is fine to share. Do not disclose nonpublic company or client information.

The final perspective is for people responsible for posting on behalf of an organization or company from the brand account. For those who are responsible for creating and sharing brand social media content, there are additional considerations to ensure that the content that is created helps to meet business objectives and follows laws and regulations. Before posting or commenting as a brand on a social media account ask, D*oes it speak to my target market?* Social media is unique from traditional marketing and requires a different perspective to be effective. Be sure to focus on your target's wants and needs, not yours. *Does it add value?* Social media only works if people view and share it. Make your content educational, insightful, or entertaining to grab interest and draw engagement. *Does it fit the social channel?* Don't post content ideal for Twitter on Instagram or Reddit. Each channel has its own culture and community. Make sure each post fits the channel's environment, mission, and policies or standards. *Is it authentic and transparent?* Trying to trick people into clicking a link or making a purchase will get you nowhere. Don't hide or exclude any relevant information.

There are other questions to ask when posting on behalf of a brand. Is it real and unique? Bots can automate tasks and be a great time saver, but use them for the right actions. Don't use auto-responses and create anything that could be perceived as spam. Is it positive and respectful? It may be fine to talk trash about competitors or complain about customers in the office, but not in social media. Don't belittle the competition or customers. Does it meet codes of conduct? As professionals, we are part of trade associations that set standards of conduct. Be sure you are meeting these ethical standards such as the AMA, AAAA, or PRSA's Code of Ethics. Does it meet all laws and regulations? Government has been catching up with social media and has issued regulations and laws you must follow. See guides on requirements like FTC endorsement, native ad, and review guidelines plus relevant standards in other countries and local laws like the California bot disclosure. *Does it meet the social media policy?* Most likely your brand or a client's brand has a social media policy. Ensure you follow your own company's standards.

The last consideration in all social media action from a personal, professional, or brand perspective has to do with listening. Research has shown that listening can influence up to 40 percent of a leader's performance.[76] Listening improves relationships, and social media is based on relationships with friends, colleagues, and customers. Thus, the last question to ask before posting or commenting in any personal, professional, or brand perspective is Am I listening *twice as much as I am talking?* Do you fully understand the person, organization, or situation you are commenting about? We have two ears and one mouth for a reason. Taking the time to listen has saved many a person or brand from putting their foot in their mouth and given valuable insight into creating successful social media efforts.

Consumer Data Privacy and Security

One final topic to consider is consumer data collection. As a social media professional, you will have the ability to collect and purchase an enormous amount of information about consumers. Deciding what to collect, what to sell, what to buy, and what to do with that information is an important legal and ethical issue. While this topic is much broader than social media and goes into digital marketing, e-commerce, customer relationship management (CRM), and even the general business practices of any organization, it is useful to mention in the context of social media. Main topics to consider in relation to social media strategy include privacy policies, behavioral targeting, data brokers, and data security.

For the Federal Trade Commission's perspective and standards in the United States, see their report "Privacy & Data Security Update (2016)" at FTC.gov.[77] In general, Europe tends to have stricter consumer protection rules, especially with the European Union (EU) General Data Protection Regulation (GDPR) mentioned in chapter 13.[78] Yet in 2020 a landmark privacy law took effect in the United States. The **California Consumer Protection Act (CCPA)** grants privacy powers to consumers in the United States granting the right to know what information companies collect about them and to opt out of having their data shared or sold.[79] For a summary of the five new rights granted, see table 15.3. It gives rights to consumers protecting their personal information to see what has been collected by companies and gives them the ability to force companies to delete that data and forbid them from sharing it with third parties.

Organizations should have privacy policies and data security standards. A **privacy policy** is a statement that defines an organization's policy on collecting and releasing information about a visitor or user.[80] It is important to note that having a privacy policy does not guarantee privacy protection. A privacy policy explains what information is collected, how

Table 15.3. Five New Rights Granted by California Consumer Privacy Act (CCPA)

1. Right to request disclosure of business's data collection and sales practices (specific categories)
2. Right to request a copy of specific personal information collected previous 12 months
3. Right to have this information deleted (with some exceptions)
4. Right to request personal information not be sold to third parties
5. Right to not be discriminated against for exercising these new rights

Source: Catherine D. Meyer, James R. Franco, and Fusae Nara, "Countdown to CCPA #3: Updating Your Privacy Policy," PillsburyLaw.com, July 8, 2019, https://www.pillsburylaw.com/en/news-and-insights/ccpa-privacy-policy.html.

it is used, and whether it is kept confidential or shared or sold to other firms, researchers, or sellers like data brokers. A survey of US internet users found that 52 percent incorrectly believed the statement, "When a company posts a privacy policy, it ensures that the company keeps confidential all the information it collects on users." Many policies are just legal documents that disclose how customer data is managed.[81] Even then privacy policies often use vague language about what is collected and how it is used. Another survey found that only 31 percent report that they understand how companies can share their personal information.[82] As a consumer it is best to read all privacy policies before using a website, service, or app. As a business there are now new stricter regulations and all online privacy policies must be updated to meet CCPA standards.

As mentioned in chapter 8, TikTok users complained that their videos were being used in TikTok ads on other social platforms without consent or payment. Yet everyone who signed up for TikTok agreed to their terms of service whether they read the small print or not, which included:

> You or the owner of your User Content still own the copyright in User Content sent to us, but by submitting User Content via the Services, you hereby grant us an unconditional irrevocable, non-exclusive, royalty-free, fully transferable, perpetual worldwide licence to use, modify, adapt, reproduce, make derivative works of, publish and/or transmit, and/or distribute and to authorise others users of the Services and other third-parties to view, access, use, download, modify, adapt, reproduce, make derivative works of, publish and/or transmit your User Content in any format and on any platform, either now known or hereinafter invented.[83]

These terms are similar to what other apps and social platforms have included in their small print. California's new data privacy law (CCPA) in addition to GDPR privacy protection and disclosure requirements, should change the way companies disclose and what they do with people's data.

As with all legal matters, organizations should consult with their lawyers and the specific laws, but experts indicate that CCPA standards will enable anyone to ask a company to disclose what data they are collecting by using a website and require a button on sites for consumers to opt out of data collection and selling. They will also have to delete data if a customer asked them to and they cannot treat those customers differently like charging higher prices because they have done so. Even though CCPA only applies to California citizens, national and regional companies may create separate systems with different standards, effectively making it a national standard. Other states' laws could follow, eventually leading to federal law.[84]

Who buys and sells this consumer data? **Data brokers** are businesses that collect consumers' personal information and sell it to other organizations.[85] Data brokers collect information about consumers from public and nonpublic sources such as courthouse records, website cookies, and loyalty card programs. In the United States there is no regulation that requires data brokers to share the information they have on consumers. Large data brokers like Acxiom, which is said to collect an average of 1,500 pieces of information on more than 200 million US citizens, have started self-regulation efforts.[86] Acxiom published a website where consumers can opt out from the use of their marketing data.[87] The buying and selling of consumer information has become very profitable. It has been reported that data brokering is now a 200-billion-dollar industry.[88]

Other concepts to consider that are relevant to paid social media include behavioral targeting. **Behavioral targeting** is used by advertisers to customize messages based on web-browsing behavior, such as web pages visited or searches made.[89] This can help improve the relevance and effectiveness of social media ads. This is better for marketers, but it is also important to note that some consumers have viewed this as creepy. Recent criticism includes consumers complaining that Facebook listens to their conversations to place customized ads in their feed. Yet this is a behavioral targeting technique the company denies.[90] It has been revealed that Facebook has also allowed third-party companies like Cambridge Analytica to collect private information from their users. Facebook CEO Mark Zuckerberg was called to testify before the US Congress over these allegations. Big data has enabled an

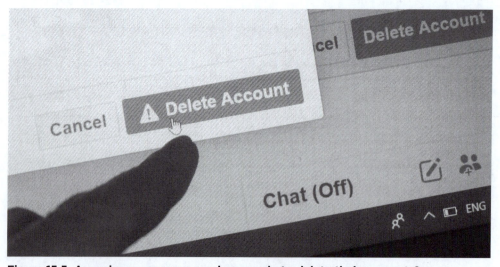

Figure 15.5. Are privacy concerns causing people to delete their accounts?

© Memitina / iStock Photo

enormous amount of consumer data that can be leveraged in many ways. But just because you can doesn't always mean you should.

Another consideration on this topic is data security. **Data security** refers to the measures organizations take to ensure digital privacy to prevent unauthorized access to computers, databases, and websites.[91] Data security is a growing concern of most organizations. This responsibility most likely rests with business information technology (IT) departments, yet marketers, advertisers, and public relations professionals must ensure that they know what measures are in place to communicate to consumers. Also, with the rise in high-profile data breaches at Target, Yahoo, eBay, and Equifax, brands need social media to communicate to worried consumers in crisis communication plans. No matter which country or countries your organization is doing business in, you should ensure that the company has strong and compliant privacy policies and data security measures in place.

This chapter just touched the surface of social media law, ethics, and etiquette. For formal legal advice, consult organization lawyers, official documents, and more in-depth resources. We must also consider growing evidence of the negative effects of social media use. New evidence, studies, and social media founder testimonies are just beginning to come out. Is social media addictive, bad for our health and our society? For further consideration of these important questions see "Additional Exercises," number 2, at the end of this chapter. The message of this chapter is that what you put out into the public helps to shape society. As Bill Bernbach said, you can choose to vulgarize and brutalize society, or you can choose to help lift it to a higher level. As discussed in chapter 13 with GDPR and Seth Godin's concept of permission marketing, it comes down to ensuring that there is a fair tradeoff. Marketing should approach data and privacy from a perspective of providing real value and only collecting what you need.

Theoretically Speaking: Elaboration Likelihood Model

Most marketing communication is designed to persuade; this includes advertising or public relations in social media. Thus it is helpful to understand theories of persuasion that may influence social media strategy. A key theory of persuasion is the Elaboration Likelihood Model (ELM) first developed by John T. Cacioppo and Richard E. Petty in the 1980s.[92] The **Elaboration Likelihood Model** is a dual process theory that proposes there are two routes to persuasion—the central route and peripheral route.[93]

Cacioppo and Petty indicated the persuasion level of a message can impact the attitude of a consumer who receives the message and explained that there are two routes to persuasion or this attitude change. The central route of persuasion requires longer thinking or elaboration. This requires motivation, which can come from relevant messages, high involvement, strong arguments, and little distraction. In the peripheral route of persuasion, the person does not spend time with the message—they don't elaborate on the meaning. Yet this route can still be persuasive by eliciting thought that doesn't require as much brainpower, such as experience, popularity, peer pressure, authority, attractiveness, or scarcity. Thus the central route applies to audiences with high motivation and the ability to think about the message. They focus on the quality of the message arguments and this can lead to lasting attitude change. The peripheral route is for audiences who have low motivation or lack the ability to think about the message. It involves more superficial processing that is more about attractiveness or surface features.[94]

How does ELM apply to social media? Consider the product, service, and target audience, which may indicate the need to emphasize one route over the other. Buying a new car is usually a high-motivation decision and requires deep processing because there is a lot of money involved in the decision. Messages for a car may take the central route. On the other hand, buying a pack of gum is usually a low-motivation decision. There is not a lot on the line. Thus a gum message may take a more superficial approach following the peripheral route focused on looks and surface features.

You may think of these as more rational versus more emotional persuasion appeals. This said, consumers don't buy cars simply on strong arguments and rational appeals. Many also fall in love with the way a car looks, sounds, or the image it has. They buy with both their head and their heart. Categories of products may vary as well. Jewelry can be very expensive but tends to appeal more to emotional decision making, but will also contain a rational component to ensure quality and craftmanship. At the end of the day, the best message route for brand strategy is usually a combination of both central and peripheral routes. Or different social media content may be chosen to highlight rational (central route) or emotional (peripheral route) messages at various times and places. What is an example of a recent brand social media post you saw that appealed to your heart and mind? Which was primary and which was secondary? Find another example where these appeals are switched.

Chapter 15 Checklist

Social media can change quickly. Visit Post Control Marketing (http://www.postcontrol marketing.com) for updates, but also use this chapter checklist to briefly check how social media statistics in this chapter have changed since publication.

- ✓ How has social media law changed? Have the FTC or other country and local laws been updated or added? Are there additional regulations that must be followed to ensure that social media marketing is not deceptive and/or protects consumer rights? Has GDPR, CCPA, and other regulations changed the targeting and tracking capabilities of social media campaigns? Have any government or trade organizations responded with new regulations to address the possible negative health effects of social media use?
- ✓ How have ethical considerations changed? Have the trade associations updated their codes of ethics around social media use? Is there a trade association for social media professionals and do they have a code of ethics? Have there been any high-profile cases where an organization or agency has violated the codes of ethics like "Wal-Marting Across America"?
- ✓ Have social media policy best practices changed? Look for the latest guides in writing a social media policy. Does more have to go into them because of increased social

SOCIAL PLAN PART 15

Checking the Plan for Law and Ethical Considerations

Your social media strategy and plan is done. You are going to present it and get it approved and then start implementing it. Before moving forward, ensure that you have considered all the legal requirements and ethical considerations. Report results of these considerations in these areas:

1. Look up the most recent FTC or other governing authority regulations for social media. Review the requirements and the brand social media plan. Does it meet the requirements?
2. Identify the most relevant trade association and read their code of ethics. Does the social media plan meet the expectations of professional conduct?
3. Does the organization or business have a social media policy? If not, write one based on best practices and brand standards. If the brand has a social media policy, review it and revise based on the latest legal regulations and ethical standards.
4. Consult business or organization lawyers to review any plans or policies for formal legal advice to ensure compliance before executing the final plan.
5. Finally, as a social media professional who may be implementing the social plan for a brand, also consider your own personal brand. Are you prepared to be active in social media from the personal, professional, and brand perspectives? Ensure that you have standards, systems, or plans in place to keep these different worlds working together.

For a condensed version of the social plan see appendix A: Three-Part Social Plan.

media use and risks? What does a typical brand social media policy look like today? How has GDPR and CCPA impacted organization privacy policies and social media practice?

KEY CONCEPTS

ad blocker
Federal Trade Commission (FTC)
International Consumer Protection and
Enforcement Network (ICPEN)
FTC Endorsement Guides
social media policy
attribution
user–generated content policy
Creative Commons
Digital Millennium Copyright Act (DMCA)
flog
social bot

California Bot Disclosure Law
ethics
etiquette
professionalism
personal branding
California Consumer Protection Act (CCPA)
privacy policy
data brokers
behavioral targeting
data security
Elaboration Likelihood Model

QUESTIONS FOR DISCUSSION

1. Go back to Bill Bernbach's quote at the beginning of this chapter. Find an example of a brand vulgarizing society with their social media. Find another brand that is helping to lift society to a higher level in social media. What are the main differences?
2. Revisit the "Wal-Marting Across America" case study. Has the Wal-Mart brand or other public relations firms done anything like that since the crisis? Have other brands or advertising agencies done something similar in a different social media context?
3. Is the use of fake followers really that prevalent? What percentage of the followers on top brand or celebrity Twitter and Instagram accounts are fake? How can you tell?
4. Go back to the box: The FTC Takes Action. If you were an employee at a business and found out that they purchased fake followers, subscribers, and views to gain new clients, what would you do? What if you were the one asked to do it? What if you were an employee at a cosmetics company and you received an email from the CEO instructing you to leave positive customer reviews and vote down negative ones to increase sales? Would you do it? Would you question it? Would you report it to the FTC?

ADDITIONAL EXERCISES

1. For this exercise, go online and find the published social media policies for three to five organizations. You may want to concentrate on one industry or simply pull from a wide variety of businesses and organizations. Make a list of the key sections from each policy and look for common categories. From this, make a list of required categories to include in a social media policy. From your research, create a template for a brand social media policy and write your own guide to creating it. If you like what you have created, seek an outlet to publish it. What blog or publication would find it to be of value?
2. Is social media addictive, bad for our health and our society? We increasingly see headlines such as "Social Media Anxiety Disorder, Explained. It's a Real Thing,"[95] "Facebook Admits Social Media Can Harm Your Mental Health,"[96] "Addiction for Fun and Profit: Facebook and Other Silicon Valley Companies Strive to Keep Users Hooked. Does that Make them Evil?"[97] and "Troll Factories, Bots and Fake News: Inside the Wild West of Social Media."[98] Research the growing evidence about the negative effects of social media. What are the latest developments and studies? Should something be done and by whom? What has happened since the Cambridge Analytica scandal? Have new federal regulations emerged after Facebook CEO Mark Zuckerberg testified before the US Congress?

Notes

1. "William Bernbach Quotes," BrainyQuote.com, accessed November 19, 2019, https://www.brainyquote.com/quotes/authors/w/william_bernbach.html.

2. Mark Ritson, "Brands Face a Rising Threat from Ad Avoidance," BrandStrategyInsider.com, August 19, 2015, https://www.brandingstrategyinsider.com/2015/08/brands–threat–avoidance.html#.WZL244qQyV5.

3. "Ad blocker," Techopedia.com, accessed November 19, 2019, https://www.techopedia.com/definition/23090/ad-blocker.

4. Matthew Cortland, "2017 Adblock Report," PageFair.com, February 1, 2017, https://pagefair.com/blog/2017/adblockreport/.

5. Irfan Ahmad, "Global Ad Blocking Behavior 2019 [Infographic]," SocialMedia Today.com, April 2, 2019, https://www.socialmediatoday.com/news/global-ad-blocking-behavior-2019-infographic/551716/.

6. "Ad blocker," Techopedia.com.

7. Jack Marshall, "Forbes Tests New Tactics to Combat Ad Blocking," WallStreetJournal .com, May 13, 2016, https://www.wsj.com/articles/forbes-tests-new-tactics-to-combat-ad-blocking-1463133628.

8. "New York Times' Digital Subscriptions Continue to Drive Growth," Forbes.com, May 4, 2017, https://www.forbes.com/sites/greatspeculations/2017/05/04/new-york-times-digital-subscriptions-continue-to-drive-growth/#6532da97295c.

9. Trefis Team, "New York Times Is Thriving on Growing Digital Subscriptions," Forbes.com, February 11, 2019, https://www.forbes.com/sites/greatspeculations/2019/02/11/new-york-times-is-thriving-on-growing-digital-subscriptions/#17f42f6f6c91.

10. "Now that You're Here. . . ," Contribute.TheGuardian.com, accessed November 19, 2019, https://contribute.theguardian.com/uk?countryGroup=us&REFPVID=j6dqw4wmynx9tmbkvc3j&INTCMP=gdnwb_copts_memco_banner.

11. "William Bernbach Facts," Biography.YourDictionary.com, accessed November 19, 2019, https://biography.yourdictionary.com/william-bernbach.

12. "Protecting Consumers Worldwide," ICPEN.org, November 19, 2019, https://www.icpen .org/.

13. "Advertising FAQ's: A Guide for Small Business," FTC.gov, April 2001, https://www.ftc.gov/tips-advice/business-center/guidance/advertising-faqs-guide-small-business.

14. "Advertising FAQ's," FTC.gov.

15. Mitchell J. Katz, Michael Ostheimer, and Mamie Kresses, "FTC Staff Reminds Influencers and Brands to Clearly Disclose Relationship: Commission Aims to Improve Disclosures in Social Media Endorsements," FTC.gov, April 19, 2017, https://www.ftc.gov/news-events/press-releases/2017/04/ftc-staff-reminds-influencers-brands-clearly-disclose.

16. "The FTC's Endorsement Guides: What People Are Asking," FTC.gov, May 2015, https://www.ftc.gov/tips-advice/business-center/guidance/ftcs-endorsement-guides-what-people-are-asking#intro.

17. "FTC's Endorsement Guides," FTC.gov.

18. "Enforcement Policy Statement on Deceptively Formatted Advertisements," FTC.gov, December 22, 2015, https://www.ftc.gov/public-statements/2015/12/commission-enforcement-policy-statement-deceptively-formatted.

19. "Native Advertising: A Guide for Business," FTC.gov, December 2015, https://www.ftc.gov/tips-advice/business-center/guidance/native-advertising-guide-businesses.

20. "Consumer Review Fairness Act: What Businesses Need to Know," FTC.org, February 2017, https://www.ftc.gov/tips-advice/business-center/guidance/consumer-review-fairness-act-what-businesses-need-know.

21. "Online Reviews and Endorsements: Advice for Business," Gov.UK, March 4, 2016, https://www.gov.uk/government/publications/online-reviews-and-endorsements-advice-for-businesses.

22. "The Deceptive Marketing Practices Digest, Volume 1," CompetitionBureau.gc.ca, June 10, 2015, http://www.competitionbureau.gc.ca/eic/site/cb-bc.nsf/eng/03946.html.

23. "Social Media," ACCC.gov.au, accessed November 19, 2019, https://www.accc.gov.au/business/advertising-promoting-your-business/social-media.

24. Sarah Marsh, "Social Media Stars Breaching Rules on Promoting Brands, Watchdog Says," TheGuardian.com, October 5, 2017, https://www.theguardian.com/media/2017/oct/05/social-media-stars-breaching-rules-on-promoting-brands-watchdog-says-instagram-twitter.

25. "CSGO Lotto Owners Settle FTC's First-Ever Complaint against Individual Social Media Influencers," FTC.gov, September 7, 2017, https://www.ftc.gov/news-events/press-releases/2017/09/csgo-lotto-owners-settle-ftcs-first-ever-complaint-against.

26. Sam Sabin, "A Year After Major Actions, FTC's Influencer Marketing Guidelines Still Overlooked," MorningConsult.com, October 4, 2018, https://morningconsult.com/2018/10/04/a-year-later-ftcs-influencer-marketing-guidelines-still-largely-ignored/.

27. Margaret Rouse and Wendy Schuchart, "Social Media Policy," SearchCompliance.TechTarget.com, August 2011, http://searchcompliance.techtarget.com/definition/social-media-policy.

28. Forbes Human Resources Council, "Why Your Business Needs a Social Media Policy and Eight Things It Should Cover," Forbes.com, May 25, 2017, https://www.forbes.com/sites/forbeshumanresourcescouncil/2017/05/25/why-your-business-needs-a-social-media-policy-and-eight-things-it-should-cover/#73273b0a5264.

29. Jylian Russell, "How to Write a Social Media Policy for Your Company," Hootsuite.com, July 29, 2019, https://blog.hootsuite.com/social-media-policy-for-employees/.

30. "Social Media Policy," GM.com, accessed November 18, 2019, https://www.gm.com/social-media-policy.html.

31. "Sharing Mayo Clinic: For Mayo Clinic Employees," Sharing.MayoClinic.org, https://sharing.mayoclinic.org/guidelines/for-mayo-clinic-employees/.

32. "Social Media Guidelines: 13 and Older," NYC Department of Education, accessed November 19, 2019, https://www.schools.nyc.gov/school-life/rules-for-students/digital-citizenship/social-media-guidelines-for-students-over-13.

33. "Social Media Guidelines for DOE Staff," NYC Department of Education, accessed November 19, 2019, https://infohub.nyced.org/reports-and-policies/policies/social-media-guidelines-for-doe-staff.

34. Russell, "How to Write a Social Media Policy."

35. Forbes Human Resources Council, "Why Your Business Needs a Social Media Policy."

36. "Attribution," Merriam-Webster.com, accessed November 19, 2019, https://www.merriam-webster.com/dictionary/attribution.

37. Alex York, "The Ultimate User-Generated Content Guide," SproutSocial.com, October 5, 2016, https://sproutsocial.com/insights/user-generated-content-guide/.

38. "How to Legally Re-Use Social Media Posts: How to Legally Repurpose User-Generated Content from Social Media," Tradablebits.com, September 21, 2015, https://tradablebits.com/blog/how-to-legally-repurpose-user-generated-content-from-social-media/.

39. "4 Clauses to Have if You Host User-Generated Content," TermsFeed.com, October 23, 2016, https://termsfeed.com/blog/4-clauses-host-user-generated-content/.

40. "User Generated Content Policy," CustomerService-Macys.com, accessed November 19, 2019, https://www.customerservice-macys.com/app/answers/detail/a_id/388/~/user-generated-content-policy.

41. "Our User Content Policy," Pier1.com, accessed November 19, 2019, https://www.pier1.com/user_content_policy.html.

42. Barry Feldman, "The 9 Best User-Generated Content Platforms for Driving Engagement and Sales," ConvinceAndConvert.com, accessed November 19, 2019, https://www.convinceandconvert.com/digital-marketing/best-user-generated-content-platforms/.

43. Craig Silverman, "Practice Ethical Curation and Attribution," AmericanPressInsitute.com, September 24, 2014, https://www.americanpressinstitute.org/publications/reports/strategy-studies/ethical-curation-attribution/.

44. Pawan Deshpande, "Content Curation & Fair Use: 5 Rules to Being an Ethical Content Curator," ContentCurationMarketing.com (blog), January 25, 2013, http://www.content curationmarketing.com/content-curation-fair-use-5-rules-to-being-an-ethical-content-curator/.

45. Dhariana Lozano, "How to Properly Re-Post User-Generated Content on Social Networks," SocialMediaToday.com, September 2, 2016, http://www.socialmediatoday.com/social-business/how-properly-re-post-user-generated-content-social-networks.

46. "About the Licenses," CreativeCommons.org, accessed November 19, 2019, https://creative commons.org/licenses/.

47. "HIPAA Social Media Rules," HIPAAJournal.com, March 12, 2018, https://www.hipaa journal.com/hipaa-social-media/.

48. Neil Vigdor, "Elon Musk Bids Twitter Farewell—Briefly," NYTimes.com, November 1, 2019, https://www.nytimes.com/2019/11/01/business/elon-musk-twitter.html.

49. Ann E. Marimow, "President Trump Cannot Block His Critics on Twitter, Federal Appeals Court Rules," WashingtonPost.com, July 9, 2019, https://www.washingtonpost.com/local/legal -issues/president-trump-cannot-block-his-critics-on-twitter-federal-appeals-court-rules/2019/07/ 09/d07a5558-8230-11e9-95a9-e2c830afe24f_story.html.

50. "Executive Summary Digital Millennium Copyright Act Section 104 Report," Copyright .gov, accessed August 15, 2017, https://www.copyright.gov/reports/studies/dmca/dmca_executive .html.

51. "Ethical Standards Advisory ESA-20," PRSA.org, September 2015, https://www.prsa.org/ docs/default-source/about/ethics/eas/ethical-standards-advisory-ethics-and-social-media.pdf?sfvrsn =be47b4cb_2.

52. David Hagenbuch, "Followers for Sale," MindfulMarketing.com, August 1, 2015, http:// www.mindfulmarketing.org/mindful-matters-blog/followers-for-sale.

53. Andrew Tate, "Buying Instagram Followers? Our Experiment Reveals the Truth . . . ," AdExpresso.com, December 27, 2016, https://adespresso.com/academy/blog/buying-instagram -followers-our-experiment-reveals-the-truth/.

54. Susan Krashinsky, "Bell to Pay $1.25-Million Penalty for Fake Reviews," TheGlobeAndMail .com, October 14, 2015, https://www.theglobeandmail.com/report-on-business/industry-news/ marketing/bell-to-pay-125-million-penalty-for-fake-reviews/article26806629/.

55. Beatrice Cole, "International Effort to Tackle Misleading Online Reviews," Gov.uk, July 31, 2017, https://www.gov.uk/government/news/international-effort-to-tackle-misleading-online -reviews.

56. Greg Finn, "Paying for Fake Product Reviews? Amazon May Sue You," MarketingLand.com, June 2, 2016, http://marketingland.com/paid-fake-review-amazon-may-now-sue-179583.

57. Crys Wiltshire, "The Fake Followers Epidemic," gShift.com, May 25, 2017, https://www .gshiftlabs.com/social-media-blog/the-fake-followers-epidemic/.

58. "5 Epic Social Media Automation Fails: Bots Just Aren't People," Cultivate -Communications.com, March 17, 2015, https://www.cultivate-communications.com/2015/03/ 5-epic-social-media-automation-fails-bots-just-arent-people/.

59. "Socialbot," Techopedia.com, accessed November 19, 2019, https://www.techopedia.com/ definition/27811/socialbot.

60. Eksith Rodrigo, "Bank of America Bot Cares about You," eksith.wordpress.com, July 7, 2013, https://eksith.wordpress.com/2013/07/07/bank-of-america-bot/.

61. Natalie Petouhoff, "What Is a Chatbot and How Is It Changing Customer Experience?" Salesforce.com, April 25, 2019, https://www.salesforce.com/blog/2019/04/what-is-a-chatbot.html.

62. Jenn Chen, "Social Media Automation Rules No Brand Should Break," SproutSocial.com, April 18, 2017, https://sproutsocial.com/insights/social-media-automation/.

63. "Senate Bill No. 1001, California Legislative Information," September 28, 2019, https://leginfo.legislature.ca.gov/faces/billTextClient.xhtml?bill_id=201720180SB1001.

64. Robert Bateman, "How to Comply with California's Bot Disclosure Law," TermsFeed.com, September 26, 2019, https://www.termsfeed.com/blog/ca-bot-disclosure-law/.

65. Simon Kemp, "Digital in 2019," wearesocial.com, 2019, https://wearesocial.com/global-digital-report-2019.

66. "Most Popular Social Networks Used by Fortune 500 Companies in 2017," Statista.com, accessed November 19, 2019, https://www-statista-com.ezproxy.messiah.edu/statistics/626872/fortune-500-corporate-social-media-usage/.

67. Kimberlee Morrison, "Survey: 92% of Recruiters Use Social Media to Find High-Quality Candidates," Adweek.com, September 22, 2015, http://www.adweek.com/socialtimes/survey-96-of-recruiters-use-social-media-to-find-high-quality-candidates/627040.

68. "Ethic," Merriam-Webster.com, accessed November 19, 2019, http://www.merriam-webster.com/dictionary/ethic.

69. "Etiquette," Merriam-Webster.com, accessed November 19, 2019, http://www.merriam-webster.com/dictionary/etiquette.

70. "Professionalism," Merriam-Webster.com, accessed November 19, 2019, http://www.merriam-webster.com/dictionary/professionalism.

71. Rachel Nauen, "Number of Employers Using Social Media to Screen Candidates at All-Time High, Finds Latest CareerBuilder Study," CareerBuilder, PRNewsWire.com, June 15, 2017, https://www.prnewswire.com/news-releases/number-of-employers-using-social-media-to-screen-candidates-at-all-time-high-finds-latest-careerbuilder-study-300474228.html.

72. Nauen, "Number of Employers Using Social Media."

73. Ryan C. Martin, Kelsey Ryan Coyier, Leah M. VanSistine, and Kelly L. Schroeder, "Anger on the Internet: The Perceived Value of Rant-Sites," *Cyberpsychology, Behavior, and Social Networking* 16, no. 2 (February 2013): 119–122.

74. Ellen Rolfes, "Why Ranting Online Doesn't Help Manage Anger," *PBS Newshour*, PBS.org, February 28, 2014, http://www.pbs.org/newshour/updates/many-rants-online/.

75. Kirstie Brewer, "What Your Social Media Presence Says about You," TheGuardian.com, April 6, 2016, https://jobs.theguardian.com/article/what-your-social-media-presence-says-about-you/.

76. Travis Bradberry, "Why Successful People Are Great Listeners," World Economic Forum, October 6, 2017, https://www.weforum.org/agenda/2015/10/why-successful-people-are-great-listeners/.

77. "Privacy & Data Security Update (2016)," FTC.gov, January 2017, https://www.ftc.gov/reports/privacy-data-security-update-2016#how.

78. "What Will the GDPR Mean for B2B Marketing Professionals?" Kingpin, May 2017, http://kingpincomms.com/wp-content/uploads/2017/04/Kingpin_GDPR-eBook-20172-002.pdf.

79. Adam Janofsky, "California Lawmakers Pass Only Minor Changes to Privacy Measure," WSJ.com, September 16, 2019, https://www.wsj.com/articles/california-lawmakers-pass-only-minor-changes-to-privacy-measure-11568626204.

80. "Privacy Policy," BusinessDictionary.com, accessed November 19, 2019, http://www.businessdictionary.com/definition/privacy-policy.html.

81. Aaron Smith, "Half of Online Americans Don't Know What a Privacy Policy Is," Pew Research.org, December 4, 2014, http://www.pewresearch.org/fact-tank/2014/12/04/half-of-americans-dont-know-what-a-privacy-policy-is/.

82. Brian Mastroianni, "Survey: More Americans Worried about Data Privacy than Income," CBSNews.com, January 28, 2016, https://www.cbsnews.com/news/truste-survey-more-americans-concerned-about-data-privacy-than-losing-income/.

83. Garett Sloane, "TikTok Users Are Surprised to Find Themselves in Ads for the App," AdAge.com, October 7, 2019, https://adage.com/article/digital/tiktok-users-are-surprised-find -themselves-ads-app/2204996.

84. Jeff John Roberts, "Here Comes America's First Privacy Law: What the CCPA Means for Business and Consumers," September 13, 2019, https://fortune.com/2019/09/13/what-is-ccpa -compliance-california-data-privacy-law/.

85. "Data Broker (Information Broker)," TechTarget.com, September 2013, http://whatis .techtarget.com/definition/data-broker-information-broker/.

86. Steve Kroft, "The Data Brokers: Selling Your Personal Information," *60 Minutes*, CBSNews .com, March 2014, https://www.cbsnews.com/news/the-data-brokers-selling-your-personal -information/.

87. "Privacy—About the Data," AboutTheData.com, accessed November 19, 2019, https:// aboutthedata.com/.

88. "How Much Is Your Personal Information Worth?" WebPageFX.com, April 16, 2015, https://www.webpagefx.com/blog/general/what-are-data-brokers-and-what-is-your-data-worth -infographic/.

89. "Behavioral Targeting," BlueFountainMedia.com, accessed November 19, 2019, https:// www.bluefountainmedia.com/glossary/behavioral-targeting/.

90. Amit Chowdhry, "Facebook Reiterates that It Does Not Listen to Conversations through Your Phone for Ad Targeting," Forbes.com, October 31, 2017, https://www.forbes.com/sites/ amitchowdhry/2017/10/31/facebook-ads-microphone/#e123b34534d3.

91. "Data Security," Techopedia.com, accessed November 19, 2019, https://www.techopedia .com/definition/26464/data-security.

92. H. Allen White, "Elaboration Likelihood Model," OxfordBibliographies.com, last modified February 23, 2011, http://www.oxfordbibliographies.com/view/document/obo-9780199756841/ obo-9780199756841-0053.xml.

93. "Elaboration Likelihood Model," OxfordBibliographies.com, last modified February 23, 2011, https://www.oxfordbibliographies.com/view/document/obo-9780199756841/obo -9780199756841-0053.xml.

94. John T. Cacioppo and Richard E. Petty, "The Elaboration Likelihood Model of Persuasion," *Advances in Consumer Research* 11, no. 1 (1984): 673–675; Sneha Mishra, "Elaboration Likelihood Model," BusinessTopia.net, accessed November 19, 2019, https://www.businesstopia.net/ communication/elaboration-likelihood-model.

95. Helaina Hovitz, "Social Media Anxiety Disorder, Explained. It's a Real Thing," TeenVogue .com, September 8, 2017, https://www.teenvogue.com/story/social-media-anxiety-disorder.

96. David Z. Morris, "Facebook Admits Social Media Can Harm Your Mental Health," Fortune.com, December 16, 2017, http://fortune.com/2017/12/16/facebook-admits-social -media-can-harm-your-mental-health/.

97. Will Oremus, "Addiction for Fun and Profit: Facebook and Other Silicon Valley Companies Strive to Keep Users Hooked. Does that Make Them Evil?" Slate.com, November 10, 2017, http:// www.slate.com/articles/technology/technology/2017/11/facebook_was_designed_to_be_addictive _does_that_make_it_evil.html.

98. Bob Abeshouse, "Troll Factories, Bots and Fake News: Inside the Wild West of Social Media," Aljazeera.com, February 8, 2018, https://www.aljazeera.com/blogs/americas/2018/02/troll -factories-bots-fake-news-wild-west-social-media-180207061815575.html.

Appendix A:
Three-Part Social Plan

A blueprint for creating an integrated social media strategy or plan has been laid out in the "Social Plan" (parts 1–15) at the end of each chapter. What follows is a condensed version of that process. Marketers, advertisers, and public relations professionals can use this simplified, three-step approach to develop a complete, integrated social media strategy for any brand, product, service, or organization. Work through each part, 1 through 3, to build a social media plan to be presented, approved, and activated.

1. Brand Summary and Social Analysis

For the first part of the social media plan, write a summary of the organization's history, mission, business objectives, current situation, and marketing campaign; define the target audience; perform a social media audit; and report results and insights gained.

- Gather a snapshot of the organization's history, mission, and vision.
- Detail recent brand performance over time, industry trends, and key competitors including a SWOT graphic summary (see figure A.1).
- Explain the current marketing communications campaign theme/tagline/look and recent efforts for the brand and main competitors.
- Define a target audience with multiple bases of segmentation including specific demographic and psychographic variables.
- Identify overall business objectives, not social media specific tactics, following SMART (specific, measurable, attainable, realistic, time bound) guidelines.
- Perform a social media audit of all possible social channels (not just current brand or competitor accounts), report results (see table A.1), and describe the insights gained.

	Helpful	Harmful
Internal	**S** Strengths	**W** Weaknesses
External	**O** Opportunities	**T** Threats

Figure A.1. SWOT Analysis (Matrix) Graphic Template

2. Big Idea and Social Channels

Create a social media big idea with legs that integrates with traditional marketing. Then select social media platform channels by category that fit target audience and big idea. Use the social media story template to plan possible big idea content.

- Summarize insights from the social media audit and add consumer research on the target audience from primary and secondary sources including their social media usage statistics.
- Explain how the insights led to a social media big idea with a theme/hashtag across social media channels. Consider how the idea can be told as a larger brand story, leveraging all five acts of storytelling.
- Select social media channels by category that are most appropriate for target audience, big idea, and business objectives (see table A.2). Include user statistics that match target audience and describe how content/culture of each platform fits the big idea.
- Suggest current social media channels that are no longer needed and should be removed or how the strategy on those existing channels needs to be changed.
- Consider how current traditional advertising, public relations, digital marketing, promotions, brand characters, and brand taglines will be integrated into the new social effort.

3. Final Social Media Plan and Presentation

Add social media integration beyond marketing communication, examples of social content for the big idea in each social channel, a content calendar, determine social media metrics

Table A.1. Social Media Audit Template

Who	Where Channel/Environment	What Content/Sentiment	When Date/Frequency	Why Purpose/Performance
Company				
Consumer				
Competitor				

Table A.2. Questions for Selecting Social Media Plan Channels

Users match target audience?	Yes/No	Demographics
Media type matches idea content?	Yes/No	Type
Existing brand account/page?	Yes/No	Changes
Existing brand community?	Yes/No	Opportunities
Competitor brand presence?	Yes/No	Strengths/Weaknesses
Paid social advertising options?	Yes/No	Options

to support business objectives, and estimate a social media budget. Collect all previous information into a final social media plan report.

- Take the plan beyond marketing, such as how social media research could support the business, identify projects or functions that could use crowdsourcing, devise a strategy to engage and reward brand evangelists, and/or plan a cross-functional social care team (consider topics in part IV, chapters 11–13).
- Finalize the plan by collecting all information from the previous two parts into one cohesive social media strategy. Start with a big picture of the current situation problem, target audience, and business objectives leading up to the social audit insights and the big idea solution and executions in the selected social media channels. Justify social channels added and removed with user statistics and content description.
- Write a buyer persona as a basis for creating the social media content (see chapter 12 under content marketing). Illustrate the big idea with at least one example in each social platform of written content in visual context of the social media environment where the content would appear. Create an example content calendar for how the plan will be executed (see table A.3).
- Add measurement by linking business objectives with metrics for each social channel to determine KPIs following the social media metrics template (see table A.4).
- Create a final oral presentation of the report to sell the plan to organization management. To go further, estimate the social media budget following the social media budget template (see table A.5).

Follow this example social media plan format:

1. Provide an overview of brand, main competitor, and current marketing communication activities including a SWOT graphic summary (see figure A.1).
2. Identify overall business objectives, define target audience, and describe their social media use.
3. Include the social media audit results in a table and describe insights gained (see table A.1).
4. Explain social media strategy big idea with theme/hashtag and how it integrates with traditional media including digital marketing, advertising, and PR.
5. Provide social media platforms added and removed with selection rationale considering user statistics, culture, and content.

Table A.3. Social Media Content Calendar

Social Media Channel Target/Persona:	Mon. (time) Title/Theme: Assets: Tags/Keywords:	Tue. (time) Title/Theme: Assets: Tags/Keywords:	Wed. (time) Title/Theme: Assets: Tags/Keywords:	Thu. (time) Title/Theme: Assets: Tags/Keywords:	Fri. (time) Title/Theme: Assets: Tags/Keywords:	Sat. (time) Title/Theme: Assets: Tags/Keywords:	Sun. (time) Title/Theme: Assets: Tags/Keywords:

Table A.4. Social Media Metrics Template

Social Media Channel	Objective 1:*	Objective 2:*	Objective 3:*	Objective 4:*
	KPI:	KPI:	KPI:	KPI:
	KPI:	KPI:	KPI:	KPI:
	KPI:	KPI:	KPI:	KPI:
	KPI:	KPI:	KPI:	KPI:

*Ensure objectives follow SMART guidelines (specific, measureable, achievable, relevant, and time bound) and refer to business objectives to connect social media activity to organization mission and goals to measure ROI.

6. Create a buyer persona (see chapter 12), write and design content in appropriate formats for each social platform, and include a content calendar with optimal posting dates/times, keywords, calls to action, and links (see table A.3).
7. Include other sections important to the individual organization such as a social media and privacy policy, crisis communication and event plan, influencer/advocate guidelines and disclosure requirements, or software and discipline integration recommendations.
8. Identify metrics by social platform and business objective using the metrics table (see table A.4) to show how success will be measured and efforts optimized while considering specific analytics software tools and methods for tracking.
9. Estimate costs with a budget using a method described in chapter 14 and following the social media budget template (see table A.5). Indicate which social media platforms (e.g., Facebook) and programs (e.g., Influencers) will require/include ad spending.

Once the formal written report is complete, the presentation is given, and the plan is approved, consider the legal and ethical guidelines discussed in chapter 15. For

Table A.5. Social Media Budget Template

Budget Category Type/Description	In-House Expense Fixed/Percentage	Outsource Expense Fixed/Percentage	Total Category Fixed/Percentage
Content Creation	($ per hour x hours	(# pieces content x $	**$ %**
Writing	per month)	per piece/project)	$ %
Graphics			$ %
Video			$ %
Social Advertising	(N/A)	($ per day x days per	**$ %**
(social channel 1)		month)	$ %
(social channel 2)			$ %
(social channel 3)			$ %
Social Engagement	($ per hour x hours	($ per hour x hours per	**$ %**
(social channel 1)	per month)	month)	$ %
(social channel 2)			$ %
(social channel 3)			$ %
Software/Tools	(N/A)	($ per month)	**$ %**
Monitoring			$ %
Scheduling			$ %
Analytics			$ %
Promotions/Contests	($ per campaign)	($ per campaign)	**$ %**
(social channel 1)			$ %
(social channel 2)			$ %
(social channel 3)			$ %
Total	**$ %**	**$ %**	**$**

implementation, what social media policies, guidelines, systems, and/or training need to be put into place?

Specific social media strategy elements will vary based on organization and situation, but the key elements of a plan include many of the elements discussed above. You can think of each as significant subhead sections for a final social media plan report and significant components of a final social media plan presentation to key stakeholders:

1. **Brand, Industry, and Competitor Overview** (SWOT, current marketing description)
2. **Business Objectives and Target Audience** (target social media use)
3. **Social Media Audit** (results and insights gained)
4. **Social Strategy Big Idea** (theme with digital marketing, advertising, and PR integration)
5. **Recommended Social Platforms** (add or remove with platform stats)
6. **Creative Content and Calendar** (buyer persona, written/designed content, content calendar)
7. **Policies, Guidelines, and Requirements** (varies per organization needs but can include social media/privacy policy, crisis communication/event plan, influencer/

advocate guidelines/disclosure requirements, or software/discipline integration recommendations)
8. **Social Media Analytics** (metrics by social platform and business objective, measurement and optimization plan including software tools and tracking methods)
9. **Social Media Budget** (overall estimate by category and platforms/programs that require ad spend)

As a final note, be sure to provide an overall introduction and conclusion or executive summary to your complete plan recommendation.

Appendix B:
Social Media Tools and Resources

What follows is a list with links to more than three hundred sites and apps to improve your social media efforts and knowledge. Use these to complete the social media plan and execute the strategy. Links are divided into ten categories: Social Media Monitoring and Metrics; Online Data Collection and Analytics; Social Media Content Creation and Data Visualization; Social Content Scheduling and Automation; Social Media and Digital Media Research; Trade Associations, Awards, and Conferences; Social Media News and Insights; Social Media and Content Marketing Podcasts; Social Media and Digital Marketing Training and Certification; and Social Media Channels. A short description of each site follows the name before the URL. This is a great start, but social media tools can change quickly. Discover more and new resources as they are introduced by visiting https://www.post controlmarketing.com/links.

Social Media Monitoring and Metrics

Acuity (video monitoring and analytics): acuityads.com
Agora Pulse (social media management tool): www.agorapulse.com
Agora Pulse Free Tools (Facebook barometer, Twitter report card, Facebook page contests): agora pulse.com/free-social-media-marketing-tools
Any Clip (AI video intelligence/management): anyclip.com
Awario (social media brand monitoring): awario.com
Bazaarvoice (brand ratings and reviews platform): bazaarvoice.com
BirdEye (customer review management) birdeye.com
Brandwatch (social listening and analytics): brandwatch.com
Brand24 (social media monitoring): brand24.com
Buzzsumo (content analytics): buzzsumo.com
Cision (social monitoring and analytics): www.cision.com/us/products/monitoring/social/
Clarabridge (customer experience management and analytics): www.clarabridge.com
Critical Mention (media monitoring): www.criticalmention.com
CrowdRiff (AI image recognition discover/manage UGC): CrowdRiff.com

Digitmind (social media management): digimind.com

Fanpage Karma (social media management): fanpagekarma.com

GIPHY (library of animated GIFs): giphy.com

Google Alerts (monitoring): google.com/alerts

GRYTICS (Facebook Group analytics and management): grytics.com

Hootsuite (social dashboard, scheduling, reporting): hootsuite.com

How Sociable (social media monitoring): howsociable.com

HYP3R (location-based social listening): hyp3r.com

Iconosquare (analytics and management): iconosquare.com

Khoros (social media management): khoros.com

Klear (influencer marketing platform): klear.com

Meltwater (social media monitoring and analytics): meltwater.com

Meltwater Impact (free content report): impact.meltwater.com

Mention (social media monitoring and publishing): mention.com

Netbase (social analytics): netbase.com

Nielsen Social (social content ratings): www.nielsensocial.com

NUVI (monitoring, analysis, reporting): www.nuvi.com

Oktopost (B2B social media management): oktopost.com

Oracle Social Cloud (monitoring, analytics, engagement): www.oracle.com/us/solutions/social

Pattern89 (AI driven paid social): pattern89.com

Podium (customer messaging and review platform): podium.com

Reputology (review monitoring and management): reputology.com

ReviewTrackers (online review management): reviewtrackers.com

Rival IQ (social media analytics): rivaliq.com

Salesforce: Social Studio (social media marketing and management): marketingcloud.com/products/
social-media-marketing/social-studio

Social Bakers (social media management): socialbakers.com

Social Blade (social media statistics): socialblade.com

Social Mention (real-time search and analysis): socialmention.com

Social Searcher (real-time social search): social-searcher.com

Socially Devoted Meter (analyze response rate): socialbakers.com/resources/socially-devoted

Sprinklr (unified customer experience management): sprinklr.com

Sprout Social (social media management): sproutsocial.com

SumAll (social media automation): sumall.com

SumoRank (analyze best Facebook page content): sumorank.com

Talkwalker (social analytics and monitoring): talkwalker.com

Talkwalker Social Analytics Search (track campaigns and hashtags): talkwalker.com/social-media
-analytics-search

TrueSocialMetrics (social media analytics): truesocialmetrics.com

Twitonomy (Twitter analytics and monitoring): twitonomy.com

Unmetric (social intelligence and analytics): unmetric.com

Unruly (social video insight): unruly.co

Viralwoot (social scheduler and analytics): viralwoot.com

Yext (search experience monitoring and management): yext.com

Yext Free Listings Scan (location data analysis): yext.com/resources/business-scan

Zoho Social (social media management): zoho.com/social

Online Data Collection and Analytics

Alexa (website statistics and analysis): alexa.com

Bottlenose (data analysis): bottlenose.com

Chartbeat (content intelligence and analytics): chartbeat.com

Comscore (cross-platform measurement): comscore.com

Conversion Fly (online tracking and optimization): conversionfly.com

Cyfe (all-in-one online monitoring dashboard): www.cyfe.com

Dataminr (monitors real-time brand social conversations) dataminr.com

Datarama (cross channel analytics/insights): datorama.com

Delmondo (AI marketing analytics): delmondo.co/snapchat-analytics-software

Drip (e-commerce CRM): drip.co

Facebook Analytics (multichannel analytics): analytics.facebook.com

Facebook Audience Insights (Facebook, Instagram audience analytics): facebook.com/business/insights/tools/audience-insights

Facebook Page Cost Calculator (Facebook ad cost tool):shiftcomm.com/facebook-page-cost-calculator

Foursquare Analytics (location-based insights): enterprise.foursquare.com/solutions/analytics

Google Analytics (website analytics): www.google.com/analytics

Google Analytics UTM Tracking URL Builder (online tracking): chrome.google.com/webstore

Google Campaign URL Builder (track custom campaigns): ga-dev-tools.appspot.com/campaign-url-builder

Google Search Console (measure/improve search traffic): search.google.com/search-console

Google Tag Manager (tracking): www.google.com/analytics/tag-manager

Google Tools (online data analysis): www.thinkwithgoogle.com/tools

Google Trends (real-time online search analysis): www.google.com/trends

Hotjar (website heatmaps, funnels, feedback) hotjar.com

IBM Cognos Analytics (AI business intelligence): https://www.ibm.com/products/cognos-analytics

iSpionage (online competitor research): ispionage.com

Keyhole (real-time hashtag and influencer analytics): keyhole.co

Keyword Tool (keyword research): keywordtool.io

Kiss Metrics (behavioral analytics and engagement): kissmetricshq.com

Kred (influence score and platform): kred.com

Leadpages (landing page creator, opt-in tools): leadpages.net

LinkedIn Analytics: linkedin.com/help/linkedin/answer/4499

Manageflitter (Twitter tools and analytics): manageflitter.co

Moz Link Explorer (Inbound link tool): moz.com/researchtools/ose

Nexalogy (discover social conversations and insights): nexalogy.com

Omgili (discussion, news, blog search): omgili.com

Pinterest Analytics: analytics.pinterest.com

Quantcast (website audience measurement): quantcast.com

RiteTag (trending hashtags): ritetag.com/hashtag-search

Searchmetrics (enterprise content marketing): searchmetrics.com

SEMrush (online competitive intelligence): www.semrush.com

Serpstat (SEO platform): serpstat.com

SharedCount (URL shares and likes tracking): www.sharedcount.com

Shopping Insights (online shopping trends): shopping.thinkwithgoogle.com

SimilarWeb (website stats and analytics comparison): similarweb.com

Snaplytics (automated story publishing and analytics): snaplytics.io
Soovle (search suggestions): soovle.co
Tableau (data analysis/visualization): tableau.com
TrendKite (PR analytics): trendkite.com
Trendspottr (real-time viral content, influencers): trendspottr.com
Tweetreach (free Twitter analytics): tweetreach.com
Twitter Advanced Search: twitter.com/search-advanced
Twitter Analytics: analytics.twitter.com
Ubersuggest (keyword suggestion tool): ubersuggest.io
Union Metrics (social marketing analytics): unionmetrics.com
UVRX (social search): uvrx.com/social.html
WordStream (keyword tool): wordstream.com/keywords
Yoast (SEO tool): yoast.com
YouGov Ratings (measures popularity and sentiment—UK): yougov.co.uk/ratings
YouTube Analytics: support.google.com/youtube/answer/92725
YouTube Trending: www.youtube.com/feed/trending
Visio Sparks (social media counts checker): visiospark.com/shared-counter

Social Media Content Creation and Data Visualization

Accelerated Mobile Pages Project (create fast websites, stories, ads, email): www.ampproject.org
Adobe Kuler (color tool): color.adobe.com/create/color-wheel
Adobe Spark (create social media content, stories): spark.adobe.com
Animaker (animated video tool): animaker.com
Animoto (video creation tool): animoto.com
Answer the Public (content ideas tool): answerthepublic.com
BeLive (live streaming video software): be.live
BIGVU (video creation tool): bigvu.tv
Bot Builder (set up and manage conversations): cai.tools.sap/bot-builder
Botletter (Messenger updates and drip campaigns): botletter.com
Camtasia (screen recording/video editing): techsmith.com/video-editor
Canva (design tool): www.canva.com
Chartbuilder (create charts): quartz.github.io/Chartbuilder
Chhirp (record audio for Twitter): cordproject.co/chhirp
Compressor by Pitchengine (automated social post creation): c.tiny.pr
Crello (design tool for social posts): crello.com
Curalate (visual commerce platform): curalate.com
Datawrapper (create charts and maps): datawrapper.de
DesignEvo (create custom logo designs): designevo.com
DesignWizard (online graphic design software): designwizard.com
Easelly (infographic tool): www.easel.ly
Ecam (live video production): ecamm.com
Emotional Marketing Analyzer (headline improvement): aminstitute.com/headline
Facebook Creative Hub (create Facebook ads): facebook.com/ads/creativehub
Fastory (mobile landing pages, microsites, ad creation): fastory.io
Free Stock Photo Sites: blog.hootsuite.com/20-free-stock-photo-sites-social-media-images

Funnelytics (visual marketing funnel tool): funnelytics.io

Gifs (gif maker): gifs.com

Good Data (business intelligence tool): gooddata.com

Google Data Studio (data visualization): datastudio.google.com

Google Fonts: www.google.com/fonts

Google Image: images.google.com

Grammarly (proofreading and editing): grammarly.com

Hashtagify (Twitter and Instagram hashtag suggestions): hashtagify.me

Headline Analyzer (optimize headlines): coschedule.com/headline-analyzer

Hemingway Editor (improve writing): hemingwayapp.com

HubSpot Blog Ideas Generator (content ideas): hubspot.com/blog-topic-generator

Infogram (create charts, maps, graphics): infogram.com

Knowem (username and trademark database): knowem.com

LibreStock (free stock image search): librestock.com

Loomly (social media calendar and publishing): loomly.com

Lumen5 (social video creation): lumen5.com

Microsoft Bot Framework (build and manage bots): dev.botframework.com

Namechk (check usernames and URLs): namechk.com

NodeXL (social analysis and visualization): nodexl.com

Opal (marketing collaboration platform): workwithopal.com

Over (social image, type, graphic tool): madewithover.com

Pexels (free photo site): pexels.com

Phonto (add text to photos): phon.to

Phrasee (AI content copywriting) phrasee.co

PicMonkey (photo editing, design): picmonkey.com

PicPlayPost (multiple media story creation): www.mixcord.co/partners/picplaypost.html

Piktochart (infographic maker): piktochart.com

Pixlr (photo editing): pixlr.com

Placeit (create mockups): placeit.net

Portent Content Idea Generator (title maker): portent.com/tools/title-maker

Power BI (business intelligence): powerbi.microsoft.com

Promo (video creation): promo.com

Recite (visual quote creator): recite.com

Relay (resize, remix designs across social): relaythat.com

Right Relevance (content discovery tool): rightrelevance.com/

Ripl (animated video creation): ripl.com

Rocketium (create BuzzFeed-style videos): rocketium.com

Screencast-O-Matic (screen recording): screencast-o-matic.com

Smartmockups (create product/post screen shots): smartmockups.com

Stencil (social media image creation): getstencil.com

Story Slicer (edit social video): storyslicer.us

Streamlabs (video streaming software): streamelements.com

Tiny PNG (image compression): tinypng.com

Tweetroot (create Twitter word clouds): rubbledev.com/app/tweetroot-for-twitter

TwistedWave (audio editor): twistedwave.com

Typito (video creation): typito.com/go

Typorama (social graphic creation): apperto.com/typorama

Unsplash (free license photos): unsplash.com

Videolicious (automatic video creation): videolicious.com

vMix (live streaming video production): vmix.com

Word Swag (add text to photos): wordswag.co

Social Content Scheduling and Automation

Adobe Experience Manager (cross-channel content management): adobe.com/marketing-cloud/enterprise-content-management.html

AdStage (paid marketing reporting and automation): www.adstage.io

Alltop (news and information aggregator): alltop.com

Bitly (link management platform): bitly.com

Buffer (schedule and track social posts): bufferapp.com

Contentgems (content discovery): contentgems.com

ContentStudio (content discovery and management): contentstudio.io

CoSchedule (cross-channel marketing calendar): coschedule.com

dlvr.it (automated social posting): dlvr.it

DrumUp (content curation tool): drumup.io

Edgar (social media automation and scheduler): meetedgar.com

Flipboard (content curation tool): flipboard.com

Google Photos (free photo storage): google.com/photos

Google Programmatic (automatic online ad buying): thinkwithgoogle.com/programmatic-guide

IFTTT (cross-app task automation): ifttt.com

Later (plan, schedule social posts): later.com

List-O-Matic (list management): accessify.com/tools-and-wizards/developer-tools/list-o-matic

MissingLett_r (automated social campaigns): missinglettr.com

Nuzzel (news feed, curation): nuzzel.com

OptinMonster (auto lead generation): optinmonster.com

Outbrain (native ad platform): outbrain.com

PixelMe (URL shortener and retargeting): pixelme.me

Post Planner (content recommendations): www.postplanner.com

Scoop.It! (content marketing automation): scoop.it

Short Stack (create contests, giveaways, landing pages): www.shortstack.com

Slack (team collaboration): slack.com

SocialOomph (social discovery and automation): www.socialoomph.com

Social Warfare (WordPress social sharing automation): warfareplugins.com

Tailwind (Pinterest/Instagram discovery and scheduling): tailwindapp.com

TINT (user-generated content platform): tintup.com

TweetBot (Twitter client): tapbots.com/tweetbot

TweetDeck (Twitter client): tweetdeck.en.softonic.com

Twillio (Messaging and SMS automation): twilio.com

Twittimer (schedule cross-platform social posts): twittimer.com

Uberflip (B2B content creation): uberflip.com

Woobox (create contests, giveaways, campaigns): woobox.com

Zapier (automate workflows across apps): zapier.com

Zendesk (social customer service system): www.zendesk.com

Social Media and Digital Media Research

Affinio (audience interest analysis): www.affin.io
Facebook IQ (consumer and ad insights): facebook.com/iq
Forrester (social media research findings): www.forrester.com/Social-Media
Gallup (social media research reports): www.gallup.com
Global Web Index (consumer survey data insights): www.globalwebindex.net
Insights from Adobe (marketing research): https://cmo.adobe.com/trends/insights-from-adobe.html
Interbrand Best Brands (global ranking of brands): interbrand.com
IRI Worldwide (predictive analytics) iriworldwide.com
Kantar Media SRDS (insights for media planners and buyers): srds.com
Millward Brown BrandZ Reports (global brand equity ranking): millwardbrown.com/brandz
Mintel (global market research): mintel.com
Nielsen Social Media Reports (social media research reports): www.nielsensocial.com
Pew Research Center (US social research reports): www.pewinternet.org
Roper Center (public opinion research): www.ropercenter.uconn.edu
Simmons (consumer survey research): simmonssurvey.com
Social Explorer (easy access to US demographic data): www.socialexplorer.com
Social Media Collective (social media research reporting): socialmediacollective.org
Sprinklr Business Index (compare brand social performance): businessindex.sprinklr.com
Statista (research statistics portal): www.statista.com
Think with Google (online consumer research insights): thinkwithgoogle.com
YouGov BrandIndex (brand perception ranking): brandindex.com

Trade Associations, Awards, and Conferences

Brand Innovators (marketer conference): brand-innovators.com/events
Content Marketing World (content marketing conference): www.contentmarketingworld.com
INBOUND (content marketing conference): www.inbound.com
INTEGRATE (IMC conference): integrate.wvu.edu/
Online Media Marketing Awards (online marketing awards): www.mediapost.com/ommaawards
The Shorty Awards (social media awards): shortyawards.com
Social Media Marketing World (social media conference): www.socialmediaexaminer.com/smmworld
Social Media Strategies Summit (social media conference): socialmediastrategiessummit.com
Social Media Week (social media conference): socialmediaweek.org
Summit (customer experience conference): summit.adobe.com/na
SXSW (new media/technology conference): sxsw.com
SXSWedu (conference and competition): www.sxswedu.com
The Webby Awards (Internet awards): www.webbyawards.com

Social Media News and Insights

Amy Porterfield (online marketing expert): amyporterfield.com
Australia ACCC (social media regulation—Australia): accc.gov.au/business/advertising-promoting
    -your-business/social-media

Canadian Competition Bureau Guides (social media regulation—Canada): www.competitionbureau .gc.ca

Chris Brogan (online marketing expert): chrisbrogan.com/blog

Christopher S. Penn (online marketing expert): christopherspenn.com

Content Marketing Institute (content marketing experts): contentmarketinginstitute.com/blog

Convince & Convert (social media experts): www.convinceandconvert.com

The Digital Garage (online learning): digitalgarage.withgoogle.com

FTC Consumer Reviews (social media regulation—US): www.ftc.gov/tips-advice/business-center/ guidance/consumer-review-fairness-act-what-businesses-need-know

FTC Disclosures (social media regulation—US): www.ftc.gov/tips-advice/business-center/guidance/ ftcs-endorsement-guides-what-people-are-asking

FTC Native Advertising (social media regulation—US): www.ftc.gov/tips-advice/business-center/ guidance/native-advertising-guide-businesses

Gartner Digital Marketing (digital marketing experts): blogs.gartner.com/digital-marketing

Grow (social media expert—Mark Schaefer): www.businessesgrow.com

Hubspot's Inbound Hub (content marketing experts): blog.hubspot.com

ICPEN Guidance (social media regulation—international): icpen.org/initiatives

Jeff Bullas (online marketing expert): jeffbullas.com

Marketing Profs (digital marketing experts): www.marketingprofs.com

Mashable (digital news): mashable.com

RazorSocial (social media B2B experts): www.razorsocial.com/blog

Scott Monty (digital marketing expert): scottmonty.com

Social Media Examiner (social media experts): www.socialmediaexaminer.com

Social Media Explorer (social media news): www.socialmediaexplorer.com

Social Media Law Bulletin (social media law insights): www.socialmedialawbulletin.com

Social Media Marketing Magazine (social media news): www.smmmagazine.com

Social Media Today (social media news): socialmediatoday.com

Social Mouths (social media experts): socialmouths.com/blog

UK CMA Guidance (social media regulation—UK): gov.uk/government/publications/ online-reviews-and-endorsements-advice-for-businesses

YouTube Video Creators (YouTube video expert): www.youtube.com/videocreators

Social Media and Content Marketing Podcasts

Amy Porterfield: amyporterfield.com/category/podcast

The Art of Online Business Podcast: rickmulready.com/category/aoobpodcast

Behind the Numbers: An eMarketer Podcast: emarketer.com/articles/topics/emarketer-podcast

Buffer Podcast: buffer.com/podcast

The Business of Story: convinceandconvert.com/podcasts/shows/business-of-story-podcast

The Content Experience: convinceandconvert.com/podcasts/shows/content-experience-show

Content Inc.: contentmarketinginstitute.com/content-inc-podcast

Experience This!: convinceandconvert.com/podcasts/shows/experience-this

The Full Monty: scottmonty.com/p/podcast.html

Influence Pros: convinceandconvert.com/podcasts/shows/influence-pros-podcast

The Marketing Book Podcast: www.artillerymarketing.com/marketing-book-podcast

The Marketing Companion: businessesgrow.com/podcast-the-marketing-companion-2

Marketing Marvels: convinceandconvert.com/podcasts/shows/marketing-marvels-podcast

Marketing Smarts Podcast: marketingprofs.com/topic/all/marketing-smarts
Social Media Examiner: socialmediaexaminer.com/shows
Social Pros Podcast: convinceandconvert.com/podcasts/shows/social-pros-podcast
This Old Marketing: contentmarketinginstitute.com/pnr-with-this-old-marketing-podcast

Social Media and Digital Marketing Training and Certification

Adobe Education Exchange: edex.adobe.com
Adobe Software (certification): training.adobe.com/training/courses
Blogging University (WordPress): dailypost.wordpress.com/blogging-university
Canva Design School: designschool.canva.com
Cision (certification and accreditation): cision.com/us/resources/university-program
Code Academy: codecademy.com
Constant Contact Social Media 101: blogs.constantcontact.com/social-media-quickstarter
Conversion Marketing (certification): ConvertedU Leadpages: convertedu.com/courses
Facebook Blueprint (certification): facebook.com/blueprint
Google Analytics Academy (certification): analyticsacademy.withgoogle.com
Google Partners (Adwords certification): support.google.com/partners
Hootsuite Academy (certification): hootsuite.com/education
HubSpot Academy (certification): academy.hubspot.com
LinkedIn Learning (learn software from Adobe Creative Cloud, Google, and LinkedIn): linkedin
    .com/learning
Meltwater Masterclass: meltwater.com/masterclass/resources
Microsoft Advertising (certification): about.ads.microsoft.com/en-us/resources/training/courses
Microsoft Dynamics 365 (certification): microsoft.com/en-us/dynamics365
Pinterest Academy (training): https://business.pinterest.com/pinterest-academy
Professional Certified Marketer—Digital Marketing (certification): ama.org/events-training/
    Certification/Pages/digital-marketing-certification.aspx
Salesforce Trailhead (badges and certification): trailhead.salesforce.com or academic-alliance.salesforce
    .com/business-specialist
Snapchat Explore (certification): forbusiness.snapchat.com/blog/introducing-explore/
Social Media Examiner (training videos): youtube.com/user/socialmediaexaminer/videos
The Trade Desk Trading Academy (certification): thetradedesk.com/products/thetradingacademy
Twitter Flight School (badge): twitterflightschool.com
Yoast Academy (badge and certification) yoast.com/academy
YouTube Certified (certification): support.google.com/youtube/answer/7380223
YouTube Creator Academy: creatoracademy.youtube.com

Social Media Channels

Overdrive Interactive's Social Media Map: ovrdrv.com/social-media-map
Wikipedia List of Social Networking Sites: en.wikipedia.org/wiki/List_of_social_networking_websites

Glossary

A/B testing is where two or more variants of a piece of content are shown to users at random and statistical analysis determines which performs better.

Account planning is designed to bring the consumer's perspective into the process of developing creative advertising and public relations messages and executions.

Actionable insight is a true understanding of people in the target audience and situations related to the product or service that can be used to meet objectives of a marketing effort.

Active voice is a sentence where a subject performs an action directly, using a verb to show the action.

Ad blocker is a program that removes online ads from a website user's desktop and mobile experience.

Adobe Education Exchange is an online site offering free courses, workshops, and teaching materials for Adobe Creative Suite.

Advertising is the placement of announcements and persuasive messages in time or space purchased in mass media.

Advertising agency is hired by organizations to conceive, produce, and manage paid commercial messages through TV, outdoor, radio, print, digital, and social marketing to promote products and services.

Advocates are super-fans and brand loyalists who engage with a brand because they love it and may not have a large sphere of influence.

AIDA model is a hierarchy of effects model that indicates how marketing, advertising, and sales people should move consumers through the stages of awareness, interest, desire, and action.

Algorithm is a formula or set of steps used for solving a problem such as how to rank content to decide what is seen in social media feeds.

Amazon Reviews is a feature on Amazon.com that allows users to submit reviews and ratings to the web page of each product sold on the e-commerce site.

Analysis paralysis is when a decision is never made because there are too many options or it is thought of as overcomplicated.

Analytics is the process of discovering and communicating meaning from data.

Art directors are the professionals who execute or coordinate the type, photos, and illustrations used in advertising design.

Artificial intelligence is computer systems performing tasks that normally require human intelligence.

Attention is the selective narrowing or focusing of consciousness and observance on something.

Attention economics deals with the problem of getting consumers to consume advertising and public relations messages.

Attribution is giving original authors credit for their content.

Automation is software that does things without human intervention.

Behavioral targeting is used by advertisers to customize messages based on web-browsing behavior such as web pages visited or searches made.

Big data refers to massive amounts of data so large or complex they are difficult to process using traditional data processing applications.

Big idea is a driving, unifying force behind brand marketing efforts.

Blog is an abbreviated version of weblog, which describes websites that contain a reverse chronological order of entries or posts featuring diary-type commentary or stories on specific subjects that range from personal to political.

Blogger is a blog-publishing service founded in 1999 that allows free user accounts hosted at the subdomain of blogspot.com.

Bottom line is the line at the bottom of a financial report showing profit or loss.

Boycott is when consumers avoid purchasing a company's products as a show of disapproval.

Brand is a name, design, or symbol that identifies one seller's product or services from others.

Brand ambassadors are influencers who are rewarded or hired by the brand for long-term relationships.

Brand community is a group of people with social relations structured around being admirers of a brand.

Brand equity is a set of metrics used to measure the value of a brand.

Brand positioning is the way consumers view a brand compared to competitors.

Brand style guide is a document that defines a brand and makes it understandable and replicable through visual and content style.

Brand voice is the personality used in brand communication that usually remains consistent.

Broadcasting is a general message delivered to a large group.

Buycott is when consumers purchase a company's products in show of support.

Buyer persona is a semifictional portrayal of the ideal customer based on real data.

BuzzFeed is a social news and entertainment company founded in 2006 that collects and creates viral content from around the web.

California Bot Disclosure Law requires a bot to be disclosed when it is used to incentivize a purchase or sale of goods or services in a commercial transaction or to influence a vote in an election.

California Consumer Protection Act (CCPA) grants privacy powers to consumers in the United States, granting the right to know what information companies collect about them and to opt out of having their data shared or sold.

Canva Design School is an online education site offering free training courses in design and using their software.

Chatbots are computer programs that simulate human conversation for customer service or information acquisition and distribution.

Check-in is defined as self-reported positioning to share one's physical location through a social-networking service.

Cision University Program offers free training courses and professional certification.

Collaborative tagging can be used to analyze trends and determine popularity of content over time as different sources converge.

Commonsense market segmentation is when managers use a single segmentation criterion, such as age, to split consumers into homogeneous groups.

Community marketing is when companies don't directly control the conversation in social media but facilitate the discussion with the help of loyal customers.

Company wikis can bring together global divisions and partners who may not be in the same building, city, or country.

Competency trap is repeating what was successful in the past and overlooking important opportunities for future success.

Consumer-brand relationship is a line of theoretical research that proposes repeated interactions between a brand and customers can begin to reflect characteristics of relationships between people.

Content calendar is a way to plan and visualize how content will be distributed during a specified period.

Content curation is a process of gathering information relevant to a specific topic or area of interest to present to others.

Content marketing is a strategic marketing approach focused on creating and distributing valuable, relevant, and consistent content to attract and retain a defined audience, ultimately to drive profitable customer action.

Content marketing manager plans, creates, and measures all digital content including social media and other content such as eBooks, email, search, and display ads to drive traffic to brand websites.

Converged media is the combining or blurring of paid (advertising), owned (brand channels), and earned media (public relations).

Conversation is an informal talk involving two people or a small group of people.

Conversational commerce (c-commerce) is when businesses connect with people via messaging to drive purchases.

Copywriters are the writers of advertising or publicity copy.

Corporate communications involves managing internal and external communications aimed at corporate stakeholders.

Corporate social responsibility (CSR) is when companies consider the impact they have on all aspects of society, including economic, social, and environmental.

Creative brief is a strategic document used to develop creative content for strategies and campaigns.

Creative Commons provides licenses as an alternative way for creators to retain copyright while allowing others to copy, distribute, and make some use of their work.

Creative process is a method for developing ideas that follows the stages of gathering raw material, looking for relationships, letting the unconscious mind work, birth of the idea, and refinement.

Crisis communication is attempting to reduce the damage to a company's reputation by third party sources due to an unexpected event.

Crowdfunding is using small amounts of capital from a larger group of people to finance a new business venture.

Crowdsourcing takes a job normally performed by a professional, such as an employee, and outsources it to a large group of people through an open call.

Customer co-creation is simply the joint creation of value by the company and customer.

Customer lifetime value is a concept that shifts focus from short-term profit to long-term profit from the continuing relationship with a customer.

Customer relationship management is using systems to better manage data and interactions with customers and potential customers with a focus on long-term relationships.

Customer service is the process of ensuring customer satisfaction, often while performing a transaction, taking a sale, providing post-purchase support, or returning a product or service.

Customer service system is a combination of technological structure and organizational networks designed to provide services that satisfy customers.

Customer stickiness is simply the increased chance to utilize the same product or service that was bought before.

Daily active users (DAUs) is the total number of unique people who interact with an app or web page in day.

Dark social is web traffic with no referral data because the link was shared through unmeasurable social media.

Data brokers are businesses that collect consumers' personal information and sell it to other organizations.

Data-driven market segmentation is when managers analyze more complex sets of variables to split consumers into homogeneous groups.

Data security refers to the measures organizations take to ensure digital privacy to prevent unauthorized access to computers, databases, and websites.

Demographic variables include information such as age range, gender, geographic location, ethnic background, marital status, income, and education.

Digg is a social news website founded in 2004 that aggregates news and publishers' streams via peer evaluation of voting up content, and also supports easy sharing of content to other social platforms such as Twitter and Facebook.

Digital market research involves using new digital media to collect results through methods such as online surveys, online focus groups, online communities, bulletin boards, and social media sites.

Digital marketing agency is hired by organizations to conceive, produce, and manage brand assets through digital media including websites and mobile and digital ads to promote products and services.

Digital marketing specialists are the professionals who handle online activities for a brand, such as web development, online advertising, search engine optimization, paid search, and e-commerce.

Digital Millennium Copyright Act (DMCA) updated US copyright law to apply to the development of electronic commerce, distribution of digital works, and protection of copyright owners' rights.

Diversity marketing strives to target audiences with marketing communication that is sensitive to individual attitudes and practices.

Drip marketing automates sending a series of communications on a schedule or by consumer trigger actions.

E-commerce describes activities related to the buying and selling of goods and services over the internet.

Elaboration Likelihood Model is a dual process theory that proposes there are two routes to persuasion—the central route and peripheral route.

Emotional cognition is a psychological phenomenon in which a person or group influences the emotions and behavior of another through conscious or even unconscious emotions.

Employee advocacy is the promotion of a business by its workforce, usually through social media.

Employer branding is efforts focused on attracting, engaging, and retaining talent.

Engagement is involvement, interaction, intimacy, and influence between an individual and a brand.

Engagement rate measures the amount of interaction social content earns relative to other audience figures such as reach.

Ethics studies ideas about good and bad behavior.

Ethnography is investigation of a group or culture based on immersion and/or participation to gain comprehensive understanding.

Etiquette is the proper way to behave.

Evangelism marketing is a form of word-of-mouth marketing in which marketers develop relationships with customers who strongly believe in a product or service and who voluntarily advocate for the brand.

Evergreen content is content that doesn't go out of date. It involves a topic that will always be relevant to your audience regardless of current trending topics, news, or season.

External factors consist of a variety of factors outside the organization that marketers typically don't have direct control over.

Facebook is an online social-networking service founded in 2004 where users create profiles, connect to other users as "friends," and exchange messages, photos, and video.

Facebook Blueprint is Facebook's free and paid online courses and certifications for marketing on Facebook, Instagram, Facebook Messenger, and WhatsApp.

Facebook Insights is the tool to track organic and paid performance on Facebook pages.

Facebook Live, first made available to the public in 2016, is a live video streaming feature added to the Facebook mobile app for any user to broadcast live video.

Facebook Messenger is the instant messaging service application that enables sending multimedia content with optional encryption through Facebook accounts.

Facebook Portal is a line of smart devices that enable video chat with Facebook friends through Facebook Messenger or WhatsApp and offers smart voice service.

Facebook Watch is a video-on-demand service built into Facebook that combines video sharing with premium content.

Family life cycle is the stages people pass through from childhood to retirement that usually represent different needs and desires.

Fauxpology is an apology that seems to express remorse but doesn't acknowledge any wrongdoing.

Federal Trade Commission (FTC) is responsible for protecting consumers in the United States from unfair trade practices, including deceptive advertising and the use of social media for marketing communication.

Firmographics is data used to segment organizations into meaningful categories for business-to-business marketing.

Five Ws are questions used for basic information gathering used by journalists to find out the who, where, what, when, and why of a story.

Flame war is a series of angry, disparaging comments exchanged by two or more people in an online argument.

Flog is a paid-for, fake blog.

Folksonomy is a simple form of shared vocabularies created through tagging in social bookmarking systems.

Forums are online discussion sites where people hold conversations on related topics via posted messages.

Four Cs can be explained as consumer not product, cost not price, convenience not place, and communicate not promote.

Four Ps divides the marketing mix or function into four interconnected parts: product, price, promotion, and place (distribution).

Foursquare is a personalized local search-and-discovery-service mobile app founded in 2009 that enables users to find friends and read recommendations.

Friendster (founded in 2002 and shut down in 2015) was one of the original social network service websites allowing users to make contacts with other members and share online content and media with them.

FTC Endorsement Guides explain that marketers or advertisers and influencers promoting or endorsing products are responsible for clearly and conspicuously disclosing material connections that affect the weight or credibility consumers give to an endorsement in social media.

Gamification is the application of elements of games, such as point scoring and competition, to marketing to encourage brand loyalty and engagement.

General Data Protection Regulation (GDPR) sets legal protection guidelines for any company that collects and processes the personal data of European Union citizens.

Generational targeting is when marketers target broader age groups such as baby boomers, generation Xers, or millennials because they may have similar desires compared to previous generations.

Geocaching is an outdoor game where people use GPS on a mobile device to hide and then seek containers called geocaches at locations marked by coordinates.

Geofencing is setting up a virtual perimeter for a real-world geographic area and using a smartphone's GPS to trigger a message or customize content.

Geosocial is a type of social networking in which user-submitted location data allow social networks to connect and coordinate users with local people, businesses, or events.

Geotagging is when geographical identification information is added to media such as a picture, video, or social media post.

Goal is something that a person or group is trying to achieve.

Golden Circle is a concept that seeks to discover a person's or organization's purpose by asking why, how, and what, starting with why in the center of three concentric circles.

Google Ads Certification are free online training and certifications in Google Ads search, display, video and shopping ads.

Google Analytics Academy is an online education site offering free training and professional certifications for Google Analytics.

Google My Business is a listing that ensures that businesses show up in searches and includes social media features such as updates, comments, photo sharing, ratings, and reviews.

Hashtag hijacking is when the original positive intent of a hashtag is hijacked to promote negatives of the brand.

Having legs means a campaign theme can be executed in many ways, in many different media, for a long period of time.

Homegrown monitoring is using search engines and going to each social media platform to find and manually track and analyze brand social media conversation.

Hootsuite Academy is an online education site offering free and paid training courses and professional certifications.

HubSpot Academy is an online education site offering free and paid training courses and professional certifications.

Human-centric marketing is where brands behave like humans, treating customers as friends.

Image recognition or computer vision is software that can recognize people, animals, and other objects.

Impressions are the number of times a piece of content is displayed.

Influencer marketing focuses on leveraging key leaders to advocate on behalf of a brand to reach the larger market.

Influencer relations managers identify, build, and manage mutual relationships with relevant celebrity, macro, and micro influencers to create and share brand social media content.

Influencers bring expertise to a specific area, have a sizable group of engaged followers, and usually share brand messages for compensation.

Information superhighway describes a telecommunications infrastructure used for widespread, rapid access to information.

Instagram is an online mobile social-networking service founded in 2010 that enables users to take photos and videos and share them on a variety of social networking platforms.

Instagram Insights is the tool that details metrics on how people are viewing brand Instagram organic and paid content.

Instagram Live is a live video–streaming feature added to the Instagram mobile app in 2016 for any user to broadcast live video.

Instagrammable is an object, scene, or moment deemed worthy of sharing, usually as a photo or video.

Integrated marketing communications (IMC) seeks to align and coordinate all marketing communications delivered to consumers to present a cohesive whole that persuades consumers to purchase.

Intelligent virtual assistants add human interface to software to answer questions and respond to commands.

Interactive marketing is the ability to address the customer, remember what the customer said, and then address the customer in a way that illustrates that the organization remembers what the customer told them.

Internal factors are the factors that occur within an organization and impact the approach and success of operations.

Internal marketing promotes the firm and its policies to employees as if they are customers of the firm.

International Consumer Protection and Enforcement Network (ICPEN) is an organization composed of consumer protection authorities from more than sixty countries.

Internet of Things (IoT) is the network of physical objects with embedded technology that includes an IP address for internet connectivity to communicate with the external environment.

IP convergence means using the Internet Protocol (IP) as the standard transport for transmitting all information such as video, data, music, and TV teleconferencing.

iTunes, released in 2001, is the Apple media player used to play, download, and organize digital audio and video on computers in the macOS and Microsoft Windows operation systems and mobile devices, including iPhone, iPod Touch, and iPad.

Jobs to be done theory shifts the focus of marketing from demographics and product attributes to the functional, social, and emotional reasons customers buy products to get a "job" done or make progress to a larger goal.

Journalist social media content developer uses their journalism skills to promote news brands or create news-style content for corporate brands in social media.

KPI is a key indicator used as a type of performance measurement.

Landing page is a specially designed page with a main goal to generate sales or capture leads from a campaign.

LinkedIn is a business-focused social-networking service founded in 2003 that allows users to create professional profiles of work experience and form connections with other professionals.

LinkedIn Analytics is the tool that provides insights into company page performance for organic and paid brand actions.

LinkedIn Learning is an online education site offering paid training courses and certifications for software, creative, and business skills.

Listicle is short-form writing based on an often numerical theme structure with added copy to be published as an article.

Live streaming video is simply compressed video content sent over the internet and displayed in real time.

Long tail refers to the large number of products that sell in small quantities, as contrasted with the small number of best-selling products.

Machine learning is when computers learn from experience by modifying processes from new input.

Macro-influencers have between 100,000 and one million followers and usually gained their fame through the internet.

Market is defined as a place where products are bought and sold.

Market segmentation is a process of grouping potential customers into sets that are homogeneous in response to elements of the marketing mix.

Marketing communications coordinates promotional messages delivered through channels like print, radio, television, and personal selling.

Marketing department is the department in an organization that promotes the business and drives sales of products and services.

Media richness theory states that media differ in the degree of richness they possess—the amount of information they allow to be transmitted in a given time.

Mega-influencers have more than one million followers and are often considered celebrities who may be more famous than influential.

Meltwater Masterclass is free online training for monitoring and analyzing social media.

Memes are ideas expressed as visuals, words, and/or videos that spread on the internet from person to person.

Metrics are standards of measurement by which efficiency, performance, or progress can be assessed.

Microblogging is a form of traditional blogging where the content is smaller in both file size and length of content.

Micro-influencer marketing is when brands partner with people who have smaller followings on social media to promote products in an authentic way versus sponsored ads.

Micro-influencers include people with 1,000 to 100,000 followers and focus on a specific niche as industry experts or topic specialists.

Micro-moments are the hundreds of real-time, goal-oriented, mobile actions that influence consumer decisions and preferences.

Mission statement is a written declaration of an organization's core purpose and focus that tends to remain unchanged over time.

Mobile first strategy started as designing websites for smaller smartphone and tablet devices but has expanded to delivering a mobile first customer experience.

Mobile marketing includes advertising delivered via mobile devices and use of mobile technology to create personalized promotion.

Mobile media is a personal, interactive, internet-enabled, and user-controlled portable platform for the exchange of information.

Mommy blogger is a mother who blogs about her children, motherhood, parenting, and other related topics. Note that some bloggers find this term condescending.

Monthly active users (MAUs) is the total number of unique people who have interacted with an app or website in a month.

Multichannel marketing uses multiple channels to communicate with customers, but each channel does not communicate with the others.

Nano-influencers have fewer than 1,000 followers and have influence within their community.

Narrowcasting is a specialized message delivered to small group.

Native advertising is paid marketing that delivers useful, targeted content along with and in a form that looks like the social media site's or app's non-ad content.

Natural language generation (NLG) takes non-language inputs and generates spoken language.

Natural language processing (NLP) finds linguistic patterns to analyze and synthesize speech.

Net Promoter Score (NPS) is a measure of customer experience to determine the presence of brand promoters, passives and detractors.

News aggregation uses software to collect all new syndicated web content from many newspapers, magazines, and blogs into one page.

Newsjacking is the strategy of injecting a brand into breaking news through social media or content marketing to get the brand noticed.

Nonprofit marketing is strategies to spread the message of a nonprofit brand and solicit donations and volunteers to meet organization objectives.

Objective is a goal, something you are trying to achieve, expressed in specific terms.

Observation is a form of qualitative research that involves the systematic collection of data where researchers use all of their senses to examine people in natural settings and situations.

Omnichannel marketing integrates multiple channels, exchanging information for a seamless and consistent customer experience.

One percent rule (1% rule) or the 90-9-1 principle states that in collaborative sites such as blogs and forums, 90 percent of users view the content, 9 percent contribute infrequently, and only 1 percent actively create new content.

Online reputation management (ORM) refers to strategies to influence public opinion of an individual's or organization's reputation online through digital and social media.

Operations are jobs tasked with converting inputs such as materials, labor, and information into outputs such as goods, services, and value-added products that can be sold for a profit.

Organic reach is the number of unique people who saw a social media post through unpaid distribution.

Over-the-top media services (OTT) are streaming media TV services offered directly to viewers over the internet, bypassing cable, broadcast, and satellite platforms.

Paid reach is the number of unique people who saw a post as a result of paid distribution.

Parasocial relationship is the emotional bond or feeling of real friendship felt by one person but not the other through the intimacy of social media.

Pareto principle (80/20 rule) states the roughly 80 percent of sales come from 20 percent of customers.

Passive voice is a sentence where the action verb or object of a sentence is emphasized over its subject.

Perceptual map is a marketing research technique that plots consumers' views about a brand, product, or service on a horizonal and vertical axis of different attributes.

Periscope is a live video streaming mobile app founded in 2015 and integrated into the microblogging social media service Twitter.

Permission marketing is when sales prospects must first explicitly agree to receive marketing communication.

Personal branding is a practice where people market themselves and their careers like brands.

Pinterest is a web and mobile social network founded in 2010 that enables visual discovery, collection, and sharing and serves as a storage tool.

Pinterest Academy is free online training about marketing on Pinterest.

Pinterest Analytics is the tool that provides data on organic and paid pin performance.

Podcast is a series of episodes of audio or video content delivered digitally that are often subscribed to and downloaded through web syndication or streamed online through a computer or mobile device.

Point of view is the angle of considering things, as in writing from first-, second-, or third-person view of a story.

Predictive analytics helps understand future performance based on current and historical data.

Prescriptive analytics helps determine the best solution among various choices.

Primary research is new research to answer specific questions, and can include questionnaires, surveys, or interviews.

Privacy policy is a statement that defines an organization's policy on collecting and releasing information about a visitor or user.

Private wikis provide access to a business's most up-to-date collective knowledge.

Professional monitoring is using one or multiple software tools to track and analyze brand social media conversation in one or multiple social media platforms.

Professionalism is the skill, good judgment, and polite behavior expected from a person trained to do a job.

Programmatic advertising is the automated buying and selling of advertising media targeting specific audiences and demographics placed through artificial intelligence and real-time bidding.

Programmatic direct is ads purchased via a publisher-owned application program interface.

Psychographic variables consist of internal factors such as values, attitudes, interests, lifestyle, and behavior.

Public relations creates and maintains the goodwill of the public, such as customers, employees, and investors, through nonpaid forms of media.

Public relations agency is hired by organizations to conceive, produce, and manage unpaid messages to the public through media to change public actions by influencing opinions.

Public relations executives are the professionals who focus on nonpaid forms of brand communication such as media relations, event planning, speeches, and crisis communication.

Publics are the audiences identified to receive messages from an organization.

Pull marketing attempts to attract the customer to brand communication by providing valuable content, usually delivered via social media.

Pull strategy aims marketing efforts at the end consumer to persuade the consumer to request the products from retail channels.

Purchase funnel is a model that illustrates a customer journey toward purchase from awareness to interest, desire, and action.

Push marketing is focused on interrupting potential customers, usually through the purchase of ads.

Push strategy is a manufacturer enticing other channel members to carry a product.

QR code is short for quick response code and is a two-dimensional bar code that provides quick and easy access to online information through a smartphone camera.

Quora is a question-and-answer website founded in 2009 where questions are submitted and answered by its community of users.

Ratings are a measurement of how good or bad something is, but expressed specifically on a scale that is a relative estimate or evaluation.

Reach is the number of unique people who see a piece of content.

Real-time bidding (RTB) is auction-based ad transactions placed on real-time impressions in open and private marketplaces.

Real-time marketing is systematically responding to consumers with dynamic, personalized content across channels that is relevant in the moment.

Reddit is a social news and entertainment company founded in 2005 and acquired by Condé Nast Publications in 2006.

Referral traffic is the number of website visits by people clicking on a hyperlink from another website.

Research and development (R&D) is the process where often departments of engineers or scientists are charged with new product development and design.

Return on investment (ROI) is measuring the profitability of an investment as a ratio between the net profit and cost of investment.

Reviews are reports that give someone's opinion about the quality of a product, service, or performance.

RSS (rich site summary) is a convenient way for people to listen to and read what others are saying and writing.

Rule of thirds is a principle that divides an image or layout into thirds horizontally and vertically to place elements in a more appealing, balanced way.

Salesforce Trailhead is an online education site offering free training and professional credentials.

Search engine marketing (SEM) is improving the visibility of a website in search engine results pages through paid advertising.

Search engine optimization (SEO) is improving the visibility of a website in unpaid (organic) web search engine results.

Secondary research discovers information previously researched for other purposes that is publicly available.

Sentiment analysis is identifying and categorizing opinions in a piece of text, determining if the attitude expressed is positive, negative, or neutral.

Share of voice is your brand social media mentions divided by total competitive brand social media mentions.

Silo syndrome is when a department or function, such as marketing, develops its own culture and has trouble working with other functions such as operations, customer service, or sales.

Situation analysis is a collection of methods used to analyze an organization's environment that impacts an organization's ability to achieve its objectives.

Slack provides a quick employee communication platform for messaging, sharing files, searches, and apps.

Slogan is a sentence or long phrase that expresses a company or products goal.

SMART objectives are specific, measurable, achievable, relevant, and timely.

Snapchat is a photo- and video-sharing messaging service founded in 2011 in which media and messages are only available for a short time before disappearing.

Snapchat Explore is Snapchat's free training for how to use Snapchat's advertising solutions to meet business objectives.

Social bookmarking is an online service where users can save, comment on, and share bookmarks of web documents or links.

Social bot is a computer program used in social media networks to automatically generate messages, simulating conversation.

Social capital is defined as actual or virtual resources collected by an individual or group by mutual association and recognition.

Social capital theory is a broad concept recognizing the power of an individual to exert influence on a group or individual to mobilize resources.

Social care is the efforts employees make through social media to care for customers.

Social commerce is the use of social networks for online buying and selling via e-commerce transactions.

Social conversation analysis is the study of the group talk produced in ordinary human interactions collected from the vast amounts of social media conversation data.

Social influence is any process from which a person's attitudes, opinions, beliefs, or behavior are altered or controlled by a form of social communication.

Social interaction is the process of reciprocal stimulation or response between two people.

Social knowledge platforms or networks are internet-based information exchanges where users can ask questions and get answers from real people.

Social media is interactive computer-mediated technologies that facilitate the creation and sharing of information, ideas, and other forms of expression via virtual communities and networks.

Social media advertising is advertising that relies on social information or networks in generating, targeting, and delivering paid marketing communications.

Social media agency is hired by organizations to conceive, produce, and manage the presence of a brand through social media channels such as social networks, messaging apps, blogs and forums, podcasts, ratings, and reviews.

Social media analysts focus on social media measurement by developing systems, processes, and reporting methods that gathering and analyzing social media data to make better informed decisions and optimize strategies, tactics, and content.

Social media audit is a systematic examination of social media data.

Social media command center is a branded social media monitoring room acting as a central, visual hub for social data.

Social media community managers create and foster social media communities built around a brand through direct engagement as a person advocating for the brand on social media channels.

Social media coordinators plan, implement, and monitor a brand's social media strategy to meet organizational objectives, working with content creators, internal departments, and external partners to measure and improve performance.

Social media copywriters plan, create, and analyze channel-specific brand social media written content, building content calendars, writing guidelines, and finding internal and external sources.

Social media feedback cycle is social media connecting post-purchase social media conversation back to the purchase process, where social media is the product of operations based on the expectation given in marketing communication.

Social media freelancers provide the services of specific social media roles on a project or campaign basis versus as a full-time employee.

Social media graphic designers create and maintain visual brand assets and find and create appropriate images and graphics for various social media channel content.

Social media listening is collecting data from brand social mentions and broader relevant conversations to improve strategy.

Social media marketing cycle is a model for the customer journey that includes influential post-purchase customer social media, putting the customer at the center of the process where marketer participates in a brand community through engagement in customer touchpoints.

Social media marketing managers manage the creation and execution of an organization's social media strategy which can include the overall brand presence and specific campaigns.

Social media monitoring is identifying and responding to brand mentions in social media to improve customer engagement.

Social media organization models are the five ways social media is categorized within an organization, including decentralized, centralized, hub and spoke, multiple hub and spoke, and holistic.

Social media policy is an organization's standards for conduct regarding the way its employees post content in social media as part of their jobs or as private individuals.

Social media press release is an easy-to-scan document containing text and multimedia elements that are simple to share and that offers links to a collection of relevant information.

Social media research involves using various tools and techniques to collect and analyze data from social media networks or platforms.

Social media specialists focus on implementation of social media strategy writing social copy, scheduling social content, and tracking social media KPIs while staying up to date on the latest trends in social media.

Social media strategic plan defines how an organization will use social media for communication to achieve measurable business objectives in conjunction with other marketing channels and the social platforms and tools it will use to achieve this.

Social media strategists plan an organization's social media strategy, ensuring the strategy connects to larger objectives and integrates marketing, advertising, and public relations.

Social media video specialists capture, edit, and produce videos for brand assets and specific social media channel content.

Social messaging is instant messaging or chat applications created around social networks for communication on mobile phones, with fewer limits and more features than traditional texting.

Social network is any website where one connects with those sharing personal or professional interests.

Social presence theory states that media differ in the degree of social presence (acoustic, visual, and physical contact) they allow between two communication partners.

Social proof is the concept that if larger numbers of people endorse something then other people are more likely to believe that it is correct, influencing their attitudes and actions.

Social selling is a process of developing relationships through social media as part of the sales process.

Solopreneur is an entrepreneur who runs their business without full-time employees.

Stakeholders are any people who have an influence or interest in an organization's success.

Strategic business unit (SBU) is a fully functional and distinct unit that develops its own strategic vision and direction.

Strategic campaign is a focused, tactical effort to meet one aspect or specific objective of a plan, often on a shorter time frame.

Strategic plan details the specific tactics that will be used to help meet specific objectives over time.

Strategic thinking means taking a broad, long-range approach and thinking systematically.

Strategy is the high-level connection between an effort or function and organization requirements.

Super-fans are a company's most active online consumers who answer forum questions, write in-depth blog posts, and provide valuable feedback without collecting a fee.

Surprise and delight is a form of marketing to attract and nurture customers through unexpected rewards.

Swarm is described as a lifelogging community with social networking features to keep track of places users have been.

SWOT analysis (or SWOT matrix) is a process and visual overview for identifying an organization's strengths, weaknesses, opportunities, and threats to analyze the internal and external factors impacting success.

Tagging is the way social-bookmarking programs organize links to resources.

Tagline is a short memorable phrase repeated in marketing messages to a company or product.

Target audience is a group of people identified as the intended recipient of a communications message.

Target market is identified in business and marketing plan objectives and represents a group of people who share common wants or needs that an organization serves.

TikTok is a social media short-form video app for creating and sharing lip-sync, comedy, and talent videos.

Traditional market research involves face-to-face or traditional media methods, such as focus groups, in-depth interviews, shop-alongs, ethnographic observation, intercepts, and telephone and mail surveys.

TripAdvisor is an online travel company founded in 2000 that provides hotel booking and reviews of travel-related content with travel forums.

Trolls are users who intentionally post inflammatory, extraneous messages in online communities to provoke emotional responses.

Tumblr is a blogging platform and social-networking website founded in 2007 that allows users to post multimedia content in a short-form blog.

Twitch is a live video streaming platform focused on live video game streaming.

Twitter is an online social-networking service founded in 2006 that enables users to send short, character-count-limited messages.

Twitter Analytics is the tool that measures organic and paid impact for brand account performance on Twitter.

Twitter Cards enable users to attach rich photos, videos, and media experiences to tweets and to drive traffic to websites.

Twitter Chats are when an organization or individual talks live with others about a topic during a preplanned time using a hashtag.

Twitter Flight School is Twitter's free online training for marketing on Twitter.

User-centric means having more control, choices, or flexibility where the needs, wants, and limitations of the end user are taken into consideration.

User-generated content is any photo, video, post, or comment published through a social media platform by an unpaid contributor.

User-generated content policy is an organization's standards for rights granted to use consumer-created content in brand marketing.

Uses and gratifications theory proposes that audiences are active in media consumption and that they consciously select media content to satisfy their various needs.

Value proposition is the value a company promises to deliver to customers, telling them what it stands for, how it operates, and why it deserves their business.

Video blog (vlog) is a combination of video, images, and text that can be thought of as a form of web television.

Video podcast is a series of video clips or web television series delivered digitally that are often subscribed to and downloaded or streamed online through a computer or mobile device.

Vision is an organization's reason for existence, where it is headed, and what impact it wants to make in the world.

Web 2.0 is the common term used to designate the collective technology changes in the way web pages were made and used that took them beyond the static pages of earlier websites.

WhatsApp is a free, cross-platform instant messaging service that allows encrypted multimedia communication through mobile cellular numbers.

White space (negative space) is the area found between design elements that enables them to stand out.

Wiki is a website that allows collaborative editing by multiple contributors.

WikiLeaks is an international nonprofit that collects news leaks and classified media by anonymous sources and publishes them on its website.

Wikipedia is a collaboratively edited, free internet encyclopedia founded in 2001 and supported by the nonprofit Wikimedia Foundation.

WikiWikiWeb was the first website to use a wiki style of programming in 1995.

Wisdom of the crowd is the collective opinion of a group rather than a single expert.

Word-of-mouth communication is when people share information about products or promotions with friends and is one of the oldest forms of marketing.

WordPress is a free, open-source blogging and content-management system founded in 2003.

Yahoo! Answers is a community question-and-answer website or social-knowledge platform founded by Yahoo! in 2005.

Yelp is a website and mobile app founded in 2004 that publishes crowdsourced ratings and reviews about local businesses.

YouTube is a video-sharing website founded in 2005 that enables users to upload, view, and share user-generated and corporate-media video.

YouTube Analytics provides data on YouTube brand channel organic and paid video performance.

YouTube Creator Academy is an online education site offering free training courses on creating and optimizing YouTube videos and channels.

YouTube Live is a live video streaming feature added to the YouTube website and mobile app to broadcast live video.

Index

Page references for figures and tables are italicized.

About the Author

Keith A. Quesenberry is a marketing professor, researcher, and consultant at Messiah University, where he teaches social media, digital marketing, marketing principles, and integrated marketing communications in the undergraduate and MBA programs and was integral in launching a digital marketing certificate. He also teaches emerging media, social media strategy, and campaigns in the graduate Integrated Marketing Communications program at West Virginia University. He previously taught communications and business classes in the Center for Leadership Education at Johns Hopkins University and key courses in the Advertising and Public Relations Department at Temple University. Prior to teaching, he spent nearly twenty years in marketing and advertising as an associate creative director and copywriter at advertising agencies such as BBDO and Arnold Worldwide. His client experience spanned from startups to Fortune 500s such as Delta Air Lines, ExxonMobil, PNC Bank, Campbell's, and Hershey.

His advertising campaigns have earned awards such as the One Show, National ADDYs, and London International Awards, and have been featured in the trade publications *Ad Age*, *Adweek*, *Brandweek*, and *Lurzer's International Archive*. His social media campaigns have been recognized by the industry, including a PRSA (Public Relations Society of America) Bronze Anvil for word-of-mouth and an OMMA (Online Media, Marketing, and Advertising) Award. He is also a contributing author to *Harvard Business Review, Entrepreneur, PR Week,* and *Social Media Today*. His articles have been recognized as "Top 40 Content Marketing" and "Top 5 Visual Marketing" articles of the year, "5 Most Viral Marketing Posts from the Pros," and featured on the *Harvard Business Review* "Weekly Hotlist."

Quesenberry has made expert appearances on MSNBC TV and NPR, and has been quoted in *Harvard Business Review*, the *New York Times*, the *New Yorker, Entrepreneur, Forbes, PR Week, European Business Review, International Business Times, MS Money, Variety*, and on MSN, Fox News, Fox Business, Yahoo News, *Heidi Cohen's Actionable Marketing Guide, Marketing Land, SpinSucks*, Business of Story podcast and AFP. His research has been published in journals including *Journal of Interactive Marketing, Journal of Marketing Theory and Practice, Journal of Current Issues and Research in Advertising, International Journal of Integrated Marketing Communications, Journal of Biblical Issues in Business, Journal of Advertising Education, Journalism and Mass Communication Educator,* and in *Ad Age* Research Reports. His research has also been presented at national conferences for the American Marketing Association, the American Academy of Advertising, and the Association for Education in Journalism and Mass Communication.

He has also contributed to other books, including *Leadership in the Creative Industries: Principles and Practice*, written by Karen Mallia; *Readings in Account Planning*, edited by Hart Weichselbaum; *The New Advertising: Branding, Content and Consumer Relationships in the Data-Driven Social Media Era*, edited by Ruth E. Brown and Valerie K. Jones; and *Creative Strategy in Advertising*, written by Bonnie L. Drewniany and A. Jerome Jewler. He blogs at www .postcontrolmarketing.com.